Praise for
The Voice of Evidence in Reading Research

"This comprehensive resource compels all of us . . . to understand the critical role research and evidence play in determining what works in improving reading instruction and student achievement in reading. Armed with evidence of what works and with research-based reading programs and instructional strategies, knowledgeable and skilled educators and administrators will meet the goal of every child reading well by the end of third grade."
> —**Sandra Feldman,** President, American Federation of Teachers

"An extraordinary collection [by] the finest educational and neurological researchers . . . This book will surely become required reading for any and all who claim to care about the quality of reading instruction in America."
> —**J. Thomas Viall,** Executive Director, The International
> Dyslexia Association

"Outstanding and just what the field needs. It should be required reading in every School of Education."
> —**Benita Blachman, Ph.D.,** Trustee Professor of Education and
> Psychology, Syracuse University

"As a parent who raised a son with reading difficulties, I have dedicated my life to ensuring students receive scientific research-based reading instruction to prevent academic failures. [This] is a significant contribution to promoting 21st-century lifelong learners who will require proficient reading skills."
> —**Norma S. Garza,** Member, National Reading Panel; Chair,
> Brownsville READS!; Member, President's Commission on
> Educational Excellence for Hispanic Americans

"Provides a much-needed bridge between reading research and reading instruction . . . The focus is, appropriately, on all children, including those who struggle to learn and read."
> —**James H. Wendorf,** Executive Director, National Center for
> Learning Disabilities

The Voice of Evidence
in Reading
Research

Edited by

Peggy McCardle, Ph.D., M.P.H.

and

Vinita Chhabra, M.Ed.

Child Development and Behavior Branch
National Institute of Child Health and Human Development
National Institutes of Health
U.S. Department of Health and Human Services
Bethesda, Maryland

·P A U L·H·
BROOKES
PUBLISHING CO ®

Baltimore • London • Sydney

Paul H. Brookes Publishing Co.
Post Office Box 10624
Baltimore, Maryland 21285-0624

www.brookespublishing.com

Royalties from the sale of this book will be donated to the Children's Inn at NIH,
a private, non-profit residence for pediatric patients and their families at the
Clinical Center, National Institutes of Health.

Typeset by International Graphics Services, Newtown, Pennsylvania.
Manufactured in the United States of America by
The Maple Press Co., York, Pennsylvania.

10   9   8   7   6   5   4   3

Library of Congress Cataloging-in-Publication Data

The voice of evidence in reading research / edited by Peggy McCardle and
Vinita Chhabra.
         p.   cm.
Includes bibliographical references and index.
ISBN 1-55766-672-5
1. Reading—Research—United States.   2. Evidence.   I. McCardle, Peggy
D.   II. Chhabra, Vinita.
LB1050.6.V65 2004
428'.4'072—dc22   2003068583

British Library Cataloguing in Publication data are available from the
British Library.

Contents

About the Editors

Peggy McCardle, Ph.D., M.P.H., Associate Chief, Child Development and Behavior Branch, and Director of the research program called Language, Bilingual, and Biliteracy Development and Disorders; Adult, Family, and Adolescent Literacy in the Center for Research for Mothers and Children, National Institute of Child Health and Human Development (NICHD), National Institutes of Health (NIH), U.S. Department of Health and Human Services, 6100 Executive Boulevard, Room 4B05, MSC 7510, Bethesda, MD 20892-7510. Dr. McCardle holds a bachelor's degree in French, a doctorate in linguistics, and a master's degree in public health. Early in her career, Dr. McCardle was an elementary school teacher. She has held both university faculty positions and hospital-based clinical positions and has published articles addressing various aspects of developmental psycholinguistics as well as issues in public health. At the NIH she served as a scientific review administrator and as a senior advisor to the Deputy Director for Extramural Research in the Office of the NIH Director before joining the NICHD in 1999. In addition to serving as Associate Chief of the NICHD's Child Development and Behavior Branch, Dr. McCardle serves as Director of the branch's research program called Language, Bilingual, and Biliteracy Development and Disorders; Adult, Family, and Adolescent Literacy, which includes three interagency-funded research networks: the Biliteracy Research Network (Development of English Literacy in Spanish-Speaking Children), the Adult Literacy Research Network, and the new Adolescent Literacy Research Network. She also served as the NICHD liaison to the National Reading Panel, is on the steering committee of the National Literacy Panel for Language Minority Children and Youth, and leads or serves on various interagency working groups.

Vinita Chhabra, M.Ed., Research Scientist, National Reading Panel (NRP), National Institute of Child Health and Human Development (NICHD), National Institutes of Health, U.S. Department of Health and Human Services, 6100 Executive Boulevard, Room 4B05, MSC 7510, Bethesda, MD 20892-7510. Ms. Chhabra has a master's degree in educational psychology and a background in special education, with an emphasis in reading disabilities. She has worked in the public school system, completing cognitive and educational assessments and recommending children for special education programs. She also has worked as an evaluator at the NICHD–Yale Center for the Study of Learning and Attention, conducting assessments of children with possible reading disabilities and attention-deficit/hyperactivity disorder and evaluating reading research data at the Yale University Department of Pediatrics. She has worked with the NRP since its inception and was responsible for researching and conducting searches of literature in reading for the NRP and coordinating and editing materials for the NRP report. She is heading the dissemination activities for the NRP and works as a liaison to joint educational activities with the National Institute for Literacy and the U.S. Department of Education. In addition, Ms. Chhabra assists the NICHD's Child Development and Behavior Branch in adolescent and family literacy initiatives, with a focus in motivation in reading and literacy. She has co-authored articles dealing with reading disabilities and is completing her doctorate in educational psychology at the University of Virginia.

About the Contributors

Coleen D. Carlson, Ph.D., Associate Research Professor, Psychology Department, University of Houston, and Associate Director, Texas Institute for Measurement, Evaluation, and, Statistics, 100 TLCC Annex, Houston, TX 77204. Dr. Carlson's research interests include measurement development and psychometric evaluation, advanced statistical methods, program evaluation, and early literacy and language development in English- and Spanish-speaking students.

Jane G. Coggshall, Doctoral Candidate, Educational Administration and Policy Program, University of Michigan School of Education, 610 East University Avenue, Ann Arbor, MI 48109. After graduating with honors from Princeton University, Ms. Coggshall taught middle school mathematics for 3 years in New York City. Her research interests include organizational theory, educational policy making, and teaching improvement and assessment.

Harris Cooper, Ph.D., Professor of Psychology, Program in Education, Duke University, Box 90739, Durham, NC 27708-0739. Dr. Cooper is Professor of Psychology and Director of the Program in Education at Duke University. He is also editor of the American Psychological Association's journal *Psychological Bulletin,* which publishes research syntheses.

Linnea C. Ehri, Ph.D., Distinguished Professor of Educational Psychology, Graduate Center of the City University of New York, 365 Fifth Avenue, New York, NY 10016. Dr. Ehri's research has contributed to the understanding of how beginners learn to read and spell words. Dr. Ehri has received research awards from the American Educational Research Association, the International Reading Association, the National Reading Conference, and the Society for the Scientific Study of Reading (SSSR). She is a past president of SSSR and was a member of the National Reading Panel.

Jack M. Fletcher, Ph.D., Professor of Pediatrics and Associate Director, Center for Academic and Reading Skills, The University of Texas Health Science Center at Houston, 7000 Fannin, UCT 2487, Houston, TX 77005. For the past 25 years, Dr. Fletcher, a child neuropsychologist, has conducted research on many aspects of the development of reading, language, and other cognitive skills in children. He has worked extensively on issues related to learning and attention problems, including definition and classification, neurobiological correlates, and, most recently, intervention.

Barbara R. Foorman, Ph.D., Professor of Pediatrics and Director, Center for Academic and Reading Skills, The University of Texas Health Science Center at Houston, 7000 Fannin, Suite 2443, Houston, TX 77030. Dr. Foorman directs many federal grants, is on the editorial boards of many journals, and has been actively involved in outreach to the schools and to the general public.

David J. Francis, Ph.D., Professor of Quantitative Methods and Chair, Department of Psychology, University of Houston, and Director, Texas Institute for Measurement, Evaluation, and Statistics, Houston, TX 77204. Dr. Francis is a fellow of Division 5 (Evaluation, Measurement, and Statistics) of the American Psychological Association and a member of the American Educational Research Association, the American Psychological Society, American Statistical Association, the International Neuropsychological Society, the National Association of Bilingual Education, and the National Council on Measurement in Education. He serves on the Independent Review Panel for the National Assessment of Title I, the National Advisory Committee for the National Center for Educational Accountability, and the National Technical Advisory Group of the What Works Clearinghouse for the U.S. Department of Education and is a member of the National Literacy Panel for Language Minority Youth and Children.

Claude Goldenberg, Ph.D., Professor and Associate Dean, College of Education, The California State University, Long Beach, 250 Bellflower Boulevard, Long Beach, CA 90740. Dr. Goldenberg has taught junior high school in San Antonio, Texas, and first grade in a bilingual elementary school in the Los Angeles area. He is involved in a number of research projects focusing on Latino children's academic development, home and school influences on Latino children's academic achievement, and the processes and dynamics of school change. He is a member of the National Literacy Panel on Language Minority Youth and Children.

John T. Guthrie, Ph.D., Professor and Director of Maryland Literacy Research Center, Department of Human Development, University of Maryland, 3304 Benjamin Building, College Park, MD 20742. Dr. Guthrie investigates the reading engagement and motivation of children and adolescents. He has designed and implemented a teaching framework, Concept-Oriented Reading Instruction, that increases engagement and reading achievement for students in the later elementary grades. He has published more than 150 articles and book chapters, edited more than 10 books, and received multiple research awards.

Nicole M. Humenick, Graduate Research Assistant, Department of Human Development, University of Maryland, 3304 Benjamin Building, College Park, MD 20742. Ms. Humenick's research interests include reading motivation and engagement and literacy development.

Michael L. Kamil, Ph.D., Professor, School of Education at Stanford University, 123 Cubberly Hall, 485 Lasuen Mall, Stanford, CA 94305. Dr. Kamil was a member of the National Reading Panel and the RAND Reading Study Group and is a member of the National Literacy Panel on Language Minority Children and Youth. He is Chair of the Planning Committee for the Reading Framework of the 2007 National Assessment of Educational Progress and is the lead editor of *Handbook of Reading Research, Volume III* (Lawrence Erlbaum Associates, 2000). In addition, he has edited, authored, or coauthored more than 100 books, chapters, and journal articles.

Barbara K. Keogh, Ph.D., Professor Emerita, Graduate School of Education, and Professor, Department of Psychiatry and Behavioral Sciences, University of California, Los Angeles, School of Medicine, 760 Westwood Plaza, Los Angeles, CA 90024. Dr. Keogh's research has focused on children with learning disabilities or developmental problems and their families. She is the author of *Temperament in the Classroom: Understanding Individual Differences* (Paul H. Brookes Publishing Co., 2003).

W. Einar Mencl, Ph.D., Senior Research Scientist, Haskins Laboratories, 270 Crown Street, New Haven, CT 06511. Dr. Mencl is an experimental psychologist whose background includes work in auditory perception, cognition, and neural network modeling. His current research applies functional neuroimaging techniques to investigate brain function.

Cecil G. Miskel, Ed.D., M.S., Professor of Educational Administration and Policy, University of Michigan School of Education, 610 East University Avenue, Ann Arbor, MI 48109. With grants from the Office of Educational Research and Improvement and the Spencer Foundation, Dr. Miskel has recently completed extensive 5-year investigations of reading policy at the national level, including Reading First, and in nine states. He is particularly interested in examining what factors bring reading to the top of the policy agenda, the processes involved in producing reading policy, and the people, organizations, and their relationships active in the policy arena. Professor Miskel is now writing two books focusing on reading policy.

Louisa C. Moats, Ed.D., Director of Literacy Research and Professional Development, Sopris West Educational Services, 4093 Specialty Place, Longmont, CO 80504. Dr. Moats has written many articles, chapters, and books on the professional development of teachers of reading, including *Speech to Print* and its workbook (Paul H. Brookes Publishing Co., 2000, 2003). She has worked as an elementary school teacher, resource teacher, learning specialist, college and graduate school instructor, practicing psychologist, researcher, and writer. She heads the program *LETRS: Language Essentials for Teachers of Reading and Spelling* at Sopris West.

Robin D. Morris, Ph.D., Associate Dean for Research and Graduate Studies & Regents and Professor of Psychology, Georgia State University, Post Office Box 4038, Atlanta, GA 30302-4038. Dr. Morris has focused his scholarly and clinical work on the biological and environmental causes of reading problems, reading disabilities, dyslexia, and other learning, attentional, and developmental problems in children and adults with a variety of disorders.

Andrew C. Papanicolaou, Ph.D., Professor and Director, Division of Clinical Neurosciences, Department of Neurosurgery, The University of Texas Health Science Center at Houston, 1333 Moursund, Suite H114, Houston, TX 77030. Dr. Papanicolaou, a neuropsychologist, has conducted extensive research in human neurophysiology, studying the neural bases of language, memory, and emotions with both healthy volunteers and patients.

Sharolyn D. Pollard-Durodola, Ed.D., M.S., M.A.T., Assistant Professor, Department of Educational Psychology, Texas A & M University, College Station, TX 77843-4225. Dr. Pollard-Durodola is an assistant professor at Texas A & M University in Special and Bilingual Education Programs. Her research interests include the study of the development of early literacy in Spanish and English, vocabulary acquisition (Spanish and English), teacher preparation, and classroom observation systems.

Kenneth R. Pugh, Ph.D., Research Scientist, Yale School of Medicine; Senior Scientist, Haskins Laboratories, 270 Crown Street, New Haven, CT 06511. Dr. Pugh's primary research interests are in the areas of cognitive neuroscience and psycholinguistics. His research program examines the neurobiology of language development with a particular emphasis on reading and reading disability and employs combined behavioral and functional neuroimaging techniques. He also directs the National Institutes of Health–funded Yale Reading Study.

Kelle Reach, M.A., Doctoral Student, Department of Psychology, University of Missouri–Columbia, 217 McAlester Hall, Columbia, MO 65211. Ms. Reach is a doctoral student in child clinical psychology at the University of Missouri–Columbia.

Valerie F. Reyna, Ph.D., Director, Informatics and Decision-Making Laboratory, University of Arizona College of Medicine; Director, Division of Learning, Technology, and Assessment, Arizona Research Laboratories; and Professor of Surgery, Medicine, Biomedical Engineering, Women's Studies, Mexican American Studies, and Public Health, Arizona Health Sciences Center, Post Office Box 245031, 1620 North Warren Avenue, Tucson, AZ 85724-5031. Dr. Reyna prepared her chapter while serving as senior research advisor in the U.S. Department of Education, Office of the Assistant Secretary and the Institute of Education Sciences. She is the author of numerous publications concerning learning and cognition and is a fellow of the American Academy for the Advancement of Sciences, the American Psychological Association, and the American Psychological Society.

William M. Saunders, Ph.D., Research Psychologist, The California State University, Long Beach, 250 Bellflower Boulevard, Long Beach, CA 90740. Dr. Saunders is Director of the Getting Results Network, an external provider that helps schools improve teaching, learning, and achievement through goal setting, assessment, professional development, and administrative and teacher leadership. Dr. Saunders is also Co-principal Investigator on several research projects. His areas of focus include school change, elementary school education, assessment, and instruction for English language learners.

Timothy Shanahan, Ph.D., Professor of Urban Education and Director, Center for Literacy, University of Illinois at Chicago, 1040 West Harrison, MC 147, Chicago, IL 60607. Dr. Shanahan's research focuses on the relationship of reading and writing, school improvement, and reading assessment. He was a member of the National Reading Panel and is chair of the National Literacy Panel for Language Minority Children and Youth and the National Early Literacy Panel.

Bennett A. Shaywitz, M.D., Professor of Pediatrics and Neurology, Yale University School of Medicine, and Co-director, NICHD–Yale Center for the Study of Learning and Attention, 333 Cedar Street, New Haven, CT 06510. Dr. Bennett A. Shaywitz is a member of the Institute of Medicine of the National Academy of Sciences and recipient of the 2003 Distinguished Alumni Award from Washington University in St. Louis.

Sally E. Shaywitz, M.D., Professor of Pediatrics, Yale University School of Medicine, and Co-director, NICHD–Yale Center for the Study of

Learning and Attention, 333 Cedar Street, New Haven, CT 06510. Dr. Sally E. Shaywitz is a member of the Institute of Medicine of the National Academy of Sciences, was a member of the National Reading Panel, and is the author of *Overcoming Dyslexia: A New and Complete Science-Based Program for Reading Problems at Any Level* (Alfred A. Knopf, 2003).

Panagiotis G. Simos, Ph.D., Associate Professor, The University of Texas Health Science Center at Houston, 1333 Moursund, Suite H114, Houston, TX 77030. Dr. Simos, a cognitive neuroscientist, uses functional brain imagining techniques, such as magnetoencephalography, to study the neurological bases of language and memory functions, including reading.

Mengli Song, Ph.D., Research Scientist, American Institutes for Research, 1000 Thomas Jefferson Street, NW, Washington, D.C., 20007. Dr. Song's research interests include education policy and politics, program evaluation, quantitative methodology, and social network analysis.

Steven A. Stahl, Ed.D., Professor of Curriculum and Instruction, University of Illinois at Urbana-Champaign, 395 College of Education, 1310 South Sixth Street, Champaign, IL 61820. Dr. Stahl taught courses in reading education at the University of Illinois at Urbana-Champaign and was Co-director of the Center for the Improvement of Early Reading Achievement. Prior to pursuing doctoral studies at the Harvard Graduate School of Education, he was a special education teacher in New York and Maine. He conducted research in many aspects of reading education and had a long-standing interest in beginning reading instruction and vocabulary instruction.

Robert W. Sweet, Jr., Professional Staff Member, Committee on Education and the Workforce, U.S. House of Representatives, 2181 Rayburn House Office Building, Washington, D.C., 20515. For 20 years Mr. Sweet served as a high school teacher, educational textbook salesman, and teacher trainer for McGraw-Hill and Holt, Rinehart & Winston. In 1981 Mr. Sweet joined the Reagan Administration and held positions at the U.S. Department of Education, the National Institute for Education, and the White House. Under President George H.W. Bush he was Administrator for Juvenile Justice and was Associate Director for the Children's Bureau at the U.S. Department of Health and Human Services. He is a professional staff member on the U.S. House Committee on Education and the Workforce and focuses on improving reading instruction in the United States. He was the primary author of the Reading First initiative and helped define the term *scientifically based research*, now noted in law more than 100 times.

Joseph K. Torgesen, Ph.D., Robert M. Gagne Professor of Psychology and Education and Director, Florida Center for Reading Research, Florida State University, 227 North Bronough Street, Suite 7250, Tallahassee, FL 32301. Dr. Torgesen's research interests include instructional methods for the prevention and remediation of reading disabilities and assessment practices for the early identification of children at risk for reading difficulties.

Foreword

The chapters collected in *The Voice of Evidence in Reading Research* suggest a number of key themes that can be seen as the crucial links among their rather varied topics. Four of these themes are mentioned explicitly by at least a couple of the contributors: communication, collaboration, cumulativity, and convergence. The fifth theme, which is only occasionally hinted at in these pages but which I would argue is at least as important, is comity (social harmony). If sufficient comity can be combined with the other four characteristics of this enterprise, chances of improving reading outcomes would indeed be greatly improved.

COMMUNICATION

This entire volume itself represents a commitment to the importance of broader communication, both about the knowledge base for improving reading and about the rationale for having developed and for using that knowledge base. Such efforts are crucial, and it is reassuring that we have gotten beyond assuming that publishing papers in research journals discharges our responsibilities to communicate. As the informative chapter about policy by Mengli Song, Jane G. Coggshall, and Cecil G. Miskel makes clear, knowledge by itself is rarely enough to change things for the better. Even knowledge that is widely shared among researchers will have only limited effect. Even knowledge that is shared by researchers with policy makers will have an effect only if "receptor sites" have been prepared by heightened attention to the problems that the knowledge can help address.

In light of that insightful analysis about the contingencies determining whether research knowledge is likely to be useful, it is not surprising that much public discussion misrepresents the nature of the "reading crisis" in U.S. schools so as to prepare those receptor sites more effectively. In international comparisons, U.S. children do not on average perform badly in the early years; if international comparisons are taken as our guide, the reading crisis is one of adolescent literacy, not one of first- to fourth-grade literacy. Data from the NAEP suggest the reading crisis could as well be called the achievement gap—the much poorer performance on reading outcomes of children living in poverty, of children from ethnic and linguistic minority families, and of children attending schools in large urban districts is the most worrying finding from NAEP. Of course, the fact that many children learn to read well is not an excuse for inaction in a society committed to universal literacy, access to further education, employability, and engagement in the responsibilities of citizenship. It is, though, useful to define the challenge in a way that can best direct our resources to it.

A single-minded emphasis on poor reading outcomes has a cost, and the cost is comity. Focusing with such laserlike intensity on problems distracts us from the fact that effective reading instruction is going on in a lot of classrooms—even in many classrooms serving the children most at risk of reading failure, quite a few of whom do learn to read. Such a focus also leads to overly simplistic statements about the incompetence of teachers, or the inadequacies of teacher preparation programs, or the failure of urban school districts. Those overly simplistic statements lead, in turn, to new alignments in which teachers and those involved in teacher education, professional development, and curriculum selection—the groups that most urgently need to be recruited to participation in reform—might well conclude that they are being blamed. The challenge of effective communication to policy makers is, then, that it may involve saying things in a way that undermines effective communication with practitioners. If the policy makers are convinced, then perhaps it is now time to turn our attention to forms of communication with practitioners that invite their collaboration in reform rather than alienating them from it.

COLLABORATION

Summary reports like the National Research Council report *Preventing Reading Difficulties in Young Children* (Snow, Burns, & Griffin, 1998) or the *Report of the National Reading Panel* (National Institute of Child Health and Human Development [NICHD], 2000) represent collaboration of the most selfless sort—researchers taking time from their own research agendas to contribute to a group effort; the researchers in question are usually insufficiently recognized, often unremunerated, and sometimes attacked, as a result. Many of them extend their generous contributions to the field by then reworking and elaborating the group's findings in ongoing efforts at effective communication, as Linnea C. Ehri, Steven A. Stahl, Michael L. Kamil, and Timothy Shanahan did for Section III of this book.

In addition to collaboration among researchers, though, collaboration between researchers and practitioners was crucial to the original production of much of the research reviewed in this volume. The contributions of practitioners to the experimental research focused on by the National Reading Panel (NRP) are particularly noteworthy, since we have not as a field developed robust mechanisms to incorporate practitioners as active agents in experimental undertakings. Most often, teacher collaborators are the recipients of training in a method or an intervention, rather than co-designers of the treatment. Teachers are too often viewed as wanting answers rather than as wanting to help formulate the questions. Of course some researchers have at times truly collaborated with empowered teachers functioning as data collectors, as originators of good ideas, as professionals with a knowledge base—but that truly collaborative approach to classroom research has been more generally characteristic of qualitative researchers than of those implementing interventions. Extending the medical clinical trial metaphor that Robin D. Morris uses in Chapter 7, many teachers have been treated more like the hypodermic syringe in which the novel drug is delivered than like the doctor selecting patients for the trial, administering the treatment, keeping track of side effects, and simultaneously managing the patient's other medical problems. The need for comity dictates that we extend to the practitioner community the lessons we as researchers have learned about successful collaboration with each other: Shared agency, mutual respect, and going out together for dinner and drinks after a long day's work all help.

CUMULATIVITY

The accumulation of findings across studies is a key process in science. Science is an inherently collaborative process in that the work of any individual almost certainly builds upon that of many others and in that the value of a discovery, finding, or reinterpretation derives from its relation to the history or the consequence of that novel idea. Thus, even when scientists are not literally collaborating by carrying out research or writing together, they are collaborating intellectually by reading their predecessors' and colleagues' work, and by contributing to a public record so as to make their own work useful to current and future members of their field.

This sketch of how science works is, of course, an idealization. But it is a worthy idealization—and it is one that has been insufficiently honored within educational research. Interestingly, precisely in the area of reading there have been recurrent efforts to summarize the state of the art—starting (in the United States) with Huey's book, *The Psychology and Pedagogy of Reading,* first published in 1908. Huey documented the wide array of approaches to teaching reading that were then in use—alphabetic, phonic, phonetic, word, and sentence-based methods. Huey preferred the word-based methods because they seemed best matched to what was known about word reading at the time—given Cattell's very influential finding, published in 1886, that whole words were read as quickly as single letters. Of course we now understand why that paradoxical effect does not suggest that readers can ignore letters within words—but the basis for that reinterpretation would not emerge for another several decades. It is important to realize that whole-word methods of teaching reading were not introduced for reasons of stupidity or obstinacy: They were a response to an important finding about the reading process, as well of course as a response to dissatisfaction with the spelling methods and the phonics methods then in use. That dissatisfaction derived in part from the boring and unnatural texts they presented and in part from the observation that they (like all other methods of teaching reading ever developed) failed with a certain proportion of students.

We now understand that universal success is too high a standard to set for any reading method. As researchers, as advisors to school districts, as educators in teacher preparation or professional development programs, we need to play the probabilities. Approaches that are more likely to work with more children are the ones we want—and the accumulation of findings over different studies, carried out in different settings and by different researchers are absolutely crucial to knowing which approach to reading instruction on average works best.

Of course, we must also recognize that (as Keith Stanovich pointed out in his June 2002 address to the Society for the Scientific Study of Reading [Stanovich, 2003]) teachers do not worry about probabilities, they worry about kids. A good teacher wants a solution that works for every child in the class, and an effect size of 0.4 or 0.8 or even 1.5 is not very convincing if Sally and Sami and Sergio are still struggling. Fortunately, there are efforts underway, inventoried by Peggy McCardle and Vinita Chhabra in the final chapter of this volume, to extend the process of accumulating evidence about reading development and instruction to include second language readers, adolescents, and adults with low literacy skills. The accumulation of evidence needs, of course, to be institutionalized—so that it indeed becomes a resource not just for estimating the impacts of various treatments, but also for deciding which approaches work best with which children, and under what circumstances.

CONVERGENCE

Vinita Chhabra and Peggy McCardle emphasize in Chapter 1 the importance of converging evidence as a basis for action, and the chapters in Section II, on research methods, all similarly make the point that a single study, a single method, or a single finding is a weak basis for action. Indeed, the findings of the experimental studies reviewed by the NRP were so convincing in part precisely because they converged with findings and conclusions from prospective longitudinal studies, from correlational studies, from psycholinguistic and cognitive theory, from neurobiological approaches (such as those reviewed in Section V), and with the conclusions of experienced and effective practitioners. Multiple sources strengthen the impact of convergence, and ease the challenges of communication and of collaboration.

A valuable potential source of convergent evidence, one which we as a field have not yet developed, is the wisdom of practice. By *wisdom of practice* I mean something quite different from accumulated anecdotes—the plural of anecdote is not evidence, as the saying goes. But documentation of the specific practices that work in generating particular identifiable results, and that address the instructional priorities confirmed as important by research, could help a wider array of teachers engage in pedagogy that converges with research-based evidence. For example, nothing in the National Reading Council report (Snow et al., 1998) or the NRP report (NICHD, 2000) helps teachers design efficient and enjoyable ways of teaching digraphs, effective procedures for first graders who write a lot but cannot read, ways of organizing peer reading that keep kids engaged, ways of using children's literature to teach vocabulary, or ways of integrating spelling instruction with phonics instruction. Experienced teachers have solved all of these problems probably thousands of times. But there is no mechanism for any of their solutions to be evaluated, compared, or even communicated to other teachers who might test them. Seeking convergence across findings from different research efforts is key to developing a robust basis for drawing conclusions. Similarly, seeking convergence among teachers on the nature of methods that work within real classrooms to teach phonological awareness, phonics, fluency, vocabulary and comprehension in coherent ways within a comprehensive reading program is a key contribution to developing a robust basis for improved practice.

COMITY

Comity has too often been the missing element in discussions about reading—thus, the constant references to the "reading wars." A prerequisite to comity is the presupposition that anyone who takes the trouble to study or teach reading, from whatever perspective, is interested in improving the lives of children. I happen personally to believe that claim, which makes practicing comity a bit easier. But I would urge my colleagues who find the claim naïve, idealistic, and lacking credibility nonetheless to try for a while acting as if they believe it anyway. Comity is a public display, not necessarily a moral commitment.

In fact, I urge comity for entirely practical, not moral, reasons. As I argued above, comity is necessary if we are going to exploit the advances of communication, collaboration, cumulativity and convergence because without comity, we run the risk that communities of practitioners, whose participation in the collaborative, cumulative enterprise is crucial, will turn against it. Teachers are potential collaborators as knowledge producers, not just knowledge users. Schools of education are potential sites for accumulating knowledge, not just for critiquing it. Urban school districts are potential partners in communicating research-based information to practitioners and to parents and policy makers. Comity is a prerequisite, though.

The authors of the chapters collected in this volume have demonstrated their commitment to communication, to collaboration, to the importance of cumulativity and convergence in research. An equal commitment to comity, from them and their readers, will maximize the value of their contributions.

Catherine Snow, Ph.D.
Henry Lee Shattuck Professor of Education
Harvard Graduate School of Education

REFERENCES

Huey, E.B. (1968). *The psychology and pedagogy of reading.* Cambridge, MA: MIT Press. (Original work published 1908)

National Institute of Child Health and Human Development (NICHD). (2000). *Report of the National Reading Panel. Teaching children to read: An evidence-based assessment of the scientific research literature on reading and its implications for reading instruction: Reports of the subgroups* (NIH Publication No. 00-4754). Washington, DC: U.S. Government Printing Office. Also available on-line: http://www.nichd.nih.gov/publications/nrp/report.htm

Snow, C.E., Burns, M.S., & Griffin, P. (Eds.). (1998). *Preventing reading difficulties in young children.* Washington, DC: National Academies Press.

Stanovich, K.E. (2003). Understanding the styles of science in the study of reading. *Scientific Studies of Reading, 7,* 105–126.

A Tribute to G. Reid Lyon

At a time when children in the United States are failing to learn to read at shocking and unacceptable rates, Peggy McCardle and Vinita Chhabra have brought together many of the nation's leading reading researchers and policy makers to argue that adherence to objective scientific evidence in reading instruction and professional development can reverse this trend. *The Voice of Evidence in Reading Research* is a timely and important book. I see far too frequently the terrible consequences of reading failure for the emotional, educational, and occupational outcomes of individuals who struggle to decipher and comprehend print.

Of the millions of children with disabilities currently receiving special education in the United States, almost two thirds of them are in the category of having Specific Learning Disability. While there are 13 categories of disability that make children eligible for special education under the current amendments to the Individuals with Disabilities Education Act (IDEA), students with learning disabilities constitute the largest group of America's children with disabilities receiving special education. Within this heterogeneous group of students, reading disabilities are the overwhelming reason why students are identified as having learning disabilities and receive special education services.

Thanks to the leadership, passion, and vision of G. Reid Lyon, we now know how children learn to read and why many children fail to acquire these critically important skills. Scientists responding to his transformational leadership have amassed clear, convincing, and converging evidence to guide needed changes in classroom instruction throughout our great country. However, this research has not yet found its way into the classrooms and to the teachers who work so hard every day to educate America's children.

Dr. Lyon has elevated the importance of teaching reading, and his courage to bring rigorous science into education has brought the discussion about reading to its current emphasis on the need for teachers to use scientific, evidence-based, empirically proven practices.

This book is a major step on the journey to improve reading instruction in America's schools. President George W. Bush has relied on Dr. Lyon's advice to inform him and shape his approach to the most significant education reforms enacted in more than 35 years, including the passage of the No Child Left Behind Act of 2001. Teachers, parents, administrators, policy makers, and all who care about America's future would be well served to read this book and implement the research that has been eloquently articulated by the scientists and others who have contributed to this book.

Many of the students currently identified as having a learning disability are not, in fact, "disabled." They are students who could have learned to read if they had been taught by highly qualified, well-trained teachers using scientifically based instructional strategies. These students are casualties of an instructional system that has not relied on scientifically based instructional strategies. Dr. Lyon has helped me and many others to understand this. He has articulated to America that the right to learn to read is a fundamentally important civil right, and the failure to learn to read is a public health problem requiring our immediate attention.

In our search for what works in teaching children to read, this book is an excellent resource for those who share Dr. Lyon's passion and courage to improve reading outcomes for America's students. I have been blessed by his friendship for more than 30 years, and I am honored to have an opportunity to introduce you to his leadership. America's children deserve a better education delivered by highly qualified, well-trained teachers. This book can help us achieve that laudable goal.

Robert H. Pasternack, Ph.D.

Acknowledgments

We acknowledge the leadership of the National Institute of Child Health and Human Development (NICHD) for their enthusiasm in supporting this book. In particular we wish to thank NICHD Director Dr. Duane Alexander, a long-time supporter of research in the behavioral sciences who has also been specifically supportive of research in reading and reading instruction and the many new initiatives and interagency partnerships that have been developed in these areas since the early 1990s. We also thank Dr. Anne Willoughby, Director of NICHD's Center for Research for Mothers and Children, for her overall support of literacy research and for her excellent help in editing chapters. We acknowledge the help of Linda Lord of NICHD's Child Development and Behavior Branch; as we moved through the writing and editorial process, her support and feedback were invaluable.

Thanks also to the staff of Paul H. Brookes Publishing Co. for their thoughtful insight and support throughout the publishing process and for their patience and encouragement. Working with you was wonderful.

And finally, we thank our husbands, Commander Robert Martschinske (U.S. Navy) and Major Lewis Rhodes (U.S. Marine Corps), who gave us their constant long-distance support while they faced far more serious crises than those facing the two of us. They are our inspiration.

For more than a decade, Dr. G. Reid Lyon, Ph.D., Chief of the Child Development and Behavior Branch of the National Institute of Child Health and Human Development, of the National Institutes of Health, has demonstrated a continuous commitment to upholding the ideals of the science behind learning to read. The research developed under his leadership has been instrumental in providing children the best opportunities to be good readers and to be successful in life. Dr. Lyon has dedicated his life to making life better for children.

This book is dedicated to him and to the children who are benefiting and who will benefit from his efforts.

I

Overview

This volume has as its goal to provide a clear explanation of the methods used for reading research that can provide solid, convergent evidence on which to base practice in the classroom. In addition, this volume provides actual findings that have direct applicability in the classroom, brain research that shows changes attributable to reading instruction, and information about how policies get made and the role research can play in that arena. Section I provides the background for all of this information, outlining the history of reading research as it has affected both national legislation and national educational policies regarding how reading is taught. The chapters in this section set the stage for the rest of the volume.

In Chapter 1, Vinita Chhabra and Peggy McCardle outline the importance of research evidence of effective instructional practices and the federal role in guiding and supporting the development of such evidence. Chhabra and McCardle define the term *convergent evidence* and explain why that concept is important to those seeking to use evidence as a base for practice. They provide a brief history of the role of the National Institute of Child Health and Human Development (NICHD) in reading research and discuss two national reports that have had major legislative and policy impact: *Preventing Reading Difficulties in Young Children* (Snow, Burns, & Griffin, 1998) and the *Report of the National Reading Panel* (NICHD, 2000).

Chapter 1 also delineates the role of Dr. G. Reid Lyon, to whom this volume is dedicated, in leading research initiatives and building a federal infrastructure across funding agencies that has resulted in a convergence of evidence that can and is being translated into classroom practice. In Chapter 2, Robert W. Sweet, Jr., outlines a history of reading research and practice. He discusses the influence of this research in molding educational policy, specifically in reading, and gives both the source and definition of the term *scientifically based reading research.* Sweet, in his position as Professional Staff Member of the Committee on Education and the Workforce in the U.S. House of Representatives, is extremely knowledgeable about the interaction of research and legislation and discusses the impact of reading research on educational legislation, as well as how this research is being implemented.

REFERENCES

National Institute of Child Health and Human Development (NICHD). (2000). *Report of the National Reading Panel. Teaching children to read: An evidence-based assessment of the scientific research literature on reading and its implications for reading instruction. Reports of the sub-groups* (NIH Publication No. 00-4754). Washington, DC: U.S. Government Printing Office. Also available on-line: http://www.nichd.nih.gov/publications/nrp/report.htm

Snow, C.E., Burns, M.S., & Griffin, P. (Eds.). (1998). *Preventing reading difficulties in young children.* Washington, DC: National Academies Press.

1

Contributions to Evidence-Based Research

Vinita Chhabra and Peggy McCardle

The ability to read is both necessary and crucial for children's academic success. The importance of success in reading for lifelong achievement must not be underestimated; how well a child learns to read may determine future opportunities, including not only career possibilities but also his or her ability to accomplish the basic activities of daily life (e.g., reading a newspaper, obtaining a driver's license or identification card, paying bills). Without a doubt, teachers play a vital role in developing and nurturing children's reading skills in the classroom.

One of the most critical components of implementing effective reading instruction is using an approach that is based on scientific evidence, that is, using programs and approaches that are proven to be successful. Using scientific research in teaching children to read and write is essential for ensuring the best academic and life opportunities for our children. Dr. G. Reid Lyon has been a catalyst for progress in reading research and in promoting the implementation of research-based methods in reading instruction. He knows that if children do not learn to read, they will have difficulty succeeding in life (2001), which is one reason that this book is dedicated to him. Dr. Lyon and a cadre of researchers have worked, and continue to work, to provide reading research findings that can inform instruction.

This volume seeks to prepare members of the educational community to evaluate the quality of research studies so that they can decide for themselves which studies are trustworthy and provide sound evidence. It addresses the methods used to obtain research evidence and why those methods are important. To this end, this

3

book shows practitioners, researchers, and educators the series of pragmatic steps that have shaped reading research, reading instruction, and educational policy in the past and present and will shape future research efforts.

ROLE OF THE FEDERAL GOVERNMENT

The federal government has played a significant role in furthering the research base on reading. Rigorous research on reading development and disorders has been actively sought and supported by the National Institute of Child Health and Human Development (NICHD) and the U.S. Department of Education. The NICHD has continuously funded research on human development, learning, and behavior, including research on reading development, reading disabilities, and reading instruction, since 1965.

In 1991, when NICHD Director Dr. Duane Alexander recruited Lyon, a psychologist and a researcher, reading and reading disabilities research became a central research focus (as it continues to be not only for the Child Development and Behavior Branch that Lyon heads but also for multiple interagency partnerships led by the NICHD). These partnerships have often involved the U.S. Department of Education and more recently also have included other agencies within the U.S. Department of Health and Human Services, as well as the National Science Foundation and the National Institute for Literacy. In his years at NICHD, Lyon has succeeded in convincing many state governments, Congress, and the White House that the failure to learn to read reflects an educational and public health problem. Children who do not learn to read have a much harder time succeeding in school and in the workplace, which in turn affects emotional health, economic security, and overall well-being. And NICHD-supported research has demonstrated that by providing effective instruction, we can significantly reduce the number of individuals who cannot read.

RESEARCH SUPPORTED BY THE NATIONAL INSTITUTE OF CHILD HEALTH AND HUMAN DEVELOPMENT

There has been a great deal of research on reading over the past 20 years. Much of this reading research has been supported by the NICHD. Indeed, NICHD has led the way in establishing rigorous standards of replicability and clear, rigorous methodologies for the study of the development of reading and the effectiveness of instructional approaches and for the development and testing of reading interventions. Bringing research investigators together in informal networks where they share their research designs and methods, compare studies, and develop collaborations among the various studies on a particular topic, such as typical reading development, reading interventions, and effectiveness of instruction, has not only been a highly productive approach but also is being adopted as a standard for research in additional areas of reading and education research. As of 2004, Dr. Lyon's research program, the Human Learning and Learning Disabilities Research Program within NICHD's Child Development and Behavior Branch, supports a large network of researchers from multiple disciplines, including psychology, child development, developmental and cognitive neuroscience, education, speech and language development and disorders, pediatrics, neurology, genetics, and epidemiology. The goal of these studies is to answer these key questions: How do children learn to read? Why don't some children learn to read? And what can we do about it? These questions have been studied for 20 years through NICHD-funded research sites in North America, Europe, and Asia. The following is an overview of the significant events that have occurred under Dr. Lyon's leadership in the area of reading and reading disabilities research; each of these events has had a profound positive and continuing effect on how educators teach children to read.

Since 1985, researchers have been working to determine the factors that place children at risk for reading difficulties so that researchers and educators can better predict which children need more intensive preventive interventions to succeed in the area of reading and thereby succeed in education in general. As of 2004, this work is underway at 12 sites throughout the United States and Canada. More than 12,000 children (including more than 1,400 good readers) are being studied to develop early identification methods that will allow educators and researchers to pinpoint children during kindergarten and first grade who are at risk for reading failure.

But research enabling identification of children at risk for reading failure is only the beginning—these identification and prediction studies have provided the foundation for prevention and early (kindergarten through grade 3) intervention studies. Specifically, NICHD-supported researchers are studying the instructional procedures that can be applied to correct reading difficulties at the earliest possible time. As of 2003, more than 10,000 youngsters are participating in longitudinal early reading intervention studies in eight states (Colorado, Florida, Georgia, Massachusetts, Michigan, New York, North Carolina, and Texas) as well as in Toronto and Australia. These studies have involved the participation of more than 1,500 teachers working in more than 900 classrooms in more than 250 schools.

CONVERGING EVIDENCE

Reading research has followed real children, in real classrooms, for long periods of time. It has employed strong and rigorous research methods from a variety of disciplines, has contributed to the development of assessment strategies to identify children at risk for reading failure, and has evaluated the effectiveness of different types of instructional intervention with children who have difficulty learning to read. Researchers and teachers alike know that one size never fits all, and this is certainly true for children learning to read. That is one reason that so many children needed to be studied, in so many different places, with so many different schools and teachers. And that is why not just one study but multiple studies have been conducted. When many studies are conducted over time with a wide cross-section of children, and the studies obtain highly similar results, researchers become more confident that the findings reflect a true picture of reading development, reading difficulties, and the effects of different types of reading instruction. This converging evidence is critical as a basis of policy and in making sound instructional decisions. Teachers should not be asked to change their classroom practice based on a single study or a good idea that has not been thoroughly and rigorously tested. There is now such converging evidence for early reading instruction. That is the message that Lyon has been presenting to Congress and to state legislators, educators, and policy makers. For example, he has testified to Congress on the importance of reading and learning disabilities and the research findings on these topics many times since 1997 (e.g., *Education Research: Is What We Don't Know Hurting Our Children?*, 1999; *Hearing on Learning Disabilities and Early Intervention Strategies*, 2002; *Hearing on Measuring Success: Using Assessments and Accountability*, 2001; *Hearing on Options for the Future of the Office of Educational Research and Improvement*, 2000; *Hearing on Title I (Education of the Disadvantaged) of the Elementary and*

Secondary Education Act, 1999; *Literacy: Why Children Can't Read,* 1997; *Overview of Reading and Literacy Initiatives,* 1998).

Though much research evidence has accumulated about reading, one of the most critical aspects of research in general is the ability to examine findings from multiple studies and look at converging evidence about a particular issue (in this case, how to teach reading). In response to this need, in 1998 a National Research Council panel of experts produced a report on reading in children. This report, *Preventing Reading Difficulties in Young Children* (Snow, Burns, & Griffin, 1998), presented an overview of then current research literature and the consensus of some of the nation's top experts in reading, language development, and child development. The panel emphasized the importance of learning to read and the conditions necessary to learn to read, of providing early intervention for those children who for whatever reasons are not learning to read, and of ensuring high-quality reading instruction for all children. This information was then converted into a guide for parents, teachers, and child care providers called *Starting Out Right: A Guide to Promoting Children's Reading Success* (Burns, Griffin, & Snow, 1999). In addition, the National Research Council report captured the attention of Congress and was in fact the basis of the federal definition of scientifically based reading research, which was central to the Reading Excellence Act of 1998.

This was a very important report, but Lyon had taught the U.S. Congress to ask for data, and members of Congress wanted more specific answers to what types of instruction work for different types of learners. Congress thus asked that the NICHD, in consultation with the U.S. Department of Education, establish a second panel to answer the specific question about the most effective methods or approaches to reading instruction. This group, the National Reading Panel (NRP), worked for 2 years, and in April 2000 presented the *Report of the National Reading Panel: Teaching Children to Read* (NICHD, 2000) to Congress. The NRP presented an objective review and analysis of relevant reading research studies that passed rigorous requirements for research design, research methods, and peer-reviewed publication. Essentially, the panel's analyses determined that systematic instruction in the components of reading—phonemic awareness, phonics, fluency, vocabulary and comprehension—was effective in teaching children to read. Teaching phonemic awareness and phonics is crucially important when teaching young children to read. But, as the NRP indicated, phonemic awareness and phonics are only one part of learning to read and reading instruction. The NRP's analyses also determined that instruction in fluency, vocabulary instruction, and comprehension, is essential to good reading instruction and development. Lyon pointed out the following in testimony to the House Committee on Education and the Workforce, Subcommittee on Education Reform: "Through scientific inquiry, we have identified the elements of an optimal reading program. We know how to measure a child's progress toward reading with fluency and comprehension" (*Hearing on Measuring Success: Using Assessments and Accountability*, p. 10).

The NRP report (NICHD, 2000) set the precedent for high standards of research quality in evaluating reading research and what has been scientifically proven to work in reading instruction. As a result, the Partnership for Reading was created in 2000, an unprecedented collaborative effort of the National Institute for Literacy, the U.S. Department of Education, and the NICHD to make evidence-based reading research available to educational organizations, teachers and educators, parents, policy makers, and others with an interest in helping children learn to read well (The Partnership for Reading, 2002). Congress, in the No Child Left Behind Act of 2001 (PL 107-110), specifically recognized the Partnership, whose mandate to use evidence-based research as the basis for making decisions about reading instruction was advanced by the Partnership's production of parent and teacher documents based on work and the findings of the NRP (NICHD, 2000). The Partnership's efforts include a diverse set of public awareness, professional development, and program replication activities that follow the high standards of scientific research in reading. Through the Partnership for Reading, dissemination materials have been developed to guide teachers and parents about effective methods of reading instruction; these guides outline the skills and abilities children need to master at each stage of development (from birth through third grade) to become proficient readers (The Partnership for Reading, 2001, 2003a, 2003b, 2003c). The findings of the NRP also formed the basis for President George W. Bush's Reading First initiative, which resulted in the No Child Left Behind legislation. The NRP report is one of the most influential and controversial documents to date to guide reading instruction and educational policies.

Although it is crucial for researchers to publish their findings in peer-reviewed journals so that other researchers can replicate, confirm or reject, and build on those findings to extend knowledge, that information must also be provided to those who will use it in our nation's classrooms. It is, however, not realistic to think that reports will be written specifically for teacher implementation for every research study or even for every major national report. Indeed, teachers need to have access to those reports and peer-reviewed journals to read the information first hand, to decide for themselves how good the evidence is. That is the goal of this volume—to explain the research process and specific research findings related to literacy instruction so that teachers, reading specialists, education administrators, new researchers, and others will be better able to judge how much confidence to place in a study and to determine whether the study's methods seem to fit the research questions being asked.

OVERVIEW OF THIS VOLUME

In this volume, policy, methodological design, and classroom implementation issues related to reading research are reviewed. Section I examines the status of reading in the United States, with a particular focus on how federal policies related to reading instruction have been implemented and changed over time. Section II provides an overview and explanation of the design methods that have been used in reading research; in particular, this part of the book explains why evidence is so critical in educational practices and how to evaluate studies to determine whether solid evidence has been provided for a particular proposed method or approach to teaching reading. Section III explains the evidence-based practices that teachers are asked to implement and how the need to teach each component of reading (phonemic awareness, phonics, fluency, and vocabulary and comprehension) was established. Section IV focuses on the actual implementation of practices in the classroom, in other words, the "how to." Section V examines some of the brain bases and methodologies used for understanding processes involved in development of reading and reading disabilities. The final part, Section VI, reviews the status of research findings that are implemented in policy and how the research base and policies resulting from research continue to move forward. Thus, this volume aims to review not only relevant policies but also *how* and *why* these research-based educational policies have come to be and why it is so critical that development and implementation of educational policies based on scientifically sound research continue to be a focus in the United States.

REFERENCES

Burns, M.S., Griffin, P., & Snow, C.E. (Eds.). (1999). *Starting out right: A guide to promoting children's reading success.* Washington, DC: National Academies Press.

Education research: Is what we don't know hurting our children? Hearing before the House Committee on Science, Subcommittee on Basic Research, 106th Cong. (1999, October 26) (testimony of G. Reid Lyon). Also available on-line: http://www.nichd.nih.gov/crmc/cdb/r_house.htm

Hearing on learning disabilities and early intervention strategies: How to reform the special education referral and identification process before the House Committee on Education and the Workforce, Subcommittee on Education Reform, 107th Cong. (2002, June 6) (testimony of G. Reid Lyon). Also available on-line http://edworkforce.house.gov/hearings/107th/edr/idea6602/lyon.htm

Hearing on measuring success: Using assessments and accountability to raise student achievement before the House Committee on Education and the Workforce, Subcommittee on Education Reform, 107th Cong. (2001, March 8) (testimony of G. Reid Lyon). Also available on-line: http://edworkforce.house.gov/hearings/107th/edr/account3801/lyon.htm

Hearing on options for the future of the Office of Educational Research and Improvement before the House Committee on Education and the Workforce, Subcommittee on Early Childhood, Youth and Families, 106th Cong. (2000, May 4) (testimony of G. Reid Lyon).

Hearing on Title I (Education of the Disadvantaged) of the Elementary and Secondary Education Act before the House Committee on Education and the Workforce, 106th Cong. (1999, July 27) (testimony of G. Reid Lyon). Also available on-line: http://edworkforce.house.gov/hearings/106th/fc/esea72799/lyon.htm

Literacy: Why children can't read. Hearing before the House Committee on Education and the Workforce, 105th Cong. (1997, September 3) (testimony of G. Reid Lyon).

National Institute of Child Health and Human Development (NICHD). (2000). *Report of the National Reading Panel. Teaching children to read: An evidence-based assessment of the scientific research literature on reading and its implications for reading instruction: Reports of the subgroups* (NIH Publication No. 00-4754). Washington, DC: U.S. Government Printing Office. Also available on-line: http://www.nichd.nih.gov/publications/nrp/report.htm

No Child Left Behind Act of 2001, PL 107-110, 115 Stat. 1425, 20 U.S.C. §§ 6301 *et seq.*

Overview of reading and literacy initiatives: Hearing before the Senate Committee on Labor and Human Resources, 105th Cong. (1998, April 28) (testimony of G. Reid Lyon). Also available on-line: http://www.nichd.nih.gov/publications/pubs/jeffords.htm

The Partnership for Reading. (2001). *Put reading first: Helping your child learn to read. A parent guide: Preschool through grade 3.* Washington,

DC: Author. (Available from ED Pubs, 800-228-8813, Post Office Box 1398, Jessup, MD 20794-1398, edpuborders@edpubs.org; also available on-line: http://www.nifl.gov/partnershipforreading/publications/Parent_br .pdf)

The Partnership for Reading. (2002). *The Partnership for Reading: Bringing scientific evidence to learning* [Brochure]. Washington, DC: Author.

The Partnership for Reading. (2003a, Spring). *A child becomes a reader: Proven ideas from research for parents. Birth to preschool* (2nd ed.). Washington, DC: Author. (Available from ED Pubs, 800-228-8813, Post Office Box 1398, Jessup, MD 20794-1398, edpuborders@edpubs.org; also available on-line: http://www.nifl.gov/partnershipforreading/publications/pdf/low _res_child_reader_B-K.pdf)

The Partnership for Reading. (2003b, Spring). *A child becomes a reader: Proven ideas for from research for parents. Kindergarten through grade 3* (2nd ed.). Washington, DC: Author. (Available from ED Pubs, 800-228-8813, Post Office Box 1398, Jessup, MD 20794-1398, edpuborders@edpubs .org; also available on-line: http://www.nifl.gov/partnershipforreading/ publications/pdf/low_res_child_reader_K-3.pdf)

The Partnership for Reading. (2003c, June). *Put reading first: The research building blocks for teaching children to read. Kindergarten through grade 3* (2nd ed.). Washington, DC: Author. (Available from ED Pubs, 800-228-8813, Post Office Box 1398, Jessup, MD 20794-1398, edpuborders@edpubs .org; also available on-line: http://www.nifl.gov/partnershipforreading/ publications/PFRbookletBW.pdf)

Snow, C.E., Burns, M.S., & Griffin, P. (Eds.). (1998). *Preventing reading difficulties in young children.* Washington, DC: National Academies Press.

2

The Big Picture

Where We Are Nationally
on the Reading Front
and How We Got Here

ROBERT W. SWEET, JR.

One day, it will be as unusual to find an educational strategy, instructional practice, or program that has not been validated by scientific evidence as it is to find a doctor who uses leeches to cure a fever. This book provides hope for parents, teachers, and all who want the most effective instruction for children under their care, and it offers a road map to achieve it. This is not just an esoteric debate among researchers, professors of education, or federal, state, and local policy makers. The decisions that are collectively made will affect generations to come. We must choose wisely for the sake of our children and the future of America. Now is the time for action.

THE READING DEFICIT

It goes without saying that failure to learn to read places children's futures and lives at risk for highly deleterious outcomes. It is for these reasons that the NICHD [National Institute of Child Health and Human Development] considers reading failure a national public health problem. (*Hearing on Measuring Success: Using Assessments and Accountability*, 2001)

The first half of the 20th century was the era of the family drug store. It was before the arrival of the so-called "miracle drugs," such as antibiotics, that we all take for granted today. Robert's Drug Store, in Lisbon Falls, Maine, advertised with the catchy phrase "Robert's

Reliable Remedies Realize Results." Perhaps the store wasn't quite sure what the results would be, but it sure sold a lot of medical remedies.

Looking back on that time, one wonders just what research validation, if any, backed those remedies. That scenario is not unlike what has happened in education in the 20th century. There have been many "secret formulas" for teaching reading, but unfortunately for our children, few of these approaches have been based on sound scientific evidence.

Medicine has made giant strides since the time of Robert's Drug Store. Now clinical trials are a requirement, not an option. In November 2002, the Council for Excellence in Government sponsored a conference titled "Rigorous Evidence: The Key to Progress in Education? Lessons from Medicine, Welfare, and Other Fields." Medical researcher Dr. Stephen Goodman summed up what had been learned from the findings of clinical trials in the field of medicine. As he put it emphatically, "It is everything we know!" Although research in education has generally lagged behind medical research, in the field of reading we now have definitive answers to some age-old problems that, if applied, could transform classroom education and virtually eliminate illiteracy in America.

Why then, are more than one third of fourth-grade students unable to read simple books and an increasing number of adults unable to read a newspaper or a bus schedule? America is a free nation, whose citizens contribute through taxes or private tuition one half trillion dollars annually to educate 53 million students from kindergarten through twelfth grade. Although America has 3 million teachers, whose average salary is more than $45,000 per year and 45% of whom have degrees beyond a bachelor's degree, we are unable to teach these students to read, spell, and write effectively (National Center for Education Statistics [NCES], 2001). More than one third, and in the case of minority students, two thirds, of students in school cannot read with clarity and fluency (NCES, 1999). This is in spite of the fact that specific knowledge about how to teach these struggling students to read is now available and could be provided to every first-grade teacher in America. Why is it that the colleges of education do not arm teachers with this vital information before they enter the classroom to teach our children?

Providing answers to these questions and offering solutions are main objectives of this book. Teachers and the public have a right to know the truth about why we continue to have a reading deficit in America, and they also have a right to know that there is an effective solution.

For the latter part of the 19th and certainly all of the 20th century, there has been a raging debate over how children and adults learn to read. This includes disagreement about the most effective methods of teaching that skill. Unfortunately, many teachers today believe that being able to read is really not a skill at all but rather an innate ability that children are born with. This theory has been soundly refuted by research, yet it continues to be the dominant view perpetuated among educators (Moats, 2000).

There have always been master teachers who can teach any typically developing child to read. These teachers understand the structure of the English language and have developed techniques to convey the essential knowledge to students of all ages about the 26 letters of the English alphabet, the 44 or so sounds they represent, and the 70 or more ways to spell them (Spalding, 2003). While debates raged in academe, these master teachers just closed their schoolroom doors and did what they do best. They taught all children, regardless of age, ethnic background, poverty level, or ability, to read fluently and with comprehension.

The United States is, after all, a nation of immigrants. In the early 1800s, America was a nation of some 5 million people, hailing from a host of nations and speaking many of the tongues on this planet, most speaking the language of their homeland. When Noah Webster completed the *American Dictionary of the English Language* in 1828, he standardized a spelling system for the new nation and then developed teaching materials to assist parents, children, and teachers to quickly and effectively teach all children and adults to read, write, spell, and speak English (Unger, 1998). For more than 100 years, until the early 1900s, the *Blue-Backed Speller* and the *McGuffey Readers* were the staples of the one-room schoolhouse and were used to teach all children and adults who attended the school to read.

By the dawn of the 20th century, America's economy was bustling, and fortunes were being made by many an entrepreneur. Certainly life was simpler then, but the ability to speak, read, write, and spell a common language provided the glue that held our society together. The doors of opportunity were open to all regardless of native language, ethnic origin, or homeland.

However, from the early 19th century, a debate had been raging among educators about reading instruction. Some believed that the traditional alphabetic approach (e.g., as presented in Noah Webster's *Blue Backed Speller*) was sufficient. Other influential educators, such as Horace Mann, John Dewey, Colonel Francis Parker, and G. Stanley Hall, strongly believed in the new method or word approach that relied on sight word memory.

As American schools became publicly funded, teacher education schools known as Normal Schools, named after the European *école normale*, or model school, became the vehicle to reform public education (Ravitch, 2000). The new method, commonly referred to as the look-and-say method, became the staple of these schools, following the new progressive approach to learning advocated by John Dewey (Blumenfeld, 1973). By 1930, this new method of teaching reading had firmly taken root, and publishers quickly produced instructional materials, such as the Dick and Jane readers, to reflect its new approach.

From 1930 until the publication of Rudolph Flesch's (1955) exposé *Why Johnny Can't Read*, schools of education and the teachers they educated applied the unproven sight word approach to millions of children. By the time the federal government began to more fully fund education in the early 1960s, millions of children had missed out on learning to read fluently in the early grades, and the remedial education industry began in earnest. Annual reports emerged on how many children could not read or were "functionally illiterate." To this day, the number of students unable to read escalates.

Since 1963, much of the focus of reading instruction subsidized by the federal government has been on members of minority communities, primarily because these individuals were deemed most vulnerable and at risk. Now the percentage of minority students unable to read is greater than it was at the beginning of the 20th century. According to the U.S. Bureau of Education, in 1890 the percentage of Black Americans who could not read was 57.1%. For the next 40 years there was a steady decline in illiteracy among Black Americans, with only 16.3% unable to read in 1930 (Blumenfeld, 1996). In contrast, *The Nation's Report Card: Reading 2002* (Grigg, Daane, Jin, & Campbell, 2003) showed that 45% of Black eighth-grade students and 43% of Hispanic eighth-grade students were reading "below *Basic*," which denotes "partial mastery of prerequisite knowledge and skills that are fundamental for proficient work at each grade" (p. 9). Millions of students unnecessarily remain illiterate because the new method advocated 150 years ago remains embedded in our schools in 2004.

Learning to read was considered to be a natural process that did not need the discipline of careful instruction or attention to learning the alphabetic principle. Instead, students would be given a limited list of commonly used words to memorize in each grade, thus gradually increasing their reading vocabulary year by year (Gray, 1951). Some students were able to do this, but many could not. Because teachers used a mixture of instructional practices to supplement these new methods, the problem of limited literacy for many students who had been in school for years did not quickly manifest itself. But by mid-century, increasing numbers of students were falling behind.

In his classic exposé of the American system of reading instruction, *Why Johnny Can't Read,* written in 1955, Dr. Rudolph Flesch put his finger on the cause of illiteracy and offered a simple solution:

> Teach the children the 44 sounds of English and how they are spelled. Then they can sound out each word . . . and read it off the page. . . . The ancient Egyptians learned that way, and the Greeks and the Romans, and the French and the Germans, and the Dutch and the Portuguese, and the Turks and the Bulgarians and the Estonians and the Icelanders and the Abyssinians—every single nation throughout history that used an alphabetic system of writing. We have thrown 3,500 years of civilization out the window and have gone back to the Age of Hammurabi. (Flesch, 1955, back cover, p. 5)

By 1965 the federal government had begun subsidizing remedial reading, beginning with the Great Society programs initiated in the Johnson administration. According to the Congressional Research Service (as cited in Bailey & Mosler, 1968), federal funding for Title I of the Elementary and Secondary Education Act of 1965 (PL 89-10) was just under $1 billion, most of which was specifically targeted at improving the reading and mathematics skills of poor children. To be eligible, students had to be at least two grade levels behind in reading and mathematics. Four decades later, the total cumulative expenditure for Title I has exceeded $140 billion. With the reauthorization of the Elementary and Secondary Education Act of 1965, now called the No Child Left Behind Act of 2001 (PL 107-110), the annual appropriation for Title I included in the Act rose to more than $12 billion (U.S. Department of Education, 2001a, 2001b). Yet, the number of students unable to read at grade level in the targeted areas is now more than 50% and in some groups as high as 66% (Grigg et al., 2003).

Publishing companies have continued to sell textbooks that are based on the false premise that students learn to read naturally. Many teachers are still being trained in a method of instruction that is failing millions of students. It manifests itself as what has commonly been called the "whole language" approach, although its unique practices are similar to those used throughout much of the earlier 20th century. To disguise the true nature of this instructional methodology, it is now called "a balanced approach." Consider that nearly 3 million students are placed in the specific learning disabilities category of special education simply because they have not learned to read (President's Commission on Excellence in Special Education, 2002). Illiterate prisoners, welfare recipients unable to read simple instructions on a medicine bottle, school dropouts who have given up on school because they cannot read their assignments, immigrants who desire to learn the language of their adopted land, and special education students who are placed in lifetime career paths simply because they have not been taught to read are all being shortchanged all because the education industry refuses to adopt the clear findings of scientific research supporting specific instructional practices that could reverse the terrible blight of illiteracy in America.

Major textbook companies seem unwilling to incorporate the findings of reading research into the textbooks they sell or to spend the funds needed to validate their reading programs before they are sold to schools, although there are some notable exceptions (see *Phonics Products for School* on The National Right to Read Foundation's web site, http://www.nrrf.org/prodschl.html). At the same time, schools of education are turning out more than 125,000 teachers each year (NCES, 2001), many of whom are unprepared to teach students to read effectively.

But that is not the end of the story. There are hopeful signs on the horizon. There is a solution to the poor reading skills that have increasingly plagued America's students. To implement this solution, however, some hard choices must be made and some deeply held beliefs will need to be abandoned. It is time to act decisively, for the sake of the children.

THE CHALLENGE AHEAD

On May 25, 1961, President John F. Kennedy challenged the nation to send a man to the moon by the end of the decade. His inspiration captured the imagination and dreams of the nation, and coupled with the practical means to accomplish the task, this goal was achievable. Thus, on July 20, 1969, just 6 months ahead of the goal President Kennedy had set, Neil Armstrong stepped onto the surface of the moon with the immortal words, "One small step for man, one giant leap for mankind." Life on earth has not been the same since.

In his September 8, 2001, radio address to the nation, President George W. Bush made clear his determination to provide all the tools necessary for every child to learn to read. He set a goal that "no child should be left behind" because he or she cannot read:

> Reading is, after all, the most basic educational skill, and the most basic obligation of any school is to teach reading. Yet earlier this year, tests showed that almost two-thirds of African American children in the 4th grade cannot read at a basic level, and reading performance overall is basically unimproved over the past 10 years.
>
> The ability to read is what turns a child into a student. When this skill is not taught, a child has not failed the system; the system has failed the child. And that child is often put on a path to frustration and broken confidence.
>
> The methods we use to teach reading are critically important. First, we will have diagnostic tests to identify early reading problems in grades K through 3. Second, we will correct those problems with intervention to give children the best possible help. Third, we will support reading instruction based on sound research, with a central role for phonics. And we'll make sure that every teacher is well-trained in these proven methods.
>
> All of this can serve an important goal I have set for our country, to ensure that every child is able to read by the end of third grade. (The White House, 2001)

On January 8, 2002, the President signed the No Child Left Behind Act of 2001 into law. The good news is that for the first time, the U.S. Congress codified the essential components of reading instruction, confirming the findings of decades of research and writing them into law (The White House, 2002). Like the goal to reach the moon within a decade, the goal President Bush has set is achievable. It is a matter of will and of applying what research says about how one learns to read, as it is carefully and laboriously detailed in this book.

THREE DECADES OF RESEARCH IN READING INSTRUCTION

The findings of the research in reading instruction, much of it conducted over a 30-year period with funding from the National Institute of Child Health and Human Development (NICHD), are clear and unequivocal. Since the early 1990s, this research program has been skillfully developed and managed by Dr. G. Reid Lyon, Chief of the Child Development and Behavior Branch. The breadth and depth of this research, conducted at more than 40 sites in the United States and in other nations, has been the subject of much discussion and debate, but there has not been any serious challenge to the veracity and validity of these findings in reading research.

These findings have been independently validated by such eminent researchers as Dr. Keith Stanovich (2000) and Dr. Marilyn Adams (1990). Moreover, as early as the 1960s, Dr. Jeanne Chall (1967, 1983, 1996) had already reached similar conclusions. Later, in her book *The Academic Achievement Challenge: What Really Works in Classrooms*, published just after her death, she challenged educators this way:

> We must have some agreement as to what constitutes "enough research evidence" on an issue to conclude for or against a practice. If we do not have some understanding of what constitutes enough evidence for "best practices," we will continue to exhaust and perhaps demoralize ourselves studying the same questions over and over again. This, in a sense, is what has happened with the research on reading instruction in the early grades. . . . However, when many school systems suffered a loss in early reading achievement in the 1990s, they turned to the skills that they had rejected earlier, explaining that now it was all right to do so because we now have sufficient evidence of its value. The evidence existed from a much earlier date. (2000, p. 182)

Unfortunately, the victims of this continued educational malpractice are many, and behind the statistics are real children. Despite the overwhelming evidence on how to teach reading, many colleges of education still refuse to adequately prepare prospective teachers for the classroom with information about valid, evidence-based instructional practices.

THE NATIONAL RIGHT TO READ FOUNDATION

In 1993, The National Right to Read Foundation (NRRF; http://www.nrrf.org) was established to promote evidence-based instruction in reading. The findings of the NICHD-sponsored research studies were just beginning to be reported. NRRF made the dissemination of this information the immediate and urgent focus of its efforts to advance the cause of evidence-based reading instruction. Testimony was presented to many state legislatures, which were concerned about students' low levels of reading achievement. Many states, including Arizona, California, Georgia, Nevada, New Jersey, North Carolina, Ohio, and Texas, passed legislation to require that reading instruction that included a strong explicit, systematic phonics component be used in their schools. Many articles were written about the need for systematic instruction in phonemic awareness and phonics in publications such as *Investor's Business Daily* (Robinson, 1997), *National Review* (Ponnuru, 1999), *Parents* magazine (Levine, 1996), *Policy Review* (Sweet, 1997), and *Time* (Collins, 1997).

READING EXCELLENCE ACT

When the reading deficit was called to the attention of the nation in President Clinton's State of the Union Address in 1996 (The White House, 1996), it was the first time that reading instruction became the focus of the federal government in such a specific and high profile way. President Clinton announced that 40% of fourth-grade students could not read at grade level. His administration proposed $2.6 billion to encourage volunteers across America to read to students and thus encourage more attention to improving reading skills.

However, the House Committee on Education and the Workforce, under the leadership of then Chairman William F. Goodling, held several hearings on the national reading deficit and determined that the solution was to provide teachers with training in the most up-to-date research findings on reading instruction and to encourage them to voluntarily apply these findings in the classroom. The final proposal that passed the House with broad bipartisan support in late fall of 1998 was the Reading Excellence Act. It provided $260 million annually to states to establish programs to offer professional development and purchase instructional materials and diagnostic assessment instruments to implement what was termed *scientifically based reading instruction*. This term was first defined in law in the Reading Excellence Act and was carefully written to reflect the manner by which valid research is conducted by the National Science Foundation, the National Institutes of Health, and the National Academy of Sciences. Scholars from across the nation had been asked to review this definition, and after many months of discussion, modifications, and review, it was agreed upon. The definition, as presented in the Reading Excellence Act, follows:

The term 'scientifically based reading research'—

(A)　means the application of rigorous, systematic, and objective procedures to obtain valid knowledge relevant to reading development, reading instruction, and reading difficulties; and

(B)　shall include research that—

　　(i)　employs systematic, empirical methods that draw on observation or experiment;

　　(ii)　involves rigorous data analyses that are adequate to test the stated hypotheses and justify the general conclusions drawn;

　　(iii)　relies on measurements or observational methods that provide valid data across evaluators and observers and across multiple measurements and observations; and

　　(iv)　has been accepted by a peer-reviewed journal or approved by a panel of independent experts through a comparably rigorous, objective, and scientific review. ("Reading and Literacy Grants to State Educational Agencies," Title II (C) Sec. 2252 (5) [20 U.S.C. § 6661a])

This began a movement that ultimately led to the inclusion of more than 110 references to the term *scientifically based research* in the No Child Left Behind Act of 2001 (PL 107-110, 20 U.S.C. § 7801, Subchapter IX, "General Provisions"; *The Reauthorization of the Office of Educational Research and Improvement,* 2002).

Although the Reading Excellence Act, which became law in October 1998, was only funded for 3 years, it laid a solid foundation for Reading First, which was part of the No Child Left Behind Act of 2001. Since the definitions of *scientifically based research* and *reading* had been vetted through many meetings in both the Senate and the House, and had been agreed to by the Clinton administration, it was simply a matter of including these definitions in other legislation that followed.

NATIONAL RESEARCH COUNCIL CONSENSUS REPORT

A National Research Council consensus report, *Preventing Reading Difficulties in Young Children* (*PRD;* Snow, Burns, & Griffin, 1998), signaled an attempt to end the so-called "reading wars" that had been raging for decades. The report was supported by the NICHD and the U.S. Department of Education.

The broad consensus that came from well-respected researchers representing diverse viewpoints on reading instruction lent credibility to the report, and it has not received any credible challenges to its veracity and objectivity. The conclusion that was reached is summarized in the following passage:

> All members agreed that reading should be defined as a process of getting meaning from print, using knowledge about the written alphabet and about the sound structure of oral language for the purpose of achieving understanding. All thus also agreed that early reading instruction should include direct teaching of information about sound-symbol relationships to children who do not know about them. And that it must also maintain a focus on the communicative purposes and personal value of reading. (Snow et al., 1998, p. vi)

NATIONAL READING PANEL REPORT

Building on the conclusions of *PRD* (Snow et al., 1998), the National Reading Panel (NRP) report was published by the NICHD in April 2000. This panel was established as follows:

> In 1997, Congress asked the "[NICHD] Director, . . . in consultation with the Secretary of Education, to convene a national panel to assess the status of research-based knowledge, including the effectiveness of various approaches to teaching children to read." The panel was charged with providing a report that "should present the panel's conclusions, an indication of the readiness for application in the classroom of the results of this research, and, if appropriate, a strategy for rapidly disseminating this information to facilitate effective reading instruction in the schools." (Congress, as cited in NICHD, 2000, p. 1-1)

Dr. Donald N. Langenberg, then chancellor of the University of Maryland, chaired the panel. In his testimony before Congress after the release of the report, he stated,

> In what may be the Panel's most important action, it developed a set of rigorous methodological standards to screen the research literature relevant to each topic. These standards are essentially those normally

used in medical and behavioral research to assess the efficacy of behavioral interventions, medications or medical procedures. (*Hearing on the Importance of Literacy*, 2000)

The report of the NRP (NICHD, 2000) has had a profound impact on public policy in America. It was the most rigorous and comprehensive review of reading research literature ever undertaken, and it provided clear and unequivocal evidence that, indeed, early reading instruction could be conducted effectively for all children, if teachers were provided the training necessary to implement the findings of the research. Six NRP subgroups reviewed those studies that were considered by the panel to be methodologically sound: alphabetics, methodology, comprehension, teacher education, fluency, and technology. Copies of the full report have been sent to virtually every school district in America, and the distribution continues through the Partnership for Reading (discussed later). The significance of this report cannot be overemphasized; it became the basis of the Reading First legislation initiated by President George W. Bush and was included in the No Child Left Behind Act of 2001.

Both *PRD* (Snow et al., 1998) and the NRP (NICHD, 2000) report made it clear that a comprehensive approach to reading instruction is necessary if all children are to learn to read efficiently and effectively. The essential components include explicit, systematic instruction in phonemic awareness, phonics, fluency, vocabulary development, and comprehension strategies. Millions of dollars have been spent on research to determine the principles that efficient, effective reading instruction should include. The NRP report focused on the quality of research findings, distilled the essence of those findings, and publicized them nationally.

READING FIRST AND EARLY READING FIRST

In his election campaign, President George W. Bush made it clear that the number of students passing through U.S. schools and yet lacking the essential skill of reading was unacceptable. He made improvement in reading instruction one of his top priorities. Just after his inauguration, President Bush took action by calling a meeting at the White House, where he and the First Lady discussed with researchers and teachers from around the nation their desire that all children learn to read.

Shortly thereafter, work began on developing the Reading First and Early Reading First initiatives, and throughout 2001 the Congress debated how to structure federal legislation that would provide professional development, instructional materials, and diagnostic instruments all based upon the findings of scientifically based reading research for those schools most in need. At the same time there was considerable debate about how to encourage schools to adopt the findings of scientific research in reading instruction without imposing the use of a specific textbook. That was accomplished by establishing the essential components of reading instruction as identified in the NRP (NICHD, 2000) report as a central requirement for all schools to implement. It placed the burden on states and local school districts to select instructional materials that include all the essential components of reading instruction and to provide professional development for teachers in how to effectively teach all students the skill of reading.

The Reading First and Early Reading First legislation was written in the House early in 2001. Just before Senator Jim Jeffords switched political parties, he agreed to introduce the House version of Reading First in the Senate, and it passed through subcommittee virtually unchanged before he left his Chairmanship of the Senate Committee on Health, Education, Labor and Pensions. This made the task of reconciling the wording between the House and Senate bills in Conference a much easier task. There were many small differences that had to be worked out, but those elements of the legislation that took the principles of the NRP (NICHD, 2000) report and translated them into law remained intact. The definitions of *reading* and *scientifically based research* remained intact as well (see PL 107-110). The major differences between what was introduced in the House and in the Senate were how the money would be delivered to the states and local schools and what portion would be available for incentive grants. Inclusion of the essential components of reading instruction was a part of the bipartisan, bicameral agreement reached on the language of the legislation in the fall of 2001, and thus the conference report passed both the Senate and the House before the end of the first session of the 107th Congress.

The U.S. Department of Education has been actively working with states to implement Reading First and to ensure that their applications are consistent with the clear intent of the law. As of October 1, 2003, approximately $1.9 billion in 2002 funding had been distributed to all 50 states to implement the Reading First program. States receive Reading First grants to provide professional development to kindergarten through third-grade teachers in the essential components of reading instruction and to issue money for competitive subgrants to local school districts who use the funds to purchase screening and diagnostic assessments to determine which students are at risk of reading failure and instructional materials based upon the findings of scientifically based reading research. The FY 2004 budget submitted to the Congress includes an increase of $75 million over the FY 2003 funding levels (U.S. Department of Education, 2003). There can be no more excuses for failure.

One important component of the Reading First law is the independent external evaluation that reviews how well states and local school districts are increasing the number of students who can read fluently and evaluates whether all the essential components of reading instruction are being taught consistently and explicitly. This process will hold schools accountable for properly implementing the Reading First program. The funding for this evaluation is provided in a sufficient amount for the review to be completed effectively. Results will be used to improve the implementation of Reading First and to ensure that all students are learning to read.

NATIONAL RESEARCH COUNCIL REPORT ON SCIENTIFIC RESEARCH IN EDUCATION

Coincidental with the development of the Reading First legislation, a national discussion emerged about the meaning of the term *scientifically based research,* its impact on federal education research, and how that research could be moved from the university to the classroom. The implications of this discussion are critical because the field of education has not been noted for rigorous, quantitative research. Many within the education community have rejected the notion that research in education is comparable to research in medicine or welfare reform. (See Chapter 7 for a more detailed discussion of the parallel between medical clinical trials and education.) Indeed, the editors of the report of the National Research Council called *Scientific Research in Education* concluded,

> Ultimately, we failed to convince ourselves that, at a fundamental level beyond the differences in specialized techniques across the individual sciences, a meaningful distinction could be made among social,

physical, and life science research, and scientific research in education. At times we thought we had an example that would demonstrate the distinction, only to find our hypothesis refuted by evidence that the distinction was not real. (Shavelson & Towne, 2002, p. 51)

This National Research Council study was commissioned by the U.S. Department of Education and the National Educational Research Policy and Priorities Board. The findings of the distinguished study panel that was chaired by Richard J. Shavelson, of the School of Education at Stanford University, were one more affirmation that research in education could be done in a rigorous and objective manner, with the resulting knowledge base providing guidance for teachers, administrators, and parents who want the most effective instruction for children under their care. The report asserted that the development of a "scientific culture" within the education research community was an essential and necessary objective (Shavelson & Towne, 2002).

Development of a scientific culture implies that clear, objective methods of inquiry must be applied to answer questions and validate theories of instruction in our schools. That process is now underway. It took medicine more than one hundred years to accept the need for clinical, randomized field trials. The same must be done in education, and it must be done now. There is still considerable debate by some naysayers on whether the findings of *PRD* (Snow et al., 1998) or the NRP (NICHD, 2000) report are reliable enough to translate into classroom practice. (See Chapter 11 for a detailed discussion of the major criticisms of the NRP report.) Unfortunately, colleges of education are reluctant to accept new, scientifically valid findings if these findings run contrary to commonly held beliefs about reading instruction.

EDUCATION SCIENCES REFORM ACT OF 2002

During the 107th Congress, there were ongoing efforts to reauthorize the Office of Educational Research and Improvement. The complicated array of programs that were included under this office made it difficult for Congress to agree on significant reforms. However, under the leadership of Congressman Mike Castle and House Committee on Education and the Workforce Chairman John A. Boehner, once again Congress reached a bipartisan, bicameral agreement, even though it was an election year, to establish the Education Sciences Reform Act of 2002 (PL 107-279). President Bush signed it into law on November 5, 2002. The Institute of Education Sciences, which replaces the Office of Educational Research and Improvement, requires federally funded research to meet high standards of quality based on the definition of "scientifically based research standards" (PL 107-279, Title I, § 102[18]). The establishment of the Institute of Education Sciences, with a director appointed for 6 years, provides the opportunity for the development of a "scientific culture" as recommended by the National Research Council. More than 10 randomized field trials funded by the Institute of Education Sciences are currently underway and more are to come, with the objective of building a base of sound, reliable knowledge that is drawn from the findings of scientific inquiry using methods of research that are consistent with those employed in other disciplines.

THE PACE QUICKENS

Beginning in 2002, shortly after the No Child Left Behind Act of 2001 became law, the education community accelerated its discussion about the ramifications of evidence-based research and its implications for the future, particularly as it applies to federal programs.

In their book *Evidence Matters: Randomized Trials in Education Research* (2002), Drs. Fred Mosteller of Harvard University and Robert Boruch of the Wharton School of the University of Pennsylvania provided an historical review of randomized field trials in welfare, job training, health-risk reduction, delinquency prevention, mentoring, nurse visitation programs, voucher-based school choice programs, and class size. This excellent review raised legitimate questions about the ethical, methodological, financial, and political implications of randomized field trials, in particular about how they affect education research. There is no doubt, however, that there is a future for this kind of rigorous, systematic research. Even when ethical questions are taken into consideration, there are strong reasons to move in this direction:

> It is worth repeating the simple ethical argument in favor of experiments: if the tested policy does real harm, it is far better to find this

out in a small-scale trial rather than to inflict harm unwittingly on a large population. (Mosteller & Boruch, 2002, p. 194)

More debate on the place for randomized field trials is underway now, and that will and should continue. Certainly there is a place for descriptive studies, but attention to systematic inquiry on the impact of programs and methods of instruction in education is long overdue. A February 28, 2002, article in *The Economist* magazine argued clearly that the widely used "whole language" approach to reading instruction in the United States since the 1980s has not been benign:

A case in point is the "whole-language" approach to reading, which swept much of the English-speaking world in the 1970s and 1980s. Whole-language holds that children learn to read best by absorbing contextual clues from texts, not by breaking individual words into their component parts and reassembling them, a method known as phonics. Unfortunately, the educational theorists who pushed the whole-language notion so successfully did not wait for evidence from controlled randomized trials before advancing their claims. Had they done so, they might have concluded, as did an analysis of 52 randomized studies carried out by the U.S. National Reading Panel in 2000, that effective reading instruction requires phonics. ("Try it and See," p. 73)

In 1993 the Cochrane Collaboration (http://www.cochrane.org) was formed to make available an international registry of randomized field trials in health care research. This registry consists of a regularly updated collection of evidence-based health care databases that provide high quality information to people providing and receiving care and to those responsible for research, teaching, funding, and administration of health care at all levels. More than 300,000 experimental health care studies have been reviewed by the Cochrane Collaboration to date. In stark contrast, however, the field of education research has no comparable registry of randomized field trials in education and social science research studies.

One way to evaluate experimental studies in the social sciences, and in particular education, would be to systematically review the cumulative evidence that becomes available through randomized field trials in education and compile them in a data base with public access. A step in that direction was taken by some of the founders

of the Cochrane Collaboration with the establishment of the international Campbell Collaboration, formally inaugurated in 2000 at a
meeting of 80 scholars from four countries. According to the Campbell Collaboration web site,

> The systematic reviews of research evidence prepared and maintained
> by contributors to the Campbell Collaboration's Review Groups will
> be designed to meet the needs of those with a strong interest in high
> quality evidence on "what works." These include members of the
> public who want to keep abreast of the best evidence on the effects
> of social and educational policies and practices, service providers,
> policy makers, educators and their students, and professional research-
> ers. Campbell systematic reviews will be published electronically so
> that they can be updated promptly as relevant additional evidence
> emerges, and amended in the light of criticisms and advances in meth-
> odology. (http://www.campbellcollaboration.org)

The formation of this collaboration was an important step in
providing a cumulative source of evidence-based data that can be
used by educators and policy makers at the local, state, and federal
levels. One of the problems faced by federal lawmakers is the lack
of objective information about the success or failure of federal education programs. Too often studies such as those required by the Title
I program under the U.S. Department of Education only measure
process, not outcome. During the debate on the reauthorization of
the Elementary and Secondary Education Act in 2001, members of
Congress from both political parties complained that there was little
evidence to rely on that demonstrated outcomes, either positive or
negative. Too often attacks on programs are made with little evidence to substantiate claims, and conversely, ineffective programs
are repeatedly reauthorized without evidence of positive results to
support them. Members of Congress and their staff are continually
bombarded by theories, ideas, or products that are touted as solutions
to problems, real or imagined, but these proposals are seldom accompanied by evidentiary support. This will change only when we all
demand to see the evidence and when we all know what valid,
reliable evidence looks like when we see it.

WHAT WORKS CLEARINGHOUSE

The passage of the No Child Left Behind Act of 2001 placed more
demands on states and local school districts to produce results, particularly in improving reading and math scores for all students. In

an effort to meet these demands, the Office of Educational Research and Improvement, predecessor to the Institute of Education Sciences, quietly began to work on transforming the federal role in education research. Seminars were held on the implications of scientifically based research.

As a result, in August of 2002, the decision was made to develop a What Works Clearinghouse. This clearinghouse would

> Summarize evidence on the effectiveness of different programs, products, and strategies intended to enhance academic achievement and other important educational outcomes (U.S. Department of Education, 2002)

An $18.5 million contract was drawn up for a special joint venture to assist the What Works Clearinghouse in its goals to establish an educational interventions registry to identify potentially replicable programs, products, and practices that have proven to enhance important student outcomes and to synthesize the scientific evidence related to their effectiveness. This contract was awarded to the Campbell Collaboration, the American Institutes for Research, Aspen Systems, Caliber Associates, and the Education Quality Institute. This consortium includes nationally recognized leaders in the field of rigorous reviews of scientific evidence and will, working with the What Works Clearinghouse as its Technical Advisory Group, carry out the goals of the What Works Clearinghouse.

NATIONAL RESEARCH COUNCIL COMMITTEE ON RESEARCH IN EDUCATION

If better evidence is to be obtained, it will require additional training for individuals within the research community, more attention to systematic data collection and analysis, and a peer review system that is objective and rigorous. The National Research Council (http://www.nationalacademies.org/nrc/) created an expert panel, the Committee on Research in Education, to identify ways to improve scientific research in education. At the initial meeting in November 2002, three primary objectives were established to guide the work of this new panel:

- Advancing an improved understanding of a "scientific" approach to addressing educational problems;
- Engaging the field of education research in action-oriented dialogue about how to further the accumulation of scientific knowledge; and

- Coordinating with, supporting, and promoting cross-fertilization among NRC efforts in education research. ("The Focus and Scope of CORE," n.d.)

The report was slated to be completed sometime in 2003 and should shed additional light on the nature of education research and how all the tools at the disposal of researchers can be used in the most effective way possible to identify and improve education practices.

COALITION FOR EVIDENCE-BASED POLICY

Another essential part of improving education research is providing funds to support it. Congress has agreed, on a bipartisan basis, that funding high-quality research in education is an appropriate federal role. With the increased attention to evidence-based research since 1998, when the definition of *scientifically based reading research* was first included in the Reading Excellence Act, a number of private sector organizations are initiating action as well. One such organization is the Council for Excellence in Government. It was founded in 1983 and is nonpartisan, nonprofit, and national in scope. The board's bipartisan membership is comprised of leading policy makers and scholars from a broad range of policy areas. The Council established the Coalition for Evidence-Based Policy and held a meeting in Washington, D.C., on November 18, 2002, titled "Rigorous Evidence: The Key to Progress in Education? Lessons from Medicine, Welfare, and Other Fields." A series of recommendations was presented at the conference that merit consideration. The Coalition stated the following:

> Over the past 30 years the United States has made almost no progress in raising the achievement of elementary and secondary school students, according to the National Assessment of Education Progress, despite a 90 percent increase in real public spending per student. Our nation's extraordinary inability to raise educational achievement stands in stark contrast to our remarkable progress in improving human health over the same time period—progress which, as discussed in this report, is largely the result of evidence-based government policies. . . .
>
> Effective implementation of the scientifically-based research concept could have a major and enduring impact on the effectiveness of U.S. elementary and secondary education. . . .

Federal, state and local governments spend more than \$330 billion per year on public elementary and secondary education, and religious and independent schools spend an additional \$30 billion. This vast enterprise encompasses thousands of educational interventions (curricula, strategies, practices, etc.), the vast majority of which have been implemented without a basis in rigorous evidence. (*Bringing Evidence-Driven Progress to Education*, 2002, pp. 1–2)

The Coalition's report also made other significant recommendations for ways the federal role in education can be strengthened and improved (see http://www.excelgov.org/usermedia/images/uploads/ PDFs/coalitionFinRpt.pdf).

THE PARTNERSHIP FOR READING

In the No Child Left Behind Act of 2001, the Congress established a very important role for the National Institute for Literacy. This law directs the institute, the Secretaries of Education and Health and Human Services and the Director of the NICHD to

(1) Disseminate information on scientifically based reading research pertaining to children, youth, and adults;

(2) Identify and disseminate information about schools, local educational agencies, and State educational agencies that have effectively developed and implemented classroom reading programs that meet the requirements of [Reading First]; and

(3) Support the continued identification and dissemination of information on reading programs that contain the essential components of reading instruction supported by scientifically based research that can lead to improved reading outcomes for children, youth and adults. (§1207[a][1–3])

According to the No Child Left Behind Act, "essential components of reading instruction" include the following: "explicit and systematic instruction in phonemic awareness; phonics; vocabulary development; reading fluency, including oral reading skills; and reading comprehension" (§1208[3][A–E]).

The collaboration, known as The Partnership for Reading, is committed to implementing this charge to disseminate information. Tools are provided for teachers to evaluate their reading programs to see whether and in what ways they are consistent with the findings of research as defined in the No Child Left Behind Act. In addition The Partnership for Reading published and widely distributed *Put Reading First: The Research Building Blocks for Teaching Children to Read* (The Partnership for Reading, 2001b, 2003b). This easy-to-read booklet is an excellent primer that describes in less technical language the practical classroom application of the five essential components of reading instruction based on the findings of the NRP (NICHD, 2000) report. Two parents' guides are also available for parents who want to prepare their children for formal instruction in learning to read (The Partnership for Reading, 2001a, 2003a).

NATIONAL CENTER FOR
READING FIRST TECHNICAL ASSISTANCE

Beginning in 2004 the National Center for Reading First Technical Assistance, funded under the Reading First program will provide ongoing, high-quality technical assistance to states, districts, and schools by the country's leading experts in the implementation of scientifically based reading instruction. The National Center will provide leadership in the field of implementing scientifically based reading instruction and will coordinate with other federally funded entities (both those funded through Reading First and those funded through other sources, including the What Works Clearinghouse). According to the U.S. Department of Education key components of this project include the following:

- *High-quality resource on scientifically based reading research:* The experts connected to the National Center will be uniquely qualified to answer the challenging questions related to the implementation of Reading First. The National Center will also respond to new issues that emerge as implementation proceeds and the field advances.

- *Identification of scientifically based instructional assessments, programs, and materials:* The National Center will provide criteria for the evaluation of the scientific base and effectiveness of instructional assessments, programs, and materials and modify these criteria as the next generation of assessments and programs are developed.

- *Capacity building:* One of the areas of greatest need related to the implementation of Reading First specifically and scientifically based reading instruction in general is the need to develop expertise in this field at all levels. States, districts, and schools will not be able to depend solely on contracting out for reading experts; they will need to develop their own internal capacities. This project provides national leadership in building this vital expertise. Activities include classroom teacher education academies; academies for educators and coaches; and training for administrators at the school, district, and state levels. A critical element of this training will be instructing teachers and administrators how to monitor their own progress in implementing scientifically based reading instruction, as well as the reading progress of their students.

- *Consultative assistance to individual states and districts:* The National Center will work with individual states and districts that need assistance in identifying, selecting, implementing, monitoring, and evaluating scientifically based reading instruction. Although many issues will be common across states and districts, the National Center will provide assistance within a local context as needed. This may include connecting scientifically based reading instruction to state standards and assessments, aligning Reading First programs with other state or local reading initiatives, or addressing issues connected to a specific population of students.

- *Regional technical assistance centers:* To ensure that high-quality technical assistance is provided to states, districts, and schools across the country, the activities of the National Center will be implemented through at least three regional centers. In addition to having an area of deeper focus and specialization, each regional center will provide a broad range of services.

- *Preservice development:* The National Center will support states as they work with institutions of higher education to evaluate and improve preservice programs to ensure that potential teachers are trained in scientifically based reading research and the essential components of reading instruction.

- *Primary materials:* The National Center will be the major source of materials for use by states, districts, and schools implementing

Reading First programs. These materials may include publications, resource lists, interactive technology, videos, training modules and implementation guides.

Every possible means of support is now available to insure that Reading First is effectively implemented. This 5-year, $35 million contract is evidence that teachers who are serious about applying scientifically based reading research in the classroom have the tools to succeed.

COMPULSORY TREATMENT OF STUDENTS

It is important to note that there is certainly great complexity in how the human brain processes the printed word, providing the ability to understand its clear meaning. Teaching a child to read, however, is not a complicated process and does not require years to accomplish. The findings of decades of careful research, as chronicled in this book, provide reading teachers with a rock solid foundation upon which to build their instructional practices. There are many problems in life for which there appear to be no answers, but teaching a child to read is not one of them.

A word of caution is needed here. Our children are being given educational "treatment" of one kind or another from the first day they enter school. The fact is that the wrong instruction can harm a child, sometimes irreparably. Carol Fitz-Gibbon, a Campbell Collaboration participant from Durham University, in England, estimated that school education amounts to about 15,000 hours of compulsory treatment ("Try It and See," 2002). It is also estimated that for most children, about 100 hours of reading instruction that is solidly based on the findings of research, is sufficient to teach them to read (see, e.g., the study of the Spell Read Phonological Auditory Training method by Rashotte, MacPhee, & Torgesen, 2001).

In her booklet *Reading Made Easy with Blend Phonics for the First Grade,* master first-grade teacher Hazel Logan Loring confirmed how much time it takes to teach most students to read:

> English is a wondrous and varied means of communication, but at the heart it is simple and consistent. We can provide the basic tool that a person can develop and expand all through life to enjoy a means of communication to express the most complex thoughts and feelings,

and to understand those of fellow human beings. I found I could provide this tool adequately in its simplest form to my school children in daily half-hour sessions in the first semester of the first grade. (1980, p. 2)

Loring was able to teach her students the essential foundational reading skills in approximately 35 hours, assuming that a semester is 15 weeks long. As she explained,

By starting in September, students have gained a working knowledge of the 44 phonetic elements in the English language and an overall concept of its basic structure before winter vacation. While their knowledge may not be 100% perfect, it will be sufficient so that they can, with the teacher's continuing help as needed, utilize the phonic key to unlock 85% of the words in the English language. The other 15%, while largely regular, contain phonetic irregularities which sometimes require a little extra help from the teacher. (Loring, 1980, p. 2)

Most first-grade classes now have up to 2 hours each day for reading instruction, or a total of 150 hours in one semester. From that point on, building a vocabulary and reading to learn is a lifelong process whose purpose is the accumulation of knowledge about science, history, art, music, literature, and the world beyond humankind's vision. Reading allows the imagination to soar and creativity to blossom. But for those who miss this essential foundation, the future is bleak indeed.

NATIONAL INSTITUTE OF CHILD HEALTH AND HUMAN DEVELOPMENT

What follows now is an appropriate acknowledgement of the contribution of the research findings of the NICHD to the body of knowledge available to teachers, parents, college professors, and the general public about how to teach a child or an adult to read. This research offers a prescription for the successful treatment of our children as they are taught to read.

No reading research movement of this magnitude is without its catalyst. In looking back to the last quarter of the 20th century, there is no question that the NICHD (one of the many institutes of the National Institutes of Health), through the funding of high-quality research into the reading process, reading instruction, and reading disability, has had a profound impact on public policy and classroom practice.

The NICHD is not just an agency in Washington, D.C., dictating public policy from a lofty bureaucracy. Nor is it one person, although since 1991, the leadership of Dr. G. Reid Lyon, Chief of NICHD's Child Development and Behavior Branch, has been nothing short of astounding. Lyon has eschewed the ideological battlefield and concentrated on methodically and rigorously pursuing the scientific basis of reading instruction. And he has had the support of the U.S. Congress and the President of the United States.

The NICHD reading research network under Lyon's leadership, outlined earlier in this chapter, has continued since 1965, when the language and reading research program was initiated. By 1997, it had produced over 2,000 refereed journal articles and books. Many more have been produced since then. In the mid-1990s Dr. Lyon was called to meet with then Texas Governor George W. Bush to discuss the reading crisis in that state and what had been learned about reading development and reading instruction from the NICHD research. Questions were raised about why so many children were not learning to read. As Dr. Lyon shared the compilation of findings from NICHD's many years of research on reading instruction with Governor Bush, it became clear that there were solutions to prevent and/or remediate reading failure. Children could be taught this vital and complex skill if they were provided with the comprehensive instruction that had been clearly identified and validated through years of research. Policies were initiated in Texas during Governor Bush's administration that are beginning to pay off now. When Governor Bush became President, he called on Dr. Lyon again to help translate the research findings into public policy. Reading First and Early Reading First are based on the findings of years of research, including many studies funded by the NICHD. As of 2004, the implementation of Reading First and Early Reading First has been underway for just over 2 years. There continues to be resistance to change, but there are many signs of hope. At the beginning of the 21st century, educators and policy makers have an opportunity to reverse the decline in the reading skills for all Americans and to reach the day when every child and every adult can read with proficiency.

MOVING FROM RESEARCH TO PUBLIC POLICY

It seems appropriate to quote selected portions from testimony that Dr. Lyon has provided to Congress since the late 1990s because the impact he has had on public policy in reading instruction has been profound. His message has been clear and unequivocal, and Congress has acted upon that information with the passage of the No Child Left Behind Act and the implementation of Reading First. That is good news for America's children.

Illiteracy Is a Public Health Issue

NICHD considers that teaching and learning in today's schools reflect not only significant educational concerns but public health concerns as well. . . . Specifically, in our NICHD-supported longitudinal studies, we have learned that school failure has devastating consequences with respect to self-esteem, social development, and opportunities for advanced education and meaningful employment. . . .

The educational and public health consequences of this level of reading failure are dire. Of the ten to 15 percent of children who will eventually drop out of school, over 75 percent will report difficulties learning to read. Likewise, only two percent of students receiving special or compensatory education for difficulties learning to read will complete a four-year college program. Surveys of adolescents and young adults with criminal records indicate that at least half have reading difficulties. . . . Approximately half of the children and adolescents with a history of substance abuse have reading problems. (*Hearing on Measuring Success: Using Assessments and Accountability,* 2001)

Teachers Are Not Prepared

Unfortunately, several recent studies and surveys of teacher knowledge about reading development and difficulties indicate that many teachers are underprepared to teach reading. Most teachers receive little formal instruction in reading development and disorders during either undergraduate and/or graduate studies, with the average teacher completing only two reading courses. (*Overview of Reading and Literacy Initiatives,* 1998)

Our NICHD-supported early intervention studies have taught us that very few practicing teachers are aware of research-based best instructional practices. As such, we must consider developing comprehensive school-based training programs that are coherent, easily accessible, and meaningful to teachers. (*Hearing on Title I [Education of the Disadvantaged] of the Elementary and Secondary Education Act,* 1999)

The Findings of Scientific Research in Reading Are Clear

It must be concluded that too little education research conducted over the past century has been based on scientific principles that have proven successful in expanding our knowledge in other arenas critical to child health and development. . . . The scientific process has proven itself in every scientific discipline including physics, biology chemistry, psychology, neuroscience, medicine, and even reading development, reading disorders, and reading instruction. . . . Educational research is at a crossroads. The educational academic community can choose to be part of the modern scientific community or it can isolate itself and its methods from mainstream scientific thought and progress. (*Education Research: Is What We Don't Know Hurting Our Children?,* 1999, p. 7)

AMERICA AT THE CROSSROADS

This book provides one more body of evidence to reassure the public that we can solve one of the most intransigent educational problems in America, the inability to read. Research on reading instruction, perhaps more than any other area of education, is ready for application in the classroom. To do that will require that many deeply held beliefs be set aside in favor of what the evidence has proven beyond a reasonable doubt. It will require schools of education to convey to prospective teachers the valuable knowledge that has been accumulated in reading research and make it practical for classroom instruction. It will require that professional organizations give more than lip service to the findings of research and find ways to educate teachers already in the classroom to the value of research-based practices. It will demand that publishers revise the textbooks they present to school districts and state textbook adoption committees to make certain that reading instruction is consistent with a comprehensive approach and not based on false assumptions. It will require policy makers at local, state, and federal levels to require accountability for results, not just for process.

We stand at a crossroads in education. We can either turn a blind eye to the evidence or do an about-face and apply what we know to education practices. In a nation with as much promise as America and with more resources than any other nation on earth, we must no longer allow nearly half of our children to suffer from educational malnutrition. We have a marvelous opportunity before us. Let us seize the moment.

REFERENCES

Adams, M.J. (1990). *Beginning to read: Thinking and learning about print.* Cambridge, MA: MIT Press.

Bailey, S., & Mosler, E. (1968). *ESEA: The Office of Education administers a law.* Syracuse, NY: Syracuse University Press.

Blumenfeld, S. (1973). *The new illiterates.* New Rochelle, NY: Arlington House.

Blumenfeld, S. (1996). *The whole language/OBE fraud.* Boise, ID: The Paradigm Co.

Bringing evidence-driven progress to education: A recommended strategy for the U.S. Department of Education. Report of the Coalition for Evidence-Based Policy. (2002, November). Retrieved October 23, 2003, from http://www.excelgov.org/usermedia/images/uploads/PDFs/coalitionFin Rpt.pdf

Chall, J. (1967). *Learning to read: The great debate.* New York: McGraw-Hill.

Chall, J. (1983). *Learning to read: The great debate* (Updated ed.). New York: McGraw-Hill.

Chall, J. (1996). *Learning to read: The great debate* (3rd ed.). New York: McGraw-Hill.

Chall, J. (2000). *The academic achievement challenge: What really works in classrooms.* New York: Guilford Press.

Collins, J. (1997, October 27). How Johnny should read. *Time,* pp. 78–82.

Elementary and Secondary Education Act of 1965, PL 89-10, 20 U.S.C. §§ 241 *et seq.*

Education research: Is what we don't know hurting our children? Hearing before the House Committee on Science, Subcommittee on Basic Research, 106th Cong. (1999, October 26) (testimony of G. Reid Lyon). Also available on-line: http://www.nichd.nih.gov/crmc/cdb/r_house.htm

Education Sciences Reform Act of 2002, PL. 107-279, 20 U.S.C.

Flesch, R. (1955). *Why Johnny can't read.* New York: HarperCollins.

Grigg, W.S., Daane, M.C., Jinn, Y., & Campbell, J.R. (2003). *The nation's report card: Reading 2002.* Washington, DC: National Center for Education Statistics. Also available on-line: http://nces.ed.gov/pubsearch/pubsinfo.asp?pubid=2003521

Gray, W. (1951). *Guess who: The new basic readers.* Glenview, IL: Scott Foresman.

Hearing on measuring success: Using assessments and accountability to raise student achievement before the House Committee on Education and the Workforce, Subcommittee on Education Reform, 107th Cong. (2001, March 8) (testimony of G. Reid Lyon). Also available on-line: http://edworkforce.house.gov/hearings/107th/edr/account3801/lyon.htm

Hearing on the importance of literacy before the House Committee on Education and the Workforce, 106th Cong. (2000, September 26) (testimony of Donald N. Langenberg). Also available on-line: http://edworkforce.house.gov/hearings/106th/fc/literacy92600/langenberg.htm

Hearing on Title I (Education of the Disadvantaged) of the Elementary and Secondary Education Act before the House Committee on Education and the Workforce, 106th Cong. (1999, July 27) (testimony of G. Reid Lyon). Also available on-line: http://edworkforce.house.gov/hearings/106th/fc/esea72799/lyon.htm

Levine, A. (1996, October). Parents report on America's reading crisis. *Parents,* 63–68.

Loring, H.L. (1980). *Reading made easy with blend phonics for the first grade.* Troy, MI: Author. Also available on-line: http://www.donpotter.net/ed.htm

Moats, L.C. (2000, October). *Whole language lives on: The illusion of "balanced" reading instruction.* Washington, DC: Thomas B. Fordham Foundation. Also available on-line: http://www.edexcellence.net/library/wholelang/moats.html

Mosteller, F., & Boruch, R. (2002). *Evidence matters: Randomized trials in education research.* Washington, DC: Brookings Institution Press.

National Center for Education Statistics. (NCES). (1999). *NAEP 1998: Reading report card for the nation and the states* (NCES Publication No. 1999-500). Washington, DC: Author. Also available on-line: http://nces.ed.gov/pubsearch/pubsinfo.asp?pubid=1999500

National Center for Education Statistics (NCES). (2001, January). *Digest of education statistics 2000.* Washington, DC: Author. Also available on-line: http://nces.ed.gov/pubsearch/pubsinfo.asp?pubid=2001034

National Institute of Child Health and Human Development (NICHD). (2000). *Report of the National Reading Panel. Teaching children to read: An evidence-based assessment of the scientific research literature on reading and its implications for reading instruction: Reports of the subgroups* (NIH Publication No. 00-4754). Washington, DC: U.S. Government Printing Office. Also available on-line: http://www.nichd.nih.gov/publications/nrp/report.htm

National Research Council, Committee on Research in Education. (n.d.). *The focus and scope of CORE.* Retrieved October 23, 2003, from http://www7.nationalacademies.org/core/Focus_of_CORE.html

The National Right to Read Foundation. (n.d.). *Phonics products for school.* Retrieved October 23, 2003, from http://www.nrrf.org/prodschl.html

No Child Left Behind Act of 2001, PL 107-110, 115 Stat. 1425, 20 U.S.C. §§ 6301 *et seq.*

Overview of reading and literacy initiatives: Hearing before the Senate Committee on Labor and Human Resources, 105th Cong. (1998, April

28) (testimony of G. Reid Lyon). Also available on-line: http://www.nichd .nih.gov/publications/pubs/jeffords.htm

The Partnership for Reading. (2001a). *Put reading first: Helping your child learn to read. A parent guide: Preschool through grade 3.* Washington, DC: Author. (Available from ED Pubs, 800-228-8813, Post Office Box 1398, Jessup, MD 20794-1398, edpuborders@edpubs.org; also available on-line: http://www.nifl.gov/partnershipforreading/publications/Parent_br .pdf)

The Partnership for Reading. (2001b). *Put reading first: The research building blocks for teaching children to read. Kindergarten through grade 3.* Washington, DC: Author.

The Partnership for Reading. (2003a, Spring). *A child becomes a reader: Proven ideas from research for parents. Kindergarten through grade 3* (2nd ed.). Washington, DC: Author. (Available from ED Pubs, 800-228-8813, Post Office Box 1398, Jessup, MD 20794-1398, edpuborders@edpubs .org; also available on-line: http://www.nifl.gov/partnershipforreading/ publications/pdf/low_res_child_reader_K-3.pdf)

The Partnership for Reading. (2003b, June). *Put reading first: The research building blocks for teaching children to read. Kindergarten through grade 3* (2nd ed.). Washington, DC: Author. (Available from ED Pubs, 800-228-8813, Post Office Box 1398, Jessup, MD 20794-1398, edpuborders@edpubs .org; also available on-line: http://www.nifl.gov/partnershipforreading/ publications/PFRbookletBW.pdf)

Ponnuru, R. (1999, September 13). Fighting words. *National Review, 51*(17), 34, 36, 38.

President's Commission on Excellence in Special Education. (2002, July 1). *A new era: revitalizing special education for children and their families.* Washington, DC: U.S. Department of Education, Office of Special Education and Rehabilitative Services. Also available on-line: http:// www.ed.gov/inits/commissionsboards/whspecialeducation/reports.html

Rashotte, C.A., MacPhee, K., & Torgesen, J.K. (2001). The effectiveness of a group reading instruction program with poor readers in multiple grades. *Learning Disabilities Quarterly, 24,* 119–134.

Ravitch, D. (2000). *Left back.* New York: Simon & Schuster.

Reading Excellence Act, PL 105-277, 112 Stat. 2681-337, 2681-393, 20 U.S.C. § 6661a *et seq.*

The reauthorization of the Office of Educational Research and Improvement: Hearing before the House Committee on Education and the Workforce, Subcommittee on Education Reform, 107th Cong. (2002, February 28) (testimony of Grover Whitehurst). Also available on-line: http:// edworkforce.house.gov/hearings/107th/edr/oeri22802/whitehurst.htm

Robinson, M. (1997, January 27). Will this help Johnny to read? *Investor's Business Daily.*

Shavelson, R.J., & Towne, L. (Eds.). (2002). *Scientific research in education.* Washington, DC: National Academies Press.

Snow, C.E., Burns, M.S., & Griffin, P. (Eds.). (1998). *Preventing reading difficulties in young children.* Washington, DC: National Academies Press.

Spalding, R. (2003). *The writing road to reading.* New York: HarperCollins.

Stanovich, K. (2000). *Progress in understanding reading: Scientific foundations and new frontiers.* New York: Guilford Press.

Sweet, R. (1997). Don't read, don't tell: Clinton's phony war on illiteracy. *Policy Review,* 38–42. Also available on-line: http://www.nrrf.org/dontread-donttell.htm

Try it and see. (2002, February 28). *The Economist, 362,* 73.

Unger, H.G. (1998). *The life and times of Noah Webster: An American patriot.* New York: John Wiley & Sons.

U.S. Department of Education. (2001a). *FY 2002 budget summary: Appendix 1. Total expenditures for education in the United States.* Retrieved October 23, 2003, from http://www.ed.gov/offices/OUS/Budget02/Summary/totalexp.html

U.S. Department of Education. (2001b). *FY 2002 budget summary: Appendix 2. Detailed budget table by program (updated 9/5/01).* Retrieved October 23, 2003 from http://www.ed.gov/offices/OUS/Budget02/Summary/appendices.html

U.S. Department of Education. (2002, August 7). *U.S. Department of Education awards contract for "What Works Clearinghouse"* (Press release). Retrieved October 23, 2003, from http://www.ed.gov/news/pressreleases/2002/08/08072002a.html

U.S. Department of Education. (2003, February 3). *FY 2004 budget summary.* Retrieved October 23, 2003, from http://www.ed.gov/about/overview/budget/budget04/summary/edlite-section1.html

The White House. (1996, January 23). *State of the Union address of the President.* Retrieved October 23, 2003, from http://clinton6.nara.gov/1996/01/1996-01-23-president-state-of-the-union-address-as-delivered.html

The White House. (2001, September 8). *President emphasizes education reform in radio address.* Retrieved October 23, 2003, from http://www.whitehouse.gov/news/releases/2001/09/20010908.html

The White House. (2002, January 8). *President signs landmark education bill* (Press release). Retrieved October 23, 2003, from http://www.whitehouse.gov/news/releases/2002/01/20020108-1.html

II

Reading Research
that Provides Evidence

The Methods

Teachers are currently being asked to use scientific, evidence-based practices in their classrooms, to incorporate scientifically proven techniques into their teaching repertoires. School administrators, specialists, or master teachers also are often called upon to help make decisions for schools or school systems about what are the best curricula, instructional approaches, and programs for teaching children to read. At the same time, there is a plethora of claims that everything now available is research based. Therefore, teachers and others—school administrators, teacher educators, and new research investigators—need to be able to recognize what actually constitutes good solid evidence and to make informed decisions about research. To do this, these individuals need to know how research is done, what the differences are among research designs, and why a researcher chooses one method over another, and they must be able to recognize when a study is well done and when it is not. That is why this section discusses research methods. These chapters were specifically written to guide those who need to be able to read research literature and judge its value so that these individuals can decide for themselves or help others decide what really does constitute solid evidence and what studies they can trust regarding something as important as teaching children to read.

In Chapter 3, Valerie F. Reyna offers a brief overview of why scientific evidence is important to teaching. She answers several important questions: Why is scientific research important? Are randomized experiments really necessary? What is the role of professional experience? Fletcher and Francis (Chapter 4) explain how to ask research questions and which research methods fit which questions. They address common myths about what actually makes a study scientific and what to look for in research reports. This chapter should better enable nonresearchers to determine the potential value of research studies based on the methods used to answer the questions being posed.

Because children grow and change rapidly over time, researchers study that change over time in longitudinal studies. In Chapter 5, Keogh gives clear examples of different approaches to longitudinal research, such as prospective and retrospective studies. She discusses longitudinal studies of reading, providing guidance on what longitudinal research can and cannot tell us.

When many studies address the same topic and find the same things, a scientist can have more confidence in the findings. But it is not always easy to combine research findings across studies—often researchers do this for us, using methods specifically developed for this purpose. Harris Cooper and Kelle Reach, in Chapter 6, explain meta-analysis, how it is done, and how it can help educators and researchers make evidence-based decisions about educational issues.

The debate about evidence has often included the comparison of educational intervention research with medical clinical trials. In the last chapter in this section (Chapter 7), Robin D. Morris addresses this comparison directly, indicating why we can and should use medical models to evaluate curricula and instructional programs, and lays out clearly the characteristics of a well-done clinical trial. The chapters in this section will not only facilitate the understanding of the remaining chapters of this volume but also will enhance the reader's ability to read and judge for him- or herself the value of additional research reports.

3

Why Scientific Research?

The Importance of Evidence in Changing Educational Practice

VALERIE F. REYNA

Landmark legislation (No Child Left Behind Act of 2001, PL 107-110) has mandated the use of instructional approaches in education that are supported by evidence of effectiveness from scientific research. In this chapter, I present the rationale for this mandate and address concerns about its feasibility. The issues I discuss are foundational to educational practice and transcend the particulars of laws and politics. My aim is to demystify what is meant by *scientific research* and *scientifically based practice* and to provide some simple guidelines for judging the quality of evidence.

EVIDENCE MATTERS

Research evidence is essential for identifying effective educational practice. Research—when it is based on sound scientific observations and analyses—provides reliable information about what works and why and how it works. This information is essential to designing effective instruction and to demonstrating that it is, in fact, effective. Responsible decisions about what is good for students, therefore, require scientific evidence.

Dr. Reyna can be contacted via e-mail at vreyna@u.arizona.edu. She prepared this chapter while serving as a senior advisor in the U.S. Department of Education, first for the Assistant Secretary of the Office of Educational Research and Improvement and then for the Director of the Institute of Education Sciences. The views expressed herein do not necessarily represent those of the U.S. Department of Education.

Responsible decisions about education must rest on evidence regardless of who is making the decisions: parents, educators, administrators, or policy makers. Government has a role to play in making scientific evidence clear and comprehensible to the public, but the public must demand such evidence. Anyone who vouchsafes an opinion about policy or practice, and has the power to affect children's lives, must take responsibility for seeking out the relevant evidence.

However, evidence is not sufficient. Educational decisions are also guided by considerations other than facts, such as values, but without facts, even the best-intentioned practices can be ineffective or even harm students. One might value excellence but would still need to know the facts about which practices promote excellence in learning. Emotional appeals to support an educational program because it "promotes excellence" could be misguided if scientific evidence shows that the program is actually ineffective. Although evidence is not sufficient to make educational decisions—values are also important—it is necessary as a minimum foundation for informed decisions.

If scientific evidence is not used to make educational decisions, then what is the alternative? Historically, across many fields of practice, the alternatives to scientific evidence have been appeals to tradition, philosophy, superstition, anecdote, or intuition (the latter is are sometimes cloaked as reflective practice or reasoned professionalism; see Table 3.1). Traditions can be a sound basis for practice, but their effectiveness must be demonstrated rather than assumed. Adopting practices solely because "that's the way we have always done it" or because "it worked for the teacher down the hall" is not defensible, although these have often been the only options available to practitioners and policy makers.

Modern educational theory stresses the need for educators to reflect on their philosophies of learning. Philosophies of learning,

Table 3.1. Why scientific research?

Research is the only defensible foundation for educational practice.

If not scientific evidence, then what?

    Tradition—Is the way we always did things but that is not enough
    Philosophy—Offers appealing rhetoric but is often lacking evidence
    Superstition—Gives the illusion of correlation
    Anecdote—Is not representative
    Intuition—Is unreliable without additional study

despite an absence of evidence, can seem compellingly plausible. However, a good story (e.g., plausible speculation about how learning happens) and a true story are not the same thing. For example, based on a Rousseauian philosophy that learning happens naturally, some educators believe that children can learn to read on their own without much instruction. Unfortunately, reading, unlike speech, requires much more than a "spontaneous apprenticeship" (Miller, 1976). A philosophy or belief system is not the same as observable evidence.

Superstitions are sometimes linked to observations, as when a ballplayer hits a home run while wearing a particular shirt or cap and then superstitiously wears that "lucky" shirt or cap for the rest of the season. Humans and other animals often act as though coincidental events, such as wearing a shirt and hitting a home run, are causally connected, especially when the events involve rewards or positive outcomes (Nisbett & Ross, 1980; Schwartz & Reisberg, 1991). Thus, it can seem compellingly clear that a new educational technique caused a positive learning outcome in a student simply because the outcome followed the use of the technique, but the connection between events could be purely coincidental. (A controlled scientific experiment, discussed later in this chapter, can establish whether the connection is real.)

Anecdotes (stories about individual cases) can also be very compelling psychologically, but it is well known that single cases can be misleading and unrepresentative (e.g., Nisbett & Ross, 1980), and therefore do not constitute a reliable basis for practice. The appeal of tradition, philosophy, superstition, anecdote, and intuition *in the absence of evidence* illustrates that human judgment is not consistently objective. (Intuition is discussed in the next section.) For example, human thinking is confirmatory, so the scientific method is an artificial approach that disciplines the bias to support hypotheses rather than refute them. Trying to disconfirm hypotheses is a hallmark of the scientific method. Science assumes that humans cannot be counted on to be objective, which is why the scientific method is necessary to approach that ideal as closely as possible. These five alternatives to scientific evidence—tradition, philosophy, superstition, anecdote, and intuition—antedated the scientific method and reflect subjective as opposed to objective approaches.

In medicine, these five alternatives used to be the foundation for practice. However, modern medicine has rejected those options in favor of clinical research trials, which have dramatically improved medical outcomes. There is no reason why educational practice should not be approached with the same standards of quality and scientific rigor as those in medicine (see Chapter 7). As in medicine, educational outcomes are important in themselves; they are also vital to economic development, national security, and national standing in the world. Because these concerns are of national scope and importance, government should provide assistance in both generating research evidence to answer critical questions about effective practice and in making reliable scientific evidence available and accessible to a wide range of decision makers.

IS SCIENTIFIC RESEARCH REALLY NECESSARY?
CAN'T EXPERIENCED TEACHERS TELL WHAT WORKS?

Psychological research has shown that human intuitions about what works in learning are fallible and are sometimes exactly the opposite of what has actually been shown to be effective. For example, challenging texts, that is, those that are difficult to understand (though ultimately comprehensible), are often retained better than texts that are easy to understand (Bjork, 2002). Making material too easy can facilitate initial learning, but it inhibits the kind of long-term retention that is more practical in the real world. Research on intuitions about learning explains how ineffective practices persist despite vast personal experience (Nelson, 1998). Vast personal experience does not necessarily impart conscious insight into what works. That is, teachers might believe a practice works despite directly observing children's repeated failure using that practice. Research has shown that learners themselves believe that certain strategies are effective despite personal experience with failure using those strategies (and vice versa). Intuitions about learning are often based on cues (e.g., the text is easy to understand) that turn out to be unreliable. Intuitions can be unreliable even about straightforward outcomes, such as dying. For example, well-intentioned medical practitioners bled patients for centuries without realizing that the practice was harmful. Learning outcomes are more subtle and difficult to track. Thus, intuitions can seem like a direct window on the mind, but they should not be the basis of classroom practice unless they have been rigorously studied. The unreliability of intuitions based on personal experience is why scientific research is a necessity, not a luxury (Reyna, 1993).

ISN'T PROFESSIONAL EXPERIENCE VALUABLE?

Professional experience is very valuable. Sometimes scientific evidence is simply unavailable and professionals must use their best judgment about what works. Professionals' intuitions about what works, based on years of classroom experience, might be the only source of ideas about how to help a particular student. As I have discussed, despite being based on experience, those intuitions could nevertheless be wrong. However, conditions can be created that help make professional intuitions more reliable. In general, conditions that make learning more effective for students also make learning from experience more effective for teachers. These conditions include the following:

- *The opportunity to observe the outcomes of practice:* Valid assessment of learning is key. Without valid feedback about whether students have learned, it is impossible to know whether practices have been effective.

- *The opportunity to observe the connection or contingency between specific practices and specific outcomes:* Many factors affect a student's academic achievement. In order to know what works, the practitioner has to be able to uniquely connect what he or she did to student outcomes.

One reason that research is necessary is that everyday life jumbles up causes and effects, making it very difficult to trace back from outcomes to what we did that might have caused those outcomes. Is the student's learning due to the textbook, the instruction, parental involvement, motivation, or some combination of these factors? Many factors are operating in a student's life at the same time. In everyday life, it is difficult to tell what caused what. That is why we do experiments.

WHAT TYPES OF QUESTIONS DO EXPERIMENTS ADDRESS?

Experiments answer the question of what works, but they can also be used to test hypotheses about how it works. A set of hypotheses about how something works is called a *process* model. For example, it was known for years that aspirin worked to reduce pain, but there was no viable process model of how that effect was achieved. Process models of learning explain *how* successful practices and techniques work. Such process models of learning, derived from experimental evidence, are most commonly found in cognitive and developmental psychology (e.g., Bjorklund, 1995; Schwartz & Reisberg, 1991; Siegler, 1991). A process model might explain successful educational outcomes in terms of motivation, attention, storage of presented information in memory, retrieval of that information from memory, or other learning processes. Process models of learning have been applied occasionally in education, but fulfilling the goal of substantially increasing student learning, as emphasized in the No Child Left Behind Act of 2002, requires everyone who makes important decisions about students to be familiar with the process of learning. In order to improve academic achievement, the *science of learning* must be treated as an essential element of educational practice and policy, regardless of the academic discipline of those who conduct research on learning and regardless of other parochial concerns that interfere with helping students learn.

ARE RANDOMIZED EXPERIMENTS REALLY NECESSARY?

The National Academy of Science's Committee on Scientific Principles for Education Research (Shavelson & Towne, 2002) distinguished three types of questions: description, causation (what works), and process or mechanism (see Table 3.2). Randomized experiments are *essential* for determining causation (what works). In a classic between-groups randomized experiment, students are randomly assigned to groups (say, by flipping a coin). If there are

Table 3.2. Different questions, different methods

Mechanism (process): How does it work?
  Method: Randomized experiments that test hypotheses about mechanism
Causation: Does it work?
  Method: Randomized experiments
    Gold standard for determining cause and effect
  Method: Quasi-experiments with statistical controls
    Can use existing school data
    Can be misleading about cause and effect
Description: Tell about it (observations).
  Method: Correlational studies without statistical controls
    Often misleading about cause and effect
  Method: Case studies
    Single case study can lead to mistaken generalizations

enough students in each group, the experimental group (the one getting the practice that you want to evaluate) and control group (the one getting something you want to compare that with, say standard practice) are comparable in every way except the difference in practice. Under these conditions of truly random assignment to groups and adequate sample size in each group, randomization ensures that any difference in outcome can be uniquely attributed to the difference in practice. Any other method for answering the question of what works is inferior because it does not allow you to infer cause and effect. Within-subjects designs with all students getting all interventions, and in which the order in which interventions are given is counterbalanced, are equally sound designs that similarly control for alternative explanations of outcomes. In a within-subjects experiment, each participant in the study acts as his or her own control.

Nonexperimental studies that show only evidence of correlation between practices and outcomes are much better than no evidence at all, but it is important to remember that correlations do not prove causation. Correlational studies identify practices that are more likely to be effective (especially if obvious counterexplanations are controlled for statistically). These studies can also be foundational to the next step, such as an experimental study. History, however, provides examples of sophisticated quasi-experiments (correlational studies with statistical controls) that turned out to be misleading once the results of experimental studies were known. One recent example is hormone replacement therapy, which was once thought to protect postmenopausal women from heart attack and strokes. Randomized experiments, however, revealed that this treatment actually increased the risk of heart attack, stroke, and certain kinds of cancer. No matter how carefully a researcher attempts to control for counterexplanations, there may always be other, uncontrolled factors that are actually responsible for the outcomes in a quasi-experiment or other correlational study. Thus, schools should make use of their voluminous data linking instructional programs and student achievement (i.e., the data that they already have in local files) and statistically control for factors such as socioeconomic status, but should reserve some doubt about cause-and-effect conclusions.

Unlike true experiments, under the best of circumstances— systematic, objective observation—descriptive studies permit no conclusions about cause and effect or educational effectiveness. Statistical survey data, when properly sampled, can be used to make descriptive statements about the world, such as the percentage of students who do not graduate from high school or who speak a language other than English at home. Description can point out the existence and magnitude of problems that are worthy of further study. Descriptive data are consistent with many different speculations about cause and effect, and speculations are not evidence. Descriptive data also do not provide evidence about the processes or mechanisms of learning; again, speculations are not evidence. For example, classroom observations made under the best of circumstances (with systematic and reliable observers) do not even permit generalization to other classrooms. Unless a representative sample of classrooms is observed systematically and reliably, descriptive statements (let alone cause-and-effect statements) that apply to one classroom may not apply to others. Other chapters in this book cover such topics as how researchers reliably measure various constructs (see Chapter 6), how internal and external validity are achieved (see Chapter 4), and how researchers try to control various factors in order to be able to conclude that some factor played a causal role in the outcome (see Chapter 4).

AREN'T RANDOMIZED CONTROL TRIALS UNETHICAL? IF YOU THINK A PRACTICE IS EFFECTIVE, HOW CAN YOU MORALLY WITHHOLD IT FROM THE CONTROL GROUP?

Some critics of experimental methods claim that it is unethical to withhold treatment from control groups, even when the "treatment" is an unproven intervention (see Table 3.3). Randomized experiments

Table 3.3. Concerns about experiments

Many want access to a new program; random assignment to groups is fair.

Not everyone can have access to a new intervention immediately, so random initial access (e.g., flipping a coin to see who gets into which group) is fair. Some (experimental group) get access now; the rest (control group) get standard practice and receive the new intervention later.

Do not use placebo (no-treatment) controls.

What would you use instead of new program? Use that standard practice for control group.

First, do no harm.

It is not clear that new is always better, so experimental study is necessary before administering a new intervention.

The experiment stops if significant difference is found between the control group and the experimental group receiving the new, targeted intervention.

often use standard practice (what students would get if the new practice were not adopted) as the control condition. Therefore, all groups are getting something; instruction or treatment is not being withheld from anyone. An alternative design is to use a wait-list control group. Resources usually do not permit everyone to get a new practice right away, regardless of research considerations. Some students get it first, while others must wait. Randomly determining who gets the new practice now and who gets it later (and therefore serves as the control group now) is a fair and unbiased way to decide how to allocate limited resources.

Conducting randomized experiments *is* the ethical choice. Ignorance, especially confident ignorance, is unethical. Although we might think that a practice is beneficial, not only could we be wrong, but research has also shown that we are often systematically wrong (based solely on our intuitions) about what is actually beneficial. When patients have a deadly disease, randomized experiments are used to determine whether a medical practice is effective. Even when life and death are at stake, and we believe a new treatment might be effective in saving lives, society recognizes that the randomized experiment is the only way to tell for sure. Just as standard practices can turn out to be harmful, new practices can also turn out to be ineffective or harmful, despite appearing to be promising. This is why it would not be ethical to simply give the new treatment, be it medical or educational, to everyone without testing it first. Medical trials are stopped as soon as the treatment has been shown to be superior (or harmful) based on specific guidelines, and similar stopping rules for educational experiments can be adopted.

IS KNOWING WHAT WORKS GOOD ENOUGH?

Knowing what works in educational practice is not enough. It is important to know how and why something works in order to generalize that practice effectively to other contexts and populations. You cannot tell whether a study's findings will apply generally just by whether the study mimics what happens in real classrooms. For example, laws of learning that apply very broadly across different groups of people and different study materials were discovered under artificial conditions using artificial materials: nonsense syllables (Schwartz & Reisberg, 1991). Ebbinghaus first described these laws of learning in 1885, and they remain as true today as when they were discovered. For example, distributed study is more effective than massed study for long-term retention; spreading your studying out over time, with breaks in between, is more effective than cramming the same amount of studying together without breaks. Basic research about *mechanisms of learning* is necessary to understand what is important to maintain about a practice across contexts to achieve the same effects and what is inconsequential and thus can be varied. Knowing the mechanisms of learning tells you whether different populations are likely to be affected in the same way as those originally studied. Children, classrooms, neighborhoods, cultures, and school contexts differ; researchers and educators need to understand how much can be changed before the effectiveness that may have been found for a specific practice or program is diminished or limited. However, superficial differences among children, classrooms, neighborhoods, cultures, and school contexts do not guarantee differences in mechanisms of learning. Despite the intuitive appeal of the familiar slogan "one size does not fit all," some educational practices are broadly effective; they can be generalized widely across contexts and populations. This is why underlying mechanisms of learning, not superficial differences, are key. Knowing how and why something works answers the question, "Does this instructional practice generalize and to whom?" For other important problems facing the nation, such as curing cancer, experience has shown that basic research on mechanisms of effectiveness pays off in producing more and better treatments. The same rules of science apply to educational practices.

CONCLUSIONS

Educational research could be greatly improved and made more relevant to classroom practice by adhering to some venerable rules of scientific methods (Campbell & Stanley, 1963; Cronbach, 1982):

1. Use interventions that are based on empirically tested theories of learning and cognition.

2. Study a sufficient number of students; an increase from a few students to 25–30 per group may be sufficient to ascertain statistically significant differences between groups.

3. Use random assignment or well-matched comparison groups.

4. Use a clearly specified intervention, and monitor its implementation.

5. Use valid and reliable outcome measures.

Parents, practitioners, policy makers, and other decision makers can use these five rules to weed out much of the cant and commentary that passes for educational research (see Table 3.4). As the discussion about anecdotes and intuitions reveals, methodologically sound evidence about what works is not a luxury. Such evidence is a necessity because many common beliefs about what is helpful for students have turned out to be tragically wrong, just as many common beliefs in medicine turned out to be wrong when they were tested scientifically. We cannot afford to lurch from fad to fad in education while students are left behind, ill equipped to participate in a democracy or hold a meaningful job. Scientific evidence provides the opportunity for cumulative progress that builds systematically on what is known in order to help individual students achieve success and to develop an educated populace, which is essential for national security and prosperity.

Table 3.4. What we don't know and why: Common shortcomings of research studies in education

Many studies produce no real evidence of effectiveness because of poor designs and lack of controls.

- A common mistake is to use descriptive methods to answer causal or process questions.
- Control groups are virtually absent from the educational literature, despite urgent need for effectiveness data.
- Many studies simply gather few data, unsystematically, with multiple sources of bias.

    Only a few students are studied, observations are subjective and not validated, or there is no control group or a poorly matched one.

Many studies that produce evidence of effectiveness still have shortcomings.

- Philosophies and practices differ across effective programs: Lack of grounding of hypotheses in empirically based theory
- Not clear what about the program is effective and what is counterproductive: What is the "active ingredient" that creates effectiveness and what could be thrown away.
- Measures are not standardized.

Many studies are not published or are not reported in peer-reviewed journals.

- Expert peer reviewers can catch mistakes and weed out unsupported claims.

Many studies have no objective evidence of student learning.

REFERENCES

Bjork, R.A. (2002). *Bridging the science of cognition to educational research and practice.* Invited address presented at the pre-application meeting of the Cognition and Student Learning Grant Program, February 19, 2002.

Bjorklund, D.F. (1995). *Children's thinking: Developmental function and individual differences* (2nd ed.). Pacific Grove, CA: Brooks/Cole.

Campbell, D.T., & Stanley, J.C. (1963). *Experimental and quasi-experimental designs for research.* Boston: Houghton Mifflin.

Cronbach, L. (1982). *Designing evaluations of educational and social programs.* San Francisco: Jossey-Bass.

Miller, G.A. (1976). *Spontaneous apprentices: Children and language.* New York: Seabury Press.

No Child Left Behind Act of 2001, PL 107-110, 20 U.S.C. §§ 6301 *et seq.*

Nelson, T.O. (1998). Metacognitive food for thought in educational theory and practice. In D.J. Hacker, J. Dunlosky, & A. Graesser (Eds.), *Metacognition in educational theory and practice* (pp. ix–xi). Mahwah, NJ: Lawrence Erlbaum Associates.

Nisbett, R., & Ross, L. (1980). *Human inference: Strategies and shortcomings of social judgment.* Upper Saddle River, NJ: Prentice-Hall.

Reyna, V.F. (1993). Theory and reality in psycholinguistics. *Psychological Science, 4,* 15.

Schwartz, B., & Reisberg, D. (1991). *Learning and memory.* New York: W.W. Norton.

Shavelson, R.J., & Towne, L. (Eds.). (2002). *Scientific research in education.* Washington, DC: National Academies Press.

Siegler, R.S. (1991). *Children's thinking* (2nd ed.). Upper Saddle River, NJ: Prentice-Hall.

4

Scientifically Based Educational Research

Questions, Designs, and Methods

JACK M. FLETCHER AND DAVID J. FRANCIS

Since the late 1990s, there has been extensive discussion of the scientific basis of educational research. The most common level of discourse characterizes "real" science as quantitative, and pits this against research utilizing observational or qualitative methods. Research in education is considered scientific if it represents an experiment in which some manipulation occurs and the effect of this manipulation is evaluated by formal assessments of student performance. The most common context for this interpretation of "real" science involves large-scale field trials in which, for example, two methods for teaching reading are compared and their effectiveness is evaluated by collecting scores on tests of students' reading ability. In contrast, nonscientific research is depicted as qualitative, reflecting use of descriptive or observational methodologies, especially ethnographies and case studies. When these methods are used to evaluate the effectiveness of two reading programs, the focus is on the impact on the teacher and students. The researchers might interview teachers or students, observe lessons, and provide narrative summaries of the researchers' perception of their experiences and the success of the programs.

This qualitative–quantitative dichotomy is false and a poor characterization of the nature of the scientific enterprise. In this chapter, we discuss the nature of scientific research in education. The starting point for this discussion is the recent report from the National Research Council, *Scientific Research in Education*, which addresses these issues in some detail (Shavelson & Towne, 2002; see also Feuer,

Towne, & Shavelson, 2002, and Levin & O'Donnell, 1999). Using this report as a guide, we begin with a brief discussion of the nature of scientific inquiry and principles of science. Then we address common misconceptions about scientific inquiry in education, noting specifically that the principles that make research "scientific" are the same in education as in other areas of science, including the natural sciences. We describe features that are unique to research involving humans, including educational research. Some of the factors that have diluted the role of scientific research in education are addressed. We conclude with a discussion of how scientific research in education can be fostered for the benefit of students, teachers, and schools.

WHAT IS SCIENTIFIC INQUIRY?

The principles of scientific inquiry are universal and can be found in all areas of human inquiry. The single most important part of scientific research is the question that leads to the investigation. Methods alone do not make a particular study scientific. In many discussions of quantitative versus qualitative research in education (see Levin & O'Donnell, 1999), there is a mixing of mechanisms of observations (qualitative versus quantitative) and the design of the study (conditions under which observations are made and participants are assigned to those conditions). The key to strong inference in any research is the design, not the method of observation. Depending on the nature of the underlying question, one approach to inquiry may lend itself to stronger inferences than another; that is, one approach may do more to reduce uncertainty about the phenomenon of interest in the population of interest. However, the fact that certain approaches might be better suited to answering a particular type of question does not render other approaches unscientific. Across a broad array of approaches, studies can be scientific if they adhere to basic principles of scientific inquiry. It all starts with the question to be investigated, which leads to the method of observation and design and a set of reasoned inferences.

Scientific research is a process of reasoning based on the interplay of theories, methods, and results. A scientist develops a theory and uses it to formulate hypotheses. To evaluate the hypotheses, a study is designed. The methods used in the study depend on the hypotheses, and these methods result in findings. The scientist then integrates what is found from this particular study into the body of knowledge that has accumulated around the research question. As such, scientific research is a cumulative process that builds on understandings derived from systematic evaluations of questions, models, and theories.

The knowledge base in scientific inquiry accumulates both vertically through increases in knowledge and horizontally as knowledge is integrated from different areas of investigation. In this respect, there may be research specific to a discipline in which knowledge grows vertically, reflecting the sheer accumulation of findings and understanding about a particular question. For example, knowledge has accumulated rapidly over the past 30 years around the question of how children learn to read (Fletcher & Lyon, 1998; Stanovich, 2000). The key question has involved the relation of language and reading (Liberman, Cooper, Shankweiler, & Studdert-Kennedy, 1967). Knowledge about this question accumulated slowly at first but accelerated more rapidly as the results of different studies began to show concurrence around answers to the initial set of questions. What was critical in the reading area was the horizontal accumulation of knowledge, in which researchers asking different questions about reading, usually in other disciplines, began to obtain results that could be integrated with research on reading development. For example, studies of the heritability of reading problems, brain function, and cross-cultural factors all suggested that phonological processing and its relation to oral language development were important components of understanding reading in each of these discipline-specific areas.

Many of the recent advances in understanding reading have reflected attempts to integrate this information across disciplines. But the accumulation of scientific knowledge can be a slow, plodding, and circuitous process (Shavelson & Towne, 2002). Often an area seems to have advanced, but the initial insight or set of findings has not held up to repeated scrutiny. Thus, scientific knowledge is developed and honed through the scientific enterprise, reflected in a community of scientists who interact around particular questions. This enterprise involves specific attempts to refute and contest specific findings, to replicate studies, and to look for convergence across different sources of information. It is important to recognize that this process is expected and built into the training of many scientists, as it is fundamental to the scientific process itself. The scientific process does not encompass the contesting of findings based on *ad hominem* arguments, which occurs when criticisms become personalized and the researcher and/or his or her motivations become the focus of objections rather than the research (see discussion in Stanovich, 2000). More often, critique of research fulfills an important part of the scientific enterprise and is not personalized. Science advances through careful examination and criticism, including examination of theory, method, findings, interpretation, and assumptions. More generally, scientific knowledge emerges through long-term, sustained efforts involving systematic replication and refutation. The need to sustain research efforts is true in all areas of science. Although specific insights may lead to a new area of investigation or even to new theory, even these types of insights have a basis in the accumulating body of knowledge.

FUNDAMENTAL PRINCIPLES OF SCIENTIFIC RESEARCH

In the National Research Council report *Scientific Research in Education* (Shavelson & Towne, 2002), a series of principles that apply to all areas of science were systematically outlined (see Table 4.1). These principles are discussed in the subsections that follow.

Empirical Investigation of Significant Questions

The principles of scientific research begin with the need to focus on a question that is considered to be significant and that can be answered *empirically*, that is, through systematic observation and the accumulation of evidence. Scientific knowledge results when a consensus forms around the interpretation of that evidence (Krathwohl, 1985). To reiterate, the most fundamental principle of scientific inquiry is the central importance of the question. Everything else that occurs in scientific research reflects the question. In fact, in advising on

Table 4.1.   Six guiding principles of scientific research

Pose significant questions that can be investigated empirically.
Link research to relevant theory.
Use methods that permit direct investigation of the question.
Provide a coherent and explicit chain of reasoning.
Replicate and generalize across studies.
Disclose research to encourage professional scrutiny and critique.

Reprinted from Shavelson, R., & Towne, L. (Eds.). (2002). *Scientific research in education* (p. 52). Washington, DC: National Academies Press.

statistical analyses, John Tukey, the world-renowned statistician, pointed out that an approximate answer to the right question is preferable to an exact answer to the wrong question (Tukey, 1962). Strong methodological inquiry on questions that are not important may be technically competent but will not contribute to scientific inquiry.

The empirical underpinnings of scientific investigation distinguish scientific inquiry from other forms of inquiry. Although philosophers debate the meaning of the term *empirical*, Shavelson and Towne defined it as knowledge "based on experience through the senses, which in turn is covered by the generic term observation" (2002, p. 58). Thus, by *empirical* we mean the attempt to systematically collect observations that can be verified, replicated, and otherwise scrutinized. Other academic disciplines, such as history, or other areas of human inquiry, such as psychoanalysis, have features that appear scientific. But because many of the methods of observation cannot be consistently verified, refuted, or otherwise scrutinized, these areas of inquiry are not adequately characterized as scientific. For example, in history or psychoanalysis, the fundamental test of truth is whether the explanation makes sense. Historians or psychoanalysts may rely on citations of manuscripts, reports of patient experience, or even records from the time of interest. But because these observations are collected in a way to make them coherent explanations of events that have already occurred, it is difficult to describe them as entirely scientific. They are less like science than what occurs in biology or even social and behavioral sciences like education or psychology. However, it would be a mistake to characterize history or psychoanalysis as completely nonempirical or nonscientific as the difference is really one of degree. Thus, in history or psychoanalysis, some data are collected that are empirical, such as an authentic document from the time period of interest in history or a transcription of a dream in psychoanalysis. Similarly, in archeology or physical anthropology, some data are empirical, such as evidence of approximate date through radiocarbon dating or DNA evidence obtained from a tissue sample. But much in these fields of study rests on the construction of an explanation from data that are often incomplete and on the surface, difficult to refute or replicate. An experiment cannot be designed that would verify the researcher's inference, though ideas might be generated that lead to alternative explanations or to reexamination of the data in light of new data. Insofar as the events of interest have occurred in the past, the events do not lend themselves to direct observation or control by the researcher. The inability of the researcher to control the events of interest makes refutation of explanations more ambiguous in these areas of inquiry.

Research Coupled with Theory

Another fundamental principle of science involves the importance of linking research to theory. Scientific research is typically guided by a conceptual framework, model, or theory that helps generate the research question. The model also helps to suggest potential answers to the questions that emerge. Thus, the theory drives the questions that are asked, which in turn determine the design, methods for data collection, and the interpretation of the results. These designs and methods typically permit direct investigation of the question. The evaluation of any research study depends on all of these major elements: the value of the question, the suitability of the research design or data collection methods to answering the question, and the scientific rigor with which the methods are applied and the study is carried out. The relationship of the question and methodology must be explicit and well justified. Any report of the study provides a detailed description of the method, participants, measures, data collection procedures, and data analyses to permit replication and a determination of the extent to which claims about knowledge can be supported.

It is important to recognize that these procedures are followed in all types of research, including, for example, research that is completed by an anthropologist using ethnographic methods of observation. In ethnographic research, there is again a focus on the question. The question drives the design and methods of observation. Rigorous observational research is concerned with the interpretive accuracy of observation—achieving over time a progressively closer "fit" between the observer's patterns of attention on the one hand and on the other hand the crucial details of action and meaning that are manifested in the research site. The observer visits the site repeatedly to ascertain (in repeated learning trials) how to see and interpret what is going on there. The assumption is that over time, the researcher's attention will focus increasingly on those details of action and meaning that are relevant to those being observed. This is why the overall duration of observation in a field site is considered an index of data quality.

One test by which the researcher attempts to verify the accuracy of his or her honing in on locally relevant details in the research setting is *triangulation* across data sources that vary in their epistemic status: For example, the researcher's observation notes may be compared with interview comments from research subjects and with site documents (e.g., memos, announcements on bulletin boards, minutes of meetings). Consistency of information on a given topic or line of interpretation across these diverse data sources provides evidence that the observer's observational notes and the inferences drawn from them were not simply idiosyncratic. In other words, the process of analytic data triangulation demonstrates what Donald Campbell called *convergent validity* (see the discussion in Erickson, 1986). Thus, the researcher uses a variety of approaches in identifying information concerning phenomena of research interest, and there is an attempt to summarize, organize, and/or tabulate this information in a way that demonstrates the validity of the analytic conclusions that have been drawn in the study.

Methods Permitting Direct Investigation

In more strictly scientific inquiries, the design permits a manipulation of the conditions of observation based on the theory in question in a way that allows measurement of the impact of the manipulation on the observations themselves. In such cases, the ability of the researcher to manipulate and control the conditions of observation and to measure the impact of those manipulations reduces ambiguity about the interpretation of the results and reduces uncertainty about phenomena of interest. But even in these cases, the critical element is the question of interest, which in turn dictates the design and methods of data collection. In science, research questions must be asked in a way that allows for empirical investigation. Descriptive or observational research in social sciences is empirical even when an experimental manipulation is not part of the research. This type of research can be replicated and generalized, depending on the question and the methodology.

Chain of Reasoning

In scientific research, a coherent and explicit chain of reasoning is provided that is subject to replication. In evaluating this chain of reasoning, it is important to consider whether the assumptions that underlie any inferences were clearly identified and justified. Similarly, the standards used to evaluate the relevance and coherence of the evidence must be explicit. Strong claims require that alternative hypotheses be identified, evaluated, and either retained as plausible or rejected as untenable based on the standards of evaluation established for the field. It should be clear to other scientists how links between the actual data and the research question were made. The design must be appropriate for the question under investigation, which is to say that the design must be capable of supporting the kinds of inferences that the question engenders. (Research design is discussed more later in this chapter and in Chapter 3.)

Replication and Generalization

Note that it is impossible to conduct research without concerns about how the phenomena of interest are observed and about the replicability or repeatability of such observations. These concerns are measurement issues, even though these terms may be interpreted or operationalized somewhat differently in qualitative and quantitative research settings. Similarly, even studies of a single individual involve implicit classifications that would lead to the selection of a particular individual for study. The data are empirical and involve decisions about measurement and classification. Such features characterize both quantitative and qualitative research in education and in other sciences.

　　Scientific research is completed in ways that permit others to repeat the study to see whether they find similar results (replication) or to manipulate aspects of the design to try to predict the outcome (generalization). Thus, for example, a researcher might repeat a reading intervention study in a district similar to the original district in which the study was completed (replication). Alternatively, the researcher might implement the reading intervention study in a district where the learning context is quite different (e.g., all schools receiving Title I funding) to see whether the results are similar (generalization). These different kinds of studies would be repeated around the initial study's claims of knowledge.

Disclosure of Research

Another important principle of scientific inquiry is that the findings of each study would be scrutinized and evaluated by the scientific community through presentations and papers, the latter typically critiqued by groups of scientists, representing peer review. These principles are apparent in all areas of science, including education. Peer review is a critical part of the scientific process (Towne, Fletcher, & Wise, in press). It has two primary purposes, one of which is to ensure that the highest quality research is identified. The other purpose is to help develop a field through systematic and public review of research findings. Peer review is an important part of the professional development of scientists. A strong peer review process helps ensure that the quality of research is continually scrutinized and that a field develops strong scientists. The purpose is not to criticize or guess the motives of the scientist or to simply "shoot down" research. It is to subject the research to scrutiny and the possible refutation of the results as an ongoing part of the scientific enterprise. In this respect, peer review must be as objective and reliable as is possible for an enterprise that involves human interactions and personal investments in the enterprise itself.

DESIGN CONSIDERATIONS

As discussed in Chapter 3, the report from the National Research Council (Shavelson & Towne, 2002) distinguishes between three general classes of research design whose use depends on the question:

1. Description (What is happening?)

2. Cause (Is there a systematic effect?)

3. Mechanism (Why or how does the effect occur?)

Regardless of what type of design is used, its role in science is to help answer questions as validly, objectively, accurately, and economically as possible (Kerlinger, 1979). In the subsections that follow, we discuss a number of issues related to the design of educational research studies.

Importance of Research Design

The heart of research design is the assessment of variability in the phenomenon of interest. Whenever a phenomenon is observed, it is measured in some way. The measurements will not be uniform but instead will vary across the observations. Some of the variability is systematic, reflecting a pattern that exists naturally (e.g., reading levels in first graders) or the effects of some manipulation (e.g., reading intervention) or contextual variable (e.g., schools that are receiving Title I funds versus schools that are not) or related factors. With any research design, the goal is to 1) maximize systematic variability, or the variability that might result from the variables of interest or the specific treatment manipulation; 2) minimize error variance, which might result from weaknesses in the observation tool or failure to deliver the treatment in precisely the same way to all participants; and 3) control extraneous or unknown sources of variability, such as characteristics of study participants or school context, that would lead to variability in study outcomes unrelated to the treatment. Kerlinger (1979) referred to these as the MAXMIN-CON principle of experimental design—maximize systematic variance, minimize error variance, and control extraneous variance.

Researchers operationalize the MAXMINCON principle in their research design through the selection of subjects, conditions, and measures and through implementation of the design conditions. A research design involves specification of the means by which the units of observation (e.g., students, teachers, classrooms, schools, districts) come to be observed—in other words, the selection of those students, teachers, or classrooms that the researchers want to study must be clearly explained. Decisions must be made whether to restrict the sampling to subjects homogenous with respect to certain characteristics or whether to allow those characteristics to vary in the sample and to control for those characteristics during analysis. These two strategies allow investigators to control extraneous sources of variability in their research. In addition, the design involves the conditions under which observations are made and the method of assigning students or teachers to the conditions being studied (e.g., a new instructional program or approach, the conditions used as controls or comparison groups). Thus, the questions that the researcher asks about the design involve how participants are selected from the population of interest, the conditions under which the participants are to be observed, the number of times and context in which the participants are observed, and how the participants are assigned to the conditions of observation. This is true, for example, both for a randomized clinical trial of the efficacy of two reading programs and for an ethnographic study of the impact of different reading programs on teachers and students in a particular school.

Validity

The reason that the design is so important is that the quality and rigor of the design supports the quality of inferences that will be able to be made from the study. To reiterate, knowledge results when there is a consensus of judgments among experts in a field that a particular relationship exists (Krathwohl, 1985). The accumulation of knowledge about a particular phenomenon is determined by the set of knowledge claims for which consensus has been established. These knowledge claims develop from the collection of individual studies conducted in an area. Scientific knowledge differs from knowledge in other areas because the consensus is formed based on the interpretation of evidence from different studies that involve direct, replicable observations (Krathwohl, 1985). This consensus depends on rules that are universal and designed to prevent the formation of arbitrary consensus. Although numerous rules have been put forward, three basic rules that govern the scientific process are integrity, skepticism, and replication. The chain of evidence that emerges around a specific knowledge claim depends upon the research design. There are very specific issues that must be addressed in evaluating a research design. These are usually summarized in terms of internal and external validity, statistical conclusion validity, and the construct validity of cause and of effects (Cook & Campbell, 1979).

For *internal validity*, the critical question is the extent to which the design reduces uncertainty about the relationship of cause and effect. In any research design, the goal is to understand whether a change in behavior, an outcome, is caused by a specific activity or intervention. Even in descriptive studies, the reason for conducting the study is to eventually understand what causes the phenomenon, even when the design itself does not have adequate internal validity to support a strong causal claim. Thus, it is common to evaluate different kinds of research designs according to the number of assumptions that must be made to support strong causal conclusions (Shavelson & Towne, 2002). From the viewpoint of internal validity, investigators can make the strongest claims about causation if it is possible to randomly assign participants to conditions because randomization reduces the number of assumptions that must be made (Levin & O'Donnell, 1999). If participants cannot be randomly assigned to conditions, then additional assumptions have to be made. For example, in a study of the effects of two different reading programs, if students, teachers, and schools cannot be randomly assigned to the curricula, then it is possible that a source of bias will emerge.

In designs in which full randomization is not possible, often called *quasi-experimental designs*, the effects of the intervention may be confounded with how participants are assigned to conditions. For example, if all schools in the study that are high performing receive one intervention and all schools that are low performing receive the other intervention, the outcomes of the study might be predicted simply by knowing the characteristics of the schools. To deal with this, a researcher would likely want to ensure that the two curricula were implemented both in some of the high-performing and in some of the low-performing schools, and that there was not bias in terms of deciding how these assignments were made. If the assignment of the schools was negotiated, for example, based on teachers and principals agreeing to use a certain program and random assignment was therefore not possible, then the best possible design would be a quasi-experimental study. In this design, it would be important to identify and measure possible sources of bias. The internal validity of a quasi-experimental study is not as strong as the internal validity of a study in which students, teachers, and schools are randomly assigned to interventions because there is a stronger possibility that unknown sources of bias are present (Levin & O'Donnell, 1999). The possible presence of unobserved sources of bias is just one reason studies need to be replicated so that convergent evidence can be obtained.

External validity involves the extent to which the findings of a study can be generalized. In other words, are the findings of the study specific to the situation in which the research occurred, or can the explanation be generalized to other instances? The key evidence for generalizability comes from systematic evaluation of the study design with respect to sample selection and the choice of settings and instruments, and from systematic evaluation of study results to ensure that they are replicable across the settings, participants, and assessments that make up a specific study. If findings are specific to one setting or if factors are operating in the study design that influence the selection of participants and interventions, then the results of the study may have weak external validity and poor generalization.

Balancing internal and external validity in the same study can be difficult. The two tend to work against each other. As noted previously, randomization is the key to strong internal validity because it allows chance to enter a study in a controlled fashion. Randomization is also the only method of controlling all possible extraneous variables, but randomization does not mean that the groups will be equivalent on all possible variables—it just means that the groups will be equivalent in the long run. It does not rule out all threats to internal validity, but it does produce immunity to the most common threats. In addition, randomization does not ensure external validity, although it helps eliminate sources of bias that are specific to the design that might affect internal validity. In fact, if the study is conducted in a highly controlled fashion with highly selected participants, schools, and interventions, internal validity may be high but external validity could be reduced.

In some situations, random assignment is not possible. It could be impractical; excessively expensive; unethical; or artificial, resulting in low external validity. The interest of the researcher may be only in a particular group, such as language-minority students or girls. Sometimes random assignment is not ethical. No one would suggest randomly assigning humans to smoke or to drink alcohol, which is why most of the research on smoking and alcohol use is quasi-experimental. What is important is that a variety of research designs be employed, reflecting different kinds of questions and the integration of information across these different domains of inquiry.

Statistical conclusion validity was introduced by Cook and Campbell (1979) as a way of characterizing the statistical treatment of the data that is collected within a study with a particular research design. The critical issue is whether the statistical evidence implies a "true" relationship, not necessarily a cause–effect relation. Statistical evidence, in and of itself, is incapable of establishing relations among putative causes and effects, but statistical evidence provides the support for inferences about cause and effect. Cause–effect relations are scientific conclusions that are built up from statistical conclusions. For scientific conclusions to be supported, the data must be analyzed correctly. In the absence of valid statistical conclusions, the prospects for reaching valid scientific conclusions about relations of interest are most remote. The threats to statistical conclusion validity are straightforward. They involve, not surprisingly, answering the wrong the question or using the wrong statistics for the right question. In studies in which a large amount of data is collected without a strong question and the data are simply analyzed to show statistically significant results, there is weak statistical conclusion validity. Similarly, if the conditions under which the statistical tests are to be applied are violated, statistical conclusion validity may be threatened. Finally, having a sample size that is small relative to the amount and quality of the data that are collected may lead individuals to reject potential explanations and relations. Investigators often fail to reach valid statistical conclusions because they do not fully understand statistical inference, do not understand the limitations of a statistical procedure (e.g., sensitivity to violations of assumptions), or fail to take into account the operating characteristics (power and robustness) of their procedures and designs.

Construct validity of cause and of effects are concepts introduced by Cook and Campbell (1979) in their original extension of Campbell and Stanley (1963). These terms describe aspects of validity related to the labeling of interventions and outcomes, respectively. These terms simply refer to the evidence that interventions and treatments are accurately measured and specified. In discussing the results of experiments, researchers label interventions and outcomes in theory-relevant terms. Evidence that can be brought to bear on the accuracy of these labels with respect to the underlying (latent) dimension(s) captured by the intervention operations and the underlying (latent) dimension(s) captured by the outcomes stands as evidence of the construct validity of cause and of effects. In some expositions of the experimental research literature, construct validity of cause and of effects are both viewed as aspects of external validity because they help to delineate the dimensions along which the results of the study can be expected to be generalized. If the evidence is weak, the external validity of the study will be weakened, even if the study has strong internal validity.

Summary of Design Considerations

By way of summary, it is helpful to think about five questions pertinent to research design. These questions are relevant to internal, external, and statistical conclusion validity:

- Who will be assessed or observed?

- What will be assessed or observed?

- When and how often will assessments or observations take place?

- Under what conditions will assessments or observations take place, and what are the means by which units and conditions become paired (assignment)?

- How will the assessments or observations be analyzed to address the research questions?

In the end, the goal is to have a research design that is appropriate for the questions and in which internal validity, external validity, and statistical conclusion validity all support the inferences made by the researcher.

PUBLIC SCRUTINY

As mentioned in the section of this chapter on research principles, another significant consideration in science is the importance of reporting research publicly in journals and other scientific venues (Feuer et al., 2002). This encourages professional scrutiny, critique, and replication or generalization. Criticism is essential to the scientific process. Scientists argue about findings, and the contentiousness of science is often surprising to outside observers. But scientists typically understand that the extent to which new findings can be reviewed, contested, and accepted or rejected by other scientists depends upon accurate, comprehensive, and accessible reporting of results. This includes clear specification of the question, the design, the methods of data collection, and the chain of reasoning.

Peer review is at the heart of scientific inquiry. Other scientists typically evaluate the claims that their colleagues make, whether in journals, grant applications, or other venues. Critics of peer review often point out that it is not "perfect review" (Finn, 2002). This observation is highly relevant. If the community is not ethical and open, it will subject itself to claims of cronyism. In addition, peer review can be conservative and should not be the sole determinant of the allocation of funds (Chubin, 1994; Horrobin, 2001). But any enterprise involving human endeavors must maintain strong ethical principles, and the participating individuals need to be as objective as possible. Others have also raised issues that concern the reliability of judgments made by peer reviewers, and these concerns are used to improve the peer review process (Cicchetti, 1991). So, although peer review is not perfect, better ways of making decisions about knowledge claims have not been identified.

COMMON MISCONCEPTIONS OF SCIENTIFIC QUALITY AND RIGOR IN EDUCATIONAL RESEARCH

What Is Scientific Research?

In recent years, education research has been barraged by different claims about what is scientific and what is not (Feuer et al., 2002). For example, some have claimed that experimental research is more "scientific" than descriptive or qualitative research. This claim is not correct. As we indicated previously, the type of design or method alone does not render the study scientific. Rather, scientific inquiry reflects a chain of reasoning. The type of design or method that is used depends upon the research question. It is entirely possible to conduct rigorous, scientific studies that are largely descriptive or qualitative. Studies are scientific when

1. There is a clear set of answerable questions that motivate the design

2. The methods are appropriate to answer the question

3. Competing hypotheses can be refuted on the basis of evidence

4. The studies are explicitly linked to theory and previous research

5. The data are systematically analyzed with the appropriate tools

6. The results are made available for review and criticism

Similarly, it is sometimes claimed that research in education is fundamentally different from research in the natural sciences. This claim is also not true (Feuer et al., 2002). Scientific research occurs in education, psychology, biochemistry, astrophysics, cultural anthropology, mathematics, and other areas. In these different disciplines, scientists seek understanding of phenomena such that the understanding conforms to a set of rules for defining evidence and knowledge. Science poses empirical and testable hypotheses that can be refuted. Studies are designed to test and rule out competing hypotheses. The observational methods are linked to theory and can be publicly assessed. There is recognition of the importance of designs, and there are criteria for judging the quality of research, such as internal and external validity and statistical conclusion validity, regardless of what discipline is conducting the research.

Distinct Features of Education Research

Education research does have some distinct features (Shavelson & Towne, 2002) that set it apart from other forms of scientific inquiry. Any research involving humans presents a unique set of considerations that are not present in the natural sciences. It is difficult to design and implement research studies that have strong internal and external validity when the research involves humans and when it concerns phenomena that are multiply determined and that differ widely across human participants. Conducting research on humans in schools means that there are likely to be many threats to internal and external validity. The level of certainty of the research conclusions therefore is often lower than in the physical sciences. Research on humans often requires more observations with larger samples to reach certainty because the measurement tools involve observations of human behavior. Human behavior is observed with greater error than are phenomena in the physical sciences. This is inherently a measurement problem that makes it especially important to understand the measurement characteristics of the instruments that are being used to collect the observations and the extent to which there are errors in those measurements.

Context has an influential role in educational research, which can also complicate the research and its interpretation and can make results and conclusions less generalizable across other contexts. Therefore, researchers in education make greater use of statistical methods but also rely more heavily on systematic replication to understand the limits of a particular scientific inference. Converging evidence across different contexts is critical. This means that several studies, which may use different methods but all of which are investigating aspects of the same problem, contribute to the same inference.

Educational research is also relatively young, having occurred only for approximately the past 100 years. In fact, the history of research in the social and behavioral sciences generally is still a relatively recent phenomenon (Shavelson & Towne, 2002). Those who have attempted to do research have been battered by differences in beliefs about the value of scientific research. Skepticism concerning the value of scientific research in education has been present since the very beginning. To illustrate, consider this recommendation about the results of an extensive evaluation of different reading curriculums conduced by the National Institute of Education, a precursor to the federal education research agency now known as the Institute of Education Sciences. It was suggested that the National Institute for Education should emphasize ethnographic and case study approaches because the audience is "teachers [who don't] need statistical findings of experiments to decide how best to teach children" and because these teachers "decide such matters on the basis of complicated public and private understandings, beliefs, motives, and wishes" (Glass & Camilli, 1981).

Although there have been a variety of opinions about the particular scientific research in education that teachers would or would not find useful, simply emphasizing a particular research design will not help them reach the best understanding about certain questions. If a teacher wants to know, for example, which methods of reading instruction work best with certain types of students, the teacher, like the scientist, is best informed by studies that use research designs that address the question of what works best. In this respect, the studies would involve random assignment as much as possible and at different levels in the model: child, teacher, classroom, school, and district. If the question involves a description of how the students and teachers felt when the new curriculum was introduced, random assignment to conditions is not critical, but random selection from the population of interest is critical so that results can be generalized to that population of interest. In fact, the strongest possible approach to this question would be to blend the methodologies and conduct a randomized trial addressing the question of what works while simultaneously interviewing students, teachers, and principals about what happened when a particular intervention was introduced to the school. The descriptive approach of interviewing participants would help address the external validity of the study. It would also provide insights into what is happening or how it is happening. In other words, just understanding that one curriculum results in better outcomes than another curriculum does not establish the mechanism whereby this takes place. Research to enable investigators to understand mechanisms can involve both experimental and descriptive research. Again, the critical issue is the question.

Some individuals in education have adopted epistemologies that devalue scientific research, often highlighting other forms of assessment or inquiry that should not be described as scientific (St. Pierre, 2000). The best way to understand these different epistemologies is to focus on the question that is of interest. For some areas of known inquiry, like history or philosophy, scientific methods may not be optimal. But that does not mean that scientific approaches to human inquiry should be devalued or simply ignored.

ENHANCING EDUCATIONAL RESEARCH

Although it is common to depict educational research as "broken," especially at the federal government level, it is probably better to portray it as "broke." The amount of financial support for educational research is meager compared, for example, with that given to biomedical or defense-related research, and there has been a tendency for sources of support to diminish over time. This reflects the lack of consumer support for educational research, leading to infrequent implementation of educational research in schools, especially after the research is completed. Moreover, many suspect that policy makers support only the research that is relevant to their agendas. To a certain extent, lack of application of research reflects the low quality of many educational research studies and the tendency to conduct studies that are driven by method, agendas, or the availability of resources as opposed to the study question. As such, even trustworthy research findings have been difficult to translate to applied classroom practices. Teachers usually rely on practical experience and on craft knowledge, as opposed to the type of knowledge that emerges from the scientific enterprise. Consequently, there is a tendency in education to embrace fads rather than to identify and implement policies in instructional practices based on empirical data (Carnine, 2000; Vaughn & Dammann, 2001).

There is no question that experience and practical knowledge can contribute to an enhanced understanding of instruction in schools. But this should not be the only type of knowledge that is used. Strong claims about the knowledge base in education should be evaluated. The best methods for evaluation involve science. There needs to be a stronger link between craft knowledge and scientific knowledge. The knowledge claims that emerge in education should be evaluated through research to enhance the generalizability of these claims. In the absence of scientific research, internal validity is weak, fads dominate, and findings and conclusions cannot be generalized beyond the original context.

CONCLUSIONS

We hope that in the future, scientific research in education will continue to make inroads and influence educational practice. We may someday see a time when policy makers and those who work in schools not only embrace scientific knowledge but also rely on it to make decisions. To do this, state and federal governments need to encourage and support activities that result in more high-quality researchers interacting with schools in a practical manner. This will be facilitated if research institutions funded by federal and state entities have experienced researchers in administrative and management positions. To inspire public confidence, these institutions need to develop rigorous and transparent review processes, including evaluations of the integrity of any forms of peer review that are used. The research programs need to be insulated from political interference, which often reflects short-term interests of a particular administration. The research programs need to be coherent, reflecting programs addressing issues that are initiated not only by the agencies but also by investigators, teachers, parents, and students. Initiatives need to be coordinated across different institutions to increase the community of researchers. State and federal governments need to invest in research and need to expect accountability for funds that are expended on the research. This means that it is incumbent on the researchers to help translate the research into practical applications in schools. Although in other areas, science for the sake of science is certainly reasonable, this may be less true in the educational sciences, where there is an expectation that the results can be implemented in ways that enhance schools and their missions. This applied focus is often not a problem because many researchers who ask questions about education are interested in science for purposes of application. In the long run, a rigorous educational research program can only benefit students, and this is the ultimate goal of educational research.

REFERENCES

Campbell, D.T., & Stanley, J.C. (1963). *Experimental and quasi-experimental designs for research.* Chicago: Rand McNally College Publishing Co.

Carnine, D. (2000). *Why education experts resist effective practices (and what it would take to make education more like medicine): A report of the Thomas B. Fordham Foundation.* Washington, DC: Thomas B. Fordham Foundation. Retrieved October 23, 2003, from http://www.edexcellence.net/foundation/publication/publication.cf m?id=46

Chubin, D.E. (1994). Grants peer review in theory and practice. *Evaluation Research, 18,* 20–30.

Cicchetti, D.V. (1991). The reliability of peer review for manuscript and grant submissions: A cross-disciplinary investigation. *Behavioral and Brain Sciences, 14,* 119–135.

Cook, T.D., & Campbell, D.T. (1979). *Quasi-experimentation: Design and analysis issues for field settings.* Chicago: Rand-McNally.

Erickson, F. (1986). Qualitative methods in research on teaching. In M. Wittrock (Ed.), *Handbook of research on teaching* (3rd ed., pp. 119–161). New York: Macmillan.

Feuer, M.J., Towne, L., & Shavelson, R.J. (2002). Scientific culture and educational research. *Educational Researcher, 31,* 4–14.

Finn, C.E., Jr. (2002). The limits of peer review. *Education Week, 21,* 30, 34.

Fletcher, J.M., & Lyon, G.R. (1998). Reading: A research-based approach. In W. Evers (Ed.), *What's gone wrong in America's classrooms* (pp. 49–90). Stanford, CA: Hoover Institution Press.

Glass, G.V., & Camilli, G. (1981). *"Follow Through" evaluation.* Washington, DC: National Institute of Education. (ERIC Document Reproduction Service No. ED244738)

Horrobin, D.F. (2001). Something rotten at the core of science? *Trends in Pharmacological Sciences, 22,* 1–22.

Kerlinger, F.N. (1979). *Behavioral research: A conceptual approach.* Austin, TX: Holt, Rinehart and Winston.

Krathwohl, D.R. (1985). *Social and behavioral science research: A new framework for conceptualizing, implementing, and evaluating research studies.* San Francisco: Jossey-Bass.

Levin, J.R., & O'Donnell, A.M. (1999). What to do about educational research's credibility gaps? *Issues in Education, 5,* 177–229.

Liberman, A.L., Cooper, F.S., Shankweiler, D.P., & Studdert-Kennedy, M. (1967). Perception of speech code. *Psychological Review, 74,* 731–761.

Shavelson, R., & Towne, L. (Eds.). (2002). *Scientific research in education.* Washington, DC: National Academies Press.

St. Pierre, E.A. (2000). The call for intelligibility in postmodern education research. *Educational Researcher, 29,* 25–28.

Stanovich, K.E. (2000). *Progress in understanding reading.* New York: Guilford Press.

Towne, L., Fletcher, J.M., & Wise, L. (in press). *Peer review of education research proposals.* Washington, DC: National Academies Press.

Tukey, J.W. (1962). The future of data analysis. *Annals of Mathematical Statistics, 33,* 1–67.

Vaughn, S., & Dammann, J.E. (2001). Science and sanity in special education. *Behavior Disorders, 27,* 21–29.

5

The Importance of Longitudinal Research for Early Intervention Practices

BARBARA K. KEOGH

The current emphasis on evidence-based decisions in education has important implications for both policy makers and practitioners. This emphasis is critical in educational programs, in which real children, some of whom may have special needs, are sometimes taught with methods that lack solid evidence of effectiveness. Too often, decisions about how to work with students at risk or those with developmental or learning problems have been made on strongly held beliefs reflecting positions of advocacy or special interests. Indeed, the history of special education is filled with controversial programs that lack evidence of treatment validity yet are enthusiastically implemented and defended (Silver, 1986). Jacobson and Mulick noted that interventions range from "validated treatments to fad, dubious, or pseudoscientific treatments" (2002, p. 11), the former based on research meeting acceptable standards of evidence, the latter based on questionable empirical or untestable theoretical foundations. The move toward educational programs founded on solid research evidence reflects the leadership of the National Institute of Child Health and Human Development (NICHD) and G. Reid Lyon, director of NICHD's Child Development and Behavior Branch, and points a welcome direction for working with all students, including those considered at-risk and those with special needs. (See Chapters 2 and 18 for more about the work of the NICHD and Lyon.)

Arguing for evidence-based decisions is not simple, however, as there is evidence and then there are data that are passed off as evidence. A critical question has to do with what constitutes evidence.

The research literature is filled with empirical studies—that is, studies that provide data. However, empirical methods do not necessarily lead to sound data, and data do not necessarily equate to evidence. Data may be tangential, even irrelevant, to the topic being studied or may be flawed because of methodological decisions and procedures. Kraemer distinguished between information and data, noting that "every bit of data comprises Signal (relevant information about the subject of interest) and Noise (irrelevant information . . . random error of measurement)" (1994, pp. 266–267). As a consequence, data may inform research questions or decisions about educational programs by providing relevant evidence, or data may be noise in the system, muddying findings and threatening the validity, reliability, and interpretation of the findings. (See Chapter 4 for more about empirical research, method selection, and validity and reliability.)

Consider the nature of evidence necessary to document the efficacy of instructional programs or clinical treatments, as these are issues of importance when educational, psychological, or medical interventions are implemented. The current push for accountability means that clinicians and educational practitioners are increasingly required to provide evidence of program effectiveness. That is, they are required to gather data that link program practices to specified outcomes. This is a laudable goal but one that is not always easily achieved. Which data should be gathered? With what methods and measures? How often and in what time frame? Some educators argue that a single objective exam at the completion of high school may provide data that do not accurately reflect students' learning in those years of schooling. Similarly, the results of standardized tests of intelligence may not provide valid evidence of the impact of early intervention programs because program effects are frequently broad or not easily measured by such tests, as seen in more positive parent–child interactions or in children's improved social relationships with peers. The critical question, of course, is whether changes in measured outcomes can be linked to the content and the methods of intervention or instructional programs.

Focusing on questions of treatment validity, a critical question in intervention research, Jacobson and Mulick asked in everyday language:

> Was there a change in behavior or in a measurable state that we can plausibly attribute to what we set in motion? Could we do it again

in much the same way? Is this set of causal relations consistent with established (i.e., true) general principles relevant to the particular situation? (2002, p. 11)

These are reasonable and straightforward questions that are relevant in many educational situations and that deserve consideration by practitioners and researchers alike. These questions cannot be answered with arguments based primarily on strongly held beliefs but, rather, require replicable data that can be translated into evidence. We need to know what are the long-term, not just the immediate or transitory, effects of instructional programs; this need underscores the importance of longitudinal research.

DATA, EVIDENCE, AND RESEARCH METHODS

Empirical researchers face well-known and common problems related to data, and thus, to evidence. There are numerous threats to the adequacy of data that limit interpretation and generalizability of findings: inappropriate or weak research designs, definition of the population of interest, sample criteria and selection, measurement and instrumentation, fidelity of implementation, and analytic methods. These threats force researchers and educators to ask if the data collected constitute evidence. And, does the evidence inform the topic under consideration?

Consider questions of study samples and sampling procedures. Because it is usually impossible to study whole populations, such as all children entering first grade in the United States in a given year, all individuals identified as having a learning disability, all high school students who drop out, or all children in early intervention programs, researchers must necessarily select individuals who presumably represent the condition being studied, that is, individuals who represent a larger population. The definition of the population is thus of real importance because the inclusionary and exclusionary criteria determine sample selection. Some populations are well defined, for example, the population of individuals with conditions such as fragile X syndrome or Williams syndrome, which are defined by particular genetic markers. In such cases, individuals are eligible to be included in a study sample only if their genetic makeup meets the criteria defining that condition.

In contrast, target populations themselves may be so broadly defined and so overinclusive that they may include many different subpopulations and collect such a heterogeneous array of individuals that they threaten adequate sampling and limit the accuracy and power of the research methods. Consider the many definitions of the term *risk* when targeting students for particular early reading interventions. Many different individuals may be gathered under the risk rubric, such as children living in poverty, children with developmental delays, and children with parents dealing with alcoholism or mental illness. These differences among the population of children at risk may result in heterogeneous samples that affect research studies or evaluations of intervention program effects. Researchers studying reading and reading specialists working with students at risk may reach different conclusions about intervention efficacy because the students studied represent different kinds of risk.

Problems in sampling are also salient in work with students with learning disabilities. Although the category *specific learning disabilities* contains the largest number of school-age children receiving special education services, the criteria for identification of a learning disability are imprecise and vary geographically, resulting in a heterogeneous population. Criteria defining learning disabilities in California may differ from those in New York or Missouri, thus yielding different data. This, of course, means that subjects in a given sample may be representative of the population in a particular state or school district or even in a certain school but may provide limited information about learning disabilities as a condition in the larger population of students. Identification and referral of children with learning disabilities may also be influenced by the resources available or even by the attitudes and beliefs of teachers and administrators in a given school or school district. Some educators are more knowledgeable than others about which behaviors and problems suggest a learning disability. As a consequence, students in one school may be referred for evaluation, whereas students with similar problems in another school may be overlooked. Yet, many research studies and the majority of efforts to document the effectiveness of intervention programs are based on samples of school-identified students, resulting in well-known problems in generalization (Keogh & MacMillan, 1983; see Chapter 4 for further discussion of generalization of research findings).

Also to be considered is the selection of control or comparison groups in empirical studies, as these groups, too, are subject to sampling problems. Comparison groups may be as heterogeneous as the study samples and may be different in different schools and school districts. Indeed, it is likely that some students who would be considered part of a control or comparison group in a given school district might be selected as study targets in another, as the criteria for identification differ according to district. Current concern for students with attention-deficit/hyperactivity disorder (ADHD) is illustrative. In school, whether a student is referred as possibly having ADHD depends in part on the teacher, as the classroom is usually where the process of identification starts. Clearly teachers differ in their tolerance for students' behavior, with some finding ADHD-like behaviors upsetting and serious and as reason for referral and others viewing the same behaviors as minor problems or irritations. A consequence of these differences in teachers' views is that some children may become part of ADHD study samples, whereas others with similar behaviors may be found in normal comparison groups. The point to be emphasized is that reliance on school- or clinic-identified samples for theoretical or program efficacy research poses serious problems in interpreting data and in generalizing across studies.

In addition, definitions and operational criteria also change over time, such that samples selected in one time period may be different from those selected at another time. Consider the differences in study populations and samples when the operational definition of mental retardation changed from one to two standard deviations below the mean on IQ tests. Note, too, the drop in the 1970s in the number of individuals identified as having mental retardation when learning disabilities was designated as a category of special needs. Hack, Klein, and Taylor (1995) pointed out that infants born before neonatal intensive care was available had higher mortality rates than those with similar conditions now, suggesting that low birth weight children born before 1960 and those born after 1960 may represent different populations. Possible differences in cohorts, of course, raise questions about comparability and generalizability of data and thus questions about evidence.

Issues of inclusionary and exclusionary criteria are critical in both population and sample decisions. At one level the question is whether the population accurately represents the concepts and constructs being tested. At another level the question is whether the sample represents the target population.

EVIDENCE FROM
CROSS-SECTIONAL AND LONGITUDINAL DESIGNS

Empirical researchers use both cross-sectional and follow-up, or longitudinal, designs to gather evidence of program effects. Cross-sectional designs provide data that map conditions at a particular time point, whereas longitudinal designs provide data over time. The choice of design reflects the nature of the specific questions being asked as well as considerations of resources and feasability.

Cross-Sectional Designs

Cross-sectional designs are those in which data are collected at single time points. Such designs provide valuable evidence about prevalence, about specific conditions, and about normative age expectancies, such as the number and proportion of preschoolers with language delays at ages 3, 4, or 5 years or the number and proportion of middle school boys reading below the 20th percentile. Those statistics are important in identifying problems that require attention. What cross-sectional data do not reveal is whether the same children evidence language delays or reading problems at different ages or whether identifying criteria result in the selection of different individuals at different time points. These problems, of course, limit inferences about the development and stability or duration of conditions, and these inferences thus require longitudinal designs.

Longitudinal Designs

In longitudinal designs, the researcher is faced with a number of critical decisions that carry long-term consequences, as decisions made early in the study cannot be changed. Who should be studied? What data should be collected? When, how, and how often should these data be gathered? What analytic strategies should be applied? These questions are important in all empirical research, but they become particularly pertinent when studying individuals over time, which is the core of longitudinal research. By definition, follow-up designs require gathering data at least at two time points, although some researchers suggest that a minimum of three time points are necessary for a study to be considered longitudinal. However, the terms *follow-up* and *longitudinal* are often used interchangeably, as is the case in this chapter.

Longitudinal studies may be prospective or retrospective; that is, they may use follow-up or follow-back designs. There are advantage and disadvantages to both. Consider a study of early identification of children at risk for difficulty with reading achievement. Information on a whole cohort of children might be collected in the first month of first grade and then again at the end of third grade and the children's progress monitored as they advance through the grades. Alternatively, achievement scores at the end of third grade might be used to identify children who are below grade level in reading and their earlier records reviewed to pinpoint progress and problems. In both examples, information collected at the early time point is historical, whether the research requires data to be collected forward or backwards in time. The choice of design relates to the purpose of the research and to available resources.

Prospective Designs   Prospective studies are those in which individuals are selected and followed over time. The number and timing of follow-ups vary by study, some limited to single pre- and postintervention measures over a short time period, others following the same individuals for many years. Follow-up studies with at least three points are often used to assess developmental progress and processes, and data collection may follow a predetermined fixed schedule. In general, there is agreement that there should be at least a 1-year interval between time points for data collection but that time of follow-ups may vary, for example, with more measures taken at times of likely rapid growth or change, such as 2 and 3 years old, when language development is marked, or early adolescence, when physical changes unfold. Follow-up designs that are based on two data collection points are widely used to test interventions or treatments.

The advantages of prospective designs are that it is often possible to describe paths to particular outcomes and to identify conditions and influences on those outcomes. The disadvantages are that prospective designs, especially those that cover many years, are expensive in terms of time and resources; that there will be sample attrition; that data gathering techniques and measures may not be comparable over time; and that the findings are time-bound—that is, they reflect particular economic, social, and political conditions that are cohort specific. (See Friedman, Haywood, & Livesey, 1994; Lerner, Hauser-Cram, & Miller, 1998; and Robins, 1979, for detailed discussions.)

Rutter (1981) described two models that are often used in prospective research. The first and most commonly used is a *real-time prospective study*. In this model, a sample is selected and studied at later time points, minimally at Time 1 and at Time 2. The number of follow-up data points and the time interval(s) between data points may be relatively short or may cover many years. Individuals in such studies may be unselected, that is, included in the study based only on age or other broad demographics, as in the large-scale Kauai study by Werner, Bierman, and French (1971). Individuals may also be selected because they represent a particular known condition, such as low birth weight infants (Hack et al., 1995) or preschoolers with developmental delays (Bernheimer & Keogh, 1988).

Rutter's (1981) second prospective model is a *catch-up prospective approach* in which the individuals in the sample are selected based on earlier information and information about their subsequent or current status is gathered. For example, children identified as learning disabled who attended a special education elementary school were followed up as young adults to assess their current status (Raskin, Goldberg, Higgins, & Herman, 1999). In a large Scottish study, Richardson and Koller (1996) followed up on the adult status of individuals identified as having mental retardation when they were children.

Both real-time and catch-up prospective studies begin to measure performance after a certain point in time, but the catch-up approach is different from a real-time prospective study in that its selection criteria are based on past events. The advantage of using a catch-up approach instead of a real-time approach is that the study is focused on individuals who are already identified as having a particular condition. The disadvantage, of course, is that there is limited possibility for inferences or generalization because some individuals with similar early characteristics may have developed without problems.

Retrospective Designs   Retrospective studies are those in which outcomes are known and individuals who exhibit those outcomes are selected for study. The paths to those outcomes are determined based on prior information gathered from records or by asking individuals to recall earlier experiences. Retrospective designs are often used when targeting individuals with specific conditions, such as poor readers at grade 5 or adolescents who are incarcerated, because such designs telescope the time period between outcome and onset and minimize data collection demands. The disadvantages include the likelihood of missing, inaccurate, or incomplete records or bias in recall leading to questionable or poor-quality data.

Rutter (1981) described one kind of *retrospective follow-back strategy* in which samples are defined by contemporary criteria and information about earlier characteristics is gathered from records or retrospective reports. In contrast to many prospective studies, in this model the outcome is known; thus, particular conditions can be targeted. For example, as part of the prospective Australian Temperament Project, Sanson, Smart, Prior, and Oberklaid (1993) identified children at age 8 who were hyperactive and/or aggressive and reviewed earlier findings to examine their development over time.

Overlapping Age Samples for Prospective or Retrospective Designs   Rutter (1981) also described a research model using *overlapping age samples* studied longitudinally for short time periods. This model allows study of a wide age range in a short time period and can be applied prospectively or retrospectively. By selecting comparable but overlapping samples of children at ages 3–6, 5–8, and 7–10, the total age span would be 3–10, but all data could be collected in a 4-year time period. Using this model in the Early Childhood Longitudinal Study, the National Center for Educational Statistics (1998) focused on two overlapping cohorts, one composed of children from birth through first grade, the other of children from kindergarten through grade 5.

EVIDENCE FROM SEVERAL PROSPECTIVE STUDIES

Each type of longitudinal study design has implications for sample selection and for data collection strategies. The present chapter focuses on evidence from prospective studies in which individuals are followed over time. Rather than provide a comprehensive review, selected studies are described as examples of research that yield evidence of effects over time. These studies reflect different sampling issues and research methods. The first are developmental studies in which relatively large samples of unselected individuals are followed. The second are longitudinal follow-ups of individuals selected for study because they are exemplars of particular conditions. The third are studies designed to test the effects of particular interventions or treatment programs over time; these kinds of designs are commonly used in educational, psychological, and medical research.

Follow-Up Studies of Development

A number of prospective longitudinal studies have been designed to document the developmental paths of individuals and to identify influences on these paths and outcomes. These studies require major commitment of resources and time and face problems of sample attrition and measurement issues. Such studies often do not provide systematic data about intervention effects but do provide critical and unique data that inform understanding of outcomes and developmental processes. Such information cannot be gathered from short-term or cross-sectional studies. Large prospective studies include the Australian Temperament Project (Prior, Sanson, Smart, & Oberklaid, 2000), the Christchurch Health and Development Study (Fergusson, Horwood, Shannon, & Lawton, 1989), the Dunedin Longitudinal Study (Silva, 1990), the New York Longitudinal Study (Thomas & Chess, 1977), and The Collaborative Perinatal Project of the National Institute of Neurological and Communicative Disorders and Stroke (Nichols & Chen, 1981). One example of a prospective longitudinal study, Werner et al.'s (1971) study of the children of Kauai, is particularly illustrative.

In 1955, Werner et al. (1971) began a prospective study of more than 800 infants born on the Hawaiian island of Kauai. These individuals have been followed at regular intervals for forty years, a truly remarkable accomplishment. Although the group as a whole came from lower socioeconomic conditions, eligibility for entry into the study was determined only by place of birth and birth date, and the subjects were not preselected to represent particular conditions. The development and life events of the participants were documented at infancy, early and middle childhood, adolescence, young adulthood, and at entry to midlife. Systematic data on more than 500 individuals identified both psychosocial and biological factors associated with individual differences in developmental paths to adulthood, and yielded evidence about risk, resilience, problems, and competencies over time (see Werner & Smith, 1977, 1989, 1992,

2001). The findings as a whole provide insights about the consequences of earlier conditions on long-term outcomes across a broad age span and document influences on individual differences in outcomes.

Follow-Up Studies of Targeted Conditions

Prospective studies are useful in studying the impact of particular conditions on subsequent development and achievement, such as low birth weight or socioeconomic disadvantage. Prospective data permit the identification of factors that contribute to or that are at least related to differences in outcomes of particular risk conditions. Hack et al. (1995) assessed the long-term developmental outcomes of low birth weight infants, and Klein (1988) focused on a group of very low birth weight infants in order to describe their cognitive development and classroom behavior when they were 5 years old and their developmental and academic achievement when they were 9 years old (Klein, Hack, & Breslau, 1989). Gallimore, Keogh, and Bernheimer (1999) followed up samples of children identified at age 3 as having developmental delays of unknown etiology. In the longest follow-up, one sample of children and their families were studied over a 20-year period, thus allowing documentation of problems and competencies from preschool to young adulthood (Keogh, Bernheimer, & Guthrie, in press).

Follow-Up Studies of Specific Interventions or Treatments

Recognition of the importance of early identification and prevention by policy makers and clinicians has resulted in increasing numbers of interventions that target particular groups or specific conditions at early ages. The most notable and ambitious example is Head Start, a broad-based, large-scale intervention aimed at preschool children considered at risk for development and achievement because of socioeconomic conditions. Current ongoing research on Head Start and other programs targets the effects of child care interventions and practices on children's development, a topic of considerable concern at both individual and policy levels (see NICHD Early Child Care Network, 1994). Other examples include but are certainly not limited to the Abecedarian Project (Campbell & Ramey, 1994;

Ramey, Bryant, Campbell, Sparling, & Wasik, 1990) and the Wood-lawn Project (Kellam, Branch, Agrawal, & Ensminger, 1975). In these studies, follow-up longitudinal designs were used to assess the impact of particular treatments or intervention programs. The period of time covered and the number of data points varied across studies, but in both studies the researchers sought evidence of treatment effects. For other examples and discussion, see *Developmental Follow-Up: Concepts, Domains, and Methods,* edited by Friedman and Haywood (1994).

In general, the evidence from many follow-up studies confirms positive effects of interventions with children at risk because of socioeconomic conditions, although findings are sometimes inconsistent and differ according to the ages of children studied, the time periods between assessments, and the nature and timing of outcomes. Two sets of studies are illustrative. An early effort to assess intervention effects involved a consortium of independent researchers from 11 different sites. Pooled data allowed test of "long-term effectiveness of early education" (Lazar & Darlington, 1982, p. 8) on more than 2,000 children in poverty. Compared with results found for control subjects, positive and long lasting effects of early intervention were found for selected measures of school competence; developed abilities (as measured by performance on achievement tests); positive self-views, attitudes, and values; and positive impact on the family but were not found for IQ. Summary follow-up evidence from the Abecedarian Project (Ramey et al., 1990) showed that infants and preschoolers who received preschool services including an early education program exceeded children in the control group in IQ and in achievement in subsequent years. At 21 years of age, the difference in average IQ was only about 5 points, but the children in the experimental group were achieving significantly higher in reading and math and had fewer grade retentions and referrals to special education (Campbell & Ramey, 1994; Campbell, Ramey, Pungello, Sparling, & Miller-Johnson, 2002).

It is important to note that follow-up studies have also documented that the positive effects of early interventions may fade over time, suggesting that young children at risk need continuing supports and opportunities for learning. Based on evidence from Head Start, a follow-up research effort, The National Transition Demonstration Study (Phillips et al., 1999) focused on the performance of more than 7,500 Head Start children in elementary school. Positive program effects were documented for the groups as a whole, and by the end of second and third grades, the children were performing close to the national average in reading and math. Comprehensive reviews of early intervention programs for children from low-income families and those with disabilities may be found, respectively, in chapters by Farran and by Hauser-Cram, Warfield, Upshur, and Weisner in the *Handbook of Early Childhood Intervention, Second Edition*, edited by Shonkoff and Meisels (2000).

LONGITUDINAL FOLLOW-UP STUDIES OF READING

Given that reading is central to academic achievement, it should not come as a surprise that a great deal of current research focuses on reading, learning to read, and problems in reading. How to teach reading has been a subject of serious, sometimes acrimonious debate, fueling the well-named "reading wars." The research literature is replete with short-term studies that test particular methods of instruction, but to date, the follow-up research has been relatively short term and the outcome measures of reading have been primarily word recognition. Less is known about reading comprehension. Nonetheless, the findings to date are encouraging. A review by Jenkins and O'Conner (2002) provided in-depth and comprehensive discussions of early reading research and findings, much of which was supported by the NICHD and the U.S. Department of Education's Office of Special Education Programs. In this chapter, a few selected follow-up studies are described briefly as examples of the research literature directed at early reading.

Wagner and colleagues (1997) followed up a random sample of 216 children from kindergarten through grade four, annually assessing aspects of phonological processing, word-level reading skills, and vocabulary. Outcome reading measures included subtests of a standard achievement test, the vocabulary subtest of a standardized IQ test, and letter-name knowledge. This was not an intervention study per se but rather was aimed at assessing relationships between phonological processing abilities and word-level reading as children advance through the grades and become skilled readers. Individual differences in phonological processing skills were found to be related to individual differences in reading at each grade level, and letter-name knowledge was found to be related to phonological awareness.

Using a prospective follow-up design, Torgesen and his colleagues (1999) identified kindergarten children who were seriously

behind their same-age peers (bottom 12 percentiles) in letter knowledge and phonological awareness. The children were randomly
assigned to one of four instructional conditions: phonological awareness plus synthetic phonics, embedded phonics, regular classroom
support, and no treatment (control). All children received individual
tutoring 4 days per week for $2^1/_2$ years, for a total of more than 90
hours of instruction. Compared at follow-up with children in other
groups, the children in the phonological awareness plus synthetic
phonics group had higher mean scores on measures of word attack
skills and word identification. There were also considerable within-
group differences, such that some children made good progress,
whereas others continued to be behind.

Foorman, Francis, Fletcher, and Schatschneider (1998) tested the
effects of early intervention programs in the development of reading
in 285 first- and second-grade children from eight schools serving
economically disadvantaged children. Three types of interventions
were implemented by general education classroom teachers trained
in the instructional methods. The three methods were direct instruction letter–sound correspondences (Direct Code), sound–spelling patterns in text (Embedded Code), and instruction in the alphabetic
code while reading (Implicit Code). Children were assessed four
times during the school year (October, December, February, and
April). The Direct Code intervention was found to be the most effective as measured by postintervention rate of reading and word recognition skills. The greatest gains were made by the children with the
poorest phonological awareness skills at study entry. The effects of
the different interventions on comprehension were similar in pattern
but weaker than the effects found in word recognition, and there
were no significant differences among interventions in vocabulary
growth or spelling.

The findings from these studies have been replicated by other
independent researchers, including those from countries other than
the United States. For example, Australian researchers Byrne and
Fielding-Barnsley (1991, 1993, 1995) followed children from preschool to elementary school, assessing the impact of a preschool
training program on subsequent reading skills. Children in the training program exceeded control children in decoding and reading comprehension but not in spelling or in automaticity.

Overall, the findings document that targeted interventions, particularly those based on direct instruction in phonological awareness, improve the early reading of children at risk. A meta-analysis

of more than 70 intervention studies conducted in the United States (Bus & Van IJzendoorn, 1999) found that phonological awareness explained about 12% of the variance in reading measured by word identification skills, leading those researchers to conclude that that phonological training has positive effects on phonological and reading skills but that, although necessary, it is not "sufficient for successful early reading" (p. 403). Questions about the long-term effects of phonologically based programs have, of course, been raised by other researchers of reading who argue for different instructional approaches (Pressley, 1998; Pressley & Rankin, 1994). Clearly there is more work to be done to determine the long-term effects of specific early interventions.

WHAT HAVE WE LEARNED FROM FOLLOW-UP INTERVENTION STUDIES?

The first and most important answer is that we have learned quite a bit from follow-up studies of early intervention, as many ongoing studies are providing solid data that translate to evidence. Individual differences among children have been widely documented and are one part of the equation that describes intervention effects. The content and timing of interventions are also part of the picture, and much as there are individual differences among children, there are significant individual differences in interventions. Some interventions are well grounded in theory, and the instructional practices are fully and correctly implemented. Other interventions may be well intentioned, but the practices lack a solid conceptual base and/ or may be poorly or inconsistently implemented. Interventions also differ in intensity and duration, with some providing daily services to children for many months or years and others limited to short-term interventions delivered several times a week. Foorman and Torgesen (2001) have identified what they believe are critical features of instructional programs for young children at risk for reading failure. These include instruction that is phonemically explicit, comprehensive, and intensive and that also provides both cognitive and emotional support. These features are consistent with a converging instructional literature (Jenkins & O'Connor, 2002) that points the way to reducing reading failure. The impact of such programs over the long term now needs to be tested, and this need thus underscores the importance of longitudinal designs.

In addition to differences in instructional programs, there are differences in how the individual characteristics of children interact with or respond to particular programs. Torgesen (2000) has found that about 2%–6% of children are "treatment resistors"; that is, they do not respond positively to well-planned and carefully implemented interventions. It is unclear whether the lack of instructional effects is due to the content and intensity of the particular program, to the length of the intervention, or to the characteristics of the students themselves. These questions, of course, add to the complexity of determining program efficacy.

Important questions emerging from longitudinal research on reading have to do with which data constitute evidence of effects over time and when follow-up should occur. The choice of outcome indicators may differ for short-term and long-term follow-ups and thus may yield different findings. Werner and Smith (2001) found differences in the competencies and problems of the individuals in their studies in different decades of life. A number of teenagers had problems that brought them into contact with educational, medical, and juvenile justice professionals, yet the majority of those teenagers were later found to be stable and productive adults in their thirties and their early forties. Follow-up studies of preschool children with developmental delays and their families have documented changes in family expectations, adaptations, and accommodations over time, thus presenting different pictures of family life and well-being at different time points (Gallimore et al., 1999). Studies of early reading interventions confirm that intense phonologically based instruction results in improved word recognition skills but does not necessarily have direct effects on reading comprehension. Studies of Head Start programs have shown that there are many immediate gains for preschool children who participate but have also found evidence of fading effects of intervention in elementary school. The point is that *when* assessment occurs as well as *what* is assessed affects findings.

It is important to note, too, that intervention effects may not be immediately apparent but rather can be documented only over longer time periods. For example, researchers in the Woodlawn Project (Kellam, Rebok, Ialongo, & Mayor, 1994) have documented "sleeper effects" at the transition from elementary to middle school following early intervention aimed at reducing aggression. Farran (2000) described long-term results of a range of early intervention programs for at-risk children. McConaughy, Kay, and Fitzgerald (2000) compared results of a school-based intervention for young children thought to be at risk for emotional problems. Moderate effects were found at the end of the first year, whereas many strong and significant effects in problem reduction and enhanced competencies were documented at the end of the second year, leading those researchers to "underscore the importance of allowing sufficient time for early prevention programs to produce changes in at-risk children's behavior" (p. 31). Taken as a whole, these findings raise questions about the timing of follow-ups and about the nature of inferences drawn from early risk indicators. Long-term predictions for groups of individuals may be made with some accuracy, but predictions about individuals within groups must be made with caution.

WHY IS LONGITUDINAL EVIDENCE IMPORTANT?

The simplest and most direct answer to the question of why longitudinal evidence is important is that follow-up studies provide evidence that cannot be gathered from cross-sectional designs. This evidence includes descriptions of the developmental paths of children at risk for negative outcomes because of particular social, familial, or personal conditions; determination of the stability or duration of problems; the effects of treatments or interventions over time; the predictive accuracy of early conditions for subsequent outcomes; and insights about continuities and discontinuities in development.

When arguing for the importance of longitudinal research, problems and limitations of follow-up designs, especially long-term studies, need to be acknowledged. By definition, longitudinal or follow-up studies require multiple data collection points; thus, the longitudinal researcher is faced with real and continuing needs for resources and research support, including personnel. Because research is conducted in a sociopolitical context, priorities and funding change over time, so resources may be diminished or curtailed during the course of a study. In longitudinal work, the individuals studied grow older, but so do the researchers, and attrition for both can be high. Assessment techniques necessarily vary because data are collected when study individuals are in different developmental periods. As a consequence, specific measures may be inappropriate across the time span of the study, and new or different measures may not be comparable. It is difficult, often impossible, to collect data on all study members at every time point; thus, data sets may be incomplete, limiting analytic methods. Repeated measures may also be compromised by practice or familiarity effects. Cohort effects can limit inferences and generalizations in different time periods.

Finally, the personal relationships between researchers and the individuals studied change over time, on the one hand encouraging continued participation but on the other hand threatening objectivity. Nonetheless, the kind of data gathered from longitudinal designs can provide unique and powerful evidence about development and experience, including the efficacy of programs of early intervention. See Keogh and Bernheimer (1998) and Robins and Rutter (1990) for further discussion.

SOME PERSONAL COMMENTS

I began this chapter arguing for a distinction between data and evidence, suggesting that data and evidence are not always the same thing. Fortunately, since the early 1990s many research programs have provided data that do translate to evidence and thus that allow clinicians and policy makers to make informed decisions. The NICHD has been one of the important players in this research effort. The NICHD, part of the National Institutes of Health, which has traditionally supported medically and developmentally oriented research, has contributed substantially to the understanding of educational issues and problems, and the impact has been major. The NICHD has initiated and supported both cross-sectional and longitudinal programs of research on reading and learning disabilities (Lyon, 1995) and as a whole the research is notable for its scope, for its high quality, and for its success in bringing scientists from different disciplines to address educational problems. Importantly, the NICHD agenda includes research directed at many aspects of reading and reading problems and interventions and instructional programs for early readers and readers who are struggling. Many of the research projects that the NICHD supports rely on follow-up strategies to test particular interventions with children at risk.

Much of the success of this research program is due to the foresight, energy, and commitment of G. Reid Lyon. It has been my good fortune to know and work with Dr. Lyon over the years, and I have watched with admiration his many accomplishments. He has put together a network of highly competent researchers who are addressing problems from different perspectives and, importantly, who talk to each other. He has insisted on rigorous research methods and on the application of powerful analytic strategies. The result is an accumulating body of high-quality evidence on which to base decisions about policies and practices in early intervention.

REFERENCES

Bernheimer, L.P., & Keogh, B.K. (1988). The stability of cognitive performance of developmentally delayed children. *American Journal on Mental Retardation, 92,* 539–542.

Bus, A.G., & Van IJzendoorn, M.H. (1999). Phonological awareness and early reading: A meta-analysis of experimental training studies. *Journal of Experimental Psychology, 91,* 403–414.

Byrne, B., & Fielding-Barnsley, R. (1991). Evaluation of a program to teach phonetic awareness to young children. *Journal of Educational Psychology, 83,* 451–455.

Byrne, B., & Fielding-Barnsley, R. (1993). Evaluation of a program to teach phonetic awareness to young children: A 1-year follow-up. *Journal of Educational Psychology, 85,* 104–111.

Byrne, B., & Fielding-Barnsley, R. (1995). Evaluation of a program to teach phonetic awareness to young children: A 2- and 3-year follow up. *Journal of Educational Psychology, 87,* 488–503.

Campbell, F., & Ramey, C. (1994). Effects of early intervention on intellectual and academic achievement: A follow-up study of children from low income families. *Child Development, 65,* 684–698.

Campbell, F.A., Ramey, C.T., Pungello, E.P., Sparling, J., & Miller-Johnson, S. (2002). Early childhood education: Young adult outcomes of the Abecedarian Project. *Applied Developmental Science, 6,* 42–57.

Farran, D.C. (2000). Another decade of intervention for children who are low income or disabled. In J.P. Shonkoff & S.J. Meisels (Eds.), *Handbook of early childhood intervention* (2nd ed., pp. 487–509). Cambridge, UK: Cambridge University Press.

Fergusson, D.M., Horwood, L.J., Shannon, F.T., & Lawton, J.M. (1989). The Christchurch Child Development Study: A review of epidemiological studies. *Paediatric and Perinatal Epidemiology, 3,* 278–301.

Foorman, B.R., Francis, D.J., Fletcher, J.M., & Schatschneider, C. (1998). The role of instruction in learning to read: Preventing reading failure in at-risk children. *Journal of Educational Psychology, 90,* 37–55.

Foorman, B.R., & Torgesen, J. (2001). Critical elements of classroom and small-group instruction promote reading success in all children. *Learning Disabilities Research and Practice, 16,* 203–212.

Friedman, S.L., & Haywood, H.C. (Eds.). (1994). *Developmental follow-up: Concepts, domains, and methods.* San Diego: Academic Press.

Friedman, S.L., Haywood, H.C., & Livesey, K. (1994). From the past to the future of developmental longitudinal research. In S.L. Friedman & H.C. Haywood (Eds.), *Developmental follow-up: Concepts, domains, and methods* (pp. 3–26). San Diego: Academic Press.

Gallimore, R., Keogh, B.K., & Bernheimer, L.P. (1999). The nature and long-term implications of early developmental delays: A summary of evidence from two longitudinal studies. In L.M. Glidden (Ed.), *International review of research in mental retardation* (Vol. 22, pp. 106–136). San Diego: Academic Press.

Hack, M., Klein, N.K., & Taylor, H.G. (1995). Long-term developmental outcomes of low birth weight infants. *The Future of Children, 5,* 176–196.

Hauser-Cram, P., Warfield, M.E., Upshur, C.C., & Weisner, T.S. (2000). An expanded view of program evaluation in early childhood intervention. In J.P. Shonkoff & S.J. Meisels (Eds.), *Handbook of early childhood intervention* (2nd ed., pp. 487–509). Cambridge, UK: Cambridge University Press.

Jacobson, J.W., & Mulick, J.A. (2002). Clinicians: "Scientist practitioners say the darnedest things" or is that shinola? *Psychology in Mental Retardation and Developmental Disabilities, 28,* 11–14.

Jenkins, J.R., & O'Connor, R.E. (2002). Early identification and intervention for young children with reading/learning disabilities. In R. Bradley, L. Danielson, & D.P. Hallahan (Eds.), *Identification of learning disabilities: Research to practice* (pp. 99–184). Mahwah, NJ: Lawrence Erlbaum Associates.

Kellam, S.G., Branch, J.D., Agrawal, K.C., & Ensminger, M.D. (1975). *Mental health and going to school: The Woodlawn Program of assessment, early intervention, and evaluation.* Chicago: University of Chicago Press.

Kellam, S.G., Rebok, G.W., Ialongo, N., & Mayor, L.S. (1994). The course and malleability of aggressive behavior from early first grade into middle school: Results of a developmental epidemiologically-based preventive trial. *Journal of Child Psychology and Psychiatry, 35,* 259–282.

Keogh, B.K., & Bernheimer, L.P. (1998). Issues and dilemmas in longitudinal research: A tale of two studies. *Thalamus, 16,* 5–13.

Keogh, B.K., Bernheimer, L.P., & Guthrie, D. (in press). Children with developmental delays twenty years later: Where are they? How are they? *American Journal on Mental Retardation.*

Keogh, B.K., & MacMillan, D.L. (1983). The logic of sample selection: Who represents what? *Exceptional Education Quarterly, 4*(3), 84–96.

Klein, N.K (1988). Children who were very low birth weight: Cognitive abilities and classroom behavior at five years of age. *Journal of Special Education, 22,* 41–54.

Klein, N.K., Hack, M., & Breslau, N. (1989). Children who were very low birth weight: Developmental and academic achievement at nine years of age. *Journal of Developmental and Behavioral Pediatrics, 10,* 32–37.

Kraemer, H.C. (1994). Special methodological problems of childhood developmental follow-up studies: Focus on planning. In S.L. Friedman & H.C. Haywood (Eds.), *Developmental follow-up: Concepts, domains, and methods* (pp. 259–276). San Diego: Academic Press.

Lazar, I., & Darlington, R. (1982). Lasting effects of early education: A report from the consortium for longitudinal studies. *Monographs of the Society for Research in Child Development, 47*(Serial No. 195), 1–151.

Lerner, R.M., Hauser-Cram, P., & Miller, E. (1998). Assumptions and features of longitudinal designs: Implications for early childhood education. In B. Spodek, O.N. Saracho, & A.D. Pellegrini (Eds.), *Yearbook on early education* (Vol. 8, 1113–1138). New York: Teachers College Press.

Lyon, G.R. (1995). Research initiatives in leaning disabilities: Contributions from scientists supported by the National Institute of Child Health and Human Development. *Journal of Child Neurology, 10*(Suppl. 1), S120–S126.

McConaughy, S.H., Kay, P.J., & Fitzgerald, M. (2000). How long is long enough?: Outcomes for a school-based prevention program. *Exceptional Children, 67,* 21–34.

National Center for Educational Statistics. (1998). *Early Childhood Longitudinal Study.* Washington, DC: Author.

NICHD Early Child Care Network. (1994). Child care and child development: The NICHD study of early child care. In S.L. Friedman & H.C. Haywood (Eds.), *Developmental follow-up: Concepts, domains, and methods* (pp. 378–396). San Diego: Academic Press.

Nichols, P.L., & Chen, T.-C. (1981). *Minimal brain dysfunction: A prospective study.* Upper Saddle River, NJ: Lawrence Erlbaum Associates.

Phillips, M.M., Ramey, S.L., Ramey, C.T., Lanzi, R.G., Brezausek, C., Katholi, C.R., et al. (1999). *Head Start children's entry into public school: A report on the National Head Start/Public School Early Childhood Transition Demonstration Study.* Birmingham: The University of Alabama at Birmingham, Civitan International Research Center.

Pressley, M. (1998). *Reading instruction that works: The case for balanced teaching.* New York: Guilford Press.

Pressley, M., & Rankin, J. (1994). More about whole language methods of reading instruction for students at-risk for early reading failure. *Learning Disabilities Research and Practice, 9,* 156–167.

Prior, M., Sanson, A.V., Smart, D., & Oberklaid, F. (2000). *Pathways from infancy to adolescence: The Australian Temperament Project 1983–2000.* Melbourne: Australia Institute of Family Studies.

Ramey, C., Bryant, D., Campbell, F., Sparling, J., & Wasik, B. (1990). Early intervention for high-risk children: The Carolina Early Intervention Program. *Prevention in Human Services, 7,* 33–57.

Raskin, M.H., Goldberg, R.J., Higgins, E.L., & Herman, K.L. (1999). Patterns of change and predictors of success in individuals with learning disabilities: Results from a twenty-year longitudinal study. *Learning Disabilities Research and Practice, 14,* 35–49.

Richardson, S.A., & Koller, H. (1996). *Twenty-two years later: Causes and consequences of mental retardation.* Cambridge, MA: Harvard University Press.

Robins, L.N. (1979). Follow-up studies. In H.C. Quay & J.S. Werry (Eds.), *Psychopathological disorders of childhood* (pp. 484–513). New York: Wiley.

Robins, L.N., & Rutter, M. (1990). (Eds.). *Straight and devious pathways from childhood to adulthood.* Cambridge, UK: Cambridge University Press.

Rutter, M. (1981). Longitudinal studies. In S.A. Mednick & A.E. Baert (Eds.), *Prospective longitudinal research: An empirical basis for primary prevention* (pp. 326–336). London: Oxford University Press.

Sanson, A., Smart, D., Prior, M., & Oberklaid, F. (1993). Precursors of hyperactivity and aggression. *Journal of the American Academy of Adolescent Psychiatry, 32,* 1207–1216.

Shonkoff, J.P., & Meisels, S.J. (Eds.). (2000). *Handbook of early childhood intervention* (2nd ed.). Cambridge, UK: Cambridge University Press.

Silva, P.A. (1990). The Dunedin multidisciplinary health and developmental study: A fifteen-year longitudinal study. *Pediatric and Perinatal Epidemiology, 4,* 96–127.

Silver, L.B. (1986). The "magic cure": A review of the current controversial approaches for treating learning disabilities. *Journal of Learning Disabilities, 20,* 408–503, 451.

Thomas, A., & Chess, S. (1977). *Temperament and development.* New York: Brunner/Mazel.

Torgesen, J.K. (2000). Individual differences in response to early interventions in reading: The lingering problem of treatment resisters. *Learning Disabilities Research and Practice, 15,* 55–64.

Torgesen, J.K., Wagner, R.K., Rashotte, C.A., Rose, E., Lindamood, P., Conway, T., et al. (1999). Preventing reading failure in young children with phonological processing disabilities: Group and individual responses to instruction. *Journal of Educational Psychology, 91,* 1–15.

Wagner, R.K., Torgesen, J.K., Rashotte, C.A., Hecht, S.A., Barker, T.A., Burgess, S.R., et al. (1997). Changing relations between phonological processing abilities and word-level reading as children develop from beginning to skilled readers: A 5-year longitudinal study. *Developmental Psychology, 33,* 468–479.

Werner, E.E., Bierman, J.M., & French, F.E. (1971). *The children of Kauai: A longitudinal study from the prenatal period to age ten.* Honolulu: University of Hawaii Press.

Werner, E.E., & Smith, R.S. (1977). *Kauai's children come of age.* Honolulu: University of Hawaii Press.

Werner, E.E., & Smith, R.S. (1989). *Vulnerable but invincible: A longitudinal study of resilient children and youth.* New York: Adams, Bannister, & Cox.

Werner, E.E., & Smith, R.S. (1992). *Overcoming the odds: High risk children from birth to adulthood.* Ithaca, NY: Cornell University Press.

Werner, E.E., & Smith, R.S. (2001). *Journeys from childhood to midlife.* Ithaca, NY: Cornell University Press.

6

What Is a Meta-Analysis and How Do We Know We Can Trust It?

HARRIS COOPER AND KELLE REACH

Parents, educators, and education policy makers have grown weary of watching fads and fashions sweep over school and teaching practices, especially in the teaching of basic skills. Many have grown cynical about educational innovations. They have come to expect that today's hot trend in education will be abandoned tomorrow. They know that many educational innovations have little sound evidence for effectiveness.

Recent initiatives have been undertaken to change this situation. These initiatives attempt to incorporate research-based practices into education. The legislative directives contained in the No Child Left Behind Act of 2001 (PL 107-110) are one example of such initiatives, as is the formation of the Institute for Education Science's What Works Clearinghouse (http://www.w-w-c.org). The What Works Clearinghouse aims to disseminate scientific evidence about effective teaching methods that will serve as a foundation for increasing the achievement of America's children (see Chapter 2 for further discussion of the What Works Clearinghouse). Particularly in the area of reading instruction, the federal government has placed an emphasis on providing federal funds to programs that have demonstrated empirically that they are successful in teaching reading skills to students. The Reading First initiative encourages recipients to apply for federal funds to incorporate teaching practices that are

The authors thank Amanda Cuca, Elizabeth Cody, and Nicole Whyte for editorial assistance.

established using scientific reading research in order to provide children with the essential knowledge and skills necessary for successful reading development in kindergarten and beyond (U.S. Department of Education, 2002; see Chapter 2 for further discussion of this program).

But, how do we know what the scientific evidence says about reading practices? Translating individual research reports from varied sources into better reading instruction is no easy task. Integrating the results of multiple studies requires the use of methods specific to the task of research cumulation. Advancing knowledge of reading instruction depends greatly on the methods used to assimilate various individual findings into a coherent and unified set of research-based recommendations.

NARRATIVE REVIEWS AND RESEARCH SYNTHESES

Across most social science disciplines, the traditional means of integrating empirical research has been to utilize narrative review procedures, a process in which multiple studies investigating the same topics are collected and then described in order to provide a summary statement about the topic of interest. In the area of reading instruction, narrative reviewers would describe successively each study of a particular instructional practice and then draw a conclusion about the approach based on the reviewers' interpretation of what was found in the literature as a whole.

Research reviews conducted in a narrative manner, however, have received much criticism. Opponents of the narrative review have suggested that this method and its resulting conclusions are imprecise in both process and outcome. In particular, narrative reviews have been cited as lacking explicit standards of proof (Johnson & Eagly, 2000; Rosenthal, 1984). Readers and users of narrative reviews do not know what standard of evidence was used to decide whether a set of studies supported the conclusion that a policy or practice was or was not effective. The rules used by the reviewer are rarely known to anyone but the reviewers themselves. It is difficult to describe what pattern of findings across studies was used to support or refute the effectiveness of the schooling or teaching technique.

Another disadvantage to narrative reviews is that individual studies are not given different amounts of credibility based on how well or how poorly they were carried out. Finally, narrative reviews, by their very nature, fail to result in statements regarding the overall magnitude or statistical significance of the relations under investigation. They cannot answer the question "What was the impact of the policy or practice on reading achievement?" or "Was the effect larger or smaller than that of other policies or practices?"

Because of concern about the potential for error and imprecision in narrative reviews, social science methodologists have developed more rigorous alternatives that possess definable and clearly evident standards. A systematic *research synthesis* employs a collection of methodological and statistical techniques designed to integrate the results of empirical studies. These techniques make explicit and standardize the procedures used to combine primary research. For example, the criteria for deciding whether a study was conducted well enough to be included in the synthesis are explicitly stated prior to starting the collection of relevant research. These criteria might include methodological issues, such as whether the control group and experimental group were comparable on pertinent dimensions (e.g., grade level, gender, socioeconomic status). In making the decision to include research, the research synthesist consistently applies these criteria to all studies, regardless of whether the results supported or refuted the effectiveness of the policy or practice. In later stages, data from the research report are recorded using predesignated coding decisions. Meta-analytic statistical methods, which are one component of the larger synthesis, are applied to summarize the data and provide a quantitative description of the cumulative research findings. Thus, systematic research synthesis and the statistical integration of study results (i.e., meta-analysis) are conducted with the same structure and rigor as is data analysis in primary scientific studies.

Meta-analysis is most appropriate when the question of interest involves the specific effects of a particular policy or instructional practice. Furthermore, in order for a statistical synthesis to be conducted, it is necessary for at least two studies to exist that examined the same relationship between the variables of interest. Without this, a quantitative research synthesis cannot be completed. Further complicating this requirement is that even if a body of research exists, the level of completeness and accuracy of existing primary research reports can be poor, diminishing the reliability of the data to be used in the meta-analysis. The resulting meta-analysis is limited if only inaccurate or incomplete data are available. Finally, a more general caution to the use of meta-analysis is that it is no substitute for wisdom (Wachter & Straf, 1990). No statistical method can generate theories or hypotheses that do not already exist, nor can it tell us what questions are important to study. A successful meta-analysis requires the integration of both statistics and human insight. Meta-analysis, however, is not a complete solution to the problems faced by research synthesis. Indeed, meta-analysis is unsuited to addressing certain kinds of questions. For example, theoretical critiques and qualitative research cannot be analyzed using meta-analytic techniques. An educator interested in describing the historical development of reading education in the schools would not find meta-analysis useful for achieving such a goal.

In summary, a clear distinction can be made between two types of research reviews: 1) narrative or traditional reviews and 2) research syntheses incorporating meta-analysis. The former type of review allows a historical description or theoretical assessment of the content of relevant experiments. The latter type of review attempts to statistically summarize past empirical research so as to draw overall conclusions based on investigations of related or identical policies or programs. Outcomes of meta-analyses allow statements with the potential for addressing the magnitude of the effects of policies and practices in quantitative terms. Synthesized reviews in education include evaluations of the effectiveness of varying reading methods (e.g., phonics; Ehri, Nunes, Stahl, & Willows, 2001), examinations of reading instruction for special groups (e.g., learning disabilities; Fuchs, Fuchs, Mathes, Lipsey, & Eaton, 2000), and evaluation of programs such as summer school or other tutoring classes (Cooper, Charlton, Valentine, & Muhlenbruck, 2000; Erlbaum, Vaughn, Hughes, & Moody, 2000).

In this chapter, we intend to provide the reader with the ability both to comprehend and evaluate current research syntheses with meta-analyses and to understand how the results of meta-analyses might apply to education. We begin with a description of the history of research synthesis. Next, we describe the processes by which research syntheses and meta-analyses are conducted. An analysis of the credibility of these techniques is then provided. Finally, the use of research synthesis in education is discussed.

To augment our discussion, we use as examples results from a research synthesis examining the effects of participation in remedial summer school on achievement outcomes, with particular attention to effects on reading (Cooper et al., 2000). As noted previously, syntheses relevant to reading research are available, and readers are encouraged to seek out this work and apply the discussion herein to understand the conclusions for their own use. For additional coverage of issues surrounding research synthesis and meta-analyses, we recommend texts by Cooper (1998), Cooper and Hedges (1994), Hedges and Olkin (1985), and Lipsey and Wilson (2001).

HISTORICAL BACKGROUND

The first known synthesis of statistical results from a set of studies was conducted by Karl Pearson (1904) at the beginning of the twentieth century. In this synthesis, Pearson used a correlation coefficient (a new technique at that time). The correlation coefficient is a statistical index describing the degree to which two variables are related. A correlation of +1 means that two variables relate exactly—as one variable increases; the other also increases in perfect proportion. Alternatively, a correlation of −1 indicates that as the value of one variable increases, the other decreases in perfect proportion. A correlation coefficient of 0 signifies that there is no relation between the two variables. Generally, correlation coefficients for most relationships fall between 0 and ±1. In his research, Pearson calculated a correlation coefficient for each of 11 independent studies examining the evidence on a vaccine against typhoid. He then averaged the correlation coefficients from the 11 studies to obtain one statistic and concluded, based on this statistic, that other vaccines were more effective.

Following this initial effort, the methods of meta-analysis remained largely dormant until the late part of the 20th century, when other reviewers synthesized research in their area. They had much larger sets of independent studies than Pearson's original 11. The focuses of these research syntheses were as varied as interpersonal expectations and behavior (Rosenthal & Rubin, 1978), the effectiveness of psychotherapy (Smith & Glass, 1977), and the validity of employment tests for black and white workers (Hunter, Schmidt, & Hunter, 1979). One of these early researchers, Gene Glass, coined the term meta-analysis and defined it as "the statistical analysis of a large collection of analysis results from individual studies for purposes of integrating the findings" (1976, p. 3). One of Glass's earliest attempts to demonstrate meta-analysis involved studies examining the relation between class size and academic achievement (Glass & Smith, 1979). In this research, Glass and Smith (1979) gathered hundreds of correlation coefficients from studies that had examined the relationship between the number of students in a class to the class's overall achievement. The meta-analysis demonstrated that the overall correlation was negative, indicating that as class size decreased, the achievement of the class increased.

Following this reapplication of Pearson's technique, others began developing meta-analytic techniques in texts written to guide such procedures. Although meta-analysis was not without criticism, empirical demonstrations showed that narrative reviews often led to inaccurate or imprecise characterizations of the accumulated research results; this revelation supported the use of meta-analysis (Cooper, 1979; Cooper & Rosenthal, 1980). Other procedures involved in research syntheses also were increasingly examined and placed within the context of a scientific process. Social scientists began to consider research synthesis "a type of research in its own right—one using a characteristic set of research techniques and methods" (Feldman, 1971, p. 86).

Other developments occurred that advanced research synthesis and meta-analysis as specific and distinctive scientific procedures. This growth included such advancements as the provision of a wide range of procedural techniques with rigorous statistical proofs (Hedges & Olkin, 1985) and the dissemination of these techniques from psychology and education to other disciplines, especially social policy (Light, 1983) and the medical sciences (see *Statistics in Medicine*, 1987, Volume 6, Issue 3). These developments led Greenberg and Folger to state that "if the current interest in meta-analysis is any indication, then meta-analysis is here to stay" (1988, p. 191).

More recently, researchers have written several books on meta-analysis. The topic is addressed generally (e.g., Cooper, 1998; Hunter & Schmidt, 1990; Lipsey & Wilson, 2001), from the perspective of particular research designs (e.g., Eddy, Hasselblad, & Shachter, 1992; Mullen, 1989), in relation to particular software packages (e.g., Johnson, 1989; Wang & Bushman, 1999), and in envisioning future developments in research synthesis (e.g., Cook et al., 1992; Wachter & Straf, 1990). A comprehensive treatment of research synthesis was published in *The Handbook of Research Synthesis* (Cooper & Hedges, 1994). This book included 32 chapters contributed by specialists in information science, computer software, and statistics as well as by experts in the use of research synthesis for psychology, medicine, education, and public policy.

COMPONENTS OF A RESEARCH SYNTHESIS

Cooper (1982) presented a five-stage model that viewed research synthesis as a data gathering exercise and, as such, applied to it criteria similar to those employed to judge primary research. Similar to primary research, a research synthesis involves

- Problem formulation

- Data collection (the literature search)

- Data evaluation

- Data analysis and interpretation (the meta-analysis)

- Applied presentation and use of conclusions

In the subsections that follow, we describe the purposes of each stage, with particular attention to the data analysis, or meta-analysis, stage.

Problem Formulation

A research synthesis, as with any research project, begins by defining the question (or questions) of interest. In order to accomplish this initial goal, the variables of interest must be identified. In defining these variables, the resulting description is sometimes broad, allowing for multiple operational definitions of the same variables across studies, and sometimes quite specific, in order to focus on an easily identifiable concept definition. The operational definition is a "cookbook" description of the observed events that characterize each variable. For example, in reading instruction, the topic of interest might be whether a particular approach to teaching reading is or is not effective, with the variables of interest identified as type of approach to teaching reading and students' subsequent reading achievement. The instructional approach might be broadly defined, for example, as instructional techniques using the phonics approach or as attending a summer reading program, or it might be narrowly defined, for example, the ABC Phonics Program or the XYZ Summer Learning Institute. Likewise, the outcomes of interest might be broadly defined, for example, total scores on a reading achievement test, or narrowly defined, for example, accurate recognition of certain phonemes.

Literature Search

Once the variables have been distinguished and operationalized, the relevant studies must be identified and obtained. One advantage of systematic research synthesis procedures over traditional narrative reviews is that the former use multiple, complementary search strategies to obtain the most representative set of relevant research, both published and unpublished (Cooper, 1998; Lipsey & Wilson, 2001). Although it is unlikely that the goal of obtaining all relevant research will be achieved, the use of comprehensive search strategies directed toward such an end serves to reduce bias in the results of the obtained literature.

One issue that research synthesists grapple with is whether to include unpublished research, including dissertations, educational reports, and conference proceedings. One pertinent reason for excluding unpublished literature is that it might be of lesser quality than published research. Research, however, often is not published for reasons other than quality (Cooper, DeNeve, & Charlton, 1997). One important reason that research goes unpublished is that it has failed to demonstrate statistically significant findings; this phenomenon is referred to as *publication bias.* This unpublished research often remains in investigators' "file drawers." The failure to publish non-significant findings results in a systematic exclusion from published research of those studies that might show that a particular program or practice had little or no effect. Thus, estimates of effect in the published literature may make relationships appear stronger than if all estimates were available to the synthesis. Primarily for this reason, it is general practice in research synthesis to include both published and unpublished studies.

Carrying out a comprehensive literature search requires the use of multiple search strategies. For example, in a synthesis of research on the effectiveness of homework (Cooper, 1989, pp. 37–39), the author conducted multiple database searches (e.g., ERIC, PsycINFO, U.S. Government Printing Office's *Monthly Catalog*) and also searched reference sections of both relevant primary research and prior narrative reviews of the homework literature. These two search strategies generally are used as the initial approaches for developing a collection of relevant research. Other search strategies are complementary, as they fill gaps in the literature by identifying additional sources (particularly those that are unpublished) that would not have been located with only database or reference section searches. In the Cooper (1989) synthesis, one complementary approach involved reviewing conference proceedings from the American Educational Research Association convention for poster sessions or symposiums that focused on homework. In addition, Cooper sent letters of inquiry explaining the research topic and requesting any information on studies that had been done to 13 active homework researchers, 25 deans of the most productive colleges of education, 53 state agencies that dealt primarily with education, and more than 100 directors of research and evaluation in selected school districts across the United States. All of these approaches are valuable and complementary ways to uncover both published and unpublished studies for use in the research synthesis.

Gathering Data from Research Reports

In order to extract and record the necessary information from research reports, research synthesists use trained personnel applying standardized coding procedures. This method is analogous to collecting data on a survey questionnaire or, more directly, to the content analysis of documents (Weber, 1990).

For all studies included in a research synthesis, regardless of the topic, certain characteristics of studies are recorded. These include information about the research report itself (e.g., author, year of publication) and specifics of each individual study (e.g., sample size, study results). In addition, information specific to the current topic under review is included. For example, if the research topic of interest is the effects on reading achievement following participation in a summer program, the research synthesist would want to record information from each study about the length of summer school, the curriculum, the size of classes, and the experience of teachers. Features of the outcome variables (e.g., standardized tests, tests of reading subskills) would also be of interest. The important features coded for summer school programs clearly would be different from those of interest when the focus of the review is a specific phonics-based instructional technique.

Thus, coded information may be both of a general nature (i.e., common to all research syntheses) and specific to the substantive topic of interest. Stock (1994) offered a more exhaustive discussion of how to construct a coding document for a research synthesis. Ideally, the coding manual will allow thorough, unambiguous, and reliable extraction of all relevant data in a research report.

Statistical Analyses

As mentioned previously, one central advantage of research synthesis over traditional narrative techniques involves the use of statistical methods (i.e., meta-analysis) to summarize research results. These methods generally lead to more precise and reliable conclusions about a research base than does the narrative integration of research. This subsection focuses on a discussion of those methods using examples from a research synthesis on summer school conducted by the first author and others (Cooper et al., 2000). This research synthesis addressed the question, "What is the impact of summer school on students in need of academic remediation?" Two more specific questions in this synthesis were "What is the impact of summer school on students in need of reading remediation?" and "Does remedial summer school have a different impact on students' reading and mathematics achievement?"

Imagine that the research synthesist wishes to answer the first question just noted, "What is the impact of summer school on students in need of academic remediation?" Multiple methods could be used to address this question. We begin with a discussion of the vote-count method.

Vote-Count Method   The vote-count method begins by taking each report and classifying the statistical findings into one of three categories (Bushman, 1994): 1) statistically significant findings that indicate summer school was effective in improving academic outcomes, 2) statistically significant findings that indicate summer school had no effect on improving academic outcomes, and 3) nonsignificant findings (i.e., the null hypothesis cannot be rejected). Simply put, the pile with the greatest number of reports ("votes") would prevail.

Although this vote count of significant findings is intuitively appealing and frequently used by narrative reviewers, the strategy is unduly conservative. With traditional inferential statistics, it would be expected that chance alone should produce only about 5% of all reports falsely indicating that participation in summer school resulted in better academic outcomes. Therefore, depending on the number of studies, 10% or less of positive and statistically significant findings might indicate a real difference due to summer school participation. The vote-counting strategy, however, requires that a minimum 34% of findings be positive and statistically significant before the hypothesis is ruled a winner. Thus, the vote counting of significant findings could, and often does, lead to the suggested abandonment of policies, practices, and programs when in fact no such conclusion is warranted.

Hedges and Olkin (1985) described an alternative way to perform vote counts in research synthesis that avoids being overly conservative. This improved procedure involves 1) counting the number of positive and negative results, regardless of significance, and 2) applying a simple test to determine if one finding appears in the literature more often than would be expected by chance. This procedure, however, is not without its own weaknesses because it fails to weight a study's contribution by its sample size. Thus, studies with vastly differing sample sizes are considered equal contributors to the overall decision (e.g., a study with 100 participants is given weight equal to a study with 1,000 participants) even though the study with the larger sample provides a more precise estimate of the effect. Similarly, the magnitude of the effect in each study is disregarded. For example, a study that resulted in only a small improvement in academic outcome following summer school is given equal consideration to a study showing a large negative effect. Still, the vote count of directional findings can be an informative complement to other meta-analytic procedures and may serve a useful purpose when only directional information about study results is available.

In the Cooper et al. (2000) synthesis of summer school research, the vote count of directional findings identified 103 evaluations revealing positive effects on academic achievement and 12 with negative effects. Although this is generally persuasive evidence of a positive effect of summer school, it clearly does not give the level of precise information educational policy makers would like and, in fact, is available in the studies.

Effect Sizes As an alternative to vote-counting procedures, meta-analysts utilize effect sizes as a statistic to describe the cumulative findings from both individual studies and, when combined across all studies of interest, the collection of relevant research. Cohen defined an effect size as "the degree to which the phenomenon is present in the population, or the degree to which the null hypothesis is false" (1988, pp. 9–10). A meta-analyst 1) calculates an effect size for the outcomes of every study; 2) averages these effect sizes to estimate general magnitudes of effect; and 3) compares effect sizes to discover if variations in outcomes exist and, if so, which features of comparisons might account for them. Estimates of effect size provide the most essential information from studies, as they allow a statement about the relative magnitude of study outcomes and can be combined across studies. Estimates of effect size, however, are not consistently reported in primary research; thus, a meta-analyst must approximate or calculate the effect size from other statistics present in a research report (see Rosenthal, 1984, for many of these approaches).

Two effect size metrics are most applicable to the education literature. The first, called the d index by Cohen (1988), is a scale-free measure (i.e., the index does not depend on what scale was used to assess the variables) of the separation between two group means. The two groups might be students needing reading remediation who either went to summer school or did not. Calculating the basic d index for any comparison involves dividing the difference between the two group means by either their average standard deviation or the standard deviation of the control group. This procedure results in a measure of the difference between the two group means expressed in terms of their common standard deviation. For example, a d index of 0.25 indicates that one quarter of a standard deviation separates the two means.

There is a way to translate the standardized mean difference metric that is a bit more informative for educational practitioners. This translation is called U_3, or the distribution overlap. For example, a d index of 0.30 is associated with a U_3 measure of 61.8. This means that the average student (the student at the 50th percentile) in the group with the higher mean outperformed 61.8% of students in the group with the lower mean. We illustrate the use of U_3 shortly.

The second effect size metric well suited to research in education is the r index, or the correlation coefficient. Typically, the r index is used to express the relationship between two continuous variables, such as a continuous measure of the amount of classroom instruction in reading that students receive and their reading achievement scores. The decision to use a particular effect size metric is determined by which fits best with the characteristics of the variables under consideration.

Averaging Effect Sizes and Measures of Dispersion The most descriptive outcomes of a meta-analysis are the average effect sizes and the related measures of dispersion (e.g., confidence intervals) that accompany them. One advantage to the calculation of effect sizes is that they can be weighted across comparisons to permit studies yielding more precise estimates—that is, those with larger sample sizes—to contribute more to the overall combined effect. Both unweighted and weighted procedures are typically used to calculate average effect sizes across comparisons. In the unweighted procedure, each effect size is given equal weight in calculating the average effect. In the weighted procedure, each effect size is first weighted by its sample size, which gives greater weight to effect sizes that are more precise estimates because they are based on larger samples.

For example, using the meta-analysis of summer school evaluations, the unweighted overall estimate of effect size was $d = +0.32$. The weighted estimate of the effect size was $d = +0.26$, with a 95% confidence interval of $+0.22 < d < +0.30$. Because zero is not contained in this interval, we can be relatively confident that summer school had a positive effect on achievement. When the effect of summer school was examined on measures of reading achievement alone, the weighted estimate of effect was $d = +0.22$. Using U_3, this means that averaging across all the summer school evaluations, the average student who went to summer school did better on the post–summer-school measure of reading achievement than 58.7% of the students who did not attend. Thus, we see that summer school had positive effects on achievement in general and reading achievement in particular. Many texts, including Cooper and Hedges (1994), Hedges and Olkin (1985), Lipsey and Wilson (2001), and Shadish and Haddock (1994), have provided procedures for calculating the appropriate weights and estimating confidence intervals.

Moderator Analysis Moderator analysis is an approach to examining variance in effect sizes by looking at variables (i.e., moderators) that may affect the strength and/or direction of the relationship under examination. That is, these analyses examine why all studies do not result in the same effect size. It is expected that there are variations in studies, beyond just sampling error, that influence their results. These variables might be related to study characteristics (e.g., whether students were randomly assigned to attend summer school), participant characteristics (e.g., how far below grade level students were reading prior to attending summer school), characteristics of the program (e.g., length of summer school classes), or other pertinent variables (e.g., whether standardized tests or tests of more specific reading skills were used as outcome measures). Before conducting these analyses, however, the synthesist must first conduct a homogeneity analysis, which compares the amount of variance in an observed set of effect sizes with the amount of variance that would be expected by sampling error alone. If there is greater variation in effects than would be expected by chance, then variables potentially moderating the outcomes can be examined.

One important benefit of conducting a meta-analysis is that the synthesist can ask questions about potential moderators of an effect even if no individual study has included that particular variable. For example, a meta-analyst can ask whether the relation between remedial summer school participation and reading test scores differs between students in special education programs and students in regular education. This can be accomplished by comparing the groups' average effect sizes even if no single study has included both groups. The results of such a comparison of average effect sizes can suggest whether this student characteristic would be important to look at in future research and/or as a guide to policy.

After calculating the average effect sizes for different subgroups of studies, the meta-analyst statistically tests whether the variation among studies is reliably associated with different magnitudes of effect. Three statistical procedures for examining variation in effect sizes appear in the literature. The first approach makes use of statistical procedures typically employed with primary research data, such as analysis of variance (ANOVA) or multiple regression. The effect sizes are designated as the dependent variable; study features (i.e., potential moderators) serve as independent or predictor variables. This approach has been criticized based on the questionable tenability of the underlying assumptions.

The second approach compares the variation in obtained effect sizes with the variation expected due to sampling error (Hunter & Schmidt, 1990). This approach involves calculating not only the observed variance in effects but also the expected variance, that is, the amount of variance expected based on the fact that researchers took just a particular sample and another sample might be different from it. A formal statistical test of the difference between these two values is typically not carried out. Rather, the meta-analyst adopts a critical value for the ratio of observed-to-expected variance to use as a means for rejecting the null hypothesis. A separate aspect of this approach to meta-analysis includes adjusting effect sizes to account for methodological artifacts such as sampling error, range restrictions, or unreliability of measurements.

The final approach relies upon a statistical procedure analogous to ANOVA but employing different assumptions. Comparisons are grouped by study features, and the average effect sizes for these groups are tested to determine if they are homogenous (i.e., if the various average effect sizes could plausibly have been drawn from the same population). If this hypothesis is rejected, the grouping variable remains a plausible potential moderator of effect.

It is relatively simple to carry out a homogeneity analysis using a computer statistical package. The formulas and techniques for homogeneity analysis are described in Cooper (1998), Cooper and Hedges (1994), Hedges and Olkin (1985), Lipsey and Wilson (2001), Rosenthal (1984), Wang and Bushman (1999), and Wolf (1986).

Without the aid of statistics, a narrative research reviewer would simply group the studies by their shared feature, examine the statistical significance of outcomes across studies, and decide intuitively (using a hidden "cognitive algebra") whether the feature was associated with variation in outcomes. At best, this method is imprecise. At worst, it leads to incorrect inferences. In contrast, meta-analysis employs a formal, explicit method for testing whether different features of studies explain variation in their outcomes. If reliable differences do exist, the average effect sizes corresponding to these differences will take on added meaning and will help the synthesist offer research-based recommendations.

Although this discussion has highlighted frequently used meta-analytic procedures, there are other methods that are beyond the scope of this chapter. Some of those not included herein (e.g., combining p levels from significance tests) are becoming increasingly outdated as other, more functional methods are developed. For example, researchers are developing different statistical models for estimating how much variance should be expected in effect sizes (Shadish & Haddock, 1994).

In sum then, a meta-analysis might contain varying sets of statistics, including, but not limited to 1) a frequency analysis (i.e., vote count) of positive and negative directional results, 2) estimates of average effect sizes with confidence intervals, and 3) moderator analyses examining study features that might influence study out-comes.

In the Cooper et al. (2000) meta-analysis of summer school, the synthesists looked at subject area as a moderator of summer school effects. As we mentioned previously, the average weighted effect size for reading achievement was $d = +0.22$. The average weighted effect of summer school on mathematics achievement was $d = +0.30$. When these two average effects were compared with one another, it was found that even though summer school had significant positive effects on both reading and mathematics achievement, its effect on mathematics was larger than its effect on reading. The synthesists speculated that students generally experience greater loss of math skills over summer than reading skills, probably because they con-tinue to have some reading practice in summer but rarely practice math. Thus, the synthesists suggested that the difference may have more to do with what is happening with the control group (that is, with the students who did not attend summer school) than with the quality or the impact of summer reading instruction itself.

TRUSTWORTHINESS OF META-ANALYSIS

Can educators trust the findings of a meta-analysis? We think so. The procedures and techniques of research synthesis have been developed to be similar to accepted methods for conducting trustwor-thy primary research (Cooper, 1982). The analogy between research synthesis and primary research is summarized in Table 6.1. This table presents the five stages of research synthesis and applies to each stage evaluative criteria that are similar to those employed to assess the trustworthiness of primary research. Thus, concepts used to evaluate the value of primary research can also be applied to secondary analyses.

In Table 6.1 the concept of threats to inferential validity (Camp-bell & Stanley, 1966) is applied to research synthesis. Numerous points are identified at which the validity and trustworthiness of a synthesis might be compromised. These might occur not only at various stages of the processes but also might result from consistent deficiencies in the set of studies that form the database of reviewed reports. Contained in Table 6.1 is a view and process for research

Table 6.1. The integrative review conceptualized as a research project

			Stage of research		
Stage characteristics	Problem formulation	Data collection	Data evaluation	Analysis and interpretation	Public presentation
Research question asked	What evidence should be included in the review?	What procedures should be used to find relevant evidence?	What retrieved evidence should be included in the review?	What procedures should be used to make inferences about the literature as a whole?	What information should be included in the review report?
Primary function in review	Constructing definitions that distinguish relevant from irrelevant studies	Determining which sources of potentially relevant studies to examine	Applying criteria to separate valid from invalid studies	Synthesizing valid retrieved studies	Applying editorial criteria to separate important from unimportant information
Procedural differences that create variation in review conclusions	Differences in included operational definitions Differences in operational detail	Differences in the research contained in sources of information	Differences in quality criteria Differences in the influence of nonquality criteria	Differences in rules of inference	Differences in guidelines for editorial judgment
Sources of potential invalidity in review conclusions	Narrow concepts might make review conclusions less definitive and robust. Superficial operational detail might obscure interacting variables.	Accessed studies might be qualitatively different from the target population of studies. People sampled in accessible studies might be different from target population of people.	Nonquality factors might cause improper weighting of study information. Omissions in study reports might make conclusions unreliable.	Rules for distinguishing patterns from noise might be inappropriate. Review-based evidence might be used to infer causality.	Omission of review procedures might make conclusions irreproducible. Omission of review findings and study procedures might make conclusions obsolete.

From Cooper, H. (1982). Scientific guidelines for conducting integrative research reviews. *Review of Educational Research, 52,* 291–302; reprinted by permission. Copyright © 1982 American Educational Research Association.

synthesis that is far more scientific (e.g., systematic, rigorous, open to criticism) than is the case for narrative research reviews.

It is important to recognize that using rigorous and systematic rules for synthesizing a collection of studies does not ensure that the resulting inferences will be reliable. For example, during the formulation of a problem, threats to the validity of a synthesis could occur if the synthesist does not consider distinctions in definitions of policies or programs that are viewed as important by others in the field. The validity of a literature search could be affected by reliance on a few selective sources of research reports or by publication bias. The validity of data evaluation and coding can be threatened if information from research reports is missing or if the coders extracting information are poorly trained.

In some of these situations, there exist opportunities to correct flawed methodologies. For example, search methods may need to be expanded if a literature search has identified only a few relevant studies. Another threat to the validity of systematic reviews is missing data in primary research reports. This may occur, for instance, if a report does not adequately describe the components of a reading program. One approach to solving this problem is to directly contact the original study authors and request more information. DuBois, Holloway, Valentine, and Cooper (2002) utilized this approach in a meta-analysis of the effectiveness of youth mentoring programs. They had some success in contacting the primary authors. They did find, however, that success in both contacting authors and retrieving data was dependent on the amount of time that had passed since original publication of the research report; there was very little success when reports had been published more than 10 years prior. This approach was successful, particularly with more recent research, in adding data to the meta-analysis that would have been otherwise unavailable, thus increasing the representativeness of the data set.

Standard reliability assessments, similar to those used in primary research, can also be applied to assess the extent to which study information has been reliably extracted from research reports. This involves employing procedures akin to those used in assessing interrater reliability in other research domains (e.g., Lipsey & Wilson, 2001; Orwin, 1994). Briefly, this would require having two (or more) reviewers independently code some subset of the studies and then deriving a reliability assessment based on these duplicate ratings. A second strategy involves having two reviewers independently code all of the studies in the review. Disagreements then may be resolved in conference or by using a third reader. This procedure raises the effective reliability of codes to very high levels.

Research synthesists must also consider the quality of the research reports that they are relying on in their review. A research synthesis is only as good as the studies that go into it. If only poor-quality studies have been conducted on the topic at hand, the synthesis cannot yield particularly interpretable findings. Of course, this holds true whether traditional narrative review procedures or meta-analysis techniques are employed. One solution to this problem is to test study quality as a moderator of effects. This may show whether high- and low-quality studies result in the same estimate of a policy or practice's effect. Indices of study quality may include variables such as use of random assignment, representative sampling procedures, or measurement reliability (Berlin & Rennie, 1999; Jüni, Witschi, Bloch, & Egger, 1999). If significant influences are identified, meta-analysts then may adjust their inferences accordingly and/or statistically control for the presence or absence of these features when examining other substantive influences on study outcomes (Lipsey & Wilson, 2001).

For example, the meta-analysis of the effectiveness of summer school programs (Cooper et al., 2000) demonstrated that studies using a one-group pretest–posttest (within-subjects) design revealed a more positive effect of summer school than studies that used a nonequivalent control group (nonrandomized between-subjects) design. Studies that employed random assignment of students (randomized between-subjects design) produced an average effect that fell between these two values. In this example, study design, one index of quality, explained some variation in the results and thus would be an important consideration when interpreting meta-analytic findings.

These limitations, when thoroughly addressed by meta-analysts, should not detract from the trustworthiness of research synthesis. It is important, however, for the discerning reader to evaluate each individual synthesis for its attempts to address these potential sources of insufficiency. In sum then, although systematic research synthesis helps us obtain more trustworthy results across a cumulative literature, it is not a guarantee. Most importantly, using systematic and open procedures to accumulate evidence makes it much easier to determine where the synthesist might have gone wrong and to continuously improve on the effort.

USE OF RESEARCH SYNTHESES IN EDUCATION

Research is not complete until results are shared with the community interested in the findings. We have already alluded to some of the issues related to public presentation of research syntheses in previous sections. For example, the research synthesist must take care to interpret and report effect sizes in such a manner as to be understandable to the intended audience. In addition, there are two potential sources of bias in findings that might emerge during public presentation. First, ignoring evidence suggesting that potential features of studies might influence a main finding can jeopardize the trustworthiness of conclusions presented by the research synthesist. Second, the synthesis techniques employed may fail to be comprehensible to the reader. That is, the synthesist must provide enough information so that readers can understand and critically assess the methods, strengths, and weaknesses of the research synthesis. Halvorsen (1994) and Light, Singer, and Willett (1994) presented numerous suggestions regarding effective ways to present the results of meta-analyses to a broad audience.

There are specific characteristics of educational research that may influence the perception of diminished value for empirical evidence in setting policy and guiding practice. Specifically, three aspects of educational research often affect the application of systematic review conclusions.

First, policies, programs, and guidelines for practice are carried out in real-world contexts. Each of these environments presents intricacies that influence whether a policy or practice produces the desired results in that particular setting. Recognizing and accounting for such nuances of setting in primary research, particularly within a single study, is a difficult task. Thus, studies that appear quite similar may produce different results for subtle reasons. Alternatively, a program that is recommended and feasible in a research context may not be viable under real-world circumstances.

Second, for both ethical and practical reasons, educational research is frequently carried out using designs that do not permit strong causal inferences. For example, a school district interested in observing the educational benefits of summer school attendance might randomly assign some at-risk children to participate in remedial summer school programs and other at-risk children to receive no intervention. Such a decision, however, likely would be met with disapproval from the individual schools and parents of the excluded students, who would be concerned about the possibility of negative consequences for withholding any remedial opportunities from students clearly in need of such assistance (see Chapter 3 for further discussion of this issue). This reality means that explanations for the outcome of a study other than the effectiveness of the policy or practice itself will remain plausible. One solution to this dilemma would be to "wait-list" students in the control group until the end of the research study and then at that time provide them with an equivalent remedial education program.

Third, the outcome of any single study is probabilistic in nature, based as it is on samples drawn from populations. Therefore, when many studies on the same topic have been conducted, variation in their outcomes (in the direction as well as the magnitude of effects) is not surprising. Indeed, such variation is expected given changes in study design due to differences that appear when conducting research among varying groups and settings. Often, this uncertainty is mistakenly labeled as conflicting results.

CONCLUSIONS

Systematic research synthesis is not a perfect solution to the problems faced by educational researchers. Syntheses conducted in a rigorous and transparent manner can, however, make important contributions to educational policy and practice. Furthermore, research synthesis offers a concise and practical means of summarizing a vast body of literature. In turn, this permits recommendations about the value of existing programs and translates this information into informative statements to guide future practice and research.

Using proper synthesis procedures also does more than simply ameliorate the problems associated with the traditional narrative review. Systematic research synthesis transforms many difficulties into strengths. Variation in the setting, design, and sampling characteristics of individual studies are sources of disturbance when studies are examined individually and narratively. These variations often prevent summative statements about multiple studies, especially when those studies examine policies and practices. Conversely, when multiple studies, each restricted in their representation of context, design, and sample, are treated as data in cumulative analysis, they can contribute jointly to confident and general, but properly contextualized, conclusions.

Because of the current emphasis in education to provide research-based and empirically supported programs, there is great potential value in the use of systematic research synthesis. Educators will have an advantage when basing policy and teaching methods on programs that are supported both by findings in the primary research domain and those that withstand further scrutiny with systematic synthesis procedures.

REFERENCES

Berlin, J.A., & Rennie, D. (1999). Measuring the quality of trials. *Journal of the American Medical Association, 282,* 1083–1085.

Bushman, B.J. (1994). Vote-counting procedures in meta-analysis. In H. Cooper & L.V. Hedges (Eds.), *The handbook of research synthesis* (pp. 193–213). New York: Russell Sage Foundation.

Campbell, D.T., & Stanley, J.C. (1966). *Experimental and quasi-experimental designs for research.* Chicago: Rand McNally.

Cohen, J. (1988). *Statistical power analysis in the behavioral sciences.* Mahwah, NJ: Lawrence Erlbaum Associates.

Cook, T.D., Cooper, H.M., Cordray, D.S., Hartmann, H., Hedges, L.V., Light, R.J., et al. (1992). *Meta-analysis for explanation: A casebook.* New York: Russell Sage Foundation.

Cooper, H.M. (1979). Statistically combining independent studies: A meta-analysis of sex differences in conformity research. *Journal of Personality and Social Psychology, 37,* 131–146.

Cooper, H.M. (1982). Scientific guidelines for conducting integrative research reviews. *Review of Educational Research, 52,* 291–302.

Cooper, H. (1989). *Homework.* New York: Longman.

Cooper, H.M. (1998). *Synthesizing research: A guide for literature reviews* (3rd ed.). Thousand Oaks, CA: Sage Publications.

Cooper, H., Charlton, K., Valentine, J.V., & Muhlenbruck, L. (2000). Making the most of summer school: A meta-analytic and narrative review. *Monographs on Child Development, 65*(1). Malden, MA: Blackwell Press.

Cooper, H., DeNeve, K., & Charlton, K. (1997). Finding the missing science: The fate of studies submitted for review by a human subjects committee. *Psychological Methods, 2,* 447–452.

Cooper, H., & Hedges, L.V. (1994). *The handbook of research synthesis.* New York: Russell Sage Foundation.

Cooper, H.M., & Rosenthal, R. (1980). Statistical versus traditional procedures for summarizing research findings. *Psychological Bulletin, 87,* 442–449.

DuBois, D.L., Holloway, B.E., Valentine, J.C., & Cooper, H. (2002). Effectiveness of meta-analytic programs for youth: A meta-analytic review. *American Journal of Community Psychology, 30,* 157–197.

Eddy, D.M., Hasselblad, V., & Shachter, R. (1992). *Meta-analysis by the confidence profile method.* San Diego: Academic Press.

Ehri, L.C., Nunes, S.R., Stahl, S.A., & Willows, D.M. (2001). Systematic phonics instruction helps students learn to read: Evidence from the National Reading Panel's meta-analysis. *Review of Educational Research, 71,* 393–447.

Erlbaum, B., Vaughn, S., Hughes, M.T., & Moody, S.W. (2000). How effective are one-to-one tutoring programs in reading for elementary students at risk for reading failure? A meta-analysis of the intervention research. *Journal of Educational Psychology, 92,* 605–619.

Feldman, K.A. (1971). Using the work of others: Some observations on reviewing and integrating. *Sociology of Education, 4,* 86–102.

Fuchs, D., Fuchs, L.S., Mathes, P.G., Lipsey, M.E., & Eaton, S. (2000). A meta-analysis of reading differences between underachievers with and without the learning disabilities label: A brief report. *Learning Disabilities: A Multidisciplinary Journal, 10,* 1–3.

Glass, G.V. (1976). Primary, secondary, and meta-analysis of research. *Educational Researcher, 5,* 3–8.

Glass, G.V., & Smith, M.L. (1979). Meta-analysis of research on class size and achievement. *Educational Evaluation and Policy Analysis, 1,* 2–16.

Greenberg, J., & Folger, R. (1988). *Controversial issues in social research.* New York: Springer-Verlag.

Halvorsen, K.T. (1994). The reporting format. In H. Cooper & L.V. Hedges (Eds.), *The handbook of research synthesis* (pp. 425–438). New York: Russell Sage Foundation.

Hedges, L.V., & Olkin, I. (1985). *Statistical methods for meta-analysis.* San Diego: Academic Press.

Hunter, J.E., & Schmidt, F.L. (1990). *Methods of meta-analysis: Correcting error and bias in research findings.* Thousand Oaks, CA: Sage.

Hunter, J.E., Schmidt, F.L., & Hunter, R. (1979). Differential validity of employment tests by race: A comprehensive review and analysis. *Psychological Bulletin, 86,* 721–735.

Johnson, B.T. (1989). *DSTAT: Software for the meta-analytic review of research literatures.* Mahwah, NJ: Lawrence Erlbaum Associates.

Johnson, B.T., & Eagly, A.H. (2000). Quantitative synthesis of social psychological research. In H.T. Reis & C.M. Judd (Eds.), *Handbook of research methods in social and personality psychology* (pp. 496–528). New York: Cambridge University Press.

Jüni, P., Witschi, A., Bloch, R., & Egger, M. (1999). The hazards of scoring the quality of clinical trials for meta-analysis. *Journal of the American Medical Association, 282,* 1054–1060.

Light, R.J. (Ed.). (1983). *Evaluation studies review annual* (Vol. 8). Thousand Oaks, CA: Sage Publications.

Light, R.J., Singer, J.D., & Willett, J.B. (1994). The visual presentation and interpretation of meta-analyses. In H. Cooper & L.V. Hedges (Eds.), *The handbook of research synthesis* (pp. 439–453). New York: Russell Sage Foundation.

Lipsey, M.W., & Wilson, D.B. (2001). *Practical meta-analysis.* Thousand Oaks, CA: Sage Publications.

Mullen, B. (1989). *Advanced BASIC meta-analysis.* Mahwah, NJ: Lawrence Erlbaum Associates.

No Child Left Behind Act of 2001, PL 107-110, 115 Stat. 1425, 20 U.S.C. §§ 6301 *et seq.*

Orwin, R.G. (1994). Evaluating coding decisions. In H. Cooper & L.V. Hedges (Eds.), *The handbook of research synthesis* (pp. 139–162). New York: Russell Sage Foundation.

Pearson, K. (1904). Report on certain enteric fever inoculation statistics. *British Medical Journal, 3,* 1243–1246.

Rosenthal, R. (1984). *Meta-analytic procedures for social research.* Thousand Oaks, CA: Sage Publications.

Rosenthal, R., & Rubin, D. (1978). Interpersonal expectancy effects: The first 345 studies. *Behavioral and Brain Sciences, 3,* 377–415.

Shadish, W.R., & Haddock, C.K. (1994). Combining estimates of effect size. In H. Cooper & L.V. Hedges (Eds.), *The handbook of research synthesis* (pp. 261–282). New York: Russell Sage Foundation.

Smith, M.L., & Glass, G.V. (1977). Meta-analysis of psychotherapy outcome studies. *American Psychologist, 32,* 752–760.

Stock, W.A. (1994). Systematic coding for research synthesis. In H. Cooper & L.V. Hedges (Eds.), *The handbook of research synthesis* (pp. 125–138). New York: Russell Sage Foundation.

U.S. Department of Education (2002). *Executive Summary of the No Child Left Behind Act of 2001.* Retrieved October 23, 2003, from http://www.ed.gov/nclb/overview/intro/execsumm.html

Wachter, K.W., & Straf, M.L. (Eds.). (1990). *The future of meta-analysis.* New York: Russell Sage Foundation.

Wang, M.C., & Bushman, B.J. (1999). *Integrating results through meta-analytic review using SAS software.* Cary, NC: SAS Institute.

Weber, R.P. (1990). *Basic content analysis* (2nd ed.). Thousand Oaks, CA: Sage Publications.

Wolf, F.W. (1986). *Meta-analysis: Quantitative methods for research synthesis.* Thousand Oaks, CA: Sage Publications.

7

Clinical Trials as a Model for Intervention Research Studies in Education

ROBIN D. MORRIS

Since the late 1990s, numerous discussions have strongly supported or ridiculed and rejected the idea of the need to study educational programs and interventions in ways analogous to the manner in which medical interventions are studied and evaluated. Should we really use medical research models to evaluate a reading program or science curriculum's effectiveness as we do a new screening test for cancer, a smoking prevention program, a new surgical intervention for heart attacks, or a new drug designed to reduce high blood pressure? Such studies in medicine are called *clinical trials* and are used to ensure that any new medical screening procedure, prevention program, surgery technique, or new drug is not only safe for the patients involved but also effective in the manner planned, in other words, that it works. Are we really suggesting clinical trials in education?

Physicians, who work every day with their patients, are very aware of the limits of their knowledge and abilities in taking care of these patients and generate many new ideas regarding how they can improve care and the quality of patients' health and lives. Unfortunately, such new ideas may be right or wrong or partially both. Practices may appear curative, yet what is observed may not be real but may only appear that way due to chance or to some unspoken or unknown biases of the developer. If these ideas or treatments are not carefully evaluated before being widely used, then patients may not get better; may be injured; or, in the worst case, may die.

This issue is even more complicated given that the new treatment or procedure may work for only some people and not others;

therefore, careful evaluation in a wide range of patients is required. Some new ideas for treatment or intervention may also be significantly more costly than those currently in use but may provide only minimally better effectiveness compared with the old approaches, so there may be questions regarding cost–benefit relationships. Is it better to have a less expensive intervention that can be widely provided to everyone even though it has limited efficacy, or should there also be a much more expensive option that may, due to cost, be available only to limited groups of people? And how should this information about efficacy and cost affect treatment decisions? How much of an improvement in intervention or treatment outcome should there be to justify the costs involved? How do researchers ensure that the evidence for using the expensive intervention is as unbiased in its evaluation as humans can make it and that the public is not being exploited by self-serving evaluations by a medical group looking for income? Without the systematic evaluations involved in clinical trials, which use scientific approaches and methodologies specifically developed to address such ideas, questions, and potential biases, medicine would still be full of "snake oil." Clinical trials have all of the strengths and limitations of good science (see Chapter 4) but really are designed to ask the question of what works, to investigate how various intervention approaches compare, and to address and understand the many human biases or other factors that may affect evaluation of interventions and care of patients.

Teachers, who work every day with children, are aware of the limits of their knowledge and abilities in teaching. Based on their experience, teachers generate many new ideas regarding how to improve their teaching and the quality of children's learning, knowledge, and true understanding of the world around them. Unfortunately, just as in medicine, such new ideas may be right or wrong or partially both. What may appear to be improvements in learning resulting from implementation of those new ideas may actually be the result of some unspoken or unknown bias of the developer. If these ideas are not carefully evaluated before being widely used, then children may learn more slowly than expected or may not learn up to their potential. In the worst case, children may not develop critical life-long knowledge or abilities, such as how to read and may even drop out of school due to their learning struggles.

This issue is even more complicated given that the new instructional approaches may work for some children but not for others; therefore, the new approaches require careful evaluation in a wide range of children and schools. Also, some new instructional ideas may be significantly more costly than the older approaches, both in time and money, but may provide only minimally better learning improvement. So, again, as with medical treatments, cost–benefit issues may come into play. As in medicine, there is a question of whether it is better to have less expensive approaches available to everyone even though they have limitations in their efficacy or whether much more expensive and time-consuming options should be in place that are available only to limited groups of teachers and children, even if these more expensive options have not been shown to be that much more effective than the less expensive or less efficient approaches. How much of an improvement in instructional outcomes justifies the costs involved? How do educators ensure that the evidence for using the new instructional approach is as unbiased in its evaluation as humans can make it and that the public is just not being exploited by self-serving evaluations by an educational consultant or a publisher looking for income?

By now it should be apparent that there are legitimate parallels to be drawn between medical and educational research. Without the systematic evaluations involved in educational trials (there is no need to call the trials *clinical* in education, as there are really no medical patients involved), which use scientific approaches and methodologies to address ideas, questions, and potential biases, teachers would continually have to make decisions about which instructional approaches are the "snake oils" of education. Educational trials, just like medical clinical trials, should benefit from the strengths and take into account the limitations of good science (see Chapter 4) and should be designed to ask the questions of what works for teachers and their students, how well it works, and what factors have an impact on its effectiveness. At the same time, these studies should be designed to address and enable researchers to understand those human biases and other factors that may affect evaluation of various instructional practices and the teaching and care of children.

OPPOSITION TO THE USE
OF CLINICAL TRIALS IN EDUCATION

So why is there opposition to employing such methodological approaches used in medicine in educational research? One of the most specific critiques is that this approach uses the scientific method, which is thought to be not appropriate for addressing such educational questions. This epistemological or philosophical criticism of how one should understand the world comes from a range of educators, some from humanistic orientations who believe that any systematic evaluation of teachers or children is so inherently flawed and full of errors as to render it useless and others who consider classroom learning situations to be so complex and to contain so many important and unique variables that science cannot integrate all of the information in any useful manner. Finally, some educators suggest that only phenomenological or experiential studies of individual teachers or children are credible and that nothing learned in one classroom can be generalized to any other classroom; yet, the majority of these individualized or case studies fail a basic tenet of the scientific method, namely the applicability of lessons learned from one situation to another (generalization).

These points of view are concerned that the scientific process dehumanizes teachers, children, and the learning process and is neither a valid nor a holistic representation of the educational environment or processes being experienced by teachers and children. Educators who implicitly or explicitly subscribe to these frameworks typically reject most science-based evidence out of hand, even though many educational researchers who value the scientific process for understanding instructional processes and children's learning feel equally strongly about the importance of the core values, ideals, and interests of teachers and children. Embracing the scientific method does not eliminate caring and sensitivity. On the contrary, some see ensuring effective education as a highly caring activity.

Unfortunately, those who embrace the antiscience orientation do not provide alternative approaches that are public for deciding whether a new instructional idea is valid or more useful than current practice. What these parties offer is opinion based on how some teachers' experience an instructional approach and feel about its value to children and teachers. It is important to realize that such different worldviews are not inherently good or bad or right or wrong. These different approaches to understanding the world, however, do influence many educators' views of how instructional knowledge and practices should be developed, evaluated, or shared.

Another common response in opposition to using educational trials for evaluating instructional ideas and practices is purely conceptual, in that such trials are based on the medical model and its core "dis-ease" model. Others who voice a similar kind of opposition are concerned with the problems involved with diagnoses, which have an educational analog in special education category labels, which focus on deficiencies rather than strengths or attributes and which frequently are seen as having a lasting negative impact on children to whom these diagnostic labels are assigned. Unfortunately, those who object to the medical or the disease model may have limited understanding of what these terms mean even in the medical world.

What is really meant by *disease?* Numerous definitions have been proposed, but as Kendell commented, "It is not so much a definition we lack as an adequate one" (1975, p. 10). Kendell's review of the concept of disease suggests that the term developed as a description of pain and suffering when there was no clear injury but over the years became more connected with the idea of some biological (e.g., anatomical, histological, physiological, cellular, genetic) process. But, as Kendell pointed out,

> The concept of an abnormality or a lesion is quite straightforward so long as one is concerned with a departure from a standard pattern. But as soon as we begin to recognize that there is no standard pattern of structure and function, and that even healthy human beings and all their constituent tissues and organs vary considerably in size, shape, composition and functional efficiency, it becomes much less obvious what constitutes a lesion, where normal variation ends and abnormality begins. (p. 11)

It appears that many educators who reject the use of a conceptual research framework exemplified by medical clinical trials implicitly link the disease model with a lesion, a pathogen, or damage, which explains their opposition. No one wants to suggest that educational researchers should use such a deficit model as the basis for understanding instructional approaches, teachers, or children. Unfortunately, opponents of educational trials have taken the current focus on accountability and consequences for poorly performing schools as confirming evidence for a conceptual focus on deficits or "diseased" schools, and this notion has strengthened their opposition to such a framework.

Over the 20th century, newer concepts of disease have become prevalent in medicine that can be easily adapted to education. One of these is the statistical concept of disease that was developed to better understand processes such as hypertension, which has appeared to have complex genetic foundations and to be influenced by a person's response to environmental stress and which has had a somewhat normal statistical distribution in the general population. Probably also important in the development of more modern concepts of disease was the increasing awareness of the complex interplay between biological and environmental factors that affected, for example, blood pressure, and that was predictive of increased mortality.

This conceptualization is not that different from modern conceptualizations of children's learning, which can easily be considered to be the results of an interplay between children's biological aptitudes and learning and instructional environments and which are frequently described in terms of a distribution of achievement levels (an analog of blood pressure measurement). In this framework, there are children who fall far from the average achievement levels (or whatever the domain of interest is), just as there are individuals who fall far from the average blood pressure levels. Doctors know that adults whose blood pressure deviates further and further from the average are at increasing risk for different health and quality-of-life outcomes, just as educators know that children whose achievement levels deviate further and further from the average are at increasing risk for different academic and quality-of-life outcomes.

This framework represents a continuum model in that no naturally occurring boundary demarcates when someone has a disease or does not—rather, there is an increased level of risk for being considered different (at an advantage or disadvantage) the further from the average one falls. Clearly, the decision of which outcomes are considered advantageous or disadvantageous is dependent on many cultural and social factors and not always an easy or consistent determination. Should educators consider children's learning similarly, so the further students fall from the average, the more likely they are to be at an educational advantage or disadvantage in their lives? And taking this line of reasoning even further, just for the sake of argument, could educators consider some children who are not learning at near-average rates to have a lack of ease (or "disease") in their learning, and ultimately in their lives? The causes of such a lack of ease in achievement or learning could be due to anything from a child's underlying genetic and related brain functions (biological attributes) to the child's past or present learning environments, including the types of instructional programs or curricula to which the child may have been exposed. This is clearly a very complex picture.

This basic concern regarding the identification of differences among children and the potential of negative labeling of any identified differences that may put children at increased risk is particularly relevant to understanding the goals of educational trials and research studies of educational interventions. One of the primary goals of such research is to better describe those factors that systematically affect children's learning and achievement outcomes. Such factors might be related to biological functioning; for example, children with severe sickle cell anemia may have multiple small strokes and may in general (there are always exceptions) score lower on some academic measures compared with those children who don't have sickle cell anemia. It could be that the lower academic performance is due to the disease or that the medications used to treat it affect children's attention and memory functioning, or it could be that the poor performance occurs because these children miss more school days than the other children. Yet another factor may be related to the environment; for example, the instructional program being followed by the teachers may cause children who receive explicit instruction to perform better on the outcome measure of interest as compared with those children who do not receive explicit instruction. And always it could be that these factors all contribute and that no single factor is responsible. It is important to realize that interactions between a child's biological attributes and instructional environments are probably more prevalent than we realize.

When examining all of these factors affecting educational outcomes, it is far too easy to make value statements regarding these differences, such that children who are different, whether they have sickle cell anemia or are performing poorly because they have not had explicit instruction, are negatively valued. Educators and educational researchers must remember that such determinations are sociocultural decisions and not relevant to the questions being asked, as such value labels do not affect the scientific results. Unfortunately, there is an apparent bias in humans to not only detect but also to label any differences in their observations and environment. We should also remember that such value labels can be reversed in certain situations; for example, the sickle cell trait can protect children from malaria in tropical environments, and this protection can be seen as a positive attribute.

CAN THE SCIENTIFIC CONCEPTS
AND METHODOLOGIES USED IN CLINICAL
TRIALS BE USEFUL IN EDUCATIONAL TRIALS?

Arguments about the usefulness of a clinical trials approach and the clarification of more modern medical and disease models may or may not convince critics of such approaches that there are important similarities between the complex biological and environmental interactions in modern medicine and modern education. Regardless, it is hard for these critics to argue that the complexities of instructional interventions are of a higher order than those involved in prevention or treatment in modern medicine. Both areas focus on understanding complex biological or environmental (interventions) conditions that can effect change, either in the underlying biological system in medicine or in learning in education. Both areas are completely dependent on their ability to create positive changes in their unique areas of interest, either health or academic achievement in a narrower focus but quality of life in the broadest conceptualization. Given that medicine has seen significant advances in its ability to improve human conditions through its increasingly sophisticated research and clinical trials for developing evidence-based medicine, it is difficult not to consider that such an approach, adapted to the educational environment and questions, would also have strong potential for advancing knowledge. In fact, the underlying scientific methods and approaches involved in clinical trials, when compared with the requirements of educational trials, are conceptually quite similar, if not identical. The real differences are in the present level of theoretical development and measurement capabilities and, of course, the level of past and present federal and institutional support for such research.

As described in Chapter 4, science is a process that requires the use of strong logic and systematic observations to answer clearly developed questions in a public process. Probably one of the most important aspects of the scientific process is its public nature, which invites other scientists to carefully review the core questions (or ideas or hypotheses), rationale and logic, the methods used, data analysis, and the interpretation of results of those studies performed by their peers. This peer-review process, which drives the iterative, process-oriented nature of science, is one of the strengths of science. By providing all of the details of a study in a peer-reviewed research journal at a level of detail that would allow others to replicate the study, researchers enable their fellow scientists to independently confirm or refute the results of any research study by repeating it. This level of detail also allows other researchers to modify a procedure in a systematic way so that they can ask new questions that add to the understanding of the original results. Thus, if someone has proposed a new instructional program, researchers can perform an educational trial to evaluate how much the program improves some achievement outcome of interest and can publish the exact description of their study so that there can be peer review. Another researcher, not as emotionally invested in the instructional program as its developer and who may have a different theoretical orientation or model, can then independently repeat the same study in other schools or classes and determine whether the results are consistent with those of the original study. As more and more researchers replicate the study and come to consistent findings, there is increasing converging evidence that the instructional approach works under the conditions that were initially set to evaluate it as suggested by the original study.

No one study by itself provides the fully convincing evidence that is needed to validate any instructional approach. Scientific inquiry is a cumulative process that gathers strength through peer review, criticism, systematic replication, evaluation of variations, and the very public process that allows all interested parties to understand the true nature of the questions being asked, the methods being used, and the quality of the results obtained. Without this public peer-review process of publishing results, there would also be no process available to refute findings or correct errors in research findings or concepts. If different researchers come to very different conclusions from those of the original research on which they based their studies, then those original findings need to be questioned. Unfortunately, this peer-review process and the systematic scientific process are very conservative, and new ideas and research findings that are widely divergent from current mainstream views may be summarily rejected without the necessary careful evaluation. When this happens, science stops. Therefore, a balance must be sought between the steady, reliable process of replication and confirmation and pushing ahead with testing new, innovative ideas and approaches—but then the cycle must confirm these new ideas and approaches through peer review and replication or confirmation.

CRITICAL COMPONENTS OF EDUCATIONAL TRIALS

Educational trials are designed to ask not only which instructional programs work but also how different instructional approaches compare in outcomes. The trials are also designed to make the findings public so that peer review and iterative scientific confirmation or corrective processes can take place. To convey the potential power of educational research trials, an example of the thinking behind the design of such a trial is described in the subsections that follow. Because reading instruction is presently such a critical but widely debated area of education, I use a fictional example from this area to better describe some of the issues involved in an educational trial designed to compare different approaches to reading instruction.

The Role of Theory

The first step in an educational trial is to start with theory. For example, this fictional study begins with three different theoretical models regarding how reading should be taught. These different theoretical models have been derived from teachers' experiences and their practical knowledge and from a review of the previous research on reading and reading instruction (existing scientifically based knowledge). One question that is frequently asked of this phase of study development is why researchers need theoretical models. The quick answer is that the models provide a framework that directs the study. Without theory, a researcher would not know the important child, teacher, or program attributes on which to focus. Without theory and related conceptual models, a researcher would have to study everything related to the children involved, their teachers, and the instructional programs, which is an impossible endeavor. At this stage, the researcher rules out certain attributes and focuses on others. For example, children's hair color or weight are probably not critical factors in understanding the basis of an instructional program in reading and thus can be discarded as potential study variables. Those critics who say that education is too complex to study may actually be implying that educational researchers do not have adequate educational theories to focus their research; such a criticism may have some validity in many areas of education.

Theory helps to guide the research through the kinds of questions it generates and provides the study with structure and direction.

Clearly presenting the underlying theory is also an important component of the public process of science. It tells others the basic logic behind an instructional program and the research questions being asked about it and provides clear predictions about what researchers should find if the theory is valid before the study is actually even done. In this way, theory helps keep researchers virtuous, as they cannot claim after the study is completed that simply any results they find are consistent with their theory. Note that refuting a theory is as important as supporting it and that a theory can never be proven in any one study because evidence from multiple studies to validate the theory's correctness has to accumulate over time. In this framework, even the fictional study I am describing can only add to the available evidence in support of one or more of the theories. It cannot prove them, although it may refute them if findings are opposite from what was predicted by the theory. The real question, though, is whether the educational trial was designed well enough to really answer the questions posed and make any valid conclusions in either direction. The quality of the study design is a key factor in answering this question.

The Role of Study Design and Randomization

In an educational trial, after the theory has been identified, study design is selected (see Chapter 4 for more on study design). One of the highest quality designs for evaluating the effectiveness of the three hypothetical instructional programs derived from three different theoretical models regarding reading development is called a *randomized controlled trial*. In this design, children, probably from a wide range of different schools and classrooms, would be randomly assigned to one of the three instructional programs or to a control condition (discussed later in this chapter), and teachers would be randomly assigned to teach them, all being equally well trained to teach any of the programs effectively. Randomization is a critical process for addressing questions about the effectiveness of various reading programs, as it helps to reduce sampling biases that could systematically influence the study's findings. Randomization means that the decision regarding which children should be taught by which reading approach is not made based on any a priori knowledge about the children or their abilities; it is made randomly. The same is true for teachers; they are not assigned to teach a particular program based on their experiences with it. Why is this so important? Because there is an underlying assumption that if there were clear evidence on which to make such assignments based on child or teacher characteristics to maximize reading outcomes, then there would be no need for the study. Unfortunately, many people in education believe that they intuitively know how to make such assignments based on their experiences, even though they are not able to make their criteria explicit or public, and they have no evidence to validate such beliefs or their consequences. A research study could be easily designed to evaluate how effective such child or teacher assignments are in affecting reading outcomes, but that is not the question being asked in this hypothetical study.

Random assignment to the different reading or control conditions also ensures that there is no hidden bias in forming the various groups of children that is due to some unknown process or child characteristics. For example, if all of the children who are the best readers were assigned to only one reading program because they were in the same class and had the same schedule or if all children from families who read with their children at home for 2 hours every night ended up in the same reading program because those parents knew which teacher to ask for in the study, then there would be systematic bias in the results from the study. Random assignment of teachers and children is designed to reduce systematic bias and to improve the chances that all groups of children who are taught in one of the four programs (the three instructional methods that are being examined and one control) are more similar to each other than not. In other words, there is equal opportunity for any child to be taught in any of the programs, and the greater the number of children in each sample, the more diversity there will be and the better will be the generalization of the results to other children in other schools who were not in this study. Large samples of randomly assigned children in each program are also necessary statistically to ensure that the resulting data analysis has enough power and is valid for the questions being addressed.

The same logic holds for why teacher selection is randomized. Clearly, teachers who may have taught one of the reading programs for years might feel that they should be the instructor of choice for that one program, as they know it the best and would provide the best example of its capabilities. This is a complicated decision that has to be made in each study. It might be possible to develop another study in which very experienced teachers in each of the individual programs are assigned to teach just that program with which they have experience. Even then it may be very difficult to match the teachers on their years of program-specific teaching experience, the number and kinds of children they have taught, or even the level of instructional program integrity they achieve. Such factors might introduce bias so that it is not the reading programs but the differences among the teachers who taught the programs that influence the outcomes. Such a study would not answer the question regarding which reading program might be most effective when taught by teachers who have limited experience with the program or are just learning it. Random assignment addresses this issue more effectively, in that all teachers in all of the programs in the study receive systematic training and ongoing instructional integrity checks and have not had years of experience with the programs investigated by the study.

Many situations in schools do not allow for easy randomization, and because of that some researchers are forced to use quasi-experimental designs with already-defined groups such as a specific classroom or school, sets of second-grade teachers, or children receiving special education services. Such predefined groups pose significant problems in research design, analysis, and interpretation, and more sophisticated statistics are needed to model any potential group differences that may be identified. The greatest threats to the validity of the findings of such a quasi-experimental study are the potential unknown biases within each group that systematically affect outcomes in a manner that misleads the interpretation of results. Unfortunately, these quasi-experiments are much more common in educational research than are true randomized experimental designs. Quasi-experimental studies require greater converging evidence across more studies before confidence in the findings are solidified.

The Role of Sampling Strategies

The characteristics and quality of one's research samples are other important considerations in an educational trial. What kinds of children, teachers, classrooms, or schools do investigators want to include? Part of the answer to this question might be found in the theoretical model. If the model suggests that the proposed reading instruction is most effective for children who are learning English as a second language, the investigators would probably want to make sure that they had a large, diverse sample of such children but also a large and diverse sample of those children who spoke English as their primary language for comparison. The logic of this sampling strategy is that in order to really evaluate whether the theoretical model is correct about the program's better impact on children learning English as a second language, there needs to be a comparison group of children without those core characteristics. On the other hand, the theoretical model may not make any predictions regarding whether girls or boys, or children from different races or socioeconomic backgrounds, may respond better. In such cases, ensuring that both groups (children who are learning English as a second language and children who are native speakers of English) included diverse samples of children with a variety of such demographic characteristics is required.

Similar theoretically driven sampling questions would have to be addressed regarding teacher characteristics, classroom attributes, and nature of the school or district. Unfortunately, to systematically consider all of these sampling issues frequently requires the development of very large, multi-site studies to ensure that the various considerations can be adequately met. This is another reason that many small-scale educational studies with samples of convenience do not provide the kind of scientific evidence necessary to ensure confidence in the results or generalization to children and teachers in other schools and districts.

The Role of Control Groups

Let's imagine that we have decided on a well-developed sampling strategy and randomized assignment at all levels of the fictional study. At this point, one of the key issues is the nature of the control group(s). This quickly becomes as much an issue of ethics as one of experimental design. First, what does the control group do? In the simplest framework, a curriculum control can be used, which means that the students in the control group will continue to receive whatever reading program the school is doing already. Of course, this is a problem if what the school is doing is similar to or overlaps with one of the three experimental reading programs. For this hypothetical study, let's assume that this is not the case so that we do not have to deal with that problem. It is important to ensure that the children in the control condition receive similar amounts of instructional time as provided in the other three programs and receive instruction at the same level of intensity, such as in small groups of 5, in full classroom activities, via computers, or with the use of peer reading. That is, there needs to be some way to equate the amount of instructional time and intensity across the three experimental reading programs and the control condition; doing so is a very difficult task. Remember, all of the teachers in this trial would also be randomly assigned to the control instructional program, so they could be teaching any one of the four conditions.

The Role of Teacher Training and Monitoring Instructional Integrity

An important consideration in educational research is the level of development of each instructional program, including the knowledge, skills, or materials needed by each teacher to use it in the way it was theoretically designed to be delivered to the children. Although many traditional reading programs have been used for years and have well-developed teacher training and professional development components in addition to well-organized teaching materials to help in instruction, teachers still may require an amount of experience using such a reading program before they might be considered to be using it in the way it was designed to be delivered. Therefore, if one is developing a new instructional program, its level of development in many aspects may be limited compared with those that have been available for years, and the creators' ability to train other teachers to use it may also be restricted. Because of such potential differences in reading program development, their level of specificity, or the ease of training, it is critical to have program-specific training criteria that develop each teacher's ability to use the program effectively up to a required level before the teacher is included as part of any educational trial. Because there still may be differences following such training in any one teacher's proficiency and effectiveness in using any of the specific reading programs, measures of teacher-specific implementation within reading groups are needed to help to analyze how such differences may affect the study outcomes.

One of the most important and related components of any educational trial design is an instructional program integrity monitoring system. Such monitoring systems typically require an independent observer to watch and systematically rate each teacher instructing children using a specific reading program, and the rating would be designed not only to provide an overview of the quality of the implementation of the specific program but also probably to include ratings of the effectiveness of the teacher in using the program. Such rating systems are conceptually and practically very hard to develop (see Chapter 13). These observational systems require their own evaluations to ensure that they are measuring the most important information reliably (i.e., to ensure that other raters would rate the situation similarly). If data on quality monitoring are available, it may be possible, using various statistical techniques, to make adjustments to the reading outcome data to address potential differences in program provision by various teachers so that a more balanced evaluation of the impact of the actual reading programs, and not these teacher differences, can be made.

Although all teachers would be trained to a specified proficiency level in all of the four groups they could be involved in, two of the biggest problems in educational trials are "drift," in which teachers begin to stray from the specific critical requirements of each instructional program, and "instructional confabulation," in which teachers mix up the various components, using methods from a different approach than the one to which they have been assigned. Another common problem is that the teachers may be differentially effective in using one of the programs compared with another; this could be considered a weakness of using a design in which all teachers are trained to teach all reading programs. A follow-up study, critical of this design decision, could alternatively take only teachers who were experts in each specific reading program and investigate the impact of only this one design change on the reading program outcomes. This is the elegance of using scientifically driven methodologies: The validity of criticism can actually be evaluated in a systematic and public process.

Based on the findings from these two educational trials, educators would have a better understanding of how teacher experience affects student reading outcomes within each of the evaluated programs. Of course, teachers need the types of information provided by each of these designs because teachers—particularly new teachers—do not typically come to schools highly experienced in any specific reading program and because there are still many levels of experience and effectiveness even in teachers who know a particular approach. One of the important roles of educational trials is to provide information that systematically helps to explain the differential outcomes, what researchers call variance, that teacher experience and effectiveness bring to different reading programs. Using these same data, one might even ask another question: Are there differences among the reading programs in the impact of teacher experience and effectiveness on outcomes? That is, teacher experience and effectiveness levels might not be very important factors in influencing one program's reading outcomes, whereas in another program these levels might play very important roles. Then the follow-up questions are what makes the programs different in this regard, and might it be related to the level of explicitness and scripting, quality of the training programs, or some other factor? Or is the difference related to some interaction with teacher personality characteristics or past teaching experiences? This is the powerful beauty of science: Each new finding leads to more questions and ideas, and each new question allows for a more complex understanding of the true nature of the phenomena being observed and studied.

If the goal is to evaluate the effectiveness of each of the three instructional programs in comparison with the control condition and with each other, there needs to be some systematic and independent evaluation of treatment integrity on an ongoing basis, with corrective instruction to each teacher, to both document drift and confabulation and predict reading outcomes. One would infer, everything else being equal, that those teachers who showed less drift and provided more program-specific instruction would, if the program were effective, exhibit better outcomes, which could explain some of the reading variability children might show at the end of the study.

The Role of Outcome Measurement

At this point in the hypothetical study, the theory to drive the research questions has been developed and the instructional programs have been derived from them. A sampling strategy has been selected at the level of children, teachers, classrooms, and/or schools or districts. In addition, the teachers have been trained to criterion on all instructional programs and an integrity monitoring system is in place. The next component of the discussion is related to outcome measurement, a very extensive topic and one that is complex both conceptually and practically. The important question is what the different foundational theories from the different instructional programs suggest are the important constructs or characteristics that should be assessed or documented in order to evaluate the impact of the different instructional programs. This consideration can include any measurement approach, including systematic observations ranging from qualitative-descriptive methods or more hypothesis-generating methods to those that are founded in a more empirical approach to measurement, such as psychometric tests or functional physiological measures (e.g., functional magnetic resonance imaging). Again, decisions regarding the most important features to measure are guided by theoretical formulations, but at the same time it is important to include measures that address alternative theoretical frameworks and/or could provide evidence that would refute the theory.

In most educational trials, investigators would expect to collect some of these measures before any intervention begins, just to obtain observations regarding the characteristics of the children, teachers, classrooms, and so forth before any experimentally induced changes can occur. During the instructional period, a researcher may want to repeat some of the observations or measures multiple times to monitor the level of change over time. This is an important concept given that some instructional programs may influence reading development more quickly than others or that there may be stages in which certain types of changes occur. Without repeated measurement, particularly including a baseline or pre-instruction measurement, understanding the level or rate of change that is occurring would be very difficult. Other measures of importance are those that assess those factors, such as language facility, that might influence the rate of change in learning and the ultimate level of reading development attained.

The decision of which measurements are used is quite complex. A decision about how to evaluate reading, which would be considered a core and critical area to measure in this particular hypothetical study, is itself very complicated even at the conceptual level. In addition, it is difficult to find well-developed, reliable, and valid measures to use. Part of this complexity is because children at different levels of reading development require different kinds of assessments. One cannot give 5-year-olds a 20-line narrative text to read and then ask them questions about their understanding of what they have just read. At the same time, one has to consider whether to assess reading accuracy at the single word, single sentence, or connected text levels; or reading fluency using single words, single sentences, or connected text; or reading comprehension, which includes prior knowledge, memory abilities, and higher-order language processes that need to be considered in its evaluation. Will the evaluation be based on silent or oral reading? Will the evaluation use psychometric measures or more qualitative measures or authentic reading materials? Will students read at instructional or at challenge levels? Will the evaluation monitor errors, reading speed, or relevant a priori knowledge of the content of the text? Will there be independent, one-to-one individualized assessments or class-presented measures in a group? Given that these are not all of the questions regarding reading evaluations that need to be answered, it not surprising that there is frequently significant debate about the adequacy of any decisions made among those peer researchers who would have made different choices. Because of this, what frequently happens is that a researcher may include some reading measures that they would not independently choose but that are used by many other researchers just so that the researcher is able to compare some of the results more directly with outcomes from other studies.

A final measurement issue is that all such measures contain some error, so they all represent imperfect estimates of a child's reading level. Also, all measures can be influenced by the examiner. This is one of the reasons that teachers who are actually teaching the instructional programs should never be the evaluators of reading outcomes in such a study; they can easily, and without awareness, introduce their own biases about the children's reading abilities into the results. Having an independent and experienced examiner evaluate the children's reading blindly (without knowing which reading program each child is in) helps to control for such potential bias and other unknown influences. Of course, such examiners may not obtain the maximal reading level from children they do not know, but this limitation would be true for all children across all programs and thus would be considered a nonbiasing factor. One of the goals of a high-quality educational trial is to address any such potential biases through design and methodological options to protect the study results from these biasing influences. Although no research study is capable of controlling for all bias or errors, the job of the researcher is to design a study that reduces their influence as much as possible so that the study results are independent of such factors.

In other words, good educational trial designs and methods try to reduce error or influences that may affect the results.

Implementing the Actual Trial

After all of these decisions regarding the study have been made; all of the resulting procedures and measures have been developed, evaluated, and shown to be reliable and valid; and schools, teachers, and students have been recruited based on the sampling strategy, then it is time to actually perform the trial. Because much of the development of the educational trial until this point has been based in strong theoretical and methodological decisions, its flawless execution is required to ensure the study can meet its potential in answering the questions originally posed. Unfortunately, the reality of doing research in schools almost always causes unexpected challenges that threaten to interfere with the study's lofty goals. For example, systemic changes may occur in some schools or with some teachers or children during the study that do not allow the study to be completed in the manner originally proposed. A local factory that employs many of the children's parents might close, and many of the children, and their families may move away during the school year; a teacher may get sick, and there could be a long period of substitute teachers who have not been trained in the reading program being provided; a child may miss more than 40 school days for unknown reasons; or between November and January, one classroom could have an influx of 10 new children who have missed significant portions of the instructional program being provided. This is the reality of educational trials. Researchers do not have complete control over their environments or their subjects, but this is a common problem in all human-oriented, applied research in the behavioral, social, and medical sciences. How successfully researchers either plan for change or are able to adapt their original design and methods to these situations and their influences is a critical factor in determining the ultimate study quality and validity.

The Role of Data Analysis and Statistics

Once the researchers actually start to systematically collect measures, data analysis can begin. Statistical analyses are mathematically based approaches to understanding systematic relationships among data measures. In our hypothetical study, they would be used to address the question of whether the reading differences found at the end of the educational trial could be due only to chance.

One might ask what chance has to do with all this. Remember that all observational measures and all tests and measures have error within them and that because of that, there is always a chance that any average differences in reading outcomes between reading programs may just be due to measurement error. Also, other chance errors may occur in the study and influence its outcomes. Statistical analyses have been designed to evaluate the probability that the results found are due only to chance or not.

It should be noted that any reading differences found among the instructional programs, no matter how large, could always be the results of random chance and not due to the experimental manipulation involved in using the different reading programs. Because of this, no research study results, no matter how well designed and performed, can ever be considered as irrefutable proof of any theory. Only through the accumulation of evidence from many different studies that result in convergent findings about a theory and its questions does confidence increase regarding the validity of the answers (see Chapter 4).

Statistical analyses might also be used to better understand the impact of various factors on the reading outcomes. For example, investigators may want to know whether students from different socioeconomic backgrounds respond differentially to the intervention programs or whether there is a relationship between school absences and reading outcomes or between reading accuracy and reading fluency measures and how much of these relationships are due to chance associations. A speaker at a conference that I attended in the mid-1970s suggested that the use of statistics was a form of public and social control over the behavior of researchers as they represent publicly determined and widely accepted approaches to understanding one's data. Because statistical methods provide probabilistic answers to the questions of chance differences or associations, there is always the issue of interpretation, and that is where many differences of opinion occur.

The interpretation of results from educational trials is rarely as clear as one might expect, given all of the thought and careful planning that go into them. For example, imagine that even though statistical analyses suggest that there is a significant difference between the reading outcomes of two of the studied instructional programs and that the probability that this difference is due to chance alone is less than 1 of 1,000, the difference between the average reading scores for the two groups of children who participated in these programs was less than half a point on a reading accuracy test. In this case, there is a statistical difference, but do we really want to suggest that the difference found has any practical meaning in an educational setting? If the same results had a probability that the difference observed is due to chance alone is 5 of 100, but the difference found was more than 20 points, would we interpret the results differently? Of course, the interpretation of results is again directed by different theoretical frameworks that may or may not have directed the educational trial; whether the original formulation and its resulting questions are supported or not by the results is the ultimate question of interest.

ENHANCING INTERVENTION RESEARCH

There is nothing particularly medical about the conceptual framework or research methodology used in clinical trials. They represent an approach to applied human research that focuses on interventions that try to make changes in a particular domain of human functioning. In the case of most clinical trials, the interventions are typically focused on domains of functioning that are primarily biological, although even in medicine, many current interventions are focused on behavior, such as smoking cessation interventions. The same underlying concepts and methods are easily applied to evaluating interventions within educational trials that are focused on changes in learning and achievement outcomes or other relevant behaviors, such as teacher competencies. The nature of such trials, regardless of the domain of focus, is on designing internally and externally valid experimental evaluations of interventions that can effect positive change in the domain or outcome of interest. Such research trials are a public process in which scientific approaches to understanding the phenomena of interest are used to advance knowledge. The best trials are presented in such detail that they can be easily reviewed, critiqued, and replicated by other researchers, and it is through such replication and convergence of findings that science and knowledge advance. This is just as true in education as it is in medicine. The potential role for educational trials to increase the public's and educators' confidence in the effectiveness of current educational approaches cannot be underestimated.

REFERENCE

Kendell, R.E. (1975). *The role of diagnosis in psychiatry.* Oxford, England: Blackwell Scientific Publications.

III

Evidence-Based Practices that Teachers Are Asked to Implement

Three of the four chapters in this section may at first appear to duplicate the major sections of the *Report of the National Reading Panel* (National Institute of Child Health and Human Development [NICHD], 2000) and are in fact authored by either members or consultants of the NRP. So why present these chapters here? Because they do contain additional new information on the major components of reading. Furthermore, these chapters not only illustrate the research methods presented in Section I but also clearly lay out the major essential ingredients of teaching reading. Each of these parts is necessary, and no single component of reading—phonemic awareness, phonics, fluency, vocabulary, or comprehension—is sufficient by itself to produce reading success. Thus the chapters in Section III, taken together, offer the essential ingredients of successful reading instruction. And these are the practices that teachers are being asked to implement under the auspices of the No Child Left Behind Act of 2001 (PL 107-110).

In Chapter 8, NRP member Linnea C. Ehri presents the findings of the NRP meta-analyses on phonics and phonemic awareness (NICHD, 2000) along with additional data. Ehri underscores the importance of phonics as an important part of a comprehensive reading program. Steven A. Stahl, who served as a consultant to the NRP, provides a chapter (Chapter 9) on reading fluency. In it, he not only discusses the foundations of teaching reading fluency and the NRP findings but also presents research findings from his own recent research that builds on the NRP findings. He also offers approaches to teaching reading fluency in the classroom. Michael L. Kamil, also a panel member, discusses in Chapter 10 the practices that the NRP cited as effective in the teaching of vocabulary and comprehension strategies. Comprehension is a crucially important area and indeed is the ultimate goal of reading—to understand and learn from what one reads. Finally, in Chapter 11, NRP member Timothy Shanahan explains that those critical of the NRP report generally attacked not the panel's findings but its process. Shanahan also describes a scientific reexamination of the findings that in fact reconfirmed the panel's findings.

REFERENCES

National Institute of Child Health and Human Development (NICHD). (2000). *Report of the National Reading Panel. Teaching children to read: An evidence-based assessment of the scientific research literature on reading and its implications for reading instruction. Reports of the subgroups* (NIH Publication No. 00-4754). Washington, DC: U.S. Government Printing Office. Also available on-line: http://www.nichd.nih.gov/publications/nrp/report.htm
No Child Left Behind Act of 2001, PL 107-110, 115 Stat. 1425, 20 U.S.C. §§ 6301 *et seq.*

8

Teaching Phonemic Awareness and Phonics

An Explanation of the National Reading Panel Meta-Analyses

LINNEA C. EHRI

Teaching beginners to read is complex. Effective instruction is needed on many fronts. My colleagues and I on the National Reading Panel (NRP) reviewed the findings of many experiments to assess the contribution of two alphabetic components of beginning reading instruction, teaching phonemic awareness and teaching systematic phonics. The statistical technique meta-analysis was used to reach conclusions. The purpose of this chapter is to summarize our approach, our findings, and their implications for beginning reading instruction. (For the complete reports, see Ehri, Nunes, Stahl, & Willows, 2001; Ehri, Nunes, Willows, et al., 2001; National Institute of Child Health and Human Development [NICHD], 2000.)

HOW ALPHABETIC KNOWLEDGE CONTRIBUTES TO READING ACQUISITION

Instruction in phonemic awareness and systematic phonics is thought to be essential for learning to read in English and many other languages because their writing systems are alphabetic. Beginners cannot become skilled readers if they do not know the system. Letters and combinations of letters (graphemes) in the spellings of words represent the smallest units of sound (phonemes) in the pronunciations of words. Phonemic awareness instruction teaches beginners to analyze and manipulate phonemes in speech, for example, how

153

to break the spoken word *teach* into three phonemes, /t/-/i/-/č/,[1] or how to blend these phonemes to say the whole word. Systematic phonics instruction teaches beginners letter–sound (grapheme–phoneme) correspondences and how to use these to decode and spell words. Because the writing system in English is more complex and variable than the writing systems in some other languages, it is harder to learn. This makes alphabetics instruction even more important to teach because children will have difficulty figuring out the system on their own.

A primary goal of alphabetics instruction is to teach students to read words in or out of text. There are several ways to read words (Ehri, 1991, 1994), all of which require knowledge of the alphabetic system. Unfamiliar words may be read by decoding, that is, by converting letters into sounds and blending them to form recognizable words, for example, pronouncing the three graphemes *sh, i,* and *p* and blending them to say "ship," or pronouncing the onset (initial consonants) and rime (vowel and following consonants) *sl* and *eep* and blending them to say "sleep." Another way to read unfamiliar words is by analogy, that is, by applying knowledge of the sounds of familiar words to read unfamiliar words, for example, applying the known word *rock* to read the new word *smock* by blending *sm* with the shared ending *-ock.* Another way to read unfamiliar words in context is by prediction using letters plus information in the text; for example, in the sentence, *For breakfast, he poured milk on his c* . . . , the final word might be *cereal, corn flakes,* or *Cheerios.* Guessing words based on partial letters, however is less reliable than and often inaccurate as compared with processing letters fully to identify words. Systematic phonics programs teach students to read words by attending to all of the letters as they represent the word's pronunciation.

Whereas unfamiliar words may be read in one of these ways, familiar words are read from memory by sight, which involves looking at the word and immediately recognizing it because it has been read before and stored in memory. People used to think that readers learned to read sight words by memorizing their visual shapes. However, research has led to a rejection of this idea. Now researchers know that sight word learning depends upon the application of letter–

---

[1]In this chapter, phonemes are represented by International Phonetic Alphabet symbols. For more information, go to the web site of the International Phonetic Association: http://www.arts.gla.ac.uk/IPA/ipa.html.

sound correspondences. These provide the glue that holds the words in memory for quick reading (Ehri, 1992). Becoming a skilled reader of sight words requires knowledge of phonemic segmentation, letter–sound correspondences, and spelling patterns to bond the complete spellings of specific words to their pronunciations and meanings in memory (Ehri, 1980, 1992, 1998; Perfetti, 1992; Rack, Hulme, Snowling, & Wightman, 1994; Reitsma, 1983; Share, 1999). For example, readers learn *brush* by forming connections between the graphemes *b-r-u-sh* and corresponding phonemes in the word's pronunciation along with the word's meaning. A skilled reader is able to read familiar words accurately and quickly because all of the letters have been secured in memory. In contrast, a weak reader reads words less accurately and more slowly and may even misread similarly spelled words such as *short, shirt,* and *sheet* because only some of the letters are connected to phonemes in memory. Words remain poorly connected when readers habitually guess words from partial letters and contextual cues without analyzing how all of the letters in spellings match up to phonemes in pronunciations (Ehri & Saltmarsh, 1995; Stanovich, 1980).

Alphabetics instruction is thought to help students not only recognize words but also comprehend text. Readers must be able to read most of the words in a text to understand its meaning. Although necessary, being able to read all of the words may not be sufficient because comprehending a text requires other abilities such as knowing the meanings of words, possessing relevant world knowledge, and being able to remember the text already read. Thus, word reading skill is one of several factors influencing comprehension.

Alphabetics instruction enables students to write words. Unfamiliar words may be written by creating spellings that represent sounds in the words. Familiar words are written by retrieving correct spellings from memory. As students acquire phonemic segmentation skill, knowledge of grapheme–phoneme correspondences, and familiarity with common spelling patterns and as they practice reading and writing words, they become better able to remember correct spellings (Griffith, 1991).

In sum, alphabetic instruction is thought to contribute in helping students learn to read because it teaches them phonemic awareness and use of letter–sound relations to read and spell words. Researchers have found that phonemic awareness and letter knowledge are the two best school-entry predictors of how well children will learn to read during the first 2 years of instruction (Share, Jorm,

Maclean, & Matthews, 1984). Let us take a closer look at experimental evidence regarding the effectiveness of these forms of instruction.

META-ANALYSIS OF PHONEMIC AWARENESS INSTRUCTION

What Is Phonemic Awareness Instruction?

Phonemes are the smallest units composing *spoken* language. English consists of about 41–44 phonemes, depending upon one's dialect. Phonemes combine to form syllables and words. Some words, such as *a* or *oh*, are made up of only one phoneme. Most words are blends of phonemes, such as *go* with two phonemes or *stop* with four phonemes. Phonemes are different from graphemes, which are units of *written* language that represent phonemes in the spellings of words (Venezky, 1970, 1999). Graphemes may consist of one letter, such as *p*, *t*, or *e*, or multiple letters, such as the digraphs *ch*, -*ck*, and *ea* or the trigraph -*igh*; each grapheme symbolizes one phoneme.

Phonemic awareness (PA) is the ability to focus on and manipulate phonemes in spoken words (Liberman, Shankweiler, Fischer, & Carter, 1974). Simply discriminating phonemes in words, for example, recognizing that *tan* sounds different from *Dan*, is not PA. The following tasks have been used to assess children's PA (the first six are quoted from NICHD, 2000, p. 2-10):

1. Phoneme *isolation*, which requires recognizing individual sounds in words, for example, "Tell me the first sound in *paste*" (/p/)

2. Phoneme *identity*, which requires recognizing the common sound in different words, for example, "Tell me the sound that is the same in *bike, boy,* and *bell*" (/b/)

3. Phoneme *categorization*, which requires recognizing the word with the odd sound in a sequence of three or four words, for example, "Which word does not belong? *bus, bun, rug*" (rug)

4. Phoneme *blending*, which requires listening to a sequence of separately spoken sounds and combining them to form a recognizable word, for example, "What word is /s/ /k/ /u/ /l/?" (*school*)

5. Phoneme *segmentation,* which requires breaking a word into its sounds by tapping . . . or counting the sounds or by pronouncing and positioning a marker for each sound, for example, "How many phonemes in *ship*?" (3 phonemes: /š/ /ɪ/ /p/)

6. Phoneme *deletion,* which requires recognizing what word remains when a specified phoneme is removed, for example, "What is *smile* without the /s/?" (*mile*)

7. *Onset–rime* manipulation, which requires isolation, identification, segmentation, blending, or deletion of onsets (the single consonant or blend that precedes the vowel in a syllable) or rimes (the vowel and following consonants), for example, *j-ump, st-op, str-ong*

PA instruction entails teaching beginners to perform one or several of these tasks. Students may be taught to manipulate spoken phonemes only (e.g., "Say the separate sounds in *jump*"), or students may be taught to manipulate phonemes using letters (e.g., "Say and write the separate sounds in *jump*"). Sounds are ephemeral, short-lived, and hard to grasp, whereas letters provide concrete, visible symbols for phonemes. Because of this, one might expect children to have an easier time acquiring PA when they are given letters to manipulate. Also, because letters bring children closer to the transfer tasks of applying PA in reading and spelling, one would expect transfer to be greater when PA is taught with letters.

Phonemic Awareness Meta-Analysis

We searched electronic databases and reference lists to locate all of the experimental studies testing the effectiveness of PA instruction. Studies had to exhibit several properties to qualify for our meta-analysis: They had to teach some form of PA to one group of students and had to include a control group that did not receive PA instruction; they had to measure the impact of PA instruction on reading; and they had to be published in peer-reviewed journals that utilized other researchers to screen articles for quality. We sought guidance from a previous meta-analysis (Bus & van IJzendoorn, 1999).

The final set of studies numbered 52. From these, 96 cases comparing PA instruction with a control condition were derived. When a study examined effects separately for different age or grade levels or compared different types of PA instruction with a control group, we treated these as separate comparison cases.

Characteristics Analyzed   We were interested in whether PA instruction helped students acquire PA and whether this affected their reading and spelling ability. Several measures were combined to assess reading, including word reading, pseudoword reading, reading comprehension, oral text reading, reading speed, and miscues. The spelling measure combined scores on invented spelling and correct spelling tests. Some studies examined whether PA instruction affected students' performance in math. Showing that math scores did not improve would indicate that any benefits of PA instruction were not explained by Hawthorne effects, that is enhanced performance resulting from the motivating effects of receiving special attention and trying harder on all tasks.

To determine whether PA instruction helped different types of students under different conditions, three reader groups were distinguished: typically achieving readers who did not have any reading problems; children below second grade who were at risk for developing reading difficulties as indicated by low PA, low reading, or low SES; and low-achieving readers in second through sixth grades who were reading below grade level.

Studies varied in the way that instruction was delivered. Some studies taught single forms of PA, such as blending or segmenting, whereas other studies taught combinations of PA skills. Some studies taught children to manipulate phonemes using letters, whereas other studies limited instruction to spoken phonemes. The instructional delivery unit varied across studies. Students were tutored individually or were taught in small groups (i.e., two to seven students) or in whole classrooms. The instructors were classroom teachers, researchers or their assistants, or computers. Also, the length of instruction varied across comparisons.

We recorded how rigorously each study was designed and conducted: whether treatment groups were assigned randomly, whether fidelity to treatment was checked, whether control groups received an alternative treatment or were left untreated, and how many students were sampled. In addition, we used assessments of design rigor published by another researcher (Troia, 1999).

Effect Sizes   To see whether instruction with PA was more effective than instruction without PA, we calculated a statistic called *effect size* by subtracting the mean of the control group from the mean of the PA treatment group and dividing by a pooled standard deviation. The DSTAT statistical package (Johnson, 1989) was used to determine weighted effect sizes and to test the influence of moderator variables. Effect sizes of studies with larger numbers of students were weighted more heavily.

Effect size tells one whether the treatment group achieved a higher score than the control group. It presents the effect of PA instruction as a number. Figure 8.1 portrays how to interpret this statistic. If the effect size is zero, there was no effect. The PA group and the control group read equally well at the end of instruction. If the effect size is a positive number, the PA group read better than

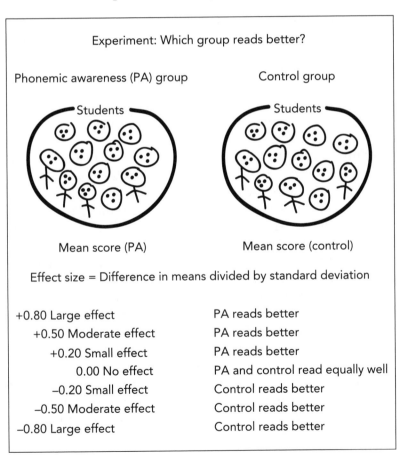

Figure 8.1. How to interpret effect size statistics.

the control group. If the effect size is a negative number, the PA group did worse than the control group. Researchers interpret 0.20 as a small effect, 0.50 as a moderate effect, and 0.80 as a large effect (Cohen, 1988).

Effect sizes were calculated on three types of measures taken after PA instruction ended: 1) PA measures to verify that PA was taught effectively, 2) reading measures to see whether PA skills helped children read, and 3) spelling measures to see whether PA skills helped children spell. In this chapter, I focus primarily on reading outcomes and report only selected effect sizes involving PA and spelling outcomes. (See Ehri, Nunes, Willows, et al., 2001, for the complete report.)

Findings Table 8.1 displays the entire pool of reading effect sizes across all studies in the database. The great majority of effect sizes were positive, indicating that students receiving PA instruction showed higher reading scores than the control group in most studies. The mean effect size was +0.53. This was statistically greater than zero and falls in the moderate range. We concluded that PA instruction helps children learn to read more effectively than no PA instruction.

Positive effects were also obtained on the other two outcomes. The mean effect size on posttests measuring PA was large, +0.86, indicating that instruction was highly effective in teaching PA. The mean effect size on spelling was +0.59, indicating that PA instruction moderately boosted spelling ability. In contrast, the mean effect size on math performance was close to zero and not significant (+0.03). This shows that the benefits of PA instruction were limited to literacy outcomes and are not explained by Hawthorne or halo effects.

The next step in the analysis was to pull out subsets of studies from the larger pool and calculate average effect sizes at the end of training for these studies. This allowed us to see whether the benefits of PA instruction held under more specific conditions, called *moderator variables*. Table 8.2 lists effect sizes on reading outcomes for the moderator variables and the number of comparisons contributing to each subset. Of course, the greater the number of comparisons in the subset, the more reliable is the effect size because it represents the average of a greater number of studies. In Table 8.2, an asterisk indicates that the effect size was statistically greater than zero,

Table 8.1.   Pool of mean effect sizes of phonemic awareness (PA) instruction on reading outcomes (N = 96) examined in the National Reading Panel report (NICHD, 2000)

Levels of effect sizes	Observed effect sizes (at end of instruction)
4.3	4.33
4.2	4.21
3.6	3.60
2.2	2.29
2.1	2.10, 2.17
1.6	1.61, 1.61, 1.64, 1.67
1.5	1.53, 1.56, 1.58
1.4	
1.3	1.30
1.2	1 .22, 1.22
1.1	1.11, 1.17, 1.17, 1.18
1.0	1.00, 1.05, 1.06, 1.07, 1.09
0.9	0.90, 0.92, 0.96, 0.97, 0.97, 0.98, 0.99
0.8	0.82, 0.86
0.7	0.71, 0.71, 0.71, 0.72, 0.73
0.6	0.60, 0.62, 0.62, 0.65, 0.67, 0.68
0.5	0.50, 0.51, 0.52, 0.52, 0.53, 0.54, 0.56, 0.57
0.4	0.42, 0.42, 0.42, 0.44, 0.47, 0.47, 0.47, 0.48, 0.49, 0.49
0.3	0.30, 0.31, 0.33, 0.35, 0.35, 0.39
0.2	0.20, 0.21, 0.22, 0.22, 0.23, 0.27, 0.27, 0.27, 0.28, 0.28
0.1	0.11, 0.13, 0.13, 0.14, 0.15, 0.17, 0.18, 0.19
+0	0.05, 0.07, 0.08
−0	−0.05, −0.05, −0.06
−0.1	−0.10, −0.19
−0.2	
−0.3	−0.37

whereas *ns* means that the effect size was not statistically greater than zero.

In interpreting effects of the moderator variables, some caution is needed. When effect sizes are larger for some levels of a moderator than for others, concluding that the moderator caused the difference remains tentative. This is because hidden factors may be confounded with the moderator and may explain the difference. Another caution involves the comparisons contributing to any effect size. Moderator effects are calculated on only some of the studies, only those in which they occurred or those that reported the involvement of the

Table 8.2. Mean effect sizes produced by phonemic awareness (PA) instruction on reading outcomes except where specified

Moderator variables and levels	Number of cases	Mean effect size
Characteristics of reading outcomes		
Time of posttest		
End of training	90	0.53*
First follow-up	35	0.45*
Second follow-up	8	0.23*
Test of word reading		
Experimenter devised	58	0.61*
Standardized	37	0.32*
Test of pseudoword reading		
Experimenter devised	47	0.56*
Standardized	8	0.49*
Reading comprehension	20	0.34*
Other outcomes		
Phonemic awareness	72	0.86*
Spelling	39	0.59*
Math achievement	15	0.03 ns
Characteristics of participants		
Grade		
Preschool	7	1.25*
Kindergarten	40	0.48*
First grade	25	0.49*
Second through sixth grade	18	0.49*
Reading level		
Normally achieving	46	0.47*
At risk	27	0.86*
Low achieving	17	0.45*
Socioeconomic status		
Low	11	0.45*
Mid- to high	29	0.84*
Language of instruction		
English	72	0.63*
Other	18	0.36*
Characteristics of PA instruction		
Skills taught		
One skill	32	0.71*
Two skills	29	0.79*
Three or more skills	29	0.27*
Blend and segment only	19	0.67*
Use of letters		
Letters manipulated	48	0.67*
Letters not manipulated	42	0.38*

Moderator variables and levels	Number of cases	Mean effect size
Delivery unit		
Individual child	32	0.45*
Small groups	42	0.81*
Classrooms	16	0.35*
Length of instruction (hours)		
1–4.5	17	0.61*
5–9.3	23	0.76*
10–18	19	0.86*
20–75	25	0.31*
Characteristics of instructors		
Classroom teachers	22	0.41*
Researchers and others	68	0.64*
Computers	8	0.33*
Characteristics of study design		
Random assignment	46	0.63*
Fidelity checked	31	0.43*
Control group		
Treated controls	54	0.65*
Untreated controls	36	0.41*
Troia overall ranking of rigor		
High (1–12)	19	1.00*
Middle (13–24)	14	0.61*
Low (25–36)	23	0.58*

Source: Ehri, Nunes, Willows, et al., 2001.
Note: * indicates that effect size was statistically greater than zero at $p < .05$; ns indicates that effect size was not statistically greater than zero.

moderators, not all of the studies. This means that different studies may have contributed to effect sizes for different moderators, so one cannot assume that the same studies are being compared when moving to a different moderator.

Inspection of the column of mean effect sizes associated with moderator variables in Table 8.2 reveals that the vast majority (those marked with an asterisk) were significantly greater than zero. This suggests that PA instruction was effective across a variety of conditions and characteristics.

From Table 8.2, it is apparent that PA instruction affected reading not only when measured at the end of instruction but also beyond, with follow-up tests ranging from 2 to 30 months. PA instruction improved various types of reading on standardized tests and tests created by researchers. Reading skills showing positive effects included the ability to read words and pseudowords and to comprehend text.

The effects of PA instruction on reading were examined at various grade levels (see Table 8.2). Most of the second- through sixth-grade comparisons (i.e., 14 of 18) involved low-achieving readers, so findings apply mainly to these students rather than to second through sixth graders in general. The impact of PA instruction on reading was similar for kindergartners, first graders, and second through sixth graders. The effect size for preschoolers was much larger statistically, but it was based on fewer comparisons, only seven, and in these cases reading was assessed with very simple word recognition tests.

The benefits of PA instruction for various types of students were also examined. Students at risk of becoming poor readers and students with low achievement in reading are known to have greater difficulty manipulating phonemes in words than are typically achieving readers (Bradley & Bryant, 1983; Juel, 1988; Juel, Griffith, & Gough, 1986). We examined whether PA instruction improved these students' PA. Results were positive. All three groups showed significant effects on outcome measures of PA skill: typically achieving readers (+0.93), at-risk readers (+0.95), and low-achieving readers (+0.62). Transfer of PA instruction to reading also occurred in all three groups as shown in Table 8.2. Children at risk showed statistically larger transfer effects on reading than typically and low-achieving readers, whose effect sizes were moderate.

Transfer of PA instruction to spelling differed among the reader groups. Effect sizes were large and did not differ statistically for at-risk readers (+0.76) and typically achieving readers (+0.88), indicating that PA instruction strongly benefited spelling for these students. However, the effect size was small and not statistically different from zero for low-achieving readers (+0.15), indicating that more than PA instruction is needed to improve their spelling.

Socioeconomic status (SES) made a difference. Large effect sizes on the PA outcome measures were observed among low SES (+1.02) and middle to high SES groups (+1.07). Also, reading outcomes benefited from PA instruction at both SES levels, although the effect size was statistically greater among the middle to high SES students (see Table 8.2). Because most studies of low-achieving readers did not report students' SES, these results pertain mainly to typically developing and at-risk readers.

Studies of PA instruction were conducted not only in English-reading countries but also in countries reading languages other than English. Results revealed that PA instruction exerted a much larger impact on English-reading students (see Table 8.2). One possible reason may be that the writing system of English is not as transparent in representing phonemes as are the writing systems of many of the other languages, so explicit PA instruction may make a bigger contribution to clarifying phoneme units and their linkage to graphemes in English.

Studies varied in the particular PA skills that were taught. Some studies taught one type of PA, whereas others taught two PA skills or more than two skills. On both PA and reading outcomes, instruction in one or two skills produced statistically greater effect sizes than instruction in more than two skills (see Table 8.2). Of special interest were effects of blending and segmentation instruction, both of which are thought to play a central role in learning to read and spell words. Blending phonemes helps children decode unfamiliar words. Segmenting words into phonemes helps children form connections to remember how to read and spell words. A number of studies taught children to blend and segment phonemes. As evident in Table 8.2, teaching these two PA skills produced greater benefits in reading than a multiple-skills approach did. These findings support the special value of blend-and-segment instruction.

Another feature expected to enhance the effectiveness of PA instruction involved the use of letters (graphemes) to teach PA. In some studies, children learned to manipulate phonemes using tokens marked with letters, whereas in other studies, children only spoke the sounds or they manipulated phonemes with blank tokens. Letters were expected to improve children's acquisition of PA because, as mentioned previously, they provide concrete, lasting symbols for sounds that are short-lived and hard to grasp. To test this expectation, we restricted the analysis to younger children and excluded older lower-achieving readers. This was because almost all studies with older readers taught PA with letters, thus precluding a fair comparison of the effects of letters versus no letters with these students. Results showed that the younger children acquired PA better with letters than without letters, supporting expectations. Teaching PA with letters was also expected to help children in reading more than teaching PA without letters because reading requires the processing of letters and sounds. From Table 8.2, it is apparent that PA instruction with letters produced an effect size that was almost twice as large as the effect size without letters on reading outcomes. These findings support the importance of including letters to teach PA.

It is commonly believed that tutoring is the most effective way to deliver instruction because tutors can tailor their teaching to individual needs. Results of our analysis, however, did not support this. Findings showed significantly greater effect sizes when PA was taught to small groups than when it was taught to individual students or classrooms (see Table 8.2). This was true for both PA and reading outcomes. Small groups may have been more effective because students paid more attention, because they wanted to do as well as their peers, or because their learning was helped by watching their peers.

It is common wisdom that the more time spent teaching a skill, the greater the learning. Time spent teaching PA varied across comparisons, from 1 hour to 75 hours. We grouped the comparisons into four time blocks to determine whether longer proved better. Results failed to support expectations. Effect sizes were significantly smaller in studies in which the most time was spent teaching PA (i.e., 20–75 hours) than in studies in which moderate amounts of time were spent (i.e., 5–18 hours). This was true for both PA and reading outcomes. These findings suggest that PA instruction does not need to be lengthy to exert its strongest effect on reading.

Classroom teachers are the primary purveyors of reading instruction, so it is important to verify that they can teach PA effectively. Results showed that the effect sizes produced by classroom teachers were large on PA outcomes (+0.78) and moderate (+0.41) on reading outcomes. Very likely this underestimates the impact of PA instruction on reading in actual classrooms. In these experiments, reading was only measured as an outcome. Teachers did not intervene to help children use their PA skills to read. If transfer to reading occurred, it was unassisted. This contrasts with normal classroom instruction, in which teachers not only teach PA but also teach children how to apply it in their reading and give their students practice doing this. Under the latter circumstances, much bigger effects on reading would be expected.

Another question of interest was whether effects of PA instruction were evident in the most rigorously designed experiments, that is, those using random assignment, those checking teachers' fidelity to instruction, and those giving the control group a special treatment rather than no instruction. In all cases, mean effect sizes were significantly greater than zero and moderate to large in size (see Table 8.2). This shows that the best-designed experiments yielded strong effects.

Troia (1999) published a critique of PA instruction studies in which he rated the methodological rigor of 28 of the 52 studies in our database. We adopted Troia's rigor rankings and grouped the studies into high, middle, and low rankings. We found that effect sizes for the most rigorous studies were statistically larger than effect sizes for the less rigorous studies (see Table 8.2). These findings again confirm that the best-designed experiments yielded the strongest effects.

In sum, findings of the meta-analysis were positive. The benefits of PA instruction were replicated multiple times across experiments and thus provide solid support for the claim that PA instruction is more effective than alternative forms of instruction or no instruction in teaching PA and in helping students learn to read and spell. Effects of PA instruction were greater under some circumstances than under others. These findings support the value of teaching PA to students.

META-ANALYSIS OF SYSTEMATIC PHONICS INSTRUCTION

What Is Systematic Phonics Instruction?

Phonics is a method of instruction that teaches students correspondences between letters in written language and phonemes in spoken language and how to use these correspondences to read and spell words. Phonics instruction is *systematic* when all of the major letter–sound correspondences are taught and are covered in a clearly defined sequence. This includes short and long vowels and vowel and consonant digraphs consisting of two letters representing one phoneme, such as *oi, ea, sh,* and *th.* Also, phonics instruction may include blends of letter sounds that represent larger subunits in words such as consonant pairs (e.g., *st, bl*), onsets, and rimes.

Over the years educators have disagreed about how beginning reading should be taught. Some have advocated starting with a systematic phonics approach, whereas others have argued for a whole word approach or a whole language approach. Disagreement has centered on whether teaching should begin with explicit instruction in letter–sound correspondences; whether it should begin with memorizing whole words; or whether initial instruction should be meaning centered, with letter–sound correspondences taught incidentally in context as needed.

The purpose of our phonics review was to determine whether there is experimental evidence showing that systematic phonics instruction helps children learn to read more effectively than unsystematic phonics instruction or instruction teaching little or no phonics. Also of interest was whether phonics instruction is more effective under some circumstances than others and for some students more than others.

Several different approaches have been used to teach phonics systematically (Aukerman, 1971, 1984; Harris & Hodges, 1995). These include synthetic phonics, analytic phonics, phonics through spelling, embedded phonics, and analogy phonics. These approaches differ in several respects. Synthetic phonics programs use a part-to-whole approach that teaches children to convert graphemes into phonemes (e.g., to pronounce each letter in *stop*, /s/-/t/-/ɑ/-/p/, and then to blend the phonemes into a recognizable word). Analytic phonics uses a whole-to-part approach that avoids having children pronounce sounds in isolation to figure out words. Rather, children are taught to analyze letter–sound relations once the word is identified. For example, the teacher might write the letter *p* followed by several words: *put, pig, play,* and *pet.* He or she would help students to read the words and to recognize that they all begin with the same sound that is associated with *p.* Phonics-through-spelling programs teach children to segment and write the phonemes in words. Embedded phonics teaches children to use letter–sound correspondences along with context cues to identify unfamiliar words they encounter in text. Analogy phonics teaches children to use parts of written words they already know to identify new words. For example, children are taught a set of key words that are posted on the wall (e.g., *tent, make, pig*) and then are taught to use these words to decode unfamiliar words by pronouncing the shared rime and blending it with the new onset (e.g., *rent, bake, jig*). Some systematic phonics programs are hybrids that include components of two or more of these approaches.

Phonics programs may differ in several other important ways, for example, how many letter–sound relations are taught and how they are sequenced, whether phonics generalizations are taught; whether PA is taught; what pace of instruction is used; whether learning activities include oral drill and practice, reciting phonics rules, or filling out worksheets; whether children read decodable text in which the vocabulary is limited mainly to words containing familiar letter–sound associations; whether phonics instruction is embedded in or segregated from the literacy curriculum; whether the teaching approach involves direct instruction in which the teacher takes an active role and students passively respond; or whether a constructivist problem-solving approach is used (Adams, 1990; Aukerman, 1981).

Phonics versus Other Methods   Evaluating the effectiveness of systematic phonics instruction has been addressed many times in the literature. The best known effort was Jeanne Chall's (1967) comprehensive review of beginning reading instruction covering studies up to the mid-1960s: *Learning to Read: The Great Debate.* Her basic finding was that early and systematic instruction in phonics led to better achievement in reading than later and less systematic phonics instruction. This conclusion has been reaffirmed in many research reviews conducted since then (e.g., Adams, 1990; Anderson, Hiebert, Wilkinson, & Scott, 1985; Balmuth, 1982; Dykstra, 1968).

At the time of Chall's (1967) original review, the contrast between phonics instruction and the alternative "look–say" methods was considerable. In the look–say approach, children were taught to read words as wholes, and they practiced reading words until they had acquired perhaps 50–100 in their sight vocabularies. Only after this, toward the end of first grade, did phonics instruction begin.

More recently, whole language approaches have replaced the whole word method as the most common alternative to systematic phonics programs. The shift has involved a change from very little letter–sound instruction to a modicum of letter–sound correspondences taught unsystematically. Whole language teachers are not told to wait until a certain point before teaching children about letter–sound relationships. Typically, they provide some instruction in phonics, usually as part of invented spelling activities or through the use of graphophonemic prompts during reading (Routman, 1996). Their approach, however, is to teach it unsystematically in context as the need arises. Observations suggest that in whole language classrooms, instruction in consonant letter–sound correspondences may be taught but that instruction in vowel letter–sound correspondences occurs infrequently (Stahl, Duffy-Hester, & Stahl, 1998).

In our meta-analysis, the effectiveness of systematic phonics instruction was compared with various types of nonphonics or unsystematic phonics instruction given to control groups. In some studies, controls received whole language instruction, whole word instruction, or some type of basal program consisting of structured books and materials. If studies included more than one control group, we selected the control group receiving the least phonics instruction.

This chapter and our meta-analysis refer to control treatments in various ways, as unsystematic phonics, nonphonics, or no phonics.

A question of particular interest to the NRP was when phonics instruction should begin. Some countries such as New Zealand and the United Kingdom introduce children to reading and writing at the age of 5 in full-day programs. In the United States, formal reading instruction typically begins in first grade. When phonics instruction is introduced after first grade, students have already acquired some reading ability presumably from another method. To exert an impact on older students may be harder because it may require them to change their way of processing print. Our database included studies that introduced phonics to students from kindergarten through sixth grades. We expected that phonics instruction would prove more effective in kindergarten and first grades than in later grades.

Phonics Meta-Analysis

Our method for the phonics meta-analysis was very similar to that used in the PA review. We searched the literature for experiments comparing the effectiveness of systematic phonics instruction with instruction providing unsystematic phonics or no phonics instruction. Studies had to be published after 1970 in refereed journals. Studies had to teach phonics in English and measure reading as an outcome. Studies had to involve interventions that might be found in schools; they could not be short-term laboratory studies teaching very limited alphabetic processes. In contrast to the PA review, studies were restricted to those teaching phonics in English. Studies that were included in the PA meta-analysis were not included here even if they might have qualified according to our other criteria.

From the 38 studies that met our qualifications, 66 treatment–control group comparisons were derived. Different age or grade levels and different types of phonics treatment and control groups within a study provided separate comparisons. Studies were coded for several characteristics to permit the analysis of moderator variables.

Characteristics Analyzed Phonics instruction is considered particularly beneficial to children with reading problems because poor readers have exceptional difficulty decoding words (Rack, Snowling, & Olson, 1992). A question of interest was whether phonics instruction helps to prevent reading failure in at-risk beginning readers and to remediate reading difficulties in older poor readers. In the analysis, we distinguished typically achieving readers and three categories of poor readers. At-risk readers were kindergartners and first graders judged to be at risk for future reading difficulties because of poor letter knowledge, poor PA, poor reading skills, or enrollment in low-achieving schools. Low-achieving readers were children above first grade who were below average in their reading. Students with a reading disability were children who were above first grade in most cases and who were below grade level in reading but at least average cognitively.

Performance on six outcomes was analyzed: decoding regularly spelled real words, decoding pseudowords, reading real words that included irregularly spelled words, comprehending text, reading connected text orally, and spelling words correctly or according to developmental criteria (Morris & Perney, 1984; Tangel & Blachman, 1995). Outcomes were measured at various times: at the end of instruction, at the end of the first school year if the program was taught for more than one year, and after a delay that ranged from 4 months to 1 year to assess long-term effects of instruction. In analyzing effects of moderator variables, we used performance at the end of instruction or at the end of the first year.

Effect Sizes   The DSTAT program (Johnson, 1989) was used to calculate effect sizes and test whether they were statistically greater than zero. Effect sizes across the six outcome measures were averaged to create one overall effect size indicating the general impact of phonics instruction on learning to read. Spelling was included because it is known to be highly correlated with reading (Ehri, 1997). Spelling measures contributed 16% of the effect sizes, whereas reading contributed 84%. (For a more complete reporting of findings, see Ehri, Nunes, Stahl, et al., 2001.)

Findings   The entire pool of effect sizes is presented in Table 8.3. Inspection of these values reveals that most were positive, indicating that in most of the studies, the group receiving phonics instruction read better than the control group.

Table 8.4 reports mean effect sizes for various subsets of studies. It is apparent that effects of systematic phonics instruction on reading were statistically greater than zero and moderate in size, regardless of whether effects were measured at the end of the program or at the end of the first year. The mean effect size at the end of training was +0.41, which is slightly lower than the mean effect size of PA instruction, +0.53. These findings indicate that systematic phonics

Table 8.3. Pool of mean effect sizes of systematic phonics instruction on overall reading outcome examined in the National Reading Panel Report (NICHD, 2000)

Levels of effect sizes	Observed effect sizes		
	End of instruction (1 year)[a]	End of instruction (> 1 year)[b]	Follow-up[c]
3.7	3.71		
2.2	2.27		
2.1			
2.0			
1.9	1.99		
1.8			
1.7			
1.6			
1.5			
1.4	1.41, 1.42		
1.3			
1.2			
1.1	1.19		
1.0			
0.9	0.91		
0.8	0.84		
0.7	0.70, 0.72, 0.73, 0.76	0.75	0.86
0.6	0.60, 0.60, 0.61, 0.62, 0.63, 0.63	0.64, 0.67	
0.5	0.50, 0.50, 0.51, 0.53, 0.53	0.52, 0.54	0.56
0.4	0.43, 0.44, 0.45, 0.47, 0.48, 0.49		
0.3	0.32, 0.33, 0.33, 0.36, 0.37, 0.38, 0.38, 0.39	0.36	0.32, 0.33, 0.38
0.2	0.20, 0.21, 0.24, 0.24, 0.25, 0.27	0.24, 0.28	0.28
0.1	0.12, 0.13, 0.14, 0.16, 0.19	0.17	
+0	0.00, 0.01, 0.03, 0.04, 0.04, 0.04, 0.07, 0.09	0.00	
−0	−0.07		
−0.1	−0.11		
−0.2	−0.20, −0.25		
−0.3	−0.33		
−0.4	−0. 47		−0.47

[a]Instruction lasted 1 year or less ($n = 62$).
[b]Instruction lasted between 2 and 4 years ($n = 10$).
[c]Follow-up tests were administered from 4 months to 1 year after instruction ended ($n = 7$).

Table 8.4. Mean effect sizes produced by systematic phonics instruction

Moderator variables and levels	Number of cases	Mean effect size
Characteristics of reading outcomes		
Time of posttest		
End of training	65	0.41*
End of training or first year	62	0.44*
Follow-up	6	0.27*
Characteristics of participants		
Grade levels		
Kindergarten and first grade	30	0.55*
Second through sixth grades	32	0.27*
Grade and reading ability		
Kindergarten at risk	6	0.58*
First grade normally achieving	14	0.48*
First grade at risk	9	0.74*
Second through sixth grade normally achieving	7	0.27*
Second through sixth grade low achieving	8	0.15 ns
Second through sixth grade with reading disability	17	0.32*
Outcome measures		
Kindergarten and first graders		
Decoding regular words	8	0.98*
Decoding pseudowords	14	0.67*
Reading miscellaneous words	23	0.45*
Spelling words	13	0.67*
Reading text orally	6	0.23*
Comprehending text	11	0.51*
Second through sixth grade		
Decoding regular words	17	0.49*
Decoding pseudowords	13	0.52*
Reading miscellaneous words	23	0.33*
Spelling words	13	0.09 ns
Reading text orally	6	0.24*
Comprehending text	11	0.12 ns
Socioeconomic status (SES)		
Low SES	6	0.66*
Middle SES	10	0.44*
Characteristics of phonics instruction		
Delivery unit		
Individual child[a]	8	0.57*
Small groups	27	0.43*
Classrooms	27	0.39*

(continued)

Table 8.4. *(continued)*

Moderator variables and levels	Number of cases	Mean effect size
Type of program—all grades[a]		
Synthetic	39	0.45*
Larger phonic units[b]	11	0.34*
Miscellaneous	10	0.27*
Type of program—kindergarten and first grades		
Synthetic	20	0.58*
Larger phonic units[b]	5	0.46*
Miscellaneous	8	0.27*
Type of control group		
Basal	10	0.46*
Regular curriculum	16	0.41*
Whole language	12	0.31*
Whole word	10	0.51*
Miscellaneous	14	0.46*
Characteristics of study design		
Assignment to groups		
Random assignment	23	0.45*
Use of existing groups	39	0.43*
Sample size		
20–31	14	0.48*
32–52	16	0.31*
53–79	16	0.36*
80–320	16	0.49*

Source: Ehri, Nunes, Stahl, et al., 2001.
Note: * indicates that effect size was significantly greater than zero at $p < .05$; ns indicates that effect size was not significantly different from zero.
[a]There were 6 comparisons not included, two because a combined method was taught, and four that did not measure reading at the end of instruction but only after a delay.
[b]This effect size was adjusted to reduce the impact of one atypically large outlier, +3.71, emerging from the study by Tunmer and Hoover (1993). The adjustment involved substituting the next largest effect size in the set.

helps children learn to read more effectively than do programs with little or no phonics instruction. In Table 8.4, as in Table 8.2, an asterisk indicates that the effect size was statistically greater than zero, whereas *ns* means that the effect size was not statistically greater than zero.

Inspection of the column of effect sizes associated with moderator variables in Table 8.4 reveals that the vast majority (those marked with an asterisk) were significantly greater than zero. This suggests that systematic phonics instruction was effective across a variety of conditions and characteristics.

Phonics instruction facilitated reading acquisition in both younger and older readers. Effect sizes were statistically greater than zero in both cases but were statistically larger among kindergartners and first graders than among second through sixth graders. These findings indicate that phonics instruction exerts its greatest impact early.

In most of the studies, phonics instruction lasted 1 school year or less. In three studies, however, phonics instruction began in kindergarten or first grade with at-risk readers and continued for 2 or 3 years (Blachman, Tangel, Ball, Black, & McGraw, 1999; Brown & Felton, 1990; Torgesen et al., 1999). Mean effect sizes at the end of each grade level were moderate, and their strength was maintained across the grades: kindergarten $d = +0.46$; first-grade $d = +0.54$; and second-grade $d = +0.43$. This shows the value of starting phonics early and continuing to teach it for 2–3 years.

The students who received phonics instruction varied in age/grade and reading ability. Kindergartners and first graders, particularly those at risk, typically began phonics instruction as nonreaders or as novice readers with much to learn, whereas children in second through sixth grades had already been exposed to reading instruction and had made at least some progress by the time that phonics instruction was introduced. Most of the comparisons with older students (78%) involved low-achieving readers or students with reading disability. Table 8.4 shows mean effect sizes for comparisons grouped by grade and reading ability. Effects were statistically significant for all but one group. They were moderate to large for at-risk and typically achieving readers in kindergarten and first grade. Effect sizes were significant but smaller for second- through sixth-grade typically achieving readers and students with reading disability. These findings indicate that phonics instruction improves reading ability more than nonphonics instruction not only among beginning readers but also among typically progressing readers above first grade and older readers with reading disability. In contrast, phonics instruction did not enhance reading among low-achieving readers.

The aim of phonics instruction is to help children acquire alphabetic knowledge and use it to read and spell words. Table 8.4 displays effect sizes for the six different literacy outcomes. Results are reported separately for younger and older students. Among beginners, phonics instruction produced significant effects on all six measures, with effects ranging from moderate to large on five measures. Among older readers, a different picture emerged. Effects on decoding were moderate, and effects on reading miscellaneous words were small to moderate. Effects on spelling and reading comprehension, however, were not statistically greater than zero. These findings reveal stronger effects on measures of decoding regularly spelled words and pseudowords than on the other four measures, which is not surprising because phonics instruction focuses on teaching students to decode unfamiliar words. The absence of significant effects among older students on spelling and reading comprehension may result from the greater need for specific instruction targeting comprehension strategies and background knowledge and for spelling instruction focused on learning individual words.

Studies reporting the SES of participants were examined. Effects favoring phonics instruction were moderate in size for children of low SES and middle SES (see Table 8.4), indicating that phonics instruction helps both low and middle SES children learn to read.

Studies differed in the size of groups receiving instruction: individuals being tutored, small groups, or classrooms. Results revealed that phonics instruction was effective for all three group sizes, and effect sizes did not differ statistically among the sizes (see Table 8.4). These findings contrast with the result of the PA review indicating that PA instruction was more effective with small groups than with the other group sizes. The phonics findings suggest that classroom instruction may be no less effective than tutoring, a possibility that is important given the expense and impracticality of delivering instruction individually. Of course, if the studies that utilized tutoring were limited to students with serious reading problems, this might explain why the effect size was not larger.

Effects were examined for three types of systematic phonics programs. One category (39 comparisons) was synthetic phonics, which involved teaching students to sound out letters and blend the sounds into recognizable words. Another category (11 comparisons) involved teaching children to analyze and blend larger phonic units of words such as onsets, rimes, and spelling patterns along with phonemes. The miscellaneous category (10 comparisons) included a spelling program, traditional phonics basal programs, and some researcher-devised instruction that focused on word analysis procedures. As evident in Table 8.4, effect sizes in all three categories were statistically greater than zero and did not differ statistically from each other, indicating that all types were more effective than nonsystematic or no phonics programs. These findings indicate that as long as phonics programs are systematic, a variety of approaches are effective.

Because phonics instruction exerted its greatest impact on beginning readers, we compared effect sizes for the three types of programs in kindergarten and first grade. All three types produced effects statistically greater than zero (see Table 8.4). However, effects were much bigger for synthetic and larger phonic unit programs than for miscellaneous programs. Statistical tests revealed that synthetic programs yielded a significantly greater effect size than miscellaneous programs ($p < .05$). Whereas three of the eight effect sizes for miscellaneous programs were zero or negative, no synthetic or larger phonic unit program yielded any effect sizes this low. Although larger phonic unit programs showed moderate effects, this category had only five comparisons, and four of these involved tutoring. In contrast, 85%–88% of the synthetic and miscellaneous comparisons were conducted with small groups or with classrooms. These findings indicate that synthetic phonics is especially effective as a method that classroom teachers can use to teach beginners to read. (This analysis was conducted after the NRP findings were published, so it does not appear in the earlier reports, e.g., Ehri, Nunes, Stahl, et al., 2001; NICHD, 2000.)

The type of instruction administered to control groups varied. In some cases, students received unsystematic or incidental phonics, whereas in other cases students received no phonics. Control groups were categorized as one of five types based on labels or descriptions provided by authors: basal, regular curriculum, whole language, whole word, miscellaneous. Basal programs were those already in use at schools. The *regular curriculum* label covered cases in which controls received the regular class curriculum in use at the school with no further specification of its contents except that it did not teach phonics systematically. Programs classified as whole language were based on authors' characterizations. These included big books (Holdaway, 1979) and language experience programs. Whole language programs were taught to control groups primarily in first grade (67% of the comparisons). Whole word programs emphasized teaching a sight vocabulary by having students memorize whole words before incidental phonics instruction began. The miscellaneous category was applied to control groups whose instruction did not fit the other categories. This included programs teaching traditional spelling, teaching academic study skills, and providing tutoring in academic subjects.

The positive effect sizes reported in Table 8.4 indicate the extent that phonics-instructed groups outperformed each type of control group. Results revealed that effect sizes were statistically greater for groups receiving systematic phonics instruction than for all types of control groups (see Table 8.4). None of the effect sizes differed statistically among the types of controls. These findings show that systematic phonics instruction produced superior performance in reading compared with all types of unsystematic phonics or no phonics instruction.

Studies in the database varied in methodological rigor. Some studies randomly assigned students to treatment and control groups, whereas other studies administered treatments to groups that already existed. Some studies sampled a large number of students, whereas others worked with fewer students. From Table 8.4, it is apparent that more rigorous designs involving random assignment and larger samples yielded effect sizes that were as large as if not larger than effect sizes for other less rigorous designs. These findings confirm that the positive effects of phonics instruction on reading did not arise primarily from weakly designed studies.

In sum, findings of the meta-analysis support the conclusion that systematic phonics instruction helps children learn to read more effectively than nonsystematic phonics or no phonics instruction. The impact of phonics instruction on reading was significantly greater in the early grades (kindergarten and first grades), when phonics was the method used to start children out, than in the later grades (second through sixth grades), after children had made some progress in reading, presumably with another method. The method of teaching phonics in the early grades made a difference, with synthetic phonics showing especially strong effects. These results reveal that early instruction in systematic phonics is especially beneficial for helping children learn to read, particularly when a synthetic approach is used.

Several possibilities might explain why effect sizes were smaller when phonics instruction was introduced beyond first grade. One is that other aspects of reading besides decoding become increasingly important contributors to reading in the later grades. This is suggested in a comparison of effect sizes drawn from the NRP's report (NICHD, 2000). Whereas phonics instruction produced an effect size of +0.27 in second through sixth graders, fluency instruction produced an effect size of +0.47, and various forms of comprehension strategy instruction produced effect sizes greater than +0.80. This suggests that phonics instruction beyond first grade must be coupled with other forms of effective reading instruction in order to achieve maximum impact.

Another explanation is that when phonics instruction is introduced after students have already acquired some reading skill, it may be more difficult to step in and influence how they read because doing so requires changing students' habits. For example, to improve accuracy, students may need to suppress the habit of guessing words based on context and minimal letter cues, to slow down, and to examine spellings of words more fully when they read them. Using phonics instruction to remediate reading problems may be harder than using phonics at the earliest point to prevent reading difficulties.

There is currently much interest in whether systematic phonics instruction is effective for children who are learning English as a second language (ELL). Unfortunately, most of our studies either provided no information about this population of individuals or intentionally excluded these students from the sample. Results of only one study (Stuart, 1999) pertained to ELL students; 86% of Stuart's sample consisted of ELL students. The effect size she observed was large (+0.73), indicating that phonics instruction helps ELL kindergartners learn to read more effectively than a whole language approach. More research is needed to replicate and extend this finding.

Implications for Teaching Reading

What does strong systematic phonics instruction look like in classrooms? Although presently we lack a sufficient research base consisting of experimental studies with control groups showing the importance of the various constituents of systematic phonics instruction, we can nevertheless identify ingredients that are likely to be important, based on theory, the available evidence, and conventional wisdom.

Phonics instruction targets several accomplishments for students. Students need to acquire knowledge of the alphabetic system. They need to acquire PA, particularly segmentation and blending. They need to learn the shapes and names of all capital and lowercase letters. They need to learn the major grapheme–phoneme correspondences. In schools where formal reading instruction begins in first grade, kindergarten teachers need to ensure that all of their students leave kindergarten with solid knowledge of letters and PA.

Phonics programs differ in how instruction is sequenced. Some teach children most of the letter–sound correspondences before they learn to read any words, whereas other programs begin word reading and writing sooner. Once children have some alphabetic knowledge, they need to practice using it to read and write. They need to learn the left-to-right direction. To read new words in or out of text, children need to be taught how to decode the words' spellings. As students practice decoding the same words, connections between letters and sounds are formed for those words in memory and students become able to read those words by sight rather than by decoding. As students practice reading words, they become able to read them automatically. This makes text reading much easier and faster. Of course, learning to read words includes bonding spellings to meanings and pronunciations in memory so that word meanings are activated automatically during text reading.

Students learn to apply their alphabetic knowledge to spell words. Novices learn to write the sounds they hear. More advanced beginners work on remembering the correct spellings of words. As students practice reading and writing words, they learn about spelling patterns that recur in words and knowledge of these regularities enhances their word reading and writing skills.

These are the key capabilities to be taught in systematic phonics programs. If you walk into a classroom during a phonics lesson, you should see one or more of these capabilities being taught or practiced.

Phonics programs include several instructional ingredients. One is a plan for teaching all of the major letter–sound correspondences. This distinguishes systematic phonics programs from casual, as-needed phonics programs that do not follow a plan and hence may not teach some correspondences. Research has indicated that vowels tend to be slighted in these casual programs.

To help children learn all of the letter–sound correspondences, some phonics programs teach mnemonic devices. For example, in the Letterland program (Wendon, 1992), the shape of K is drawn as the body of a "kicking king" whose first sound, /k/, is the sound of the letter. The shape of S is drawn as the body of "Sammy Snake." In this way, an easily remembered mediator is taught to help children connect the shape of the letter to its sound. Research shows that this makes it easier for children to learn the correspondences (Ehri, Deffner, & Wilce, 1984). In the study by Stuart (1999) using Jolly Phonics, children were taught mnemonics that involved hand or body motions linking letters to sounds.

Synthetic phonics programs teach students to transform graphemes into phonemes and to blend them to form recognizable words. Children begin with two letters and work up to longer sequences. Larger phonic unit programs teach students to read words by breaking them into letter chunks, decoding the chunks, and blending them. In larger phonic unit programs, children might be taught a set of key words whose chunks are useful for reading new words. For example, a key word might be *king*. The *-ing* would be used to read *fling*. Or, children might be taught to read *ing* as a chunk by itself.

It is essential for students to be able to apply their alphabetic and word reading skills to the reading of stories. Systematic phonics programs typically provide special texts for this purpose. The texts are written so that most words contain the letter–sound correspondences that children have been taught up to that point. For example, in a text at the easiest level, a large number of words might contain the short /æ/ vowel. At a higher level, all of the short vowels might appear in different words. At a still higher level, several long and short vowels would be present. The easiest texts have very limited language and ideas to comprehend, for example, "The cat sat on the mat." As children's word reading skills grow, however, the texts become richer conceptually and more interesting.

These are some ingredients of good phonics instruction. There are also practices that are thought to be less effective. One is the extensive reliance on worksheets to teach phonics. This should not be the primary way that phonics is taught. Teachers need to actively teach students, to explain and model the use of alphabetic principles, and to provide practice with feedback.

Another less effective technique is teaching students to recite complex spelling rules. Being able to state a rule is not equivalent to being able to use the rule. A more effective approach is to have students recognize the pattern by reading and writing words that exhibit the rule.

A third approach that is less effective is to teach phonics as a separate subject unrelated to anything else students are taught during the day. For example, children might study letter–sound correspondences for 20 minutes every morning, and then move to reading and writing instruction that bears no connection to the phonics lessons. Research shows that students will not apply their alphabetic knowledge if they do not use it to read and write (Juel & Roper/Schneider, 1985). The best phonics program is one that is deliberately integrated with reading and writing instruction.

Systematic phonics programs might exhibit the very best instructional features. However, if they are not carried out by a knowledgeable teacher, their likelihood of success is diminished. Teachers must understand how to implement a phonics program effectively and how to plan lessons and must make sure they are carried out. Teachers must hold expectations about the effects of their instruction on students. They must understand what students should know and be able to do better as a result of their teaching. To verify that their instruction is working, teachers need to use informal testing to monitor students' progress toward the expected accomplishments. Teachers need to understand how to enrich instruction for students who don't get it, and how to scaffold lessons to eliminate their problems. The job of teaching reading effectively to classrooms of students requires a high degree of professional competence indeed.

The importance of professional development to enhance teachers' effectiveness in teaching reading was underscored by the chair of the NRP, Dr. Donald Langenberg, who is a physicist and was chancellor of the University of Maryland when the NRP was preparing its report. Dr. Langenberg knew little about reading when he began his job, but he strongly believed in the panel's mission to help schools identify the best ways to teach reading based on scientific evidence. During the panel's first meeting, Dr. Langenberg was given a publication by the American Federation of Teachers (1999) titled *Teaching Reading* Is *Rocket Science: What Expert Teachers of Reading Should Know and Be Able to Do.* He was especially interested in the booklet because his business is rocket science. Two years later when he presented the NRP report (NICHD, 2000) to the U.S. Congress, he mentioned this book in his speech but complained that its title was misleading. As a physicist chairing this panel for 2 years, he had come to realize that teaching reading is really much *harder* than rocket science (*Hearing on the Importance of Literacy,* 2000).

To conclude, educators and policy makers must recognize the place of phonics in a beginning reading program. The goal of making every child a reader is not easy. There is no magic pill to make it happen. Systematic phonics instruction by itself does not help students acquire all of the processes they need to become successful readers. Phonics needs to be combined with other forms of instruction to create a comprehensive reading program. Other sections of the NRP report (NICHD, 2000) indicated the importance of instruction to teach fluency, vocabulary, and reading comprehension strategies. In a meta-analysis of instructional studies employed with students having a learning disability, Swanson (1999, 2000) observed significantly larger effect sizes on reading outcomes when direct skills instruction was combined with comprehension strategy instruction than when each was administered separately to students. By emphasizing all of the processes that contribute to growth in reading, teachers have the best chance of making every child a reader.

REFERENCES

Adams, M.J. (1990). *Beginning to read: Thinking and learning about print.* Cambridge, MA: MIT Press.

American Federation of Teachers. (1999, June). *Teaching reading is rocket science: What expert teachers of reading should know and be able to do* (Item No. 372 6/99). Washington, DC: Author.

Anderson, R.C., Hiebert, E.F., Wilkinson, I.A.G., & Scott, J. (1985). *Becoming a nation of readers.* Champaign, IL: Center for the Study of Reading.

Aukerman, R. (1971). *Approaches to beginning reading.* New York: Wiley.

Aukerman, R. (1981). *The basal reader approach to reading.* New York: Wiley.

Aukerman, R. (1984). *Approaches to beginning reading* (2nd ed.). New York: Wiley.

Balmuth, M. (1982). *The roots of phonics: A historical introduction.* New York: McGraw-Hill.

Blachman, B., Tangel, D., Ball, E., Black, R., & McGraw, D. (1999). Developing phonological awareness and word recognition skills: A two-year intervention with low-income, inner-city children. *Reading and Writing: An Interdisciplinary Journal, 11,* 239–273.

Bradley, L., & Bryant, P. (1983). Categorizing sounds and learning to read: A causal connection. *Nature, 30,* 419–421.

Brown, I., & Felton, R. (1990). Effects of instruction on beginning reading skills in children at risk for reading disability. *Reading and Writing: An Interdisciplinary Journal, 2,* 223–241.

Bus, A., & van IJzendoorn, M. (1999). Phonological awareness and early reading: A meta-analysis of experimental training studies. *Journal of Educational Psychology, 91,* 403–414.

Chall, J.S. (1967). *Learning to read: The great debate.* New York: McGraw-Hill.

Cohen, J. (1988). *Statistical power analysis for the behavior sciences* (2nd ed.). Mahwah, NJ: Lawrence Erlbaum Associates.

Dykstra, R. (1968). The effectiveness of code- and meaning-emphasis in beginning reading programs. *The Reading Teacher, 22,* 17–23.

Ehri, L. (1980). The development of orthographic images. In U. Frith (Ed.), *Cognitive processes in spelling* (pp. 311–338). London: Academic Press.

Ehri, L. (1991). Development of the ability to read words. In R. Barr, M. Kamil, P. Mosenthal, & P. Pearson (Eds.), *Handbook of reading research* (Vol. II, pp. 383–417). New York: Longman.

Ehri, L.C. (1992). Reconceptualizing the development of sight word reading and its relationship to recoding. In P. Gough, L. Ehri, & R. Treiman (Eds.), *Reading acquisition* (pp. 107–143). Mahwah, NJ: Lawrence Erlbaum Associates.

Ehri, L. (1994). Development of the ability to read words: Update. In R. Ruddell, M. Ruddell, & H. Singer (Eds.), *Theoretical models and processes of reading* (4th ed., pp. 323–358). Newark, DE: International Reading Association.

Ehri, L.C. (1997). Learning to read and learning to spell are one and the same, almost. In C.A. Perfetti & L. Rieben (Eds.), *Learning to spell: Research, theory, and practice across languages* (pp. 237–268). Mahwah, NJ: Lawrence Erlbaum Associates.

Ehri, L.C. (1998). Grapheme-phoneme knowledge is essential for learning to read words in English. In J.L. Metsala & L.C. Ehri (Eds.), *Word recognition in beginning literacy* (pp. 3–40). Mahwah, NJ: Lawrence Erlbaum Associates.

Ehri, L., Deffner, N., & Wilce, L. (1984). Pictorial mnemonics for phonics. *Journal of Educational Psychology, 76,* 880–893.

Ehri, L., Nunes, S., Stahl, S., & Willows, D. (2001). Systematic phonics instruction helps students learn to read: Evidence from the National Reading Panel's meta-analysis. *Review of Educational Research, 71,* 393–447.

Ehri, L., Nunes, S., Willows, D., Schuster, B., Yaghoub-Zadeh, Z., & Shanahan, T. (2001). Phonemic awareness instruction helps children learn to read: Evidence from the National Reading Panel's meta-analysis. *Reading Research Quarterly, 36,* 250–287.

Ehri, L., & Saltmarsh, J. (1995). Beginning readers outperform older disabled readers in learning to read words by sight. *Reading and Writing: An Interdisciplinary Journal, 7,* 295–326.

Griffith, P. (1991). Phonemic awareness helps first graders invent spellings and third graders remember correct spellings. *Journal of Reading Behavior, 23,* 215–233.

Harris, T.L., & Hodges, R.E. (Eds.). (1995). *The literacy dictionary: The vocabulary of reading and writing.* Newark, DE: International Reading Association.

Hearing on the importance of literacy before the House Committee on Education and the Workforce, 106th Cong. (2000, September 26) (testimony of Donald N. Langenberg). Also available on-line: http://edwork force.house.gov/hearings/106th/fc/literacy92600/langenberg.htm

Holdaway, D. (1979). *The foundations of literacy.* Sydney, Australia: Ashton-Scholastic.

Johnson, B. (1989). *DSTAT: Software for the meta-analytic review of research literatures.* Mahwah, NJ: Lawrence Erlbaum Associates.

Juel, C. (1988). Learning to read and write: A longitudinal study of fifty-four children from first through fourth grade. *Journal of Educational Psychology, 80,* 437–447.

Juel, C., Griffith, P., & Gough, P. (1986). Acquisition of literacy: A longitudinal study of children in first and second grade. *Journal of Educational Psychology, 78,* 243–255.

Juel, C., & Roper/Schneider, D. (1985). The influence of basal readers on first grade reading. *Reading Research Quarterly, 20,* 134–152.

Liberman, I., Shankweiler, D., Fischer, F., & Carter, B. (1974). Explicit sylla-ble and phoneme segmentation in the young child. *Journal of Experimental Child Psychology, 18*, 201–212.

Morris, D., & Perney, J. (1984). Developmental spelling as a predictor of first grade reading achievement. *Elementary School Journal, 84*, 441–457.

National Institute of Child Health and Human Development (NICHD). (2000). *Report of the National Reading Panel. Teaching children to read: An evidence-based assessment of the scientific research literature on reading and its implications for reading instruction: Reports of the subgroups* (NIH Publication No. 00-4754). Washington, DC: U.S. Government Printing Office. Also available on-line: http://www.nichd.nih.gov/publications/nrp/report.htm

Perfetti, C. (1992). The representation problem in reading acquisition. In P. Gough, L. Ehri, & R. Treiman (Eds.), *Reading acquisition* (pp. 107–143). Mahwah, NJ: Lawrence Erlbaum Associates.

Rack, J., Hulme, C., Snowling, M., & Wightman, J. (1994). The role of phonology in young children learning to read words: The direct-mapping hypothesis. *Journal of Experimental Child Psychology, 57*, 42–71.

Rack, J., Snowling, M., & Olson, R. (1992). The nonword reading deficit in developmental dyslexia: A review. *Reading Research Quarterly, 27*, 29–53.

Reitsma, P. (1983). Printed word learning in beginning readers. *Journal of Experimental Child Psychology, 75*, 321–339.

Routman, R. (1996). *Literacy at the crossroads.* Portsmouth, NH: Heinemann.

Share, D. (1999). Phonological recoding and orthographic learning: A direct test of the self-teaching hypothesis. *Journal of Experimental Child Psychology, 72*, 95–129.

Share, D., Jorm, A., Maclean, R., & Matthews, R. (1984). Sources of individual differences in reading achievement. *Journal of Educational Psychology, 76*, 1309–1324.

Stahl, S., Duffy-Hester, A., & Stahl, K. (1998). Everything you wanted to know about phonics (but were afraid to ask). *Reading Research Quarterly, 35*, 338–355.

Stanovich, K. (1980). Toward an interactive-compensatory model of individual differences in the development of reading fluency. *Reading Research Quarterly, 16*, 32–71.

Stuart, M. (1999). Getting ready for reading: Early phoneme awareness and phonics teaching improves reading and spelling in inner-city second language learners. *British Journal of Educational Psychology, 69*, 587–605.

Swanson, H.L. (1999). Reading research for students with LD: A meta-analysis of intervention outcomes. *Journal of Learning Disabilities, 32*, 504–532.

Swanson, H.L. (2000). What instruction works for students with learning disabilities? Summarizing the results from a meta-analysis of intervention studies. In R. Gersten, E. Schiller, & S. Vaughn (Eds.), *Contemporary special education research: Syntheses of the knowledge base on critical instructional issues* (pp. 1–30). Mahwah, NJ: Lawrence Erlbaum Associates.

Tangel, D., & Blachman, B. (1995). Effect of phoneme awareness instruction on the invented spelling of first-grade children: A one-year follow-up. *Journal of Reading Behavior, 27,* 153–185.

Torgesen, J., Wagner, R., Rashotte, C., Rose, E., Lindamood, P., Conway, T., et al. (1999). Preventing reading failure in young children with phonological processing disabilities: Group and individual responses to instruction. *Journal of Educational Psychology, 91,* 579–593.

Troia, G. (1999). Phonological awareness intervention research: A critical review of the experimental methodology. *Reading Research Quarterly, 34,* 28–52.

Tunmer, W., & Hoover, W. (1993). Phonological recoding skill and beginning reading. *Reading and Writing: An Interdisciplinary Journal, 5,* 161–179.

Venezky, R. (1970). *The structure of English orthography.* The Hague: Mouton.

Venezky, R. (1999). *The American way of spelling.* New York: Guilford Press.

Wendon, L. (1992). *First steps in Letterland.* Cambridge, UK: Letterland Ltd.

9

What Do We Know About Fluency?

Findings of the National Reading Panel

STEVEN A. STAHL

O nce, fluency was considered the "neglected goal" of reading (Allington, 1983), but no longer. Fluency is one of the five goals of reading stressed in the Reading First program incorporated into the No Child Left Behind Act of 2001 (PL 107-110). This legislation is the blueprint for elementary education in the United States for the next several years. Because fluency is a major part of this legislation, it will get major attention.

Although there is recognition at least among policy makers of the importance of fluent reading, there is much confusion about what fluency is and how to achieve it in both classrooms and remedial settings. The purpose of this chapter is to review what is known about fluent reading and to discuss effective approaches for promoting fluency.

Several models of reading development suggest that fluency is a crucial component of effective reading. Chall (1996), for example, suggested that reading develops through a series of six stages. There are two that precede fluency: *emergent literacy* (not Chall's term for this stage), in which children first develop concepts foundational to reading such as phonological awareness, concepts of print, and knowledge of the alphabet; and *decoding*, in which children learn

This project was supported by the Interagency Education Research Initiative, a program of research managed jointly by the National Science Foundation, the Institute of Education Sciences in the U.S. Department of Education, and the National Institute of Child Health and Human Development (NICHD) in the National Institutes of Health. Funding for the project was provided by NICHD Grant No. 1-RO1-HD40746 and by the National Science Foundation.

to read words accurately, either through decoding or word-calling. The third stage is *confirmation and fluency*, in which the child consolidates (Ehri, 1998) the knowledge of decoding to develop fluent reading and reading becomes more conversation-like. The child learns to integrate knowledge of sound–symbol relationships, sight words, and knowledge of the language conventions of connected text to create a smooth reading. In Chall's model, fluent word recognition is necessary for children to be able to learn from text, as might be expected in grades 4 and higher.

WHAT IS FLUENCY?

Conventionally, for reading to be fluent, it should be 1) accurate (without too many miscues), 2) at a reasonable rate, and 3) prosodic (read with enough expression that it sounds like language) (Kuhn & Stahl, 2003; National Institute of Child Health and Human Development [NICHD], 2000). Teachers assume that those who sound like they are struggling with the text, making many miscues, hesitating, and repeating words and phrases are struggling readers and that those who read the text comfortably are comprehending accurately. For the most part, these assumptions are correct. Reading, however, is more complex. Sometimes children can be reading accurately but do not understand what they read (Carpenter & Paris, in press; Pinnell et al., 1995). Some children can read haltingly but still get a significant amount of the text's meaning (Pinnell et al., 1995).

Traditionally, oral reading accuracy, usually as measured on an informal reading inventory (Johns, 1993), has been used as a general measure of children's reading skill. However, Pinnell et al. (1995), in the oral reading study of the National Assessment of Educational Progress (NAEP), found that among the fourth graders tested on this special study, overall oral reading accuracy was not significantly related to comprehension. (Pinnell et al. did, however, find that the number of significant miscues, or significant differences between the text and what a child read, was strongly related to the child's comprehension.) Carpenter and Paris (in press) and Schwanenflugel, Kuhn, Meisinger, Bradley, and Stahl (2003) found that oral reading accuracy was related to comprehension only in first and second grades, with the correlations in third grade and beyond dropping to nearly zero. Thus, oral reading accuracy may be important only in the early grades, with other factors such as vocabulary and comprehension strategy use becoming important later on (see also Stahl & Hiebert, in press).

In contrast to oral reading accuracy, oral reading rate remains important throughout the elementary years. Several theories of reading (Chall, 1996; LaBerge & Samuels, 1974) stress that word recognition should become automatic. If children can recognize words quickly and automatically, then word recognition does not interfere with comprehension, and children can understand any text within their language ability. As competent readers, we recognize words that we see only rarely, such as *quixotic, mandolin,* and *recumbent,* without much thought, whether we know their meanings or not. Reading rate was strongly associated with comprehension in the fourth-grade oral reading portion of the NAEP study (Pinnell et al., 1995) and elsewhere (e.g., Shinn, 1992).

Teaching children simply to say isolated words faster does not seem to improve reading comprehension. A number of studies have examined teaching children to say words that they know faster (Fleisher, Jenkins, & Pany, 1979–1980; Levy, Abello, & Lysynchuk, 1997; Spring, Blunden, & Gatheral, 1981). Although all of these studies found that children's passage reading fluency improved, none found differences in comprehension between the study group and control group. In contrast, preteaching words that children do not know seems to improve comprehension (e.g., Blanchard, 1981; Tan & Nicholson, 1997). Studies of repeated and assisted reading of connected text, not isolated words, do show strong effects on measures of comprehension as well as on measures of fluency. The National Reading Panel (NRP), in their review of guided oral reading procedures, found that "competent reading requires skills that extend beyond the single-word level to contextual reading, and that this skill can best be acquired by practicing reading in which the words are in a meaningful context" (NICHD, 2000, p. 3-11). Approaches that do this are discussed next.

INSTRUCTIONAL APPROACHES FOR DEVELOPING FLUENCY

Various approaches have been designed for developing fluency. Some have been developed for use in remedial or one-to-one situations, such as the method of repeated reading (e.g., Samuels, Schermer, & Reinking, 1992) or various forms of assisted reading (e.g., Heckelman, 1986). Others have been designed for whole-class or small-group use (e.g., Rasinski, Padak, Linek, & Sturtevant, 1994; Stahl, Heubach, & Cramond, 1997). All were designed as alternatives to traditional "round robin" reading, in which children in a small group take turns reading short sections of the text, discussing it as they go.

Round Robin Reading

Before discussing the alternatives, it is worthwhile to discuss why round robin reading, although not totally ineffective, is less effective than the alternatives. One factor, found across a wide variety of studies (e.g., Berliner, 1981; Leinhardt, Zigmond, & Cooley, 1981; Taylor, Frye, & Maruyama, 1990), is that the more time children spend practicing reading text at an appropriate level, the more they will gain in reading skill. This should be common sense. If people practice any skill, they will be better at that skill. Classroom observation studies have found that the more time children spend "with eyes on text," or doing engaged reading, the better readers they become (Berliner, 1981). In round robin reading, because of the turn taking, only one child can be assumed to be reading at any given moment. If there are five others in the group, these children might be doing many things other than attending to the text. In fact, there is ample evidence that this is the case (e.g., Durkin, 1993). Some have complained that round robin reading forces low-performing children to perform publicly or that it is boring for the child. I believe that the major problem is that it wastes instructional time. In round robin reading, children spend too much time waiting for others to finish reading or doing seatwork (Stallings, 1980). One older observational study (Gambrell, Wilson, & Gantt, 1981), conducted during a period in which round robin reading predominated, found that children read an average of 6 minutes per day, with low-achieving readers often reading less than 2 minutes per day. Any approach that would increase time spent reading should have positive effects on achievement.

Round robin reading is just one approach that can provide children with feedback about their reading performance. This feedback is an important component of effective reading instruction (McCoy &

Pany, 1986). Teachers, however, vary considerably in their ability to provide this feedback effectively (Pflaum & Pascarella, 1980). This feedback might include correcting word recognition miscues (McCoy & Pany, 1986) or cuing children to use their knowledge of words to decode unknown words in context (Clay, 1993). Many instructional approaches to oral reading are more efficient than round robin reading at providing this feedback and enabling children to gain reading practice.

National Reading Panel Fluency Report

The NRP (NICHD, 2000) examined the effects of a number of approaches that provided some sort of alternative to round robin reading. The panel used the term *guided oral reading* to refer to practices that "emphasize repeated reading or guided oral reading practice," including procedures such as "repeated reading (Samuels, 1979), neurological impress (Heckelman, 1969), radio reading (Greene, 1979), paired reading (Topping, 1987), and a variety of similar techniques" (NICHD, 2000, p. 3-11). Beginning with a corpus of more than 16,000 studies, the panel narrowed its analysis to 14 studies of the immediate effects of different programs on passage reading. Typically, these studies measured some aspect of fluency or comprehension with particular passages and then monitored changes in this performance from one reading to another. These studies did not necessarily measure transfer to more general reading or to reading of noninstructed passages. Not surprisingly, these studies generally found that children improved in their reading fluency or comprehension when reading the same text repeatedly. This overall finding is interesting because the repeated reading conditions varied considerably between studies. Repeated reading, with one to seven repetitions, when combined with listening or previewing a text, seems to be effective for first graders as well as for struggling fifth graders. These results are encouraging, but as the panel reported, "It certainly cannot [be inferred] that repeated reading or other guided repeated oral reading procedures would be effective in raising reading achievement on the basis of these studies alone" (p. 3-16).

The NRP (NICHD, 2000) also examined 16 experimental studies that included a control group as well as a pre-and posttest. By including a control group, which presumably received an equivalent amount of time in traditional round robin reading, one can examine whether the guided oral reading procedure produced better results than might be expected by chance alone.

In this analysis, the NRP (NICHD, 2000) found 49 comparisons that measured comprehension in 12 of the studies. The average effect size in this analysis was +0.35. This is considered a moderate effect size. In other words, an average child in the experimental group scored as well as a child in the 64th percentile of the control group. This is a noticeable but not a large effect. The panel also found 35 comparisons that measured fluency in 10 studies, using measures such as standardized measures of rate and accuracy or an informal reading inventory. The average effect size was +0.44, again a moderate effect size. On measures of fluency, the average child in the experimental group scored as well as a child in the 67th percentile of the control group. Again, this effect is noticeable but not large. For measures of word recognition, the panel found 11 comparisons in eight studies for an average effect size of +0.55. For aggregate or full-scale reading measures, the effect size from four comparisons in four separate studies was +0.50. Again, all of these effects are moderate.

That the effects on measures of reading comprehension are lower than those for fluency measures is not surprising. Reading comprehension is less directly related to fluency training than are more direct measures of fluency. Transfer is always more difficult to find. However, the findings seem robust and encouraging.

What Is Guided Oral Reading?

In the NRP report (NICHD, 2000), the term *guided oral reading* covers a great many different procedures. Thus, it is difficult to tell which one to recommend. Within the studies reviewed are repeated reading approaches, both individual and group; assisted reading such as neurological impress; and tutor-based techniques such as paired reading, peer tutoring, and cross-age tutoring, as well as listening while reading, and oral reading previewing. These approaches are described briefly in the following subsections to show the diversity of approaches devised to develop fluency.

Repeated Reading The method of repeated reading was one of the first approaches developed to improve fluency. Based on La-Berge and Samuels' (1974) model of automaticity, repeated reading was intended to improve children's automatic recognition of words in text so that less cognitive effort has to be expended on word recognition and more attention can be devoted to comprehension. Literally, repeated reading means that students read the same text repeatedly until a desired level of fluency is attained. A typical clinical version of the method of repeated reading is the one used in the tutoring done at the University of Georgia Reading Clinic:

1. The teacher should choose a passage to read that is slightly above the child's instructional level but one that the child might be interested in reading. Grade-level materials may be used for a child reading significantly below grade level.

2. The teacher takes a 100-word excerpt from this passage. (Different lengths may be used, but the math is more difficult.)

3. The child reads the passage aloud, while the teacher times him or her using a stopwatch or a wristwatch with a sweeping second hand. The teacher can choose to make an audiotape recording of the child's reading. As the child reads, the teacher marks all of the miscues that the child makes. The teacher marks the child's speed and error rate on a chart.

4. The teacher reviews the miscues with the child, using the audiotape or discussion.

5. The child rereads the passage, and the teacher makes an audiorecording, if desired. The teacher marks the child's errors and time on the chart.

6. The child and teacher continue Steps 4 and 5 until the child achieves a speed of 100 words per minute with zero or one miscue per 100 words. If this takes more than seven tries, the teacher might want to discontinue and use an easier passage. Repeated reading of a passage usually takes more than one clinic session. The teacher charts each attempt.

7. The teacher selects another 100-word passage at the same level. When the child can read a passage relatively fluently on the

first reading, the teacher provides a more difficult passage. It is important for the teacher to progressively challenge the child so that reading improvement can be made.

Another version of repeated reading, although not tested in any of these studies, can be used in whole classes or in small groups. In this variation, children begin reading orally from multiple copies of the same text on cue. After 3 minutes, the teacher calls "time" and children mark where they stopped with a pencil. After the reading, the teacher or the children can bring up words that gave the children difficulty. The teacher then repeats the procedure two more times, with the children marking how far they got in 3 minutes each time. Presumably, children get further each time; thus, this approach provides motivation and practice in reading (Stahl, 2003).

In the versions of repeated reading described here, children are monitored to ensure that they are on task, and they are given explicit guidance. I have seen repeated reading used as a mere exhortation for children to read a text repeatedly, either in class or at home. Without the teacher monitoring whether the reading is getting done or checking which words are providing difficulty, it is unclear whether this approach is effective (see Kuhn & Stahl, 2003).

Assisted Reading The first version of assisted reading had the unfortunate name of *neurological impress*, from its roots in theories of reading best now forgotten. In neurological impress reading, a child and a tutor read the same text simultaneously, with the tutor sitting behind the child reading into the child's dominant ear, with both the tutor and child pointing to the words at the same time. More contemporary versions keep the simultaneous reading but discard the precarious sitting and pointing arrangements. Typically, the tutor and child read the same text repeatedly, using the simultaneous reading technique. With each repetition, the tutor softens his or her voice so that the child becomes more dominant and independent in reading. The point in assisted reading is that the child has a model of fluent reading rather than just rate and accuracy criteria to aspire toward.

Assisted reading includes more than just neurological impress reading. Some authors (e.g., Chomsky, 1978) have modified assisted reading using audiotapes to provide the model for the child. Chomsky worked with a small group of children who had had extensive instruction in decoding but did not apply their phonics knowledge to their oral reading. She made audiotapes of books written somewhat above the students' reading level available to these children. The children were asked to listen repeatedly to the tapes until they were able to render the text fluently. The children selected their own books and set their own pace for the assisted repeated readings. They were instructed first to listen to an entire book or chapter from a book before selecting a portion that they wanted to practice. They were then to read along orally while repeatedly listening to those parts of the story they wanted to rehearse. In addition, Chomsky and a research assistant worked with each child on a weekly basis both to monitor progress and to engage the learner in further analysis of the text through language games. Children read each book as many as 20 times until the book had been mastered. Children gained 6 months in oral reading and 7 months in comprehension over the 10-month study. There was no control group. The gain, however, was less than might be expected over the time of the study, suggesting that although these children made an absolute gain, they were still reading and comprehending text below the level of their peers. Carbo (1978) found somewhat greater gains using audiotapes especially recorded at a somewhat slower rate than normal conversational speech.

One of the primary concerns regarding such read-along techniques is that there is no way to ensure active engagement on the part of the learners. Just having children listen to audiotapes with the instruction to follow along is not likely to have much of an effect. Indeed, a number of classroom observation studies (e.g., Evans & Carr, 1985; Leinhardt et al., 1981) have found that time spent listening to audiotapes in class does not significantly affect achievement. In Carbo's (1978) and Chomsky's (1978) studies, however, students were held responsible for being able to read the text fluently, so it appeared that they did actively participate in the process. As with repeated reading, the level of monitoring and guidance provided seems to make a difference.

Tutor-Based Reading Approaches   The three tutor-based techniques of paired reading, peer tutoring, and cross-age tutoring involve some degree of both assisted and repeated reading. In all three approaches, someone other than a teacher delivers the instruction.

In paired reading (Topping, 1995) a more capable reader, usually an adult, works one-to-one with a struggling reader. A paired reading session begins with the tutor and tutee choosing a book together. The book need be only of interest to the tutee. There should be no readability limits (although the experience of my research assistants, teaching assistants, and me is that children rarely choose material that is far too difficult). The tutor and tutee begin by reading in unison. The child signals the tutor, by touching the tutor or by raising a hand or some other prearranged signal, when he or she wants to read solo. This continues until the child makes an error. Errors are corrected by the tutor providing the word, repeating the sentence in unison with the child, and returning to paired reading, until the child again signals a desire to read solo again. Paired reading has been used in the classroom and by parents. Paired reading, although represented in the NRP report (NICHD, 2000) by one study (Miller, Robson, & Bushell, 1986), differs from the other guided oral reading approaches because it involves only minimal repetition. Instead, tutor and tutee go all of the way through a text without practice for fluency.

Peer and cross-age tutoring approaches can involve repetition. Peer tutoring involves children in the same class, whereas cross-age tutoring involves children tutoring younger children. In some peer tutoring approaches (e.g., Simmons, Fuchs, Fuchs, Hodge, & Mathes, 1994; Simmons, Fuchs, Fuchs, Mathes, & Hodge, 1995), the peer tutors are given fairly structured instructions in how to carry out the tutoring, parts of which are scripted. In other approaches, a teacher supervises both tutor and tutee so that tutoring may differ depending on the needs of the child. Sometimes in cross-age tutoring, the tutors are given books and asked to practice reading them so that they can read the book to a younger child. Especially in cross-age tutoring, but somewhat in peer tutoring as well, it is expected that the tutor as well as the tutee will make gains in reading. Thus, for a second-grade struggling reader practicing to read a book such as *Green Eggs and Ham* to a kindergartner, it is expected that the repeated reading involved in the practicing would lead to gains in reading skill. It is also expected that the kindergartner might learn from the reading but possibly not as much as the tutor does. Because the older children's peers view working with younger children as desirable, cross-age tutoring also allows the older children to fend off ridicule for reading "easy" books (Stahl, 2003).

A Mulligan Stew? Of the 16 studies involved in the NRP meta-analysis of the effects of guided oral reading (NICHD, 2000), 2 appeared to involved repeated reading, 5 involved assisted reading, 1 involved children reading along with prepared audiotapes, 5 involved tutoring, and 2 involved other or combined approaches. Thus, although the finding of a positive effect on fluency is robust when combining the effect sizes of all of the different approaches into a single effect size, with each approach represented by a small number of studies, it is difficult to get guidance as to what approaches to choose.

Kuhn and Stahl (2003) reviewed fluency-oriented approaches but used a broader range of studies. Whereas the NRP meta-analysis (NICHD, 2000) was confined to experimental or quasi-experimental studies published in peer-reviewed journals, Kuhn and Stahl looked at more of the literature as a whole. Kuhn and Stahl examined three groups of studies—those dealing with repeated reading, those dealing with assisted reading in clinical settings, and those examining classroom approaches to fluency development. In addition, because there were too few studies with adequate controls and statistics for meta-analysis to be appropriate, Kuhn and Stahl used vote counting (Light & Pillemer, 1984) to examine trends. This broader range of studies, although not as scientifically rigorous as a whole, can support the general findings of the NRP. Vote counting classifies comparisons within studies as either significantly favoring the treatment, significantly favoring the control group, or finding no significant difference between the two approaches (see Chapter 6 for further description of vote counting). Meta-analysis is more sensitive than vote counting to small differences that might not be statistically significant in individual studies but that might show an overall trend if accumulated between studies (Glass, McGaw, & Smith, 1981).

Basically, Kuhn and Stahl (2003) found that fluency instruction generally seems to be effective, confirming the general finding of the NRP (NICHD, 2000). Nearly all of the studies examined showed that children made absolute gains when involved in some sort of fluency-oriented instruction. Sometimes, however, as in the Chomsky (1978) study cited previously, the gains were less than might be expected given the amount of time spent in instruction. Children with reading problems, such as the children in many of these studies, rarely make 1 month's progress in 1 month's time (their inadequate progress is the reason they are behind their peers), and they may have made more progress in fluency instruction than they made in other types of instruction. However, for children with reading problems to reach their peers' achievement (the goal of remedial instruction), the children need to make accelerated progress (see Chapter 15 and Clay, 1993). It is not clear whether these treatments were successful in helping the children make such progress. In addition, it is unclear whether any success might have occurred because of specific instructional features or because fluency instruction involves children reading increased amounts of text. That is, it is not known why repeated or assisted reading approaches worked. It could be that there were some features of the instruction that were important, or the instructional methods used could have worked simply by providing more practice reading. Potentially, other approaches could do the same thing without repeated reading.

Kuhn and Stahl (2003) also found that assisted approaches, such as listening while reading, seem to be more effective than nonassisted approaches, such as repeated reading. Kuhn and Stahl found 15 studies that examined repeated reading using a control-group design. Of these 15 studies, 6 found effects favoring the repeated reading treatment, 8 found no significant difference between the treatment and control, and 1 found an effect favoring the control. From this pattern, one cannot claim that repeated reading in itself is effective in improving reading achievement. Kuhn and Stahl speculated that one reason for the lackluster effects of repeated reading approaches may be that these approaches used might not have included adequate monitoring and guidance.

In contrast to the weak findings on repeated reading, Kuhn and Stahl (2003) found seven studies that examined the effects of assisted reading on fluency measures using a control group. Of these seven, five found significant treatment effects and two found that the differences between the treatment and control were not statistically significant. This suggests that assisted reading might be a useful approach for improving fluency. Again, the results for comprehension measures mirrored those for fluency measures. The difference between repeated and assisted reading may be due to the amount of guidance provided. In assisted reading, a teacher is monitoring the reading. In many of the repeated reading studies, children were reading on their own and may not have been devoting the same amount of attention to reading that they would have with more active monitoring.

Repetition? If repeated reading does not seem to lead to improved fluency and comprehension but assisted reading does, is repetition necessary? Kuhn and Stahl (2003) found several studies that compared repeated and nonrepeated reading. Homan, Klesius, and Hite (1993), Mathes and Fuchs (1993), Rashotte and Torgesen (1985) and van Bon, Boksebeld, Font Freide, and van den Hurk (1991) found no difference in effects between repeated readings of a small number of texts and nonrepetitive reading of a larger set of texts. These findings suggest that the amount of time spent orally reading connected text, not the repetition, may lead to the positive effect on fluency and comprehension.

Difficulty Kuhn and Stahl (2003) also examined the relative difficulty of the passages. Some authors (e.g., Clay, 1993) have argued that having students read and reread relatively easy passages improves their fluency. It can also be argued that the rereadings scaffold children's word recognition abilities so that the children can read more difficult material.

Mathes and Fuchs (1993) compared the use of easy and difficult materials and found no effect for the difficulty of materials. However, they also did not find a difference between a repeated reading treatment and a control condition. Rashotte and Torgesen (1985) used relatively easy reading materials and also failed to find significant differences between their repeated reading treatment and a control condition. The remainder of the studies used materials at or above the child's instructional level. Six of the eleven remaining studies found differences favoring the treatment group. Kuhn and Stahl's (2003) best guess was that more difficult materials lead to greater gains in achievement, but more research is needed on this question.

Whole-Class Reading Approaches

The majority of studies just discussed involved one-to-one instruction, either given in a clinical or remedial setting or in a whole-class peer or cross-age tutoring setting. There have been several promising approaches to whole-class fluency development, one of which (Rasinski et al., 1994) was included in the NRP report (NICHD, 2000). Another approach, fluency-oriented reading instruction (FORI; Stahl et al., 1997), was evaluated without a control group. For this reason and because it was not published in a peer-reviewed journal, it was not included in the NRP report. A current study is conducting that evaluation. The results of the first year of the multi-year study are promising and are presented in the subsection that follows.

Both of these whole-class approaches (Rasinski et al., 1994; Stahl et al., 1997) and others (Hoffman, 1987; Reutzel & Hollingsworth, 1993) were tested in second-grade classrooms. Second grade was chosen because of the importance of fluency development at that grade, at which point children have learned to decode but are not yet confronted with the large amounts of text in third grade and higher or with the added demand of learning specific content (Chall, 1996). Although these whole-class approaches may not be directly applicable to older children, they can be easily adapted to older struggling readers reading at a late first- or early second-grade level. Chall (1996) assumed that the need for fluency development was basically over by third grade; data from the FORI study (Schwanenflugel et al., 2003) suggest that children may continue to develop in automaticity past third grade.

Fluency-Oriented Reading Instruction   Stahl et al. (1997) used repeated readings in a second-grade classroom program to help develop fluent and automatic word recognition in second graders. The resulting program, FORI, has three aspects—a redesigned basal reading lesson, a free-reading period at school, and a home reading program.

Figure 9.1 contains a lesson plan developed for FORI. In this plan, the class is broken into two groups: students reading at or above grade level and those approaching grade level. This has been done to illustrate how the basic lesson plan can be adapted for different types of children. By showing a 5-day sequence, the plan illustrates how the various components of the program fit together. For a child approaching grade level, the home reading program can be modified to provide more practice, if needed. For a child reading above grade level, all of the time spent reading at home can be given to reading books of the child's choice. Also, echo reading (in which the teacher reads part of the story and the class or a group echoes it back) is probably not needed for all children but might provide essential support for children with reading problems.

The FORI reading lesson uses stories from the children's second-grade basal reading text. This text would be difficult for children reading below grade level. With the support provided by the program, however, children who entered second grade with some basic reading ability could profit from a conventional second-grade text.

For students reading at or above grade level

	Monday	Tuesday	Wednesday	Thursday	Friday
Basal lesson	**Teacher introduces story.** Teacher reads story to class and discusses it with students. Teacher reviews key vocabulary and gives comprehension and other story-focused exercises. *Option:* Teacher develops graphic organizers. *Option:* Students do activities from class text.	**Students read and practice story.** *Option:* Students do partner reading.	**Students read and practice story.** *Option:* Students do partner reading.	**Students do extension activities,** such as writing in response to the story.	**Students do extension activities,** such as writing in response to the story. *Option:* Teacher keeps running records of children's reading.
Choice reading	Students read a book of their choosing.	Students read a book of their choosing.	Students read a book of their choosing.	Students read a book of their choosing.	Students read a book of their choosing.
Home reading	Students read 15–30 mins. in a book of their choosing.	Students read the story to parents or other reader.	Students read 15–30 mins. in a book of their choosing.	Students read 15–30 mins. in a book of their choosing.	Students read 15–30 mins. in a book of their choosing.

For students approaching grade-level reading

	Monday	Tuesday	Wednesday	Thursday	Friday
Basal lesson	**Teacher introduces story.** Teacher reads story to class and discusses it with students. Teacher reviews key vocabulary and gives comprehension and other story-focused exercises. *Option:* Teacher develops graphic organizers. *Option:* Teacher uses prepared audiotape.	**Students read and practice story.** *Option:* Teacher and students do echo reading.	**Students read and practice story.** *Option:* Students do partner reading.	**Students do extension activities,** such as writing in response to the story. *Option:* Students do partner reading. *Option:* Students do activities from class text.	**Students do extension activities,** such as writing in response to the story. *Option:* Students do activities from class text. *Option:* Teacher keeps running records of children's reading.
Choice reading	Students review the story and read a book of their choosing.	Students read a book of their choosing.	Students read a book of their choosing.	Students read a book of their choosing.	Students read a book of their choosing.
Home reading	Students read 15–30 mins. in a book of their choosing.	Students read the story to parents or other reader.	Students read the story to parents or other reader.	Students read the story to parents or other reader.	Students read 15–30 mins. in a book of their choosing.

Figure 9.1. Fluency-oriented reading instruction (FORI) divided into two instructional groups. (Note: Both groups use reading material appropriate to grade level.)

On the first day of the FORI reading lesson, the teacher begins by reading the story aloud to the class and discussing it. This discussion puts comprehension at the forefront, so that children are aware that they were reading for meaning. Following this, the teacher reviews key vocabulary and conducts comprehension exercises and other activities focused around the story itself. On the second day, the teacher can choose to use echo reading. Other times, this review and comprehension work involves having children read and practice part of the story. Then, the story is sent home after the second day of the lesson for the child to read with his or her parents or with other readers listening. For children who struggle, the story is sent home additional times during the week. Children who do not have difficulty with the story do other reading at home on these days.

On the second day, the children reread the story with a partner, do echo reading, or practice the story in some other manner. In partner reading, one partner reads a page while the other monitors the reading. Then they switch roles until finishing the story. In echo reading, the teacher takes aside children who need extra support. The teacher reads a small portion of the story (a sentence, paragraph, or more), and the children echo it back. This gives these students added exposure to the vocabulary and content of the story prior to their reading it at home and with a partner.

On the third and fourth days, children receive additional practice as well as activities that provide more work on the vocabulary and comprehension of the story. This is also a time when decoding instruction is provided. At the end of the 5-day cycle, the teacher does extension activities, such as writing in response to the reading or activities that extend the comprehension of the story.

Although this basal lesson is an important part of the program, it is not the only reading that children do. Later during each day, time is set aside for children to read books that they chose. For children approaching grade level, this period could be used to review the new story as well. These books are usually easy to read and are read for enjoyment. Children sometimes read with partners during this period, as well. This time ranged from 15 minutes in the beginning of the school year to 30 minutes by the end.

Also, children are required, as part of their homework, to read at home. Outside reading is monitored through reading logs, and teachers make sure that the children in this program read at home an average of 4 days per week for at least 15 minutes per day.

In the first study (Stahl et al., 1997), this program was carried out by 4 teachers in two schools during the first year and was expanded to

10 teachers in three schools for the second year. The results from both years were positive. In both years, children gained on average nearly 2 years in reading growth in the second-grade year, as measured by an informal reading inventory. What is more gratifying are the effects that this intensive reading experience had on struggling readers. Over 2 years, all but 2 of the 105 children who began the second-grade year reading at a primer level or higher were reading at a second-grade level or higher at the end of the year.

Although these results were impressive, without a control group, one cannot say for certain that they are more extraordinary than what is customarily achieved in second grade, especially with talented teachers. To replicate this study and extend it, Stahl et al. (2003) are conducting a 5-year large-scale examination of FORI. In the first 2 years, they have been working with nine schools and 28 teachers in three sites. One third of these teachers have been applying FORI as outlined previously, one third have been using a wide-reading variation, and one third serve as a control. The wide-reading variation is similar to the basic FORI, but instead of reading one book repeatedly over the course of the week, children read three books, with similar supports for the reading. This variation was included to test whether the effects for FORI found by Stahl et al. (1997) were due to the specific program or whether they were due to increased amount of reading of connected text. Furthermore, Kuhn (2000) found that children in a small-group program who read a different book each day outperformed children who read one book repeatedly on a measure of comprehension. The purpose of Stahl et al.'s (2003) wide-reading variation was to replicate this finding using a larger sample.

Generally Stahl et al. (2003) found that both fluency-oriented approaches outperformed the control, at least for children reading at the pre-primer level or higher. Those children who were reading below that level were given a remedial program based on Lovett, Warren-Chaplin, Ransby, and Borden's (1990) program and Reading Mastery (SRA/McGraw-Hill). The children in the remedial group made significant growth. Most children in this group started as virtual nonreaders, but by the end of the first year, these children performed as well as average children did at the beginning of the school year. Thus, the remedial program allowed the children in the remedial group to get into the "reading system" and, with an accelerated program the following year, a chance to catch up. The analysis presented here is a work in progress, and the final presentation might differ somewhat.

Stahl et al. (2003) did two types of analysis. Because two of the control groups were involved in school improvement programs, the comparison was no longer a treatment versus control but was the FORI treatment versus another treatment. The school improvement program was fairly intensive. It involved hiring a reading coach who worked with the second-grade teachers, purchasing thousands of books, and placing an overall emphasis on reading that was lacking in previous years. In comparison, the FORI treatment was fairly minimal, involving two short in-service sessions at the beginning of the year and continuing contact throughout the year. Thus, the comparisons using the concurrent control group (the one observed at the same time as the treatment groups) are fairly conservative, because the control group was also getting added attention. Therefore, my colleagues and I also compared the children with a historical control group, which consisted of children in the same schools assessed the previous spring. I present the results from both sets of comparisons.

To evaluate our program, Stahl et al. (2003) used three types of measures: a standardized measure of reading comprehension (The Psychological Corporation, 2001), a standardized measure of oral reading accuracy and rate (Wiederholt & Bryant, 2001), and standardized measures of isolated word reading and decoding (Torgesen, Wagner, & Rashotte, 1999). On the analyses using the concurrent control group, my colleagues and I used a time by condition by remediation interaction to test the effects of the program. We used this analysis because we had data from the fall, winter, and spring for nearly all subjects and this analysis allowed us to examine the rate of growth of both remedial (those below pre-primer) and nonremedial students. We found a significant effect for this factor both on the measure of isolated word recognition, $F(4, 556) = 3.46$, $p = .0024$, and on the measure of oral reading, $F(4, 556) = 2.794$, $p = .0026$. The effect for the comprehension measure was not statistically significant, but the effect for time by condition (including both remedial and nonremedial students in the analysis) approached statistical significance, $F(2, 280) = 2.90$, $p = .0056$. This fairly conservative analysis suggests that the fluency-oriented program was fairly effective, at least in improving children's rapid word recognition in context and in isolation.

The results from the comparisons involving the historical controls reinforce this finding. The analyses using the historical controls were simpler, involving a comparison between the two treatments and the two control groups. Stahl et al. (2003) found significant overall effects for the different conditions on all measures—isolated word recognition, $F (3,495) = 6.26$, $p < .001$; oral reading rate and accuracy, $F (3, 483) = 36.04$, $p < .001$; and comprehension, $F (3, 496) = 4.32$, $p = .005$. For the measure of reading isolated words, the wide-reading group outperformed the repeated reading group, the historical control group, and the concurrent control group—which performed similarly to each other. For the measure of oral reading, the wide-reading group outperformed the repeated reading group and the concurrent control group, who performed similarly to each other. All other groups significantly outperformed the historical control group. For the comprehension measure, again the wide-reading group outperformed the other groups, but only the difference between it and the concurrent control group was statistically significant. The wide-reading group, although randomly chosen, had the highest pretest scores, so its strong performance in the spring posttest is not surprising.

These analyses are preliminary, but they indicate that FORI is successful. The two variations, repeated and wide reading, were similar to each other in their effects, suggesting that the increased amount of reading and the support given during that reading are what underlie the success of the two approaches. The repeated reading approach is easier to implement. Therefore, my colleagues and I will be expanding this approach in the next year of the study.

THE ROLE OF PRACTICE

One consistent finding from the process–product studies of effective teaching (Berliner, 1981), to the experimental work reviewed by the NRP (NICHD, 2000), to Kuhn and Stahl's (2003) study is that the amount of reading that children do influences their achievement, at least as long as the children are guided and monitored during that reading. But not all practice is equally effective.

One of the most controversial findings from the NRP report (NICHD, 2000) was the finding that nonmonitored reading, in the form of sustained silent reading (SSR) or similar approaches, was not shown to be effective in the experimental studies that the panel reviewed. In SSR, a period of time is set aside daily for children to read books of their choosing. At this time, the teacher is supposed to model reading as well. Although one cannot prove with experimental studies that a practice is not effective, in the absence of positive findings one might recommend other practices until positive, experimental evidence can be found.

The failure to find positive effects from SSR may be due to two factors. First, the NRP (NICHD, 2000) looked only at experimental evidence. In this area, the best studies are not experimental but are correlational (see Krashen, 2001). Studies such as those by Anderson, Wilson, and Fielding (1988) and Taylor et al. (1990), among many others, have found that the amount of reading that children do correlates strongly with children's gains in reading. Correlations between variables do not establish that one variable causes the other; this is why correlational studies were not used by the NRP. This is an area, however, that is difficult to study experimentally. If one group is given a period of time for SSR and the other is not, one is not sure whether and how much the children in the SSR program are actually reading. Many SSR advocates do not allow teachers to check up on children or recommend that teachers read their own books during this time to be a model of a reader. Without teacher monitoring, it is unclear whether children are reading or not.

One set of experimental studies that do find positive effects for practice in reading are the "book flood" studies. Elley and his colleagues (Elley, 2000; Elley & Mangubhai, 1983) in a series of studies have found that increasing the amount of reading material available to children and teaching teachers how to encourage children to use that material can dramatically improve children's reading achievement. This work was done with second-language learners, generally in the South Pacific, so it was outside of the purview of the NRP (NICHD, 2000).

One failing of SSR is that teachers may not monitor their children's reading. We have observed SSR in a number of classrooms and found that children are often not reading during that time or are reading material that is inappropriate for their reading level. One pair of children observed in a study (Stahl, Suttles, & Pagnucco, 1996) were taking turns talking and turning pages in a shared book, looking as if they were sharing reading. When I came close enough to listen to what they were saying, however, I heard them talking about what they were going to do that weekend. In other observations, I have seen children read books that were very easy or very difficult for them, neither of which would aid in their reading development.

Although the research reviewed by the NRP (NICHD, 2000) does not support the use of SSR, common sense suggests that children should have some time during the day to read books of their own choosing, if only for motivational purposes (see Turner, 1995). However, I suggest that teachers actively monitor children's reading, both by going around the room to make sure that children are on task and by asking questions about what children are reading, and encourage children to read books of an appropriate level. Effective teachers can cajole children to read books that will engage them and develop their reading abilities. In short, reading practice may be useful for children, but like guided oral reading, the practice needs to be actively monitored and guided by the teacher and should involve reading books of an appropriate level of difficulty.

PUTTING THIS ALL TOGETHER

There is evidence from a number of sources that educators can re-engineer instruction, both in remedial environments and in whole-class environments, to improve children's fluency. Several characteristics typify effective fluency-oriented instruction.

Although many successful approaches used repeated readings of a single text, repetition does not seem to be necessary. Instead, it seems necessary to increase the amount of reading that children do at an appropriate level. Successful programs can do this not only through repeated reading but also through assisted reading using a variety of texts. The key seems to be providing practice.

Effective approaches monitor children's reading and provide guidance during repeated and assisted reading. The contrast is clear in assisted approaches such as using audiotaped reading, which is effective when the teacher makes students responsible for reading what was on the audiotape (e.g., Chomsky, 1978) as opposed to using listening-while-reading stations, which do not seem to have any effects on achievement (e.g., Leinhardt et al., 1981). The absence of teacher monitoring and guidance may underlie the lack of effects found for repeated reading by Kuhn and Stahl (2003). Teachers' active intervention is vital for children to improve their reading achievement.

Children should be given support in reading relatively difficult material, rather than repeatedly reading easy material. Reading difficult materials, even those at a child's frustration level, with appropriate scaffolding through repeated reading and/or teacher assistance can improve children's reading achievement. Again, the teacher scaffolding is important so that children can read those materials successfully.

Although fluency—accuracy, rate, and prosody—is an important component of effective reading, it is not sufficient to make a child a reader. Children need to know the language of the text, especially the word meanings in the text; they need to be able to integrate the words into a coherent message (Kintsch, 1998); and they need to have strategic knowledge so that they can match their comprehension with their purposes for reading (Paris, Lipson, & Wixson, 1983). Our studies suggest that fluency is most important in first and second grades, with other aspects of reading gaining importance in third grade and higher. Disfluent reading can limit children's comprehension, but more than fluency is needed to make a child a successful reader.

Fluency can and should be taught as part of an effective reading program. Fluency, however, is just one part of such a program. A truly effective reading program includes work in phonological awareness and decoding instruction in kindergarten and first grade and work in vocabulary and comprehension in all grades, and it provides children with the supported, scaffolded, and monitored practice needed to become fluent readers.

REFERENCES

Allington, R.L. (1983). Fluency: The neglected reading goal. *The Reading Teacher, 37,* 556–561.

Anderson, R.C., Wilson, P.T., & Fielding, L.G. (1988). Growth in reading and how children spend their time outside of school. *Reading Research Quarterly, 23,* 285–303.

Berliner, D.C. (1981). Academic learning time and reading achievement. In J.T. Guthrie (Ed.), *Comprehension and teaching: Research reviews* (pp. 203–226). Newark, DE: International Reading Association.

Blanchard, J.S. (1981). A comprehension strategy for disabled readers in the middle school. *Journal of Reading, 24,* 331–336.

Carbo, M. (1978). Teaching reading with talking books. *The Reading Teacher, 32,* 267–273.

Carpenter, R., & Paris, S.G. (in press). *Informal reading inventories and comprehension* (Research report). Ann Arbor: University of Michigan, Center for the Improvement of Early Reading Achievement.

Chall, J.S. (1996). *Stages of reading development* (2nd ed.). Fort Worth, TX: Harcourt-Brace.

Chomsky, C. (1978). When you still can't read in third grade: After decoding, what? In S.J. Samuels (Ed.), *What research has to say about reading instruction* (pp. 13–30). Newark, DE: International Reading Association.

Clay, M.M. (1993). *Reading Recovery: A guidebook for teachers in training.* Portsmouth, NH: Heinemann.

Durkin, D. (1993). *Teaching them to read* (6th ed.). Boston: Allyn & Bacon.

Ehri, L.C. (1998). Grapheme-phoneme knowledge is essential for learning to read words in English. In J.L. Metsala & L.C. Ehri (Eds.), *Word recognition in beginning literacy* (pp. 3–40). Mahwah, NJ: Lawrence Erlbaum Associates.

Elley, W.B. (2000). The potential of book floods for raising literacy levels. *International Review of Education, 46*, 233–255.

Elley, W.B., & Mangubhai, F. (1983). The impact of reading on second language learning. *Reading Research Quarterly, 19*, 53–67.

Evans, M.A., & Carr, T.H. (1985). Cognitive abilities, conditions of learning and the early development of reading skill. *Reading Research Quarterly, 20*, 327–350.

Fleisher, L.S., Jenkins, J.R., & Pany, D. (1979–1980). Effects on poor readers' comprehension of training in rapid decoding. *Reading Research Quarterly, 15*, 30–48.

Gambrell, L.B., Wilson, R.M., & Gantt, W.N. (1981). Classroom observations of task-attending behaviors of good and poor readers. *Journal of Educational Research, 74*, 400–404.

Glass, G.V., McGaw, B., & Smith, M.L. (1981). *Meta-analysis in social research.* Thousand Oaks, CA: Sage Publications.

Heckelman, R.G. (1986). N.I.M. revisited. *Academic Therapy, 21*, 411–420.

Hoffman, J. (1987). Rethinking the role of oral reading. *Elementary School Journal, 87*, 367–373.

Homan, S., Klesius, P., & Hite, S. (1993). Effects of repeated readings and nonrepetitive strategies on students' fluency and comprehension. *Journal of Educational Research, 87*, 94–99.

Johns, J.L. (1993). *Informal reading inventories.* DeKalb, IL: Communitech International Incorporated.

Kintsch, W. (1998). *Comprehension: A paradigm for cognition.* Cambridge, UK: Cambridge University Press.

Krashen, S. (2001). More smoke and mirrors: A critique of the National Reading Panel report on fluency. *Phi Delta Kappan, 83*(2), 119–123.

Kuhn, M.R. (2000). *The effects of repeated reading and non-repeated reading on comprehension and fluency.* Unpublished doctoral dissertation, University of Georgia.

Kuhn, M.R., & Stahl, S.A. (2003). Fluency: A review of developmental and remedial practices. *Journal of Educational Psychology, 95*(1), 3–21.

LaBerge, D., & Samuels, S.J. (1974). Toward a theory of automatic information processing in reading. *Cognitive Psychology, 6*, 293–323.

Leinhardt, G., Zigmond, N., & Cooley, W. (1981). Reading instruction and its effects. *American Educational Research Journal, 18*, 343–361.

Levy, B.A., Abello, B., & Lysynchuk, L. (1997). Transfer from word training to reading in context: Gains in reading fluency and comprehension. *Learning Disabilities Quarterly, 20*, 173–188.

Light, R.J., & Pillemer, D.B. (1984). *Summing up: The science of reviewing research.* Cambridge, MA: Harvard University Press.

Lovett, M., Warren-Chaplin, P.M., Ransby, M.J., & Borden, S.L. (1990). Training the word recognition skills of reading disabled children. *Journal of Educational Psychology, 62*, 769–780.

Mathes, P.G., & Fuchs, L.S. (1993). Peer-mediated reading instruction in special education resource rooms. *Learning Disabilities Research and Practice, 8,* 233–243.

McCoy, K.M., & Pany, D. (1986). Summary and analysis of oral reading corrective feedback research. *The Reading Teacher, 39,* 548–554.

Miller, A., Robson, D., & Bushell, R. (1986). Parental participation in paired reading: A controlled study. *Educational Psychology, 6,* 277–284.

National Institute of Child Health and Human Development (NICHD). (2000). *Report of the National Reading Panel. Teaching children to read: An evidence-based assessment of the scientific research literature on reading and its implications for reading instruction: Reports of the subgroups* (NIH Publication No. 00-4754). Washington, DC: U.S. Government Printing Office. Also available on-line: http://www.nichd.nih.gov/publications/nrp/report.htm

No Child Left Behind Act of 2001, PL 107-110, 115 Stat. 1425, 20 U.S.C. §§ 6301 *et seq.*

Paris, S.G., Lipson, M.Y., & Wixson, K.K. (1983). Becoming a strategic reader. *Contemporary Educational Psychology, 8,* 293–316.

Pflaum, S.W., & Pascarella, E.T. (1980). Interactive effects of prior reading achievement and training in context on the reading of learning-disabled children. *Reading Research Quarterly, 16,* 138–158.

Pinnell, G.S., Pikulski, J.J., Wixson, K.K., Campbell, J.R., Gough, P.B., & Beatty, A.S. (1995). *Listening to children read aloud: Data from NAEP's integrated reading performance record (IRPR) at grade 4.* Washington, DC: National Center for Education Statistics.

The Psychological Corporation. (2001). *Wechsler Individual Achievement Test—II.* San Antonio, TX: Author.

Rashotte, C.A., & Torgesen, J.K. (1985). Repeated reading and reading fluency in learning disabled children. *Reading Research Quarterly, 20,* 180–188.

Rasinski, T.V., Padak, N., Linek, W., & Sturtevant, B. (1994). Effects of fluency development on urban second-grade readers. *Journal of Educational Research, 87,* 158–165.

Reutzel, D.R., & Hollingsworth, P.M. (1993). Effects of fluency training on second graders' reading comprehension. *Journal of Educational Research, 86,* 325–331.

Samuels, S.J., Schermer, N., & Reinking, D. (1992). Reading fluency: Techniques for making decoding automatic. In S.J. Samuels & A.E. Farstrup (Eds.), *What research says about reading instruction* (2nd ed., pp. 124–144). Newark, DE: International Reading Association.

Schwanenflugel, P., Kuhn, M.R., Meisinger, B., Bradley, B., & Stahl, S.A. (2003, April). *An examination of the attentional resource model and the development of reading fluency.* Paper presented at biennial meeting of the Society for Research in Child Development, Tampa, FL.

Shinn, M.R. (1992). Curriculum-based measurement of oral reading fluency: A confirmatory analysis of its relation to reading. *School Psychology Review, 21,* 459–479.

Simmons, D.C., Fuchs, L.S., Fuchs, D., Hodge, J.P., & Mathes, P.G. (1994). Importance of instructional complexity and role reciprocity to classwide peer tutoring. *Learning Disabilities Research and Practice, 9,* 203–212.

Simmons, D.C., Fuchs, L.S., Fuchs, D., Mathes, P.G., & Hodge, J.P. (1995). Effects of explicit teaching and peer tutoring on the reading achievement of learning disabled and low performing students in regular classrooms. *The Elementary School Journal, 95,* 387–408.

Spring, C., Blunden, D., & Gatheral, M. (1981). Effect on reading comprehension of training to automaticity in word-reading. *Perceptual and Motor Skills, 53*(3), 779–786.

Stahl, S.A. (2003). No more "madface": Motivation and fluency. In D.M. Barone & L.M. Morrow (Eds.), *Research-based practices in early literacy.* New York: Guilford Press.

Stahl, S.A., Bradley, B., Smith, C.H., Kuhn, M.R., Schwanenflugel, P., Meisinger, E., et al. (2003, April). *Teaching children to become fluent and automatic readers.* Paper presented at the annual meeting of the American Educational Research Association, Chicago.

Stahl, S., Heubach, K., & Cramond, B. (1997). *Fluency-oriented reading instruction.* Athens: GA, and Washington, DC: National Reading Research Center and U.S. Department of Education, Office of Educational Research and Improvement, Educational Resources Information Center.

Stahl, S.A., & Hiebert, E.H. (in press). The "word factors": A problem for reading comprehension assessment. In S.G. Paris & S.A. Stahl (Eds.), *Current issues in reading comprehension and assessment.* Mahwah, NJ: Lawrence Erlbaum Associates.

Stahl, S.A., Suttles, C.W., & Pagnucco, J.R. (1996). The effects of traditional and process literacy instruction on first graders' reading and writing achievement and orientation toward reading. *Journal of Educational Research, 89,* 131–144.

Stallings, J.A. (1980). Allocated academic learning time revisited, or beyond time on task. *Educational Researcher, 8*(11), 11–16.

Tan, A., & Nicholson, T. (1997). Flashcards revisited: Training poor readers to read words faster improves their comprehension of text. *Journal of Educational Psychology, 89,* 276–288.

Taylor, B.M., Frye, B.J., & Maruyama, G.M. (1990). Time spent reading and reading growth. *American Educational Research Journal, 27,* 351–362.

Topping, K. (1995). *Paired reading, spelling, and writing: The handbook for teachers and parents.* London: Casell.

Torgesen, J., Wagner, R., & Rashotte, C. (1999). *Test of Word Reading Efficiency.* Austin, TX: PRO-ED.

Turner, J.C. (1995). The influence of classroom contexts on young children's motivation for literacy. *Reading Research Quarterly, 30,* 410–441.

van Bon, W.H.J., Boksebeld, L.M., Font Freide, T.A.M., & van den Hurk, A.J.M. (1991). A comparison of three methods of reading-while-listening. *Journal of Learning Disabilities, 24,* 471–476.

Wiederholt, J.L., & Bryant, B.R. (2001). *Gray Oral Reading Tests (GORT-4)* (4th ed.). Austin, TX: PRO-ED.

10

Vocabulary and Comprehension Instruction

Summary and Implications of the National Reading Panel Findings

MICHAEL L. KAMIL

There have been two recent, large-scale efforts to summarize the research on comprehension and comprehension instruction. The first of these was the work of the National Reading Panel (NRP) (National Institute of Child Health and Human Development [NICHD], 2000). The second effort was the work of the RAND Reading Study Group (2002). The RAND effort built on the work of the NRP to formulate a plan for a program of research in reading comprehension. The RAND report gives the rationale for this effort:

> Recent research on reading instruction has led to significant improvements in the knowledge base for teaching primary-grade readers and for ensuring that those children have the early-childhood experiences they need to be prepared for the reading instruction they receive when they enter school. Nevertheless, evidence-based improvements in the teaching practices of reading comprehension are sorely needed. Understanding how to improve reading comprehension outcomes, not just for students who are failing in the later grades but for all students who are facing increasing academic challenges, should be the primary motivating factor in any future literacy research agenda. (p. ix)

Although this work is important in presenting a detailed compilation of what is known about reading comprehension, it is not exclusively focused on instruction. The RAND (2002) report detailed the need for research in basic processes of comprehension, new formats for assessment, social and cultural factors, and the specific needs of second-language learners. Because the report focused on the importance of new research rather than a systematic review of the existing research, it is most useful in this current context as important background. It provides a broad picture of the entire range of issues in comprehension research, but it provides less in the way of guidance about specific instructional practices.

In contrast to the RAND (2002) report, the NRP report (NICHD, 2000) reviewed the research on comprehension instruction in three areas: vocabulary instruction, comprehension strategy instruction, and preparing teachers to teach comprehension. In this chapter, those three sets of NRP findings are summarized.

VOCABULARY

As early as 1925, in the *Twenty-Fourth Yearbook of the National Society for Studies in Education,* this quotation appeared: "Growth in reading power means, therefore, continuous enriching and enlarging of the reading vocabulary and increasing clarity of discrimination in appreciation of word values" (Whipple, 1925, p. 76). Further evidence for the importance of vocabulary is often attributed to Davis (1942), who presented evidence that reading comprehension comprised two skills: word knowledge (vocabulary) and reasoning. Although there have been questions regarding the notion that reading can be separated into skills, the finding that vocabulary is strongly related to general reading achievement is unchallenged.

A Theory of Vocabulary

Vocabulary occupies an important position in learning to read. As a learner begins to read, vocabulary encountered in texts is mapped onto the oral vocabulary that the learner brings to the task. That is, the reader is taught to translate the (relatively) unfamiliar print words into speech because it is expected that the speech forms are easier to comprehend because they are familiar. Understanding text by applying letter–sound correspondences to printed material only occurs if the word read orally is a known word in the learner's oral vocabulary. If the word read orally is not in the learner's vocabulary, then the learner will not be able to understand the word's meaning. Thus, vocabulary seems to occupy an important middle ground in learning to read. Oral vocabulary is key when a beginning reader makes the transition from oral to written forms, whereas reading vocabulary is crucial to the comprehension processes of a skilled reader.

Despite the clear importance of vocabulary, research since the 1980s has focused more on overall comprehension than on vocabulary. This appears to be a function of the more inclusive nature of many contemporary models of comprehension instruction, which seem to incorporate at least some vocabulary instruction. Even in traditional methods of teaching reading, lesson formats always include vocabulary instruction.

Research has shown that reading ability and vocabulary size are related (e.g., Anderson & Freebody, 1979; Stanovich, Cunningham, & Feeman, 1984), but the *causal* link between increasing vocabulary and an increase in reading ability has been difficult to demonstrate (Stanovich, 2000).

Why this demonstration should be so difficult is sometimes obscured by the imprecise nature of the definitions of vocabulary and comprehension. Both involve the meaning of the text, albeit at different levels. Vocabulary is generally tied closely to individual words, whereas comprehension is more often thought of in much larger units. Comprehension of larger units requires the processing of the words. Precisely separating the two processes is difficult, if not impossible, making it difficult to tell where one ends and the other begins.

Vocabulary Size

A long history of research supports the importance of vocabulary, but there has been a trend over the years to deemphasize the teaching of vocabulary (Biemiller, 2001; Nagy & Anderson, 1984). Why would something so important be neglected instructionally? A large part of the reason was the demonstration that the size of students' vocabularies was far greater than what could possibly be expected from instruction. Nagy and Anderson (1984) examined printed text for grades 3–9. They estimated that good readers read approximately 1,000,000 words per year. Clearly, not all of these words are unique, but the sheer numbers led to the conclusion that students could never be taught that many words. Instructionally, there seems to be no choice but to rely on students' learning vocabulary from context. Consequently, more reliance has been placed on students' own learning from context. The NRP review (NICHD, 2000), however, showed that although learning from context is important, direct instruction of vocabulary is effective in improving both vocabulary and comprehension. The implication is that *both* direct, explicit instruction *and* learning from context are important.

Measurement of Vocabulary

How is vocabulary measured? This is a difficult question, because researchers distinguish between many different kinds of vocabulary. Receptive vocabulary is the vocabulary that a person can understand when it is presented in text or as others speak, whereas productive vocabulary is that vocabulary a person uses in writing or when speaking to others. It is generally believed that receptive vocabulary is much larger than productive vocabulary because a person often recognizes words that he or she would rarely use. Vocabulary is also subcategorized as oral or reading vocabulary, in which oral vocabulary is essentially the same as receptive vocabulary, whereas reading vocabulary refers to words that are recognized in print. Sight vocabulary is a subset of reading vocabulary that does not require explicit word recognition processing. Conclusions about some of these different types of vocabularies often do not apply to all types.

Because there are so many definitions or designations of vocabulary, the format for assessing or evaluating vocabulary is important in both practice and research. Receptive vocabulary can be assessed by asking the learner to select a definition for a word from a list of alternatives or to select a word, given the definition. In many cases, such as with standardized tests, this method is used for efficiency in testing. A second method is to have the learner generate a definition for a word. Because this requires judgment about the response, it is often deemed less efficient than a recognition method. Most often, receptive vocabulary is measurably larger than productive vocabulary.

Another difficulty with the measurement of vocabulary is that we can only test a relatively small number of words, and those words must be representative of a larger pool of vocabulary items. In short, educators and researchers can never know exactly how large a vocabulary an individual has. Instead, they often measure only specific vocabulary items that they want the individual to know, for example, in the context of a reading or a science lesson. Standardized tests attempt to deal with this by selecting words that cover a wide range of expected familiarity.

Selection of the Research Studies
for the National Reading Panel Review

For the NRP review (NICHD, 2000) of research on vocabulary, searches of the on-line ERIC and PsycInfo databases were initiated using the search terms *vocabulary* and *instruction* and *reading* and *research* and *method*. From the resulting set, studies were removed if they were not reports of research studies and were not experimental or quasi-experimental studies. Studies were also removed if they dealt with college students or adult learners, with reading in languages other than English, or exclusively with individuals diagnosed with learning disabilities or other special populations.

Three meta-analyses (Fukkink & de Glopper, 1998; Klesius & Searls, 1990; Stahl & Fairbanks, 1986) and two literature reviews on vocabulary instruction research (Blachowicz & Fisher, 2000; Nagy & Scott, 2000) were also used to supplement the electronic searches. These procedures yielded a total of 50 studies that were candidates for further analysis. The 50 studies were coded in a Filemaker database, using the categories established by the NRP (NICHD, 2000), and analyzed.

VOCABULARY INSTRUCTION FINDINGS

The analysis of the vocabulary instruction studies found support for a variety of methods. Effective methods emphasized the multimedia aspects of learning, richness of context in which words are to be learned, active engagement in learning vocabulary, and increasing the number of exposures to words that learners will receive. The major findings and implications from the vocabulary database are summarized in the following subsections.

Repetition and Rich Support
for Learning Vocabulary Items Are Important

One clear finding from the data set is that there is a large improvement in vocabulary when students encounter vocabulary words
often. Although not surprising, this finding does have direct implications for instruction. Not only do students need to encounter target
vocabulary items frequently, but they also should be given items
that are likely to appear in many other contexts. This does not mean,
however, that students should be taught only high-frequency words,
particularly when the students may already know those with the
highest frequency. Rather, the targeted words should be those that
occur often enough to be useful in reading.

The context in which a word is learned is critical. Lists are
generally less effective than connected text for learning most vocabulary. If vocabulary is organized by categories, however, it is learned
more easily than if vocabulary is presented in a list that has no such
context (e.g., Meyerson, Ford, & Jones, 1991). Students learn words
better if they are actively engaged in the task of inferring vocabulary
meanings from context rather than simply being given the definition
(e.g., Jenkins, Matlock, & Slocum, 1989).

Vocabulary Tasks and Instruction
Should Be Restructured When Necessary

It is often assumed that students who do not learn vocabulary words
need more practice. Research has shown, however, that it is often
the case that students simply do not understand the task involved.
For example, simply asking students for the definition of a word
might be confusing to the students. Asking the students to give an
example of the word or to use it in a sentence might be easier.
Revising learning materials or designing instruction to meet the
needs of learners often facilitates vocabulary learning (Gordon,
Schumm, Coffland, & Doucette, 1992). Once students know what
is expected of them in a vocabulary task, they often learn rapidly.
Restructuring tasks seems to be particularly effective for low-achieving students or at-risk students (e.g., Schwartz & Raphael, 1985).

Group Learning Formats
May Be Helpful for Vocabulary Instruction

Structuring the delivery of vocabulary instruction to include group learning formats has found empirical support. Examples of group learning formats that were successful include learning vocabulary in pairs, peer tutoring, and reciprocal teaching strategies (Eldredge, Quinn, & Butterfield, 1990; Malone & McLaughlin, 1997). One possible explanation for this is that students may learn vocabulary items when they are simply listening to other students respond.

Vocabulary Learning Should
Entail Active Engagement in Learning Tasks

Findings consistently show that having students actively participate in learning vocabulary words is best (e.g., Dole, Sloan, & Trathen, 1995). Successful examples of active engagement in tasks included a variety of methods, such as having students make mental pictures of the definitions, act out the definitions with sign language, use the word in writing tasks, and actively attend to context clues to infer word meanings.

Computer Technology Can
Be Used to Help Teach Vocabulary

Research demonstrates the benefits of computer technology for vocabulary instruction (Davidson, Coles, Noyes, & Terrell, 1991; Heller, Sturner, Funk, & Feezor, 1993). Research suggests that animations of target words may help to augment vocabulary learning (Higgins & Cocks, 1999). Multimedia presentations may be particularly effective for helping second-language learners (e.g., Chun & Plass, 1996; Knight, 1994).

Vocabulary Should Be Taught Directly

Direct instruction of vocabulary should be included in reading lessons. There is a need for instruction of those vocabulary items that are required for a specific text to be read as part of the lesson. Such instruction can help to make the translation of print to speech meaningful by introducing the items orally (Brett, Rothlein, & Hurley, 1996). All of the studies reviewed by the NRP (NICHD, 2000) that examined direct instruction of vocabulary found that both comprehension and vocabulary improved as a result of the direct instruction.

One crucial question is which words should be taught directly. Although the research provides no empirical data on this issue, some researchers have begun to develop methods to answer this question. One promising approach has been developed by Beck, McKeown, and Kucan (2002), who suggested that vocabulary words fall into tiers, based on frequency of use. They noted that teaching highly frequent words (Tier 1 words) is probably not worth the effort because students are likely to know them already. Beck et al. also suggested that teaching the least frequent words (Tier 3) is of little benefit to students until they encounter these words in the text. Words that fall in between those two extremes should be the content of explicit vocabulary instruction. Beck et al. reasoned that students are likely to encounter these words often enough to make the investment in learning them worthwhile. Definitive research has yet to evaluate these promising suggestions.

Vocabulary Can Be Acquired Through Incidental Learning

Incidental learning of vocabulary through listening, other reading instruction, and storybook readings was found to improve comprehension. Two factors that have been found to affect learning outcomes include the frequency of the word encounters and the instructional techniques involved with the repeated readings of texts (Dickinson & Smith, 1994; Senechal, 1997). Not all vocabulary has to be taught explicitly.

Summary of Vocabulary Findings

Perhaps the most striking finding of the NRP review of research (NICHD, 2000) is the finding that explicit instruction of vocabulary is highly effective. As noted previously, this runs somewhat counter to much of the prevailing practice in instruction. Although there is not definitive evidence about how to decide which words should be taught, there are promising suggestions. In addition, the NRP review revealed the importance of instructional methods that entail active engagement with word learning, multiple repetitions, and the use of computers and multimedia presentations. These are all features that can easily be incorporated in most conventional instruction.

COMPREHENSION STRATEGY INSTRUCTION FINDINGS

Comprehension is the ultimate goal in reading instruction. The amount and type of comprehension instruction has been the focus of concern for a long time. Durkin's (1978–1979) studies of reading instruction showed that teachers spent very little time teaching comprehension; only 20 minutes of comprehension instruction was observed in 4,469 minutes of reading instruction. Even when Hodges (1980) reanalyzed the data, she found only a minimally greater amount of time spent in comprehension instruction. Duffy, Lanier, and Roehler (1980) described teachers as spending time in assigning activities, supervising and monitoring students, assessing what the students were doing, and providing feedback when the students made errors. The teachers did not demonstrate the strategies or processes that should be used in comprehension.

Research on direct instruction of comprehension strategies that could help students improve their reading comprehension began in the late 1970s and has thrived since then. Researchers and educators have long been interested in what people think about thinking, in how a person's knowledge develops, and in how what a person knows about his or her own thought processes affects reading comprehension. The focus on what is known about cognition has led to the development of practical strategies for improving student's comprehension.

Typically, direct instruction of cognitive strategies employed during reading consists of the following (Palincsar & Brown, 1984; Paris & Oka, 1986; Pressley, Almasi, Schuder, Bergman, & Kurita, 1994):

1. Readers developing self-awareness of those cognitive processes that are amenable to instruction

2. A teacher modeling the action(s) that readers can take to enhance their own cognitive processes during reading

3. Readers practicing those strategies with teacher assistance until readers achieve a gradual internalization and independent mastery of those processes

With this background, the NRP analyzed 203 studies of comprehension strategy instruction and found that there was research evidence for the efficacy of 8 strategies. These strategies are described in the following subsections.

Comprehension Monitoring

The strategy of comprehension monitoring consists of readers becoming aware of how well they understand what they are reading. When readers realize they do not understand, they have to employ appropriate fix-up strategies to correct their understanding of the text. This is not a natural process, so students must be taught how to monitor their comprehension. Comprehension monitoring instruction provides readers with steps that they can take to resolve reading problems as they arise. Steps may include formulating what the difficulty is, restating what was read, looking back through the text, and looking forward in the text for information that might help to resolve a problem (Bereiter & Bird, 1985). According to Rosenshine, Meister, and Chapman (1996), the earliest uses of the term comprehension monitoring can be found in Gagne (1977) and Weinstein (1978).

Cooperative Learning

Cooperative or collaborative learning is both a social organization for instruction and a strategy. It involves breaking the class into smaller groups of students to work together on clearly defined tasks. When those tasks are related to comprehension activities, cooperative learning becomes a powerful strategy for comprehension. One of the conditions that is important is that the tasks must require the participation of all of the students in the group. One format for collaborative learning was used by Klingner, Vaughn, and Schumm (1998). Students were taught to work together to translate "teacher-talk" about strategies to "kid-talk" in order to facilitate learning. Collaborative learning could be a vehicle for teaching many different types of strategies. As Klingner et al. (1998) pointed out, the majority of direct teaching, reciprocal teaching, and transactional strategy instruction programs have taken place in resource rooms or other remedial settings in small groups rather than in large classrooms.

Graphic Organizers

Graphic organizers are visual or spatial representations of text. They help students visualize the relationships among various elements in the text by changing them from pure text to text plus graphics. For stories, graphic organizers have been used as story maps. For content areas, they have been called semantic maps, concept maps, or semantic organizers.

Because graphic organizers are constructed during reading or after reading, they have the benefit of focusing readers' attention on the important structural elements in the text. When used after reading, they have the added benefit of improving the writing of summaries (e.g., Bean & Steenwyk, 1984).

Story Structure

Story structure denotes the organization of narrative story text into common components. These components are often given as setting, initiating events, internal reactions, goals, attempts, and outcomes. Because all stories can be analyzed in terms of these components, the reader can comprehend stories better with knowledge of these components than without such knowledge (e.g., Greenewald & Rossing, 1986; Singer & Donlan, 1982).

The underlying story structure strategy involves identifying the content of the story and how it is organized structurally. In addition, the reader can learn to infer causal and other relationships in the story. Using this strategy helps the reader develop deeper understanding of stories and allows him or her to construct more coherent memory representations of the story.

Questioning

Perhaps the most common form of comprehension assessment involves asking and answering questions. The analysis of the comprehension strategy research (NICHD, 2000) showed support for two strategies involving questions: question answering and question generation.

Question Answering   Students are often asked to answer questions about what they have read. The questions are posed either in the text or before or after the passage to be read. At other times, teachers ask the questions. Students, left to their own devices, have a difficult time answering questions. Strategy instruction in how to answer questions helps students comprehend better by assisting them in locating the information in the text. In the cases where questions are given before reading, students can be taught to answer them while reading and thus improve their comprehension of the text (e.g., Richmond, 1976). Students can also be taught that answering a question does not always depend on finding the answer in the text and that they can combine information from the text with their prior knowledge (e.g., Raphael & Pearson, 1985). Because questions are the dominant form of comprehension assessment, this strategy is particularly important for students who have difficulty in answering questions.

Question Generation   Question answering is a relatively passive strategy in that students are limited by the questions that someone else poses. If students are to become independent, active readers, they need to learn to ask and answer their own questions. Generating questions helps readers engage text by asking, and answering, questions that lead to the construction of better memory representations. Question generation should also increase readers' awareness of whether they understand the text. Teachers can use students' generation of questions to assess readers' success or failure in comprehension.

Question generation can be used independently or as part of multiple strategy instruction, as in reciprocal teaching. In fact, a meta-analysis of the research on question generation (Rosenshine et al., 1996) concluded that there was strong support for question generation as a strategy for improving reading comprehension.

Summarization

Summarizing serves two functions. It forces the reader to concentrate on the main ideas in the text instead of details, and it forces readers to process the text by excluding irrelevant information and generalizing across examples of similar concepts.

Few students are taught explicitly to summarize what they read. Consequently, few students develop the necessary skills to prepare good summaries. Summarizing is effective in improving comprehension (e.g., Rinehart, Stahl, & Erickson, 1986). Not only does it lead to improved reading comprehension, but that improvement can transfer to other situations. When asked to summarize, students have to pay closer attention to the text while they read. They also have to return to the text to reread as they prepare the summary. This leads to increased engagement with the text. The benefits may derive from students spending more time reading the text and determining what they did and did not comprehend when they read the text initially.

Multiple Strategies

Although there are clear improvements in comprehension as a result of using any of the strategies noted so far, it is the case that skilled readers often use more than one strategy. In multiple strategy instruction, students are taught how to adapt the strategies and use them flexibly, according to the reading task (Pressley, Gaskins, Wile, Cunicelli, & Sheridan, 1991). Cooperative learning or peer tutoring may be used as a part of multiple strategies instruction.

One of the most well-known examples of multiple strategy instruction is reciprocal teaching (Palincsar & Brown, 1984). In reciprocal teaching, the teacher models and explains what strategies are and when to use them. Readers are guided in applying and practicing strategies while reading a passage. Ultimately students practice and implement each strategy independently. One feature of reciprocal teaching is that students assume the role of teacher as well as that of student. This feature is not the central characteristic of the strategy; rather, it may be a key element in learning what the strategies are and how they work.

Summary of Comprehension Strategy Instruction Findings

The NRP review (NICHD, 2000) found that there was research support for the teaching of eight comprehension strategies. Seven can be taught as independent strategies that students can use to improve their reading, whereas the eighth strategy is actually a combination of two or more of the other seven. Although there are still many questions surrounding the implementation of these strategies in instruction, the evidence is sufficiently strong that they do help students improve in reading comprehension.

PREPARING TEACHERS TO
TEACH COMPREHENSION STRATEGIES

In the foregoing discussions of vocabulary and comprehension, much emphasis is placed on the role of the teacher and how the teacher needs to arrange instruction. When it comes to direct instruction, teachers must have a solid background in what is to be taught and how it should be done. Moreover, in real classroom settings, the entire program of instruction has to be managed, rather than one or two elements as in many of the research studies on comprehension. The NRP (NICHD, 2000) thought that the question of preparing teachers to teach comprehension strategies was sufficiently important to warrant a separate examination.

There have been two major approaches to comprehension strategy instruction: direct explanation (DE) and transactional strategy instruction (TSI). Each of these has different underlying philosophies and different needs for teacher expertise. To illustrate those differences, four studies are described: for DE, Book, Duffy, Roehler, Meloth, and Vavgrus (1985) and Duffy et al. (1987), and for TSI, Anderson (1992) and Brown, Pressley, Van Meter, and Schuder (1996).

Direct Explanation

The DE approach was designed to improve upon the standard direct instruction approach to strategy instruction used in most of the earlier studies, in which students were simply taught to use one or several strategies. Duffy et al. (1987) argued that standard direct instruction was insufficient because it did not attempt to provide students with an understanding of the reasoning and mental processes involved in reading strategically. In DE, teachers do not teach individual strategies but focus instead on helping students to 1) view reading as a problem-solving task that necessitates the use of strategic thinking and 2) learn to think strategically about solving reading comprehension problems. The focus in DE is on developing teachers' ability to clearly explain the reasoning and mental processes involved in successful reading comprehension, in an explicit manner, hence the use of the term *direct.* The implementation of DE requires specific and intensive teacher development on how to teach the traditional reading comprehension skills found in basal readers *as strategies,* for example, teaching students the skill of how to find the main idea by casting it as a problem-solving task and reasoning about it strategically.

The results of the two investigations of the DE approach to comprehension strategy instruction suggest that although this approach is clearly useful for increasing student awareness of the need to think strategically while reading, the effects on actual reading comprehension ability are less clear-cut. Book et al. (1985) did not measure student reading performance at all, and Duffy et al. (1987) found mixed results on a standardized measure of reading performance. It should be noted, however, that many of the lessons in the Duffy et al. study were oriented toward acquisition of word-level processes and not to what are usually considered comprehension processes.

Transactional Strategy Instruction

The TSI approach includes the same key elements as the DE approach but takes a different view of the role of the teacher in strategy instruction. Whereas the emphasis in DE is on teachers' ability to provide explicit explanations, the TSI approach focuses more on the ability of teachers to facilitate discussions in which students 1) collaborate to form joint interpretations of text and 2) explicitly discuss the mental processes and cognitive strategies that are involved in comprehension. In other words, although TSI teachers do provide their students with explicit explanations of strategic mental processes used in reading, the emphasis is on the interactive exchange among learners in the classroom, hence use of the term *transactional.*

In both DE and TSI, teachers explain specific strategies to students and model their use. Both approaches include the use of systematic practice of new skills, as well as scaffolded support, in which teachers gradually withdraw the amount of assistance they offer to students. Perhaps the most salient distinction to be made between DE and TSI is the manner in which the different emphases of the two approaches (explanation versus discussion) result in differences in the level of collaboration among students. The DE approach may be called noncollaborative, because strategy instruction is primarily conducted by the teacher. In contrast, the TSI approach is more collaborative, although explicit teacher explanation is still important. TSI is designed for learning to occur primarily through the collaborative transactions among the students during classroom discussion.

Summary of Preparing Teachers to Teach Comprehension

General guidelines for teachers that derive from the research evidence on comprehension instruction with typical children include the suggestion that teachers help students by explaining fully what it is they are teaching: what to do, why, how, and when; by modeling their own thinking processes; by encouraging students to ask questions and discuss possible answers among themselves; and by keeping students engaged in their reading by providing tasks that demand active involvement. The current dearth of comprehension instruction research at the primary grade level should not lead to the conclusion that such instruction should be neglected during the important period when children are mastering phonics and word recognition and developing reading fluency.

In evaluating the effectiveness of strategy instruction in the classroom, the primary focus should not be on the students' performance of the strategies themselves. Rather, the appropriate assessment is of the students' reading achievement plus other outcome measures, such as how interested students are in reading and how satisfied teachers are with their instructional methods. Implementation of effective comprehension instruction is not a simple matter; substantial preparation is usually required to become successful at teaching comprehension.

There is a need for greater emphasis in teacher education on the teaching of reading comprehension. Such instruction should begin at the preservice level, and it should be extensive, especially with respect to how to teach comprehension strategies.

The NRP report noted the following:

> Every one of these studies [that examined strategy instruction] reported significant differences, and although none of them reported effect sizes, they provided enough information so that effect sizes could be calculated for most of the studies. The effect sizes were [positive and] substantial, suggesting that these initial attempts to provide effective instruction for teachers in reading comprehension strategy training are promising and worth following up. . . .
>
> Of course, any evaluation of these instructional approaches is limited by the fact that these studies cannot easily be compared. They differed in terms of specific purpose, teacher preparation method, intervention, type of student (age, reading level, etc.), control group, and other characteristics. Nevertheless, [at the very least,] the studies [seem to] indicate that instructional methods that generate high levels of student involvement and engagement during reading can have positive effects on reading comprehension. Also, these studies [indicate that training] teachers [to] use such methods leads to students' awareness of strategies and use of strategies, which can in turn lead to improved reading comprehension.
>
> These findings beg the question as to what it is, in fact, that makes for effective strategy instruction. Is it the teacher preparation? (If so, how extensive does it have to be? Would the teachers maintain their instructional effectiveness without the supports inherent in an ongoing study?) Is it the use of direct explanation and/or collaborative discussion when teaching students? Is it the particular strategies that are taught? Is it a combination of some or all of these possibilities or of other factors not mentioned here? (NICHD, 2000, pp. 4-124 to 4-125)

These questions should be addressed in future research.

NATIONAL READING PANEL FINDINGS: IMPLICATIONS FOR PRACTICE

The evidence from the comprehension strategy research, as reviewed by the NRP (NICHD, 2000), suggests that students learn best when teachers explain fully what it is that they are teaching. Teachers should tell students what they are expected to do. When appropriate, teachers should model their own thinking processes for students. Teachers should also encourage students to ask questions and discuss possible answers and problem solutions among themselves. Most powerfully, students should be taught how to develop their own questions rather than simply answer those provided by the teacher or the text. Teachers should keep students engaged in their reading by providing tasks that demand active involvement.

Instruction in reading comprehension strategies should be incorporated into content area instruction. Specific strategies may be realized somewhat differently in different content areas. That is, knowing how to ask a question in history is probably very different from knowing how to ask a question in science. Teachers should work to help students modify the appropriate strategies so that the strategies are most effective in each content area.

Strategies should not be taught as ends in themselves. Students should realize that the goal is comprehension, not the application of strategies. Teachers must be careful to emphasize this point by assessing reading and learning in appropriate contexts rather than by assessing the appropriate selection or application of a strategy.

Despite the fact that most of the research on comprehension strategy instruction is in upper elementary and high school grades, comprehension instruction should not be neglected in the primary grades. It is important to emphasize the need for focusing on comprehension during the period when children are mastering phonics and word recognition and developing reading fluency.

The research on preparing teachers to teach comprehension was conducted as professional development. Because the research shows the efficacy of instruction in complex strategies, teachers must be prepared to teach them. Consequently, there should be greater emphasis in teacher education on the teaching of reading comprehension. Such instruction should begin during preservice programs, it should be extensive, and it should continue as professional development for in-service teachers.

CONCLUSION

The findings of the NRP (NICHD, 2002) provide strong, research-based guidance for instruction in vocabulary and comprehension strategies. Knowing the methods and procedures is not, in itself, sufficient. Teacher education and professional development are required if teachers are to provide students with high-quality instruction so that they learn to read well. Although it is clear that more research is needed, educators can make dramatic improvements in reading instruction by applying what is currently known.

REFERENCES

Anderson, V. (1992). A teacher development project in transactional strategy instruction for teachers of severely reading-disabled adolescents. *Teaching & Teacher Education, 8*(4), 391–403.

Anderson, R., & Freebody, P. (1979). *Vocabulary knowledge* (Tech. Rep. No. 136). Urbana-Champaign: University of Illinois at Urbana-Champaign, Center for the Study of Reading.

Bean, T.W., & Steenwyk, F.L. (1984). The effect of three forms of summarization instruction on sixth graders' summary writing and comprehension. *Journal of Reading Behavior, 16*(4), 297–306.

Beck, I.L., McKeown, M.G., & Kucan, L. (2002). *Bringing words to life: Robust vocabulary instruction.* New York: Guilford Press.

Bereiter, C., & Bird, M. (1985). Use of thinking aloud in identification and teaching of reading comprehension strategies. *Cognition & Instruction, 2,* 131–156.

Biemiller, A. (2001). Teaching vocabulary: Early, direct, and sequential. *The American Educator, 25*(1), 24–28.

Blachowicz, C., & Fisher, P. (2000). Vocabulary instruction. In M. Kamil, P. Mosenthal, P.D. Pearson, & R. Barr (Eds.), *Handbook of reading research* (Vol. III). Mahwah, NJ: Lawrence Erlbaum Associates.

Book, C., Duffy, G.G., Roehler, L.R., Meloth, M.S., & Vavgrus, L.G. (1985). A study of the relationship between teacher explanation and student metacognitive awareness during reading instruction. *Communication Education, 34*(1), 29–36.

Brett, A., Rothlein, L., & Hurley, M. (1996). Vocabulary acquisition from listening to stories and explanations of target words. *Elementary School Journal, 96,* 415–422.

Brown, R., Pressley, M., Van Meter. P., & Schuder, T. (1996). A quasi-experimental validation of transactional strategies instruction with low-achieving second-grade readers. *Journal of Educational Psychology, 88*(1), 18–37.

Chun, D., & Plass, J. (1996). Facilitating reading comprehension with multimedia. *System, 24,* 503–519.

Davidson, J., Coles, D., Noyes, P., & Terrell, C. (1991). Using computer-delivered natural speech to assist in the teaching of reading. *British Journal of Educational Technology, 22,* 110–118.

Davis, F.B. (1942). Two new measures of reading ability. *Journal of Educational Psychology, 33,* 365–372.

Dickinson, D.K., & Smith, M.W. (1994). Long-term effects of preschool teachers' book readings on low-income children's vocabulary and story comprehension. *Reading Research Quarterly, 29,* 104–122.

Dole, J.A., Sloan, C., & Trathen, W. (1995). Teaching vocabulary within the context of literature. *Journal of Reading, 38*(6), 452–460.

Duffy, G., Lanier, J.E., & Roehler, L.R. (1980). *On the need to consider instructional practice when looking for instructional implications.* Paper presented at the Reading Expository Materials Conference, University of Wisconsin–Madison.

Duffy, G., Roehler, L., Sivan, E., Rackliffe, G., Book, C., Meloth, M., et al. (1987). Effects of explaining the reasoning associated with using reading strategies. *Reading Research Quarterly, 23*(3), 347–368.

Durkin, D. (1978–1979). What classroom observations reveal about reading comprehension instruction. *Reading Research Quarterly, 14,* 481–533.

Eldredge, J.L., Quinn, B., & Butterfield, D.D. (1990). Causal relationships between phonics, reading comprehension, and vocabulary achievement in the second grade. *Journal of Educational Research, 83*(4), 201–214.

Fukkink, R.G., & de Glopper, K. (1998). Effects of instruction in deriving word meaning from context: A meta-analysis. *Review of Educational Research, 68*(4), 450–469.

Gagne, R.M. (1977). *The conditions of learning* (3rd ed). New York: CBS College Publishing.

Gordon, J., Schumm, J.S., Coffland, C., & Doucette, M. (1992). Effects of inconsiderate versus considerate text on elementary students' vocabulary learning. *Reading Psychology, 13,* 157–169.

Greenewald, M.J., & Rossing, R.L. (1986). Short-term and long-term effects of story grammar and self-monitoring training on children's story comprehension. *National Reading Conference Yearbook, 35,* 210–213.

Heller, J.H., Sturner, R.A., Funk, S.G., & Feezor, M.D. (1993). The effect of input mode on vocabulary identification performance at low intensity. *Journal of Educational Computing Research, 9*(4), 509–518.

Higgins, H.C., & Cocks, P. (1999). The effects of animation cues on vocabulary development. *Reading Psychology, 20,* 1–10.

Hodges, C.A. (1980). Toward a broader definition of comprehension instruction. *Reading Research Quarterly, 15,* 299–306.

Jenkins, J.R., Matlock, B., & Slocum, T.A. (1989). Two approaches to vocabulary instruction: The teaching of individual word meanings and practice in deriving word meaning from context. *Reading Research Quarterly, 24*(2), 215–235.

Klesius, J.P., & Searls, E.F. (1990). A meta-analysis of recent research in meaning vocabulary instruction. *Journal of Research and Development in Education, 23,* 226–235.

Klingner, J.K., Vaughn, S., & Schumm, J.S. (1998). Collaborative strategic reading during social studies in heterogeneous fourth-grade classrooms. *Elementary School Journal, 99*(1), 3–22.

Knight, S. (1994). Dictionary: The tool of last resort in foreign language reading? A new perspective. *Modern Language Journal, 78*(3), 285–299.

Malone, R.A., & McLaughlin, T.F. (1997). The effects of reciprocal peer tutoring with a group contingency on quiz performance in vocabulary with seventh- and eighth-grade students. *Behavioral Interventions, 12,* 27–40.

Meyerson, J.J., Ford, M.S., & Jones, W.P. (1991). Science vocabulary knowledge of third and fifth grade students. *Science Education, 75*(4), 419–428.

Nagy, W.E., & Anderson, R.C. (1984). How many words are there in printed school English? *Reading Research Quarterly, 19*(3), 304–330.

Nagy, W., & Scott, J. (2000). Vocabulary processes. In M. Kamil, P. Mosenthal, P.D. Pearson, & R. Barr (Eds.), *Handbook of reading research* (Vol. III). Mahwah, NJ: Lawrence Erlbaum Associates.

National Institute of Child Health and Human Development (NICHD). (2000). *Report of the National Reading Panel. Teaching children to read: An evidence-based assessment of the scientific research literature on reading and its implications for reading instruction: Reports of the subgroups* (NIH Publication No. 00-4754). Washington, DC: U.S. Government Printing Office. Also available on-line: http://www.nichd.nih.gov/publications/nrp/report.htm

Palincsar, A.S., & Brown, A.L. (1984). Reciprocal teaching of comprehension-fostering and comprehension-monitoring activities. *Cognition & Instruction, 1*(2), 117–175.

Paris, S., & Oka, E. (1986). Self-regulated learning among exceptional children. *Exceptional Children, 53*, 104–108.

Pressley, M., Almasi, J., Schuder, T., Bergman, J., & Kurita, J.A. (1994). Transactional instruction of comprehension strategies: The Montgomery County, Maryland, SAIL program. *Reading & Writing Quarterly: Overcoming Learning Difficulties, 10*, 5–19.

Pressley, M., Gaskins, I.W., Wile, D., Cunicelli, E.A., & Sheridan, J. (1991). Teaching literacy strategies across the curriculum: A case study at Benchmark School. In J. Zutell & S. McCormick (Eds.), *Learner factors/teacher factors: Issues in literacy research and instruction* (Fortieth Yearbook of the National Reading Conference, pp. 219–228). Chicago: The National Reading Conference.

RAND Reading Study Group. (2002). *Reading for understanding: Toward a R&D program in reading comprehension.* Santa Monica, CA: RAND Corporation.

Raphael, T.E., & Pearson, P.D. (1985). Increasing students' awareness of sources of information for answering questions. *American Educational Research Journal, 22*, 217–235.

Richmond, M.G. (1976). The relationship of the uniqueness of prose passages to the effect of question placement and question relevance on the acquisition and retention of information. In G.H. Mc Ninch (Ed.), *Reflections and investigations on reading: Twenty-fifth yearbook of the National Reading Conference* (pp. 268–278). Clemson, SC: National Reading Conference.

Rinehart, S.D., Stahl, S.A., & Erickson, L.G. (1986). Some effects of summarization training on reading and studying. *Reading Research Quarterly, 21*(4), 422–438.

Rosenshine, B., Meister, C., & Chapman, S. (1996). Teaching students to generate questions: A review of the intervention studies. *Review of Educational Research, 66*(2), 181–221.

Schwartz, R.M., & Raphael, T.E. (1985). Instruction in the concept of definition as a basis for vocabulary acquisition. In J.A. Niles & R.V. Lalik (Eds.), *Issues in literacy: A research perspective: Thirty-fourth yearbook of the National Reading Conference* (pp. 116–124). Rochester, NY: National Reading Conference.

Senechal, M. (1997). The differential effect of storybook reading on preschoolers' acquisition of expressive and receptive vocabulary. *Journal of Child Language, 24,* 123–38.

Singer, H., & Donlan, D. (1982). Active comprehension: Problem-solving schema with question generation for comprehension of complex short stories. *Reading Research Quarterly, 17*(2), 166–186.

Stahl, S.A., & Fairbanks, M.M. (1986). The effects of vocabulary instruction: A model-based meta-analysis. *Review of Educational Research, 56,* 72–110.

Stanovich, K. (2000). *Progress in understanding reading: Scientific foundations and new frontiers.* New York: Guilford Press.

Stanovich, K.E., Cunningham, A.E., & Feeman, D.J. (1984). Relation between early reading acquisition and word decoding with and without context: A longitudinal study of first-grade children. *Journal of Educational Psychology, 76,* 668–677.

Weinstein, C.E. (1978). Teaching cognitive elaboration learning strategies. In H.F. O'Neal (Ed.), *Learning strategies.* San Diego: Academic Press.

Whipple, G. (Ed.). (1925). *The twenty-fourth yearbook of the National Society for the Study of Education: Report of the National Committee on Reading.* Bloomington, IL: Public School Publishing Company.

11

Critiques of the
National Reading Panel Report

Their Implications for Research, Policy, and Practice

Timothy Shanahan

I was about to present a workshop at a local school. The principal, who appeared agitated, wanted to check something before we started. "Should I still tell them that you were a member of the National Reading Panel? Are you going to change your talk?" she wondered, waving a magazine with the latest critique of the panel. She was fearful of injecting yet another reading controversy into her school.

I asked, "Which of the NRP findings did the critic disagree with?"

She looked puzzled. "The article didn't say anything about the findings."

And so it goes. The National Reading Panel report (National Institute of Child Health and Human Development [NICHD], 2000) was a remarkable development in the application of research to practice in reading education. In the past, if research was referred to in reading policy, it was an idiosyncratic affair—with each researcher or practitioner making his or her own decisions about the implications of research. Educational practitioners usually lack preparation for interpreting research first hand, and the vast amounts of research now available make that impractical for anyone but full-time researchers. Not surprisingly, this vacuum has been filled by a cacophony of reading gurus elbowing for position to have their voices heard in the research interpretation choir.

The federal government has used the NRP report (NICHD, 2000)—a summary of reading research—as the basis for federal education policy. But are the reading wars truly over? It would be easy to conclude from reading the criticism of the NRP that they still rage on, no matter what anyone may claim. And most school administrators rightly do not want to infect their schools with divisive controversy. This unfortunately confers great power to those who wish to block reading improvement, at least any improvement that does not emanate from them. Under these circumstances, even errant criticism can be an impediment to reform.

This does not mean that there is not room for criticism of the NRP report (NICHD, 2000) or any report on reading research. But it is incumbent on both the critics and the respondents to the critics to act responsibly and to never lose sight of the practical implications of the report. The principal I was speaking with was surprised to find that despite the withering criticism, this particular detractor had never actually challenged the basic findings of the report.

I have carefully pored over the many critiques of the NRP findings that have appeared so far and transformed each into a laundry list of complaints. Then I reassembled this list by category of objection so that I could respond to the major concerns without tedious repetition. Overall, the most stunning result of this analysis is how rarely the critics have trained their guns on the findings of the report; most of the objections are wholly irrelevant to whether the NRP findings *should* be put into action. Despite the storm of complaints, there appears to be no reason not to apply the panel's findings to classroom instruction and many reasons for making sure that these findings guide the instruction we give our children.

THE NATIONAL READING PANEL REPORT

The NRP report (NICHD, 2000) was written at the request of the U.S. Congress and supported by the National Institute of Child Health and Human Development in cooperation with the U.S. Department of Education. The reason for commissioning this work was to settle—to the satisfaction of the government of the United States—the poisonous disagreements that had plagued reading education. These disagreements were hampering the ability of schools to adequately respond to the nation's reading needs and undermining public confidence in education.

Although the field of reading has had the benefit of many highly visible public reports, the NRP (NICHD, 2000) was the first to provide a wide-ranging, systematic review of the research literature. Unlike the previous reports, which offered focused looks at phonics

(Adams, 1990; Chall, 1967, 1983, 1996), findings from one research center (R.C. Anderson, Hiebert, Scott, & Wilkinson, 1985), or consensus reports of expert opinion (Snow, Burns, & Griffin, 1998), the NRP had to employ systematic objective methods for identifying and selecting research studies to include in its review and for analyzing these studies. The panel was prohibited from making recommendations concerning reading instruction or policy. Its task was to review the research, determine what the research findings were, and evaluate the readiness of the field to employ on a wide scale what was found.

The NRP was required to carry its work out in public. Panel meetings were open to the public and were often attended by representatives of various organizations. In addition, these meetings were audiotaped and transcribed, and the transcriptions were publicly accessible.

The questions to be answered by the panel were set by the panel itself within the requirements of Congress. These questions emerged from an analysis of a published consensus report (Snow et al., 1998); five public hearings at which approximately 400 policy makers, educators, and others gave testimony; and the panel's own expertise. Approximately 30 topics were considered for review, and the panel examined the 8 topics that received the highest number of votes from panel members.

The panel took great care to limit any bias in its work. To accomplish that, it adopted objective search, selection, and analysis procedures that adhered to the highest standards for the synthesis of scientific evidence (Cooper, 1998; Cooper & Hedges, 1994; Rosenthal, 1991; T. Shanahan, 2000). The panel could not, for instance, decide to review only studies that might support a particular program or perspective. The panel only reviewed studies published in refereed journals (meaning that the quality of the work had already been reviewed and accepted by independent experts). It also limited its analysis to studies that reported some form of an experiment. This meant that the instructional approaches under question had to be tried and evaluated in terms of whether they improved learning. Typically, experiments require participating teachers to adopt an approach not already in use, so the results are likely to be more in line with the actual situations facing schools that want to adopt a new approach. Finally, the panel required a substantial amount of evidence. Education studies tend to involve few teachers and students, so the panel sought accumulations of evidence (the repetition of findings across independent studies) to make determinations of what works.

It would be fair to describe this approach as conservative. The panel required a high degree of certainty for drawing any research-based conclusion about reading instruction. This approach lessened the chance that a major report finding would be wrong, but with high standards of evidence, it is likely that other approaches to reading instruction would work too (though there might still not be a sufficient accumulation of evidence on them to justify their widespread adoption).

Specifically, the panel examined instructional practices for phonemic awareness, phonics, oral reading fluency, encouraging children to read, vocabulary, comprehension, teacher education, and technology. The panel concluded that instruction in phonemic awareness, phonics, fluency, vocabulary, and comprehension, and increased teacher education all provided improved reading achievement for students. More specific findings about instruction were provided on each topic. For two of the topics (encouraging children to read and technology), the panel recommended more research, as it found too little valid data to draw any conclusions for educational practice.

CRITICISMS OF THE NATIONAL READING PANEL FINDINGS

Before delving into the criticism and its implications for the application of the NRP findings (NICHD, 2000) to instructional practice and public policy, it is worthwhile to note that—contrary to the commentary examined here—most of the response to the NRP has been positive. The report has enjoyed widespread acceptance in much of the field. It is widely and positively cited (e.g., Bender & Larkin, 2003; Foorman, Breier, & Larkin, 2003; Hinchman, Alvermann, Boyd, Brozo, & Vacca, 2004; Invernizzi, 2001; Kame'enui & Simmons, 2001; McCandliss, Beck, Sandak, & Perfetti, 2003; Morris, Bloodgood, Lomax, & Perney, 2003; Morrow & Asbury, 2003; Rasinski & Hoffman, 2003; Yopp & Yopp, 2003). No one who reads this chapter, which is entirely about the criticism, should be led to believe otherwise.

On a related point, the criticisms of the NRP have ranged widely in quality. On the low end, they have included name calling and have been rife with error and misinterpretation. But it would be unfair to characterize all of the criticism in this way, as some of the critics have been careful, painstaking, and thoughtful. The critics were often less interested in the practical implications of the NRP for teachers and schools than about some feared side effect, such as the impact the NRP might have on future research funding. Nevertheless, the scope of this chapter is limited to exploring the implications of the criticism for instructional practice and policy.

Criticism 1: Some Important Reading Topics Have Been Neglected

One oft-voiced complaint has been the neglect of one topic or another by the NRP. This conceptual narrowness complaint first arose in the minority report issued by Joanne Yatvin (2000), a panel member:

> At its first meeting in the spring of 1998, the Panel quickly decided to examine research in three areas: alphabetics, comprehension, and fluency, thereby excluding any inquiry into the fields of language and literature. After some debate, members agreed to expand their investigations to two other areas: computer-linked instruction and teacher preparation. . . .
>
> To have properly answered its charge, the Panel had to . . . [examine] the basic theoretical models of processes of learning that begin in infancy and continue through young adulthood. . . . The scientific basis for each of these models needed to be examined, then the effectiveness of the methods they have generated. The research on language development, pre-reading literary knowledge, understanding of the conventions of print, and all the other experiences that prepare young children to learn to read also demanded the Panel's attention. And finally, the changing needs and strategies of adolescent readers called for a review of the existing research. (pp. 1, 2)

Yatvin's factual claims about how the panel worked do not match the written record, nor does her understanding of the congressional charge match with those of the other panelists or apparently of Congress, which accepted the report. Yet, she is correct about what the panel did not study. The panel at its first meeting began exploring which topics to study, but transcripts reveal that these deliberations continued for 6 months before they were finalized. (During this time, five public hearings were held, and a great deal of debate and discussion ensued among panel members—topics were added and dropped along the way.) Ultimately, the panel finalized its search plan with a formal vote. Yatvin expressed a willingness to pursue some of the "missing issues" herself and was given preliminary approval to do so by the panel. I helped her design electronic searches on her topics (as I had done for several of the other panel searches), and the Northwest Regional Educational Laboratory conducted the searches for her. When these efforts failed to turn up studies that confirmed her beliefs about reading, she expressed discouragement and seemingly dropped the matter—until her minority report in which she denounced us for not exploring those topics. (Her criticisms of the panel omissions have grown with time. In one critique [Yatvin, 2002], she castigated the NRP for omitting the interdependence between reading and writing; the effects of the types, quality, or amounts of material children read; oral language; literature and its conventions; and how the "world apart from print affects [children's] ability to learn to read.")

Yatvin has not been alone in her concerns about what the panel left out. Pressley, Dolezal, Roehrig, and Hilden, were "taken aback by the NRP's neglect of the preschool years" (2002, p. 80) and complained about the lack of attention to writing. Allington (2002) criticized the panel for omitting motivation and out-of-school reading. Pressley has argued for 1) the inclusion of family literacy and whole language (2002a) and 2) for investigation of the influence of home experiences on literacy development, the effects of public television on reading readiness, community resources, and the effects of school reform movements on literacy (2001) and for studies that underscore the notion that there are no "quick fixes for interventions" (2000, p. 15).

All of these critics are correct that potentially important topics that could have been studied were not pursued by the NRP. As the report prominently noted,

> The panel did not consider these questions and the instructional questions that they represent to be the *only* topics of importance in learning to read. The Panel's silence on other topics should not be interpreted as indicating that other topics have no importance or that improvement in those areas would not lead to greater reading achievement. (2000, p. 1-3)

In fact, the panel had considered including approximately 30 topics—including most of those noted by the critics and several others they have not raised (T. Shanahan, 2003).

The omissions noted by the critics and by the NRP itself are real and are being taken seriously by the federal government. The research arm of the U.S. Department of Education is currently supporting a research synthesis in the fashion of the NRP (this one under the auspices of the Center for Applied Linguistics) to find out what is known about the reading and writing development of language minority students, and the National Institute for Literacy is supporting the National Center for Family Literacy in a similar examination of preschool and family literacy.

However, these criticisms of omission by their very nature say nothing about the quality of the work or the accuracy of the findings of the NRP. In other words, that the NRP lacked the resources to study all possible issues in reading is no reason to dismiss the findings that it did report. As Pressley et al. wrote, "Yes, the components the panel identified as validated should be included in primary-grades reading instruction, but there is much, much more that could and should be in the mix" (2002, p. 85).

Criticism 2: The Panel Was Too Narrow in Its Research Paradigm

A second widespread complaint has concerned the panel's decision to only examine experimental or quasi-experimental research when evaluating the effectiveness of instruction (Coles, 2001; Edmondson & Shannon, 2002; Garan, 2002; Newkirk, 2002; Pressley, 2002a; Shaker & Heilman, 2002). For example, according to Cunningham, "The experimentalism held so unswervingly by the NRP violates all common wisdom" (2001, p. 331). The National Council of Teachers of English (2003) even went so far as to pass a resolution denouncing the report, in part because of its neglect of "teacher research," despite the fact that such research is not generalizable and could not be the basis of public policy.

To practitioners and policy makers this charge may alternately seem to be an issue of fairness (why wasn't everybody's research considered?) or of validity (how could the panel know if an approach worked if it didn't consider all of the evidence?). To the critics themselves it has more often been an issue of territory or philosophy (what counts as "science"—and who in the research community will influence policy?).

A common concession from critics of the NRP's supposed scientific narrowness is this one from Purcell-Gates (2000):

> There is no doubt that experimental, and to some degree quasi-experimental, research is required to "prove" the effectiveness of an instructional approach, method, or intervention. . . . While experimental and quasi-experimental studies are the gold standard for examining program impact, there are many critical issues facing education and educators that raise other types of questions.

In other words, according to Purcell-Gates, the NRP produced sound results for the questions that it asked, but it would have benefited from evidence developed through different research approaches *if* it had raised different questions.

Similarly, though more strident in his accusations of narrowness, Cunningham's (2001) detailed analysis of the NRP findings (NICHD, 2000) was actually quite positive. Again, the claim seems to be that the NRP findings are right but that the NRP should have considered other evidence as well.

In the 1980s, debates between proponents of quantitative and qualitative research paradigms were often bitter and angry, and those have gone on over the years with various factions claiming scientific legitimacy or superiority for their positions. Critics err, however, in assuming that the NRP's reliance on experimental evidence (NICHD, 2000) is an extension of that debate. The panel took seriously the idea that its findings might establish standards of practice for educators and therefore made analytical decisions that would result in findings that could be stated with a great degree of certainty. The essential point is that not all research evidence can be used to answer all questions, as is clear from the report of the National Research Council's Committee on Scientific Principles for Education Research (Shavelson & Towne, 2002). Researchers and practitioners may draw inferences from a wide range of evidence, but they cannot do so from different forms of evidence with equal degrees of certainty. (It is this attempt at certainty that has led to the charge of timidity [Pressley, 2002b] because the NRP findings are not the result of innovative insights or originality, nor are they revelatory of the next big research trend. Instead, they are no more than a careful and objective analysis of existing research data.) The only research paradigm that allows a clear unambiguous determination of whether an instructional approach *causes* higher reading achievement for kids is the experimental paradigm, and for that reason the NRP limited its look to those kinds of studies.

In one of the most thoughtful and interesting critiques of the NRP report (NICHD, 2000), Almasi, Garas, and L. Shanahan (no relation to T. Shanahan) (2002) attempted to show the benefits of including qualitative evidence. Rather than just complain, they attempted to reanalyze the NRP results on comprehension instruction using qualitative studies. Almasi et al. sought any research articles on this topic that used qualitative methods (i.e., ethnography, case study); when this search turned up few articles, they conducted a hand search of all issues of *Reading Research Quarterly* since 1978 to find more. They identified 12 qualitative studies of reading comprehension (the NRP examined more than 200 comprehension studies, so this would represent approximately 5% additional studies). Two of these twelve qualitative articles actually appeared during or after the NRP work, so only 10 of these studies really would have been available for inclusion in the panel's original report.

Despite their own analysis that qualitative studies dominate *Reading Research Quarterly*, Almasi et al. wrote, "There simply were not that many qualitative studies of comprehension published" (2002, p. 24). My own efforts to identify relevant qualitative studies for the panel (T. Shanahan, 2003) located even fewer qualitative studies on topics such as phonemic awareness, phonics, oral reading fluency, and vocabulary teaching. Thus, even if one claims that the NRP should have included qualitative studies, there are few such studies available that are directly relevant to these topics of instruction.

After analyzing these 12 studies, Almasi et al. concluded that many of these studies were so flawed as to have not been expected to add valid or trustworthy data to the NRP review:

> We also found that several of the qualitative studies reviewed were not rigorous. . . . Many of the studies seemed exploratory in nature and occurred across such brief periods of time that prolonged engagement, persistent observation, and/or the triangulation of data sources were impossible. (2002, p. 23)

Despite these severe limitations, Almasi et al. (2002) continued to try to show that the NRP had omitted essential information that could be used to help establish public policy or standards of professional practice. To do this, they had to stretch their interpretations of some of the excellent qualitative studies included in their review. For example, from a descriptive study of a single second-grade class taught for a year by a college reading professor (Baumann & Ivey, 1997), they concluded that the integrated curriculum approach used by the professor had caused the children to become effective comprehenders. Not only did the study not provide any evidence concerning how well these students comprehended compared with other second graders, but also the study did nothing to sort out whether the improvements were due to method of instruction or to normal maturation, outside influences on learning such as parents or older siblings, or even other aspects of the daily instruction offered in this one very atypical classroom.

Baumann and Ivey (1997) did not make the causal claim that Almasi and colleagues (2002) made, and in fact qualitative researchers themselves seem to concur that such claims are not even appropriate for qualitative research (Denzin & Lincoln, 1994; Shavelson & Towne, 2002). Qualitative studies of this type can provide a rich and nuanced description of what happened in a given context but do not allow for any more than a hypothesis about causation. In fact, given the centrality of the anthropological notion of context, qualitative researchers themselves are deeply divided concerning the extent to which qualitative research findings are generalizable for application to practical prescriptions or policy mandates (Beach, Green, Kamil, & T. Shanahan, in press).

What seems evident from Almasi and colleagues' (2002) attempt is that the inclusion of qualitative studies in the NRP's analysis (NICHD, 2000) would not have had much, if any, impact on the findings. Qualitative and other kinds of research *can* tell us a lot (e.g., they can be especially useful in the hypothesis-setting stage of an investigation), but they are not particularly relevant for addressing the "what works" kinds of questions that the NRP grappled with. The use of qualitative methods to deepen researchers' understanding of how things work (rather than whether they work) is without dispute. The availability of qualitative data on any of the NRP questions could have been informative, but as Almasi et al. illustrated, there is little of this type of evidence on these questions, certainly not enough to come to any definitive conclusions about practice or policy.

Criticism 3: The Panel Should Not Have Opposed Encouraging Children to Read

Of course, the NRP did not actually oppose encouraging children to read, but it would be difficult to tell this from the critics. The NRP did examine the research evidence concerning the effects of various ways that schools might encourage children to read more. Unfortunately, the panel found very few studies on these schemes and, overall, the quality of this research was not particularly high. Given this, the panel had no findings with regard to such plans, though it did recommend that researchers turn their attention to this issue.

These criticisms have nothing to say about the validity and value of the NRP findings (NICHD, 2000) themselves. The most fundamental problem with criticism of this part of the report is that so much of it is based on a misconception of what the panel actually did. Many focus on the idea that the panel was challenging the value of reading practice or the benefits of reading. In fact, the panel only examined the impact of particular *ways* of encouraging children to read. Although some critics have claimed to be confused by this distinction (Allington, 2002), it is really pretty straightforward. If one assumes that children learn from reading, the question for teachers is what to do to encourage children to read more or to motivate non-readers to read enough to accomplish higher achievement. Just because practice is a good idea does not mean that all forms of practice would work equally well. It was that issue that the NRP examined.

This misunderstanding has led to some pretty strange claims. For example, Cunningham confusedly chastised the panel for regarding "independent silent reading as a treatment" (2001, p. 333), apparently not recognizing that the most popular way of encouraging students to read is, indeed, a program or treatment (e.g., Sustained Silent Reading [SSR]). This confusion has morphed into an internal disagreement among the critics, not about whether they should disagree with the NRP, but why. Edmondson and Shannon (2002) complained that the NRP withdrew instructional status from just letting kids read; Krashen (2001) argued that just letting kids read is better than instruction and that a finding of no difference is actually evidence for free reading in classrooms. Allington evidently agreed with everyone; though praising Krashen and Edmondson and Shannon, he concluded, "Maybe I agree with the National Reading Panel, because I don't believe that reading a book is reading instruction" (2002, p. 224).

Although I disagree with Krashen's (2001, p. 121) claim that teachers prefer just having students read instead of teaching them, I do think it is useful for readers of the criticism to understand why Krashen would claim that kids learn as much about reading from reading on their own as they do from teachers. In experiments, to say something works, a researcher must show that the method works better than something else. The finding of "no significant differences" is not very informative, because it is usually impossible to determine whether the intervention wasn't good, whether there just wasn't enough of it, and so forth. Many of the studies on encouraging reading have reported no differences with regard to reading achievement or motivation (usually when independent reading is compared with some impoverished form of teaching, e.g., just assigning random worksheets).

In addition, several critics have argued for the acceptance of correlation as evidence that *all* programs and approaches claiming to encourage reading work (i.e., the programs increase the amount that kids read and, consequently, improve achievement), because these studies show that better readers read more than poorer ones. This logic is flawed: Correlational data cannot demonstrate that one thing causes another; such data merely show that the two are associated. That is, these data cannot reveal whether the good readers read more than poor readers because they are able to or because more reading leads to better reading. Correlation does not imply causation.

Addressing this issue, Cunningham wrote,

> In its assertions about the relationship between causal claims and the need for experimental evidence, the Panel has unwittingly allied itself with the research arm of the U.S. tobacco industry, the Tobacco Institute, which has long argued that the Surgeon General or anyone else has no right to claim that smoking causes cancer because the relationship is merely correlational. (2001, p. 328)

Newkirk weighed in on this in the same vein:

> The reading report stunningly fails to find any solid evidence in support of independent reading, largely because it dismisses all correlational studies. Correlation, of course, does not demonstrate causation, but even fields like medicine and epidemiology regularly make use of it when experimentation is difficult (the effects of cigarette smoking,

for example). If proficient readers typically read extensively on their own, as the research suggests, it would seem prudent, even scientific, to develop this habit in young readers. (2002, p. 39)

It is true that medical researchers use correlational evidence for some determinations, but how this is done is much more sophisticated than what the critics seem to assume. First, correlational evidence can never be used as the sole determiner of whether something works (which is how Cunningham, 2001, and Newkirk, 2002, proposed using it in education). It can only be used to proscribe the use of something; thus, its use in the cigarette example. Second, to use correlation, it is not enough that experimentation be "difficult"; in fact, it has to be virtually impossible to do an experiment. Researchers, for instance, would not be allowed to try to induce cancer, so a direct experiment of smoking effects could not be done. Are Cunningham and Newkirk really arguing that it would be "difficult" (unethical) to encourage students to read more for the sake of research? And if that really is their position, why would they want teachers providing such encouragement? Third, it should be noted that even in the case of cigarettes, the health community was unwilling to accept correlational studies alone but required experimental studies testing the effects of nicotine on animals. Nevertheless, Allington (2002) claimed that it would be unethical to test the impact of encouraging reading.

Essentially, these critics are telling schools to accept the effectiveness of any and all incentive programs that pay children in some way to read more; any and all commercial programs that claim to encourage reading; and any and all free reading programs, book availability programs, and other reading encouragement approaches, including those that take the place of sound instruction from a professional teacher. Such critics are saying that all of these programs work and that it would be foolish and unethical to even try to find out how well they work. These claims certainly are not based on evidence and make no sense in terms of the nature or ethics of science or the practice of education.

Allington (2001, p. 28) agreed with the NRP that correlational evidence cannot answer the "chicken and egg problem," that is, "Does better reading lead to more reading? Or does more reading lead to better reading?" He then marshaled additional correlational studies on a slightly different topic (showing the relationship of average amount of school reading with achievement gains). Unfortunately, most of the studies that he cited for this claim did not separate amount of reading instruction from amount of reading, and none were able to show that the school procedures led students to read any more than the students normally would choose to. Furthermore, the study that Allington cited that did separate reading from instruction (Stallings, 1980) actually found no correlation between silent reading of the type that Krashen champions and reading gains.

Allington (2002) showed similar confusion in his failure to recognize any difference in the reading that is part of a reading lesson and the additional reading that students might be encouraged to engage in independently beyond these lessons. While chiding the NRP for finding insufficient evidence proving that these programs work, he argued that any effort to improve reading achievement should begin with the issue of the amount of reading. He continued with 11 pages of suggestions of how this might happen—never once mentioning any of the SSR, Drop Everything and Read, Accelerated Reader, or reading incentive programs that had been studied by researchers, examined by the NRP (NICHD, 2000), or that are championed by Krashen (2001, 2002) and others. Allington primarily suggested ways to increase reading within instructional lessons, which, of course, is a different issue from the one under discussion.

Krashen (2001) claimed that the panel failed to locate much of the research on SSR, an approach in which children are given time to read self-selected books within the school day with no teacher monitoring or guidance. He noted that the NRP only examined 10 such studies, and he compared the results of these studies with those of the 32 relevant studies that he claims the panel missed. This accusation is important because it challenges the integrity and validity of the NRP. Missing 32 relevant studies is not a minor error. Krashen's claim, however, is wrong. He pointed out that six of the NRP studies are on his list (but fails to note a seventh, Cline & Kretke, 1980, that is on both lists). Furthermore, eight of Krashen's studies are not actually refereed articles (i.e., they had no independent quality review) and could not be on the NRP's list for that reason. Even if the NRP had tried to include such studies, it would have had to do so systematically—meaning that the panel could not have done as Krashen did, selecting studies whose findings the panel agreed with while ignoring equivalent studies with discrepant findings. The NRP did not "miss" these eight studies. Moreover, the

NRP recognized that extra English reading time beyond instruction might have different implications for young English-language learners who may have no other opportunity to hear and use English. Thus, the NRP's examination was limited to studies of native language learners (and there is a federal panel that is considering what works with second-language learners). Krashen's approach assumes cultural differences don't matter—he puts forth six studies on the learning of English in Singapore, India, Fiji, and Malaysia.

Krashen (2000) also criticized the NRP for including studies that went beyond SSR (e.g., incentive programs, free reading time with more limited student choice), but violated his own conditions and listed studies of instructional programs from the 1950s and 1960s that required students to read literary trade books in place of basal readers. Individualized reading programs of this type, however, do not necessarily use SSR and in fact provide a great deal of reading instruction (Veatch, 1959). Krashen's choice of these studies is highly selective, including only findings that match his claims—and pointedly leaving out even more widely known, multiyear comparison studies that failed to find this supposed superiority (Bond & Dykstra, 1967/1997). Because these studies did not examine the effects of SSR and because none showed that the programs under study led children to read more, it seems unreasonable to use them as proof of the effectiveness of SSR.

That leaves one "missing" study (by Oliver, 1973). This is a minor study, but it is in the ERIC database and would have been identified in the NRP search if any of the more recent studies had cited it. Apparently researchers in this area missed this article or did not think it particularly important. In any event, had the NRP found it, it would have added one short-term (1-month) study to the ledger, this one finding no difference due to SSR. That would have given the NRP 15 evaluations of methods for encouraging reading, with only 3 of these coming out positive. Thus, even with Krashen's "corrections," there are few high-quality studies in this area. Krashen (2000, p. 48) expressed concern that the panel's report devoted only 6 pages to pleasure reading but 66 pages to phonemic awareness and nearly as many to phonics. But given the paucity of research on pleasure reading (phonemic awareness included 52 studies and phonics included 38 studies, whereas encouraging reading included only 14 studies), its relative low quality (the average encouraging reading study was roughly half the length of the average phonemic awareness study, revealing big differences in reporting thoroughness), and the fact that the panel had findings on those other topics, the page differential makes great sense.

Criticism 4: This Wasn't a Very Good Panel, It Did the Wrong Stuff, and Other People Are Going to Mess Things Up

This fourth kind of criticism of the NRP might seem silly, but a surprising amount of the criticism has taken the form of saying bad things about the panelists, making erroneous claims about what the panel did, and complaining about how the NRP findings (NICHD, 2000) will be misused. I would gladly forego analysis of this unfortunate material, given its obvious irrelevance to whether practitioners and policy makers should depend upon the NRP, but it makes up such a large portion of the criticism that I fear that neglecting it would be misleading.

Let's look at a few examples. One major concern of the critics has been the qualifications of the panelists, particularly that most of the panel members were from universities. For example, Yatvin explained that Congress had mandated that the panel be made up of "15 individuals who . . . include leading scientists in reading research, representatives of colleges of education, reading teachers, educational administrators, and parents" (Congress, as cited in Yatvin, 2002). Yatvin (2002) complained that

> NICHD stretched that definition to its limits by appointing 12 university professors. . . . Other categories were represented by one parent, one elementary school principal, and one middle school language arts teacher. . . . There was no reading teacher in the sense that I believe Congress intended.

Garan asserted that most of the panel "had never been directly involved in actually teaching children to read but came from an unusual assortment of occupations" (2002, p. 3). She also stated that only two panelists had close links to the teaching of reading. These sentiments have frequently been voiced (Allington, 2002; Toll, 2001; Yatvin, 2000). These complaints neglect the fact that several of the panelists had years of teaching and administration experience in school reading programs, teacher education, and reading curriculum design. More to the point, however, is that the panel's task was to analyze research evidence, which requires a depth of knowledge of how to read and analyze research, *not* to try to interpret panel members' personal classroom experiences. Toll (2001) was critical that the panel member selection privileged the scientist over the teacher, who has experience and expertise, but, of course, an analysis of research evidence by definition is an attempt to reveal what experience cannot.

More to the point is Yatvin's complaint:

> To have fully answered its charge, the Panel needed to assess the implications for practice growing out of research findings. As a body made up mostly of university professors, however, its members were not qualified to be the sole judges of the "readiness for implementation in the classroom" of their findings or whether the findings could be "used immediately by parents, teachers, and other educational audiences." Their concern, as scientists, was whether or not a particular line of instruction was clearly enough defined and whether the evidence of its experimental success was strong. What they did not consider in most cases were the school and classroom realities that make some types of instruction difficult—even impossible—to implement. (2000, p. 2)

This judgment of "readiness for implementation" is something that university-based scientists obviously could not carry out—if it was to be done by matching research findings with personal experience. What the panel actually did was to look at whether the interventions had worked again and again with a wide variety of students and in a wide variety of settings. The panel considered whether the success of the interventions depended upon extraordinarily expert teachers, extensive or expensive professional development programs, specialized or hard-to-access materials, and other objective features of the programs themselves. In all cases, the findings described instructional techniques and materials that are easily learned by teachers and that require materials widely available and within most school budgets. (Evidence of the applicability of the findings can be drawn from my experiences as director of reading for the Chicago Public Schools, where I applied the NRP findings (NICHD, 2000) to more than 500 schools serving a population that is 85% low income).

In another challenge to the membership of the panel, Garan wrote a statement that bordered on libelous:

> The scientific researchers on the National Reading Panel had vested interests in the outcome of the report both professionally and, unfortunately, financially. . . . While there are many connections between the

researchers for the NRP report, McGraw-Hill Publishing, and the administration of George W. Bush, isn't it possible that the researchers are not [sic] guilty of deliberate misrepresentation to promote their own financial and professional interests? (2002, pp. 77, 81)

In fact, by law, none of the panelists were allowed to have financial interests in reading programs, and all panelists were required to submit financial disclosure statements prior to being appointed to the panel. I do not know if any of the panelists have connections with President Bush, but it should be remembered that the NRP report (NICHD, 2000) was commissioned and carried out completely during President Clinton's term, while Bush was still governor of Texas.

Various other complaints have been put forth concerning the panel, including the idea that panel members got "dumber" as they worked together as a group (Allington, 2002, p. 270); that panel members were too "old" and unrecognized in the field to be credible on these topics (Allington, 2002, p. vi); that the panel consisted "primarily [of] researchers with established careers in experimental research, few of whom were grounded in instructional research" (Garan, 2001c, p. 62); that somehow we were closely associated with mandates, federal power, politicians, Republicans, publishers, standardization, accountability, intensive phonics, decodable texts, and textbook adoption (Allington, 2002, pp. 265–266 and throughout the volume); that our efforts reveal "evidence of manipulation, bias, fallacious argument, and other tactics unbecoming inquiry" (Shaker & Heilman, 2002, p. 2); and that we used "propagandist technique[s]" and were part of an "approach of disinformation that includes corrupted forms of inquiry, second-generation 'summaries' that betray even the original panel's work, and federal sponsorship of a grave erosion of scholarly communication" (Shaker & Heilman, 2002, p. 3). Whew! I am uncertain how to respond to the name-calling, guilt by association, and unsubstantiated assertions and leave the evaluation of these to the judgment of the reader.

So many errors and misinterpretations have crept into the criticism that it would be impossible to reply to all of it within the space of a chapter or within the attention span of most readers—though in terms of debating tactics, the revelation of such errors might convey a carelessness on the part of the critics that could undermine their positions. That, ultimately, is not my concern. The NRP report (NICHD, 2000) is long and complex, and trying to undermine the critics' arguments by showing that they have erred serves no greater good.

With regard to the mistakes, I am most concerned about those that suggest directly or by implication that the NRP got its mission wrong. For instance, Garan (2002) claimed that the NRP focused "on isolated skill and drill" (p. 2), that the panel's results were "based on children's performance on isolated skills" (p. 21), and that "the work of the National Reading Panel all begins and ends with the notion that reading is . . . a series of isolated skills that can be identified, measured, put together, and ultimately taught according to a prescribed, sequential formula" (p. 3). What she neglected to note is that few of the studies examined by the NRP ever looked at any teaching approach out of context and that all were validated—at least in part—with reading comprehension tests (in other words, the studies did not just look at isolated skills). The NRP never put forward any kind of sequence of teaching or direction on how schools could best orchestrate instruction. Cunningham (2001) similarly claimed that the panel evaluated the effectiveness of encouraging kids to read on fluency tests—when, to the contrary, *all* of those studies used silent reading comprehension tests as the outcome; only a few used fluency measures.

Both Cunningham (2001) and Garan (2002) claimed that there were so few comprehension studies that we did not analyze them in the same manner that we did the studies on the other topics— suggesting that the report has little to say about the teaching of reading comprehension. This is also untrue. In fact, the panel examined more studies of reading comprehension than of phonemic awareness, phonics, oral reading fluency, and encouraging students to read *combined.* These comprehension studies weren't meta-analyzed because there were so many (more than 200) and because they were so diverse that the panel lacked the time to provide the kind of detailed analysis that they deserved. The panel was only able to determine what methods of comprehension instruction worked and was unable to provide a thorough tabulation of the features of these programs that contributed to their success.

Garan (2002) and others have often claimed that the NRP results (NICHD, 2000) can only be applied to "at-risk" children, which is also untrue. The studies we examined did include children with learning problems (or potential learning problems, for younger students), but they also included typical readers. One of the interesting findings in areas such as phonemic awareness and phonics was that greater achievement gains resulted when the methods were taught in regular classrooms than when they were used solely with students with learning problems.

Garan (2002) has written an entire book expressing her antipathy for the NRP, along with several companion articles (2001a, 2001b, 2001c) along the same lines. The numbers of errors and misunderstandings about basic research methodology are too numerous to count. I'll respond to just two more. Garan suggested that the NRP supported a particular commercial program (Open Court), though we never evaluated that or any commercial program. Whether one likes or dislikes the Open Court program, it has nothing to do with the NRP. More seriously, Garan has charged that the phonics "studies were actually turned over to the graduate students of Steven Stahl, one of the panel's contributors" and stated that "it was these graduate students who analyzed the studies; the highly regarded members of the National Reading Panel did not even see the majority of [the studies]" (2002, p. 73). The suggestion here is that the phonics analysis was the result of some kind of chicanery. Nothing could be further from the truth. All of the procedures for searching for phonics articles had been designed and carried out by panel members. All of the phonics articles were read and analyzed (including all of the coding of the article features into a database) by the panel members and their assistants. At that point, the panelist leading this part of the effort was injured and was unable to complete the work without assistance. Steven Stahl, a widely known researcher and author of Chapter 9, was asked to carry out the statistical analysis of the phonics data under panel direction. Given the work that had been done up to this point by the panel on phonics and what Professor Stahl was asked to do, there was absolutely nothing underhanded, inappropriate, or biasing about his valuable—but limited— contribution.

Finally, there are dozens of complaints that warn about the potential dangers for the report's misuse or that blame the report for any numbers of misstatements about the report by politicians, media, and educators. There is no possible way that anyone who writes or speaks publicly can guarantee that his or her words will never be misappropriated, and there is no possible way that any scientist can guarantee that his or her results will never be misused. Furthermore, complaints about the misuse of the report, like the complaints about panel membership, say nothing about the value of the information in this report or its value to practice and policy.

Criticism 5: The National
Reading Panel Report Is a Fool's Errand

Potentially the most significant criticisms of the NRP are those that challenge the basic premises of the panel, as these comments could expose reasons that the NRP should not influence practice or policy. The NRP was fundamentally based upon the idea that schools should try to improve children's reading abilities and close the achievement gaps between rich and poor, black and white, and so forth. Another basic premise of the NRP was that research could provide valuable direction toward improving achievement and that it was thus necessary to make an objective public determination of the scientific research evidence on reading. A final premise of the NRP was that the research evidence had to be analyzed in a manner consistent with the highest standards for research synthesis to limit the influence of personal belief, self-interest, and other biasing factors.

Some critics have challenged these basic premises and have directly contradicted the NRP findings (NICHD, 2000). One would think that no critic would want to oppose higher reading achievement, though Allington skated precariously close when he grudgingly conceded, "I'll grant American schools could be improved, and that we could improve children's reading proficiency, but it seems to me that it's almost time for a national celebration of what we have accomplished up to this point" (2002, p. 16). He did admit that schools could try to address the "rich/poor achievement gap" (p. 16), and he even accepted the existence of research that could help with this process. It is odd that these concessions are so reluctant given that reading achievement in the United States has been stagnant since the 1970s and that racial and economic disparities are growing (Grigg, Daane, Jinn, & Campbell, 2003).

Allington (2002) challenged the entire enterprise of applying research findings of this type to instructional practice. He attacked the very idea of promoting instructional approaches that have been found to be effective in research. "The notion of 'proven programs' is simply . . . wrongheaded" (p. 18). He also asserted that using an "external expert intervention model to research how to teach reading is an enormously flawed approach" (pp. 90–91). I am uncertain what he means exactly by an "expert intervention model," but apparently it includes studies in which teachers alter their typical instructional routines in order to see if children learn more than they would have otherwise. Allington's opinion on this is widely contradicted, however. Various panels of experts have endorsed the value of such approaches (Coalition for Evidence Based Policy, 2002; What Works Clearinghouse, 2002), and major reports on reading have embraced such methodologies by recommending instructional approaches based upon them (Snow et al., 1998), as have independent scholars (including, interestingly enough, Richard Allington, 2001).

I suspect what Allington (2002) was really talking about here is that in the hands of an ineffective teacher, even a program with a strong research basis will not fare well (T. Shanahan, 2002). Toll elaborated on this idea: "The language of the NRP report reflects a discourse of change that is rooted in a belief in objective knowledge existing outside the local context and beyond any individual teacher's awareness" (2001, p. 322). Certainly, it is true that no matter how well supported by research a particular approach may be, its ultimate effectiveness can be subverted by other factors. This, however, seems to beg the point. Would schools agree to provide children lunches without balanced nutritional value simply because some students would not eat the entire lunch? It seems better to select instructional approaches that have been shown repeatedly to benefit children rather than to rely on tradition, fad, or opinion for making such choices. Typically, well-done research studies demonstrate how well an approach works when used by teachers who are comparable to those in the control conditions; furthermore, that a method has worked repeatedly suggests that others could make it work, too.

Cunningham (2001), although not challenging the idea of using research to improve reading education, does seemingly believe that policy makers should provide public support for virtually *anything* that might be done in a classroom—as long as there is no convincing negative information on that approach. After analyzing the phonemic awareness portion of the NRP report (NICHD, 2000), Cunningham acknowledged that systematic phonemic awareness instruction gives children an early advantage in learning to read but then stated,

> I contend that the burden of proof is with the Panel to show that research-based practices such as shared reading of books and play with sounds, writing with invented spelling, and teaching onsets using a variety of activities (key actions, students' names, and key foods or beverages) do not help most children develop the necessary phonemic awareness they need. (p. 332)

In other words, he is saying that the types of activities that he recommends to teachers should be supported even without any evidence that they actually help children. Moreover, he believes that these activities should be granted the same status in schools as those activities that have repeatedly been shown by research to benefit children. He casts this as a freedom-of-choice issue for teachers and teacher educators rather than as one of standards for developing higher achievement for children. In Cunningham's view, anything goes in instruction as long as there is no convincing evidence disproving its value, and Cunningham would have no method—no matter how strong the evidence that it benefits kids—take precedence over those approaches for which there is no evidence.

Another tactic that Cunningham (2001) used is to hold the NRP to an impossibly high quality standard, one that he evidently does not use in his own determinations of what works. I am less concerned about the inconsistency of this than I am by the idea of imposing a standard that is currently unattainable. Cunningham (2001) proposed that beginning reading programs must be shown to confer advantages that last to "fifth grade and beyond on the most important variables" (p. 332). In other words, if a program improves children's achievement in kindergarten or first grade, nothing can be concluded about the value of that program until students have completed at least 4 or 5 more years of schooling. I know of no educational program that could meet this high standard given all of the variables that come into play over such a long period of time (T. Shanahan & Barr, 1995). Cunningham seems to be saying that there is no benefit to applying research-based standards to instruction given the inadequacy of current research, yet even in his critical review, he champions instructional approaches that lack the level of evidence reviewed by the NRP.

A related issue has to do with the appropriateness of the synthesis methodology used by the NRP. Researchers employ many different measures of reading ability in their studies, and there are no well-established rules for combining data from these varied measures, though there are precedents. The NRP followed these precedents. Generally, the panel agreed to accept almost any test that a researcher used to measure reading or its parts. For some analyses the NRP grouped these diverse measures into a reading set—meaning that an intervention would be evaluated with regard to whether it had any consistent effect on reading measures overall. The NRP analysis also separated out each measure on the basis of conceptual criteria so that the relative impact of an intervention could be evaluated across the various kinds of measures. For example, with oral reading fluency, analyses were reported that showed the separate impacts on word reading, oral fluency or reading speed, and reading comprehension. For the phonics studies, measures such as word recognition of phonetically regular words, word recognition of phonetically irregular words, and word recognition of nonsense words were examined both together and separately.

The issue of what counts as reading is particularly problematic for studies with preschoolers or kindergartners because children at these levels usually cannot read in a conventional sense but researchers would like to know if instruction at these levels offers any learning advantage to children (e.g., would they do better with later reading?). In such cases, the so-called "reading" measures usually evaluate abilities, skills, or knowledge that have been shown by research to have a predictive relationship to later reading ability.

This approach, though widely used and accepted in the field of reading, has been under attack by the NRP critics, who believe it to be misleading. For instance, Garan (2002, p. 16), intimated, "Here now is the sleight of hand. The panel averaged these single, isolated comparisons and instead of naming this averaged outcome *skills* or growth in *isolated skills*, they named it General Reading—a misnomer!" On this basis, Garan (2001a, 2001b, 2002) challenged any finding that was not based upon reading comprehension tests that included considerable amounts of text reading—despite the fact that she was speaking of studies of young children. So, when the NRP showed that children who receive phonics instruction did better with decoding phonetically regular words, her reply was, "We all know that just because a child can, for example, decode phonetically regular words or even read fluently, such behavior does not necessarily guarantee comprehension" (2002, p. 14). That such decoding strongly increases the probability of higher comprehension is not acceptable to her. However, even when this standard is met, say with preschool studies of phonemic awareness that show later benefits in terms of beginning reading comprehension, the evidence is dismissed because not all of the studies evaluated it this way or because there are too few such studies—and she has been unwilling to acknowledge or accept the implication of the consistent pattern of outcome across the entire set of these highly correlated measures.

This measurement issue is a prime one because it is on this point that much of the small amount of criticism directed at the NRP findings (NICHD, 2000) revolves. The only direct challenges to the findings of the NRP are those proposed by K. Anderson (2000), Coles (2001), Garan (2001a, 2001b, 2001c, 2002), and Krashen (2001).

For example, both Coles (2001) and Garan (2001a, 2001b, 2001c, 2002) have challenged the idea that phonics instruction needs to be systematic, largely based on measurement issues. A major basis for their concern is that there are not enough studies of young children that include a reading comprehension test or that are longitudinal studies ending up with some kind of later measure of reading comprehension. They are unwilling to accept a small number of studies that exhibit these characteristics, even when there are many additional studies showing improved word recognition and oral reading ability as a result of this instruction and even though these abilities are highly correlated with reading comprehension and have been shown to be causally implicated in reading improvement. (The rejection of this widely accepted evidence is probably the reason so many other critics—Pressley, 2001, 2002a, 2002b; Cunningham, 2001; Almasi and colleagues, 2002; and Purcell-Gates, 2000, just to name a few—part company with Garan and Coles in these areas.)

Coles's rejection of the NRP's conclusions about phonemic awareness also depends upon the types of comparisons that were sometimes included in the NRP analysis:

> Finally, like numerous studies included in the meta-analysis, this study contains a "Compared to what?" problem. That is, it draws a comparison of instruction and no instruction, rather than of one form of instruction and another. . . . Consequently, the meta-analysis is disingenuous in its design and statistical calculations when it pits instruction against no instruction and concludes that instruction had a substantial outcome. (2001, p. 207)

What Coles (2001) failed to note is that some "reading experts" have argued that children don't need phonemic awareness training because these skills develop simply from engaging in language use or in working with songs and nursery rhymes. Under such circumstances, it is quite appropriate to show that phonemic awareness training added to a typical preschool or kindergarten regimen would be better than what would happen without this addition and it is perfectly reasonable to include them in the analysis.

Another way that Coles, Garan, and Krashen have challenged the NRP is through a seemingly detailed analysis of the actual research studies themselves—to reveal some flaw in the study or in the discussion of it by the NRP in order to impeach the evidence. The NRP examined more than 50 studies of phonemic awareness that provided direct evaluations of such instruction under controlled conditions, and Coles provided a detailed analysis of about 15% of those studies. For one, he complained that even though phonemic awareness clearly gave an advantage, another condition in the study did well, too, and therefore deserved equal attention to the phonemic awareness treatment. With another study, the complaint was that the comparison between using a basal reader and using a basal reader with a phonemic awareness component was improper—because this finding only concerns phonemic awareness in combination with basal readers. In another, he complained that phonics instruction only helped children learn faster—rather than better. These complaints are similar to those raised by Krashen (2002) and Garan (2002) about certain aspects of phonics instruction.

The problem with such complaints is that selective attention to strengths and weaknesses of studies is not in accord with the widely accepted methods of research synthesis. All research studies have flaws, some of which are more serious than others. Biased reviews of research reject evidence that does not fit a preconceived set of outcomes, and this is easy to do by selectively using research standards to get rid of the findings that one doesn't like. The key to sound synthesis is an even-handed use of research quality standards—making sure that each standard is used to make sense of both the studies that support one's position and those that challenge it. Even with that, most synthesists do not reject a particular finding due to its limitations but instead analyze the impact of the limitations. For example, the NRP examined the entire set of phonemic awareness studies using widely accepted quality standards and found that the most rigorously conducted studies had resulted in the largest effect size estimates for phonemic awareness.

It is not that Coles, Garan, or Krashen are necessarily wrong in what they say about particular studies—though frequently they are—it is simply that one cannot evaluate a research synthesis in the manner that they do in their criticism. Instead, it is essential that the critic weigh each limitation for all of the studies and show how much impact this had on the overall effect size computed for that approach.

K. Anderson (2000) was the only other critic to challenge the findings of the panel. His approach was quite different. He simply claimed to "know" many things about the effectiveness of phonics and was highly critical of the NRP for not supporting his claims. How Anderson could know what he claimed to know without research is anybody's guess, but the NRP did not find empirical evidence supporting his positions. For example, Anderson expressed outrage that the NRP showed evidence that supported many approaches to instruction (phonemic awareness, phonics, comprehension, vocabulary, guided oral reading). He was so certain that phonics was the most important aspect of instruction, conferring the greatest benefit of all, that he evidently was not particularly interested in research that supported other aspects of teaching. Anderson essentially said research is only valuable when it supports one's beliefs and that it can safely be rejected when it supports contradictory positions. The NRP, of course, had to present the research findings—and steer away from claims based solely upon panel members' personal beliefs or preferences.

This set of criticisms, unlike the others, does argue against the application of the NRP findings (NICHD, 2000) to policy or practice. Some of these claims are philosophical (e.g., the idea that because these findings did not emerge from the teacher's own experiences, they would not be useful for improving instructional practice). The other claims are largely methodological and are easier to refute on the basis of widely accepted standards and norms for synthesizing research data. Thus, as an NRP member, I continue to support the approach to research synthesis used and encourage the implementation of the findings in classrooms across the nation.

CONCLUSIONS

Just as this chapter was going to press, an important reanalysis of the NRP results was published (Camilli, Vargas, & Yurecko, 2003). This paper was not a critique of the NRP of the style reviewed here but was a serious reanalysis of the data from the phonics portion of the NRP study—the most controversial portion of the NRP report (NICHD, 2000). Camilli and colleagues took the studies identified by the NRP and reviewed them to again consider which ones actually met the criteria and which did not. This led Camilli and colleagues to drop one study that the NRP included and to add two others for coding and analysis. They recoded all of the data and reanalyzed the results, sometimes with different analytical assumptions and statistical formulae. Nevertheless, despite all of these changes, their conclusion was identical to the NRP's original conclusion on phonics: "Systematic phonics instruction did outperform treatment conditions in which a more typical or moderate level of phonics instruction was provided" (Camilli et al., 2003, p. 34). The analytic changes that Camilli made did lead to a reduction in the effect size associated with phonics, but even with that change, the results of this summary of a large number of independent phonics studies affirmed the NRP's conclusion that phonics instruction was valuable in the early grades. Camilli did suggest that these phonics results might be amplified or moderated by some other variables not considered by the NRP (e.g., tutoring, an ill-defined language variable), but it would take additional research to confirm those hypotheses.

The NRP report (NICHD, 2000) has generated a firestorm of controversy among critics who seemingly would like to prevent it from being used by teachers or policy makers. As this analysis shows, however, the critics usually have not made challenges to the NRP findings—in fact, most of the critics have expressed agreement with the findings of the report. Furthermore, the few actual challenges to applying the NRP findings have been controversial even among the critics themselves and are on shaky philosophical, logical, and methodological grounds.

REFERENCES

Adams, M.J. (1990). *Beginning to read: Thinking and learning about print.* Cambridge, MA: MIT Press.

Allington, R.L. (2001). *What really matters for struggling readers.* New York: Longman.

Allington, R.L. (Ed.). (2002). *Big brother and the national reading curriculum: How ideology trumped evidence.* Portsmouth, NH: Heinemann.

Almasi, J.F., Garas, K., & Shanahan, L. (2002, December). *Qualitative research and the report of the National Reading Panel: No methodology left behind?* Paper presented at the annual meeting of the National Reading Conference, Miami, FL.

Anderson, K. (2000, July 18). The reading wars: Understanding the debate over how best to teach children to read. *Los Angeles Times.*

Anderson, R.C., Hiebert, E.H., Scott, J.A., & Wilkinson, I.A.G. (1985). *Becoming a nation of readers: The report of the Commission on Reading.* Washington, DC: National Academy of Education.

Baumann, J.F., & Ivey, G. (1997). Delicate balances: Striving for curricular and instructional equilibrium in a second-grade, literature/strategy-based classroom. *Reading Research Quarterly, 32,* 244–275.

Beach, R., Green, J.L., Kamil, M.L., & Shanahan, T. (in press). *Multidisciplinary perspectives on literacy research* (2nd ed.). Mahwah, NJ: Lawrence Erlbaum Associates.

Bender, W.N., & Larkin, M.J. (2003). *Reading strategies for elementary students with learning difficulties.* Thousand Oaks, CA: Corwin.

Bond, G.L., & Dykstra, R. (1997). The cooperative research program in first-grade reading instruction. *Reading Research Quarterly, 32,* 348–427. (Original work published 1967)

Camilli, G., Vargas, S., & Yurecko, M. (2003). Teaching children to read: The fragile link between science and federal policy. *Education Policy Analysis Archives, 11,* 1–52.

Chall, J. (1967). *Learning to read: The great debate.* New York: McGraw-Hill.

Chall, J. (1983). *Learning to read: The great debate* (Updated ed.). New York: McGraw-Hill.

Chall, J. (1996). *Learning to read: The great debate* (3rd ed.). New York: McGraw-Hill.

Cline, R.K.J., & Kretke, G.L. (1980). An evaluation of long-term SSR in the junior high school. *Journal of Reading, 23,* 503–506.

Coalition for Evidence-Based Policy. (2002). *Bringing evidence-driven progress to education.* Washington, DC: U.S. Department of Education.

Coles, G. (2001). Reading taught to the tune of the "scientific" hickory stick. *Phi Delta Kappan, 83*(3), 205–212.

Cooper, H. (1998). *Synthesizing research* (3rd ed.). Thousand Oaks, CA: Sage Publications.

Cooper, H., & Hedges, L.V. (1994). *The handbook of research synthesis.* New York: Russell Sage Foundation.

Cunningham, J.W. (2001). [Review of the National Reading Panel report]. *Reading Research Quarterly, 36,* 326–335.

Denzin, N.K., & Lincoln, Y.S. (Eds.). (1994). *Handbook of qualitative research.* Thousand Oaks, CA: Sage Publications.

Edmondson, J., & Shannon, P. (2002). The will of the people. In R.L. Allington (Ed.), *Big Brother and the national reading curriculum: How ideology trumped evidence* (pp. 137–153). Portsmouth, NH: Heinemann.

Foorman, B.R., Breier, J.I., & Fletcher, J.M. (2003). Interventions aimed at improving reading success: An evidence-based approach. *Developmental Neuropsychology, 24,* 613–639.

Garan, E. (2001a). Beyond the smoke and mirrors: A critique of the National Reading Panel Report on phonics. *Phi Delta Kappan, 82*(7), 500–506.

Garan, E. (2001b). More smoking guns: A response to Linnea Ehri and Steven Stahl. *Phi Delta Kappan, 83*(1), 21–27.

Garan, E. (2001c). What does the report of the National Reading Panel really tell us about teaching phonics? *Language Arts, 79*(1), 61–70.

Garan, E. (2002). *Resisting reading mandates: How to triumph with the truth.* Portsmouth, NH: Heinemann.

Grigg, W.S., Daane, M.C., Jinn, Y., & Campbell, J.R. (2003). *The nation's report card: Reading 2002.* Washington, DC: National Center for Education Statistics.

Hinchman, K.A., Alvermann, D.E., Boyd, F.B., Brozo, W.G., & Vacca, R.T. (2004). Supporting older students' in- and out-of-school literacies. *Journal of Adolescent and Adult Literacy, 47,* 304–310.

Invernizzi, M.A. (2001). The complex world of one-on-one tutoring. In S.B. Neuman & D.K. Dickinson (Eds.), *Handbook of early literacy research* (pp. 459-470). New York: Guilford Press.

Kame'enui, E.J., & Simmons, D.C. (2001). Introduction to this special issue: The DNA of reading fluency. *Scientific Studies of Reading, 5,* 203–210.

Krashen, S. (2000, May 10). Reading report: One researcher's "errors and omissions." *Education Week,* 48.

Krashen, S. (2001). More smoke and mirrors: A critique of the National Reading Panel Report on fluency. *Phi Delta Kappan, 83*(2), 119–123.

Krashen, S. (2002). The NRP comparison of whole language and phonics: Ignoring the crucial variable of phonics. *Talking Points, 13*(4), 22–28.

National Council of Teachers of English. (2003, February). NCTE members urge Congress to review Reading First initiative. *The Council Chronicle, 12,* 1, 4.

McCandliss, B., Beck, I., Sandak, R., & Perfetti, C. (2003). Focusing attention on decoding for children with poor reading skills: Design and preliminary tests of the word building intervention. *Scientific Studies of Reading, 7,* 75–104.

Morris, D., Bloodgood, J.W., Lomax, R.G., & Perney, J. (2003). Developmental steps in learning to read: A longitudinal study in kindergarten and first grade. *Reading Research Quarterly, 38,* 302–328.

Morrow, L.M., & Asbury, E. (2003). Current practices in early literacy development. In L.M. Morrow, L.B. Gambrell, & M. Pressley (Eds.), *Best practices in literacy instruction* (2nd ed., pp. 43–64). New York: Guilford Press.

National Institute of Child Health and Human Development (NICHD). (2000). *Report of the National Reading Panel. Teaching children to read: An evidence-based assessment of the scientific research literature on reading and its implications for reading instruction: Reports of the subgroups* (NIH Publication No. 00-4754). Washington, DC: U.S. Government Printing Office. Also available on-line: http://www.nichd.nih.gov/publications/nrp/report.htm

Newkirk, T. (2002, April 24). Reading and the limits of science. *Education Week,* 39.

Oliver, M. (1973). The effect of high intensity practice on reading comprehension. *Reading Improvement, 10,* 16–18.

Pressley, M. (2001). *Effective beginning reading instruction.* Chicago: National Reading Conference.

Pressley, M. (2002a). *Reading instruction that works* (2nd ed.). New York: Guilford Press.

Pressley, M. (2002b). What I have learned until now about research methods in reading education. *Yearbook of the National Reading Conference, 51,* 33–44.

Pressley, M.P., Dolezal, S., Roehrig, A.D., & Hilden, K. (with the Notre Dame Reading Research Seminar). (2002). Why the National Reading Panel's recommendations are not enough. In R.L. Allington (Ed.), *Big Brother and the national reading curriculum: How ideology trumped evidence* (pp. 75–89). Portsmouth, NH: Heinemann.

Purcell-Gates, V. (2000, July). The role of qualitative and ethnographic research in educational policy. *Reading Online, 4*(1). Retrieved October 23, 2003, from http://www.readingonline.org/articles/purcell-gates/

Rasinski, T.V., & Hoffman, J.V. (2003). Oral reading in the school literacy curriculum. *Reading Research Quarterly, 38,* 510–522.

Rosenthal, R. (1991). *Meta-analytic procedures for social research.* Thousand Oaks, CA: Sage Publications.

Shaker, P., & Heilman, E.E. (2002, April). Advocacy versus authority: Silencing the education professoriate. *Substance,* 1–6.

Shanahan, T. (2000). Research synthesis: Making sense of the accumulation of knowledge in reading. In M.L. Kamil, P.B. Rosenthal, P.D. Pearson, & R. Barr (Eds.), *Handbook of reading research* (Vol. 3, pp. 209–228). Mahwah, NJ: Lawrence Erlbaum Associates.

Shanahan, T. (2002). What reading research says: The promise and limitations of applying research to reading education. In A.E. Farstrup & S.J. Samuels (Eds.), *What reading research has to say about reading instruction* (3rd ed., pp. 8–24). Newark, DE: International Reading Association

Shanahan, T. (2003). Research-based reading instruction: Myths about the National Reading Panel report. *The Reading Teacher, 56*(7), 646–655.

Shanahan, T., & Barr, R. (1995). Reading Recovery: An independent evaluation of the effects of an early instructional intervention for at risk learners. *Reading Research Quarterly, 30,* 958–996.

Shavelson, R.J., & Towne, L. (Eds.). (2002). *Scientific research in education.* Washington, DC: National Academies Press.

Stallings, J. (1980). Allocated academic learning time revisited, or beyond time on task. *Educational Researcher, 8*(11), 11–16.

Snow, C.E., Burns, M.S., & Griffin, P. (Eds.). (1998). *Preventing reading difficulties in young children.* Washington, DC: National Academies Press.

Toll, C.A. (2001). Can teachers and policy makers talk to one another? *The Reading Teacher, 55*(4), 318–325.

Veatch, J. (1959). *Individualizing your reading program: Self-selection in action.* New York: Putnam.

What Works Clearinghouse. (2002). *What Works evidence review process and the role of scientific standards.* Washington, DC: Institute of Education Sciences.

Yatvin, J. (2000). Minority view. In *Report of the National Reading Panel: Teaching children to read. An evidence-based assessment of the scientific research literature on reading and its implications for reading instruction: Report of the subgroups* (NIH Pub. No. 00-4754, pp. 1–6). Bethesda, MD: National Institutes of Health, National Institute of Child Health and Human Development.

Yatvin, J. (2002). Babes in the woods: The wanderings of the National Reading Panel [Electronic version]. *Phi Delta Kappan, 83*(5), 364–369. Retrieved October 23, 2003, from http://www.pdkintl.org/kappan/k0201yat.htm

Yopp, R.H., & Yopp, H.K. (2003). Time with text. *Reading Teacher, 57,* 284–287.

IV

Reading Research
Evidence in the Classroom

The fourth section of this volume addresses what happens for both teachers and students when reading research moves into the classroom. These chapters deal with how teachers can best develop their abilities and experiences to more effectively deliver scientifically based instruction, in terms of their own professional development, their use of their own time and creative energy, their ability to promote reading motivation, and whether they can deliver effective interventions in the classroom. Louisa C. Moats is well known for her work on professional development. In Chapter 12, she outlines context and content for professional development and clearly addresses how to prepare teachers to implement reading research findings in the classroom. Barbara R. Foorman, Claude Goldenberg, Coleen D. Carlson, William M. Saunders, and Sharolyn D. Pollard-Durodola (Chapter 13) describe a research method for classroom observation and offer implications for classroom teachers of what is learned through this approach.

But having well-trained teachers with a solid grasp of how children learn to read, the structure of language, and what instructional methods are most effective for which children is not enough in and of itself, just as no single component of reading instruction is enough without the others. Educators must also somehow maintain or instill in students a motivation to learn. John T. Guthrie and Nicole M. Humenick have dedicated research efforts to finding techniques that work in the classroom by studying students' motivation, and in Chapter 14 they present a review of the literature on reading motivation and ways that teachers can make reading more rewarding and motivating.

Even the best teacher will not succeed in teaching every child to read—some children require specific intervention because they do not develop grade-level reading skills. In Chapter 15, Joseph K. Torgesen describes the role of intervention research, using both preventive and remedial instruction, in real classrooms. He examines studies that look at various aspects of intervention such as teaching methods, delivery intensity, educational contexts, and the ability of the student. Understanding preventive and remedial instructional techniques that are most effective for students is fundamental when teaching students of all levels.

12

Science, Language, and Imagination in the Professional Development of Reading Teachers

Louisa C. Moats

One of the most widely accepted facts of modern reading psychology is that reading and writing difficulties are associated with inefficient, inaccurate, or underdeveloped language processing (Rayner, Foorman, Perfetti, Pesetsky, & Seidenberg, 2001). Specific language processes, such as speed of letter naming, accuracy of letter–sound associations, and fluency in decoding unknown words, account for individual differences in passage reading accuracy and fluency at the end of first grade and beyond. In addition, children living in poverty and children who come to school without English language proficiency experience a gap in vocabulary and background knowledge that undermines academic achievement. On school entry, economically and educationally disadvantaged children may know half as much vocabulary as children from middle-class circumstances (Hart & Risley, 1995). If these disadvantaged children are also slow to acquire basic reading skills, they will fall further behind the norm in both oral and written language proficiency. By the middle and upper elementary grades, a very large group of "garden-variety" poor readers who are not necessarily dyslexic are typically overwhelmed by the language of academic texts and the demands of academic, expository writing.

Fortunately, children who begin schooling at a disadvantage in letter, sound, word, and concept knowledge can be taught to read and write well if their teachers consistently implement a linguistically informed, structured, comprehensive, and content-rich curriculum.

This is much easier said than done, however, because it means that teachers must be knowledgeable and skilled in some very specific areas, must use validated tools for assessment and instruction, and must work in supportive contexts that help them sustain intensive effort year after year.

How do we prepare and develop linguistically informed, effective teachers who can deliver research-based programs and practices? Our 4-year study of reading instruction in high-poverty schools, called Early Interventions for Children with Reading Problems (hereafter referred to as the Early Interventions Project), led by Barbara R. Foorman, and funded by the NICHD, yielded multiple sources of data regarding effective professional development of classroom teachers and reading specialists. Data were obtained through direct classroom observations of teacher effectiveness, sampling of instructional time allocation, and measures of the relationship between these factors and student achievement (Foorman & Schatschneider, 2003). We also obtained anonymous, tape-recorded interviews with teachers (Foorman & Moats, in press); teacher surveys and questionnaires (see Chapter 13); surveys directed at the nature and level of teachers' knowledge of language and of reading instruction (Moats & Foorman, 2003); teachers' evaluations of courses and workshops; and anecdotal reports of the ambient conditions in our schools. Nine schools participated in Washington, D.C., and eight participated in Houston, and all were chronically low performing with high-poverty populations. All schools received intervention, as it was not possible to have some schools be nontreatment control schools in the context of districtwide reform. In both settings, the Early Interventions Project enabled children to achieve at or above the national average in grades K–4.

Teachers indicated in their interviews that the combination of professional development and comprehensive reading program adoption was the key to their improvement and success with students. Teachers welcomed the combination of program-specific training; information about scientific studies of reading development and reading difficulty; and information about the language structures they were teaching—phonemes, spelling, word structures, sentences, language history, discourse and genre structure, and cultural-linguistic differences among children. The application of knowledge to instructional decision making and actual practice was facilitated through coaching, mentoring, team meetings, and the creation of a supportive context in which teacher growth and student achievement were celebrated. The context, content, and processes of professional development were all critical to building and maintaining teaching teams that could implement the practices supported by reading research. This chapter discusses in detail what we taught, how we taught it, and what we learned about teaching teachers.

THE CONTEXT OF PROFESSIONAL DEVELOPMENT

Consistent Policy

Classroom teachers work in school, district, and state contexts. Policies and practices at these levels often contradict one another and may have little continuity from year to year as administrative leadership changes. One of the most common complaints from our teachers in D.C. concerned the everchanging mandates that prevented them from refining and sustaining application of practices that were effective. During the study's first year, administrators; classroom teachers from all nine participating D.C. schools; specialists; teaching assistants; and tutors all attended the same professional development workshops and courses. The common goals, vocabulary, and understandings we established across individuals with various roles allowed administrators to guide teachers with consistency and to support them in using their instructional materials. The essentials of research-based instruction—including oral language production, phoneme awareness, explicit and systematic phonics, reading fluency, vocabulary, comprehension, and writing—were defined and demonstrated for everyone, regardless of the instructional program in use.

In Houston, the context differed considerably. In Texas, as in California, the state had aligned academic achievement standards, curricular frameworks, textbooks, instructional programs, and assessments with one another; this had occurred before our study began. Teachers at the Houston site of the Early Interventions Project were thus aware of and motivated by systemic accountability. Messages about components of instruction, instructional goals, and evaluation processes were consistent across schools and from year to year. In D.C., however, no such alignment of critical systemic components existed, and teachers often felt as if district-level mandates and project-level requirements were in conflict. For example, our emphasis on teaching phonological skills in kindergarten and first grade was unique within the D.C. school system to our nine schools, as was our use of a validated screening instrument. The project staff and consultants in D.C. delivered all professional development; no district-sponsored workshops, courses, or directives existed to support our activities. At the conclusion of the project, the program that was associated with the most positive results in D.C. was jettisoned by the school district in favor of one with less robust results, probably because the tenets and practices of the one we had used remained foreign to the dominant practices in the school district.

Time

Adequate time must be allowed for professional development that is substantive and that challenges teachers to learn and apply new teaching behaviors. Teaching children how to read and write is a complex activity that is learned with knowledge, coaching, and experience (American Federation of Teachers, 1999; Learning First Alliance, 2000). One of the most often-cited reasons why the D.C. teachers rated the project's professional development highly was its time frame. Many teachers in their recorded interviews commented that they needed 2 years of professional development and teaching experience for "everything to fall into place," and they welcomed the rare opportunity to study topics in depth. The three-credit graduate courses on phonology, writing, phonics, vocabulary, and comprehension each lasted for at least a half-year and sometimes lasted longer. In addition, the D.C. teachers rated these courses highly because participants could collaborate on lessons, share insights, and demonstrate practices for and with colleagues. Teachers commented frequently that they enjoyed learning from their peers whose practical and collective wisdom they trusted. Although the courses were perceived to be challenging in ways the teachers were unaccustomed to, course enrollments were filled and attendance at workshops was high. Thus, a state-level requirement, such as California's, for teachers to attend 40 hours of summer training and 80–100 additional hours per year school in team meetings, independent study, team collaboration, and coursework would be reasonable, given the reports and behavior of our teachers.

Data-Based Decision Making

A focus on the interpretation of student assessments to inform instruction was more prevalent on the Houston side of the project because of statewide use of the Texas Primary Reading Inventory (TPRI; Texas Education Agency, 1996). Although in D.C. we trained teachers in the use of the TPRI, teachers did not use the screening data to differentiate instruction. Teachers dutifully gave the test to their students, but without principal, coach, or team facilitation and a requirement to generate a data-based instructional plan, teachers did not organize instructional groups or select instructional targets on the basis of the TPRI results.

Leadership at the School Level

The substantial school effects in our study were related to the leadership and commitment of district and building administrators. The principals whose schools outperformed the other schools in the study visited classrooms regularly, reminded teachers of the value of specific instructional practices, promoted literacy throughout the school, read with children, supported family literacy programs and outside reading programs, created a businesslike atmosphere in the school, and expected improvement at all levels. Several greeted every child entering the school building every day.

THE CONTENT AND PROCESS OF PROFESSIONAL DEVELOPMENT IN READING AND WRITING

Early identification of reading problems, preventive intervention, and progress monitoring are now widely encouraged on the basis of research reported in this volume. For new policies to be successful, however, teachers must be well informed about reading development, reading difficulties, and research-based instruction. More specifically, they must be able to judge the meaning of students' screening test results, choose which skills to emphasize and how to teach them to specific children, interpret student written and oral responses, and allocate instructional time in proportion to student need. Intentional teaching of reading, spelling, and writing requires knowledge of oral and written language structure, developmental sequences in oral and written language learning, and the ways in which speech and print can be problematic for children (Ehri, 1995). Without such knowledge, teachers cannot take responsibility for what their students learn. As one of the D.C. teachers commented, "I could read the manual and go through the lessons, but I couldn't *teach* until I understood for myself what I was teaching." On the knowledge surveys we gave to teachers, we discovered surprising misconceptions and gaps in the awareness of many teachers about language and reading instruction. We subsequently addressed these in professional development, and the subsections that follow discuss these.

Phoneme Awareness and Phonological Processing

One of the most important jobs for the teacher of beginning reading or the teacher of students with reading problems is to foster awareness of phonemes (speech sounds) in words and to help children acquire the ability to articulate, compare, segment, and blend those phonemes (Ehri et al., 2001). Knowing word meanings and differentiating confusable words depend on accurate perception of the phonological structure of the words. Children must be aware of subtle contrasts in similar-sounding spoken words, such as "shark" and "shock"; "fill," "fell," and "fail"; "fresh" and "flesh"; and "irrelevant" and "irreverent," in order to learn their meanings. Thus, teachers must recognize when and how to direct children's attention to contrasts in speech-sound sequences. More importantly, word recognition and spelling depend on rapid and accurate association of phonemes with graphemes (written letters and letter groups that represent phonemes) in the service of reading and writing whole words. These associations should be taught explicitly, cumulatively, and systematically for best results (National Institute of Child Health and Human Development, 2000), but the foundation for instruction is phoneme identity and differentiation.

Phoneme awareness instruction involves more than delivery of a set of playful activities in kindergarten. Students scoring below benchmark levels in reading and/or spelling may acquire phoneme awareness over a number of years and may need continuing clarification during instruction, even as reading skill progresses. Phoneme awareness can be taught with a variety of tasks that precede or complement letter manipulation, including phoneme counting (e.g., "How many sounds are in *sheep*?"), phoneme identification (e.g., "What is the last sound in *cab*?"), phoneme segmentation (e.g., "Let's say the sounds in *shoe:* /sh/ /ŭ/"), and phoneme deletion (e.g., "Say *steak* without the /t/")

The teacher who knows phonemes and their distinction from letters (graphemes) and letter names can demonstrate this knowledge in the context of daily classroom interactions. The effective teacher will refer to the /f/ sound, not the "ef" sound; he or she contrasts it with the voiced consonant /v/, which is articulated similarly. He or she asks for the last *sound*, not the last letter, in the words *half* and *have* when those words are exchanged in a student's spelling. He or she says, "How do we spell /v/ at the ends of words? That's right, with -*ve*!" This level of expertise was uncommon in our classrooms until we worked with teachers on the underlying concepts that enable such behavior.

Our surveys and experiences during the project and before it (Moats, 1994; Moats & Foorman, 2003), as well as the research of others (Bos, Mather, Dickson, Podhajski, & Chard, 2001; Mather, Bos, & Babur, 2001; McCutchen, Abbott, et al., 2002; McCutchen, Harry, et al., 2002), have indicated that specific concepts of word structure and speech-sound differentiation are problematic for teachers. We targeted these topics in our professional development. For example, teachers often believed that the consonant clusters in complex syllables were "one sound." Thus, about half of the teachers undercounted the number of phonemes in the word *shrimp.* With word items involving digraph and vowel team spellings, such as *sing, sawed,* and *boy,* more than a third of the teachers overcounted the number of phonemes, revealing a tendency to count letters rather than speech sounds. Phoneme identification and matching were problematic when the letter or letters used to represent a sound were different from the letter or letters that most often represent that sound. For example, about half of the teachers surveyed believed that the last sound in *nose* was /s/, not /z/, and half could not identify that /t/ ends the spoken word "walked." The concept that single phonemes, including /ng/ and /ch/, are represented in orthography with letter teams was either unknown or only partially known by a very large group of experienced teachers. These confusions influenced instruction, for it was not uncommon for teachers to be seen teaching children that each letter represented a separate sound in words such as *house* or *them* even if the teacher's manual contained directions for sound production and sound blending.

Many of our teachers in D.C. cited their learning of speech sounds as a pivotal experience in professional development. We began with a tour of the consonant and vowel inventories (i.e., the system of speech sounds) and careful differentiation of the approximately 44 phonemes of English from the 26 letters in the alphabet. We practiced production, segmentation, blending, and manipulation of consonant and vowel sounds apart from and in relation to the letters that represent them. During this exploration, we discussed dialectal and regional differences in pronunciation and the nature of phoneme awareness and its role in reading acquisition. Learning the phoneme inventory and practicing phoneme manipulation helped the teachers appreciate the challenges of phoneme awareness for children. Moreover, the experience itself impressed on teachers the nature and role of the alphabetic principle in learning to read. No teacher challenged the importance of this insight once it was apparent, and many teachers expressed dismay that they had been directed away from explicit sound-based instruction by district policy of the previous decade.

Knowledge of Orthography

Users of English orthography spell by both sound and meaning. To read the alphabetic orthography proficiently, learners must first appreciate that letters and letter groups, such as *oa, eau, igh,* and *eigh,* are the relational units that represent phonemes (Venezky, 2001). Next, to read multisyllabic words fluently, learners must recognize the syllable spelling conventions and junctures of printed syllables that permit visual "chunking" of long letter sequences and assignment of a vowel sound to specific letter patterns. To spell accurately, children must learn specific orthographic patterns, principles, and rules and typically do so in a more or less predictable sequence (Bear & Templeton, 1998; Ehri, 1995).

Many teachers we surveyed had partial or unelaborated knowledge of phonic correspondences and syllabication, and many had not had exposure to even a traditional approach to teaching phonics or spelling. When information about orthography is found in modern reading textbooks, it is often presented in unappealing, unsystematic, and unteachable lists of rules about letter sequence constraints.

Consequently, lacking awareness of either the orthographic system or its specifics, teachers may try to teach phonics with incomplete information, disconnected lists of formidable rules, and superficial strategies that mislead, such as "Find the little word in the big word" or "When two vowels go walking, the first one does the talking" (see Henry, 2003, p. 76, for an explanation of why the latter mnemonic is unhelpful).

Our surveys of teachers again suggested knowledge gaps that should be addressed directly in professional development. A large percentage did not know the concept that letter groups such as *-dge* in *edge* are correspondence units, used conventionally for sounds in specific contexts (*-dge* spells the sound /j/ after accented short vowels). About one of three teachers did not identify which of the following high-frequency words have a regular spelling: *when, does, were,* or *said.* (*When* is perfectly predictable by sound–spelling correspondences.) Teachers were weakest in knowledge of syllable spelling conventions. Fifty-five percent could recognize a closed syllable such as *up* from four choices. Fifty-one percent knew that the double *d* in *puddle* resulted from the joining of a closed syllable (*pud*) with a consonant-*le* syllable (*dle*). The links between inflections *-ed* and *-s* and their various pronunciations were not well known; about half could match the sounds of the inflections on *dogs* and *coached* to the same last sound on another word. In the case of *dogs*, teachers tended to choose a matching word that ended with the letter *s* even though the *s* in that matching word represented the voiceless /s/ instead of the voiced /z/ at the end of *dogs*. In the case of *coached*, whose final sound is /t/, teachers matched it incorrectly with *screamed* (/d/) and *filled* (/d/).

Teachers appreciated acquiring insights that helped them explain words to their students. Activities such as marking graphemes in familiar words and building words with grapheme tiles instead of tiles for single letters (e.g., building *shouting* with *sh ou t i ng*) were productive because they fostered awareness of the relational units in the sound–symbol correspondence system. Syllable sorting and classification were revelations, especially to the second- and third-grade teachers. For example, the word *happy* has four phonemes; the double *p* results from the combination of a closed syllable with the vowel *y*, needed to mark the first vowel as short. With the knowledge of this principle, teachers understood that the two *p* letters do not represent two separate speech sounds but rather an orthographic convention of syllable juncture.

Morphology and Etymology

English orthography represents both sound structures (phonemes and syllables) and meaning structures (inflections and Anglo-Saxon base words in compounds; Latin-based derivational suffixes, prefixes, and roots in lower frequency nouns, verbs, adjectives, and adverbs; and Greek-based combining forms in scientific and mathematical vocabulary). Spelling is often related to the word's language of origin (e.g., *antique, rouge, mosquito, piano*). Beyond basic phonics, the study of meaningful parts of words and where they came from assists vocabulary development, word recognition, and spelling. An expert teacher of orthography is one who can explain the spelling of almost any word with reference to its phonemes, syllables, morphemes, orthographic patterns, language of origin, usage, and meaning (King, 2000; Moats, 2000, 2003a). For example, silent letter patterns such as *kn-, wr-, -ough, -ould,* and *-igh* are remnants of Anglo-Saxon, in which those "silent" letters were sounded. The word *tube* is Anglo-Saxon, but the word *television* has three Latin-based morphemes that recur in other words and that have stable pronunciations, meanings, and spellings: *tele, vis,* and *ion*. The richness of expression in English is a consequence of its linguistic history: From our Anglo-Saxon heritage, we *walk;* from Latin and Greek, respectively, we *ambulate* across the *geography*. From Anglo-Saxon, we *live;* from Latin, we are *animate;* from Greek, we are part of *biodiversity*. Anglo-Saxon gave us *mothers* and *fathers;* Latin gave us *maternal* and *paternal* figures; Greek allows us to talk about our *genes* and *chromosomes*. (See Henry, 2003, for more about the origins of the English language and how that information can be applied to explicit instruction in decoding, spelling, and morphology.)

Where does language instruction for the teachers begin, and of what use is such knowledge? The goal of professional development is to enable teachers to explain language concepts accurately and completely. Teachers who are knowledgeable can exploit a teachable moment, for example, to link words such as *native, national, nativity,* and *nation*. If a teacher has never studied Latin or the history of the English language, however, morphology is foreign territory and the topic should be approached through its foundations. The distinction between free and bound morphemes (e.g., *fur* versus *fer*) and the distinction between inflections (*-ing, -ed, -s*) and derivational suffixes (*-al, -ment, -ful, -ity*) are important basic concepts. The insight that the spelling system of English preserves or represents morphology, often in the presence of sound pattern alternations such as *sign, signature; inspire, inspiration; legal, legislate; preside, president; and medicine, medical* (Moats & Smith, 1992), helps teachers call students' attention to word structure beyond phonics, especially during spelling.

Derivational suffixes mark the part of speech of the root or word to which they are added, and simply marking whether a suffix creates a noun, verb, adjective, or adverb is instructive for teachers. Exploration of suffixes that cause changes of pronunciation in the base words to which they are added, such as *divide, division; repeat, repetitive; peculiar, peculiarity;* and *medicine, medical,* helps teachers appreciate why word families should be taught together, why words must be pronounced when they are being learned, and why the meaningful parts are useful to discuss. Rather than memorizing lists of prefixes, suffixes, and roots, teachers enjoy selecting one productive Latin root and locating many examples of words derived from that root. They can then organize a map of those morphological relationships (see Henry, 2003, and Moats, 2000, 2003b). Realizing that multisyllabic words can be divided by either syllable division rules or by morphology is helpful for teachers who want to know the "right" way to divide a word. The answer, of course, depends on which kind of language organization is of interest: One can divide the word instruction morphologically (*in-struct-ion*), or syllabically (*in-struc-tion*).

Morphology and language history provide a narrative context for the study of words. Because teachers cannot teach children every word they need to know, the instructional goal must also include cultivation of linguistic awareness, or word consciousness. Teacher preparation itself should excite teachers about linguistic discoveries so that the same enthusiasm and interest is communicated to the children. This assertion leads to the next topic: What is the role of imagination and creativity in scientifically based reading instruction?

Engaging Teachers' Imagination in Vocabulary and Comprehension Instruction

No less important for teachers is the ability to teach word and text meaning. Novice teachers need to know that much more is involved in teaching vocabulary than matching dictionary definitions to words or giving students definitions to memorize. Likewise, there is more to teaching comprehension than asking students questions about what they read. Effective teaching pursues meaning making at both literal and inferential levels, using a variety of techniques and strategies that fit the text, the situation, and the children.

Vocabulary and comprehension are domains of instruction that defy formulaic approaches. Formulaic approaches can keep children busy but often divert them from making sense of what they read. Formulaic approaches include such activities as posting new vocabulary on the board and matching definitions to the words; ordering children to make "mind maps" regardless of whether the graphic organizer fits the structure of the content; or always taking a compulsory "picture walk" through a text to predict its outcomes, instead of sometimes using other kinds of introductions. Although such practices have their place, the key to reading comprehension instruction is intentional, creative use of questions and strategies to get the children to identify and articulate the meanings that the author intended (Beck, McKeown, Hamilton, & Kucan, 1997). Before instituting professional development based on Beck and colleagues' approach, we found that many teachers had lost sight of the purpose of their instruction. For example, they were teaching vocabulary without ever using the vocabulary in context, teaching strategies instead of focusing on the use of the strategies to garner meaning from the text, or rereading stories over and over without deepening the purpose of the rereading. We witnessed many cases of teachers embarking on text instruction without having read the text themselves. In an extreme and memorable case, one teacher remarked in a workshop, "You mean we're supposed to understand what we teach before we teach it?"

Such habits could be changed. We found that change of approach occurred after teachers explored the nature of elementary students' miscomprehensions and the difference between queries (questions designed to deepen understanding) and closed questions that usually elicited brief, unelaborated, thoughtless responses from children. For example, a query might ask, "Why do you think the author is giving us this information about the character?" whereas a closed question might ask "Who was she talking to?" An enjoyable exercise for teachers involved planning the instruction of a text together. They read the text aloud in a small group, summarized the critical meanings that they wanted students to understand, and then identified places in the text at which they intended to pose queries. Each group discussed and formulated those queries. Then, teachers shared their plans with the other groups of teachers. Lively discussions, such as those that we wanted to see in the classrooms, ensued among teachers as they sought agreement about the intentional use of a given text. Even though the teachers' manuals directed them to use specific questions and strategies, teachers did not implement these effectively until they were engaged with the material and took responsibility for what the children were learning.

Specific teaching behaviors were also practiced in the teacher classes. For example, teachers practiced using new words in spoken sentences as a text was previewed and using graphic organizers to demonstrate logical relationships in expository text. Consequently, teachers who understood the principle of teaching word meanings through multiple examples dramatically changed their verbal behavior. One reported that she learned that she should talk before writing things down for students. Another spent about 20 minutes explicating the meaning of one word through contextual examples. Another reported that for the first time, her students retained and used words from one lesson to the next.

In the text discussions, we drew teachers' attention to the metaphorical, idiomatic, and colloquial expressions that could interfere with reading comprehension. Language is by nature metaphorical, and metaphorical language is even more common in literary text than it is in everyday speech. We do not *keep time* in a physical sense, nor do we *run out of luck*. Awareness of the ubiquitous nature of metaphorical and idiomatic language was cultivated as we shared examples of children's misinterpretations and learned to anticipate them. We identified the need for contextualizing idiomatic phrases for English language learners. We discussed and modeled other comprehension skills and strategies, but no exercises had more power to focus and motivate teachers than the ones in which careful reading and questioning was modeled and practiced.

Written Expression

Progress in writing for students in D.C. and Houston was far more limited than progress in reading. A very small percentage of instructional time was spent teaching writing across classrooms, and the quality of instruction was observed to be poor. Teachers, in turn, often struggled with written expression on class assignments and expressed insecurity about their own command of written language. On the knowledge survey, 44% of the teachers chose to define a kernel or "bare-bones" sentence as a clause or a group of words with a capitalized first word and a period rather than as a subject and a predicate. Systematic teaching of children, nonetheless, requires teachers to explicate sentence, paragraph, and genre structure, as well as standard English grammar and usage—areas in which the teachers themselves were weak. To compound the issue, teachers' instructional materials for writing and grammar were far less structured, comprehensive, and integrated than their reading programs.

In our course on writing instruction, teachers were least prepared in the structured teaching of sentence and paragraph composition and were seldom organized to lead children through the stages of the writing process. Course time was devoted to setting up and organizing writing centers, practicing sentence-level skill development, using rubrics to evaluate writing, and learning to coach children through the stages of the writing process. The importance of skill development to composition quality and fluency (Berninger & Richards, 2002) was a theme reiterated throughout the course. Unfortunately we were not able to gather evidence that these interventions with teachers resulted in better classroom implementation of writing instruction.

SUMMARY OF FINDINGS ON TEACHER NEEDS

In the context of a longitudinal, 4-year study of reading instruction in low-performing urban schools (Foorman & Moats, in press; Moats & Foorman, 2003), we found modest but statistically significant relationships among teacher knowledge, teacher effectiveness, and student achievement variables. Preliminary data, obtained under difficult public school conditions, supported the common-sense assertion that teachers' knowledge and their ability to apply it affects student learning. Teachers reported in tape-recorded interviews that professional development; the presence of classroom coaches and observers; and the adoption of core, comprehensive reading programs were keys to their success. The professional development process was more comprehensive, substantive, and intensive than past district offerings. Courses and workshops, followed by classroom coaching, promoted understanding of research findings about reading acquisition, the structure of the English language, and instructional methods supported by research. Professional development sessions also aimed to engage the imagination, affect, and commitment of teachers who often seemed deflated by the aversive conditions in their schools.

We documented, through multiple-choice surveys, what teachers typically did and did not know about language structure and reading development. Responses indicated that the following understandings were elusive and needed to be addressed in class: 1) differentiation of speech sounds from letters; 2) detection of the identity of phonemes in words, especially when the spelling of those sounds was not transparent; 3) knowledge of the letter combinations (graphemes) that represent many phonemes; 4) conceptualization of functional spelling units such as digraphs, blends, and silent-letter spellings; 5) knowledge of syllable division and syllable spelling; 6) identification of the syntactic constituents of a sentence; 7) identification of students' problems with phonological, orthographic, and syntactic learning; and 8) comprehension of the ways in which the components of reading instruction are causally related to one another. Knowledge of morphology, etymology, and writing instruction were addressed more briefly because of time limitations.

Our approach to professional development emphasized both content depth and teachers' active engagement in learning. Teachers' tolerance for lecture presentations was very limited. Classes were successful when teachers prepared demonstrations for one another, read aloud with one another, worked as groups to answer questions, toured each other's classrooms, viewed videotapes of peers at work, or put themselves in the shoes of the children. Heated discussions were encouraged, even though they were sometimes tangential. Appeals to affect and imagination energized the teachers as much as insights into subject matter and the children's learning processes.

RECOMMENDATIONS FOR PROFESSIONAL DEVELOPMENT PROGRAMS

Researchers in reading development and reading disabilities have made considerable progress in early identification and treatment of dyslexia and other reading problems. The fruits of these scientific labors cannot be realized, however, unless teachers understand and are prepared to implement them. Fundamental to differentiated instruction in basic reading skill are the teacher's insight into what causes variation in students' reading acquisition and the ability to explain concepts explicitly, to choose examples wisely, and to give targeted feedback when errors occur. Knowledge of language structure, language and reading development, and the dependence of literacy on oral language proficiency are prerequisite to (but not sufficient for) informed instruction of reading.

According to our teacher surveys and interviews, teachers often need more than an instructional program and classroom experience to understand how children learn to read and how to teach language structure. Teachers who implement comprehensive, research-based reading programs usually achieve better results with their students than teachers who do not (Foorman, Francis, Fletcher, Schatschneider, & Mehta, 1998), as the programs provide essential tools. A teacher, however, delivers the program and unless he or she understands the content and principles of instruction in the teachers' manual, intentional teaching is not possible. Although general verbal ability may well be a mediating factor in how readily knowledge of language and reading instruction is acquired and how skillfully it is applied, teachers, too, deserve to be taught systematically the content they are responsible for teaching to children.

Knowledge of language and access to science-based programs of instruction are still not all that brings the best effort from teachers. Our experience and teacher interview data indicated that teachers appreciate an approach that engages their affect and imagination, is respectful of their concerns, and that shows them the connection between what is being learned and the job they have to do. Any professional would prefer such conditions to prevail in the workplace. These goals may best be accomplished with a combination of activities: directed assessment of children; discussion of those results; direct instruction about phonemes, graphemes, morphemes, syntax and grammar, semantic organization, etymology, discourse structure, and pragmatics; lesson study groups; small-group readings to summarize and respond to texts; and rehearsal of the writing skills expected of the children.

Research on teacher education in reading is a young science. Better-controlled studies should address further the many questions raised by studies such as ours. What combination and sequence of learning experiences is most effective and appropriate for new teachers? How much content knowledge should be required before teachers are even admitted to a licensing program? What level of content knowledge can be taught within a licensing program? What is typically learned after licensing? What is the difference between knowledge and skill needed by specialists and knowledge and skill needed by regular classroom teachers? What kinds of measures are valid predictors of how well a teacher is likely do in reading instruction?

And finally, policy makers must accept the financial responsibility of supporting teachers if quality counts. Sustained, embedded, substantive professional development for teachers is a necessary investment if research gains are to be realized on a wide scale.

REFERENCES

American Federation of Teachers. (1999, June). *Teaching reading is rocket science: What expert teachers of reading should know and be able to do* (Item No. 372 6/99). Washington, DC: Author.

Bear, D.R., & Templeton, S. (1998). Explorations in developmental spelling: Foundations for learning and teaching phonics, spelling, and vocabulary. *The Reading Teacher, 52,* 222–242.

Beck, I.L., McKeown, M., Hamilton, R.L., & Kucan, L. (1997). *Questioning the author: An approach for enhancing student engagement with text.* Newark, DE: International Reading Association.

Berninger, V., & Richards, T. (2002). *Brain literacy for educators and psychologists.* Amsterdam, The Netherlands: Academic Press.

Bos, C., Mather, N., Dickson, S., Podhajski, B., & Chard, D. (2001). Perceptions and knowledge of preservice and inservice educators about early reading instruction. *Annals of Dyslexia, 51,* 97–120.

Ehri, L.C. (1995). Teachers need to know how word reading processes develop to teach reading effectively to beginners. In C.N. Hedley, P. Antonacci, & M. Rabinowitz (Eds.), *Thinking and literacy: The mind at work.* Mahwah, NJ: Lawrence Erlbaum Associates.

Ehri, L.C., Nunes, S.R., Willows, D., Schuster, B., Yaghoub-Zadeh, Z., & Shanahan, T. (2001). Phonemic awareness instruction helps children to read: Evidence from the National Reading Panel's meta-analysis. *Reading Research Quarterly, 3,* 250–257.

Foorman, B.R., Chen, D., Carlson, C., Moats, L., Francis, D., & Fletcher, J. (2003). The necessity of the alphabetic principle to phonemic awareness instruction. *Reading and Writing: An Interdisciplinary Journal, 16,* 289–324.

Foorman, B.R., Francis, D.J., Fletcher, J.M., Schatschneider, C., & Mehta, P. (1998). The role of instruction in learning to read: Preventing reading failure in at-risk children. *Journal of Educational Psychology, 90,* 37–55.

Foorman, B.R., & Moats, L.C. (in press). Conditions for sustaining research-based practices in early reading instruction. *Remedial and Special Education.*

Foorman, B.R., & Schatschneider, C. (2003). Measurement of teaching practices during reading/language arts instruction and its relationship to student achievement. In S. Vaughn & K.L. Briggs (Eds.), *Reading in the* classroom: Systems for the observation of teaching and learning (pp. 1–30). Baltimore: Paul H. Brookes Publishing Co.

Hart, B., & Risley, T.R. (1995). *Meaningful differences in the everyday experience of young American children.* Baltimore: Paul H. Brookes Publishing Co.

Henry, M.K. (2003). *Unlocking literacy: Effective decoding and spelling instruction.* Baltimore: Paul H. Brookes Publishing Co.

King, D. (2000). *English isn't crazy: The elements of our language and how to teach them.* Timonium, MD: York Press.

Learning First Alliance. (2000). *Every child reading: A professional development guide.* Washington, DC: Author.

Mather, N., Bos, C., & Babur, N. (2001). Perceptions and knowledge of preservice and inservice teachers about early literacy instruction. *Journal of Learning Disabilities, 4,* 471–482.

McCutchen, D., Abbott, R.D., Green, L.B., Beretvas, S.N., Cox, S., Potter, N.S., et al. (2002). Beginning literacy: Links among teacher knowledge, teacher practice, and student learning. *Journal of Learning Disabilities, 35*(1), 69–86.

McCutchen, D., Harry, D.R., Cunningham, A.E., Cox, S., Sidman, S., & Covill, A.E. (2002). Reading teachers' content knowledge of children's literature and phonology. *Annals of Dyslexia, 52,* 207–228.

Moats, L.C. (1994). The missing foundation in teacher education: Knowledge of the structure of spoken and written language. *Annals of Dyslexia, 44,* 81–102.

Moats, L.C. (2000). *Speech to print: Language essentials for teachers.* Baltimore: Paul H. Brookes Publishing Co.

Moats, L.C. (2003a). *LETRS: Language essentials for teachers of reading and spelling* (Book 1). Longmont, CO: Sopris West Educational Services.

Moats, L.C. (2003b). *Speech to print workbook: Language exercises for teachers.* Baltimore: Paul H. Brookes Publishing Co.

Moats, L.C., & Foorman, B.R. (2003). Measuring teachers' content knowledge of language and reading. *Annals of Dyslexia, 53,* 23–45.

Moats, L.C., & Smith, C. (1992). Derivational morphology: Why it should be included in language assessment and instruction. *Language, Speech, and Hearing Services in Schools, 23,* 312–319.

National Institute of Child Health and Human Development. (2000). *Report of the National Reading Panel. Teaching children to read: An evidence-based assessment of the scientific research literature on reading and its implications for reading instruction: Reports of the subgroups* (NIH Publication No. 00-4754). Washington, DC: U.S. Government Printing Office. Also available on-line: http://www.nichd.nih.gov/publications/nrp/report.htm

Rayner, K., Foorman, B.F., Perfetti, C.A., Pesetsky, D., & Seidenberg, M.S. (2001). How psychological science informs the teaching of reading. *Psychological Science in the Public Interest, 2*(2), 31–74.

Texas Education Agency. (1996). *Texas Primary Reading Inventory.* Austin: Author.

Venezky, R. (2001). *The American way of spelling: The structure and origins of American English orthography.* New York: Guilford Press.

13

How Teachers Allocate Time During Literacy Instruction in Primary-Grade English Language Learner Classrooms

Barbara R. Foorman, Claude Goldenberg,
Coleen D. Carlson, William M. Saunders, and
Sharolyn D. Pollard-Durodola

By the end of grade 3, national and state benchmarks share the expectation that children are able to 1) read grade-level literature independently with enjoyment and interest, 2) read grade-level information text with understanding for the purpose of learning, and 3) discuss and write about those texts in grade-appropriate ways. These benchmarks are echoed in many state standards and accountability tests and in the National Assessment of Educational Progress (NAEP). Yet, results from NAEP show that 37% of fourth graders read below the basic proficiency level for grade 4 and that among minority students this percentage is an alarming 63% for African American fourth graders and 58% for Hispanic fourth graders (National Center for Educational Statistics [NCES], 2001a). Although some have questioned the validity of the NAEP proficiency levels (Linn, Baker, & Betebenner, 2002), there is no question that there are real differences in achievement among ethnic groups.

The jump in Hispanic enrollment in the school-age population in the United States from 9.9% in 1986 to 16.3% in 2001 (NCES, 2001b) has resulted in increasing numbers of English language learners (ELLs) in classrooms. Educators and researchers need to better

The study reported in this chapter was supported by a grant from the National Institute of Child Health and Human Development (NICHD), Grant No. HD39521, "Oracy/Literacy Development in Spanish-Speaking Children."

understand the conditions under which ELLs become proficient in English literacy and the role of primary-language instruction in this process (Snow, Burns, & Griffin, 1998). In addressing this need, a central question to ask is, Within and across language models, what instructional strategies are used in Spanish and in English and how do they relate to student literacy development? A first step toward answering this question is to reliably measure the language and content of literacy instruction in bilingual classrooms. Accordingly, in this chapter we describe an observational system developed to capture teachers' strategies, student engagement, and teacher and student language during reading/language arts and English language development (ELD) instruction in primary grade classrooms with large numbers of ELLs.

BACKGROUND

Given the consensus for integrating phonics and meaning emphases in teaching English literacy evident in national and state benchmarks, what are the key research findings that can inform classroom practice and teacher preparation for ELLs learning English literacy? Two distinct areas need to be considered: 1) What should be the language of instruction for ELLs? and 2) What do we know about effective instructional practices for ELLs learning to read in English?

The Controversy Over Language of Instruction

Language has been the topic of greatest controversy in the education of ELLs, and by far the most volatile issue has been the use of ELLs' primary language for academic instruction: Should ELLs be taught English skills in English from the outset of their schooling, or should they be taught academic skills in their home language? And if they are to be taught in their home language, for how long? And if they are taught in English, how much native language support (e.g., explaining or clarifying concepts in the home language) is advisable? Primary-language advocates on one extreme say that the longer, more intensively, and more effectively students learn literacy and academic skills in their home language, the better their eventual academic attainment will be in English (Thomas & Collier, 1997). In diametric opposition, advocates of English instruction say that early, sustained, and effective use of primarily English in the classroom leads to superior attainment in English (Rossell & Baker, 1996).

Studies point policy in opposite directions. Baker (1998) and Rossell and Baker (1996) concluded that evaluation studies and research support the efficacy of intensive English use to promote academic development among ELLs. Their analyses and conclusions challenge the central premise held by advocates of primary-language instruction, which is that teaching students academic skills and knowledge in their home language, then transferring those skills and knowledge to English (or some other second language), is more effective than teaching students in a language they do not understand. Two research syntheses, however, have concluded precisely the opposite: Use of students' primary language *does* produce superior achievement results in English, as compared with immersing students in English-only instruction (Greene, 1998; Willig, 1985). These syntheses thus support the central tenet of primary-language instruction and most versions of bilingual education as practiced in the United States.

But even if one were to accept the conclusions of Greene's (1998) and Willig's (1985) work, existing studies do not provide a basis for determining how much primary-language instruction is optimal. Studies claiming that the longer students are in an effective primary-language program, the better their achievement in English, have either been plagued by technical problems (e.g., Ramirez, 1992; see Meyer & Fienberg, 1992, for a full technical review) or have not published complete details of the research, thereby not permitting a full evaluation of findings (e.g., Thomas & Collier, 1997). A more recent report by Thomas and Collier (2002) presented a stronger empirical case for the benefits of increased time in primary-language instruction for ELLs. But this study reported achievement data analyzed by language model (e.g., English-only instruction, transitional bilingual education, two-way bilingual education). There are no data or analyses describing type of language use in the classroom and its relationship to student achievement.

We are left, therefore, with important gaps in our understanding of the proper role of children's primary language in their eventual attainment in English. It might be that these gaps cannot be filled in any fully generalizable way, that is, independent of the particulars of children's schools and communities. The language-of-instruction issue is certainly important, but it must be kept in perspective because it is only one of several issues educators face in teaching

ELLs (August & Hakuta, 1997; National Educational Research Policy and Priorities Board, 1999). Moreover, as Cummins pointed out, language of instruction "is not, in itself, a determinant of academic outcomes" (1999, p. 31). The nature of the instruction must be considered within the larger school and community context in which that instruction takes place.

Two-way, or dual-language, bilingual education represents an important and relatively new direction in the debate on language of instruction. Two-way programs make extensive use of ELLs' primary language, but these programs also have as their goal bilingualism, biliteracy, and high levels of academic achievement in two languages, both for ELLs and native English speakers. ELLs maintain their home language and develop English language skills, while English speakers learn a second language in addition to continuing to progress in English. Research on two-way programs in the United States is still relatively new.

Some studies suggest very positive results: ELLs in two-way programs develop high levels of English proficiency and maintain their first language at high levels; English speakers maintain high levels of English competence but also learn another language (Cazabon, Nicoladis, & Lambert, 1998; Christian, 1994; Howard & Christian, 1997; Lindholm, 1996; Thomas & Collier, 1997).

As with other types of bilingual education, there are several challenges to successful implementation of two-way programs—staffing (bilingual staff), demographics (roughly equal numbers of children from two different language backgrounds), and program development (language mix and how this changes over the grades; complex curriculum and instruction promoting high levels of achievement in two languages). Virtually nothing is known about the consequences of different configurations of staff, demographics, and program options on student outcomes (August & Hakuta, 1997). This is an area that is crucial to examine because two-way bilingual education might be a promising approach for promoting the achievement of ELLs and simultaneously promoting bilingualism and biliteracy—with all of the attendant economic, intellectual, and cultural advantages (August & Hakuta, 1997; Crawford, 1991; Peal & Lambert, 1962; Rossell & Baker, 1996).

Learning English Literacy

A review of extant research suggests the following points about the literacy development of ELLs. First, the experiences and skills that children bring to school influence their literacy development (August & Hakuta, 1997; Snow et al., 1998). Children with more exposure to print, more knowledge of print and its functions, greater phonological awareness, and knowledge of letters and sounds are much more likely to do well in becoming literate and, indeed, in succeeding in all of their academic school tasks. The fact that students come to school with a huge range of experience, knowledge, and skill presents educators with formidable challenges. To the extent that a student's cultural and/or socioeconomic background influence experiences, knowledge, and skills that in turn influence literacy development, culture and socioeconomics play a role in literacy attainment. Adjusting classroom practice to reflect and be sensitive to students' cultural and socioeconomic backgrounds can promote high levels of student engagement. August and Hakuta (1997) cited studies that seem to show that schools and classrooms are more effective when they are responsive to community culture, values, and goals (see Tharp, 1982, and Wong-Fillmore, Ammon, McLaughlin, & Ammon, 1985). However, it is unclear to what extent accommodating to students' specific cultural or socioeconomic characteristics or experiences per se improves literacy attainment.

Second, direct, explicit instruction of basic (e.g., phonological) and more advanced (e.g., comprehension, analysis) language and literacy skills promote academic and language development of ELLs (Fitzgerald, 1995; Gersten, 1985, 1996). Systematic assessment of learning, opportunities for students to practice emerging skills, teaching strategies that enhance student understanding, and home and parent involvement are all associated with higher levels of achievement for ELLs (August & Hakuta, 1997; Goldenberg, 1998; Slavin & Madden, 1999).

Third, as important as is systematic instruction in essential literacy skills, ELLs also benefit from literacy learning experiences providing opportunities for reading and writing for pleasure, communication, and other personally meaningful purposes (August & Hakuta, 1997). For example, Elley and Mangubhai (1983) reported that "flooding" classrooms with high-interest illustrated storybooks in English improved the English reading and listening comprehension of 9- to 11-year old Fijian students learning English as a second language. Fitzgerald and Noblit (2000) provided numerous examples of communicative uses of print in a first-grade classroom with ELLs, although it is difficult to know what contribution the meaning-emphasis approach made to those children's early literacy development.

Fourth, literacy instruction for ELLs must at a minimum make accommodations for students' lack of proficiency in English. Advocates of primary-language programs advocate short- to long-term academically substantive programs in the students' primary language; advocates of English immersion advocate minimal use of the primary language and extensive use of English. Despite the radically different prescriptions derived from each position, both agree that instruction for ELLs must be structured and delivered in such a way as to be comprehensible and meaningful. Indeed, this is not just an educational nicety; it is a requirement of the amendments to the Elementary and Secondary Education Act, including the No Child Left Behind Act of 2001 (PL 107-110). In English immersion situations, making instruction comprehensible requires specialized techniques (e.g., "sheltered English," Echevarria & Graves, 1998) and at least some use of the primary language. Even strong proponents of English immersion acknowledge that use of the home language might be beneficial to learners faced with the formidable challenge of learning academic content and learning English simultaneously (Baker, 1998). It is unknown whether there are optimal levels of home language use in English immersion situations. Nor is it known the degree of comprehensibility that must be attained for students to benefit from academic instruction in a language they are still learning. Some students might require a higher degree of comprehensibility than others in order to benefit from academic instruction and other learning opportunities.

Fifth, the relationship between ELLs' oral English proficiency and literacy instruction in English is unclear. Should ELLs learn to read and write English as they learn to speak and understand it? Or should ELLs acquire certain levels of oral English proficiency before being expected to deal with English print? Some researchers argue that learning to read in English while learning to speak the language is possible, even desirable. Siegel (1999) reported that of the ELLs who entered kindergarten in Vancouver, British Columbia, with very little English familiarity, 90% were at the 50th–60th national percentile in reading 18 months later in first grade. (However, more than 50% of the ELLs Siegel studied participated in government-funded after-school and Saturday "heritage" language and culture classes; Siegel's findings thus also support the proposition that primary-language instruction leads to higher levels of learning in a second language.) Geva, Yaghoub-Zadeh, and Schuster (2000) also reported success in Toronto in teaching ELLs word-recognition skills, despite the students' limited English. Some researchers argue that acquiring and using English literacy skills will actually help promote ELLs' English language development (Anderson & Roit, 1996; Elley & Mangubhai, 1983; Gersten, 1996). Others, however, contend that a certain threshold of oral English proficiency must be acquired before ELLs are taught English literacy skills (e.g., Snow et al., 1998; Wong-Fillmore & Valadez, 1986). The basic argument is that it is extremely difficult to learn to read in a language that is unfamiliar in its sounds and meanings. Therefore, ELLs should be at least minimally familiar with the target language (how familiar is unclear). Fitzgerald (1995), although sympathetic to the argument that learning to read a second language can proceed simultaneously with learning to speak it (Fitzgerald & Noblit, 2000), argued that the results of studies are too mixed and inconclusive to permit any empirically based judgment about the relationship between learning to speak and understand a language and learning to read and write it.

One way to reconcile the different positions is to treat reading as a developmental process. That is, reading is different things at different stages. In the beginning stages, reading is more dependent on phonological processing (hearing the sounds in words) and being able to associate printed letters and groups of these letters with particular sounds; in later stages, vocabulary and concept knowledge in the target language become more important for proficient reading (Chall, 1983). Particularly significant for ELLs is that the relationship between reading and language changes as students progress from stage to stage. Beginning reading places greatest emphasis on phonological processes (e.g., hearing sounds in words, associating sounds and symbols, sequential blending of sounds represented by letters) that are largely meaning-free. This is likely to be relatively easy for ELLs, who can probably begin learning to read even with minimal knowledge of English. (Note, however, that these students must still learn to hear and discriminate sounds that are specific to the language in which they are learning to read; Geva, 2000.)

Later reading stages, however, rely more on extensive vocabulary and syntactic knowledge of the language, which take longer to develop than phonological skills. Indeed, at higher grades the correlations between reading proficiency and oral language proficiency among ELLs increase, suggesting that reading and oral language proficiency become more closely related as students advance in their reading development (Fitzgerald & Noblit, 2000). At these stages, lack of vocabulary and incomplete structural knowledge of English make continued literacy progress a greater challenge than it is in the early stages of reading. The lag between the acquisition of basic reading skills (phonological and decoding skills) and the acquisition of language required for success at more advanced stages of reading present a formidable challenge for ELLs and their teachers. As August and Hakuta noted, "A major obstacle to helpful research on reading instruction for language minority children is the failure to recognize the existence of developmental changes in the reading process and in the speed and efficiency of second-language learning" (1997, p. 62). Moreover, success in later stages of reading requires greater speed and efficiency of mental processes involved in reading. Although ELLs reading in English demonstrate similar mental processes as fluent English speakers, ELLs differ from English speakers in the extent, sophistication, and speed with which they use meta-cognitive strategies required for successful reading (Fitzgerald, 1995). For example, some ELLs summarize as they read and make predictions, but they do so more slowly and less effectively than English speakers.

Sixth, reading instruction and assessment must therefore be accompanied by instruction and assessment specifically designed to promote ELD in the areas of vocabulary, syntax, morphology, and discourse. Phonological and decoding skills, even rote reading, might be relatively independent of vocabulary and syntactic knowledge. Reading *comprehension* clearly is not. Successful literacy instruction for ELLs must contain large amounts of language development and support for understanding English. Vocabulary, syntax, and discourse in English must be stressed. The addition of an English as a second language (ESL) component for ELLs as part of Success for All (Slavin & Madden, 1999), a successful early reading program for Title I schools (Borman, Hewes, Overman, & Brown, 2002), suggests that a program that is effective for English speakers is not by itself sufficient for ELLs. Accommodations must be made due to ELLs' limited language proficiency, but there are many ways of accomplishing this.

Seventh, ELLs need instruction/assistance in gaining access to what they know in their first language and applying it to reading in English. Perhaps as a function of limited English vocabulary or other aspects of the English language they are in the process of acquiring, ELLs can have difficulty gaining access to background knowledge or even using skills they have mastered in their primary language (Jiménez, 1997). Gersten (1996) has proposed "structures, frameworks, scaffolds, and strategies" such as visual organizers and story maps to help students facilitate this transfer and organize information. He proposed that teachers use various mediation/feedback functions that are comprehensible, provide assignments students can complete, and focus on meaning rather than grammar or syntax. He also encouraged the use of native language responses. With the exception of the last item, the other functions can be seen as more or less generic "recommended practices" in teaching. For ELLs, however, consistent and conscious use of these practices is important to help them develop the skills essential for continued literacy development.

In summary, although there are many areas of uncertainty and disagreement, existing research suggests several literacy practices for ELLs, among them,

1. Make connections with students' culture, background, and experiences, which can promote high levels of student engagement.

2. Use direct, explicit instruction of basic and advanced skills.

3. Provide opportunities for reading and writing for pleasure, communication, and personally meaningful purposes.

4. When ELLs receive instruction in English, make accommodations for students' lack of proficiency in English.

5. In whichever language students are learning to read, emphasize phonological aspects of reading and mapping speech to print during the early stages of literacy development. Later stages rely more on vocabulary and syntactic knowledge of the language, which takes longer to develop than phonological skills.

6. Actively promote language development and support for English.

7. Help students gain access to and apply home language knowledge to reading English.

RESEARCH ON BILINGUAL AND BILITERACY DEVELOPMENT IN PRIMARY-GRADE CLASSROOMS

We are currently engaged in a multiyear, multisite investigation called "Oracy/Literacy Development in Spanish-Speaking Children," funded by the National Institute of Child Health and Human Development and the Institute of Education Sciences. This research project involves approximately 1,400 children in kindergarten

through grade 2 in schools in two urban sites in Texas, one site in
Border Texas, and one site in urban California. Schools were selected
based on 1) their average or better achievement levels (based on
accountability data in Texas and in California; in California, schools
could enter the study based on high achievement either in English
or in Spanish) and 2) their model of reading/language arts instruction
(i.e., primary language, two-way or dual language, English immersion). In Year 1 we piloted procedures and forms with 14 participating
Title I schools, with 105 participating K–2 classrooms and 848 students. The student sample consisted of 445 girls and 403 boys and
was largely Hispanic: 808 Hispanics, 24 African Americans, 2 Asians,
3 Caucasians, and 11 students whose ethnicity data were missing.
Individual projects in this program project concern the nature of
classroom instruction, development of students' language- and
literacy-related skills, and the home and community contexts in
which the students live. Additional projects focus on measurement
issues and, for a subset of students, changes in brain activation
patterns with development of language and literacy skills.

Our project concerns the nature of classroom instruction. We
document teachers' instructional practices by making extensive
classroom observations during reading/language arts. We note teaching competencies, strategies, quality and quantity of content, student
engagement, the presence of instructional aides, and the percentage
of time devoted to Spanish and English usage by teachers and students. We also record whether instructional materials are printed or
are on the computer and whether they are in English or in Spanish.

Descriptive studies have repeatedly indicated that typical reading instruction provides insufficient engaged reading opportunities
to facilitate reading growth for many students (Gelzheizer & Meyers,
1991; O'Sullivan, Ysseldyke, Christensen, & Thurlow, 1990; Simmons, Fuchs, Fuchs, Mathes, & Hodges, 1995; Vaughn, Hughes,
Schumm, & Klingner, 1998). For example, students spend approximately two thirds of their reading periods independent of the teacher
and engaged in nonreading or indirect reading activities (Allington &
McGill-Franzen, 1989; Simmons et al., 1995) and when students are
being instructed directly by the teacher, they spend about 70% of
their time passively watching and listening to the teacher or other
students, with little or no opportunity to actually read (O'Sullivan
et al., 1990; Simmons et al., 1995). Furthermore, it appears that
students most at risk for school failure actually receive fewer engaged
reading opportunities than their higher performing peers (O'Sullivan
et al., 1990). Arreaga-Mayer and Perdomo-Rivera (1996) observed 24

students categorized as limited English proficient (LEP) in grades 3–5 in 14 classrooms in three schools for the entire school day six times over the course of a school year. The observations revealed that the most frequently coded student behaviors in both general education and ESL classrooms were no talk (96% in general education, 92% in ESL classrooms) and use of no language, oral or written (82% general, 79% ESL). Academic talk (2% general, 6% ESL) and using the English language in oral and written communication occurred infrequently (18% general, 9% ESL). The percentage of the day spent in oral engagement was 4% in general education classrooms and 9% in ESL classrooms. These results suggest few linguistic opportunities for LEP students during the school day. The low percentages of oral engagement in ESL classrooms are particularly disturbing because those classrooms are specifically designed to build English language skills.

Measuring the Language and Content of Literacy Instruction

Measuring the quantity and quality of time allotment during the reading/language arts block is critically important to understanding teaching effectiveness (Allington, 1991). Accordingly, we modified a procedure used by Scanlon and Vellutino (1996) to quantify time spent on various reading/language art behaviors and use it in primary-grade classrooms in high-poverty schools in which 95% of the students were African American (Foorman & Schatschneider, 2003). According to our modified system, observers code the instructional format and content of teaching in designated intervals within each minute. Four categories of instructional format are noted, ranging from whole class or large group, to small groups, to all students working on their own with or without the teacher monitoring. There are five subject codes—reading/language arts, ELD, social studies, science, and math—and a code for transition between subjects. ELD is often called English as a second language (ESL) and focuses on language instruction for ELLs. Within the intervals devoted to recording the subject code, both a primary and a secondary subject can be recorded. For example, when reading/language arts and ELD are integrated, both codes might appear within the observational interval. Likewise, when science instruction occurs during the ELD period, both codes can be used within the observational interval. In addition, one observation per year can be conducted in social studies, science, and math to document the extent of literacy instruction.

Finally, there are 20 content codes: oral language (including listening comprehension and instruction in the structure of English and Spanish); book and print awareness; discussion of predictable text; phonemic awareness; alphabet letter recognition and reproduction; alphabetic instruction; structural analysis; word work; vocabulary; previewing a text before reading; spelling in the context of reading; reading text (teacher reads aloud, students read aloud, students read silently); students reading their own writing; reading comprehension (during or after reading); spelling instruction; writing composition; grammar or mechanics; giving directions, passing out materials, or referring to teacher's guide; nonreading activities; and feedback (e.g., corrective feedback, praise, punitive feedback). Behaviors that do not fit into any one of these 20 content areas are marked uncodable. A more detailed description of these categories is available in the appendix to this chapter. Good interrater reliability has been achieved on this coding system in English language classrooms (i.e., > .80; Foorman & Schatschneider, 2003).

Because we are also interested in the language of instruction in bilingual classrooms, we code the language used by the teacher during each minute and the language used by the students every other minute. We adjust for the fact that teachers' language is observed twice as frequently as students' language by analyzing data as a percentage of observed time. The coding reflects Spanish only, English only, a mix of Spanish and English, or missed. "Missed" means that there was no opportunity to observe teacher or student language due to the lack of language use or the observer's inability to hear well enough to make a decision. Observers also rate student engagement by recording whether each of four students randomly selected from the class roster were engaged in on-task or off-task behaviors. Finally, within the minute, observers also note whether an instructional aide is present or absent, whether instructional materials are in print format or on the computer, and the language of the instructional materials.

In order to make precise, within-the-minute recordings, observers wear headsets attached to audiotape players that indicate when to observe and when to record. The intervals for observing and recording within odd and even minutes are described in Table 13.1. Every 20 minutes observers take a 2-minute break. Observers are trained initially in a 2-day session at the beginning of the school year using videotapes of bilingual primary-grade classrooms. Interrater reliabilities are compared and serve as the basis of focused discussions of

Table 13.1. Time-sampling system

Odd minutes	
First 15 seconds	Observe all (instructional format, content, subject, materials, aide).
Next 5 seconds	Record observation.
Next 10 seconds	Observe teacher language.
Next 5 seconds	Record teacher language.
Next 10 seconds	Observe student engagement.
Next 5 seconds	Record student engagement.
Next 5 seconds	Record instructional aide.
Next 5 seconds	Wait for next minute; no observation or recording.
Even minutes	
First 15 seconds	Observe all (instructional format, content, subject, materials, aide).
Next 5 seconds	Record observation.
Next 20 seconds	Observe teacher and student language.
Next 5 seconds	Record teacher and student language.
Next 5 seconds	Record instructional aide.
Next 10 seconds	Wait for next minute; no observation or recording.

subtle differences between content codes in various contexts. Then observers practice in actual classrooms, comparing interrater reliabilities and working to achieve agreement of at least 80%. Once data collection begins, the coordinator and observer observe the same classroom for 10% of observations. To avoid drift, observers are retrained at mid-year by the coordinator. Based on this procedure, we have obtained adequate average interrater reliabilities during our first year of data collection. Interrater reliabilities were computed as the absolute percent agreement across the 5-second recording periods that follow each of the 10- to 20-second observation intervals within the minute (see Table 13.1). Interrater reliabilities are presented in Table 13.2 for all four sites across the three waves of data collection. Mean interrater reliabilities are high (80% or higher), with one of the urban Texas sites being the lowest. Minimum interrater reliabilities reflect individual observer variation, which was addressed by mid-year retraining.

Preliminary Description of the Language and Content of Instruction

The classrooms participating in this research study were selected as representative of one of three types of models of reading/language arts instruction for ELLs. Model 1 represents instruction in the primary language (in this case, Spanish) in classes with predominantly

Table 13.2. Mean, minimum, and maximum reliabilities on timed observation codes for four sites across three waves of data collection

	Sites											
	Urban Texas 1			Border Texas			Urban Texas 2			Urban California		
	M	Min	Max	M	Min	Max	M	Min	Max	M	Min	Max
Instructional format	98.0	93.3	100.0	97.6	94.3	99.5	87.3	58.6	100.0	93.3	43.8	100.0
Content code	97.3	94.3	99.0	97.2	94.8	99.5	80.2	51.0	97.1	86.4	37.6	100.0
Primary subject	99.5	98.1	100.0	99.0	96.7	100.0	89.8	52.4	100.0	99.3	96.7	100.0
Secondary subject	99.4	98.1	100.0	100.0	100.0	100.0	98.6	92.4	100.0	97.1	75.2	100.0
Print/ computer	100.0	100.0	100.0	100.0	100.0	100.0	99.8	99.0	100.0	100.0	100.0	100.0
Material language	97.9	94.8	100.0	98.2	93.8	100.0	91.7	53.8	100.0	96.9	86.2	100.0
Teacher language	95.3	87.6	100.0	93.3	87.1	100.0	85.6	54.3	99.0	98.3	93.3	100.0
Student engagement	99.0	97.6	100.0	99.5	98.1	100.0	97.1	91.0	100.0	99.0	93.8	100.0
Student language	97.2	94.8	98.6	97.7	95.7	100.0	92.5	78.1	99.0	99.0	97.6	100.0
Instructional aide	99.6	99.0	100.0	99.0	97.1	100.0	95.7	81.4	100.0	95.3	71.4	100.0

Spanish speakers. Within Model 1 there are schools that exit students into English instruction early (e.g., first or second grade) or later (e.g., third grade or later). These late-exit programs used to be referred to as "maintenance" programs but since 1984 have been referred to within Title VII of the amendments to the Elementary and Secondary Education Act as "developmental bilingual education" to emphasize the "importance of supporting the long-term linguistic, academic, and cognitive development of English language learners" (Ramirez, 1992, pp. 19–20). Model 2 depicts reading/language arts instruction in primary language and in English in classes that are ideally balanced in proportions of native English speakers and native Spanish speakers. This model is often called two-way immersion or dual language. Model 3 represents reading/language arts instruction in English and is often called immersion.

During Year 1 of the project, observers from the four sites observed each classroom three times during the school year—in the fall (October–November), winter (February), and spring (April–May). They observed during the reading/language arts period and during the ELD period, if there was one. As can be seen in Table 13.3, 67 of the 105 participating classrooms present reading/language arts and ELD as separate instructional periods, whereas 38 integrate these periods into a single reading/language arts class. There are differences between sites with regard to these formats. For example, in the second urban Texas site and in urban California, primary-language classrooms (Model 1) use the separate-class format, whereas in the first urban Texas site and the Border Texas site, Model 1 classrooms use either the separate or the integrated formats. The format for the immersion classrooms of Model 3 also varies by site: The second urban Texas site uses the integrated format, whereas the urban California site has both integrated and separate reading/language arts and ELD classes. However, dual-language classrooms at both of these sites tend to use the separate format more than the integrated format.

Across sites, language models, and grades, the mean number of minutes per day in the reading/language arts period was 105.96 minutes ($SD = 32.50$) and in the ELD period the mean was 58.49 minutes ($SD = 40.85$). Because of the relatively large variability in instructional time, we looked at the percentages of time spent in teacher and student language and the percentage of time allocated to various instructional content areas.

Language Usage   The percentages of time during the reading/language arts period and (given parenthetically) the ELD period that

Table 13.3. Number of reading/language arts classrooms with or without additional English language development (ELD) classrooms by site, language model, and grade

Site	Language model	Grade	Reading/language arts and ELD	Reading/language arts	Total teachers
Urban Texas 1	Model 1	K	4	1	5
		1	4	2	6
		2	6	2	8
Border Texas	Model 1	K	4	4	8
		1	4	4	8
		2	2	6	8
Urban Texas 2	Model 1	K	5	0	5
		1	4	0	4
		2	4	0	4
	Model 2	K	4	0	4
		1	4	3	7
		2	2	1	3
	Model 3	K	0	2	2
		1	0	2	2
		2	0	2	2
Urban California	Model 1	K	2	0	2
		1	2	0	2
		2	2	0	2
	Model 2	K	2	0	2
		1	3	0	3
		2	2	2	4
	Model 3	K	3	1	4
		1	3	2	5
		2	1	4	5
TOTAL CLASSES			67	38	105

teachers speak in Spanish, in English, in a mix of both languages, or no language (i.e., missed) are presented in Table 13.4 by site, language model, and grade. Generally, these data fit with the language model. Instruction in Model 3's immersion classrooms is almost completely in English in grades K–2, both in reading/language arts and in ELD. Reading/language arts instruction in Model 2's dual-language classrooms is primarily in Spanish, with ELD instruction occurring almost exclusively in English from kindergarten. Instruction in Model 1's primary-language classrooms is mainly in Spanish in kindergarten, but the percentage of English instruction increases

Table 13.4. Percentage of time teachers spent with language use categorized as Spanish (SP), English (E), mixed (MIX), or missing (M) in reading/language arts and (parenthetically) English language development (ELD) by site, language model, and grade

Language model and grade	Urban Texas 1				Border Texas				Urban Texas 2[a]				Urban California			
	SP	E	MIX	M	SP	E	MIX	M	SP	E	MIX	M	SP	E	MIX	M
Model 1																
K	68 (25)	8 (42)	17 (20)	7 (13)	53 (8)	26 (53)	15 (34)	6 (4)	71 (24)	25 (45)	1 (22)	3 (9)	69 (0)	14 (98)	12 (2)	5 (0)
Grade 1	63 (19)	5 (42)	27 (27)	5 (12)	42 (4)	44 (78)	9 (11)	5 (7)	60 (26)	20 (30)	12 (27)	8 (17)	70 (0)	29 (94)	1 (1)	0 (5)
Grade 2	32 (5)	36 (78)	16 (5)	16 (13)	9 (1)	72 (88)	13 (8)	6 (4)	55 (12)	34 (63)	8 (17)	3 (9)	66 (0)	31 (98)	2 (1)	1 (1)
Model 2																
K									88 (0)	8 (84)	1 (5)	3 (6)	98 (1)	2 (97)	0 (2)	0 (0)
Grade 1									78 (0)	8 (90)	3 (3)	11 (7)	91 (0)	9 (99)	0 (0)	0 (1)
Grade 2									76 (0)	16 (97)	1 (1)	7 (3)	56 (0)	38 (99)	5 (1)	1 (0)
Model 3																
K									1	81	11	7	0 (0)	96 (97)	3 (3)	1 (0)
Grade 1									2	85	9	4	0 (0)	98 (98)	0 (0)	2 (2)
Grade 2									9	71	13	7	0 (0)	96 (93)	0 (7)	3 (0)

[a]In the second urban Texas site, there was no separate ELD class for students in the immersion program.

by grade 2, and this generally holds for both reading/language arts and ELD.

There are numerous site differences in teacher language across different language models. Model 3's immersion classrooms in urban California use all English from kindergarten through grade 2. In contrast, immersion classrooms in urban Texas use some proportion of Spanish and mixed language (i.e., 11%–21% combined across classrooms in urban Texas), and this is evident through grade 2. Likewise, urban Texas and urban California contrast somewhat in language usage in Model 2's dual-language classrooms: Both sites build English through the ELD period. However, they differ somewhat in language usage during the reading/language arts period: In urban California, instruction is almost exclusively in Spanish in kindergarten and grade 1 and then more balanced in Spanish and English in grade 2. In urban Texas, instruction remains predominantly in Spanish across the three grades.

Finally, site differences in Model 1's primary-language emphasis are consistent with an early exit model in Border Texas and a later exit model in the second urban Texas site. In Border Texas, Spanish instruction during reading/language arts drops from 53% in kindergarten to 9% in grade 2, whereas English instruction during ELD increases from 53% to 88%. This contrasts with drops from 71% to 55% in Spanish instruction during reading/language arts instruction in the second urban Texas site and corresponding increases in English during ELD from 45% to 63%. Urban California looks like a later exit or developmental bilingual education program in terms of the predominance of Spanish during reading/language instruction. The first urban Texas site seems to fall between the early exit strategy apparent in Border Texas and the later exit approach of the second urban Texas site. Spanish instruction in the first site drops from 68% in kindergarten to 32% in grade 2, with English usage during ELD rising from 42% to 78%. However, teachers use a mix of Spanish and English for instruction during both reading/language arts and ELD (5%–27%).

The corresponding description of student language is presented in Table 13.5. Percentages of student language categorized as Spanish, English, mixed, or missed are given for the reading/language arts block and, parenthetically, for the ELD block. In the second urban Texas site, there is no separate ELD class for students in Model 3's immersion classrooms. Student language during the reading/language arts block generally supports the language models, as does

Table 13.5. Percentage of time students spent with language use categorized as Spanish (SP), English (E), mixed (MIX), or missing (M) in reading/language arts and (parenthetically) English language development (ELD) by site, language model, and grade

Language model and grade	Urban Texas 1				Border Texas				Urban Texas 2[a]				Urban California			
	SP	E	MIX	M	SP	E	MIX	M	SP	E	MIX	M	SP	E	MIX	M
Model 1																
K	71 (44)	2 (21)	5 (11)	22 (24)	39 (17)	10 (10)	47 (70)	4 (2)	82 (39)	4 (27)	3 (18)	11 (16)	83 (0)	11 (89)	4 (7)	2 (4)
Grade 1	89 (54)	3 (7)	7 (32)	1 (7)	38 (4)	31 (55)	26 (37)	5 (4)	56 (32)	17 (14)	11 (31)	15 (22)	71 (0)	28 (84)	0 (16)	1 (0)
Grade 2	43 (17)	25 (62)	14 (13)	18 (8)	8 (2)	50 (71)	33 (24)	9 (3)	54 (33)	22 (38)	12 (16)	12 (13)	78 (0)	21 (87)	0 (13)	1 (0)
Model 2																
K									81 (10)	0 (54)	10 (23)	8 (13)	97 (0)	1 (90)	2 (10)	0 (0)
Grade 1									77 (0)	0 (61)	11 (26)	12 (13)	99 (0)	1 (98)	0 (0)	0 (2)
Grade 2									85 (0)	2 (51)	5 (31)	8 (18)	72 (0)	24 (94)	4 (0)	0 (6)
Model 3																
K									5	56	14	25	0 (0)	99 (97)	1 (3)	0 (0)
Grade 1									4	63	28	5	0 (0)	97 (100)	0 (0)	3 (0)
Grade 2									2	67	12	18	0 (0)	91 (87)	1 (13)	8 (0)

[a]In the second urban Texas site, there was no separate ELD class for students in the immersion program.

the teacher language. That is, in immersion classrooms, students primarily speak in English, whereas in Model 1's early and later exit classrooms and Model 2's dual-language classrooms, students primarily speak Spanish. However, in Model 1 classrooms in Border Texas, it is the mixing of Spanish and English that stands out: 26%–47% coded as mixed in reading/language arts classes and 24%–70% in ELD classes. There are further site differences in Model 1 classrooms during ELD: A relatively large percentage of Spanish is used in the second urban Texas site in all three grades and in the Border Texas site in kindergarten and grade 1 compared with low percentages of Spanish in Border Texas after grade 1 and in urban California. English is mainly used in Model 2's dual-language classrooms during ELD, but urban California's percentages are much larger than Model 3 sites: 90%–98% versus 51%–61%. Thus, when the mixing of languages is taken into account in Border Texas, one sees a distinctive difference in the ratio of Spanish to English between the Texas sites and the California site: Students in the three Texas sites use more Spanish than do students in the California site, during both reading/language arts and ELD classes.

Instructional Content   Allocation of time to instructional content was first examined by looking at frequencies of all 20 content codes described previously. To facilitate comparisons across sites, language models, and grades, the following superordinate categories were created. Few data were designated as uncodable (i.e., < 5%) or in the feedback category (i.e., medians of 0% and 3% for ELD and reading/language arts, respectively).

- Word Work—book and print awareness/conventions, alphabet letter recognition and reproduction, phonemic awareness, alphabetic instruction, structural analysis, and word work with or without text

- Oral Language—oral language/discussion, English language strategies, Spanish language strategies, and vocabulary

- Writing/Spelling—writing composition (e.g., student composition, student dictation, teacher-led writing), spelling in the context of reading (often from a speller), grammar, and students reading their own writing

- Reading Texts—teacher reading aloud, students reading aloud, students reading silently, and students singing or chanting in connection to text

- Reading Comprehension—discussions of predictable text, previewing to prepare for reading, and reading comprehension strategies for addressing literal and inferential questions and for responding with written summaries

- Nonreading Activities—chaos or other activities unrelated to reading instruction (e.g., transitions/off-task, teacher out of class, teacher checking papers or doing clerical work, discipline, interruptions due to visitors or intercom announcements)

- Direction Giving—activities related to instruction (e.g., passing out materials, referring to the teacher's guide)

The percentage of time allocated to each superordinate category was computed both for the ELD period and for the reading/language period across all three observation points. Percentages for ELD are given in Table 13.6 by site, language model, and grade. There are four notable points about the data in Table 13.6. First, irrespective of language model, teachers in urban California allocate much higher percentages of time to Oral Language instruction in each grade (ranging from 30% to 87%) than do teachers in the three Texas sites (ranging from 7% to 27%).

Second, teachers in the Texas sites tend to allocate more time to Word Work, Reading Texts, and Reading Comprehension than do teachers in the urban California site, except for kindergarten teachers in Model 3's immersion classrooms in California, who spend 37% of instructional time on Word Work. The nature of the reading activities varies within these Texas sites, with teachers in Border Texas devoting more time to Word Work and teachers in the urban sites devoting more time to working with text. The text-work varies within these two urban Texas sites, with teachers in the first site Reading Texts to or with the students, and teachers in the second site emphasizing Reading Comprehension. Urban California teachers also spent time Reading Texts to or with their students during ELD, and only one grade-level in one language model (grade 1 in

Table 13.6. Percentage of time allocated to instructional categories during English language development (ELD) class by site, language model, and grade

Site	Language model	Grade	Percentage of time during ELD						
			Word Work	Oral Language	Writing/ Spelling	Reading Texts	Reading Comprehension	Non-reading	Giving Directions
Urban Texas 1	Model 1	K	22	21	14	17	9	12	5
		1	4	17	14	34	3	11	18
		2	20	9	18	14	15	13	11
Border Texas	Model 1	K	52	27	0	0	0	2	19
		1	31	15	24	8	9	2	12
		2	24	9	25	20	7	3	11
Urban Texas 2	Model 1	K	14	23	0	19	23	9	13
		1	24	9	10	26	10	6	14
		2	14	7	3	19	32	11	15
	Model 2	K	8	28	0	12	33	12	9
		1	5	17	0	12	43	12	11
		2	0	10	10	24	31	4	21
Urban California	Model 1	K	0	70	0	4	0	7	19
		1	1	36	0	30	12	10	11
		2	0	65	0	27	0	2	7
	Model 2	K	0	81	0	9	0	5	5
		1	0	49	0	15	28	4	5
		2	0	65	0	32	0	0	3
	Model 3	K	37	35	0	7	0	3	18
		1	10	30	10	25	8	11	7
		2	0	87	0	0	0	13	0

Note: There was no ELD block for immersion classes in the second urban Texas site.

Table 13.7. Percentage of time allocated to instructional categories during reading/language arts class by site, language model, and grade

Site	Language model	Grade	Percentage of time during reading/language arts						
			Word Work	Oral Language	Writing/ Spelling	Reading Texts	Reading Comprehension	Non-reading	Giving Directions
Urban Texas 1	Model 1	K	35	14	11	16	4	6	15
		1	23	7	14	18	10	7	21
		2	17	9	18	19	18	7	12
Border Texas	Model 1	K	37	15	10	9	9	2	15
		1	28	13	18	14	9	3	16
		2	16	11	26	18	16	2	11
Urban Texas 2	Model 1	K	24	20	11	12	4	13	16
		1	16	11	9	23	13	8	19
		2	8	15	24	17	18	3	14
	Model 2	K	24	16	9	10	18	10	13
		1	11	12	15	15	21	10	14
		2	4	18	17	26	17	3	15
	Model 3	K	40	10	8	8	9	11	14
		1	24	3	18	24	9	4	17
		2	20	15	12	19	17	6	12
Urban California	Model 1	K	27	28	12	12	1	3	12
		1	9	9	36	20	6	6	14
		2	13	19	23	22	9	3	10
	Model 2	K	13	43	15	5	0	6	18
		1	10	19	9	22	13	13	11
		2	13	13	21	19	21	4	10
	Model 3	K	28	22	12	15	8	4	12
		1	22	13	20	24	8	3	10
		2	15	16	26	21	8	6	8

Model 2's dual-language classrooms) has a notable amount of time devoted to Reading Comprehension (28%).

Third, sites differ in the percentage of time allocated to Writing/ Spelling. First- and second-grade teachers in Border Texas devote one quarter of ELD time to Writing/Spelling. Teachers in the first urban Texas site allocate 14%–18% of their time to Writing/Spelling, but teachers in the other two Texas sites allocate 0%–10% of time to this category.

Fourth, classrooms in all sites are characterized by relatively low amounts of Nonreading Activities (< 13%), with Border Texas being the lowest (< 4%). Percentage of time Giving Directions varies by grade within site.

The percentages of time allocated to instructional categories during the reading/language arts period are presented in Table 13.7. First, we discuss Model 2's dual-language classrooms and Model 3's immersion classrooms in the second urban Texas site and in the urban California site. Remember, in Model 2's dual-language kindergartens, instruction is almost entirely in Spanish in kindergarten and grade 1 in these two sites. However, the percentages of time spent on Word Work, Oral Language development, Writing/Spelling, and Reading Comprehension differ between sites. Teachers in the second urban Texas site spend 24% of time on Word Work, 10% of time Reading Texts, and 18% of time on Reading Comprehension activities. In contrast, kindergarten teachers in urban California spend 43% of time on Oral Language activities, 13% on Word Work, and 5% on Reading Texts. In grades 1 and 2, the two sites look more similar.

Model 3's immersion classrooms in the second urban Texas site and the California site differ subtly in profiles of time allocation depicted at the bottom of Table 13.7. In the urban Texas site, more time is spent on Word Work (40% versus 28% in kindergarten) and Reading Comprehension (17% versus 8% in grade 2). In the urban California site, more time is spent in Oral Language and Writing/ Spelling activities in all three grades.

Model 1's primary-language classrooms exist in all four sites. To compare time allocations, it is helpful to refer to within-grade graphs. Kindergarten graphs are presented in Figure 13.1. Profiles of time allocation in kindergarten are similar for the sites in the top of the graph and for those in the bottom of the graph. An emphasis on Word Work dominates reading/language arts instruction in the urban Texas site and Border Texas (35% and 37%, respectively), although the emphasis on Reading Texts relative to working on Reading Comprehension is not apparent in Border Texas as it is in all other sites. Remember that Spanish is the primary language of instruction in kindergarten at these sites. Teachers in Border Texas, however, instruct in English 26% of the time, making their classrooms more representative of an early exit program. Kindergarten classrooms in urban California engage in more Oral Language Activities than in the other sites (28%), and kindergarten teachers in the second urban Texas site spend more time in Nonreading Activities (13%).

Time allocation in first-grade primary-language classrooms is depicted in Figure 13.2. Again, the similarities in sites in the top row and in the sites in the bottom row are notable. In the first urban Texas site and the Border Texas site, there are still significant proportions of time devoted to Word Work (23% and 28%, respectively) and increases from kindergarten in proportions of time devoted to Writing/Spelling and Reading Texts and, in urban Texas, increases in Reading Comprehension. In the bottom of Figure 13.2, the large amount of time devoted to Writing/Spelling in urban California is notable (36%). We note the decrease from kindergarten in time allocated to Word Work (15% and 9%, respectively) and note increases in Reading Texts and Reading Comprehension in both sites. All sites devote significant proportions of time to Giving Directions (14%–21%). With respect to instructional language, Spanish is used the majority of time in the first-grade classrooms in all sites but Border Texas. In that site, the ratio of Spanish to English is 42% to 44%. In the first urban Texas site, there is a relatively large degree of mixing of languages (27%).

Time allocation profiles in grade 2 primary-language classrooms are provided in Figure 13.3. Again, there are similarities in profiles between the sites in the top row and between the sites in the bottom row. In the first urban Texas site and the Border Texas site, relatively large proportions of time are devoted to Word Work, Writing/Spelling, Reading Texts, and working on Reading Comprehension and less time to Oral Language activities. In contrast, profiles for the second urban Texas site and the urban California site show more time allocation to Oral Language and less to Word Work. In addition, Texas sites differ from the California site in that the time allotted to Reading Texts versus the time given for Reading Comprehension is relatively balanced in the Texas sites compared with the California site, where more than twice as much time is spent on Reading Texts

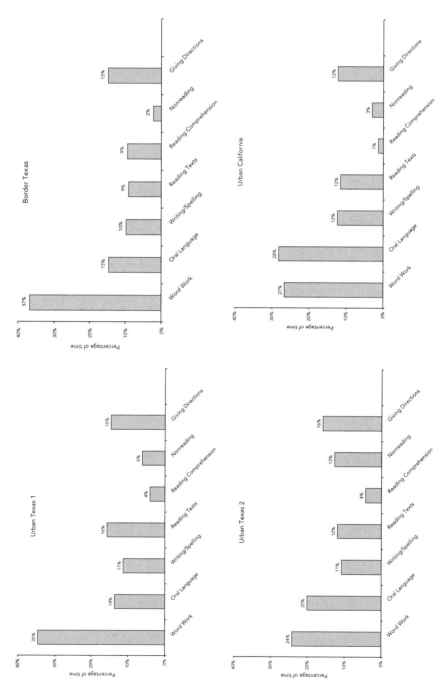

Figure 13.1 Percentage of time allocated to reading/language arts activities in kindergarten primary-language classrooms in four sites in urban Texas, Border Texas, and urban California.

314

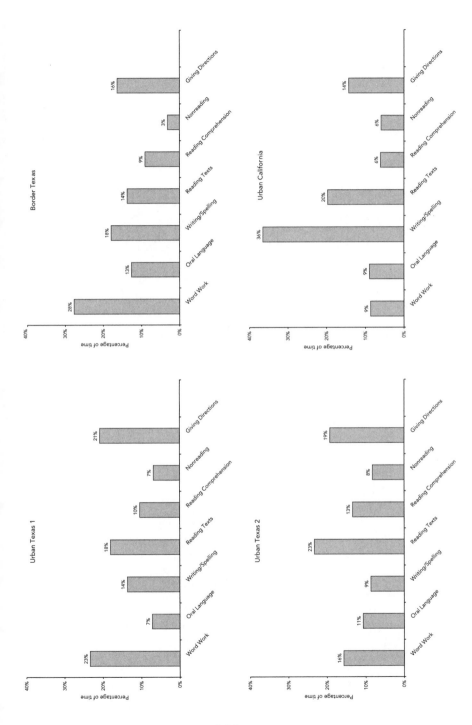

Figure 13.2 Percentage of time allocated to reading/language arts activities in grade 1 primary-language classrooms in four sites in urban Texas, Border Texas, and urban California.

315

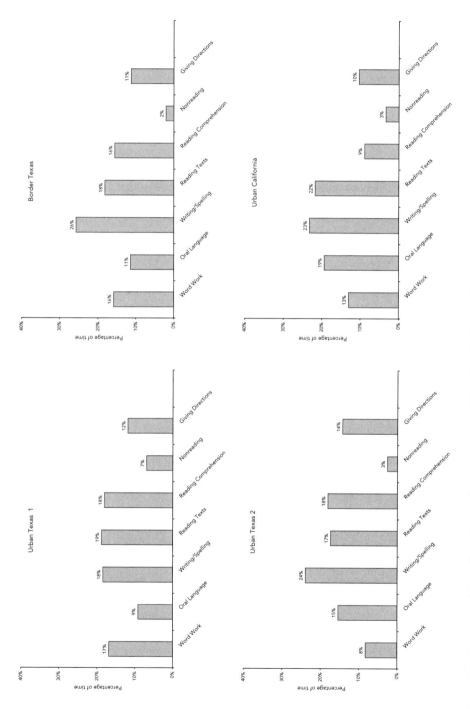

Figure 13.3 Percentage of time allocated to reading/language arts activities in grade 2 primary-language classrooms in four sites in urban Texas, Border Texas, and urban California.

316

(22%) as on Reading Comprehension (9%). A notable amount of time across sites (10%–14%) is still devoted to Giving Directions.

CONCLUSION

In this chapter we have described a reliable observational system for measuring the language and content of primary-grade classrooms with large numbers of ELLs. In addition, we provided preliminary cross-sectional data in 105 kindergarten, grade 1, and grade 2 classrooms in four sites in Texas and California engaged in three models of reading/language arts instruction: primary-language instruction in Spanish (Model 1), two-way or dual-language instruction (Model 2), and English immersion (Model 3). Percentages of teacher language classified as Spanish, English, mixed, or missed during reading/language arts classes tend to support the various language models. That is, English is used primarily in Model 3's immersion classes, both English and Spanish in Model 2's dual-language classes, and a decelerating use of Spanish and accelerating use of English in Model 1's primary-language classrooms. There are differences between sites, however, such as more mixed language in two of the Texas sites. Site differences are further accentuated when ELD classes are considered. More time is allocated to developing English skills in ELD classes in the urban California site, in contrast to the emphasis on developing reading skills in the Texas sites. In Border Texas, ELD classes consist of more opportunities for Writing/Spelling.

The pattern of student language, like that of teacher language, tends to support the language models. During the reading/language arts block, students tend to speak Spanish in Model 1's primary-language and Model 2's dual-language classrooms and English in Model 3's immersion classrooms. However, a relatively large amount of language mixing was observed, especially in the Border Texas site. During ELD classes, students tend to speak mainly Spanish in Model 1's primary-language classes in both urban Texas sites and in Model 2's dual-language classrooms in the second urban Texas site. Thus, when the mixing of languages is taken into account, a geographical difference in student language emerges: There is more use of primary language in the Texas sites compared with the California site.

When the content of literacy instruction is examined, we see some common themes emerging from the profiles of time allocation in both ELD and reading/language arts classes. First, more time tends to be allocated to Oral Language activities in the urban California site than in the Texas sites. In contrast, in the Texas sites more time tends to be allocated to the reading-related activities of Word Work and Reading Comprehension. All sites tend to spend more time Reading Texts than working on Reading Comprehension except in the second urban Texas site. Interestingly, classrooms in this second urban Texas site emphasize Reading Comprehension over Reading Texts not just in reading/language arts classes but during ELD classes as well. As we follow these students over time, it will be interesting to see how the relative trade-offs of different allocations of instructional time affect achievement outcomes. Is it better to allocate more time to building oral language skills through vocabulary instruction and discussions of text read to students or is it better to emphasize word-level decoding and comprehension of text that students read? Researchers (e.g., Fitzgerald & Noblit, 2000) have stressed the importance of building oral language skills while alphabetic knowledge is mastered so that text comprehension does not suffer later. However, no one has examined how allocation of instructional time or language use explains variability in student outcomes.

Finally, our sites were relatively similar in their percentages of time devoted to Nonreading Activities and Giving Directions (0%–14% for Nonreading Activities and 0%–21% for Giving Directions). These percentages are nowhere near the 67% of noninstructional time many researchers have noted (Allington & McGill-Franzen, 1989; Simmons et al., 1995), and this may be due to our method of sampling schools based on state accountability data. Nonreading activities have been shown to negatively relate to rating of teaching effectiveness for first-grade teachers (Foorman, Schatschneider, Fletcher, Francis, & Moats, 2003). However, the impact on student outcomes of teachers' time spent giving directions is less clear. Taylor, Peterson, Pearson, and Rodriguez observed classrooms in eight high-poverty elementary schools and concluded that "the more a teacher was coded as telling children information, the less the children grew in reading achievement" (2002, p. 278). They interpreted this finding as supporting a "student-support stance" in contrast to a "teacher-directed stance" in the classroom. There may, however, be a threshold for giving directions related to instruction beyond which student achievement is adversely affected. Furthermore, we surmise that it is not just the *quantity* of time devoted to teaching particular content that matters but that it is the *quality* of teaching that ultimately matters for student learning.

In summary, instructional practices and the language used in classrooms with large numbers of ELLs emerge as distinct variables in the data presented in this chapter, and both variables vary by site. Site differences will be informed by our analyses of home and community variables. Our next step is to look at how these classroom-level variables moderate relations between students' language and literacy proficiency at the beginning of the year and their achievement outcomes at the end of the year, taking into account contextual differences among sites. Classrooms are complex systems, and only by working with teachers to systematically gather evidence of what counts as good teaching can we improve instructional practices for all students, including ELLs.

REFERENCES

Allington, R.L. (1991). Children who find learning to read difficult: School responses to diversity. In E.H. Hiebert (Ed.), *Literacy for a diverse society* (pp. 237–252). New York: Teachers College Press.

Allington, R.L., & McGill-Franzen, A. (1989). School response to reading failure: Instruction for Chapter One and special education students in grades two, four, and eight. *The Elementary School Journal, 89*, 529–542.

Anderson, V., & Roit, M. (1996). Linking reading comprehension instruction to language development for language-minority students. *The Elementary School Journal, 96*, 295–310.

Arreaga-Mayer, C., & Perdomo-Rivera, C. (1996). Ecobehavioral analysis of instruction for at-risk language-minority students. *The Elementary School Journal, 96*, 245–258.

August, D., & Hakuta, K. (1997). *Improving schooling for language-minority children.* Washington, DC: National Academies Press.

Baker, K. (1998). Structured English immersion: Breakthrough in teaching limited-English-proficient students. *Phi Delta Kappan, 80*, 199–204.

Borman, G.D., Hewes, G.M., Overman, L.T., & Brown, S. (2002). Comprehensive school reform and student achievement: A meta-analysis. *Review of Educational Research, 73*, 125–230.

Cazabon, M., Nicoladis, E., & Lambert, W. (1998). *Becoming bilingual in the Amigos two-way immersion program* (Research Report No. 3). Washington, DC: Center for Research on Education, Diversity & Excellence and the Center for Applied Linguistics.

Chall, J.S. (1983). *Stages of reading development.* New York: McGraw-Hill.

Christian, D. (1994). *Two-way bilingual education: Students learning through two languages* (Education Practice Report No. 12). Santa Cruz, CA, and Washington, DC: National Center for Research on Cultural Diversity and Second Language Learning.

Crawford, J. (1991). *Bilingual education: History, politics, theory, and practice* (2nd ed.). Los Angeles: Bilingual Education Services.

Cummins, J. (1999). Alternative paradigms in bilingual education research: Does theory have a place? *Educational Researcher, 28*(7), 26–32.

Echevarria, J., & Graves, A. (1998). *Sheltered content instruction: Teaching English-language learners with diverse abilities.* Boston: Allyn & Bacon.

Elley, W., & Mangubhai, F. (1983). The impact of reading on second language learning. *Reading Research Quarterly, 19,* 53–67.

Fitzgerald, J. (1995). English-as-a-second-language reading instruction in the United States: A research review. *Journal of Reading Behavior, 27,* 115–152.

Fitzgerald, J., & Noblit, G. (2000). Balance in the making: Learning to read in an ethnically diverse first-grade classroom. *Journal of Educational Psychology, 92,* 3–22.

Foorman, B.R., & Schatschneider, C. (2003). Measurement of teaching practices during reading/language arts instruction and its relationship to student achievement. In S. Vaughn & K.L. Briggs (Eds.), *Reading in the classroom: Systems for the observation of teaching and learning* (pp. 1–30). Baltimore: Paul H. Brookes Publishing Co.

Foorman, B.R., Schatschneider, C., Fletcher, J.M., Francis, D.J., & Moats, L.C. (2003). *The impact of instructional practices in Grades 1 and 2 on reading and spelling achievement in high poverty schools.* Manuscript submitted for publication.

Gelzheizer, L.M., & Meyers, J. (1991). Reading instruction by classroom, remedial and resource room teachers. *The Journal of Special Education, 24,* 512–526.

Gersten, R. (1985). Structured immersion for language minority students: Results of a longitudinal evaluation. *Educational Evaluation and Policy Analysis, 7,* 187–196.

Gersten, R. (1996). Literacy instruction for language-minority students: The transition years. *The Elementary School Journal, 96,* 227–244.

Geva, E. (2000). Issues in the assessment of reading disabilities in L2 children: Beliefs and research evidence. *Dyslexia, 6,* 13–28.

Geva, E., Yaghoub-Zadeh, Z., & Schuster, B. (2000). Understanding individual differences in word recognition skills of ESL children. *Annals of Dyslexia, 50,* 123–154.

Goldenberg, C. (1998). A balanced approach to early Spanish literacy instruction. In R.M. Gersten & R.T. Jiménez (Eds.), *Promoting learning for culturally and linguistically diverse students* (pp. 3–25). Belmont, CA: Wadsworth.

Greene, J. (1998). *A meta-analysis of the effectiveness of bilingual education.* Claremont, CA: Tomas Rivera Policy Institute.

Howard, E., & Christian, D. (1997). *The development of bilingualism and biliteracy in two-way immersion students.* Paper presented at the annual meeting of the American Educational Research Association, Chicago.

Jiménez, R. (1997). The strategic reading abilities and potential of five low-literacy Latina/o readers in middle school. *Reading Research Quarterly, 32,* 224–243.

Lindholm, K. (1996). *Evaluation of academic achievement in two-way bilingual education programs.* Paper presented at the annual meeting of the American Educational Research Association, New York.

Linn, R.L., Baker, E.L., & Betebenner, D.W. (2002, June). *Accountability systems: Implications of requirements of the No Child Left Behind Act of 2001* (Center for the Study of Evaluation Technical Report 567). Retrieved October 23, 2003, from http://www.cse.ucla.edu/CRESST/Reports/TR567.pdf

Meyer, M.M., & Fienberg, S.E. (Eds.). (1992). *Assessing evaluation studies: The case of bilingual education strategies.* Washington, DC: National Academies Press.

National Center for Educational Statistics (NCES). (2001a). *Common core of data (CDD): State nonfiscal survey of public elementary/secondary education.* Washington, DC: U.S. Department of Education.

National Center for Educational Statistics (NCES). (2001b). *Fourth grade reading highlights 2000: The nation's report card.* Washington, DC: U.S. Department of Education.

National Educational Research Policy and Priorities Board. (1999, July 15–16). *Proceedings of the Improving the Education of English Language Learners: Best Practices conference.* Washington, DC: Author.

No Child Left Behind Act of 2001, PL 107-110, 115 Stat. 1425, 20 U.S.C. §§ 6301 *et seq.*

O'Sullivan, P.J., Ysseldyke, J.E., Christensen, S.L., & Thurlow, M.L. (1990). Mildly handicapped elementary students' opportunity to learn during reading instruction in mainstream and special education settings. *Reading Research Quarterly, 25,* 131–146.

Peal, E., & Lambert, W.E. (1962). The relation of bilingualism to intelligence. *Psychological Monographs: General and Applied, 76,* 1–23.

Ramirez, J.D. (1992). Executive summary. *Bilingual Research Journal, 16,* 1–62.

Rossell, C.H., & Baker, K. (1996). The educational effectiveness of bilingual education. *Research in the Teaching of English, 3,* 7–74.

Scanlon, D.M., & Vellutino, F.R. (1996). Prerequisite skills, early instruction, and success in first-grade reading: Selected results from a longitudinal study. *Mental Retardation and Developmental Research Reviews, 2,* 54–63.

Siegel, L. (1999). The Canadian experience. In *Effective instruction for English language learners: A discussion sponsored by California Education Policy Seminar and the California State University Institute for Educational Reform* (pp. 3–6). Sacramento, CA: The CSU Institute for Educational Reform.

Simmons, D.C., Fuchs, L.S., Fuchs, D., Mathes, P.G., & Hodges, J.P. (1995). Effects of explicit teaching and peer mediated instruction on the reading achievement of learning disabled and low performing students. *The Elementary School Journal, 95,* 387–408.

Slavin, R., & Madden, N. (1999). *Effects of bilingual and English-as-a-second-language adaptations of Success for All on the reading achievement of students acquiring English.* Unpublished manuscript.

Snow, C.E., Burns, M.S., & Griffin, P. (Eds.). (1998). *Preventing reading difficulties in young children.* Washington, DC: National Academies Press.

Taylor, B.M., Peterson, D.S., Pearson, P.D., & Rodriguez, M.C. (2002). Looking inside classrooms: Reflecting on the "how" as well as the "what" in effective reading instruction. *Reading Teacher, 56*(3), 270–279.

Tharp, R. (1982). The effective instruction of comprehension: Results and description of the Kamehameha Early Education Program. *Reading Research Quarterly, 17*, 503–527.

Thomas, W.P., & Collier, V. (1997). *School effectiveness for language minority students.* Washington, DC: National Clearinghouse for Bilingual Education.

Thomas, W.P., & Collier, V. (2002). *A national study of school effectiveness for language minority students' long-term academic achievement: Final Report, Project 1.1.* Santa Cruz, CA: Center for Research on Education, Diversity & Excellence (Available on-line: http://www.crede.ucsc.edu/research/llaa/1.1_final.html).

Vaughn, S., Hughes, M.T., Schumm, J.S., & Klingner, J. (1998). A collaborative effort to enhance reading and writing instruction in inclusive classrooms. *Learning Disability Quarterly, 21*, 57–74.

Willig, A.C. (1985). A meta-analysis of selected studies on the effectiveness of bilingual education. *Review of Educational Research, 55*, 269–317.

Wong-Fillmore, L., Ammon, P., McLaughlin, B., & Ammon, M. (1985). *Learning English through bilingual instruction: Final report.* Berkeley: University of California.

Wong-Fillmore, L., & Valadez, C. (1986). Teaching bilingual learners. In M.C. Wittrock (Ed.), *Handbook of research on teaching* (3rd ed., pp. 648–685). New York: Macmillan.

Appendix
Bilingual Timed Observation Codes

SUBJECT

R Reading/language arts
C Science
M Math
S Social studies
E English language development
T Transition between subjects

INSTRUCTIONAL FORMAT

1 Teacher works with whole class or large group.
2 Teacher works with 1–2 students or with small or cooperative groups (3–6 students).
3 All students work on their own, individually or in groups, with teacher monitoring.
4 All students work on their own, individually or in groups. Teacher is *not* monitoring.
5 Nonreading instruction

LANGUAGE OF INSTRUCTION

E (English) Instruction is in English.
S (Spanish) Instruction is in Spanish.
M (Mixed) Instruction is in English and Spanish.
X (Missed) No language was recorded.

CONTENT

The following content codes are listed in numerical order, not by superordinate category. Chapter 13 lists the superordinate categories and the content codes within each category.

1. **Oral language/discussion**   This oral discussion usually occurs without a written stimulus; in *kindergarten,* there may be a written stimulus, such as a calendar, picture cards, and so forth. The teacher is leading an activity that is intended to develop students' *verbal* skills. This includes a variety of activities that help to develop oral skills in the area of vocabulary, grammar, and syntax. Examples include asking children to identify things (e.g., body parts, colors, days of the week); working on directional terms; discussing the items and activities associated with a special place such as the beach; and discussing days of the week, names of months, and seasons. This can also take the form of sharing in which the teacher elicits or allows children to talk about their personal experience, tell a story, and so forth. Examples in *kindergarten* include calendar activities, singing along with a prerecorded audiotape, and so forth.

   a. *Listening comprehension*   The teacher is focused on the children's understanding of the text they are hearing. Discussion may include structural details (e.g., plot, characters) and knowledge related to what was read. This is all oral work. Children are not reading the text.

   b. *English language strategies*   Oral language instruction in English strategies focuses on teaching the structure of English (e.g., vocabulary, grammar). The teacher may state, "In English we say _____," or the class may be labeled as English as a second language (ESL) or may use a specialized curriculum.

   c. *Spanish language strategies*   Oral language instruction in Spanish strategies focuses on teaching the structure of Spanish (e.g., vocabulary, grammar). The teacher may state, "In Spanish we say _____," or the class may be labeled as a Spanish language class.

2. **Book and print awareness/conventions**   The teacher is acquainting the children with print. This includes things such

as conventions of print use and the format of a book, including title page, author, reading left to right, table of contents, and genre of book. In *kindergarten,* the teacher may emphasize the following: moving top to bottom and left to right, recognizing that printed words are separated by spaces, recognizing upper- and lowercase letters in isolation or in printed words, and recognizing the significance of capitalization and punctuation (e.g., periods, punctuation marks, quotation marks).

3. **Discussion of predictable text**   Instruction with predictable text consists of explicit discussion of patterns that are repeated in a text. The teacher draws attention to patterns. In *kindergarten,* these patterns may be rhymes, repeated phrases, and so forth.

4. **Phonemic awareness**   Instruction in phonemic awareness is all instruction that is targeted at directing the children's attention to the sounds in language and/or manipulating these sounds. These activities do *not* include explicit reference to text. In some cases, text may be presented, but the teacher is not providing explicit instruction about the link between the sounds and the text. Examples include identifying initial, middle, or ending phonemes; segmenting phonemes or syllables; substituting or deleting phonemes; and blending phonemes.

5. **Alphabet letter recognition and reproduction**   Instruction to teach children the alphabet includes reciting the alphabet, writing letters, and recognizing letters. The focus here is *not* on sounds.

6. **Alphabetic instruction**   Alphabetic instruction is any instruction that is intended to help students understand that written letters of the alphabet are used to represent the sounds in words (graphophonemic correspondences). It includes instruction in which letters make which sounds. These activities almost always involve text. Examples include giving the sound for a written letter, identifying the letter sound a word starts with, mapping two letters onto a single sound (e.g., digraph as in *sh*), mapping multiple letters onto a single sound (e.g., consonant cluster as in *tch*), mapping multiple letters onto multiple sounds (e.g., consonant blends as in *str*), focusing on isolated syllables, and teaching rules for letter–sound correspondence.

7. **Structural analysis** Structural analysis includes instruction about meaningful parts (morphemic units) of words, such as plurals, possessive, prefixes, suffixes, verb tenses, root words, derivations, and etymology.

8. **Word work** Word work is any instruction with text that works purely at the word level. This can include words on the board, on a word wall, in a book, or in other print medium. Examples of word work include blending or reading words, learning sight words, and writing words.

   a. *With connected text*

   b. *Not with connected text*

9. **Vocabulary** In vocabulary instruction, the teacher focuses on developing the children's knowledge of the meanings of words within the context of teaching reading as the vocabulary is related to *print*. Examples include giving definitions; using a word in a sentence; and focusing on synonyms, antonyms, homophones, and words with multiple meanings.

10. **Previewing a text to prepare for reading (before reading a book or a page that has not been read previously)** This preparation for reading includes all discussions of topics and issues related to something the teacher and/or students will read. For example, if the class is going to read a book about going to the beach, the teacher might ask who has gone to the beach. These discussions differ from the discussions for oral language development because the emphasis here is on knowledge that is linked to what is going to be read. This also includes picture walking, or previewing a book through illustrations.

11. **Spelling in the context of reading** Spelling covered in the context of reading does *not* include an extended spelling activity.

12. **Reading text—beyond the word level (all types of text; students may or may not see the text)**

   a. *Teacher reads aloud (alone without students).*

   b. *Students read aloud (with or without teacher).*

   c. *Students read silently.*

   d. *Students sing or chant a known pattern or song that is related to a text.*

13. **Students read their own writing**

14. **Reading comprehension (during or after reading)** The teacher is focused on the children's understanding of the text they are reading. This includes structural details (e.g., character, plot) and summarization, prediction, statement of main idea, and so forth. Also, reading comprehension activities can be direct instruction on comprehension strategies such as story mapping and may also include the class discussing knowledge related to what was read, students drawing a picture about what was read, or students creating a craft related to what was read (e.g., reading about frogs and then making a frog puppet). This does *not* include listening comprehension.

   a. *Literal, "right there in the book" questions*

   b. *Inferential questions*

   c. *Written responses to comprehension questions*

15. **Spelling instruction** Instruction in spelling is a lesson or segment of a lesson specifically focused on spelling. Often a separate speller or lists of words are used.

16. **Writing composition**

   a. *Student composition* Student composition comprises activities in which children are asked to create original stories, journal entries, recipes, essays, and so forth and express these ideas by writing them on paper. These activities may consist of drawing a picture to tell a story, scribbling, drawing pictures and labeling with a few words to tell a story, dictating a story to a teacher, and any other form of emergent writing.

   b. *Student dictation* Students write what the teacher orally recites to them.

   c. *Teacher-led instruction* Teacher is modeling/instructing students in writing forms/processes, that is, the "how to" of composition.

17. **Grammar or mechanics** In formal grammar instruction, the teacher focuses on and gives students opportunities to practice a grammatical concept or a point about mechanics, such as capitalization or punctuation. In *kindergarten*, this is different from print awareness, which is instruction that makes the student aware of what appears in print and how print works. It is a focused lesson on grammar or mechanics.

18. **Giving directions/passing out language-related materials/referring to teacher's guide (relevant to reading instruction)** Directions in this category have an instructional purpose.

19. **Nonreading activities**
    a. *Chaos in the classroom or disruptive student behavior*
    b. *Other* Other nonreading activities include discipline, off-task transitions, teacher grading papers, teacher out of classroom, and interruptions caused by visitors or intercom announcements.

20. **Feedback in response to a reading relevant comment or event**
    a. *Corrective*
    b. *Praise*
    c. *Punitive*

Uncodable Uncodable behaviors are those that do not fit in any of the above codes.

14

Motivating Students to Read

Evidence for Classroom Practices that Increase Reading Motivation and Achievement

JOHN T. GUTHRIE AND NICOLE M. HUMENICK

In their invitation to contribute to this volume, the editors challenged us with the following question: "What motivates students to read?" Our contribution to this dialogue on reading is to address this question with findings from available research. Before we can begin, however, we need to unpack the question. We are referring to teachers and others who have an opportunity to implement classroom practices and create educational environments for reading development. Our chapter does not address parents, who are also influential in motivating, and does not address the peer group, which has high influence over reading and other aspects of lifestyle, especially for adolescent students. Our aim is to provide a knowledge base to guide the decision making for a variety of educators.

We use the word *motivate* in the sense of engagement in an important task. The term *motivate* does not point toward mere frills, fun, or transitory excitement, but to a cognitive commitment toward reading to learn and to extending one's aesthetic experience. Motivation, then, is not isolated from the language or cognitive processes of reading, but gives energy and direction to them. In our discussion, *student* refers to learners ages 8–14 years. In our literature review, we found very few systematic investigations of motivation in students younger than this age range. We interpret *reading* as understanding the content of a text. Although processes of word recognition are indispensable to reading comprehension, there is little literature on motivation for word-level reading processes. We address comprehension of text in a relatively simple form, not including issues of literary criticism or synthesis of multiple texts in extended knowledge-seeking endeavors.

Finally, we interpret the question as a quest for causal relation-ships. We are interested in whether educators can design and sustain contexts in educational settings that foster long-term reading moti-vation. Therefore, we searched for experimental evidence regarding classroom conditions that are conducive to long-term motiva-tional development.

Prior to examining classroom conditions that influence motiva-tion for reading, it is important to recognize that reading motivation has many dimensions; it is not a unitary attribute. Students are not either motivated or unmotivated. Rather, students are likely to exhibit different forms of motivation for reading, as well as different levels of these forms. In a theoretical literature review with extensive statistical investigations, Wigfield and Guthrie (1997) identified at least 12 dimensions of motivation for reading. In this chapter, we want to talk about three types of reading motivation based on these 12 dimensions: external motivation, internal motivation, and self-efficacy.

External motivation is the seeking of prizes and recognition for excellence in reading. Externally motivated students focus cognitive effort on reading activities to gain incentives such as points, public praise, or money. Their motivations are external (or extrinsic) because these students depend upon teachers, peers, computers, or systems outside themselves to deliver the benefits from their read-ing activities.

Internal motivation is the seeking of benefits that the reading activity itself confers on the reader. Internally motivated readers have desires, interests, needs, and dispositions that are satisfied through various forms of reading activities. The internally (or intrin-sically) motivated student who is interested, for example, in reptiles gains new information about dinosaurs to satisfy a curiosity, and this new information is his or her reward for reading. Internally motivated readers believe that reading is valuable and embrace the goal of reading well and reading widely. They have internalized reading excellence because they are aware that reading is valued by teachers and parents and that it will benefit them in the future.

A third motivational attribute is *self-efficacy*. Students with self-efficacy believe they have the capability to read well. They approach books with confidence and tackle challenging texts or diffi-cult words with the expectation that they will master them. They have a "can-do" approach to reading and learning from text. In contrast, students with lower self-efficacy are likely to say, "I can't do it," when faced with long passages, unfamiliar text, or new expectations for learning from a book. Without the energizing value of high efficacy, students are unable to sustain the effort required to learn reading skills or to become knowledgeable through print.

To address the question of what motivates students to read, we identified 22 studies that experimentally compared conditions expected to increase motivation with conditions not expected to increase motivation. All of these studies are related to reading from text or manipulating words meaningfully. Most of the students were ages 8–14, although a few were undergraduate students. A substantial majority (73%) of the studies in our review were true experiments, and the others were quasi-experiments. In true experiments, students (the units of analysis) are randomly assigned to treatment conditions. With random assignment, there is no bias, and the groups are similar on all variables at the outset. If there is a statistically significant difference between groups on a variable following the completion of the treatment and control conditions, the experimenters can infer that the difference was attributable to the treatment. For example, in the McLoyd (1979) study of the effects of choice, which is discussed later in this chapter, students were randomly assigned to choice and no-choice conditions. Following the study, the choice group was higher on the measure of motivation than the non-choice group. There is no other explanation than the response to treatment to explain this difference. Choice increased motivation.

Of course, it is possible to measure all of the groups on a pretest before the treatment. If the groups have the same results on the pretest, this confirms the effects of randomness in assignment to treatment. Some measures, however, are reactive. That is, having the study participants take the measure affects the treatment. For example, if a study has a motivation measure as a pretest, followed by an instructional treatment involving choice, students may be sensitized to the treatment. They may think that the choice is intended to influence their motivation. In this case, the pretest and treatment interact, and the inference of causality from the treatment is weakened. Therefore, pretests are not usually used in true experiments that have a motivation-oriented treatment. Cognitive experiments in reading may also be subject to reactivity of the pretest. Any time the pretest gives a clue, or an opportunity to practice the skill or attribute being taught in the treatment condition, the pretest may interact with the treatment and thus weaken the inference of causality in the experiment.

In this review, all of the experiments, except those that are noted otherwise, contain random assignment of students to experimental conditions. This permits causal inferences from the outcomes of the study. Such an inference is necessary, if one is attempting to determine whether an instructional practice influences a dependent variable of any kind. To address the question "What motivates students to read?" it is necessary to compile and weigh the evidence from experiments with random assignment, as reported in this chapter.

Within the 22 studies identified, we made 131 experimental comparisons. Each comparison was quantified using effect size, which is the mean (average) of students' scores on the dependent variable in one experimental condition minus the mean of students' scores on the same dependent variable in a control condition divided by the standard deviation of students' scores in the control condition. For example, if one group of 8-year-old students was given a choice of which paragraph to read and a second group was not given a choice of which paragraph to read, the motivation for reading each paragraph could be compared to examine the effect of choice on motivation. If the choice group had higher scores on the dependent variable than the no-choice group, a positive effect size would be identified, indicating that the classroom practice of providing a choice of paragraph reading influenced students' motivation.

In the review, 63 effect sizes were computed for knowledge goals, 46 effect sizes for student choices, 54 for influences of texts on motivation, and 7 for collaboration in reading. This includes 39 experimental comparisons in which the treatment condition was coded in two categories. These effect sizes were moderate to high, indicating that they were substantially important instructional characteristics for improving reading, according to existing criteria in the research literature. The effect sizes are displayed in Figure 14.1. Knowledge goals in reading had an effect size of 0.72 on motivation; student choices afforded in the classroom had an effect size of 0.95 on motivation for reading; the nature of texts influenced motivation with an effect size of 1.15; and collaboration for reading influenced motivation with an effect size of 0.52. These classroom practices have each been verified experimentally as having a sizable impact on reading motivation and should be viewed as major constituents of any long-term instructional program. Next, we discuss each of the educational practices with reference to some of the evidence.

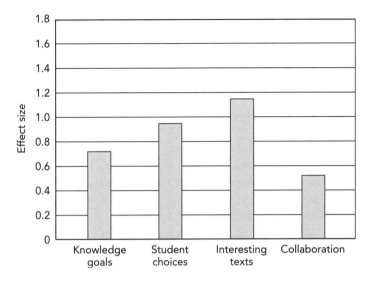

Figure 14.1. Benefits of motivational classroom practices for students' reading motivation.

INFLUENCES OF CONTENT GOALS
ON STUDENT MOTIVATION FOR READING

When students are faced with a new text in a classroom situation, they may adopt a wide range of goals and purposes for reading this text. At the same time, a wide range of teachers' practices can enable students to adopt goals and purposes for reading that are conducive to motivational development and reading improvement. Enabling students to become deeply immersed in and intrigued by the content of a passage or book is a central practice among teachers who are effective in motivating students. When students are eager to pursue the topic of a text and keen to follow the next steps of a narrative literary work, they are likely not only to read effectively but also to develop additional motivation for subsequent reading. Teachers can help students make the content of texts richly rewarding in many ways: enabling students to use their background knowledge and experience, arranging for hands-on activities that arouse curiosity that can be satisfied through reading, and modeling the behaviors of the curious reader who seeks to understand texts as fully as possible.

Emphasizing content learning during reading instruction can be accomplished with a wide range of approaches. Some teachers have extended projects in which students pursue a theme and read a variety of materials. For instance, some students have the opportunity to study a state within the United States to make a brochure that advertises the state and describes its merits or attractions to tourists and the public. Another approach is to expect students to be able to explain the meaning of a text to other individuals. This technique was studied by Benware and Deci (1984), who assigned some students to read an article about the brain in order to explain it to others. Students in the control group were given the task of reading to pass a test. Students given the goal of reading to teach others reported more interest in the content, more enjoyment in the process of reading, and a willingness to participate further in the activity (to repeat the study). They also attained higher conceptual learning from the text than the other students did. This motivational practice increased both motivational outcomes of the activity and new knowledge derived from the materials.

One frequent approach to emphasizing content goals for reading instruction that might serve to motivate students is to pursue a conceptual theme for an extended period of time. For instance, if students are studying the American colonies or westward expansion, they accumulate an understanding of the topic and develop significant accumulations of expertise. The students' sense of being in command of the topic fuels their confidence and arouses new curiosities, while providing a platform for understanding the content of new materials. This content emphasis encourages students to adopt mastery goals for reading activities and to read with purpose, rather than to merely complete assignments.

Connected to the practice of using content goals are several motivational practices, such as the use of interesting text. Interesting text has dual features of being devoted to a topic that is intriguing to the learner and having an appealing layout of text illustrations and graphics. Interesting texts naturally elicit the goal of content learning and encourage students to read for mastery of information. Students immersed in interesting texts are not consumed with anxiety about whether they are reading better or worse than their classmates and are not fearful of looking foolish. Teachers who provide conceptual themes, real-world connections to texts, a variety of topics and genre within the classroom, and tasks that allow students to expand their knowledge and experience from reading are enhancing students' intrinsic motivations for reading. These motivations propel students toward excellence in the skills of comprehension and toward high amounts of reading, which also increase comprehension.

A substantial body of investigation supports the motivational practice of using content goals for reading instruction. In one experimental study, Grolnick and Ryan (1987) gave three different groups of fifth graders the same story about health and medical care across history. Students were randomly assigned one of three different purposes for reading the story: 1) a content reading goal (students were to follow the meaning and build their own understanding of this text), 2) answering test questions correctly (students were urged to read for the purpose of attaining the highest possible test score), and 3) control (students were given few directions but were encouraged to read on their own).

The results indicated that students who read with the purpose of understanding the content were more interested in the text and gained more conceptual knowledge than students who read to attain the highest test score. The content-purpose group wrote essays that were more elaborate and captured more of the main ideas and important details than the control students in this study did. In comparison, students who were reading to excel on the test recalled facts by rote and reported feeling more pressure to perform than those in the content-purpose group. It is evident that content goals in reading increase motivation for the reading activity and simultaneously foster deep conceptual knowledge growth.

After having established rich content learning goals, teachers can continue to motivate students to read through effective feedback on the students' progress toward the goals. Butler and Nisan (1986) conducted an experiment with sixth-grade students in a word-building activity. Students were randomly assigned to a condition in which they 1) received comments about how they were doing in the task, how challenging the task was, and how their strategies were effective in succeeding in the activity; 2) were told they would be given grades; or 3) were provided no feedback in the task at all. Students receiving feedback that helped them understand how well they were succeeding and how the task could be performed effectively reported that the task was more interesting. Feedback describes students' varying levels of performance on portions of the task and gives students a sense of their progress and criteria for improving their competency. This effective feedback during reading activities enables students to perceive when they are reading competently and how their reading comprehension can be improved. This information satisfies the fundamental need for perceiving oneself as competent in an important task (Ryan & Deci, 2000).

Thus, an important part of the motivational practice of using contents goals for reading instruction is to generate informational feedback and support for the learners to enable them to see that they are attaining these interesting and valuable goals through their exercise of cognitive competency and their effort in reading (Butler & Nisan, 1986). In addition, children gain valuable feedback about their performance from their peers. Butler (1995) found that students who were given the content goal for mastering a task increased their motivation by reviewing the work of peers doing the same activity. Students with a content learning goal viewed the peers' work as more interesting and reported seeking further information more frequently than students who were given the performance goal of succeeding as much as possible to be favorably compared with other students. In other words, the strength of content learning goals in reading can be increased by appropriate attention to the work of peers as a form of feedback and a source of information for self-improvement (Butler & Nisan, 1986).

Content goals in teaching reading or English are often described as *mastery goals*. Students perceive that the teacher is emphasizing content mastery goals with the following types of statements:

"The teacher makes sure I understand the work."

"The teacher pays attention to whether I am improving."

"The teacher wants us to try new things."

"I work hard to learn."

In contrast, when teachers are emphasizing *performance goals,* students are likely to agree with the following statements:

"Students want to know how others score on assignments."

"Only a few students can get top marks."

"Students feel badly when they do not do as well as others."

Ames and Archer (1988) found that students in grades 8–11 who perceived their class to be mastery oriented were more likely to have positive attitudes toward the subject matter, to embrace challenging tasks, to use effective strategies for studying, and to attribute their success in a class to their specific learning strategies than students who perceived their class to be performance-oriented. A complementary finding was reported by Anderman, Maehr, and Midgley (1999), who found that student motivation in a performance-oriented middle school was very different from motivation in a school that focused on content mastery. In the performance-oriented school, there was a pervasive emphasis on competitive assessment of student progress, recognition of achievement for high grades, and a strong tracking program. In the mastery-oriented schools, content goals were emphasized along with a commitment to interdisciplinary projects and a focus on student interests. In the performance-oriented schools, students reported high levels of extrinsic motivation by responding affirmatively to the following kinds of statements:

"The main reason I do my work in English is because we get grades."

"I don't care whether I understand something or not in English as long I get the answers right."

That is, a mastery orientation with a content emphasis in the classroom led to interest in content, which represents intrinsic motivation for reading and learning English, whereas a performance orientation in the classroom led to an interest in gaining high grades and a competitive advantage over other students, which represents extrinsic motivation.

Similarly, Butler (1995) found that fourth and fifth graders working in mastery-oriented conditions used feedback about other students' performances to improve understanding of their tasks. In contrast, students working in performance conditions in which high scores were emphasized were more likely to use information about other students' work to improve their grades and test scores. In the performance conditions, students used information about their peers' work to "get a better grade for myself," but in the mastery conditions students used information about other students' work to "help me understand how to improve and get better on this task." Across a wide range of ages and classroom environments, the pattern is consistent showing that teachers who emphasize content goals and deep understanding enable students to become intrinsically motivated to read and comprehend, whereas teachers who emphasize performance goals of grades and extrinsic incentives increase students' attention to their performance and their standing relative to peers, which represent extrinsic motivations for reading.

Another motivation, confidence (or self-efficacy), can be increased by providing specific content goals and immediate feedback about progress. These combinations of specific goals and feedback can increase students' self-efficacy, which translates into higher effort and devotion to reading. In an experiment, Schunk and Swartz (1993) provided some students specific content goals in a writing activity with strategies and feedback. Other students were given only the general goal of composing a paragraph. Students given specific goals, and information about their progress toward the goals, had more confidence in their writing than students assigned a more global task. Schunk and Zimmerman (1997) reviewed research on goal setting and self-efficacy in a wide range of reading investigations. Children's efficacy for reading and confidence in their future success were consistently improved by providing specific goals with information about the progress toward them. Thus, the concreteness of the goal, and information about progress toward the goal of understanding, foster students' motivational processes of self-efficacy and increase their self-confidence as readers.

Content learning goals are powerful not only because they increase intrinsic motivation for reading, but also because they increase the students' comprehension and cognitive outcomes in reading activities. Grolnick and Ryan (1987) reported that when fifth-grade students in an experiment were given content learning goals for reading, they gained more conceptual knowledge than when they were given performance goals of scoring well on tests. It is likely that the content goals increased motivation, which fosters deeper comprehension and meaningful processing of text. In addition, content goals may focus students' attention on "big ideas," whereas performance goals focus students' attention on completing the task and minimizing effort necessary to get an adequate test score on the assessment. A similar finding was reported by de Sousa and Oakhill (1996) who showed that third and fourth graders who read in a condition that involved "reading like a detective to uncover clues toward meaning" (a content learning goal) used comprehension monitoring strategies more fully than students who read a normal text that did not have the detective-game activities. Students in the content learning condition comprehended more fully because they monitored the level of their understanding as they read. This benefit of content learning goals was specially marked for students with lower interest in the text. Higher interest students were likely to be monitoring their comprehension, irrespective of whether the condition involved reading like a detective or not. The conclusion is that content learning goals increased the comprehension monitoring of lower interest readers more fully than those with higher interest.

Consistent with these findings, students' recall of what they read is higher when they are given content learning goals that are likely to be motivating than when they are given performance goals that lead them to be competitive or to have no goals at all for their reading activities (Graham & Golan, 1991). Related to the cognitive benefit of content learning goals in reading is the alignment of the students' purpose with the content of the text. Students' purposes are closely related to their motivations. When students read purposefully, they are more motivated to gain understanding than when they read with limited or no purposes. If a text contains all of the information necessary for students to meet their purposes in reading, then motivations for the reading activity and the recall of the text are relatively high. In other words, when students' purposes for reading (in other words, their content learning goals) are well aligned with the subject matter in the text and the content of the materials, students' motivation and memory of new knowledge gained will be increased (Schraw & Dennison, 1994).

It should be noted that the effect of content goals on motivation may be undermined by distracting text material. If the graphic information and illustrations or specific details in the text are distracting from the main theme or are irrelevant, they reduce interest, are ignored by students, and decrease understanding of the material (Harp & Mayer, 1997).

Summarizing across a wide range of studies, the mean effect size of content knowledge goals on students' reading motivation was found to be 0.72, as shown in Figure 14.1. Furthermore, knowledge goals had an effect size of 0.87 on reading achievement and comprehension, as shown in Figure 14.2. The evidence is that using knowledge goals in reading instruction enhances students' reading motivation and achievement.

INFLUENCES OF CHOICE ON STUDENT MOTIVATION FOR READING

Teachers generally believe that choice is motivating for young readers. Surveys at elementary schools (Sweet, Guthrie, & Ng, 1998), middle schools (Zahorik, 1996), and secondary schools (Flowerday & Schraw, 2000) showed that teachers believe that providing choices of reading activities increase students' interest and time spent in reading. These are aspects of intrinsic motivation. A range of choices may include which book to read; where to do the reading within the classroom; how to respond (in writing or drawing); whether to read alone or with a partner; and especially which genre and authors

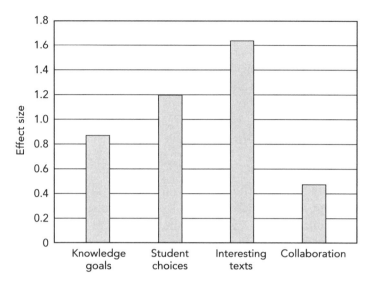

Figure 14.2. Benefits of motivational classroom practices for students' reading comprehension and achievement.

to follow. A substantial body of experimental evidence undergirds these beliefs about the power of choice to increase intrinsic motivations for reading.

McLoyd (1979) conducted an experiment on choice with second- and third-grade students. Some individuals were randomly assigned to be given a choice of which book to read, whereas other individuals were randomly assigned to participate in a reading activity without choice. The group with choice selected books from the following: *Amelia Bedelia and the Surprise Shower, George the Drummer Boy, Here Comes the Strikeout, Kittens and More Kittens, Prehistoric Monsters Did the Strangest Things,* and *You Will Go to the Moon.* A variety of topics and genres for both boys and girls were provided. In the choice condition, each child selected the book he or she preferred from the list. In the no-choice condition, the child was given a book by the experimenter that he or she had not chosen to read. All students read about 250 words of their books. They were then given free time in which they could do crossword puzzles, play Scrabble or a math game, or continue reading the book. Time spent reading during this 10-minute free period was one measure of intrinsic motivation. Number of words read during this free choice period was a second measure of intrinsic motivation for reading under these two conditions. Findings were that after the initial 250 words were read, students in the choice condition read for about 5 minutes (295 seconds), whereas students in the no-choice condition read for only about 2 minutes (131 seconds). This was a highly significant advantage for the choice condition in motivation for reading. The variable of number of words reflected this time expenditure. After the initial 250 words were read, students in the choice condition read 440 words, whereas those in the no-choice condition read 216 words in the available time, meaning that there was a highly significant advantage in motivation for the choice condition.

Reynolds and Symons (2001) reported a similar finding in which they gave third-grade students a choice of which book to read in an information-seeking activity. They were given three books on three different topics and 2 minutes to preview and select a topic. In the no-choice condition, students were given the three books for 2 minutes and then were randomly assigned a book for the task. Students were then given four questions to answer by searching in the text. Interest in the different topics and prior knowledge about the topics were controlled for statistically. Students in the choice condition spent 23% less time reading than did students in the no-choice condition, and students in the choice condition were 21% more accurate in answering questions than were students in the no-choice condition. Furthermore, the quality of the strategies used by students in the choice condition was higher than that used by students in the no-choice condition. Both of these indicators show higher intrinsic motivation for reading, favoring students who selected their reading materials. Consequently, the increase in motivation was accompanied by an increase in competence in using cognitive strategies in this information-seeking task in reading.

The role of choice in motivation for reading may influence children from diverse cultural backgrounds differently. Iyengar and Lepper (1999) theorized that Anglo-American children and Asian American children may respond to choices differently because Asian American children seek to maintain high relationships with parents or authority figures and follow their suggestions. Confirming this, Iyengar and Lepper found that Anglo-American children spent more time in a literacy activity (a measure of intrinsic reading motivation) when *they* made the choice than when the experimenter made the choice. They also found that Anglo-American children were more motivated when they made the choice compared with when their mothers made the choice for them. In contrast, Asian American children were most intrinsically motivated when choices were made for them by their mothers. They were less motivated to pursue activities of their own choice than to pursue activities chosen for them by trusted authority figures. It appears that the effect of choice on motivation is influenced by children's beliefs and values, which are embedded within their cultural experience.

When providing choice in reading activities is applied to ongoing instruction in classroom situations, it is usually integrated with other classroom practices. For example, Morrow (1992) reported on an experiment in which some students were provided a set of opportunities to choose texts and spend time with a genre they selected, whereas other students were presented with no choices in their reading activities. Students in the high-choice curriculum were able to select from a wide range of books and were able to read literary and informational texts that were not available in the no-choice condition. In other words, the practices of choice and diversity of genre were integrated into this classroom-based intervention. With the no-choice control condition, fewer genres were available and the text diversity was limited. Findings were that students in the intervention with choice and text diversity spent more time reading books after school in a free choice situation than students with no choice and low text diversity. In addition, students with the high-choice and high-diversity literacy opportunities showed higher reading comprehension, including better oral retelling of stories, text comprehension, and story rewriting, all of which measure different aspects of reading comprehension. In conclusion, when choice and text diversity were combined in a practical intervention within schools over a substantial time period, benefits were observable for intrinsic motivation, as measured by time spent reading and by cognitive competency in reading motivation, according to several indicators.

Benefits of choice in reading and literacy interactions can be shown with a variety of indicators of intrinsic motivation. For instance, Cordova and Lepper (1996) observed students in a computer-based literacy activity. Some students were provided choices about how to play a game, whereas others were given no choices about the game. Those given choice reported liking the game and believing themselves to be more competent in the game than the students in the no-choice condition reported. Many researchers use students' perceptions of their own competence as an indicator of the students' level of intrinsic motivation for tasks. Highly related to self-efficacy, perceived competence creates favorable conditions for enjoying a task, spending time with a task, and devoting effort to success. A popular indicator of motivation is students' ratings of interest. For example, Schraw, Flowerday, and Reisetter (1998) provided some students choice in a testing situation, whereas other students had no choices in the test. Those with choice rated the materials read in the test as more interesting than those with no choice. In this experiment, it should be noted that choice did not increase performance on the test itself, although it increased interest in reading the materials on the test. It appears that in classroom learning situations, choice of text increases students' comprehension as well as their motivation, whereas in a traditional test, choice does not have the opportunity to facilitate or increase comprehension. In sum, the evidence points directly to the principle that providing choice increases students' motivation for reading and enhances their comprehension of self-selected texts.

The benefit of choice on reading on motivation is shown in Figure 14.1. The graph shows that the mean effect size of student choices on reading motivation was 0.95. Furthermore, student choices in the classroom had an effect size of 1.20 on reading achievement and comprehension, as shown in Figure 14.2. Clearly this aspect of providing academically significant choices during teaching is salient for students' reading development.

CONTRIBUTION OF INTERESTING TEXTS TO READING MOTIVATION

The implication for educational practice based on the literature review conducted here is that interesting texts increase motivation for reading and comprehension of those texts. In other words, when students are reading texts that they rate as interesting to them, they report that reading such texts is enjoyable. Students often say they wish to continue reading these texts when they have free time and select them when they have an opportunity (Ainley, Hidi, & Berndorff, 2002; Cordova & Lepper, 1996; Morrow, 1992), which are indicators of intrinsic motivation.

Children are more likely to comprehend texts that they find interesting than texts they do not rate as interesting. Evidence for this was reported by Wade, Buxton, and Kelly (1999), who found that when students rated a sentence within a text to be interesting, they were more likely to recall that sentence as a part of the content of the text than if they rated the sentence as uninteresting. This positive effect of the interestingness of sentences prevailed, regardless of how important the sentence was rated by the students. In other words, important or not, interesting content within a text is recalled more highly than uninteresting content. Harp and Mayer (1997) confirmed this finding for illustrations in text. When students were given text with illustrations that were rated as interesting due to relevance to the content, the students' motivation for reading was higher than when they were given uninteresting (decorative) illustrations in the same text. Furthermore, Schraw and Dennison (1994) showed that when students were given text that was relevant to their purpose for reading, they rated the text as relatively interesting and they recalled that text more highly than other materials. In other words, recall of text segments that were interesting because of their relevance was greater than recall of uninteresting segments. The effect sizes for these impacts of text interest on comprehension and recall are substantial, as indicated in Figure 14.2.

Because interesting text is motivating and increases comprehension, it is valuable to ask, "What makes a text interesting?" Educators should identify the properties of a text that lead students to rate it as interesting. A well-documented finding is that students find a text interesting if they possess background knowledge about it (Schiefele, 1999). Of course, this does not mean that children should avoid reading about new topics important to their education, but rather that their initial interest will be higher in topic domains that are most well-matched to their prior knowledge. Having a text on a reasonably familiar topic, with its visual layout having an appropriate number of illustrations, graphics, and display features, is important to students' perceptions of how interesting the material is (Schraw, Bruning, & Svoboda, 1995). Related to this graphic layout, texts that appear to be easy to comprehend are rated as more interesting than texts that are expected to be difficult (Schraw et al., 1995). If students anticipate that they will be frustrated in their attempts to understand or complete a text reading activity, their self-efficacy is threatened and their ratings of text interest will be low.

This does not suggest that more illustrations and more vivid details are always better. Students can distinguish illustrations and facts that are distracting from those that are helpful for understanding the main ideas. For example, an illustration about a giant, fearsome gorilla in a story about gorillas' eating habits in the wild may be entertaining but is not likely to be highly informative. Advanced learners perceive such distractions as negative, rather than positive. In other words, *interest* refers to qualities of a text that help students learn from a text. It does not merely refer to the brilliance or garishness of its appearance (Harp & Mayer, 1997).

Central to the interest value of a text is its relevance to the learner. For example, if students have well-established goals about learning about llamas in the Andes, texts on llamas will be rated as more interesting than texts on another subject. If students have embraced a purpose for learning, then reading materials that enable them to fulfill that purpose are perceived as relevant and thus interesting and valuable (Schraw & Dennison, 1994). Likewise, illustrations and detail within a text that are viewed as helpful for learning the content of a text and attaining the purposes for reading will be more interesting than less relevant or less useful illustrations and graphics (Harp & Mayer, 1997). This suggests that the motivational practices of using content goals and interesting texts for reading instruction can be profitably merged. In other words, when well-developed subject matter goals are sustained in the classroom and pursued by teachers and students, then texts that are valuable for attaining these purposes will be viewed as valuable and interesting to students.

Related to goal relevance of texts are activity connections. When students perceive that reading material is connected to an activity that they have been engaged in, the reading material acquires interest and motivational value. For example, if students have recently observed an ant farm in the classroom, they will most likely be enthusiastic about reading books on ants and their homemaking and social communications. When a text is associated with concrete activities a student has recently participated in, the text takes on the interest value of the activities themselves (Sweet et al., 1998; Swan, 2003).

In the analysis of all of the experimental comparisons on motivation, the factor of interesting texts had a mean effect size of 1.15 on students' reading motivation, as shown in Figure 14.1, indicating that high text interest increased motivation for reading substantially. Furthermore, the influence of interesting texts on students' reading achievement and comprehension had an effect size of 1.64, as shown in Figure 14.2, documenting that when students were interested in the text, they comprehended it more fully.

ROLES OF SOCIAL COLLABORATION DURING READING

Providing the opportunity and expectation for collaboration during reading and writing activities increases intrinsic motivation. Regrettably, few experimental investigations have been conducted that expressly focus on the effects of collaboration on reading motivation. However, related studies can be examined in reference to this educational practice. For example, Wentzel (1993) found that sixth- and seventh-grade students who possessed goals for classroom interactions that included social collaboration achieved more highly in reading, language arts, and other subject matters than students who did not have such well-formed social goals.

In addition, students who show responsibility goals in the classroom, such as thinking about how their behavior will affect other students, trying to do what the teacher asks of them, and continuing to work even when other students are making a lot of noise, are higher achievers than students who do not possess these social responsibility attributes (Wentzel, 1993). This leads to the conclusion that when students' social motivation and goals for collaboration are high their achievement is relatively high as well.

Consistent with teachers' beliefs, the process of collaborating socially in reading and academic activities increases intrinsic motivation, whereas activities that are pursued more individually are less motivating (Sweet et al., 1998). In an experimental investigation of this issue, Isaac, Sansone, and Smith (1999) found that when students across a wide range of ages were assigned to work collaboratively on a 1-hour activity of designing a school campus, they found the task interesting and wanted to continue the activity even after it was completed. In contrast, students who were assigned to work on the same design task individually, without interaction or conversation with other students, were less likely to rate the task as interesting and not at all keen to pursue the activity after the experimental study was completed. In other words, collaborative structures increase intrinsic motivation for academic tasks. This finding is similar to that of Ng, Guthrie, Van Meter, McCann, and Alao (1998) regarding elementary school students working in more highly and less highly collaborative conditions for reading and writing activities.

Social collaboration influenced students' reading motivation with an effect size of 0.52, as shown in Figure 14.1, showing that when students worked together in reading, they were more motivated than when they worked alone. The impact of these social interactions for reading on achievement and comprehension had an effect size of 0.48, as shown in Figure 14.2, providing evidence that collaborating during reading increased students' ability to comprehend the reading materials.

A VIGNETTE FROM MYRA BUSKIRK'S CLASSROOM

The following example of the classroom practices we have been discussing was drawn from data we collected in an ongoing study supported by the Interagency Education Research Initiative (IERI), a joint program of the National Science Foundation, National Institute of Child Health and Human Development, and the U.S. Department of Education. In this study, engagement-supportive reading instruction is being implemented in 40 classrooms in four schools daily over 3 months of school. Videotapes of instruction are made regularly for research purposes, and this vignette is a faithful depiction of one videotaped lesson in Myra Buskirk's classroom.

Upon entering this fourth-grade classroom, we see the theme of the wetlands unfold. Myra's students are surrounded by posters of wetland plants and animals. At the front of the classroom is a chart listing observations of a wetland based on a recent field trip by Myra's students. Information books on the wetlands fill the classroom. Myra's students have been learning about how plants and animals survive in different environments, and their current focus is survival in the wetlands. In this classroom, the fourth graders learn reading strategies and techniques while building conceptual scientific knowledge because Myra believes it is important to integrate her reading instruction with science and social studies.

On this particular day, Myra begins her lesson by asking her students to observe a science experiment they began the day before. The children had placed celery stalks in water that was mixed with dirt and cocoa power to represent polluted water. After allowing the celery to soak over night, the students then observe the changes in the celery stalk and in the water. They discuss these changes, and Myra asks them to individually record predictions about why they think these changes occurred.

After having her students share their observations and predictions with the class, Myra opens a discussion about the wetland walk the class had taken on a previous field trip. In order to connect today's experiment with the children's prior knowledge about the wetlands, she asks the class to think of questions related to both their experiment and the plants they observed on their wetland walk. She encourages the students to turn to their neighbor and come up with one question that the two students would like to have answered. Myra gives her students the freedom to develop inquiries based on their own interests, but she keeps their focus by narrowing the topic to include only their experiment and wetland plants. She distributes information books on the wetlands for them to browse to inspire thoughtful questions.

After each pair of students has developed a question, Myra directs the attention of the class toward a chart called "Wetland Plant Questions." As the children share their own questions with the class, Myra records the questions on the chart, including the name of each paired child next to the pair's question. During the next part of the lesson, the children increasingly take control of their learning. Myra points out the large variety of information books on the wetlands, such as *Wetlands* and *Marshes and Swamps*, on the children's desks that they will use to answer their own questions. After a review of the text features found in expository books, Myra instructs the students to work in pairs to read and answer their questions. In order to ensure all of her students' success in learning from these books, Myra provides a variety of difficulty levels when selecting books for her lessons. Though the information books all share similar topical information, they span multiple reading levels so that all children can choose a text that is suitable to their reading ability.

As Myra's students begin to find answers to their own questions, the classroom begins to buzz with excitement. Children are proud to point out particularly interesting findings to their neighbors. One student even exclaims, "I just found Bobby's answer!" as she discovers the explanation to another student's question in her book, *Wetlands.* When a few students have trouble finding their own answers, Myra encourages them to help one another. The students can record their findings in any way they choose. A few children take notes as they read, whereas others write their answers after they have finished browsing. Myra only asks that the students give written explanatory answers that include enough information to fully answer their questions.

After 20 minutes of searching, reading, and note taking, the students are ready to share their new information with the entire class. As the students share their answers, Myra helps to guide them in giving a fully explained answer. Students who have not yet found their answers are assured that they will have more time to read until they are fully satisfied with their answers.

Content Goals

In this lesson, the students are focused on goals oriented toward the mastery of knowledge, in this case the ecology of wetlands. Each student develops his or her own questions that become personalized learning goals for the lesson. These questions are based on the individual interests of the children, which may be sparked by the experiment they performed, the field trip they attended, or the interesting book that caught their eye. Such content goals are intrinsically motivating. Children are intrinsically motivated to find an explanation to a question that intrigues them. Myra makes sure that the children have sufficient resources so that they understand that the goal is to discover a completely satisfying answer. A full answer to the question usually requires full understanding of multiple texts and of a complex network of knowledge by integrating information.

Myra's classroom orientation toward knowledge mastery is in stark contrast to one that emphasizes performance and competition, which are extrinsic incentives for motivation. She does not use rewards to rank one child's performance in comparison with that of another child. Instead, she posts all of the children's questions on a classroom chart and values every child's discovery of knowledge as a success. She tells the class that their goal for the lesson is to uncover knowledge so that all can learn more. Each student is therefore contributing to the class's fuller understanding of the ecological concepts found in the theme of the wetlands.

Choices

The students in Myra's classroom were enabled to make significant decisions during this lesson that affected their own learning. This element of choice encourages children to invest themselves more fully in their reading. The various supports for choice and student control increase motivation for reading.

In addition to these choices, Myra's students were given freedom at the end of the lesson to simply read the book they had chosen from beginning to end. This opportunity to read the text in depth is extremely important because it gives the children the opportunity to express their interests in related subtopics. Without the limitations of focusing on searching for the answer to a particular question, the fourth graders can read to gain valuable knowledge according to their own curiosities and to integrate conceptual understanding and factual information in the content domain.

Interesting Text

The abundance and variety of interesting texts play key roles in children's interest in reading. Number alone is not sufficient. The teacher makes it known to the students that the texts are there to help the students gain knowledge. Books are displayed on children's desks so that they are accessible to all students. Furthermore, the selection of texts is important to the students' reading motivation. Myra's texts are appealing to young students because of their vivid photographs and illustrations and the attractive layout of their information.

Social Collaboration

It is also important for students to work together to gain conceptual knowledge and to learn good reading strategies. In this lesson, students are given ample time to interact with one another to practice these skills by developing questions and searching for corresponding answers. Most students' intrinsic motivation for reading is increased when they can read together, share information, and present their knowledge to others. Although the students are assigned to work with one other partner most of the time, they are also encouraged to share their learning with other members of the class. This sharing emphasizes the collaboration of the class as a whole.

APPLICATIONS TO CLASSROOM PRACTICE

As verified in the literature review and meta-analysis and as illustrated in the preceding classroom vignette, several classroom practices increase motivation for reading. To motivate students within classrooms, teachers often combine and merge these practices. For example, many teachers provide choices among different texts to read. Consequently, the principle of affording students' choice and providing interesting texts are merged. Frequently in reading instruction, teachers who are successful in motivating learners create content goals with an overall conceptual theme. This sustains subject matter awareness and makes reading purposeful. The content goals in such a conceptual theme can be linked to the purposes and texts for reading. Simultaneously, in learning about content through reading and writing, teachers often facilitate collaboration among pairs or teams of learners. Such collaborating fosters intrinsic motivation, especially if it is connected to other classroom practices for motivation.

It is vital to recognize that as important as intrinsic motivation, extrinsic motivation, and self-efficacy are for reading comprehension, they are not sufficient for successful reading instruction. To enable students to improve in reading comprehension, teachers must foster the development of vocabulary, comprehension skills, and related writing activities. A motivated reader is not likely to automatically gain these complex cognitive competencies independently. The unmotivated reader, however, is quite unlikely to gain these reading competencies at all. Therefore, motivation is a necessary part of a comprehensive plan for reading instruction that ensures growth in reading comprehension.

CLOSING

We have explained four classroom practices in reading that improve and expand children's motivations for reading: using content goals for reading instruction, providing a range of choices in reading activities, affording students interesting texts for reading instruction, and ensuring collaboration for reading in the classroom. These practices are all supported by experimental evidence. This evidence represents a base for building long-term reading motivation in schools. It should be recognized that teachers engage in many practices intended to motivate students, including the following: reading aloud, posing questions, modeling their own curiosity, rewarding students' success, encouraging expressive reading, linking writing to reading activities, and tailoring instruction to individual student needs.

Although these may be likely to foster motivation, they have not been examined experimentally to date. We can expect that they will be investigated in the future and may be useful additions to the collection of effective research-based practices for motivation. At present, however, it is clear that reading comprehension, which requires direct teaching of such elements as vocabulary and cognitive strategies, is also increased through engagement-supporting practices in the classroom. When students are deeply engaged in text interaction and motivated to understand over lengthy periods of time, their achievement in reading comprehension increases (Guthrie & Wigfield, 2000).

REFERENCES

Ainley, M., Hidi, S., & Berndorff, D. (2002). Interest, learning, and the psychological processes that mediate their relationship. *Journal of Educational Psychology, 94*(3), 545–561.

Ames, C., & Archer, J. (1988). Achievement goals in the classroom: Students' learning strategies and motivation processes. *Journal of Educational Psychology, 80*(3), 260–267.

Anderman, E.M., Maehr, M.L., & Midgley, C. (1999). Declining motivation after the transition to middle school: Schools can make a difference. *Journal of Research and Development in Education, 32*(5), 131–147.

Benware, C.A., & Deci, E.L. (1984). Quality of learning with an active versus passive motivational set. *American Educational Research Journal, 21*(4), 755–765.

Butler, R. (1995). Motivational and informational functions and consequences of children's attention to peers' work. *Journal of Educational Psychology, 87*(3), 347–360.

Butler, R., & Nisan, M. (1986). Effects of no feedback, task-related comments, and grades on intrinsic motivation and performance. *Journal of Educational Psychology, 78*(3), 210–216.

Cordova, D.I., & Lepper, M.R. (1996). Intrinsic motivation and the process of learning: Beneficial effects of contextualization, personalization, and choice. *Journal of Educational Psychology, 88*(4), 715–730.

de Sousa, I., & Oakhill, J. (1996). Do levels of interest have an effect on children's comprehension monitoring performance? *British Journal of Educational Psychology, 66*(4), 471–482.

Flowerday, T., & Schraw, G. (2000). Teacher beliefs about instructional choice: A phenomenological study. *Journal of Educational Psychology, 92*(4), 634–645.

Graham, S., & Golan, S. (1991). Motivational influences on cognition: Task involvement, ego involvement, and depth of information processing. *Journal of Educational Psychology, 83*(2), 187–194.

Grolnick, W.S., & Ryan, R.M. (1987). Autonomy in children's learning: An experimental and individual differences investigation. *Journal of Personality and Social Psychology, 52*(5), 890–898.

Guthrie, J.T., & Wigfield, A. (2000). Engagement and motivation in reading. In M.L. Kamil & P.B. Mosenthal (Eds.), *Handbook of reading research* (Vol. III, pp. 403–422). Mahwah, NJ: Lawrence Erlbaum Associates.

Harp, S.F., & Mayer, R.E. (1997). The role of interest in learning from scientific text and illustrations: On the distinction between emotional interest and cognitive interest. *Journal of Educational Psychology, 89*(1), 92–102.

Isaac, J.D., Sansone, C., & Smith, J.L. (1999). Other people as a source of interest in an activity. *Journal of Experimental Social Psychology, 35*(3), 239–265.

Iyengar, S.S., & Lepper, M.R. (1999). Rethinking the value of choice: A cultural perspective on intrinsic motivation. *Journal of Personality and Social Psychology, 76*(3), 349–366.

McLoyd, V.C. (1979). The effects of extrinsic rewards of differential value on high and low intrinsic interest. *Child Development, 50,* 1010–1019.

Morrow, L.M. (1992). The impact of a literature-based program on literacy achievement, use of literature, and attitudes of children from minority backgrounds. *Reading Research Quarterly, 27*(3), 250–275.

Ng, M.M., Guthrie, J.T., Van Meter, P., McCann, A., & Alao, S. (1998). How do classroom characteristics influence intrinsic motivation for literacy? *Reading Psychology, 19*(4), 319–398.

Reynolds, P.L., & Symons, S. (2001). Motivational variables and children's text search. *Journal of Educational Psychology, 93*(1), 14–22.

Ryan, R.M., & Deci, E.L. (2000). Intrinsic and extrinsic motivations: Classic definitions and new directions. *Contemporary Educational Psychology, 25,* 54–67.

Schiefele, U. (1999). Interest and learning from text. *Scientific Studies of Reading, 3*(3), 257–279.

Schraw, G., Bruning, R., & Svoboda, C. (1995). Sources of situational interest. *Journal of Reading Behavior, 27*(1), 1–17.

Schraw, G., & Dennison, R.S. (1994). The effect of reader purpose on interest and recall. *Journal of Reading Behavior, 26*(1), 1–18.

Schraw, G., Flowerday, T., & Reisetter, M.F. (1998). The role of choice in reader engagement. *Journal of Educational Psychology, 90*(4), 705–714.

Schunk, D.H., & Swartz, C.W. (1993). Writing strategy instruction with gifted students: Effects of goals and feedback on self-efficacy and skills. *Roeper Review, 15*(4), 225–230.

Schunk, D.H., & Zimmerman, B.J. (1997). Developing self-efficacious readers and writers: The role of social and self-regulatory processes. In J.T. Guthrie & A. Wigfield (Eds.), *Reading engagement: Motivating readers through integrated instruction* (pp. 34–50). Newark, DE: International Reading Association.

Swan, E.A. (2003). *Concept-Oriented Reading Instruction: Engaging classrooms, lifelong learners.* New York: Guilford Press.

Sweet, A.P., Guthrie, J.T., & Ng, M.M. (1998). Teacher perceptions and student reading motivation. *Journal of Educational Psychology, 90*(2), 210–223.

Wade, S.E., Buxton, W.M., & Kelly, M. (1999). Using think-alouds to examine reader-text interest. *Reading Research Quarterly, 34*(2), 194–216.

Wentzel, K.R. (1993). Motivation and achievement in early adolescence: The role of multiple classroom goals. *Journal of Early Adolescence, 13*(1), 4–20.

Wigfield, A., & Guthrie, J.T. (1997). Relations of children's motivation for reading to the amount and breadth of their reading. *Journal of Educational Psychology, 89,* 420–432.

Zahorik, J. (1996). Elementary and secondary teachers' reports of how they make learning interesting. *Elementary School Journal, 96,* 551–564.

15

Lessons Learned from Research on Interventions for Students Who Have Difficulty Learning to Read

JOSEPH K. TORGESEN

R esearch on reading since the 1980s has been enormously productive in advancing our understanding of how children become skilled readers as well as the factors that make it difficult for some children to learn to read (Rayner, Foorman, Perfetti, Pesetsky, & Seidenberg, 2001). This research has taught us a great deal about the processes involved and the knowledge and skill required to be a good reader from first grade through high school and adulthood. Thus, this research is very helpful in specifying the kinds of knowledge and skill that children must have to be good readers, but it does not necessarily tell us directly how teachers should work with children to help them acquire this necessary knowledge and skill.

The role of intervention, or instructional, research is to examine the teaching methods that are most effective in helping children acquire all the skills, knowledge, and attitudes required to become a good reader. The task of identifying effective teaching procedures may sound relatively straightforward, but, as most teachers know, it is enormously complex (American Federation of Teachers, 1999). First, what is meant by "good reader"? One who can orally read the words in grade-level text accurately and fluently? Or, one who can

The author's research reported in this chapter was supported by Grant No. HD30988, "Prevention and Remediation of Reading Disabilities," from the National Institute of Child Health and Human Development.

identify the gist, or main idea, of an expository passage at an appropriate level of difficulty? Or, one who can combine information from several different sources and produce a synthesis that integrates information from all sources?

Clearly, the most important elements of instruction may vary depending upon how the ultimate goal of instruction is defined, and that, in turn, depends on how good reading skills are defined. If the primary goal is to enable children to attain a certain level of reading fluency by the end of third grade, investigators may find a specific set of instructional and practice procedures that are most important for achieving that goal. In contrast, if the goal is to enable students to make accurate inferences from vocabulary-rich and conceptually difficult material in seventh grade, researchers may emphasize some of the same instructional elements as in the first instance but may find others critically important as well. In other words, conclusions about the nature of effective instruction in reading depend on what researchers want children to know and be able to do when the instruction is finished.

Answers to questions about the essential features of good reading instruction may also depend on which particular children researchers are most concerned about. Whitehurst and Lonigan (1998) have recently identified two broad classes of emergent literacy skills that have a substantial impact on how easily children learn to read once they enter school. One set of skills, such as phonemic awareness and letter knowledge, is particularly important in learning to read words accurately and fluently. In contrast, the other family of knowledge and skill, encompassing a broad range of oral language ability and including such things as vocabulary and grammatical knowledge, is important for understanding language.

Most children who enter school at risk for difficulties learning to read fall into one of two broad groups. Many children enter school with adequate oral language ability but have weaknesses in the phonological domain. Their primary problem in learning to read involves learning to read words accurately and fluently (Torgesen, 1999). In contrast, many other children, coming largely from families of lower socioeconomic or minority status, enter school with significant delays in a much broader range of prereading skills (Hart & Risley, 1995; Hecht, Burgess, Torgesen, Wagner, & Rashotte, 2000). These children have weaknesses both in the broad oral language knowledge that supports reading comprehension and in the phonological and print-related knowledge required in learning to read words. Although it is possible for children to enter school weak in vocabulary but strong in the phonological skills and knowledge required in learning to read words, these children are, in fact, quite rare. This pattern of abilities is not commonly observed because the same preschool environmental conditions that affect vocabulary growth also affect the growth of print-related knowledge and skills such as phonemic awareness and knowledge of letters.

Children with general oral language weaknesses plus phonological weaknesses require instructional interventions in a broader range of knowledge and skills than those who come to school with impairments only in phonological ability. However, because both groups have weaknesses in the phonological and print-related domain, *both* kinds of children require special support in the growth of early word reading skills if they are to make adequate progress in learning to read.

Thus, depending on the entering knowledge and skill levels of the children in an intervention study, the investigators may come up with slightly different answers about the teaching methods that are essential in promoting reading growth. One frequent argument against increasing the amount and explicitness of phonics instruction in early elementary school classrooms is that not all children need the same level of instruction in this area. This is, in fact, true. Many children enter school with excellent phonological processing skills and a strong beginning understanding of the alphabetic principle. These children can discover, during interactions with print, most of the knowledge that must be acquired to become a skilled reader. As these children read, they notice useful generalizations about print–sound relationships, and they learn quite easily to recognize many words at a single glance (Share & Stanovich, 1995). Although research in the classroom suggests that initial explicit instruction in phonics is useful for all children (Snow, Burns, & Griffin, 1998), the benefits of this type of instruction are particularly strong for children who begin with weak phonological skills (Foorman, Francis, Fletcher, Schatschneider, & Mehta, 1998; Juel & Minden-Cupp, 2000).

SOME USEFUL DISTINCTIONS
AMONG INSTRUCTIONAL STUDIES

Although studies of instructional methods in reading vary in a number of important ways, three distinctions are most important for present purposes. One way that they differ from one another is in terms of the types of children included in the sample and the setting in which the instruction takes place. A great deal of research has studied reading instruction at the classroom level, in which all students in a kindergarten, first-, second-, or third-grade classroom are included in the sample of children being studied. Conclusions from this classroom-level research would apply to other classrooms that serve similar kinds of children. For example, conclusions about the essential elements or methods of instruction might vary, depending on whether students in the study came from relatively homogeneous environments or whether they came from very diverse environments.

In contrast to classroom research that examines the effectiveness of core reading curricula with whole classes of children, *intervention* research typically focuses either on children who are experiencing difficulties learning to read in the regular classroom or on children who are at risk for reading difficulties because of such things as low phonemic awareness, inadequate vocabulary, or low socioeconomic status. In this chapter, I focus on findings from the second type of instructional research, which is usually referred to as intervention research because it examines instructional methods that are designed to *intervene* to prevent or remediate reading difficulties in children who are not developing adequately in reading or prereading skills.

Types of Intervention Studies

Intervention studies can be distinguished from one another in terms of the types of questions they are designed to answer. Historically, most intervention research has focused on questions about the efficacy of one method versus another or the effectiveness of a particular method when compared with a control group that did not receive the intervention. In these studies, if one method produces better reading growth than another, it is judged to be more effective, and the authors of the study usually conclude that the method should be used with other children who have similar types of reading difficulties.

An interesting example of this type of study was reported by Iversen and Tunmer (1993), who compared the effectiveness of two different instructional methods in preventing reading problems in first-grade children identified as at risk for reading failure. One group of children received instruction following procedures that were standard for the Reading Recovery method (Clay, 1985), and another group received a method that was very similar, except that one part of the standard method was replaced by 5 minutes of very explicit phonics instruction. Children in the second group achieved about a 30% gain in their rate of reading growth compared with students who received the standard method, and the study authors concluded that the addition of a relatively small amount of very explicit phonics instruction would substantially improve the effectiveness of the Reading Recovery technique when used with first-grade children at risk for reading failure.

Swanson (1999) recently reported a comprehensive meta-analysis of this type of intervention research focusing on children with learning disabilities. This analysis identified a number of instructional practices that consistently produced significant improvement in learning as compared with standard instructional practices. For example, if learning was measured by growth in word reading ability, then methods that included direct instruction in component skills produced the most powerful effects. In contrast, if the reading outcome used in the study was a measure of reading comprehension, then methods that combined direct instruction techniques with cognitively oriented strategy instruction produced the biggest gains. These data are useful because they show that many of the elements of effective instruction for children with reading disabilities are understood, but the data are limited in another way. They provide information about which instructional approaches are more effective, but they typically do not reveal whether the most effective instructional techniques are sufficiently powerful to prevent reading problems in almost all children or to remediate the reading skills of children with established reading disabilities.

For example, one excellent and widely cited study (Lovett, Borden, Lacerenza, Benson, & Brackstone, 1994) examined the effectiveness of several carefully contrasted interventions. This study produced useful information about important elements of instruction for children with severe reading disabilities. At the conclusion of the study, however, the children's reading skills still fell in the range of severe disability. The children in the two strongest interventions began the study with scores on a measure of word reading ability below the 1st percentile, and at the conclusion of the study, their scores were still below the 2nd percentile. The same pattern was observed for a measure of reading comprehension. Although one could argue that continued application of the successful instructional techniques from this study might eventually bring the student's reading skills into the average range, in the absence of direct evidence, one simply does not know if this assumption is correct.

Clearly, a strong science of reading intervention also needs research that focuses on the conditions that must be in place to actually bring the reading skills of children with reading disabilities into the typical range. The important questions in such studies might include the following: 1) What kind of instruction, 2) delivered with what intensity, 3) for how long, 4) with what level of teacher skill, 5) for which kinds of children, and 6) in what broad educational contexts is required to prevent or remediate reading difficulties? Typically, studies that are designed to address questions about the ultimate effectiveness of instructional methods in preventing or remediating reading disabilities provide more instruction and longer follow-up reading assessments (to determine if the instructional effects have long term stability) than studies that are simply interested in determining if one method produces more rapid reading growth than another.

Prevention versus Remedial Studies

In addition to distinguishing between instructional research at the classroom and intervention level, and between studies that test specific instructional hypotheses and those that examine ultimate instructional effectiveness, it is important to distinguish between studies of preventive interventions and research on remedial interventions. The primary distinguishing characteristic between these two types of studies is that instruction in prevention studies is usually begun in kindergarten or early first grade, before children have had a chance to exhibit noticeable or significant failure in learning to read. Remedial studies, on the other hand, study methods to accelerate reading growth once children have exhibited clear difficulties in learning to read.

In practice, the distinction between prevention and remedial studies is not as clear as I have just outlined it. In a sense, there is no such thing as a true prevention study if the intervention does not begin until school starts in kindergarten. Although children selected for prevention studies in kindergarten and early first grade have not failed in learning to read, they are always selected because they are lagging behind in the development of critical prereading skills such as phonemic awareness, knowledge of letters, or oral language and vocabulary. In other words, they have already failed to learn these critical prereading skills as well as their classmates. The "preventive" instruction they receive must "remediate" their impairments in these areas if it is to be effective in preventing serious delays in the acquisition of the formal reading skills of word reading accuracy and fluency and reading comprehension. In another sense, however, interventions that are provided in kindergarten and first grade can be truly preventive. If this kind of instruction is effective, it can eliminate many of the negative consequences of true reading failure such as loss of motivation and interest in reading (Oka & Paris, 1986), loss of reading practice opportunities to build fluency (Torgesen, Rashotte, & Alexander, 2001), and limitations in the development of vocabulary that results from restricted reading experience (Cunningham & Stanovich, 1998).

In the remainder of this chapter, I provide information about the major conclusions from recent intervention research in reading. These conclusions are classified by the distinctions I have already made between the types of questions addressed in the research and whether the research has a preventive or a remedial focus.

CONTENT AND METHOD
OF INSTRUCTION FOR INTERVENTIONS

We now have a very broad scientific consensus about the types of knowledge and skill that are required to become a good reader. Both the report of the National Research Council (Snow et al., 1998) and the more recent report of the National Reading Panel (National Institute of Child Health and Human Development [NICHD], 2000) converge on very similar lists of skills that children must acquire as they learn to read. For example, it is very important that young children 1) become aware of the phonemic elements in words (phonemic awareness), 2) learn to decode words they have not seen before in print by using knowledge about relationships between letters and sounds (phonics), and 3) learn to recognize large numbers of words by sight so that they can read fluently. At the same time, children must become able to 4) instantly retrieve the meanings of an increasingly large vocabulary of words and 5) think actively while they read in order to construct meaning (use comprehension strategies). These same conclusions are also supported in an article called "How Psychological Science Informs the Teaching of Reading" (Rayner et al., 2001) that was specifically written to show how research can be used to inform the content of reading instruction for both younger and older children.

Although there is clear evidence about the kinds of skills involved in learning to read, it is clear that children can compensate somewhat for weaknesses in one area by having strengths in another area (Stanovich, 1984). Children may also vary in the amount and explicitness of instruction they require in each of the broad areas of reading or prereading skill. It is now generally understood, however, that skills and knowledge in these five areas each contribute to becoming a good reader during elementary school. Thus, it should not be surprising that prevention and intervention research since the 1980s demonstrates that at-risk and struggling readers show greater reading growth with interventions that focus directly on strengthening these components than with methods that do not address them in a comprehensive manner (Juel & Minden-Cupp, 2000; Torgesen, 2002).

For example, recent prevention research with children at risk for reading failure has provided powerfully converging evidence for the effectiveness of methods that directly teach phonemic awareness and phonics skills as compared with those that do not. One study (Torgesen et al., 1999) demonstrated that of three interventions that were tested on a sample of highly at-risk young children, the most phonemically explicit method produced the strongest growth in word reading ability. In fact, of the three interventions tested, only the most explicit and direct intervention produced a reliable difference in growth of word reading ability as compared with the ability of children who were not provided with any special interventions. This same pattern of results has been obtained in studies reported by Brown and Felton (1990); Hatcher, Hulme, and Ellis (1994); and Iversen and Tunmer (1993). Furthermore, a recent review of research on the effectiveness of comprehensive school reform models showed that Direct Instruction (Carnine, Silbert, & Kameenui, 1990) and Success for All (Slavin, Madden, & Karweit, 1989) were 2 of only 3 (of 29) models that had reliable and substantial evidence for effectiveness in schools that serve large proportions of children at risk for difficulties learning to read (Borman, Hewes, Overman, & Brown, 2002). Both of these methods provide relatively direct and systematic instruction in phonemic decoding skills.

Perhaps the most important conclusion to draw from recent intervention research is that intervention instruction should focus on the same major dimensions of knowledge and skill that are taught in the regular classroom but must be more *explicit* and *intensive* than classroom instruction to prevent or remediate reading difficulties. As Gaskins, Ehri, Cress, O'Hara, and Donnelly pointed out, "First graders who are at risk for failure in learning to read do not discover what teachers leave unsaid about the complexities of word learning. As a result, it is important to teach them procedures for learning words" (1997, p. 325).

Explicit instruction is instruction that does not leave anything to chance and does not make assumptions about skills and knowledge that children will acquire on their own. For example, explicit instruction requires teachers to directly make connections between the letters in print and the sounds in words, and it requires that these relationships be taught in a comprehensive fashion. It also requires that the meanings of words be directly taught and be explicitly practiced so that they are accessible when children are reading text (Beck, McKeown, & Kucan, 2002). Finally, it requires not only direct practice to build fluency (Mercer, Campbell, Miller, Mercer, & Lane, 2000) but also careful, sequential instruction and practice in the use of comprehension strategies to help construct meaning (Mastropieri & Scruggs, 1997).

Intervention researchers currently have a good understanding of the kinds of knowledge and skill that must be taught and have learned that this knowledge and skill must be taught explicitly and systematically to struggling readers. However, the exact mix of instructional activities that is most effective almost certainly varies depending on the individual needs of each child. Furthermore, the range of instructional methods that can be used to effectively teach specific skills to struggling readers may also be quite broad. For example, in one remedial study (Torgesen et al., 2001), my colleagues and I found that two methods that both taught phonics explicitly but that used quite different methods and distributed instructional activities very differently produced essentially the same long-term outcomes on reading growth for a sample of children with severe reading disabilities. Richard Olson and his colleagues at the University of Colorado (Olson, Wise, Johnson, & Ring, 1997; Wise, Ring, &

Olson, 1999) also demonstrated that a variety of explicit instructional methods are equally effective in accelerating reading growth for children with reading disabilities in second through fifth grades.

In addition to having findings about the advantages of explicit instruction, intervention researchers have also learned that preventive and remedial instruction must be substantially more intense than regular classroom instruction if it is to accomplish its purposes (Vaughn & Linan-Thompson, 2003). The basic problem here is that both at-risk and struggling readers must improve their reading skills *at a faster rate* than their typically achieving peers to make up the gaps in learning and skill that got them identified for intervention in the first place.

There are essentially two ways to increase intensity of reading instruction in elementary school. Either instructional time can be increased, or instruction can be provided individually or in small groups. Although increasing large-group instructional time for reading helps many children with mild risk status, the most practical method for increasing instructional intensity for small numbers of highly at-risk students is to provide small-group instruction.

On both logical and empirical grounds, there is no question that significantly reducing the size of instructional groups is necessary to accelerate the reading growth of struggling and at-risk readers. On logical grounds, children who are at risk for reading failure are already behind their peers in many essential prereading skills. Children with established reading disabilities are seriously behind their peers on many actual reading skills. If these children are to close the gap in reading so they are able to adequately read and understand grade-level material, they will require many more learning opportunities than can be provided in large groups during the regular instructional day.

On empirical grounds, meta-analyses consistently show positive effects of grouping practices that increase instructional intensity (Elbaum, Vaughn, Hughes, & Moody, 1999; Lou et al., 1996; Swanson, Hoskyn, & Lee, 1999). One interesting finding that has emerged from these analyses is that, so far, one-to-one interventions in reading have not been shown to be more effective than small-group interventions (Elbaum et al., 1999; NICHD, 2000; see also Table 8.2 in Chapter 8). Although Torgesen et al. (2001) have recently demonstrated very powerful instructional effects for one-to-one instruction (as opposed to the larger group instruction typically provided in special education resource rooms), other studies have shown similar rates of growth for children with reading disabilities in small groups of three and four children at a time (Rashotte, MacFee, & Torgesen, 2001; Wise et al., 1999).

FINDINGS ABOUT THE ULTIMATE EFFECTIVENESS OF PREVENTIVE AND REMEDIAL INSTRUCTION

How effective are current approaches at preventing reading problems in young children or in remediating reading difficulties in older children? I first answer this question with regard to research on prevention and then examine outcomes from remedial studies.

Prevention Studies

In order to answer questions about the effectiveness of current approaches to preventive interventions, one must first make several assumptions. For example, what outcome measure should be used to measure success, and what level of performance constitutes success for a preventive intervention? Within the United States, the federal No Child Left Behind Act of 2001 (PL 107-110) requires states to set reading standards that determine whether a child has attained adequate reading skills by third grade. Within each state, the effectiveness of preventive programs will ultimately be evaluated by examining the percentage of children who fail to meet these standards for adequate reading ability by the end of third grade. For example, the 2002 administration of the Florida Comprehensive Achievement Test showed that 41% of third-grade children were reading below the standard across the state. Thus Florida has a very long way to go, as do most states, before it has accomplished the goal of preventing reading problems in almost all children. However, such state-level standards cannot be used to evaluate outcomes from prevention research because they are not yet available in many states and because most prevention studies have not followed their students through third grade.

In the absence of universally applied reading outcome measures available for third-grade children, I have suggested elsewhere (Torgesen, 2000) that a reasonable standard for preventive instruction with young children is to expect reading achievement within $1/2$ standard deviation of the mean on a nationally standardized test, which corresponds roughly to the 30th percentile. I am comfortable with this standard based on current norms but recognize that as reading instruction for all children improves, increasingly higher skills will be required to achieve the 30th percentile level. As overall reading scores improve through more effective instruction, it may become the case that children with reading skills at the 30th percentile would actually be reading quite well by today's standards and would no longer be considered at risk for reading difficulties.

An alternative to using a normative standard for prevention outcomes is to determine benchmarks for specific skills that are predictive of future grade-level performance on important criterion measures (e.g., third-grade comprehensive reading assessments). The work of Roland Good and his colleagues (Good, Simmons, & Kameenui, 2001) is a notable example of this approach. Using the Dynamic Indicators of Basic Early Literacy Skills (DIBELS; Good & Kaminski, 2002), for example, they suggested that children who reach an oral reading fluency benchmark of 40 accurate words per minute on grade-level text by the end of first grade are on track for grade-level reading comprehension performance at the end of third grade. These benchmarks for absolute reading skill level, however, have not yet been applied broadly in intervention research, so they cannot be used as a standard for evaluating the success of current preventive efforts.

For the time being, and in the absence of well-established *absolute* standards of reading attainment for each grade level, I have adopted the goal for preventive programs of ensuring that children do not fall below the 30th percentile on critical word reading skills at any time during their early elementary years. In evaluating prevention studies, I have also focused on measures of word reading ability as the primary outcome, not only because these measures are more universally available in the studies examined but also because word-level reading problems are almost universally present in children at risk for reading failure. If an intervention is not effective in preventing the development of serious word reading difficulties in young children, then it is very unlikely to be effective in producing adequate performance on a reading comprehension test by grade 3 (Foorman, Francis, Shaywitz, Shaywitz, & Fletcher, 1997).

Table 15.1 provides data from six prevention studies in which it was possible to identify the percentage of children in each intervention sample who obtained scores below the 30th percentile on measures of word reading ability at the end of the intervention. The measure of word reading skill was an average of performance on measures of phonemic decoding ability and context-free word reading accuracy. From 11% to 44% of the children in these studies still

Table 15.1. Proportions of students from intervention studies with word-level reading skills below the 30th percentile at the conclusion of intervention

Study	Amount of instruction (hours)	Instructional group size (teacher–student ratio)	Sample failure rate	Population failure rate
Foorman et al., 1998	174	Whole class	35%	6%
Brown & Felton, 1990	340	1:8	29%	5%
Vellutino et al., 1996	35–65	1:1	44%	6%
Torgesen et al., 1999	88	1:1	34%	4%
Torgesen, Wagner, et al., 2003	80	1:3	11%	2%
Torgesen, Rashotte, Mathes, et al., 2003	91	1:3 or 1:5	8%	1.6%

had critical word reading skills below the 30th percentile at the conclusion of the studies. It is important, however, to remember that these children represented the 12%–18% of children most at risk for reading failure; they were not a random sample of all children. To obtain an estimate of the proportion of *all* children who would remain with weak reading skills if these interventions were applied more broadly, one can multiply the percentage of weak readers at the end of the study in the intervention sample by the proportion of the population they represent. For example, in the study conducted by Barbara Foorman and her colleagues (1998), the students who received the intervention came from the 18% most at risk for reading failure. At the conclusion of the intervention, 35% percent of this bottom 18% remained weak readers, and multiplying .18 by .35 yields a population failure rate of 6%. In Table 15.1, these population failure estimates are reported in the column on the far right.

Although there are a number of important caveats to the estimation of population failure rates reported in Table 15.1 (Torgesen, 2000), one point is well established. Intervention research has not yet discovered the conditions that need to be in place for *all* children with the most serious disabilities to acquire adequate word-level reading skills in early elementary school. However, research has clearly shown how to sharply reduce the number of children who leave first and second grades with weak skills in this area. Most of the estimates reported in Table 15.1 suggest that 4%–6% of children would still have weak word reading skills even if those interventions were applied to all who needed them.

My colleagues and I have some data from one study reported in Table 15.1 (Torgesen, Rashotte, Mathes, et al., 2003) that these estimates of the success of current prevention studies may be a bit optimistic in projecting the percentage of children who would fall below grade level on a group-administered reading comprehension test at the end of third grade. In this study, we provided intensive preventive instruction to the 20% of first-grade children most at risk for reading failure from five suburban schools in which effective classroom instruction was also provided to all children. Children received systematic and highly explicit supplemental instruction in groups of three or five for 45 minutes a day from October through May. Whereas all children in the intervention groups began the intervention with scores on a word reading accuracy measure below the 25th percentile, only 8% had scores below the 30th percentile on the same measure at the end of first grade. Using the technique from Table 15.1 to calculate the population failure rate for word level reading skills gives an estimate of 1.6% (.2 × .08).

These same children were followed through to the end of second grade (with no further intervention from us), and our estimation of the population failure rate for the word reading measure was the same for second grade as for first (Torgesen, Rashotte, Mathes, et al., 2003). In other words, there was no significant drop in performance from the end of first grade to the end of second grade on the word reading measure. However, when the outcome measure was a group-administered measure of silent reading comprehension at the end of second grade, the population failure rate (estimated percentage of the total population remaining below the 30th percentile) was 4.1% rather than 1.6%. I project that this failure rate would be even higher for a comprehensive measure of reading comprehension at the end of third grade for the simple reason that as reading material becomes more complex (with increasing vocabulary demands and more difficult concepts), the role of broad verbal ability in accounting for reading comprehension difficulties becomes larger (Adams, 1990). Forty-six percent of the children in our intervention sample had estimated verbal intelligence below the 30th percentile. Thus, although our intervention students were doing better on a measure of reading comprehension in second grade than would be predicted by an estimate of their broad verbal ability, we would expect verbal ability to play an increasingly important role as reading material becomes more complex. Although research has shown how to prevent word-level reading difficulties for almost all children, methods for substantially and permanently increasing relative verbal ability (i.e., verbal intelligence) once children enter elementary school remain to be discovered (Lee, Brooks-Gunn, Schnur, & Liaw, 1990).

Remedial Interventions

Until very recently, the research-based prognosis for children who fall significantly behind in reading growth during the first 3 years of elementary school has been relatively bleak. For example, Juel (1988) found that only one child in eight who fell in the bottom quartile in word reading ability at the end of first grade attained grade-level reading skills by fourth grade. Two other longitudinal studies (Francis, Shaywitz, Stuebing, Shaywitz, & Fletcher, 1996; Torgesen & Burgess, 1998) found essentially the same thing.

Furthermore, examinations of the effectiveness of special education in public school settings has indicated that children do not typically close the gap in reading skills and catch up with their peers (Hanushek, Kain, & Rivkin, 1998). The degree of reading impairment in children with reading disabilities tends to be stabilized by special education (children do not fall further behind) rather than being reduced. These results apply not only to traditional pull-out programs (Kavale, 1988; McKinney, 1990; Schumaker, Deshler, & Ellis, 1986) but also to inclusive education models for assisting children with reading disabilities (Zigmond et al., 1995). These results led the President's Commission on Special Education (2002) to conclude that special education has generally failed in its mission to close the gap in academic achievement between children with and without learning difficulties. At the same time, the commission identified the goal of "normalizing" the academic achievement of children with learning difficulties as one of the most important missions of special education.

Fortunately, there is strongly converging evidence from recent research on remedial interventions for older children indicating that it is possible to substantially close the gap in reading ability for many children, even after they have struggled in learning to read for several years (Lovett et al., 2000; Rashotte et al., 2001; Torgesen et al., 2001; Wise et al., 1999). The research-based interventions that support this conclusion are quite different from those that are typically provided to children with reading disabilities in public school special education programs. Not only do these interventions provide instruction that is more explicit and systematic than is frequently provided to public school students (Vaughn, Moody, & Shuman, 1998), but also the interventions that have been studied are delivered much more intensively. Whereas public school special education teachers in pull-out classrooms often are required to teach 15–20 students at one time, the interventions studied in recent research have been provided either one to one or in small groups of no more than three to five children.

After examining intervention results with five different samples of older children (ages 9–12) who were provided 50–100 hours of relatively intense (one-to-one or small-group), phonemically explicit and systematic instruction, my colleagues and I (Torgesen, Rashotte, Alexander, Alexander, & McPhee, 2003) suggested several important conclusions about current instructional capabilities. One of the samples had roughly average intelligence and had mild impairments in word reading accuracy (scores around the 30th percentile) but severe impairments in reading fluency (approximately the 2nd percentile) when the intervention began. The children in this group were given an average of 60 hours of appropriate small-group instruction, and their skills in phonemic decoding, text reading accuracy, reading comprehension, and reading fluency were brought solidly into the average range (82nd, 80th, 70th, and 48th percentiles, respectively). In other words, a relatively brief dose of appropriately intensive and explicit instruction completely closed the gap in reading skill for children who begin the intervention with mild reading impairments.

Conclusions were slightly different for two samples of children who began the intervention with moderate reading impairments (word reading accuracy around the 10th percentile) and estimated intelligence about the 30th percentile. These children began the intervention with similar levels of reading impairment, but one group received 50 hours and the other an average of 100 hours of intervention. Before intervention, both groups had reading fluency scores below the 1st percentile and reading comprehension scores around the 8th percentile. The group receiving only 50 hours of intervention attained phonemic decoding and reading comprehension skills solidly in the average range (55th and 35th percentiles, respectively), but their text reading accuracy remained below average (25th percentile) and fluency was at the 7th percentile at the end of intervention. In contrast, a similar group of children receiving 100 hours of intervention finished with phonemic decoding, text reading accuracy, and passage comprehension all solidly in the average range (77th, 39th, and 39th percentiles, respectively). Although the relative impairment of this group in reading fluency was decreased by the intervention, the gap in fluency between these children and other children the same age remained substantial (8th percentile).

Finally, my colleagues and I (Torgesen, Rashotte, Alexander, et al., 2003) reported on two samples of children with severe reading disabilities (average age: 10 years) that began an intensive intervention with word reading accuracy scores at the 2nd percentile and verbal intelligence at about the 30th percentile. These children were all identified as having learning disabilities and had been receiving special education services for an average of 16 months before they were selected for the study. Thus, they represent a group of children who had remained substantially unresponsive to reading instruction even when exposed to intervention through special education services.

One of these samples received 67.5 hours of one-to-one instruction with skilled teachers, whereas the other sample received 133 hours in a combination of one to one instruction and instruction with two students and one teacher (Torgesen et al., 2001). Both samples were selected by the same criteria, and both began instruction with the same level of reading skills. After 67.5 hours of instruction, the first sample had phonemic decoding skills in the average range (39th percentile), reading accuracy scores at the 23rd percentile, reading comprehension scores at the 27th percentile, and fluency scores at the 5th percentile. At a follow-up testing 2 years after the intervention ended and about 40% of the children in the first sample no longer qualified for special education services, reading accuracy scores had improved to the 27th percentile, comprehension to the 36th percentile, and relative fluency had declined to the 4th percentile. Thus, most of the children had been able to maintain their reading gains in accuracy and comprehension during the 2 years following the intensive intervention, but the gap in reading fluency remained substantial.

The second remediation sample, which received 133 hours of instruction was selected 3 years later from the same classrooms as the first sample. The children in this second sample were randomly assigned to two groups, and one of the groups received the same type of intervention as in the first sample of children with severe reading disabilities. The other group in the second sample substituted special fluency-oriented interventions (repeated reading of words, phrases, and passages) for some of the accuracy-oriented instruction starting midway through the intervention. Preliminary results after 45 children received intervention (of a projected total second sample of 60), showed there was no difference in outcome between the intervention that emphasized fluency and the one that did not, so their results were considered together. At the conclusion of the intervention, the children in both groups of the second sample had improved from the 3rd to the 39th percentile in phonemic decoding ability, from the 6th to the 16th percentile in text reading accuracy, from the 7th to the 19th percentile in reading comprehension, and they stayed at the 3rd percentile in reading fluency. Thus, for all reading skills except reading fluency, the children made substantial progress toward closing the gap in reading ability with average readers, but they remained below average in text reading accuracy and comprehension.

In spite of the fact that the second sample received twice as much instruction as the first sample, it actually improved less in text reading accuracy and comprehension than the first sample did. Because both the first and second samples had received very similar interventions and had been selected by the same criteria, the only explanation we are able to offer for this unexpected finding is that the latter group had even more severe reading disabilities than the first one. Our primary evidence for this assertion is that the special education classes from which the children were selected had improved substantially during the 3 years that intervened between the selection of the two samples. It was actually more difficult to find students who read poorly enough to meet our selection criteria when we selected the second sample than it was when we identified children for the first study. Teachers who had worked in both studies also noticed immediately that the children in the second sample were "much more difficult to teach" than children in the first sample.

This finding introduces another complication that must be kept in mind when looking at the results of intervention studies. The actual reading impairment a child shows at any point is always the result of an interaction between the child's degree of disability and the strength of instruction that has been provided. Children with a mild learning disability who are provided with only weak instruction (in the general education classroom or in another environment) show larger reading impairments when tested than do children with the same degree of learning disability who have had stronger instruction. By the same token, children whose severe reading impairments persist within a strong instructional environment are likely to have a more serious learning disability than those whose reading impairments persist after receiving only weak instruction. Thus, if researchers select their intervention samples from among children who have already received a good dose of appropriate and reasonably intensive instruction, the children in those samples will be more difficult to teach than children who are selected by the same reading criteria from a weaker instructional environment.

What About the Remaining Problems in Fluency?

One of the consistent findings in our remedial research for children who begin the intervention with moderate or serious impairments in word reading ability is that the interventions have not been sufficient to close the gap in reading fluency. Although the gap in reading accuracy and comprehension can be substantially or completely closed by current interventions, the gap in fluency has remained much less tractable to intervention for moderately and seriously impaired children.

When teachers or other researchers see these results, they think immediately that there must be something wrong with the interventions. Perhaps the interventions we have used emphasize phonics too much, perhaps they focus on accuracy too much, or perhaps they don't provide enough practice in reading fluency itself. We do not entirely discount these possibilities, but we also have considerable evidence that the problem may lie in the nature of reading fluency itself rather than in the interventions. First, in one study with children with severe reading impairments (Torgesen et al., 2001), one of the instructional interventions invested 50% of instructional time in reading connected text, whereas the other invested only 5%. There was no difference in fluency outcomes. Second, the intervention used with the previously described three samples of children with mild and moderate impairments (Torgesen, Rashotte, Alexander, et al., 2003) also focused considerable instructional time in text reading activities with an emphasis on both modeling and practicing fluent reading. Again, the students who began the intervention with moderate (10th percentile) word reading difficulties showed only moderate improvement in their age-based percentile ranking for fluency. Third, and probably most important, we have not observed the same differences in outcomes between reading fluency and reading accuracy in our prevention studies as have been found in the remedial studies. Figure 15.1 shows the standard scores (a score of 100 is average) for reading accuracy and fluency outcomes for the five samples that received remedial instruction (Torgesen, Rashotte, Alexander, et al., 2003), with each sample identified by their reading accuracy percentile at the beginning of the intervention. Even for the children who began the intervention at the 30th percentile in word reading ability and who achieved fluency in the average range, there is a considerable gap between their standard score for accuracy and their score for fluency.

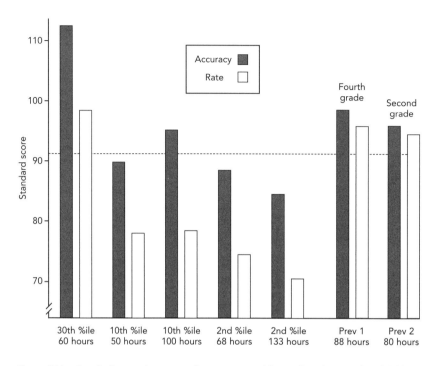

Figure 15.1. Standard scores for text reading accuracy and fluency from five samples of children in late elementary school who received effective remedial instruction (Torgesen, Rashotte, Alexander, et al., 2003) and two samples of at-risk children (Prev 1 and Prev 2) who received preventive instruction in kindergarten and first grade (Torgesen, Rashotte, Wagner, et al., 2003; Torgesen et al., 1999).

Outcomes for text reading accuracy and fluency from two prevention studies are presented on the right side of Figure 15.1. The most obvious difference between the outcomes from the prevention and remediation studies is that the gap between reading accuracy and fluency is not nearly as large for the prevention as for the remediation studies. The first prevention study (Prev 1; Torgesen et al., 1999) provided $2^1/2$ years of instruction to children in 20-minute sessions 4 days per week from the second semester of kindergarten through second grade. The children were identified as the 10% most at risk for reading failure because of low scores in phonemic awareness and letter knowledge in the first semester of kindergarten. Figure 15.1 shows the performance of children in the most effective instructional condition at the end of fourth grade, 2 years after the intervention was concluded. The children's scores for both reading accuracy and fluency are solidly in the average range.

In the second prevention study shown in Figure 15.1 (Prev 2; Torgesen, Rashotte, Wagner, Herron, & Lindamood, 2003), preventive instruction was provided during first grade to children identified at the beginning of first grade as the 20% most at risk for reading failure. The children were taught in small groups using a combination of teacher-led and computer-assisted instruction in 50-minute sessions, 4 days per week from October through May. The data in Figure 15.1 show the performance of the children from the most effective condition at the end of second grade, one year after the intervention concluded. Again, both reading accuracy and fluency scores are solidly within the average range, and the gap between these scores is very small.

We have proposed elsewhere (Torgesen et al., 2001) several possible explanations for the difficulty we have experienced in helping older children to close the gap in reading fluency after they have struggled in learning to read for several years. The most important factor appears to involve difficulties in making up for the huge deficits in reading practice the older children have accumulated by the time they reach late elementary school. These differences in reading practice emerge during the earliest stages of reading instruction (Allington, 1984; Beimiller, 1977–1978) and they become more pronounced as the children advance across the grades in elementary school. For example, Cunningham and Stanovich (1998) reported evidence suggesting enormous differences in the amount of reading done by good and poor fifth-grade readers outside of school. A child at the 90th percentile of reading ability may read as many words in 2 days as a child at the 10th percentile reads in an entire year outside of school. Reading practice varies directly with the severity of a child's reading disability, so children with severe reading disabilities receive only a very small fraction of the total reading practice obtained by children with typical reading skills.

One of the major results of this lack of reading practice is a severe limitation in the number of words the children with reading disabilities can recognize automatically, or at a single glance (Ehri, 1998; Share & Stanovich, 1995), sometimes referred to by teachers as the child's *sight word vocabulary*. This limitation of sight word vocabulary is a principle characteristic of most children with reading disabilities after the initial phase in learning to read (Rashotte et al., 2001; Torgesen, Rashotte, Alexander, et al., 2003; Wise et al., 1999).

My colleagues and I have shown elsewhere (Torgesen et al., 2001) that inefficiency in identifying single words is the most important factor in accounting for individual differences in text reading fluency in samples of children with reading disabilities. When these findings are combined with the fact that the number of less frequent words (words children are less likely to have encountered before in text) increases rapidly after about third-grade level (Adams, 1990), it is easy to see why it is so difficult for children who have failed in reading for the first 3 or 4 years of school to close the gap in reading fluency and catch up with their typically achieving peers. If successively higher grade-level passages include increasing numbers of less frequent words and typical readers are continually expanding their sight vocabularies through their own reading behavior, it should be very difficult for children, once significantly behind in the growth of their sight word vocabulary, to close the gap in reading fluency. Such catching up would seem to require an extensive period of time in which the reading practice of the children with reading disabilities is actually *greater* than that of their peers. Even if word reading accuracy is dramatically increased through the more efficient use of analytic word reading processes, reliance on analytic processes will not produce the kind of fluent reading that results when most of the words in a passage can be recognized by sight.

CONCLUSIONS

The results from the intervention research described in this chapter have several important implications for both educational practice and for future research. The first implication for practice and educational policy is that schools must work to provide *preventive* interventions to eliminate the enormous reading practice deficits that result from prolonged reading failure. One of the most important goals of preventive instruction should be to maintain the fundamental word reading skills of at-risk children within the typical range so that they can read independently and accurately. If they can read independently and accurately and they are also taught to enjoy reading, it is likely that they will experience roughly typical rates of growth in their sight word vocabularies and thus be able to maintain more nearly average levels of reading fluency as they progress through the elementary school years.

The second implication is that schools must find a way to provide interventions for older children with reading disabilities that are *appropriately focused and sufficiently intensive.* This chapter has described a number of examples of the way this type of intervention can produce dramatic improvements in older children's text reading accuracy and reading comprehension in a relatively short period of time. With this evidence in hand, educators, administrators, and parents need to work toward finding ways to bring more intensive instruction to more children, and our expectations about what constitutes reasonable progress in reading for older children with reading disabilities needs to be adjusted.

With regard to research, the two most obvious questions arising from the findings considered in this chapter are these: 1) What is the most appropriate range of intensity and amount of remedial instruction that should be available to older children with reading disabilities, and 2) how can reading practice be focused more effectively with older children to help them close the gap in reading fluency and catch up with their typically achieving peers? The first question arises from the fact that even in the most effective remedial studies, significant numbers of children remain with poor reading skills at the conclusion of the intervention. There is substantial agreement about the elements of effective instruction for children with the most common form of reading disabilities (Lovett et al., 2000; Torgesen, Rashotte, Alexander, et al., 2003), but there is much less information available about the amount and intensity of such instruction that may be required to help all children acquire adequate reading skills.

For children with reading disabilities who have limited sight word vocabularies and limited proficiency in decoding novel words, it seems that the first target of intervention should be to increase the accuracy of individual word reading skills. More accurate reading at the word level through effective application of a repertoire of word analysis skills is necessary before children can consistently add to the depth and breadth of their sight word vocabulary through independent reading (Share & Stanovich, 1995).

The most successful fluency intervention described to date, repeated reading (NICHD, 2000; see also Chapter 9), is effective because it provides the kind of repeated exposure to words that either leads to acquisition of new sight words or increases efficiency of access to words that are already in a child's sight vocabulary. Simply providing more reading opportunities for children with limited sight word vocabularies may not be sufficient to increase their sight vocabularies at an acceptable rate because at higher grade levels, the less frequent words that they are trying to learn occur at such infrequent intervals in text (Adams, 1990). Thus, an important question for future research is how to increase the efficiency of reading practice for children whose reading accuracy problems have been remediated through successful interventions. In other words, how should practice be engineered and focused so that it produces accelerated growth in the fluent word reading processes that are the most critical factor in oral reading fluency?

REFERENCES

Adams, M.J. (1990). *Beginning to read: Thinking and learning about print.* Cambridge, MA: MIT Press.

Allington, R.L. (1984). Content coverage and contextual reading in reading groups. *Journal of Reading Behavior, 16,* 85–96.

American Federation of Teachers. (1999, June). *Teaching reading* is *rocket science: What expert teachers of reading should know and be able to do* (Item No. 372 6/99). Washington, DC: Author.

Beck, I.L., McKeown, M.G., & Kucan, L. (2002). *Bringing words to life: Robust vocabulary instruction.* New York: The Guilford Press.

Beimiller, A. (1977–1978). Relationships between oral reading rates for letters, words, and simple text in the development of reading achievement. *Reading Research Quarterly, 13,* 223–253.

Borman, G.D., Hewes, G.M., Overman, L.T., & Brown, S. (2002). Comprehensive school reform and student achievement: A meta-analysis. *Review of Educational Research, 73,* 125–230.

Brown, I.S., & Felton, R.H. (1990). Effects of instruction on beginning reading skills in children at risk for reading disability. *Reading and Writing: An Interdisciplinary Journal, 2,* 223–241.

Carnine, D., Silbert, J., & Kameenui, E.J. (1990). *Direct instruction reading.* New York: Merrill.

Clay, M.M. (1985). *The early detection of reading difficulties.* Portsmouth, NH: Heinemann.

Cunningham, A.E., & Stanovich, K.E. (1998, Spring/Summer). What reading does for the mind. *American Educator, 22,* 8–15.

Elbaum, B., Vaughn, S., Hughes, M.T., & Moody, S.W. (1999). Grouping practices and reading outcomes for students with disabilities. *Exceptional Children, 65,* 399–415.

Ehri, L.C. (1998). Grapheme-phoneme knowledge is essential for learning to read words in English. In J. Metsala & L. Ehri (Eds.), *Word recognition in beginning reading* (pp. 3–40). Mahwah, NJ: Lawrence Erlbaum Associates.

Foorman, B.R., Francis, D.J., Fletcher, J.M., Schatschneider, C., & Mehta, P. (1998). The role of instruction in learning to read: Preventing reading failure in at-risk children. *Journal of Educational Psychology, 90,* 37–55.

Foorman, B.R., Francis, D.J., Shaywitz, S.E., Shaywitz, B.A., & Fletcher, J.M. (1997). The case for early intervention. In B. Blachman (Ed.), *Foundations of reading acquisition and dyslexia: Implications for early intervention* (pp. 243–264). Mahwah, NJ: Lawrence Erlbaum Associates.

Francis, D.J., Shaywitz, S.E., Stuebing, K.K., Shaywitz, B.A., & Fletcher, J.M. (1996). Developmental lag versus deficit models of reading disability: A longitudinal, individual growth curves analysis. *Journal of Educational Psychology, 88,* 3–17.

Gaskins, I.W., Ehri, L.C., Cress, C., O'Hara, C., & Donnelly, K. (1997). Procedures for word learning: Making discoveries about words. *The Reading Teacher, 50,* 312–327.

Good, R.H., & Kaminski, R.A. (Eds.). (2002). *Dynamic Indicators of Basic Early Literacy Skills* (6th ed.). Eugene, OR: Institute for Development of Educational Achievement.

Good, R.H., Simmons, D.C., & Kameenui, E. (2001). The importance and decision-making utility of a continuum of fluency-based indicators of foundational reading skills for third-grade high-stakes outcomes. *Scientific Studies of Reading, 5,* 257–288.

Hanushek, E.A., Kain, J.F., & Rivkin, S.G. (1998). *Does special education raise academic achievement for students with disabilities?* (Working Paper No. 6690). Cambridge, MA: National Bureau of Economic Research.

Hart, B., & Risley, T.R. (1995). *Meaningful differences in the everyday experience of young American children.* Baltimore: Paul H. Brookes Publishing Co.

Hatcher, P., Hulme, C., & Ellis, A.W. (1994). Ameliorating early reading failure by integrating the teaching of reading and phonological skills: The phonological linkage hypothesis. *Child Development, 65,* 41–57.

Hecht, S.A., Burgess, S.R., Torgesen, J.K., Wagner, R.K., & Rashotte, C.A. (2000). Explaining social class differences in growth of reading skills from beginning kindergarten through fourth-grade: The role of phonological awareness, rate of access, and print knowledge. *Reading and Writing: An Interdisciplinary Journal, 12,* 99–127.

Iversen, S., & Tunmer, W.S. (1993). Phonological processing skills and the reading recovery program. *Journal of Educational Psychology, 85,* 112–126.

Juel, C. (1988). Learning to read and write: A longitudinal study of 54 children from first through fourth grades. *Journal of Educational Psychology, 80,* 437–447.

Juel, C., & Minden-Cupp, C. (2000). Learning to read words: Linguistic units and instructional strategies. *Reading Research Quarterly, 35,* 458–492.

Kavale, K.A. (1988). The long-term consequences of learning disabilities. In M.C. Wang, H.J. Walburg, & M.C. Reynolds (Eds.), *The handbook of special education: Research and practice* (pp. 303–344). New York: Pergamon.

Lee, V., Brooks-Gunn, J., Schnur, E., & Liaw, F. (1990). Are Head Start effects sustained?: A longitudinal follow-up comparison of disadvantaged children attending Head Start, no preschool, and other pre-school programs. *Child Development, 61,* 495–507.

Lou, Y., Abrami, P.C., Spence, J.C., Poulsen, C., Chambers, B., & d'Appolonia, S. (1996). Within-class grouping: A meta-analysis. *Review of Educational Research, 66*(4), 423–458.

Lovett, M.W., Borden, S.L., Lacerenza, L., Benson, N.J., & Brackstone, D. (1994). Treating the core deficits of developmental dyslexia: Evidence of transfer of learning after phonologically- and strategy-based reading training programs. *Journal of Educational Psychology, 30,* 805–822.

Lovett, M.W., Lacerenza, L., Borden, S.L., Frijters, J.C., Steinbach, K.A., & DePalma, M. (2000). Components of effective remediation for developmental reading disabilities: Combining phonologically and strategy-based instruction to improve outcomes. *Journal of Educational Psychology, 92,* 263–283.

Mastropieri, M.A., & Scruggs, T.E. (1997). Best practices in promoting reading comprehension in students with learning disabilities: 1976–1996. *Remedial and Special Education, 18,* 197–213.

McKinney, J.D. (1990). Longitudinal research on the behavioral characteristics of children with learning disabilities. In J. Torgesen (Ed.), *Cognitive and behavioral characteristics of children with learning disabilities* (pp. 128–142). Austin, TX: PRO-ED.

Mercer, C.D., Campbell, K.U., Miller, M.D., Mercer, K.D., & Lane, H.B. (2000). Effects of a reading fluency intervention for middle schoolers with specific learning disabilities. *Learning Disabilities Research and Practice, 15*(4), 179–189.

National Institute of Child Health and Human Development (NICHD). (2000). *Report of the National Reading Panel. Teaching children to read: An evidence-based assessment of the scientific research literature on reading and its implications for reading instruction: Reports of the subgroups* (NIH Publication No. 00-4754). Washington, DC: U.S. Government Printing Office. Also available on-line: http://www.nichd.nih.gov/publications/nrp/report.htm

No Child Left Behind Act of 2001, PL 107-110, 115 Stat. 1425, 20 U.S.C. §§ 6301 *et seq.*

Oka, E., & Paris, S. (1986). Patterns of motivation and reading skills in underachieving children. In S. Ceci (Ed.), *Handbook of cognitive, social, and neuropsychological aspects of learning disabilities* (Vol. 2, pp. 115–145). Mahwah, NJ: Lawrence Erlbaum Associates.

Olson, R.K., Wise, B., Johnson, M., & Ring, J. (1997). The etiology and remediation of phonologically based word recognition and spelling disabilities: Are phonological deficits the "hole" story? In B. Blachman (Ed.), *Foundations of reading acquisition and dyslexia: Implications for early intervention.* Mahwah, NJ: Lawrence Erlbaum Associates.

President's Commission on Special Education. (2002). *A new era: Revitalizing special education for children and their families.* Washington, DC: U.S. Department of Education.

Rashotte, C.A., MacPhee, K., & Torgesen, J.K. (2001). The effectiveness of a group reading instruction program with poor readers in multiple grades. *Learning Disabilities Quarterly, 24,* 119–134.

Rayner, K., Foorman, B.R., Perfetti, C.A., Pesetsky, D., & Seidenberg, M.S. (2001). How psychological science informs the teaching of reading. *Psychological Science in the Public Interest, 2,* 31–73.

Schumaker, J.B., Deshler, D.D., & Ellis, E.S. (1986). Intervention issues related to the education of learning disabled adolescents. In J.K. Torgesen & B.Y.L. Wong (Eds.), *Psychological and educational perspectives on learning disabilities* (pp. 329–365). San Diego: Academic Press.

Share, D.L., & Stanovich, K.E. (1995). Cognitive processes in early reading development: A model of acquisition and individual differences. *Issues in Education: Contributions from Educational Psychology, 1,* 1–57.

Slavin, R.E., Madden, N.A., & Karweit, N.L. (1989). Effective programs for students at risk: Conclusions for practice and policy. In R.E. Slavin, N.L. Karweit, & N.A. Madden (Eds.), *Effective programs for student at risk* (pp. 355–372). Boston: Allyn & Bacon.

Snow, C.E., Burns, M.S., & Griffin, P. (Eds.). (1998). *Preventing reading difficulties in young children.* Washington, DC: National Academies Press.

Stanovich, K. (1984). The interactive-compensatory model of reading: A confluence of developmental, experimental, and educational psychology. *Remedial and Special Education, 5,* 11–19.

Swanson, H.L. (1999). Reading research for students with LD: A meta-analysis of intervention outcomes. *Journal of Learning Disabilities, 32,* 504–532.

Swanson, H.L., Hoskyn, M., & Lee, C. (1999). *Interventions for students with learning disabilities: A meta-analysis of treatment outcomes.* New York: The Guilford Press.

Torgesen, J.K. (1999). Phonologically based reading disabilities: Toward a coherent theory of one kind of learning disability. In R.J. Sternberg & L. Spear-Swerling (Eds.), *Perspectives on learning disabilities* (pp. 231–262). New Haven: Westview Press.

Torgesen, J.K. (2000). Individual differences in response to early interventions in reading: The lingering problem of treatment resisters. *Learning Disabilities Research and Practice, 15,* 55–64.

Torgesen, J.K. (2002). The prevention of reading difficulties. *Journal of School Psychology, 40,* 7–26.

Torgesen, J.K., & Burgess, S.R. (1998). Consistency of reading-related phonological processes throughout early childhood: Evidence from longitudinal-correlational and instructional studies. In J. Metsala & L. Ehri (Eds.), *Word recognition in beginning reading* (pp. 161–188). Mahwah, NJ: Lawrence Erlbaum Associates.

Torgesen, J.K., Rashotte, C.A., & Alexander, A. (2001). Principles of fluency instruction in reading: Relationships with established empirical outcomes. In M. Wolf (Ed.), *Dyslexia, fluency, and the brain* (pp. 333–355). Timonium, MD: York Press.

Torgesen, J.K., Rashotte, C.A., Alexander, A., Alexander, J., & MacPhee, K. (2003). Progress toward understanding the instructional conditions necessary for remediating reading difficulties in older children. In B.R. Foorman (Ed.), *Interventions for children at-risk for reading difficulties or identified with reading difficulties* (pp. 275–298). Timonium, MD: York Press.

Torgesen, J.K., Rashotte, C.A., Mathes, P.G., Menchetti, J.C., Grek, M.L., Robinson, C.S., et al. (2003). *Effects of teacher training and group size on reading outcomes for first grade children at-risk for reading difficulties.* Unpublished manuscript. Florida State University, Tallahassee.

Torgesen, J.K., Rashotte, C.A., Wagner, R.K., Herron, J., & Lindamood, P. (2003). *A comparison of two computer assisted approaches to the prevention of reading disabilities in young children.* Unpublished manuscript, Florida State University, Tallahassee, FL.

Torgesen, J.K., Wagner, R.K., Rashotte, C.A., Rose, E., Lindamood, P., Conway, T., et al. (1999). Preventing reading failure in young children with phonological processing disabilities: Group and individual responses to instruction. *Journal of Educational Psychology, 91,* 579–593.

Vaughn, S., & Linan-Thompson, S. (2003). Group size and time allotted to intervention: Effects for students with reading difficulties. In B.R. Foorman (Ed.), *Interventions for children at-risk for reading difficulties or identified with reading difficulties.* Timonium, MD: York Press.

Vaughn, S.R., Moody, S.W., & Shuman, J.S. (1998). Broken promises: Reading instruction the resource room. *Exceptional Children, 64,* 211–225.

Vellutino, F.R., Scanlon, D.M., Sipay, E.R., Small S.G., Pratt, A., Chen R., & Denckla, M.B. (1996). Cognitive profiles of difficult-to-remediate and readily remedeated poor readers: Early intervention as a vehicle for distinguishing between cognitive and experiential deficits as basic causes of specific reading disability. *Journal of Educational Psychology, 88,* 601–638.

Whitehurst, G.J., & Lonigan, C.J. (1998). Child development and emergent literacy. *Child Development, 69,* 335–357.

Wise, B.W., Ring, J., & Olson, R.K. (1999). Training phonological awareness with and without explicit attention to articulation. *Journal of Experimental Child Psychology, 72,* 271–304.

Zigmond, N., Jenkins, J., Fuchs, L., Deno, S., Fuchs, D., Baker, J.N., et al. (1995). Special education in restructured schools: Findings from three multi-year studies. *Phi Delta Kappan, 76,* 531–535.

V

Neuroimaging
and Brain Research

Neuroimaging is an important technique for studying the neurobiological underpinnings of reading, reading disorders, and reading intervention. Children who have been identified as being at risk for reading difficulties or who display difficulties later in the development of reading abilities have participated in noninvasive neuroimaging studies before and after interventions or while taking part in remediation programs. Neuroimaging is a tool that enhances what scientists learn in behavioral studies about how reading develops or does not develop and helps researchers and educators understand the links between brain and behavior as they continue to study reading and reading disability. The goal of these neuroimaging studies is to determine 1) differences in brain function that accompany reading disability versus reading proficiency and 2) the effects of well-designed instruction on both reading and brain development. Section V of this volume presents the brain research on reading. Reading is a complex cognitive activity that requires the coordination and integration of many skills. What educators do is literally change how the brain functions! That clearly highlights not only the excitement but also the awesome responsibility that lies in teaching children to read. And, these changes can be found in images of the brain while individuals are performing reading tasks. The science that has developed this evidence is functional neuroimaging. In Chapter 16, Andrew C. Papanicolaou, Kenneth R. Pugh, Panagiotis G. Simos, and W. Einar Mencl, four neuropsychologists who conduct neuroimaging research in reading, explain two major types of functional neuroimaging: magnetoencephalography

(MEG) and functional magnetic resonance imaging (fMRI). They also give illustrations of how these technologies are used to study reading and discuss processes that children use in compensating for reading disabilities.

In Chapter 17, Sally E. Shaywitz and Bennett A. Shaywitz demonstrate the application of fMRI technology in studying the development of reading over time. They present data from the Connecticut Longitudinal Study, in which they have followed students from kindergarten into young adulthood. The fMRI data they present demonstrate differences in brain activation in good and poor readers. In this chapter, the authors discuss the definition, history, and neurological bases of reading disabilities.

16

Functional Brain Imaging

An Introduction to Concepts and Applications

ANDREW C. PAPANICOLAOU, KENNETH R. PUGH,
PANAGIOTIS G. SIMOS, AND W. EINAR MENCL

The purpose of this chapter is to outline two representative brain imaging methods, magnetoencephalography (MEG), otherwise known as magnetic source imaging (MSI), and functional magnetic resonance imaging (fMRI), both of which are used in research on reading. We also explain how researchers establish the correspondence between images of brain *activation* patterns obtained with each of these methods and psychological *functions*. MEG and MRI provide distinct but complementary information on those brain systems that support the development and expression of complex cognitive skills such as reading. This type of information is of particular importance in understanding the neurobiology of normal cognitive development; specific impairments in children with developmental brain disorders; and the ways in which targeted interventions might alter functional brain organization in these children, resulting in enhanced cognitive performance.

BASIC CONCEPTS

Baseline Activation

Activation is what functional images of the brain show. It represents biochemical and physiological events that are categorized as the neurophysiological processes of *metabolism* and *neural signaling*.

This chapter is adapted from Papanicolaou, A.C. (1998). *Fundamentals of functional brain imaging: A guide to the methods and their applications to psychology and behavioral neuroscience.* Lisse, The Netherlands: Swets & Zeitlinger.

Metabolism includes changes in the regional rate and volume of blood, relative quantities of oxygen in the blood, rates of consumption of oxygen or glucose, and many other changes. Signaling among neurons mainly involves electrical currents that are sent between and within cells.

Some of these biochemical and physiological events are associated with electromagnetic signals that radiate from their point of origin inside the brain to its surface, where they can be recorded by special instruments. Because functional imaging does not change or affect these electromagnetic signals, it is considered *noninvasive.*

The processes of metabolism and of signaling are continuous, but the rates vary from one brain region to the other. In fact, each region has its own characteristic level of *baseline activation.* Obtaining the baseline activation profile is the easiest form of functional imaging because such profiles reflect the total amount of activation of each brain region, which remains more or less constant over time. Consequently, if one could view and measure directly the rate of metabolism or the rate of signaling of neurons in each part of the brain and plot it over time, one would likely arrive at a figure similar to Figure 16.1. Moreover, if one were to obtain, at different points in time, functional images of this activation profile, the images would be very similar, as shown in Figure 16.1.

The main use of functional images of baseline activity is to reveal malfunctions, or pathological deviations, from the expected baseline rates of metabolism and signaling of particular areas of the brain, either abnormally low (*hypoactivation*) or abnormally high (*hyperactivation*). There are two kinds of such deviations or malfunctions. The first is *chronic,* or constant over time, and the other is *phasic,* appearing intermittently at particular times. An example of chronic malfunction is Parkinson's disease, in which a particular brain area, the internal globus pallidus, is constantly hyperactive and its constituent neurons are signaling (and metabolizing) at high rates.

An example of a phasic malfunction is an epileptic discharge resulting in transient deviations from the normal level of activation of the affected structures. Such deviations may be captured in images taken when the deviations occur. The brain regions that function abnormally can then be identified by comparing those images with others taken before or after the abnormal episode.

Function-Specific Activation Patterns

Neuropsychologists are most interested in the functional images of activation patterns that are related to specific psychological

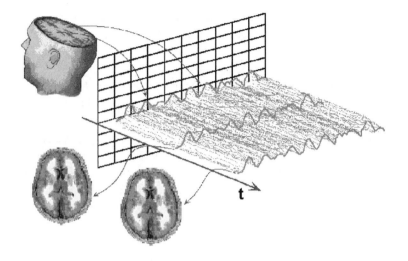

Figure 16.1. A schematic rendering of a hypothetical activation profile of a section of the brain. Each wavy line represents the degree of activation of each small region of the brain, as it changes slightly from moment to moment. This baseline profile of activation is represented here in stylized cross-section images that could have been obtained at two different points in time. Because the profile remains more or less constant over time, the functional images are almost identical. (From Pananicolaou, A.C. [1998]. *Fundamentals of functional brain imaging: A guide to the methods and their applications to psychology and behavioral neuroscience* [Fig. 2]. Lisse, The Netherlands: Swets & Zeitlinger; reprinted by permission.)

functions. This is because it seems that the correspondence between a given activation pattern and a given function reflects aspects of the neurophysiological mechanism necessary for each function.

A *function* is the process of production of a set of similar phenomena (whether subjective, e.g., perceptual experiences, or objective, e.g., movements) that serve a common purpose. A *brain mechanism* is a set of events that take place in particular brain areas in a particular order, resulting in the generation of the phenomena that define each function.

When the mechanism is operating, a particular pattern of activation occurs, but this pattern may be difficult to see because it is embedded in the global profile of the baseline activity. To separate out the activation pattern for this particular function, a laboratory situation must be set up to elicit that naturally occurring function on demand while the participant's brain activity is recorded. To do so, researchers may present stimuli of the same kind as those that naturally trigger the function and may instruct the participants to deal with the stimuli as they would under normal circumstances. The stimuli and the instructions constitute the experimental *task*. Typically, participants are asked to make an overt response (e.g., by pressing a button, by speaking out loud) to indicate that they have processed each stimulus. If the stimuli and the task instructions do elicit the function, the task is said to be *ecologically valid* and capable of activating the brain mechanism of the function.

With appropriate tasks and analytic methods in place, scientists can, in principle, isolate brain areas that are associated with specific cognitive functions and their component processes. However, it is not quite that simple. Several issues must be considered when attempting to establish a meaningful link between cognitive systems and behavioral expression, on the one hand, and the underlying neurobiological mechanisms, on the other. First, there is good evidence that specific cognitive functions are represented in multiple areas of the brain that work together; this is referred to as *functional connectivity*. Therefore, it is important to try to describe the relative timing and coordination of these different areas for specific cognitive functions. These kinds of analyses can increase the psychological relevance of the neuroimaging studies. Moreover, in the context of pediatric neuroimaging research, it is important to develop protocols that permit the examination of change within an individual over time. Finally, a better understanding is needed of variation in competence in cognitive domains such as reading, attention, or math, in relation to variation in brain circuitry. Imaging studies take on greater relevance when relevant brain–behavior correlations can be established. Essentially, researchers seek to account for individual differences in behavioral performance and individual differences in the underlying circuits that support these behaviors. In the following sections, we explain the basics of current brain imaging techniques and then consider their application to reading development and reading disability (RD).

MAGNETOENCEPHALOGRAPHY

The Nature of Activation Imaged

Signaling among neurons constitutes one of the basic forms of activation that can be imaged with the current brain imaging methods. It consists of electrochemical events that take place at the synapses and in the axons and dendrites of neurons. With the exception of the phenomenon of neurotransmitter release and uptake, which does not directly involve electrical activity, neuron activation involves flow of electrically charged particles, or ions, which results in electrical current.

If one could directly view the variation of the electrical currents at every set of cells in the brain and plot these variations as a function of time, one would obtain the typical picture of activation shown in Figure 16.1. Let us then assume that a set of cells that are typically not synchronized begin to signal in unison. This can take place, for instance, with a delay (e.g., 200 milliseconds) after the presentation of an external stimulus (e.g., a printed word). The cells' combined electrical currents will create a large deviation from the baseline level of activity. In such cases, using MEG can help provide answers to questions such as where the source of this deviation is (i.e., which part of the brain hosts the activated neurons). Needless to say, the pattern of activation of the brain itself is hidden from view. Researchers have only indirect access; they are limited to recording electromagnetic energy that can travel outside the head, as shown in Figure 16.2. This energy is called *magnetic flux.*

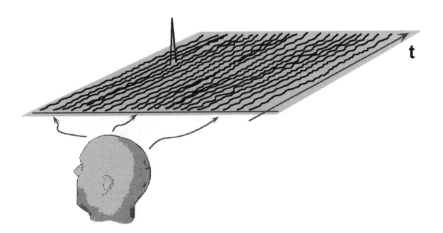

Figure 16.2. A schematic rendering of the electromagnetic signals recorded on the head surface that echo the electrical currents inside the brain. A transient deviation in electromagnetic signal intensity over a particular region of the head surface reflects the coordinated signaling activity of a large set of neurons somewhere in the brain. (From Pananicolaou, A.C. [1998]. *Fundamentals of functional brain imaging: A guide to the methods and their applications to psychology and behavioral neuroscience* [Fig.10]. Lisse, The Netherlands: Swets & Zeitlinger; reprinted by permission.)

Recording Magnetic Flux

Magnetic flux is recorded using superconducting loops of wire positioned over the head surface. With enough magnetic sensors placed over the entire head surface, the shape of the entire distribution of magnetic flux created by a brain activity source can be determined. Based on the surface flux distribution, the position and strength of the brain source (or activated brain region) that produced the flux can be estimated. The activated brain region is identified using three *fiducial points* that are defined on the participant's head surface. Usually these are clear anatomical landmarks, such as the ridge of the nose and the ear canals.

These reference points define a system of three coordinate axes (x, y, and z) that intersect somewhere near the center of the head. The position and orientation of the source of the magnetic flux is defined with reference to this coordinate system. Usually, markers are attached on these three points, and a structural MRI is taken, either before or after the MEG recording session. The positions of the markers are visible on the MRI scans, which helps the researcher determine the relative position of all brain structures with respect to the position of the source of activity. This process is known as *co-registration* of the MEG-derived active source on the structural MRI.

The Averaging Procedure

Since the early 1980s, advances in electronics and software used to reduce the contribution of extraneous sources of magnetic flux to the MEG data have made it possible to detect changes in magnetic flux associated with the presentation of a single stimulus, such as a printed word. Additional procedures are often used, however, to extract activation patterns specific to particular brain functions that are embedded in the global, baseline activation profile. In the case of MEG, such extraction is accomplished with an averaging procedure that is helpful when the amount of neural signaling for a particular function that differs from the baseline is very small. The output of this procedure is an event-related magnetic response or field (ERF), a time-varying record of magnetic flux at each of several recording locations (usually 148–300) around the head, as shown in Figure 16.3.

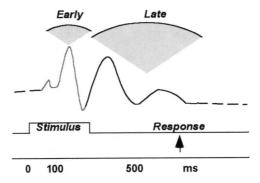

Figure 16.3. Averaged event-related magnetic field (ERF) in response to auditory or visual stimuli. Stimulus onset (set at 0 milliseconds [ms]) determines the onset of the ERF, which consists of an early (sensory) portion and a late portion. The participant's mean (behavioral) response time is indicated by the arrow.

The early portion of the ERF corresponds to activation of the sensory cortex specific to each type of stimulus (i.e., visual, auditory), enabling researchers to identify simple sensory functions. In contrast, late portions of the ERF reflect activation of the association cortex. By mapping late activity, the brain circuits that support higher cognitive functions can be studied in real time, *as* the stimulus is processed and *before* a response is made by the participant.

By analyzing the surface distribution of the averaged flux at several time points, scientists can identify the brain regions that produce the recorded magnetic activity. In this way, the source(s) that account for the recorded magnetic flux at each time point can be calculated and projected onto the structural images of the brain. Figure 16.4 shows some examples of functional images for different simple sensory functions.

The same general procedure is used to extract the activity specific to a more complex cognitive function. For example, to image the mechanism of verbal memory, the researcher may present spoken or printed word stimuli to participants with instructions to, say, identify words that occur more than once in a session. If the study is successful, the early portion of the ERF should be accounted for by sources in the primary auditory cortex, whereas the sources that account for the late portions of the ERF should outline the mechanism of the function that was produced in response to the task, in this case verbal episodic memory.

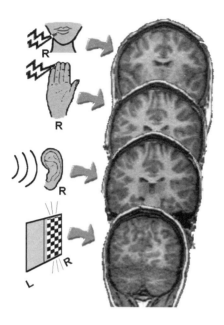

Figure 16.4. Typical magnetoencephalography (MEG) images displaying neurophysiological activity related to somatic, auditory, and visual sensation. Dark patches represent the location of the sources of magnetic flux observed briefly (< 0.1 seconds) after the presentation of a somatic stimulus (parietal cortex), an auditory stimulus (temporal cortex), or a visual stimulus (occipital cortex).

FUNCTIONAL MAGNETIC RESONANCE IMAGING

The Nature of Activation Imaged

As mentioned previously, there are two basic types of brain activation: neural signaling and metabolism. The rate of metabolism varies as much as the rate of signaling. Metabolic rate varies first from one type of tissue to another and second within a given tissue sample, depending on the amount of work the brain tissue performs. Because the main type of work neurons perform is signaling, changes in the rate of signaling are correlated with changes in the metabolic rates of neurons.

The sequence of physiological processes that are observed in functional magnetic resonance images can be summarized as follows: If a particular sample of tissue (set of neurons) engages in increased signaling, its metabolic rate increases, causing the brain to consume more oxygen; this increased oxygen consumption in turn causes lower amounts of hemoglobin (oxygenated blood) in that area. This change in the concentration of hemoglobin becomes apparent about 2 seconds after the increase in the signaling rate. Next, the reduction of hemoglobin triggers a vascular reaction resulting in an oversupply of oxygenated blood to that tissue sample 5–8 seconds later.

Recording Functional Magnetic Resonance Images

Scientists cannot directly view the levels of hemoglobin in brain tissue. The presence of hemoglobin, however, is associated with the presence of hydrogen atoms that produce electromagnetic energy. Recording these signals from hydrogen atoms enables scientists to estimate the distribution of hemoglobin throughout the brain and represent it in images. Electromagnetic energy associated with hydrogen atoms can be recorded by placing the head inside a very strong magnetic field, which is produced by an electromagnetic coil. This device is the same as the one used to obtain structural images of the rest of the body for diagnostic purposes.

Using different combinations of magnetic coils placed around the head, researchers are able to arrange the shape of the magnetic field so that every region of space or element of space (voxel) inside the MR magnet has a slightly different and unique value. Using this information, researchers are able to identify specific brain areas having abnormally high or low baseline activation. Activation that is specific to particular functions, however, requires additional procedures to be extracted from the global, baseline activation.

The Hemodynamic Response Function

Unlike the responses obtained by MEG, the blood oxygen level dependent (BOLD) response measured by fMRI reflects physiological changes that take place in the brain shortly after a particular cognitive function has already taken place. In response to a single stimulus event, this hemodynamic response function typically begins rising from baseline at approximately 2 seconds post-stimulus, rises to its peak at approximately 5 seconds, and slowly returns to baseline by approximately 16 seconds. Differences in the response magnitude between tasks or groups are assumed to reflect the relative increases (or decreases) in the underlying neural activity. Statistical analysis is employed to identify those differences that are reliable and replicable.

The Integration and Subtraction Procedure

General pattern extraction for fMRI involves the procedures of *integration* and *subtraction.* Although the stimuli during fMRI may be presented at the same rate as for MEG, in fMRI recording of the electromagnetic signals must be made over a longer time span that includes enough time to obtain the requisite number of electromagnetic signals to construct an image before, during, and/or after the participant performs a task repeatedly, as shown in Figure 16.5.

Researchers, however, are not able to see any systematic difference in the segments of the *during* patterns because that pattern is contained in and fused with the ongoing global activation or baseline activity that corresponds to all functions concurrently performed by the brain. It is assumed that the *before* and *after* periods do not include the function of interest. Thus, the *before* and *after* images should be nearly the same and the activity of the brain during those

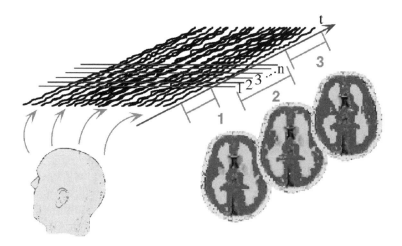

Figure 16.5. Electromagnetic signals recorded with functional magnetic resonance imaging (fMRI) over time intervals 1) before, 2) during, and 3) after the presentation of stimuli (the onset of which are indicated by horizontal lines). Signals recorded during each interval are integrated to construct a functional (or activation) image. (From Pananicolaou, A.C. [1998]. *Fundamentals of functional brain imaging: A guide to the methods and their applications to psychology and behavioral neuroscience* [Fig. 61]. Lisse, Netherlands: Swets & Zeitlinger; reprinted by permission.)

periods should also be present as background during the task performance. Because it is further assumed that the background global activation and the function-specific pattern are independent, they should be able to be separated by simple subtraction. Subtracting either the *before* or the *after* image from the *during* image, therefore, gives the activation pattern for the performance of the function.

Usually, the *before* and *after* images are not exactly the same because the baseline state of the participant rarely stays the same over long periods of time. Consequently, the subtracted image of the function-specific pattern may also be different. Therefore, these baseline and functional images are obtained several times to assess the reliability of the task-related difference relative to changes in baseline state (integration of images). How a researcher obtains a stable background activation image (also known as the problem of obtaining the appropriate control image) is of great importance, especially when complex functions are concerned.

The General Linear Model

In the vast majority of cases, the statistical significance of differences between experimental conditions (e.g., different types of stimuli, tasks, and instructions to participants) or groups are assessed using the general linear model, or GLM, a broad formalization that includes more familiar analysis techniques such as analysis of variance (ANOVA) and multiple regression (Frackowiak, Friston, Frith, Dolan, & Mazziotta, 1997; Hays, 1998; Kirk, 1982). This approach is linear in that data are modeled as a linear combination of a set of predictor variables, plus variance caused by the systematic influence of unknown variables (e.g., fatigue) or by random fluctuations of brain activity over time (which are referred to as *noise* in the activation patterns). For a single participant, these variables typically indicate which stimuli he or she received and which task the participant was performing at each point in time throughout image acquisition. Across participants, these predictor variables often include scores on behavioral tests or reflect clinical group membership or demographic status.

The vast majority of early fMRI studies employed *block* designs, characterized by the alternating presentation of one or more experimental conditions (e.g., two types of print) with a control condition (e.g., rest, fixation) across blocks. Each block of the experiment (whether it contains the experimental or the control condition) lasts for a relatively long period (typically 20–40 seconds). Within each block, multiple trials are presented, but these trials are from a single experimental condition only. In this type of design, the intensity of the electromagnetic signal measured from each brain area is averaged across the entire set of trials composing a single block. Then differences among experimental conditions, or between each experimental condition and the control condition, are assessed for each brain area separately, and a functional image reflecting these differences (or lack thereof) is constructed.

Recently, event-related designs have gained substantial popularity in the imaging field following advances in analysis methods. This technique allows the BOLD responses associated with a specific stimulus event to be examined on a trial-by-trial basis. In this case, signal intensity is integrated over a shorter period of time, usually 2–3 seconds, which is a substantial improvement over the 20- to 40-second integration time of block designs.

Across-Subjects Analysis

Computing probability values within a single participant allows generalization of results only to the population of repeated scans within that same participant. Under certain circumstances, such as in case studies, this kind of generalization may actually be useful. In the more typical situation, however, researchers wish to know whether an effect measured in the current sample can be generalized to the population from which the sample was originally drawn (e.g., the entire population of proficient readers). For practical and computational reasons, the direct test of a specific hypothesis commonly involves a two-step procedure: First the size of the effect of interest (the parameter estimate) is obtained separately for each participant, and then the reliability of these estimates is assessed across participants using GLM analyses (Holmes & Friston, 1998; Kirk, 1982; Woods, 1996).

Brain–Behavior Analysis

Primary analyses inevitably compare activation levels across tasks or groups. These are extended with brain–behavior analyses, in which the goal is to predict behavioral performance from brain activity levels. Because both behavioral performance and brain activity levels are measured (dependent) variables, the researcher can indicate whether the two are associated but cannot make claims about the true direction of causality. For each voxel, the correlation between the behavioral score and the activation level is computed across the sample. Areas where activity significantly correlates with the behavioral score exhibit (at least) a continuous linear relationship, in the sense that greater activity in a particular brain area or areas is associated with better performance on the experimental task.

Functional Connectivity Analysis

The univariate techniques just described, although useful for detecting localized effects, fail to take into account a basic characteristic of the brain, namely, that any complex function is determined by the interaction of many parts of the brain. The goal of connectivity analyses is to understand the causal influence, or *effective connectivity*, that each brain region exerts on every other (Friston, 1994; McIntosh, Nyberg, Bookstein, & Tulving, 1997). Although this influence is not measured directly, the correlations between activity measures of pairs of brain regions can be readily quantified; these correlations are measures of *functional connectivity* and serve as the basis for functional connectivity analysis.

There are two general approaches to assessing functional connectivity: within subjects and across subjects. Within-subject connectivity analyses quantify region-to-region correlations over time, often within a given task (Biswal, Yetkin, Haughton, & Hyde, 1995; Hampson, Peterson, Skudlarski, Gatenby, & Gore, 2002; Lowe, Mock, & Sorenson, 1998). A high correlation between two regions means that their activity levels tend to fluctuate up and down together over time, implying that one may affect the other (either directly or indirectly). Although within-subject connectivity analyses can theoretically provide the most direct evidence of interregional cooperation within a single brain, it also brings distinct challenges to analysis. Because the hemodynamic response function is slightly different from region to region, two regions whose signal intensities are highly correlated may not in fact exhibit a strong correlation in their BOLD time courses. Across-subject measures of functional connectivity deal with this problem by first extracting measures of activation from each participant, then computing region-to-region correlations across subjects (Horwitz et al., 1992; McIntosh et al., 1997; Pugh, Mencl, Shaywitz, et al., 2000). Strong correlations indicate that these regions tend to be activated in concert, which implies that they function together as part of an integrated functional network.

Multivariate Analysis

Analyses mentioned thus far have been either purely univariate (i.e., t-test, ANOVA) or bivariate (i.e., multiple regression, brain–behavior correlation, interregional correlation). True multivariate analyses simultaneously assess activations across a larger number of regions or the entire brain, in an attempt to understand the neural systems underlying behavior. A wide range of methods have been employed, including principal components analysis/independent components analysis (PCA/ICA) and multivariate analysis of variance (MANOVA); here, we briefly describe one particular method, partial least squares (PLS).

PLS is a regression-based method with multiple applications in neuroimaging (McIntosh, Bookstein, Haxby, & Grady, 1996; McIntosh et al., 1997; Mencl et al., 2000). Various forms of PLS are employed to assess different questions, although the underlying mathematics is similar. In short, a *data matrix* of activation values is constructed, consisting of one row for each participant and/or experimental condition and one column for each region or voxel measured. A design matrix is also created, coding predictors of interest, typically task contrasts or behavioral scores. The data are correlated with the design matrix to create a cross-correlation matrix of each region with each effect. This (typically large) set of correlations is subjected to singular value decomposition, which consolidates the covariance into a small set of components of ordered importance. Each component can be described by *brain loadings*, which identify how strongly each region participates in the component, and *design loadings*, which indicate how strongly each predictor participates in the component.

In task PLS, the goal is to identify a small set of brain-wide images that optimally discriminate the activation differences among a set of tasks (McIntosh et al., 1996). Here, the design matrix is composed of orthogonal regressors that contrast task effects. Each extracted component identifies a set of (often distributed) regions that show a similar response pattern (brain loadings) to a particular linear combination, or contrast, among the tasks (design loadings). In brain–behavior PLS, the goal is to identify a set of brain-wide images that optimally correlate with exogenous predictor variables, typically behavioral scores or demographic variables (McIntosh et al., 1996; Mencl et al., 2000). The design matrix is composed of one or more behavioral variables, and extracted components identify sets of regions that correlate similarly to the behavioral predictors and/or contrasts among the behavioral predictors. Last, seed voxel PLS builds on the bivariate approach to determining functional connectivity (McIntosh et al., 1997). One or more source regions are selected, and the activation values for these regions are entered as predictors in the design matrix. Extracted components identify sets of other regions that correlate similarly to the seed regions and identify whether these correlations are similar or different across the tasks. Each of these variants exemplifies the shift in focus from analysis of individual voxels or regions to analysis of brain-wide patterns of activity.

APPLICATIONS OF FUNCTIONAL IMAGING

A Typical Neuropsychological Study

Most psychological functions are complex, involving a series of interconnected cognitive operations, although how many depends on the particular theory being investigated. For example, it can be claimed that for a person to understand the meaning of words heard, first acoustic analysis is necessary for determining the physical features of the word stimuli, then phonological analysis is needed for identifying the language-relevant features, and finally semantic analysis (also involving memory) is used for identifying the meaning of the set of phonological features that constitute each spoken word. Now, to find the activation pattern specific to each cognitive operation, an experimental design involving more than just one control task is necessary.

An activation pattern may be recorded using a brain imaging technique while participants listen to words and indicate by means of some discriminant response that they comprehend the words' meaning. That pattern is supposed to contain activity specific to the semantic (S), the phonological (P), and the acoustic (A) processes, as well as activity due to the rest of the ongoing or baseline processes (R) performed by the brain. Therefore, the pattern obtained during the task would be a composite of subpatterns S + A + P + R.

A second activation pattern may then be recorded while the participants listen to the same words but are now told to ignore what the words mean, to attend to some of the words' phonological features instead, and to respond each time they hear a word that contains a particular phoneme combination (e.g., /rt/ as in *cart*). This second pattern is supposed to contain all of the component operation-specific patterns the first one did, except for the pattern specific to the semantic analysis operation; consequently, the second pattern would be a composite of subpatterns P + A + R.

Then, a third activation pattern can be obtained while the participants hear the same words but are told to ignore everything else about them, attend exclusively to the words' acoustic features (e.g., relative loudness), and respond each time they hear a word played at a slightly lower volume than the rest of the stimuli. In this case, the pattern is supposed to consist of only the activity specific to acoustic processing plus any additional ongoing processes that may take place concurrently, namely subpatterns A + R.

Assuming that all three experimental tasks required the same level of alertness and effort and that they were completed to the same degree of accuracy, one may subtract the second from the first (i.e., [S + P + A + R] – [P + A + R]) to obtain the activation profile specific to the semantic analysis operation (S), and the third from the second (i.e., [P + A + R] – [A + R]) to obtain the activation profile specific to the phonological analysis operation (P). To obtain the sign of the acoustic function (A), we would need an additional task involving ongoing processes (R) but not the acoustic function. We would perform the subtraction once again (i.e., [A + R] – R) to obtain the activation profile specific to the acoustic analysis operation.

It is obvious that for this scheme to work, the different functions postulated must be independent of each other, involving clearly separate mechanisms. These assumptions are not always true, and in some cases alternative (e.g., factorial, parametric) designs are desirable (Friston, Zarahn, Josephs, Henson, & Dale, 1999; Pugh et al., 1996).

Uses of Function-Specific Activation Patterns

Function-specific activation patterns can and have been used to explore possible differences in brain mechanisms of particular functions in groups of individuals that differ in some prominent physiological or psychological characteristic, for example, gender, age, or presence or absence of learning disability. Here again, the validity of the functional images and the relative difficulty in establishing validity depend on whether individuals can be assigned unequivocally to a particular category, the degree to which the mechanism of the particular function is known, and whether individuals in the compared groups can perform the same function with equal ease. We discuss in some detail two examples of this type of application of functional imaging—gender differences and differences between children with RD and typically developing children—to illustrate this application's utility and the requirements for establishing its validity.

Research findings suggest that there are reasons to hypothesize that the brain mechanisms of language involve left hemisphere structures in men and both left and right hemisphere structures in women. Such a hypothesis and others of the same type can be readily evaluated through functional imaging. The requirements for evaluating them correctly, that is, in a manner that would allow reasonable interpretation of the results, are as follows.

First, all members of each group need to possess the characteristic on the basis of which they are classified together. In this example of hemisphere use in men and women, this requirement is perfectly satisfied because gender is usually unequivocal.

The second requirement is that no other prominent characteristic distinguishes the members of the two groups. If that requirement is not met, for instance, if several men in the group have cognitive impairments and some of the women are creative writers by occupation, any difference that may be found in the brain activation patterns of the two groups could not be uniquely attributed to gender. In general, this second requirement can be met only approximately; it is always possible to find characteristics that differ between any two groups of individuals besides the characteristic that defines the group. For example, the members of the two groups could differ in height, weight, eye color, or some other trait. Thus, although it is not possible to select group members who are identical in everything except the group-defining characteristic, it is possible to select them such that they do not differ appreciably in a characteristic relevant to linguistic competence.

The third requirement is that members of both groups must be able to perform the same language task with equal ease and efficiency. Obviously the odds for doing so are better if the general level of group members' linguistic competence is approximately equal. If it is not, then to perform the same task, group members will have to exert different degrees of effort or will be more or less alert during the task. Both of these factors may affect group members' brain activation profile and either obscure, exaggerate, or modify possible differences in the language-specific activation patterns.

Each individual in each group may undergo imaging during a task believed to represent effectively the function of language. Assuming that the fidelity of these patterns is deemed satisfactory, one can examine whether the hypothesis is correct that the signs of the language mechanism in men are different from those in women. A quick way of estimating this is to average all of the patterns of men and to average all of those of the women to see whether there is an overall difference. Assuming that there is, one next has to establish whether the difference seen in the average patterns is a real or a circumstantial one. Any time that patterns are averaged, some pattern will be obtained. To verify that the patterns are not arbitrary, one can either compare the activation patterns of several individual men and women with the average patterns of their group (given that it is impossible to test all men and women on the planet) or examine whether the averaged group patterns reappear in replications of the study with the same or with different groups of individuals.

In some cases, function-specific patterns that characterize particular diagnostic groups are visibly similar across members of the group and clearly different from those of nonmembers (see Figure 16.A at http://www.brookespublishing.com/mccardlemris). But even when reliable distinctions among brain activation profiles, consistent with expectations, can be obtained, these distinctions do not necessarily imply that brain activation profiles can be used to identify a particular disorder. To claim that a particular atypical activation profile is useful in identifying a particular condition, a researcher must first demonstrate that individual participants can be correctly assigned to diagnostic categories solely on the basis of their functional images. Though as of 2004, no claims to that effect have been made directly, it is quite possible that with constant improvements in the fidelity of images, researchers may soon be able to do so.

Criteria for Establishing Function-Specific Activation Profiles

To describe the brain circuits that support any cognitive function, such as reading, in a comprehensive and accurate manner, every functional imaging method must be capable of providing the following:

1. Information regarding brain areas that show *increased levels* of neurophysiological activation during experimental tasks that exemplify the cognitive function under investigation

2. *Real-time* data regarding the temporal course of regional activation

3. Activation protocols that produce reproducible spatiotemporal activation profiles *both within and across individuals*

4. Independent confirmation, preferably from invasive functional brain mapping, that at least some components of the activation maps obtained with a particular task and data reduction protocol are *essential* for the performance of that task

5. Information on how brain activity measures relate to individual *performance* in these tasks

Although as of 2004 fMRI can address several of these criteria, only MEG has been able to address all five. Each method has limitations and advantages. The capacity to establish significant correlations between measures of brain activation and measures of behaviors only one of several pieces of evidence that establish the external validity of functional brain imaging data. Given that knowledge regarding the neurological basis of developmental conditions, such as reading or math disability, can have serious repercussions for educational policy, establishing that brain imaging procedures meet the above criteria is crucial. Several studies supporting the validity of MEG activation and analysis protocols have been successfully completed thus far (Breier et al., 2001; Breier, Simos, Zouridakis,

Wheless, et al., 1999; Castillo, Simos, Venkataraman, Breier, & Papanicolaou, 2001; Maestú et al., 2002; Simos, Breier, et al., 2002; Simos, Breier, et al., 1999; Simos, Breier, Wheless, et al., 2000; Simos, Breier, Zouridakis, & Papanicolaou, 1998; Simos, Papanicolaou, et al., 1999; Szymanski et al., 2001). Given that these studies have established the overall scientific merit of imaging procedures (in this case, MEG imaging protocols), researchers can now proceed to apply them to the study of brain function related to education.

NEUROBIOLOGICAL STUDIES OF READING AND READING DISABILITY

For neuroimaging data to be relevant to reading development, links must be established between behavioral and cognitive processes and those neural systems that support these processes. Thus, neuroimaging research must be informed by cognitive behavioral research from the outset. Behavioral studies have characterized critical cognitive processes necessary to acquire fluent reading, and how these processes are deficient in individuals with RD. The core difficulty in RD manifests itself as a deficiency within the language system and, in particular, a deficiency at the level of phonological analysis. To learn to read, a child must first develop an appreciation that sound changes in words change meaning (phonemic awareness) and must understand that written words, too, possess an internal phonological structure that is mapped onto the corresponding spoken words (alphabetic principle). As many studies have shown, phonemic awareness is largely missing in children and adults with RD (Brady & Shankweiler, 1991; Fletcher et al., 1994; Rieben & Perfetti, 1991; Shankweiler et al., 1995; Stanovich & Siegel, 1994). Phonological processing impairments persist into adulthood (Bruck, 1992; Felton, Naylor, & Wood, 1990; Shaywitz et al., 1999), and instruction in phonemic awareness promotes the acquisition of reading skills (see Chapter 8; see also Ball & Blachman, 1991; Foorman, Francis, Fletcher, Schatschneider, & Mehta, 1998; Torgesen, Morgan, & Davis, 1992; and Wise & Olson, 1995).

Neuroimaging has been employed successfully in the area of reading development, RD, and intervention (see Chapter 17; see also Pugh, Mencl, Jenner, et al., 2000., and Sarkari et al., 2002, for reviews). Studies that meet all of the criteria for scientific merit just outlined provide a highly consistent but rather basic view of the brain circuit that supports reading (Simos, Breier, et al., 2002; Simos et al., 2001; Simos, Fletcher, Foorman, et al., 2002). The following regions show increased levels of activation consistently, both within and across different individuals, and therefore are likely to constitute indispensable components of the brain circuit that supports reading: the primary visual cortex (which is necessary for the initial visual analysis of print), the association visual cortex in the ventral temporo-occipital areas, the posterior portion of the superior temporal gyrus extending posteriorly into the supramarginal gyrus (Wernicke's area), and the inferior frontal gyrus (Broca's area). With the exception of primary visual cortex, where activation is noted bilaterally for printed stimuli presented in the center of the visual field, activity in all other areas is stronger in the left hemisphere in the majority of readers who have never experienced difficulties in learning to read, regardless of age. Parts of the middle temporal gyrus, including the cortex within the superior temporal sulcus, are also observed to be involved, especially when real words (as opposed to meaningless yet pronounceable letter strings) are used as stimuli. When the same criteria of inter- and intraindividual consistency are applied, less common activation is observed in the angular gyrus.

Once researchers had established the elementary features of the activation profile associated with word recognition, several research groups designed studies to go further, addressing the neurobiological basis of reading and RD using hemodynamic imaging techniques (Pugh et al., 1996; Shaywitz et al., 1998; Simos, Breier, et al., 2002). Although the imaging protocols employed in these studies may not fulfill all of the aforementioned criteria, the study investigators sought to overcome this problem by relying on intricate experimental design and analysis techniques. The ultimate goal of these research efforts was to determine the specific role of distinct components of the brain circuit that supports reading in adults and, in some cases, children, who experience difficulty in learning to read.

Data from this set of studies indicate that at least two distinct brain circuits are involved in skilled printed word recognition. One circuit may be involved in a slow, presumably effortful process of word recognition that is responsible for the recognition of novel and uncommon words (e.g., *turpentine*). The other is a later-developing, faster circuit that processes familiar printed words (e.g., *morning*). The two circuits involve different regions in the posterior part of the left hemisphere (which in the majority of right-handed people mediates language functions in general). A key component of the slow-acting circuit is Wernicke's area, a region that is also responsible for processing spoken words. The fast-acting recognition circuit, on the other hand, consists mainly of brain areas specialized for complex visual processing in the base of the brain. In MEG studies, activity in these areas during reading tasks is observed earlier than activity in Wernicke's area (Breier, Simos, Zouridakis, & Papanicolaou, 1998, 1999; Simos et al., 2001). The two circuits operate in conjunction with another area whose primary function is the planning of speech (articulation), namely Broca's area, in the anterior part of the brain (Pugh, Mencl, Jenner, et al., 2000). A variety of technologies have contributed to these findings, including MEG; fMRI; and a third brain imaging technique, positron emission tomography, which can only be used with adult participants (Fiebach, Friederici, Muller, & Von Cramon, 2002; Helenius, Salmelin, Service, & Connolly, 1998; Pugh et al., 2000; Pugh et al., 1997; Rumsey et al., 1997; Shaywitz et al., 1998).

On the basis of the neurobiological data, Pugh, Mencl, Jenner, et al. (2000) have proposed a theory of word recognition in which word selection in the brain is determined by the faster circuit for common words and by the slower circuit for new or uncommon words. The two systems correspond (but only loosely) to the two routes of classical dual route theory (Coltheart, Curtis, Atkins, & Haller, 1993). Although imaging evidence supports the existence of dual routes, as of 2004 no compelling data suggest that the fast route involves direct activation of meaning, as proposed in some versions of dual route theory. Phonological representation of words may still be involved either in mediating the activation between orthography and meaning or as an obligatory consequence after the activation of meaning directly by orthography (Simos, Breier, et al., 2002).

With regard to the slower circuit, the neurobiological theory is consistent with the other major (dual route) theory in proposing that this slow process produces phonological representations generated by subword analysis. Previous evidence from imaging is consistent with this idea because there is a strong correlation between activation of the slower circuit and activation of Broca's area. Direct evidence supporting the critical role of the slower circuit in sub–word-level phonological analysis comes from an electrocortical stimulation study (Simos, Breier, Wheless, et al., 2000): Electrical interference with a small portion of Wernicke's area consistently impaired the patients' ability to decode pseudowords. Whereas this ability relies primarily on the slow route, the ability to read real words with exceptional spellings, which could be accomplished by the fast route, remained unaffected. There is also indirect evidence that Broca's area and at least one other component of the slower circuit (the supramarginal gyrus) support subword phonological analysis. Activity in both regions is 1) stronger for pseudoword reading than for real words; 2) stronger for uncommon words than for common words; and 3) stronger for tasks, such as rhyme judgment, that require phonological analysis (Pugh et al., 1996).

Moreover, there is also evidence that beginning and early readers show activity in Wernicke's and Broca's areas but do not show substantial activity in the faster circuit, unlike more skilled readers (Booth et al., 2001; Shaywitz et al., 2002). When present, activity in visual processing areas in the base of the brain, which shows strong left hemisphere lateralization in adults, appears to be bilaterally symmetric in children, a finding consistent with the notion of a progressive specialization of the faster circuit in the left hemisphere with reading experience (Simos et al., 2001). Moreover, several studies have reported greater activation to real words than to pseudowords within the faster system, particularly at middle and inferior temporal sites (Fiebach et al., 2002; Tagamets, Novick, Chalmers, & Friedman, 2000). In addition, as discussed later in this chapter, the faster system's activation increases with age and reading skill (Shaywitz et al., 2002). A detailed discussion of the data supporting a processing distinction between the faster and slower circuits can be found in Pugh, Mencl, Jenner, et al. (2000).

Altered Circuits in Reading Disability

Readers with no impairment (NI) and readers with RD have clear functional differences with regard to the dorsal, ventral, and anterior sites discussed thus far. In readers with RD, a number of functional imaging studies have observed left hemisphere posterior dysfunction at both dorsal and ventral sites during phonological processing tasks (Brunswick, McCrory, Price, Frith, & Frith, 1999; Paulesu et al., 2001; Pugh, Mencl, Shaywitz, et al., 2000; Rumsey et al., 1997; Salmelin, Service, Kiesila, Uutela, & Salonen, 1996; Shaywitz et al., 1998; Shaywitz et al., 2002). This disruption is reflected by a relative underactivation of these circuits specifically in processing words and pseudowords, which requires decoding; this finding suggests a disruption of these regions in readers with RD. Indeed, a study using diffusion-weighted imaging analysis has documented anomalies in the nerve fiber pathways that connect Wernicke's area with the rest of the brain, suggesting a possible mechanism for the often-seen functional anomalies, reflected, for example, in low reading scores (Klingberg et al., 2000).

The suspected functional deficit in posterior left hemisphere circuits can be observed with a high degree of consistency on a case-by-case basis, as suggested by the review of MEG data from a large group of children with severe reading difficulties imaged using protocols that meet the five criteria for scientific merit discussed previously (Sarkari et al., 2002). Underactivation in two key components of the slow circuit, Wernicke's area and the angular gyrus, is detectable as early as the end of kindergarten in children who have not reached important milestones in learning to read (Simos et al., 2003). In addition, the typical progression of activity from visual processing areas in the left hemisphere to mirror areas in the right hemisphere is reversed in children with more severe impairments. Complex statistical analyses show that intercorrelations between different component areas of the two circuits are low in readers with RD during word and pseudoword reading tasks but are strong in nonimpaired readers, suggesting a breakdown in the integrity of processing posterior left hemisphere regions (Pugh, Mencl, Shaywitz, et al., 2000; see also Horwitz, Rumsey, & Donohue, 1998, for similar findings).

Of particular importance, the suggested functional anomaly in posterior left hemisphere circuits was found only at the word reading level, for both real and pseudowords, in both adults and children. In contrast, on simple single-letter orthographic or phonological judgment tasks, no group differences were seen—either by activation analyses (Shaywitz et al., 1998) or by functional connectivity analyses (Pugh, Mencl, Shaywitz, et al., 2000). This strongly implies that left hemisphere posterior circuits, although poorly developed, are not fundamentally disrupted in readers with RD. Thus, altering the functional status of these circuits may be possible, providing that appropriate retraining procedures are implemented.

Compensatory Processing in Reading Disability

Many studies using various neuroimaging methods—MEG, fMRI, and PET—have examined phonological processing, word and nonword reading, and other tasks. These studies converge to indicate that there is a left hemisphere anomaly and a compensatory shift to anterior brain sites (Broca's area) in individuals with RD (Brunswick et al., 1999; Richards et al., 1999; Rumsey et al., 1997; Salmelin et al., 1996; Shaywitz et al., 1998; Shaywitz et al., 2002; Simos et al., 2003).

Evidence of a second apparent compensatory shift—in this case, to posterior right hemisphere regions—comes from Sarkari and colleagues (2002), who found an increase in reading-specific activation in the right hemisphere homologue of Wernicke's area that could be considered compensatory. When coupled with hypoactivation of Wernicke's area (in the left hemisphere), presence of increased activation in the corresponding right hemisphere region can accurately classify kindergarten students as being at risk for developing reading problems with greater than 75% accuracy (Simos et al., 2003).

Hemodynamic measures permitting more detailed examination of this trend indicate that hemispheric asymmetries in activity in Wernicke's area and neighboring areas (the middle temporal gyrus and the angular gyrus) vary significantly among RD and NI groups (Shaywitz et al., 1998): There was greater right than left hemisphere activation in individuals with RD but greater left than right hemisphere activation in the NI group (see also Barnes, Lamm, Epstein, & Pratt, 1994; Pugh, Mencl, Jenner, et al., 2000; and Rumsey et al., 1999). In summary, readers in the NI group show strong, functioning left hemisphere posterior circuits in word and pseudoword reading, but individuals with RD do not. Instead, individuals with RD show evidence of two apparently compensatory responses to their left hemisphere posterior dysfunction: increased bihemispheric Broca's activation and an increased functional role for right hemisphere posterior sites.

Developmental Changes in the Three Left Hemisphere Systems

As noted previously, researchers have examined developmental changes in the left hemisphere response to print stimuli in cohorts of individuals without reading impairments and individuals with dyslexia ranging in age from 7 through 17 (Shaywitz et al., 2002). The primary finding in these cross-sectional analyses was that as typically developing readers mature, there is a shift in the degree of activation from right hemisphere and frontal lobe sites toward posterior left hemisphere regions (primarily complex visual processing regions). Indeed, when multiple regression analyses examined both age and reading skill (measured by performance on standard reading tests), the critical predictor was reading skill level. The higher the reading skill, the stronger the response in left hemisphere complex visual processing regions (other areas showed age and skill-related reductions). Thus, a beginning reader on a successful trajectory employs a widely distributed cortical system for print processing, including Wernicke's area, Broca's area, and complex visual processing regions in the right hemisphere. As reading skill increases, these regions play a diminished role while left hemisphere visual processing regions begin to carry rapid printed word recognition. This notion is supported by longitudinal MEG data demonstrating a progressive specialization of cortex in Wernicke's area and left hemisphere complex visual processing regions in the initial stages of reading acquisition (see Figure 16.6).

Intervention Studies

As described previously, a large number of studies suggest left hemisphere posterior anomalies in RD along with compensatory shifts to right hemisphere posterior regions and Broca's area. Moreover, there is some evidence from fMRI studies that higher levels of reading skill are strongly associated with the development of reading-specific

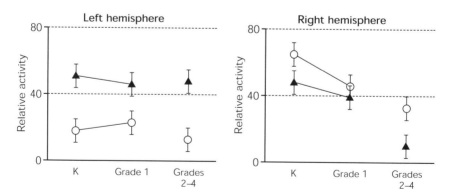

Figure 16.6. Longitudinal (kindergarten to first grade, n = 28; *source:* Simos et al., 2003) and cross-sectional data (second to fourth grade, n = 12; *source:* Papanicolaou et al., 2003; Simos, Breier, Fletcher, et al., 2000) regarding changes in the degree of activity in temporoparietal cortex during the early stages of reading acquisition and beyond. The vertical axis displays number of activity sources in Wernicke's area, normalized with respect to total brain activity to enable comparisons across groups.

responses in left hemisphere visual association areas that may be involved in processing word forms. Given this difference in developmental trajectories, researchers can begin to ask whether a given intervention, at a given age or for children with RD with a certain profile, will have the consequence of normalizing the trajectories in these children toward a consolidated left hemisphere posterior reading system.

In a recent MEG study of eight children with severe RD who underwent a brief but intensive remediation program, the most pronounced change observed on a case-by-case basis was a several-fold increase in the apparent engagement of Wernicke's area (in the left hemisphere), accompanied by a moderate reduction in the activation of the corresponding right hemisphere area (Simos, Fletcher, Bergman, et al., 2002; see Figure 16.B at http://www.brookespublishing .com/mccardlemris). This increase in left hemisphere posterior activation after intervention was reported by Temple and colleagues (2003) in a subsequent fMRI study. These types of findings provide a good starting point for large-scale investigations of remediation and neurobiological change in varied populations of struggling readers.

CONCLUSION

Neuroimaging studies cut across multiple domains, including various age groups; levels of proficiency; and research on the brain, reading development, cognition, and instruction. These studies show that the brain is involved at all ages and levels of proficiency but do not indicate that the brain has a deterministic influence that can be separated from experience. Indeed, instruction and practice seems essential for developing and strengthening the neural networks that must be in place for the brain to support complex activities such as reading. Some of these appear to be specific to reading and are not activated by other language experiences or by exposure to written language. This type of knowledge must be integrated into the broader knowledge of research on reading. At the most dramatic level, neuroimaging research shows that teaching affects the brain in positive, long-term ways that are essential for the development of reading.

REFERENCES

Ball, E.W., & Blachman, B.A. (1991). Does phoneme awareness training in kindergarten make a difference in early word recognition and developmental spelling? *Reading Research Quarterly, 26,* 49–66.

Barnes, A., Lamm, O., Epstein, R., & Pratt, H. (1994). Brain potentials from dyslexic children recorded during short-term memory tasks. *Journal of Neuroscience, 74,* 227–237.

Biswal, B., Yetkin, F.Z., Haughton, V.M., & Hyde, J.S. (1995). Functional connectivity in the motor cortex of resting human brain using echo-planar MRI. *Magnetic Resonance in Medicine, 34,* 537–541.

Booth, J.R., Burman, D.D., Van Santen, F.W., Harasaki, Y., Gitelman, D.R., Parrish, T.B., et al. (2001). The development of specialized brain systems in reading and oral-language. *Neuropsychology, 7,* 119–141.

Brady, S., & Shankweiler, D. (Eds.). (1991). *Phonological processes in literacy: A tribute to Isabelle Y. Liberman.* Mahwah, NJ: Lawrence Erlbaum Associates.

Breier, J.I., Simos, P.G., Wheless, J.W., Constantinou, J.E.C., Baumgartner, J.E., Venkataraman, V., et al. (2001). Language dominance in children as determined by magnetic source imaging and the intracarotid amobarbital procedure: A comparison. *Journal of Child Neurology, 16,* 124–130.

Breier, J.I., Simos, P.G., Zouridakis, G., & Papanicolaou, A.C. (1998). Relative timing of neuronal activity in distinct temporal lobe areas during a recognition memory task for words. *Journal of Clinical and Experimental Neuropsychology, 20,* 782–790.

Breier, J.I., Simos, P.G., Zouridakis, G., & Papanicolaou, A.C. (1999). Temporal course of regional brain activation associated with phonological decoding. *Journal of Clinical and Experimental Neuropsychology, 21,* 465–476.

Breier, J.I., Simos, P.G., Zouridakis, G., Wheless, J.W., Willmore, L.J., Constantinou, J.E., et al. (1999). Language dominance determined by magnetic source imaging: A comparison with the Wada procedure. *Neurology, 53,* 938–945.

Bruck, M. (1992). Persistence of dyslexics' phonological deficits. *Developmental Psychology, 28,* 874–886.

Brunswick, N., McCrory, E., Price, C., Frith, C.D., & Frith, U. (1999). Explicit and implicit processing of words and pseudowords by adult developmental dyslexics: A search for Wernicke's Wortschatz? *Brain, 122,* 1901–1917.

Castillo, E.M., Simos, P.G., Venkataraman, V., Breier, J.I., & Papanicolaou, A.C. (2001). Mapping of expressive language cortex using magnetic source imaging. *Neurocase, 7,* 419–422.

Coltheart, M., Curtis, B., Atkins, P., & Haller, M. (1993). Models of reading aloud: Dual-route and parallel-distributed-processing approaches. *Psychological Review, 100,* 589–608.

Felton, R.H., Naylor, C.E., & Wood, F.B. (1990). Neuropsychological profile of adult dyslexics. *Brain and Language, 39,* 485–497.

Fiebach, C., Friederici, A., Muller, K., & Von Cramon, Y. (2002). FMRI evidence for dual routes to the mental lexicon in visual word recognition. *Journal of Cognitive Neuroscience, 14,* 11–23.

Fletcher, J.M., Shaywitz, S.E., Shankweiler, D.P., Katz, L., Liberman, I.Y., Stuebing, K.K., et al. (1994). Cognitive profiles of reading disability: Comparisons of discrepancy and low achievement definitions. *Journal of Educational Psychology, 86,* 6–23.

Foorman, B.R., Francis, D., Fletcher, J.K., Schatschneider, C., & Mehta, P. (1998). The role of instruction in learning to reading: Preventing reading failure in at-risk children. *Journal of Educational Psychology, 90,* 37–55.

Frackowiak, R., Friston, K., Frith, C., Dolan, R., & Mazziotta. (1997). *Human brain function*. San Diego: Academic Press.

Friston, K. (1994). Functional and effective connectivity: A synthesis. *Human Brain Mapping, 2*, 56–78.

Friston, K.J., Zarahn, E., Josephs, O., Henson, R.N.A., & Dale, A.M. (1999). Stochastic designs in event-related fMRI. *NeuroImage, 10*, 607–619.

Hampson, M., Peterson, B.S., Skudlarski, P., Gatenby, J.C., & Gore, J.C. (2002). Detection of functional connectivity using temporal correlations in MR images. *Human Brain Mapping, 15*, 247–262.

Hays, W.L. (1988). *Statistics*. Orlando, FL: Holt, Rinehart & Winston.

Helenius, P., Salmelin, R., Service, E., & Connolly, J. (1998). Distinct time courses of word and context comprehension in the left temporal cortex. *Brain, 121*, 1133–1142.

Holmes, A.P., & Friston, K.J. (1998). Generalizability, random effects, and population inference. *NeuroImage, 7*, S34.

Horwitz, B., Grady, C.L., Haxby, J.V., Shapiro, M.B., Rapoport, S.I., Ungerleider, L.G., et al. (1992). Functional associations among human posterior extrastriate brain regions during object and spatial vision. *Journal of Cognitive Neuroscience, 4*, 311–322.

Horwitz, B., Rumsey, J.M., & Donohue, B.C. (1998). Functional connectivity of the angular gyrus in normal reading and dyslexia. *Proceedings of the National Academy Sciences of the United States of America, 95*, 8939–8944.

Kirk, R.E. (1982). *Experimental design: Procedures for the social sciences*. Belmont, CA: Wadsworth.

Klingberg, T., Hedehus, M., Temple, E., Salz, T., Gabrieli, J.D., Moseley, M.E., et al. (2000). Microstructure of temporo-parietal white matter as a basis for reading ability: Evidence from diffusion tensor magnetic resonance imaging. *Neuron, 25*, 493–500.

Lowe, M.J., Mock, B.J., & Sorenson, J.A. (1998). Functional connectivity in single and multislice echoplanar imaging using resting-state fluctuations. *NeuroImage, 7*, 119–132.

Maestú, F., Ortiz, T., Fernandez, A., Amo, C., Martin, P., Fernández, S., et al. (2002). Spanish language mapping using MEG: A validation study. *NeuroImage, 17*, 1579–1586.

McIntosh, A.R., Bookstein, F.L., Haxby, J.V., & Grady, C.L. (1996). Spatial pattern analysis of functional brain images using partial least squares. *NeuroImage, 3*, 143–157.

McIntosh, A.R., Nyberg, L., Bookstein, F.L., & Tulving, E. (1997). Differential functional connectivity of prefrontal and medial temporal cortices during episodic memory retrieval. *Human Brain Mapping, 5*, 323–327.

Mencl, W.E., Pugh, K.R., Shaywitz, S.E., Shaywitz, B.A., Fulbright, R.K., Constable, R.T., et al. (2000). Network analysis of brain activations in working memory: Behavior and age relationships. *Microscopy Research and Technique, 51*, 64–74.

Papanicolaou, A.C., Simos, P.G., Breier, J.I., Fletcher, J.M., Foorman, B.R., Francis, D.J., et al. (2003). Brain mechanisms for reading in children with and without dyslexia: A review of studies of normal development and plasticity. *Developmental Neuropsychology, 24*, 593–612.

Paulesu, E., Démonet, J.F., Fazio, F., McCrory, E., Chanoine, V., Brunswick, N., et al. (2001). Dyslexia: Cultural diversity and biological unity. *Science, 291,* 2165–2167.

Pugh, K.R., Mencl, W.E., Jenner, A.J., Katz, L., Lee, J.R., Shaywitz, S.E., et al. (2000). Functional neuroimaging studies of reading and reading disability (developmental dyslexia). *Mental Retardation and Developmental Disabilities Review, 6,* 207–213.

Pugh, K., Mencl, E.W., Shaywitz, B.A., Shaywitz, S.E., Fulbright, R.K., Skudlarski, P., et al. (2000). The angular gyrus in developmental dyslexia: Task-specific differences in functional connectivity in posterior cortex. *Psychological Science, 11,* 51–56.

Pugh, K.R., Shaywitz, B.A., Shaywitz, S.E., Constable, T.R., Skudlarski, P., Fulbright, R.K., et al. (1996). Cerebral organization of component processes in reading. *Brain, 119,* 1221–1238.

Pugh, K.R., Shaywitz, B.A., Shaywitz, S.E., Shankweiler, D.P., Katz, L., Fletcher, J.M., et al. (1997). Predicting reading performance from neuroimaging profiles: The cerebral basis of phonological effects in printed word identification. *Journal of Experimental Psychology: Human Perception and Performance, 23,* 299–318.

Richards, T.L., Dager, S.R., Corina, D., Serafini, S., Heide, A.C., Steury, K., et al. (1999). Dyslexic children have abnormal brain lactate response to reading-related tasks. *American Journal of Neuroradiology, 20,* 1393–1398.

Rieben, L., & Perfetti, C.A. (1991). *Learning to read: Basic research and its implications.* Mahwah, NJ: Lawrence Erlbaum Associates.

Rumsey, J.M., Horwitz, B., Donohue, B.C., Nace, K.L., Maisog, J.M., & Andreason, P.A. (1999). Functional lesion in developmental dyslexia: Left angular gyral blood flow predicts severity. *Brain and Language, 70,* 187–204.

Rumsey, J.M., Nace, K., Donohue, B., Wise, D., Maisog, J.M., & Andreason, P. (1997). A positron emission tomographic study of impaired word recognition and phonological processing in dyslexic men. *Archives of Neurology, 54,* 562–573.

Salmelin, R., Service, E., Kiesila, P., Uutela, K., & Salonen, O. (1996). Impaired visual word processing in dyslexia revealed with magnetoencephalography. *Annals of Neurology, 40,* 157–162.

Sarkari, S., Simos, P.G., Fletcher, J.M., Castillo, E.M., Breier, J.I., & Papanicolaou, A.C. (2002). The emergence and treatment of developmental reading disability: Contributions of functional brain imaging. *Seminars in Pediatric Neurology, 9,* 227–236.

Shankweiler, D., Crain, S., Katz, L., Fowler, A.E., Liberman, A.M., Brady, S.A., et al. (1995). Cognitive profiles of reading-disabled children: Comparison of language skills in phonology, morphology, and syntax. *Psychological Science, 6,* 149–156.

Shaywitz, S.E., Fletcher, J.M., Holahan, J.M., Shneider, A.E., Marchione, K.E., Stuebing, K.K., et al. (1999). Persistence of dyslexia: The Connecticut Longitudinal Study at adolescence. *Pediatrics, 104,* 1351–1359.

Shaywitz, S.E., Shaywitz, B.A., Pugh, K.R., Fulbright, R.K., Constable, R.T., Mencl, W.E., et al. (1998). Functional disruption in the organization of the brain for reading in dyslexia. *Proceedings of the National Academy of Sciences of the United States of America, 95,* 2636–2641.

Shaywitz, B.A., Shaywitz, S.E., Pugh, K.R., Mencl, W.E., Fulbright, R.K., Skudlarski, P., et al. (2002). Disruption of posterior brain systems for reading in children with developmental dyslexia. *Biological Psychiatry, 52,* 101–110.

Simos, P.G., Breier, J.I., Fletcher, J.M., Bergman, E., & Papanicolaou, A.C. (2000). Cerebral mechanisms involved in word reading in dyslexic children: A magnetic source imaging approach. *Cerebral Cortex, 10,* 809–816.

Simos, P.G., Breier, J.I., Fletcher, J.M., Foorman, B.R., Castillo, E.M., Fletcher, J.M., et al. (2002). Brain mechanisms for reading words and pseudowords: An integrated approach. *Cerebral Cortex, 12,* 297–305.

Simos, P.G., Breier, J.I., Fletcher, J.M., Foorman, B.R., Mouzaki, A., & Papanicolaou, A.C. (2001). Age-related changes in regional brain activation during phonological decoding and printed word recognition. *Developmental Neuropsychology, 19,* 191–210.

Simos, P.G., Breier, J.I., Maggio, W.W., Gormley, W., Zouridakis, G., Wilmore, L.J., et al. (1999). Atypical temporal lobe language representation revealed by MSI and intraoperative stimulation mapping. *Neuroreport, 10,* 139–142.

Simos, P.G., Breier, J.I., Wheless, J.W., Maggio, W.W., Fletcher, J.M., Castillo, E.M., et al. (2000). Brain mechanisms for reading: The role of the superior temporal gyrus in word and pseudoword naming. *Neuroreport, 11,* 2443–2447.

Simos, P.G., Breier, J.I., Zouridakis, G., & Papanicolaou, A.C. (1998). Identification of language-related brain activity using magnetoencephaolography. *Journal of Clinical and Experimental Neuropsychology, 2,* 706–722.

Simos, P.G., Fletcher, J.M., Bergman, E., Breier, J.I., Foorman, B.R., Castillo, E.M., et al. (2002). Dyslexia-specific brain activation profile become normal following successful remedial training. *Neurology, 58,* 1203–1213.

Simos, P.G., Fletcher, J.M., Foorman, B.R., Francis, D.J., Castillo, E.M., Davis, R.N., et al. (2002). Brain activation profiles during the early stages of reading acquisition. *Journal of Child Neurology, 17,* 159–163.

Simos, P.G., Papanicolaou, A.C., Breier, J.I., Wheless, J.W., Constantinou, J.E., Gormley, W.B., et al. (1999). Localization of language-specific cortex by using magnetic source imaging and electrical stimulation mapping. *Journal of Neurosurgery, 91,* 787–796.

Simos, P.G., Fletcher, J.M., Sarkari, S., Billingsley, R.L., Francis, D.J., Castillo, E.M., et al. (2003). *Early development of neurophysiological processes involved in normal reading and reading disability.* Manuscript submitted for publication.

Stanovich, K.E., & Siegel, L.S. (1994). Phenotypic performance profile of children with reading disabilities: A regression-based test of the phonological-core variable-difference model. *Journal of Educational Psychology, 86,* 24–53.

Szymanski, M.D., Perry, D.W., Gage, N.M., Rowley, H.A., Walker, J., Berger, M.S., et al. (2001). Magnetic source imaging of late evoked field responses to vowels: Toward an assessment of hemispheric dominance for language. *Journal of Neurosurgery, 94*, 445–453.

Tagamets, M.A., Novick, J.M., Chalmers, M.L., & Friedman, R.B. (2000). A parametric approach to orthographic processing in the brain: An fMRI study. *Journal of Cognitive Neuroscience, 12*, 281–297.

Temple, E., Deutsch, G.K., Poldrack, R.A., Miller, S.L., Tallal, P., Merzenich, M.M., et al. (2003). Neural deficits in children with dyslexia ameliorated by behavioral remediation: Evidence from functional MRI. *Proceedings of the National Academy of Sciences of the United States of America, 100*, 2860–2865.

Torgesen, J.K., Morgan, S.T., & Davis, C. (1992). Effects of two types of phonological awareness training on word learning in kindergarten children. *Journal of Educational Psychology, 84*, 364–370.

Wise, B.W., & Olson, R.K. (1995). Computer-based phonological awareness and reading instruction. *Annals of Dyslexia, 45*, 99–122.

Woods, R.P. (1996). Modeling for intergroup comparisons of imaging data. *NeuroImage, 4*, S84–S94.

17

Neurobiologic Basis for Reading and Reading Disability

SALLY E. SHAYWITZ AND BENNETT A. SHAYWITZ

In seeking and gathering evidence, scientists prefer to go directly to the source. For the fundamental understanding of reading, the unequivocal source is the brain. As obvious as this seems, the appreciation that cognition and, specifically, reading arise in the squishy gray matter of the brain is relatively recent. For centuries, the heart was considered to house the soul and the uninteresting-appearing brain was ignored (S. Shaywitz, 2003). It was the physician-scientist Galen, conducting animal experiments in the second century A.D., who demonstrated the importance of the brain for a range of functions, including cognition. From the 17th century onward, perceptive physicians began to link specific symptoms experienced by their patients to areas of brain injury. Of course, the relationships were based on observations made after the patient had succumbed to illness. At that time, a physician examining the brain might notice an area of tissue destruction and relate this specific brain region to the symptoms that had been experienced during the patient's lifetime. The very first definitive linkage of brain injury to a symptom was made by the French neurologist Paul Broca in the middle of the 19th century. Broca related his patient Tan's expressive language difficulties to a lesion in the front of the left side of Tan's brain.

Portions of this chapter appeared in and are similar to other reviews by us in Shaywitz, B., & Shaywitz, S. (2002). Dyslexia. *Continuum*, 8(5), 17–36; and in Shaywitz, S. (1998). Current concepts: Dyslexia. *The New England Journal of Medicine*, 338(5), 307–312, copyright © 1998 Massachusetts Medical Society. All rights reserved. Adapted with permission 2004. Many of the topics are elaborated in Shaywitz, S. (2003). *Overcoming dyslexia: A new and complete science-based program for reading problems at any level.* New York: Alfred A. Knopf.

Technically, this region is referred to as the left inferior frontal gyrus, or more commonly, as Broca's area. Today, this language problem, the ability to understand but not express language, is called Broca's aphasia. Later on, another neurologist, Carl Wernicke, was able to relate lesions along the upper surface of the left side of the temporal lobe to a different kind of language problem, the converse of Broca's aphasia, called Wernicke's aphasia. In this type of aphasia, the patient cannot understand language but speaks clearly although nonsensically.

This was the state of affairs in searching for evidence of the neural origins of cognitive functions such as reading and language until the 1970s, when Sir Godfrey N. Hounsfield and Allan M. Cormack used computed tomography to capture images of the living brain for the first time. CT uses a series of X-rays to build a three-dimensional image of the brain, making it possible to see the structure of the brain. Ideally, in trying to understand the neurologic nature of reading and reading difficulties, the objective is to observe not only the structure but also the *function* of the brain as an individual is reading. The technology to accomplish this, functional imaging, became available in the early 1980s and has revolutionized our search for evidence of the neural origins of reading while at the same time providing new and valuable insights into the cause of reading difficulties and effective approaches to reading interventions.

The examination of the neural basis of reading is informed by decades of neurological and behavioral research on reading and reading disability. Functional imaging is a tool; its optimal use relies on the foundation provided by previous investigators who gathered evidence of the epidemiology, origins, and cognitive influences on reading. Rather than being a separate or isolated pursuit, brain imaging studies are influenced by the large body of science that came before and that continues to emerge from laboratories around the world. In this chapter we wish to emphasize both that the neural structures and systems of the brain represent the source of the most direct evidence for the examination of reading and that brain imaging studies (including their specific hypotheses, experimental design, and interpretation) are significantly influenced by the corpus of evidence contributed by other fields investigating reading. Furthermore, we believe that the functional brain imaging of reading has matured so that there now exists a reciprocal relationship between it and other modes of investigation of reading, one continually influencing the other.

We begin by reviewing the now overwhelming and converging evidence from many lines of investigation of the fundamental characteristics of reading and reading disability, including its definition, prevalence, longitudinal course, etiology, and cognitive basis. Building on this strong foundation, we next review studies of children and adults that provide unequivocal proof that reading originates in and relies upon the complex neural systems of the brain in place for processing the sounds of language. The key, of course, is to discover how humans are able to transform the abstract squiggles and lines of print into letters and words imbued with meaning. Although the work is relatively new, great progress has been made in identifying the neural systems for reading in good readers and in identifying a disruption in these systems in struggling readers. In addition, researchers are now beginning to understand the neural mechanisms associated with the development of skilled (fluent) reading. As we discuss in this chapter, this basic knowledge is now being applied to better understand the influence of specific reading interventions on the neural circuitry for skilled reading.

DEFINITION AND PREVALENCE

Dyslexia, a developmental disorder, is characterized by an unexpected difficulty in reading in children and adults who otherwise possess the intelligence, motivation, and education considered necessary for developing accurate and fluent reading (Lyon, 1995). Dyslexia (or specific reading disability) represents one of the most common problems affecting children and adults; in the United States the prevalence of dyslexia is estimated to range from 5% to 17%, with up to 40% of school-age children reading below grade level (S.E. Shaywitz, 1998). Dyslexia is the most common and most carefully studied of the learning disabilities (LDs), affecting 80% of all individuals identified as having LD (Interagency Committee on Learning Disabilities, 1987; Lerner, 1989; S.E. Shaywitz, 1998).

EPIDEMIOLOGY

Epidemiologic data indicate that like hypertension and obesity, dyslexia fits a dimensional model: Within the population, reading and reading disability occur along a continuum, with reading disability representing the lower tail (left side) of a bell-shaped curve of normal distribution of reading ability (Gilger, Borecki, Smith, DeFries, & Pennington, 1996; S. Shaywitz, Escobar, B. Shaywitz, Fletcher, & Makuch, 1992). Good evidence, based on sample surveys of randomly selected populations of children, indicates that dyslexia affects boys and girls equally (Flynn & Rahbar, 1994; S.E. Shaywitz, Shaywitz, Fletcher, & Escobar, 1990; Wadsworth, DeFries, Stevenson, Gilger, & Pennington, 1992); the long-held belief that only boys have dyslexia reflected sampling bias in school-identified samples.

Longitudinal studies, both prospective (Francis, S.E. Shaywitz, Stuebing, B.A. Shaywitz, & Fletcher, 1996; B. Shaywitz et al., 1995) and retrospective (Bruck, 1992; Felton, Naylor, & Wood, 1990; Scarborough, 1984), indicate that dyslexia is a persistent, chronic condition; it does not represent a transient developmental lag (see Figure 17.1). Over time, poor readers and good readers tend to maintain their relative positions along the spectrum of reading ability (B. Shaywitz et al., 1995).

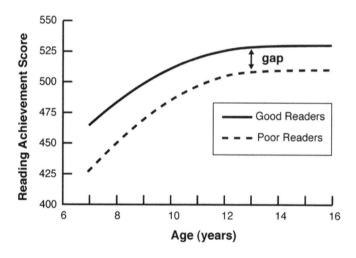

Figure 17.1. Trajectory of reading skills over time in readers with and without dyslexia. The ordinate (y axis) indicates Rasch scores (W scores) from the Reading subtest of the Woodcock-Johnson–Revised Tests of Achievement (Woodcock & Johnson, 1989) and the abscissa (x axis) shows age in years. Both readers with and without dyslexia improve their reading scores as they get older, but the gap between the two groups remains. Thus dyslexia is a deficit and not a developmental lag. (From Shaywitz, S. [2003]. *Overcoming dyslexia: A new and complete science-based program for reading problems at any level* [p. 34]. New York: Alfred A. Knopf; reprinted by permission.)

ETIOLOGY

Dyslexia is both familial (runs in families) and heritable (is inherited on genes) (Pennington, Van Orden, Smith, Green, & Haith, 1990). Family history is one of the most important risk factors; 23%–65% of children who have a parent with dyslexia are reported to have the disorder (Scarborough, 1990). Approximately 40% of siblings and 27%–49% of parents of people with dyslexia also have dyslexia (Pennington & Gilger, 1996). Family history thus provides opportunities for early identification of siblings and often for delayed but helpful identification of adults with dyslexia. Replicated linkage studies of dyslexia implicate loci (sites) on chromosomes 2, 3, 6, 15, and 18 (Fisher & DeFries, 2002). The involvement of multiple sites may mean that the inheritance of dyslexia involves many different genes (polygenic inheritance), that different cognitive pathways may lead to the same final outcome (i.e., dyslexia), or that there may be several types of dyslexia (Morris et al., 1998; S.E. Shaywitz et al., 2003).

COGNITIVE INFLUENCES

Theories of dyslexia have been proposed that are based on the visual system (Stein & Walsh, 1997) and on other factors, such as temporal processing of stimuli within the visual and auditory systems (Talcott et al., 2000; Tallal, 2000). There is now a strong consensus, however, among investigators in the field that the central difficulty in dyslexia reflects a deficit within the language system (J.M. Fletcher et al., 1994; Morris et al., 1998). Investigators have long known that speech enables its users to create an indefinitely large number of words by combining and permuting a small number of phonologic segments, the consonants and vowels that serve as the natural constituents of language. An alphabetic transcription (reading) brings this same ability to the reader, but only as the reader connects its arbitrary characters (letters) to the phonologic segments they represent. Making that connection requires an awareness that all words can be decomposed into phonologic segments. It is this awareness that allows the reader to connect the letter strings (the orthography) to the corresponding units of speech (phonologic constituents) that they represent. The awareness that all words can be decomposed into these basic elements of language (phonemes) allows the reader to decipher the reading code. In order to read, a child has to develop the insight that spoken words can be pulled apart into phonemes and that the letters in a written word represent these sounds. As numerous studies have shown, however, such awareness is largely missing in children and adults with dyslexia (Bruck, 1992; J.M. Fletcher et al., 1994; Liberman & Shankweiler, 1991). Results from large and well-studied populations of individuals with reading disability confirm that in young school-age children (J.M. Fletcher et al., 1994; Stanovich & Siegel, 1994) and in adolescents (S.E. Shaywitz et al., 1999), a deficit in phonology represents the most robust and specific (Morris et al., 1998) correlate of reading disability. Such findings form the basis for the most successful evidence-based interventions designed to improve reading (National Reading Panel, 2000).

IMPLICATIONS OF THE PHONOLOGIC MODEL OF DYSLEXIA

Basically, reading comprises two main processes—decoding and comprehension (Gough & Tunmer, 1986). In dyslexia, a deficit at the level of the phonologic module impairs a reader's ability to segment the written word into its underlying phonologic elements. As a result, the reader experiences difficulty, first in decoding the word and then in identifying it. The phonologic deficit is domain-specific; that is, it is independent of other, nonphonologic abilities. In particular, the higher-order cognitive and linguistic functions involved in comprehension, such as general intelligence and reasoning, vocabulary (Share & Stanovich, 1995), and syntax (Shankweiler et al., 1995), are generally intact. This pattern—a deficit in phonologic analysis contrasted with intact higher-order cognitive abilities—offers an explanation for the paradox that otherwise intelligent people may experience great difficulty in reading (S.E. Shaywitz, 1996).

According to the model, a circumscribed deficit in a lower-order linguistic (phonologic) function blocks access to higher-order processes and to the ability to draw meaning from text. For example, when an individual who knows the precise meaning of the spoken word "apparition" encounters the same word in text, he or she will not be able to use knowledge of the meaning of the word until he or she can decode and identify the printed word on the page and will appear not to know the word's meaning.

In addition to the accumulating evidence about the definition, prevalence, persistence, etiology, and cognitive basis of reading disability, there is now evidence about the neurobiologic basis of reading and reading disability. This unprecedented level of understanding provides insights into the reading process, supports the phonologic model, explains the manifestations of reading and reading disability across development, and adds a new level of evidence supporting approaches to reading instruction. Furthermore, such studies provide a renewed sense of urgency that effective interventions be provided without delay to children at risk of reading failure. The importance of reading instruction is supported by new neurobiological evidence suggesting that environmental factors may exert a strong influence on the ultimate reading outcome of at-risk children.

NEUROBIOLOGIC STUDIES

To a large degree these advances in understanding dyslexia have informed and facilitated studies examining the neurobiological underpinnings of reading and dyslexia. As early as 1891, the French neurologist Dejerine suggested that a portion of the left posterior brain is critical for reading. As discussed previously, at that time knowledgeable physicians examined the brains of patients who had succumbed to an illness. Often, an examination of the brain revealed an anatomic lesion that the physician would try to relate to the patient's symptoms.

Before we describe the specific anatomic findings of recent neurologic studies of dyslexia, it is helpful to review a few basics of brain anatomy: *anterior* refers to the front of the brain, *posterior* to the back. The brain is composed of four major lobes: Beginning in the front, they are the *frontal, temporal, parietal,* and *occipital* lobes, the last of which is at the very back or posterior part of the brain. These specific names of brain regions will help the reader relate these descriptions to other discussions of brain anatomy in dyslexia.

Beginning with Dejerine's (1891) work, a large literature on acquired inability to read (acquired alexia) has described neuroanatomic lesions most prominently centered in the parieto-temporal area (encompassing portions of both the parietal and the temporal lobes), which is pivotal in mapping print onto the phonologic structures of the language system or, more simply, in relating letters to sounds (Damasio & Damasio, 1983; Friedman, Ween, & Albert, 1993; Geschwind, 1965). Another posterior brain region, in the occipito-temporal area (encompassing portions of the occipital and temporal lobes), was also described by Dejerine (1892) as critical in reading. More recently, a range of neurobiologic investigations using post-mortem brain specimens (Galaburda, Sherman, Rosen, Aboitiz, & Geschwind, 1985), brain morphometry (careful measurement of brain regions; Sowell et al., 2003), and diffusion tensor magnetic resonance imaging (MRI) examining the direction of white matter fibers in the brain (Klingberg et al., 2000; Zeng, Staib, Schultz, & Duncan, 1999), support the belief that there are differences in the temporo-parieto-occipital brain regions between readers with and without dyslexia. Thus, Dejerine's original findings converge with more recent studies indicating that brain regions serving language and vision are involved in reading difficulties.

FUNCTIONAL BRAIN IMAGING

Rather than being limited to examining the brain in an autopsy specimen, or measuring the size of brain regions using static morphometric indices based on CT or MRI, functional imaging offers the possibility of examining brain function during performance of a cognitive task such as reading. In principle, functional brain imaging is quite simple. When an individual is asked to perform a discrete cognitive task, that task places processing demands on particular neural systems in the brain. To meet those demands requires activation of neural systems in specific brain regions, and those changes in neural activity are, in turn, reflected by changes in brain metabolic activity, which in turn, are reflected by changes, for example, in cerebral blood flow and in the cerebral utilization of metabolic substrates such as glucose. The term *functional imaging* has also been applied to the technology of magnetic source imaging using magnetoencephalography, an electrophysiologic method with strengths in resolving the temporal sequences of cognitive processes (see Chapter 16).

Functional magnetic resonance imaging (fMRI) promises to supplant other methods for its ability to map the individual brain's response to specific cognitive stimuli. Since it is noninvasive and safe, it can be used repeatedly; these properties make it ideal for studying children. In principle, the signal detected by MRI images changes by a small amount (typically 1%–5% intensity) in regions that are activated by a stimulus or task. The increase in signal results from the combined effects of increases in the tissue blood flow, volume, and oxygenation, though the precise contributions of each of these is still somewhat uncertain. MRI image intensity increases when deoxygenated blood is replaced by oxygenated blood, which occurs in response to stimuli, for example, reading words. A variety of methods can be used to record the changes that occur, but one preferred approach makes use of ultrafast echoplanar imaging (EPI), to produce complete images acquired in intervals substantially shorter than a second, at a rate fast enough to capture the time course of the changes in blood flow in response to neural activation and to permit a wide variety of imaging paradigms over large volumes of the brain. Details of fMRI are reviewed in several sources (Anderson & Gore, 1997; Jezzard, Matthews, & Smith, 2001), including Chapter 16.

Our research program has used fMRI to examine the functional organization of the brain for reading and reading disability, first in adults with good reading skills and those with reading difficulties, then in children. Most recently, we have used fMRI in a group of young adults who have been followed longitudinally from kindergarten to young adulthood. Some of these young adults have persistent reading disability, and some have compensated for their disability. These studies have been influenced by our knowledge of the phonologic model of reading and dyslexia. The goal is to better understand the reading process by identifying the neural underpinnings of good and poor reading and then determine if and how it may be possible to facilitate the development of those neural systems responsible for skilled reading.

Functional Magnetic Resonance Imaging in Adult Readers with Dyslexia

In an early investigation (S.E. Shaywitz et al., 1998), we studied 61 men and women, of whom 29 had dyslexia and 32 had no reading disorder, ages 16–63 years. Both groups were in the average range for IQ score. The mean standard score on a measure of nonword reading was 81 in readers with dyslexia compared with 114 in readers with no impairment, with no overlap of scores between groups. During the imaging procedure, our subjects were shown a pair of pseudowords (nonsense words) and asked whether the words rhymed, for example, *Do LEAT and JETE rhyme?* Another task required subjects to determine the meaning of words, for example, *Are CORN and RICE in the same category?*

We focused on those brain regions that previous research had implicated in reading and language (Démonet, Price, Wise, & Frackowiak, 1994; Henderson, 1986; Petersen, Fox, Snyder, & Raichle, 1990) and examined these areas for evidence of differences between the two reading groups. We found significant differences in brain activation patterns between readers with and without dyslexia. As shown in Figure 17.2, we found a disruption in the parieto-temporal component of the posterior reading system in readers with dyslexia.

Functional Magnetic Resonance Imaging in Children with Dyslexia

To determine whether these findings are the cumulative result of a lifetime of poor reading or whether they are present during the period of literacy acquisition, we used fMRI to compare children with and

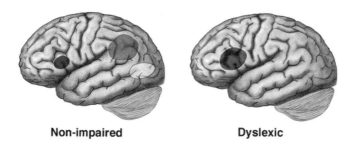

Non-impaired   **Dyslexic**

Figure 17.2.   Brain activation patterns in nonimpaired readers (*left*) and readers with dyslexia (*right*) engaged in phonological processing during a nonword rhyming task. Readers without dyslexia activate three brain regions, one anterior (front of the brain) and two posterior (back of the brain). In contrast, dyslexic readers demonstrate a relative underactivation in this posterior region and an increased activation in the anterior region. (From Shaywitz, S. [2003]. *Overcoming dyslexia: A new and complete science-based program for reading problems at any level* [p. 83]. New York: Alfred A. Knopf; reprinted by permission.)

without dyslexia during tasks that required phonologic analysis, that is, tasks that tapped the problems typically experienced by children with dyslexia in sounding out words (S.E. Shaywitz et al., 2003).

We studied 144 children, 70 readers with dyslexia and 74 readers with no reading impairments, ages 7–18 years. All children had intelligence scores in the average range. Again, as in the study of adults, we focused our subjects' attention on two tasks: judging whether two pseudowords rhymed and judging whether two real words were in the same category. Reading performance in the children with dyslexia was significantly impaired: These children's mean standard score on a measure of pseudoword reading was 85 compared with 120 in children without reading impairments. Our findings in children showed the same disruption of posterior reading systems observed in adults with reading difficulties and indicated that dysfunction in left hemisphere posterior reading circuits is already present in children with dyslexia and cannot be ascribed simply to a lifetime of poor reading. Our results converge with reports from many investigators using functional brain imaging that show a failure of left hemisphere posterior brain systems to function properly in both adults (Brunswick, McCrory, Price, Frith, & Frith, 1999; Helenius, Tarkiainen, Cornelissen, Hansen, & Salmelin, 1999; Horwitz, Rumsey, & Donohue, 1998; Paulesu et al., 2001; Rumsey et al., 1992; Rumsey et al., 1997; Salmelin, Service, Kiesila, Uutela, & Salonen, 1996; S.E. Shaywitz et al., 1998) and children (Seki et al., 2001; B.A. Shaywitz et al., 2002; Simos, Breier, J. Fletcher, Bergman, & Papanicolaou, 2000; Temple et al., 2000) with reading disability during reading tasks and during nonreading visual processing tasks (Demb, Boynton, & Heeger, 1998; Eden et al., 1996).

In anterior regions, too, we found differences in brain activation between children with and without dyslexia. Abnormalities in anterior regions in readers with dyslexia have been noted by others in children (Corina et al., 2001; Georgiewa et al., 1999) and in adults (Gross-Glenn et al., 1991; Paulesu et al., 1996). Activation in anterior regions assumed particular importance in comparisons between younger and older readers. Thus, in our sample of children ages 7–18 years, we were able to compare brain activation patterns in younger and older good and poor readers. We observed few differences in brain activation patterns between younger and older good readers. In contrast, there were significant differences in the patterns between younger and older children who were struggling readers. Older poor readers demonstrated increased activation in the right and left frontal regions and in the right posterior brain regions; we interpret these findings as reflecting areas of attempted compensation (discussed later).

These findings, acquired from an exceptionally large sample representing a broad age range across childhood, provide neurobiologic evidence of the persistence of reading difficulties across the life span. We caution that these are cross-sectional and not longitudinal studies, in which the same individuals are followed across development. However, the demonstration of the same posterior disruption in children and adults strongly suggests that children do not outgrow their reading difficulties and that the disruption that interferes with reading in childhood remains into adulthood. Thus, behavioral and neurobiological evidence converge to indicate that reading difficulties are not outgrown, do not represent a developmental lag, and remain with the child unless proven and powerful interventions are provided. We believe that this neurobiological evidence of the persistence of the neural anomaly presents an urgent call to provide children with early and intensive evidence-based reading interventions.

Our fMRI study in children has proved extremely helpful in providing a beginning understanding of the neural basis of skilled reading. Neurobiological evidence now converges with behavioral evidence to provide a deeper understanding of how children become skilled readers. Early on, a developing reader learns how to associate letters with sounds, then learns to sound out words. With time, effective instruction and the experience of repeatedly reading the same word correctly, the child forms the synaptic connections that result in increasingly accurate neural representations of that word. Eventually, an exact neural replica reflecting the word's pronunciation, its spelling, and its meaning, is formed. When that child sees the word again, all of the relevant information about that word is instantly activated—he or she knows how to pronounce it, how to spell it, and what it means. In this way, as children become more skilled, they read words accurately, rapidly and with good expression, and become fluent readers. Critically, children who become more proficient are able to recognize and read words instantly. Reading becomes automatic and is no longer effortful. Data from our brain imaging study of children provide evidence of the neurobiologic roots of skilled reading. We found a positive correlation between reading performance measured by reading tests and the brain activation patterns revealed by fMRI in the left occipito-temporal region that are shown in Figure 17.3. These findings across the full cohort of children reveal a continuum from very poor to skilled readers (S. Shaywitz et al., 1992) and indicate that the better a child reads, the more he or she shows activation in this brain region, meaning that activation of the word form area and skilled reading are directly related. These data also demonstrate that this region is disrupted in struggling readers and further suggest that unless a child receives effective reading instruction, this dysfunction will be present throughout adulthood.

Functional Magnetic Resonance Imaging in Young Adults with Childhood Histories of Dyslexia

In a recent study (S.E. Shaywitz et al., 2003) we wanted to learn whether and how two groups of young adults who were poor readers as children, a group that had compensated somewhat for reading difficulties and a group with persistent reading difficulties, differed from young adults without reading impairments. In addition, we wanted to determine if any factors distinguishing the two groups might account for their different outcomes. To this end we took

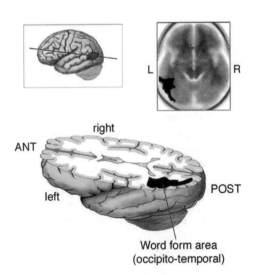

Figure 17.3. Correlation map between skill and brain activation for nonimpaired readers and readers with dyslexia. The better the child reads (as measured out of magnet), the greater the activation in the left occipito-temporal region. (From Shaywitz, S. [2003]. *Overcoming dyslexia: A new and complete science-based program for reading problems at any level* [p. 8]. New York: Alfred A. Knopf; reprinted by permission.)

advantage of the availability of a cohort who are participants in the Connecticut Longitudinal Study (CLS), a representative sample of individuals who have been prospectively followed since 1983 when they were age 5 years and who have had their reading performance assessed yearly throughout their primary and secondary schooling. Three groups of young adults were recruited from the subjects in the CLS. They were ages 18.5–22.5 years and were classified as persistently poor readers, accuracy-improved (compensated) readers, and nonimpaired readers. Persistently poor readers (n = 24) met criteria for poor reading in second or fourth grade and again in ninth or tenth grade; accuracy-improved readers (n = 19) satisfied criteria for poor reading in second or fourth grade but not in ninth or tenth grade; and nonimpaired readers (n = 27) did not meet the criteria for poor reading at any time from second to tenth grade, had a reading standard score greater than 94 (above the 40th percentile; this criterion prevented overlap with the persistently poor readers and accuracy-improved readers), and had average Full Scale IQ scores on the Wechsler Intelligence Scale for Children–Revised (WISC-R; Wechsler, 1974) lower than 130 (to avoid a control group with above-average IQ scores) (S.E. Shaywitz et al., 2003). We used fMRI to examine brain activation patterns while the subjects engaged in the two visually presented tasks described previously: pseudoword rhyming and reading real words.

During pseudoword rhyming, both groups with reading impairments (persistently poor readers and accuracy-improved readers) demonstrated the brain activation patterns we have come to expect. That is, in contrast to nonimpaired readers, both accuracy-improved readers and persistently poor readers demonstrated a relative underactivation in posterior neural systems located in the parieto-temporal and the occipito-temporal regions. During real word reading, however, the brain activation patterns for the accuracy-improved and persistently poor readers diverged. Compared with nonimpaired readers, accuracy-improved readers demonstrated relative underactivation in left posterior regions during real word reading. In contrast, activation patterns in persistently poor readers during real word reading were similar to the activation patterns of nonimpaired readers. Thus, despite the significantly better reading performance in nonimpaired readers compared with the performance of persistently poor readers on every reading task administered, left posterior reading systems were activated during reading of *real* words in both nonimpaired readers and persistently poor readers.

One reasonable explanation for these unexpected findings comes from a consideration of the hypothesis that two systems are critical in the development of skilled, automatic reading (Logan, 1997). According to Logan's theory, one system involves word analysis, operates on individual units of words such as phonemes, and processes relatively slowly; the second system operates on the whole word (word form) and processes very rapidly. Converging evidence from a number of lines of investigation indicates that the word analysis system is localized within the parieto-temporal region, whereas the automatic, rapidly responding system is localized within the occipito-temporal area, functioning as a visual word form area (Cohen et al., 2000; Cohen et al., 2002; Dehaene, Le Clec'H, Poline, Le Bihan, & Cohen, 2002; Dehaene et al., 2001; Moore & Price, 1999). This word form area appears to respond preferentially to rapidly presented stimuli (Price, Moore, & Frackowiak, 1996) and is engaged even when the word has not been consciously perceived (Dehaene et al., 2001); that is, the word form area is engaged even when the words are shown subliminally. This region may function for words in an analogous manner to the *right* hemisphere fusiform area for expertise in recognition of faces (Gauthier, 2000; Gauthier et al., 2000; Tarr & Gauthier, 2000). Our data indicate that both nonimpaired readers and persistently poor readers rely on the left occipito-temporal system for reading real words but that they engage this system differently. We hypothesize that nonimpaired readers have developed this system through phonologically based word analysis; in contrast, persistently poor readers rely more on *rote memory* for recognizing real words. And in fact, persistently poor readers perform significantly more poorly reading unfamiliar words as compared with reading familiar words, suggesting that these individuals are able to recognize memorized words but lack a strategy with which to read new or low-frequency words.

Support for this position comes also from results of an analysis of functional connectivity, that is, how the individual neural sites for reading are linked together to form a reading network (B.A. Shaywitz et al., 2002). Results indicated that nonimpaired readers demonstrated connectivity, or linkage, between the left occipito-temporal region and the left inferior frontal gyrus (Broca's area), a region associated with language. In contrast, persistently poor readers demonstrated functional connectivity between the left occipito-temporal region and right prefrontal areas often associated with working memory and memory retrieval (P. Fletcher, Frith, & Rugg, 1997; MacLeod,

Buckner, Miezin, Petersen, & Raichle, 1998), a finding consistent with the hypothesis that in persistently poor readers, the occipito-temporal area functions as a component of a memory network. These findings suggest that persistently poor readers have relied on memorizing words rather than learning to sound them out by phonologic analysis. As a consequence, these individuals may be able to recognize familiar words but are stymied when presented with new or unfamiliar words. The failure to build the use of the left occipito-temporal region through a phonologic route is associated with a lack of fluency in these readers. These findings provide further evidence of the importance of developing analytic strategies for word identification and the limitations of simply relying on a memory-based approach.

Behavioral, cognitive, and environmental influences differed among the groups (S.E. Shaywitz et al., 2003). As young adults, the three groups differed on word reading; pseudoword reading; and several measures of oral reading, including reading rate. Persistently poor readers were slower than accuracy-improved readers, who were slower than nonimpaired readers. On two measures, oral reading comprehension and prose literacy (a measure of functional reading ability), nonimpaired readers and accuracy-improved readers were not significantly different from one another, but persistently poor readers had more significant impairments than the other two groups. These data agree with previous studies of adults with childhood histories of reading difficulty (Bruck, 1998; S.E. Shaywitz et al., 1999). As young children, persistently poor readers and those who later became accuracy-improved readers came from families with lower socioeconomic status than nonimpaired readers. Furthermore, persistently poor readers, but not future accuracy-improved readers, attended more disadvantaged schools than nonimpaired readers (school disadvantage was judged by the percentage of students in the participants' schools who received subsidized meals). Although reading scores at first grade were comparable in future accuracy-improved readers and persistently poor readers, there were early differences in ability between the two groups: As early as first grade, compared with persistently poor readers, children who later became accuracy-improved readers demonstrated significantly higher Full Scale IQ scores on the WISC-R (S.E. Shaywitz et al., 2003).

A NEURAL MODEL FOR READING

Accumulating evidence from our laboratory and from laboratories around the world indicates that a number of interrelated neural systems are used in reading, at least two in posterior brain regions as well as distinct and related systems in anterior regions (see Figure 17.4). The evidence suggests that rather than having the smoothly functioning and integrated reading systems observed in nonimpaired readers, children with dyslexia have disruption of the posterior reading systems that results in these children's attempting to compensate by shifting to other, ancillary systems, for example, anterior sites, such as the inferior frontal gyrus and right hemisphere sites (B.A. Shaywitz et al., 2002). The anterior sites, critical in articulation (Brunswick et al., 1999; Fiez & Peterson, 1998; Frackowiak, Friston, Frith, Dolan, & Mazziotta, 1997), may help the child with dyslexia develop an awareness of the sound structure of the word by forming the word with the lips, tongue, and vocal apparatus and thus allow the child to read, albeit more slowly and less efficiently than would occur through a functioning, fast occipito-temporal word identifica-

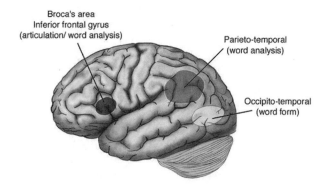

Figure 17.4.   Neural systems for reading. Converging evidence indicates three important systems in reading, all primarily in the left hemisphere. These include an anterior system and two posterior systems: 1) an anterior system in the left inferior frontal region; 2) a parieto-temporal system involving posterior portions of the superior temporal gyrus, the supramarginal gyrus, and the angular gyrus; and 3) an occipito-temporal system involving portions of the middle and inferior temporal gyrus, the middle and inferior occipital gyrus, and the fusiform gyrus. (From Shaywitz, S. [2003]. *Overcoming dyslexia: A new and complete science-based program for reading problems at any level* [p. 78]. New York: Alfred A. Knopf; reprinted by permission.)

tion system. The tendency of disabled readers to rely on subvocalization may reflect engagement of these frontal systems. The right hemisphere sites may represent the engagement of brain regions that allow the poor reader to use other perceptual processes to compensate for his or her poor phonologic skills (discussed later).

THE INFLUENCE OF TEACHING

Functional imaging studies have converged with behavioral studies in indicating that there are important differences, here neurologically based, between children with and without reading disabilities. Demonstration of these differences in children who are at the cusp of learning to read and in adults confirms the persistent nature of dyslexia. Studies have previously demonstrated that the reading of bright individuals with dyslexia becomes more accurate as these individuals mature, but that these individuals do not attain fluency or automaticity in reading (Bruck, 1992; Felton et al., 1990). Now, functional imaging provides an explanation. As noted previously, converging evidence from many laboratories implicates the left occipito-temporal region as a site for skilled, automatic reading. Failure of readers with dyslexia to activate this region explains their lack of automaticity; observation of activation of right hemisphere frontal and posterior regions—ancillary systems for word reading—provides an explanation for accurate but not automatic reading. These secondary systems can permit word decoding but do so slowly and not with the degree of automaticity characteristic of left hemisphere linguistically structured brain regions. These findings have important clinical implications: They confirm the biologic validity of reading disability; they explain the lack of automaticity, even in those readers who develop accuracy; and they emphasize the need for intervention programs for struggling readers that target the development of fluency and not just accuracy.

Our recent findings of neurobiological differences between groups of struggling readers who develop into persistently poor readers compared with others who are able to read accurately, to read unfamiliar words, and to read with good comprehension albeit slowly suggest that there may two types of vulnerable readers. These results are consistent with Olson's suggestion (Olson, 1999; Olson, Forsberg, Gayan, & DeFries, 1999) that there are two possible types of childhood reading disability: one primarily genetic, the other more environmentally influenced. That is, although both inherent and experiential factors play a role in the development of reading in all children, there appear to be groups in whom one or the other of these factors may predominate. We speculate that the accuracy-improved readers may represent children with an inherent disruption in the neural pathways for reading and that the persistently poor readers, who tend to go to more disadvantaged schools, may reflect children in whom there is a stronger environmental influence. For the persistently poor readers, who represent approximately two thirds of individuals with reading impairments in our epidemiologic sample survey, we hypothesize the neural systems that form the substrate for developing mature reading systems may be intact. Due to lack of environmental stimulation, such as effective teaching, these systems apparently fail to develop appropriately. If so, exposure to highly effective, evidence-based reading instruction should lead to the development of left posterior neural systems characterizing skilled reading.

Within this new framework of understanding, the association of an area in the brain for skilled reading (the word form area in the left occipito-temporal region) is now a neurobiological target for reading interventions to develop fluent reading. Recent studies (see below) carried out in a range of laboratories affirm both the plasticity (ability of the brain to adapt and change) of the neural systems for reading and the positive influence on these systems of effective reading instruction. In other words, there is now neurobiological evidence that what happens in the classroom is important and that how reading is taught matters. In previous studies using functional brain imaging in adults (Temple et al., 2000) and children (Richards et al., 2000; Simos et al., 2002), improvement in reading performance coincided with improvement in brain function. In the largest imaging study of a reading intervention and the first report of the effects of a reading intervention on children (B. Shaywitz et al., 2003), we used fMRI to study the effects of a phonologically based reading intervention on brain organization and reading fluency in 77 children from 6 to 9 years of age. Children received a systematic, explicit, phonologically based reading intervention 1 hour per school day for the entire school year. These children made significant gains in reading fluency and demonstrated increased activation in left hemi-sphere brain regions important for reading, including the inferior frontal gyrus and the parieto-temporal and occipito-temporal (word form) reading systems. What is particularly exciting is that taken together, these studies combining functional brain imaging with an evidence-based intervention demonstrate the importance of effective teaching and further demonstrate that phonologically based interventions affect the development of the brain systems that are critical for skilled reading.

In summary, functional neural disruption has been demonstrated in both children and adults with reading disorders, and a neural site for skilled reading and its disruption in struggling readers has been identified. Together with the demonstration that this word form area (and the development of fluent reading) develops following a systematic, intensive phonologically based intervention, this evidence provides great hope for increasing our understanding of the fundamental neural underpinnings of reading and reading disability and provides compelling evidence that researchers and educators now have the knowledge and the ability to develop these automatic systems in poor readers. These findings underscore the importance of teaching and the impact of effective reading instruction on the very brain systems responsible for skilled reading. This new and exciting level of evidence of the functional neural lesion in reading disability and its potential reparability represents, we believe, both an educational and a moral imperative to provide the type and quality of reading instruction that make it possible for virtually all children to become better readers.

REFERENCES

Anderson, A., & Gore, J. (1997). The physical basis of neuroimaging techniques. *Child and Adolescent Psychiatric Clinics of North America, 6,* 213–264.

Bruck, M. (1992). Persistence of dyslexics' phonological awareness deficits. *Developmental Psychology, 28*(5), 874–886.

Bruck, M. (1998). Outcomes of adults with childhood histories of dyslexia. In C. Hulme & R.M. Joshi (Eds.), *Cognitive and linguistic bases of reading, writing, and spelling* (pp. 179–200). Mahwah, NJ: Lawrence Erlbaum Associates.

Brunswick, N., McCrory, E., Price, C.J., Frith, C.D., & Frith, U. (1999). Explicit and implicit processing of words and pseudowords by adult developmental dyslexics: A search for Wernicke's Wortschatz. *Brain, 122,* 1901–1917.

Cohen, L., Dehaene, S., Naccache, L., Lehéricy, S., Dehaene-Lambertz, G., Hénaff, M.-A., et al. (2000). The visual word form area: Spatial and temporal characterization of an initial stage of reading in normal subjects and posterior split-brain patients. *Brain, 123,* 291–307.

Cohen, L., Lehéricy, S., Chochon, F., Lemer, C., Rivaud, S., & Dehaene, S. (2002). Language-specific tuning of visual cortex?: Functional properties of the Visual Word Form Area. *Brain, 125,* 1054–1069.

Corina, D., Richards, T., Serafini, S., Richards, A., Steury, K., Abbott, R., et al. (2001). fMRI auditory language differences between dyslexic and able reading children. *NeuroReport, 12,* 1195–1201.

Damasio, A.R., & Damasio, H. (1983). The anatomic basis of pure alexia. *Neurology, 33,* 1573–1583.

Dehaene, S., Le Clec'H, G., Poline, J., Le Bihan, D., & Cohen, L. (2002). The visual word form area: A prelexical representation of visual words in the fusiform gyrus. *NeuroReport, 13,* 1–5.

Dehaene, S., Naccache, L., Cohen, L., Le Bihan, D., Mangin, J., Poline, J., et al. (2001). Cerebral mechanisms of word masking and unconscious repetition priming. *Nature Neuroscience, 4,* 752–758.

Dejerine, J. (1891). Sur un cas de cécité verbale avec agraphie, suivi d'autopsie. *Comptes rendus de la Société de Biologie, 43,* 197–201.

Dejerine, J. (1892). Contribution à l'étude anatomo-pathologique et clinique des différentes variétés de cécité verbale. *Mémoires de la Société de Biologie, 4,* 61–90.

Demb, J., Boynton, G., & Heeger, D. (1998). Functional magnetic resonance imaging of early visual pathways in dyslexia. *Journal of Neuroscience, 18,* 6939–6951.

Démonet, J., Price, C., Wise, R., & Frackowiak, R. (1994). A PET study of cognitive strategies in normal subjects during language tasks: Influence of phonetic ambiguity and sequence processing on phoneme monitoring. *Brain, 117,* 671–682.

Eden, G.F., VanMeter, J.W., Rumsey, J.M., Maisog, J.M., Woods, R.P., & Zeffiro, T.A. (1996). Abnormal processing of visual motion in dyslexia revealed by functional brain imaging. *Nature, 382,* 66–69.

Felton, R.H., Naylor, C.E., & Wood, F.B. (1990). Neuropsychological profile of adult dyslexics. *Brain and Language, 39,* 485–497.

Fiez, J.A., & Peterson, S.E. (1998). Neuroimaging studies of word reading. *Proceedings of the National Academy of Sciences of the United States of America, 95*(3), 914–921.

Fisher, S., & DeFries, J.C. (2002). Developmental dyslexia: Genetic dissection of a complex cognitive trait. *Nature Reviews: Neuroscience, 3,* 767–780.

Fletcher, J.M., Shaywitz, S.E., Shankweiler, D.P., Katz, L., Liberman, I.Y., Stuebing, K.K., et al. (1994). Cognitive profiles of reading disability: Comparisons of discrepancy and low achievement definitions. *Journal of Educational Psychology, 86*(1), 6–23.

Fletcher, P., Frith, C., & Rugg, M. (1997). The functional anatomy of episodic memory. *Trends in Neurosciences, 20,* 213–218.

Flynn, J., & Rahbar, M. (1994). Prevalence of reading failure in boys compared with girls. *Psychology in the Schools, 31,* 66–71.

Frackowiak, R., Friston, K., Frith, C., Dolan, R., & Mazziotta, J.C. (1997). *Human brain function.* San Diego: Academic Press.

Francis, D.J., Shaywitz, S.E., Stuebing, K.K., Shaywitz, B.A., & Fletcher, J.M. (1996). Developmental lag versus deficit models of reading disability: A longitudinal, individual growth curves analysis. *Journal of Educational Psychology, 88*(1), 3–17.

Friedman, R.F., Ween, J.E., & Albert, M.L. (1993). Alexia. In K.M. Heilman & E. Valenstein (Eds.), *Clinical neuropsychology* (3rd ed., pp. 37–62). New York: Oxford University Press.

Galaburda, A.M., Sherman, G.F., Rosen, G.D., Aboitiz, F., & Geschwind, N. (1985). Developmental dyslexia: Four consecutive patients with cortical anomalies. *Annals of Neurology, 18*(2), 222–233.

Gauthier, I. (2000). What constrains the organization of the ventral temporal cortex. *Trends Cognitive Science, 4,* 1–2.

Gauthier, I., Tarr, M., Moylan, J., Skudlarski, P., Gore, J.C., & Anderson, A. (2000). The fusiform "face area" is part of a network that processes faces at the individual level. *Journal of Cognitive Neuroscience, 123,* 495–504.

Georgiewa, P., Rzanny, R., Hopf, J., Knab, R., Glauche, V., Kaiser, W., et al. (1999). fMRI during word processing in dyslexic and normal reading children. *NeuroReport, 10,* 3459–3465.

Geschwind, N. (1965). Disconnection syndromes in animals and man. *Brain, 88,* 237–294.

Gilger, J.W., Borecki, I.B., Smith, S.D., DeFries, J.C., & Pennington, B.F. (1996). The etiology of extreme scores for complex phenotypes: An illustration using reading performance. In C.H. Chase, G.D. Rosen, & G.F. Sherman (Eds.), *Developmental dyslexia: Neural, cognitive, and genetic mechanisms* (pp. 63–85). Timonium, MD: York Press.

Gough, P.B., & Tunmer, W.E. (1986). Decoding, reading, and reading disability. *Remedial and Special Education, 7,* 6–10.

Gross-Glenn, K., Duara, R., Barker, W.W., Loewenstein, D., Chang, J.-Y., Yoshii, F., et al. (1991). Positron emission tomographic studies during serial word-reading by normal and dyslexic adults. *Journal of Clinical and Experimental Neuropsychology, 13*(4), 531–544.

Helenius, P., Tarkiainen, A., Cornelissen, P., Hansen, P.C., & Salmelin, R. (1999). Dissociation of normal feature analysis and deficient processing of letter-strings in dyslexic adults. *Cerebral Cortex, 4,* 476–483.

Henderson, V.W. (1986). Anatomy of posterior pathways in reading: A reassessment. *Brain and Language, 29,* 119–133.

Horwitz, B., Rumsey, J.M., & Donohue, B.C. (1998). Functional connectivity of the angular gyrus in normal reading and dyslexia. *Proceedings of the National Academy of Sciences of the United States of America, 95,* 8939–8944.

Interagency Committee on Learning Disabilities. (1987). *Learning disabilities: A report to the U.S. Congress.* Washington, DC: U.S. Government Printing Office.

Jezzard, P., Matthews, P., & Smith, S. (2001). *Functional MRI: An introduction to methods.* Oxford, UK: Oxford University Press.

Klingberg, T., Hedehus, M., Temple, E., Salz, T., Gabrieli, J., Moseley, M., et al. (2000). Microstructure of temporo-parietal white matter as a basis for reading ability: Evidence from diffusion tensor magnetic resonance imaging. *Neuron, 25,* 493–500.

Lerner, J. (1989). Educational interventions in learning disabilities. *Journal of the American Academy of Child and Adolescent Psychiatry, 28,* 326–331.

Liberman, I.Y., & Shankweiler, D. (1991). Phonology and beginning to read: A tutorial. In L. Rieben & C.A. Perfetti (Eds.), *Learning to read: Basic research and its implications.* Mahwah, NJ: Lawrence Erlbaum Associates.

Logan, G. (1997). Automaticity and reading: perspectives from the instance theory of automatization. *Reading and Writing Quarterly: Overcoming Learning Disabilities, 13,* 123–146.

Lyon, G.R. (1995). Toward a definition of dyslexia. *Annals of Dyslexia, 45,* 3–27.

MacLeod, A., Buckner, R., Miezin, F., Petersen, S., & Raichle, M. (1998). Right anterior prefrontal cortex activation during semantic monitoring and working memory. *NeuroImage, 7,* 41–48.

Moore, C., & Price, C. (1999). Three distinct ventral occiptotemporal regions for reading and object naming. *NeuroImage, 10,* 181–192.

Morris, R.D., Stuebing, K.K., Fletcher, J.M., Shaywitz, S.E., Lyon, G.R., Shankweiler, D.P., et al. (1998). Subtypes of reading disability: Variability around a phonological core. *Journal of Educational Psychology, 90,* 347–373.

National Reading Panel. (2000). *Teaching children to read: An evidence-based assessment of the scientific research literature on reading and its implications for reading instruction. Reports of the subgroups* (NIH Publication No. 00-4754). Bethesda, MD: National Institutes of Health, National Institute of Child Health and Human Development. Also available on-line: http://www.nichd.nih.gov/publications/nrp/report.htm

Olson, R. (1999). Genes, environment, and reading disabilities. In R. Sternberg & L. Spear-Swerling (Eds.), *Perspectives on learning disabilities* (pp. 3–22). Boulder, CO: Westview Press.

Olson, R., Forsberg, H., Gayan, J., & DeFries, J. (1999). A behavioral-genetic analysis of reading disabilities and component processes. In R. Klein & P. McMullen (Eds.), *Converging methods for understanding reading and dyslexia* (pp. 133–153). Cambridge, MA: MIT Press.

Paulesu, E., Démonet, J.-F., Fazio, F., McCrory, E., Chanoine, V., Brunswick, N., et al. (2001). Dyslexia: Cultural diversity and biological unity. *Science, 291,* 2165–2167.

Paulesu, E., Frith, U., Snowling, M., Gallagher, A., Morton, J., Frackowiak, R.S.J., et al. (1996). Is developmental dyslexia a disconnection syndrome?: Evidence from PET scanning. *Brain, 119,* 143–157.

Pennington, B., & Gilger, J. (1996). How is dyslexia transmitted? In C.H. Chase, G.D. Rosen, & G.F. Sherman (Eds.), *Developmental dyslexia: Neural, cognitive, and genetic mechanisms* (pp. 41–61). Timonium, MD: York Press.

Pennington, B., Van Orden, G., Smith, S., Green, P., & Haith, M. (1990). Phonological processing skills and deficits in adult dyslexic children. *Child Development, 61,* 1753–1778.

Petersen, S.E., Fox, P.T., Snyder, A.Z., & Raichle, M.E. (1990). Activation of extrastriate and frontal cortical areas by visual words and word-like stimuli. *Science, 249,* 1041–1044.

Price, C., Moore, C., & Frackowiak, R.S.J. (1996). The effect of varying stimulus rate and duration on brain activity during reading. *NeuroImage, 3*(1), 40–52.

Richards, T., Corina, D., Serafini, S., Steury, K., Echelard, D., Dager, S., et al. (2000). Effects of a phonologically driven treatment for dyslexia on lactate levels measured by proton MRI spectroscopic imaging. *American Journal of Neuroradiology, 21,* 916–922.

Rumsey, J.M., Andreason, P., Zametkin, A.J., Aquino, T., King, C., Hamburger, S.D., et al. (1992). Failure to activate the left temporoparietal cortex in dyslexia. *Archives of Neurology, 49,* 527–534.

Rumsey, J.M., Nace, K., Donohue, B., Wise, D., Maisog, J.M., & Andreason, P. (1997). A positron emission tomographic study of impaired word recognition and phonological processing in dyslexic men. *Archives of Neurology, 54,* 562–573.

Salmelin, R., Service, E., Kiesila, P., Uutela, K., & Salonen, O. (1996). Impaired visual word processing in dyslexia revealed with magnetoencephalography. *Annals of Neurology, 40,* 157–162.

Scarborough, H. (1984). Continuity between childhood dyslexia and adult reading. *British Journal of Psychology, 75,* 329–348.

Scarborough, H. (1990). Very early language deficits in dyslexic children. *Child Development, 61,* 1728–1743.

Seki, A., Koeda, T., Sugihara, S., Kamba, M., Hirata, Y., Ogawa, T., et al. (2001). A functional magnetic resonance imaging study during sentence reading in Japanese dyslexic children. *Brain & Development, 23,* 312–316.

Shankweiler, D., Crain, S., Katz, L., Fowler, A.E., Liberman, A.M., Brady, S.A., et al. (1995). Cognitive profiles of reading-disabled children: Comparison of language skills in phonology, morphology, and syntax. *Psychological Science, 6*(3), 149–156.

Share, D.L., & Stanovich, K.E. (1995). Cognitive processes in early reading development: Accommodating individual differences into a model of acquisition. *Issues in Education: Contributions from Educational Psychology, 1*(1), 1–57.

Shaywitz, B., Holford, T., Holahan, J., Fletcher, J., Stuebing, K., Francis, D., et al. (1995). A Matthew effect for IQ but not for reading: Results from a longitudinal study. *Reading Research Quarterly, 30*(4), 894–906.

Shaywitz, B., & Shaywitz, S. (2002). Dyslexia. *Continuum, 8*(5), 17–36.

Shaywitz, B., Shaywitz, S., Blachman, B., Pugh, K., Fulbright, R., Skudlarski, P., et al. (2003). *Development of left occipito-temporal systems for skilled reading following a phonologically-based intervention in children.* Paper presented at the meeting of the Organization for Human Brain Mapping, New York.

Shaywitz, B.A., Shaywitz, S.E., Pugh, K.R., Mencl, W.E., Fulbright, R.K., Skudlarski, P., et al. (2002). Disruption of posterior brain systems for reading in children with developmental dyslexia. *Biological Psychiatry, 52,* 101–110.

Shaywitz, S.E. (1996). Dyslexia. *Scientific American, 275*(5), 98–104.

Shaywitz, S. (1998). Current concepts: Dyslexia. *The New England Journal of Medicine, 338*(5), 307–312.

Shaywitz, S. (2003). *Overcoming dyslexia: A new and complete science-based program for reading problems at any level.* New York: Alfred A. Knopf.

Shaywitz, S., Escobar, M., Shaywitz, B., Fletcher, J., & Makuch, R. (1992). Evidence that dyslexia may represent the lower tail of a normal distribution of reading ability. *The New England Journal of Medicine, 326*(3), 145–150.

Shaywitz, S.E., Fletcher, J.M., Holahan, J.M., Shneider, A.E., Marchione, K.E., Stuebing, K.K., et al. (1999). Persistence of dyslexia: The Connecticut Longitudinal Study at adolescence. *Pediatrics, 104,* 1351–1359.

Shaywitz, S.E., Shaywitz, B.A., Fletcher, J.M., & Escobar, M.D. (1990). Prevalence of reading disability in boys and girls: Results of the Connecticut Longitudinal Study. *Journal of the American Medical Association, 264,* 998–1002.

Shaywitz, S.E., Shaywitz, B.A., Fulbright, R.K., Skudlarski, P., Mencl, W.E., Constable, R.T., et al. (2003). Neural systems for compensation and persistence: Young adult outcome of childhood reading disability. *Biological Psychiatry, 54,* 25–33.

Shaywitz, S.E., Shaywitz, B.A., Pugh, K.R., Fulbright, R.K., Constable, R.T., Mencl, W.E., et al. (1998). Functional disruption in the organization of the brain for reading in dyslexia. *Proceedings of the National Academy of Sciences of the United States of America, 95,* 2636–2641.

Simos, P., Breier, J., Fletcher, J., Bergman, E., & Papanicolaou, A. (2000). Cerebral mechanisms involved in word reading in dyslexic children: A magnetic source imaging approach. *Cerebral Cortex, 10,* 809–816.

Simos, P., Fletcher, J., Bergman, E., Breier, J., Foorman, B., Castillo, E., et al. (2002). Dyslexia-specific brain activation profile becomes normal following successful remedial training. *Neurology, 58,* 1203–1213.

Sowell, E.R., Peterson, B.S., Thompson, P.M., Welcome, S.E., Henkenius, A.L., & Toga, A.W. (2003). Mapping cortical change across the human life span. *Nature Neuroscience, 6*(3), 309–315.

Stanovich, K.E., & Siegel, L.S. (1994). Phenotypic performance profile of children with reading disabilities: A regression-based test of the phonological-core variable-difference model. *Journal of Educational Psychology, 86*(1), 24–53.

Stein, J., & Walsh, V. (1997). To see but not to read: The magnocellular theory of dyslexia. *Trends in Neurosciences, 20*(4), 147–152.

Talcott, J., Witton, C., McLean, M., Hansen, P., Rees, A., Green, G., et al. (2000). Dynamic sensory sensitivity and children's word decoding skills. *Proceedings of the National Academy of Sciences of the United States of America, 97,* 2952–2957.

Tallal, P. (2000). The science of literacy: From the laboratory to the classroom. *Proceedings of the National Academy of Sciences of the United States of America, 97,* 2402–2404.

Tarr, M., & Gauthier, I. (2000). FFA: A flexible fusiform area for subordinate-level visual processing automatized by expertise. *Nature Neuroscience, 3,* 764–769.

Temple, E., Poldrack, R., Protopapas, A., Nagarajan, S., Salz, T., Tallal, P., et al. (2000). Disruption of the neural response to rapid acoustic stimuli in dyslexia: Evidence from functional MRI. *Proceedings of the National Academy of Sciences of the United States of America, 97,* 13907–13912.

Wadsworth, S.J., DeFries, J.C., Stevenson, J., Gilger, J.W., & Pennington, B.F. (1992). Gender ratios among reading-disabled children and their siblings as a function of parental impairment. *Journal of Child Psychology and Psychiatry, 33*(7), 1229–1239.

Wechsler, D. (1974). *Wechsler Intelligence Scale for Children–Revised.* San Antonio, TX: The Psychological Corporation.

Woodcock, R.W., & Johnson, M.B. (1989). *Woodcock-Johnson Psycho-Educational Battery–Revised* (WJ-R). Allen, TX: Developmental Learning Materials.

Zeng, X., Staib, L., Schultz, R., & Duncan, J. (1999). Segmentation and measurement of the cortex from 3d using coupled surfaces propagation. *IEEE Transactions on Medical Imaging, 18*(10).

VI

Policy and Research

Where Are We Today
and Where Are We Going?

The last section of this book addresses the interface of research and policy—how the two affect one another. Policies should be based on sound research and on convergent evidence but are also affected by the political climate. Research seeks to answer questions that are crucial to confirming or changing current practice via evidence of effectiveness and optimal conditions under which certain practices can be effective; in this way, research should inform policy. The last two chapters in this book address the processes through which these interactions occur. Mengli Song, Jane G. Coggshall, and Cecil G. Miskel, in Chapter 18, present information on how policy is formed. They offer a detailed discussion of people who are able to exert great influence on reading policy, and illustrate this with Dr. G. Reid Lyon as an example. Chapter 18 is an interesting culmination to a book that is dedicated to this leader in the field of reading research because this chapter traces his influence in both the research and policy arenas. Chapter 19 (by Peggy McCardle and Vinita Chhabra) serves as a coda, indicating what activities are underway whose findings will be available in coming years. McCardle and Chhabra outline new panels that are actively working or that have recently completed work and new interagency efforts that are funding research that can inform practice and policy in various age groups and special populations: preschoolers, adolescents, adults, and English language learners. In this way, Chapter 19 serves as a map to the evidence that will emerge over the coming years that can inform both practice and policy.

18

Where Does Policy Usually Come From and Why Should We Care?

MENGLI SONG,
JANE G. COGGSHALL, AND CECIL G. MISKEL

Throughout the 1990s, a veritable rash of policies on reading instruction, standards, and assessment broke out around the country. Policy makers engineered countless policies designed to alleviate a perceived crisis in reading achievement. Beginning in the Clinton administration, two prominent federal policy initiatives—the America Reads program and the Reading Excellence Act—were launched, marking the advent of a new era in national reading policy (McDaniel, Sims, & Miskel, 2001). George W. Bush's administration has added its own policies, including the Reading First and Early Reading First initiatives, key components of the No Child Left Behind Act of 2001 (PL 107-110). The reading policy contagion has spread throughout the states as well. Policy makers in most states have been actively involved in pushing their own prescriptions for the reading problem. Notable examples include the Alabama Reading Initiative, the California Reading Initiative, and Texas's Student Success Initiative, to name only a few.

Describing the causes and conditions of these particular policy initiatives is the central aim of this chapter. We use the recent development of reading policy as an example to get at the heart of the question, Where does policy usually come from? We frame our discussion with several contemporary theories of the agenda-setting process. We begin by describing the forces that shape a policy agenda, highlighting how policy makers come to recognize societal problems and place them as action items on the policy agenda. We then discuss the roles that members of the policy community and their ideas play in addressing the agenda items. Next, using Dr. G. Reid Lyon as an example from the national reading policy community, we make the case that policy entrepreneurs and influence tactics are integral to explaining where policy comes from. We conclude the paper with our reflection on why we think all the above should matter to educational researchers and practitioners (so, if you are doubtful, perhaps you may first want to read the conclusion, called "Why Should We Care?").

AGENDA SETTING

An essential aspect of the policy-making process is setting the policy agenda. The relative prominence of potential policy issues determines which issues policy makers will and will not act on. Two factors help explain why some issues are more prominent than others—problem recognition and the political environment.

Problem Recognition

Before any policy actions are undertaken, a societal condition must capture policy makers' attention and be recognized as a problem that demands action. According to Kingdon (1995), policy actors (i.e., members of the policy community) recognize societal conditions as policy problems through indicators, focusing events, or feedback. Indicators are measuring sticks that assess the magnitude of the issue. When the indicators suggest that conditions large or bad enough, or change significantly, policy makers and the public see them as problems. Attention is called to issues through focusing events such as crises or disasters, popularization of powerful symbols, or even a policy maker's own (sometimes harrowing) personal experiences. Feedback that officials receive from constituents or program evaluators can also transform a societal condition to a policy problem.

   Since the early 1990s, the issue of early reading achievement has clearly caught people's attention both in and outside of government. Perhaps the most widely cited indicator or evidence of low reading achievement was the 1994 National Assessment of Educational Progress (NAEP) reading results. The outcomes revealed that 41% of American fourth graders were reading below the basic level and only 28% were reading at or above the proficient level. These statistics sent a powerful message to education policy makers that a serious reading problem exists for America's schoolchildren. Focusing events, such as the precipitous decline in the scores of California's students on the 1994 NAEP reading test (which was so dramatic as to be deemed more than simply an indicator) and policy makers' personal struggles with children who were having difficulty learning to read, also heightened policy makers' attention to the reading achievement problem. Furthermore, feedback such as complaints from business interests that prospective employees' low levels of literacy were hindering competitiveness in the global economy raised policy makers' awareness of the problem of literacy in the United States. All of these mechanisms served to elevate the societal condition of widespread low reading achievement to a problem in need of a policy solution.

In addition to the magnitude of the condition, its nature (i.e., its causes and potential effects) influences the condition's immediacy and salience as a problem needing fixing. Stone reiterated the "old saw in political science that difficult conditions only become problems when people come to see them as amenable to human action" (1989, p. 281). If policy makers see nature, fate, accident, or the like as causing poor conditions, then the policy makers are unlikely to expend energy or political capital attempting to change these conditions. Thus, according to Stone, those who wish to influence policy would compose accounts about the specific causes of societal conditions in order to push favored policy solutions.

The causal stories told by reading policy actors around the country vary widely. For example, these policy actors have variously attributed the reading problem to poor teacher preparation, a dearth of professional development opportunities, the influx of English language learners, a lack of school readiness, an increase in television watching, a lack of parents who read to their children, inadequate access to libraries, inner-city poverty, rural poverty, and an overreliance on either whole language or phonics (e.g., Coggshall & Osguthorpe, 2002; Shepley, 2002; Young, 2002). Each of these causes implies a different solution; and Stone (1989) suggested that policy actors deliberately portray the causes of the reading problem in ways "calculated to gain support for their side" (p. 282).

Political Environment

The status of a potential policy issue on policy makers' agendas depends not only on the salience of the issue but also on the political environment of the policy domain. Kingdon (1995) outlined three major political factors that affect an issue's agenda status: the national mood, organized political forces, and events within government itself. National mood refers to the notion that a rather large number of people in a given nation are thinking about a problem along certain common lines. Policy makers' perceptions of the national mood or a swing of the mood can promote some items on their policy agendas and restrain others from rising to prominence, depending on whether the items fit with the mood. Policy makers also gauge the level of support and opposition among organized political forces (e.g., coalitions of interest groups, political elites, large groups of mobilized citizens) regarding particular policy issues, and are more likely to promote issues with stronger support from organized political forces. Finally, agendas are subject to marked changes because of events within government itself (e.g., an election, turnover of key personnel, shifts in jurisdictional boundaries, casualties in turf battles).

Where reading policy is concerned, one can easily sense a national mood that is deeply concerned with education in general and with reading in particular. Although diverse policy actors have had heated debates over such issues as the magnitude of the reading problem, appropriate methods of teaching reading, and standards and assessments, few would deny the importance of ensuring that every child can read well. As a teacher union member in Michigan aptly stated, "Being against . . . sound reading policy is like being against motherhood or democracy" (as cited in Shepley, 2002, p. 3). Thus, the importance of reading spans even partisan divides, bringing balance to organized political forces. This balance, in combination with a prevailing national mood in favor of improving reading, has made the policy makers more prone to accepting proposals for new reading policies. Moreover, both the Clinton and Bush administrations have contributed to this susceptible political environment by staunchly promoting the importance of reading achievement while the transition between the two administrations provided opportunities for different actors (e.g., political appointees and policy activists) to come on the scene. As a result, reading has acquired a prominent position on policy makers' agendas across the states as well as in the nation's capital.

POLICY COMMUNITIES AND POLICY IDEAS

The emergence of a compelling problem or developments in the political environment such as those just discussed may trigger the opening of what Kingdon (1995) called a "policy window." Staying open only briefly, the policy window represents a propitious opportunity for policy change. For policy change to actually occur, however, a compelling problem needs to be coupled with a viable solution in a politically favorable environment. An open policy window represents an opportunity for policy change; it does not represent actual policy change. Policy makers select viable solutions from a diverse array of ideas, proposals, and alternatives generated by a policy community. Policy communities are networks of specialists in a given policy area who regularly (or irregularly) interact with each other to exchange ideas, share knowledge, and formulate and reformulate policy alternatives. They are primarily composed of researchers, congressional staffers, people in planning and evaluation offices or budget offices, academics, and interest group analysts (Kingdon, 1995).

Once dominated by policy makers and a handful of education associations (Marshall, Mitchell, & Wirt, 1989; Salisbury, 1990; Thomas & Hrebenar, 1999), education policy making is now the realm of a growing number of actors of diverse natures who are committed to shaping public education (e.g., government agencies, teacher unions, educational organizations, think tanks, citizens' groups). A research team at the University of Michigan, of which we are a part, found that an advocacy explosion occurred in the national reading policy arena during the 1990s, with more than 100 government agencies and interest groups actively vying for influence on national reading policy (e.g., McDaniel et al., 2001; Song & Miskel, 2002). This explosion was mirrored in the states—the total number of reading policy actors (defined as groups or individuals acting on their own) reached 266 across the nine states that we examined. At both state and national levels, reading community members include not only government agencies such as congressional offices, legislative committees, or departments of education but also various interest groups. Those groups cover a broad spectrum: teachers' associations, administrator organizations, education associations, higher education institutions, citizens groups, businesses, foundations, think tanks, and the media. Hence, the research evidence indicates that both proliferation and diversity characterize the policy communities within the reading policy domain.

In many policy communities, academics, researchers, and analysts play a prominent role. They are especially active in the development of policy ideas and alternatives to which government actors (i.e., policy makers) often attend. As Kingdon noted, "Ideas from academic literature are regularly discussed by Hill staffers, bureaucrats, and lobbyists. Prominent academics are well known by name, and referenced repeatedly" (1995, p. 54). Nevertheless, policy makers will often only turn to the research community for proposals *after* the policy agenda has been set. Moreover, policy makers may only attend to those research findings that support their positions.

In any case, as members of the policy community interact, their ideas about the best solutions to a policy problem are proposed, shared, debated, revised, excoriated, or ignored. These policy ideas can predate the recognition of the problem. In other words, actors often have their favorite policy alternatives in mind and then look around for a problem to solve. As mentioned previously, policy actors may even construct a causal story in which a good conclusion depends on using their alternatives. For example, a reading specialist who is an expert in phonics may couch the reading problem as resulting from an overreliance on whole language as he or she attempts to win support for his or her favored program or textbook. Although there may be some truth to the specialist's causal story, the whole truth or strict evidence is almost irrelevant to this process. What is relevant is the ability of that reading specialist to sell his or her solution by telling a good story about how the approach solved the problem. Kingdon (1995) called those most adept at this process "policy entrepreneurs."

POLICY ENTREPRENEURS AND INFLUENCE TACTICS

In a dynamic policy domain such as reading, various interests generate a plethora of policy ideas, proposals, and alternatives. Floating around in the so-called "policy primeval soup" (Kingdon, 1995), some ideas prosper and are taken seriously, whereas others die an unmarked death. This selection process, however, does not occur in an entirely haphazard manner because policy entrepreneurs energetically shape the process. Either inside or outside government, policy entrepreneurs are the activists within the policy community, who vigorously invest their time, energy, and often money in advocating for their pet solutions or favorite ideas.

Kingdon (1995) described policy entrepreneurs as persistent and opportunistic. They know influential people and lobby them tirelessly. Like surfers, they wait for the perfect wave and then paddle like mad when they sense that those forces beyond their control (e.g., a swing in national mood, a change of administration) will propel their proposals forward. Without their efforts, the coupling of problems with solutions can hardly occur, and policy change will not take place even with an open window of opportunity. They are "central figures in the drama" (p. 180). Nevertheless, if an entrepreneur's ideas lack technical feasibility, sound evidence for effectiveness, or acceptable values, then no amount of paddling will get his or her proposals adopted.

Policy entrepreneurs employ a variety of influence tactics, or in Kingdon's terminology, "softening up" methods, to build acceptance for their proposals within both the policy community and the general public and to push for their favored ideas. Although policy makers may promote their ideas by introducing bills, holding congressional hearings, and making speeches, interest groups have an even wider array of tactics available for influencing policy decisions (Berry, 1977, 1997; Browne, 1998; Heinz, Laumann, Nelson, & Salisbury, 1993; Kollman, 1998; Nownes & Freeman, 1998; Rosenthal, 1993; Salisbury, 1990; Schlozman & Tierney, 1986; Thomas & Hrebenar, 1999; Walker, 1991). Scholars often distinguish between inside tactics and outside tactics. Inside tactics entail direct interactions between interest group representatives and government officials, such as contacting government officials, testifying at legislative hearings, presenting research findings, and serving on government commissions. In addition to direct contact with policy makers, interest groups may use outside tactics to influence the policy-making environment by arousing public opinion, mobilizing grass roots support, and influencing election outcomes. Specific examples include engaging the mass media, organizing telephone or letter-writing campaigns, protesting and demonstrating, and endorsing candidates for elected office.

In the national reading policy domain, Sims, McDaniel, and Miskel (2000) found that interest groups had a common toolbox of influence tactics and employed both inside and outside tactics in their attempts to influence national reading policy. Of the 14 types of influence tactics that they examined, Sims and her colleagues found that 8 were used by more than half of the groups: presenting research findings (90%), contacting government officials (87%), monitoring policy developments (83%), engaging the mass media (78%), testifying at hearings (79%), forming coalitions (75%), serving on government commissions (72%), and drafting legislation and regulations (53%).

Importantly, the two most often cited tactics for influencing national reading policy were presenting research findings and making direct contact with government officials, the importance of which participants in a study (Miskel et al., 2003) of state reading also frequently pointed out. During an interview that we conducted on state reading policy, for example, a state senator from Texas commented, "The most important [influence strategy] is contacting legislators and the commissioner and combining that with presenting research findings. If you have good research and you make contact, you probably are 80% of the way down the road." An education association representative in Michigan likewise contended during our interview that the most influential people in the state are people who lobby: "People who work in the lobby front . . . are the people that are going to help shape the way it is done; that tends to be the lobby presence."

Thus, direct contact with legislators and other policy makers, in combination with presenting solid research findings, is seen as being an extremely effective way to influence policy. Indeed, as Kingdon observed, "Inventors are less important than entrepreneurs" in determining policy outcomes (1995, p. 183).

READING POLICY ENTREPRENEURSHIP: AN EXAMPLE

One of the most active and influential policy entrepreneurs in the national reading policy domain is Dr. G. Reid Lyon of the National Institute of Child Health and Human Development (NICHD). Although he might insist that neither he nor the NICHD is in the business of making reading policy, we argue that he is a consummate reading policy entrepreneur. In addition to his expertise in psychological and educational—in particular reading—research, Lyon has a powerful formal position of leadership in the federal government as the Chief of the Child Development and Behavior Branch of the

NICHD. Both qualifications give Lyon a "claim to a hearing" (Kingdon, 1995, p. 180). His extensive network of influential friends, colleagues, and contacts within both the national and state policy levels solicit and listen to his perspectives. For example, Lyon continues to provide information and advice on reading research and its relation to reading instruction to President George W. Bush following his service as an advisor to the Governor's Business Council in Texas when Bush was the governor and his membership on the Bush administration's transition team.

Hare (2002) hailed Lyon as America's "reading czar," and Clowes designated Lyon as "the nation's leading expert on how children learn to read" (1999, p. 1). Lyon has been "credited with restoring the public's faith in phonics-based reading programs" (Amis, 2001). He has authored, co-authored, and edited more than 100 journal articles, books, and book chapters addressing learning differences and disabilities in children. Lyon has testified before the House Committee on Education and the Workforce annually since 1997 (see, e.g., *Literacy: Why Children Can't Read*, 1997; *Hearing on Title I (Education of the Disadvantaged) of the Elementary and Secondary Education Act*, 1999; *Hearing on Options for the Future of the Office of Educational Research and Improvement*, 2000), and has appeared before the Senate Committee on Labor and Human Resources (*Overview of Reading and Literacy Initiatives*, 1998) and before the House Committee on Science (*Education Research: Is What We Don't Know Hurting Our Children?*, 1999). He was consulted almost daily as the drafters of the No Child Left Behind Act of 2001 hammered out critical language in the legislation.

In the late 1990s, among those within the reading policy community, Lyon was perceived as the most influential individual, followed by then Representative Bill Goodling (R-PA); Robert W. Sweet, Jr.; Louisa Cook Moats; and Marilyn Adams (McDaniel et al., 2001). Part of Lyon's influence stems from his ability to shape the debate over the cause of the reading problem. Lyon has portrayed the issue of poor reading achievement as relating to both educational policy and public health. In his testimony before the Senate Committee on Labor and Human Resources, Lyon stated the following:

> The psychological, social, and economic consequences of reading failure are legion. It is for this reason that the National Institute of Child Health and Human Development considers reading failure to reflect

not only an educational problem, but a significant public health problem as well. (*Literacy: Why Children Can't Read,* 1997, p. 2)

Lyon has aggressively disseminated this definition of the problem through speeches in various policy forums, through his testimony before Congress, and by talking with members of the media. In making this argument, Lyon often cites NAEP data as an indication of the magnitude of the problem. He also uses NICHD findings that

> For 60% of the nation's children . . . learning to read is a much more formidable challenge, and for at least 20% to 30% of these youngsters, reading is one of the most difficult tasks they will have to master throughout their schooling. (*Overview of Reading and Literacy Initiatives,* 1998, p. 1)

If that were not enough, Lyon has pounded his message home: "If you do not learn to read and you live in America, you do not make it in life" (*Overview of Reading and Literacy Initiatives,* 1998, p. 2). Framing the problem as a public health issue has effectively heightened its status on policy makers' agendas by making low reading achievement seem even more compelling to policy makers, if not outright alarming.

In addition to testifying, publishing research, and engaging the mass media, Lyon has employed other influence tactics such as traveling throughout the country to give speeches and present research findings to members of various state legislatures. He has spoken, for example, to state assemblies in California, Connecticut, Indiana, Louisiana, Maryland, New Mexico, Texas, and Virginia. He has worked with individual school districts (e.g., Charlotte-Mecklenburg, North Carolina; Los Angeles; Sacramento, California) and with state departments of education on their reading initiatives (e.g., the Alabama Reading Initiative). He is currently working on the implementation of Reading First by talking with educators and state education experts. Lyon has also maintained regular contact with many members of the reading policy community, including the American Association of Colleges of Teacher Education, the American Federation of Teachers, the Governor's Business Council in Texas, the House Committee on Education and the Workforce, the International Reading Association, the National Research Council, and the U.S. Department of Education. With Darv Winnick, Lyon helped recruit Susan Neuman, Robert H. Pasternack, and Grover J. Whitehurst to their posts as Assistant Secretary of Education of the Office of Elementary and Secondary Education, Assistant Secretary of the Office of Special Education and Rehabilitation Services, and Director of the Institute of Education Sciences, respectively. (Neuman resigned in January 2003, and Pasternack resigned in January 2004.)

Lyon joined the NICHD at the National Institutes of Health in 1991. It was not until the mid-1990s, however, that Lyon and the NICHD became involved in the politics and policy of reading. At this juncture, NICHD-funded early reading intervention studies had substantial converging evidence that could be presented to help inform reading policies and practices. Once the NICHD became involved, it quickly became a dominant player (McDaniel et al., 2001). In fact, McDaniel and her colleagues (2001) found that other members of the reading policy community perceived the NICHD as being the most influential organization in reading policy creation. Participants described the NICHD as "particularly adept at disseminating its ideas throughout the [reading policy] network" (p. 107). It has distributed more than 200,000 copies of the National Reading Panel (NRP) report (NICHD, 2000) to individual schools and federal and state legislators, as well as 14 countries in Europe and Asia.

NICHD derives its influence from its program of research. The NICHD has been conducting research on reading since the mid-1960s. It administers more than 40 reading research sites throughout the United States, Europe, and Asia. As noted previously, it was not until NICHD-supported scientists began publishing studies of reading interventions—not just studies of normal reading development or how the brain functions during the process of learning to read—that the NICHD became involved in reading policy and politics. Classroom teachers and policy makers were perhaps unusually interested in these types of applied studies. The NICHD has continued its commitment to reading research, providing $20 million in funding to reading research in 2002 and earmarking $12 million of those funds for studies that investigate the effects of well-defined reading interventions on both reading development and brain function measured through noninvasive neuroimaging technology.

Lyon and the NICHD would not view their activity as "softening up" the policy community but as merely informing policy by disseminating their research. Nevertheless, in his 1995 testimony before the Senate Committee on Labor and Human Resources, Lyon stated,

"While this new information resulting from our research has been replicated by each of the NICHD research projects, few teachers are aware of the facts and the diagnostic and instructional methodologies that are based on these scientific findings." Thus, Lyon implicitly signaled his desire for the research to change policy and practice. Indeed, the very foundation of his advocacy is research, and the incentive for his advocacy is purposive—that is, promoting values or beliefs—rather than material or community interests (Kingdon, 1995; Wilson, 1973).

Nevertheless, in all of his speeches, testimonies, and interviews with the media, Lyon is careful not to overwhelm his audience with the gritty (but some would argue important) details of research, that is, correlation coefficients, effect sizes, and the like. He expresses his policy ideas and research findings in clear, unambiguous—even absolute—terms. One can speculate that this is why Lyon's message appeals to policy makers—they need a solution and data to support it, and he has this in spades. Diane Jean Schemo (2002) of *The New York Times* called Lyon's confident delivery "salesmanship," but it is more than that. As Kingdon (1995) suggested, policy entrepreneurs often believe that what they are "selling" is important. Furthermore, the NICHD's reputation of having a solid, rigorous research base and the longitudinal nature of its studies lend credibility to Lyon's message. As a knowledgeable media representative pointed out during an interview with us on national reading policy,

> NICHD is effective because they have 30 years of research, and it is pretty hard to argue with pretty significant research that has been replicated and replicated and held to the highest scientific standards that were medical standards, not educational standards. We have very few standards for research in education. They have been effective because they have that weight of data and because the researchers who have done that work have finally emerged to actually talk about it and connect the research to the policy implications.

Thus, as McDaniel et al. (2001) observed, the long history of quantitative and experimental studies of the NICHD has attracted the attention of policy makers and many members of the public, who now insist that only programs based on scientific research should be funded and implemented in America's classrooms.

Indeed, Lyon and the NICHD have been remarkably successful in getting their research-based policy ideas enacted into law. The

Reading Excellence Act (PL 105-277), for example, bears their stamp in the definitions of reading and of reading research. Policy makers strategically and explicitly infused the Reading Excellence Act with legislative language about the need for strong evidentiary standards and not just as a mechanism to get funds to states and local districts. Much of the same language is in Reading First and Early Reading First of the No Child Left Behind Act of 2001. Policy makers involved in writing these acts contend that the NICHD and the reports on reading research by the National Research Council (Snow, Burns, & Griffin, 1998) and the NRP (NICHD, 2000) were influential in shaping these reading policies.

In 1997, Congress charged the Director of the NICHD (Dr. Duane Alexander), in consultation with the Secretary of Education (Richard W. Riley) with convening a panel of researchers, members of higher education institutions, teachers, and parents to assess the state of reading research and to learn what interventions research had proven to work. The NRP used the National Research Council's report (Snow et al., 1998) as a starting point for its work. The NRP report (NICHD, 2000) has been very influential. The conclusions served to guide how legislators defined evidence-based reading instruction, effectively using the studies reviewed by the NRP as *the* evidence base. Although only one or two NICHD researchers were on the NRP, the NICHD provided the panel with staff support. In short, the advocacy of Dr. G. Reid Lyon and the NICHD has not only shaped the national conversation about reading but also has influenced the criteria for distributing federal funds to our nations' schools and students.

WHY SHOULD WE CARE?

So why does it matter that policy comes from problem recognition and solutions, stories about their causes, a favorable political environment, and a soup of policy ideas cooked up by a group of specialists? So what that it takes a relentless policy entrepreneur to take advantage of an open window of opportunity to accomplish policy change? How do these issues matter to classroom teachers or education researchers?

First, it is important to be aware that good ideas, programs, or proposals are not enough. Persistent policy entrepreneurs who are viewed as having legitimate knowledge are required if those solutions are to be coupled with perceived problems. This sometimes requires portraying the problem in such a way as to make the solution seem self-evident—for example, "the problem is a lack of funds for professional development," which is logically followed by "the solution is more funds for professional development."

Second, in order to build consensus for a policy proposal, the interested parties often make compromises. For instance, the drafters of Reading First would have preferred that it be written in such a way to preclude programs they deemed to have a limited independent evidentiary base, but powerful special interests kept some such programs. Furthermore, the legislators added the phrase *quasi-experimental* in conference, somewhat to the chagrin of the law's positivist drafters. Thus, multiple policy makers often reformulate policy ideas so that the policy may end up in the classroom looking very different from what its drafters first envisioned.

Third, the nature of this recent round of reading policies implies that educational practitioners will no longer be able to ignore the policy cacophony as they have in the past. In this era of heightened accountability, in which reading standards and assessments drive pedagogy and scientific evidence must undergird reading programs, teachers' practice is certain to change in response to these policies. Knowing whence these policies sprang may make them more or less palatable. That is, knowing that they did not just arise from the stroke of some politician's pen may heighten their legitimacy. Knowing that they arose afar from rational processes, however, may cast doubt on their potential effectiveness.

Fourth, to quote GI Joe, "Knowing is half the battle." An understanding of how the system works will help policy actors to make better-informed decisions and take more effective policy actions for the making of better-designed education policies. A recurrent theme in the interviews that we and our colleagues conducted with various groups and individuals in the national reading policy community is that policy actors' knowledge about the policy system and the process contributes to effective policy actions (Song, Miskel, Young, & McDaniel, 2000). The president of a professional association, for example, observed that some groups were more effective at influencing reading policy because of "being knowledgeable about how the system works or doesn't work . . . and knowing what action is going to work" (as cited in Song et al., 2000). A policy maker similarly noted that some organizations were able to make an impact because "they understand the political process and they understand how to work within that process very well in terms of leveraging support and what are the right moments when things are aligned to get movement" (as cited in Song et al., 2000).

Knowledge about the policy formation process assumes particular significance for classroom teachers and other reading professionals, who often play marginal roles in influencing policy despite their knowledge and expertise (Miskel & Song, 2002; Song & Miskel, 2002). A comprehensive understanding of how a variety of factors shape policy outcomes will help reading researchers and educators to participate more fully in the policy process. The origins of education policy ought to lay in rigorous research and insights gained from classroom practice; however, without the sparks provided by policy entrepreneurs, sound policy ideas will remain mired in the primordial soup.

Whether present and future outbreaks of reading policies have malignant, benign, or beneficial impacts may depend on the expertise and motives of the policy entrepreneurs of the moment. Given the entrepreneurs' potential influence, the consequences may be dire, if self-interests, blind ideology, or empty politics drive such entrepreneurs. Fortunately, no matter who its mouthpiece is, the voice of evidence is likely to be listened to most closely. So far, in reading policy, the voice of evidence has spoken.

REFERENCES

Amis, K. (2001, July). Bush says reading is job 1. *School Reform News.* Retrieved October 23, 2003, from http://www.heartland.org/archives/education/jul01/reading.htm

Berry, J.M. (1977). *Lobbying for the people: The political behavior of public interest groups.* Princeton, NJ: Princeton University Press.

Berry, J. (1997). *The interest group society* (3rd ed.). New York: Longman.

Browne, W.P. (1998). *Groups, interests, and U.S. public policy.* Washington, DC: Georgetown University Press.

Clowes, G.A. (1999, July). Reading is anything but natural: An interview with G. Reid Lyon. *School Reform News.* Retrieved October 23, 2003, from http://www.heartland.org/archives/education/jul99/lyon.htm

Coggshall, J.G., & Osguthorpe, R.T. (2002). *Maine reading policy: Problems, processes, and participants.* Ann Arbor: University of Michigan, Center for the Improvement of Early Reading Achievement.

Educational research: Is what we don't know hurting our children? Hearing before the House Committee on Science, Subcommittee on Basic

Research, 106th Cong. (1999, October 26) (testimony of G. Reid Lyon). Also available on-line: http://www.nichd.nih.gov/crmc/cdb/r_house.htm

Hare, M.G. (2002, September 17). 'Reading czar' has talk with educators. *The Baltimore Sun,* p. 1B.

Hearing on options for the future of the Office of Educational Research and Improvement before the House Committee on Education and the Workforce, Subcommittee on Early Childhood, Youth and Families, 106th Cong. (2000, May 4) (testimony of G. Reid Lyon). Also available on-line: http://www.nichd.nih.gov/crmc/cdb/GR_Lyon_Testimony.htm

Hearing on Title I (Education of the Disadvantaged) of the Elementary and Secondary Education Act before the House Committee on Education and the Workforce, 106th Cong. (1999, July 27) (testimony of G. Reid Lyon). Also available on-line: http://edworkforce.house.gov/hearing/106th/fc/esea72799/lyon.htm

Heinz, J.P., Laumann, E.O., Nelson, R.L., & Salisbury, R.H. (1993). *The hollow core: Private interests in national policy making.* Cambridge, MA: Harvard University Press.

Kingdon, J.W. (1995). *Agendas, alternatives, and public polices* (2nd ed.). New York: HarperCollins.

Kollman, K. (1998). *Outside lobbying: Public opinion and interest group strategies.* Princeton, NJ: Princeton University Press.

Literacy: Why children can't read. Hearing before the House Committee on Education and the Workforce, 105th Cong. (1997, September 3) (testimony of G. Reid Lyon).

Marshall, C., Mitchell, D., & Wirt, F. (1989). *Culture and education policy in the American states.* New York: Falmer Press.

McDaniel, J.E., Sims, C.H., & Miskel, C.G. (2001). The national reading policy arena: Policy actors and perceived influence. *Education Policy,* 15(1), 92–114.

Miskel, C.G., Coggshall, J.G., DeYoung, D.A., Osguthorpe, R.T., Song, M., & Young, T.V. (2003, August). *Reading policy in the states: Interests and processes. Final report for the Field Initiated Studies Grant PR/Award No. R305T990369, Office of Educational Research and Improvement, U.S. Department of Education and the Spencer Foundation Major Research Grants Program Award #200000269.* Ann Arbor: University of Michigan.

Miskel, C.G., & Song, M. (2002). *Elite policy actors and Reading First: Network structure, involvement and beliefs.* Paper presented at the annual convention of the International Reading Association, San Francisco.

National Institute of Child Health and Human Development (NICHD). (2000). *Report of the National Reading Panel. Teaching children to read: An evidence-based assessment of the scientific research literature on reading and its implications for reading instruction. Reports of the subgroups* (NIH Publication No. 00-4754). Washington, DC: U.S. Government Printing Office. Also available on-line: http://www.nichd.nih.gov/publications/nrp/report.htm

No Child Left Behind Act of 2001, PL 107-110, 115 Stat. 1425, 20 U.S.C. §§ 6301 *et seq.*

Nownes, A.J., & Freeman, P. (1998). Interest group activity in the states. *The Journal of Politics, 60*(1), 86–112.

Overview of reading and literacy initiatives: Hearing before the Senate Committee on Labor and Human Resources, 105th Cong. (1998, April 28) (testimony of G. Reid Lyon). Also available on-line: http://www.nichd .nih.gov/publications/pubs/jeffords.htm

Rosenthal, A. (1993). *The third house: Lobbyists and lobbying in the states.* Washington, DC: Congressional Quarterly Press.

Salisbury, R. (1990). The paradox of interest groups in Washington: More groups, less clout. In A. King (Ed.), *The new American political system* (2nd ed., pp. 203–229). Washington, DC: AEI Press.

Schemo, D.J. (2002). Now, the pressure begins for Bush's reading expert. *The New York Times,* p. A14.

Schlozman, K., & Tierney, J. (1986). *Organized interests and American democracy.* New York: HarperCollins.

Shepley, T.V. (2002). *Michigan reading policy: Problems, processes, and participants.* Ann Arbor: University of Michigan, Center for the Improvement of Early Reading Achievement.

Sims, C., McDaniel, J., & Miskel, C. (2000, December 2000). *The influence tactics of interest groups and national reading policy.* Paper presented at the National Reading Conference, Scottsdale, AZ.

Snow, C.E., Burns, M.S., & Griffin, P. (Eds.). (1998). *Preventing reading difficulties in young children.* Washington, DC: National Academies Press.

Song, M., & Miskel, C.G. (2002). Interest groups in national reading policy: Perceived influence and beliefs on teaching reading. *Theory and Research in Educational Administration, 1,* 77–96.

Song, M., Miskel, C.G., Young, T.V., & McDaniel, J.E. (2000). *Perceived influence of interest groups in national reading policy.* Paper presented at the Annual Meeting of the University Council for Educational Administration, Albuquerque.

Statement of Dr. G. Reid Lyon before the Senate Committee on Labor and Human Resources, 104th Cong. (1995) (testimony of G. Reid Lyon).

Stone, D.A. (1989). Causal stories and the formation of policy agendas. *Political Science Quarterly, 104,* 281–300.

Thomas, C., & Hrebenar, R. (1999). Interest groups in the states. In V. Gray, R. Hanson, & H. Jacob (Eds.), *Politics in the American states: A comparative analysis* (7th ed., pp. 113–143). Washington, DC: Congressional Quarterly Press.

Walker, J.L. (1991). *Mobilizing interest groups in America.* Ann Arbor: University of Michigan Press.

Wilson, J.Q. (1973). *Political organizations.* New York: Basic Books.

Young, T.V. (2002). *California reading policy: Problems, processes, and participants.* Ann Arbor: University of Michigan, Center for the Improvement of Early Reading Achievement.

19

The Accumulation of Evidence

A Continuing Process

PEGGY MCCARDLE AND VINITA CHHABRA

A s outlined in the first chapter of this volume, various agencies have come together since the mid-1990s in an unprecedented coordination to fund reading and literacy research, to identify gaps in the research through workshops and conferences, and to develop initiatives that address those gaps. The importance of scientifically based evidence, and in particular scientifically based reading research, is recognized and being implemented in schools across the nation, and more activities are underway to continue to develop that evidence. The research on elementary school literacy has focused heavily on reading and reading instruction in kindergarten through third grade and has largely addressed phonemic awareness, phonics, and reading decodable text. Some work—but not nearly enough—has also been done on fluency, vocabulary, and comprehension. Researchers are continuing to focus on reading development, reading disabilities, effective instruction, and intervention in school-age children, but they are also now working to develop evidence on these same major components of reading in specific age groups and special populations across the life span. Panel reports continue to play a major role in bringing the research and practice communities up to date on the state of the science in various aspects of literacy and in focusing on areas in which additional evidence is needed. In addition to the major research networks that were begun in the 1970s and 1980s, current research in reading is continuing to bring new information to the field. In this chapter, we provide an overview of the various areas in which new reports and new research evidence to inform teaching practice are expected. We begin with activities addressing English language learners because a large network of investigators have been conducting research for 3 years on preschool and school-age children whose native language is Spanish and because this topic is relevant to all age groups. Following that, we discuss activities that are underway to produce convergent evidence by age group—preschoolers, preadolescents and adolescents, and adults.

ENGLISH LANGUAGE LEARNERS

Today's world is often referred to as a global village. Even within the United States, there is a reflection of the world's diversity, as the nation continues to be a melting pot of cultures and ethnicities. The diversity within the United States includes a diversity of native languages. The 2000 U.S. Census report (U.S. Census Bureau, 2003) indicated that 45 million individuals 5 years of age and older spoke a language other than English at home and that more than 10.5 million (nearly one fourth) of these indicated that they spoke English "not well" or "not at all." The U.S. Census Bureau reported more than 380 languages and dialects spoken in the United States. Spanish is the single most commonly spoken language other than English in the United States. The 2000 U.S. Census (U.S. Census Bureau, 2001) indicated that since 1990, the Hispanic population had grown by nearly 60%; although not all of these individuals speak Spanish, many are bilingual, and for many of the children Spanish may be their first and perhaps their only language prior to school entry. Clearly, schools all over the United States are faced with the issue of teaching children whose first language is not English. For these children, learning to read is just one of the tasks they face upon school entry—often learning to speak English is also a major part of their early education. This adds to the challenge of teaching these youngsters to read.

One area that neither the National Research Council's Committee on Preventing Reading Difficulties in Young Children (Snow, Burns, & Griffin, 1998) nor the National Reading Panel (NRP) (National Institute for Child Health and Human Development [NICHD], 2000) addressed is teaching children whose first language is not English to read. Both groups noted the importance of this topic, but neither was able to undertake a thorough assessment in addition to the primary focus on reading. Congressional and public interest had been growing about how to best teach reading to this particular population. Because there was insufficient information on the best approaches to teach these children, two major efforts were undertaken—the creation of a new national panel and the funding of research.

National Literacy Panel

In 2001 the Office of Educational Research and Improvement (OERI; now the Institute of Education Sciences [IES]), with input from the U.S. Department of Education's Office of English Language Acquisition and the National Institute of Child Health and Human Development (NICHD), funded the establishment of the National Literacy Panel on Language Minority Children and Youth (Center for Applied Linguistics, n.d.). This panel was charged with developing a synthesis of the existing research literature on the development of reading and reading-related abilities in children whose first language is not English. The panel will address the relationship between spoken language abilities and literacy; the course of literacy development in students whose first language is not English; how contexts such as family, culture, community, and classroom affect literacy development; what strategies are effective for instruction and for professional development to maximize the literacy development of English language learners (ELLs); what measures and methods are optimal for assessing the literacy abilities of ELLs; and how those measures should be used (e.g., accommodations for testing) with ELLs. The panel's report will summarize what is known and can be implemented currently in the reading instruction of ELL students. The report also contains information about underresearched topics regarding ELL reading instruction.

The Research

A federal research effort was initiated in 1999 when the NICHD, in partnership with the OERI (now the IES), published a major research solicitation and funded seven major studies to answer those now-familiar reading research questions regarding Spanish-speaking children: How do children, in this case children whose first language is Spanish, learn to read English? What goes wrong when they don't, and what can we do about it? These questions are now being studied in the detail and complexity that has been applied to the study of reading development in monolingual English-speaking children. In addition, the agencies wanted to know what teacher knowledge, skills, and instructional strategies are required to ensure optimal outcomes. Over the 5 years of the currently funded initiative, from 2000 through 2004, researchers will have studied more than 5,400 children at multiple sites in eight states and Puerto Rico. To address the major questions that are the focus of this initiative, the researchers have been adapting and developing tests for use in their research. Information about these measures and publications resulting from this research can be found on the web site for the Center for Applied Linguistics (2003). The researchers have presented their research designs and some information about the tests that they have developed at professional meetings and conferences, and are now beginning to publish their initial findings in journals. Soon there will be additional evidence to inform the instruction of Spanish-speaking children in English literacy.

The Future

The special challenge of identifying and remediating reading disability in ELLs is an area that clearly remains underresearched. The U.S. Department of Education's Office of English Language Acquisition and Office of Special Education and Rehabilitation Services (OSERS), as well as the NICHD, have a special interest in encouraging research on this important topic, some of which will most likely grow out of the NICHD–IES studies of English reading in Spanish-speaking children. These agencies are also working in partnership to find ways to encourage research on biliteracy in children whose home language is any language other than English on bilingual language development, which will have implications for the education and literacy of ELL students.

PRESCHOOLERS

Another research area that was influenced by the NICHD reading research and the approach and findings of the NRP's report (NICHD, 2000) is literacy-related issues in the preschool period. Because of what is known about early reading and risk factors for reading failure, it is clear that the preschool period is important in preparing children to enter kindergarten ready to learn to read. In September 2001, the NICHD, in partnership with the National Institute of Deafness and Other Communication Disorders, the U.S. Department of Education, and several professional associations, held a workshop focused on early and emergent literacy. This workshop developed a research agenda that called for an increase in interdisciplinary studies of the social, cultural, environmental, experiential, and neurobiological factors that provide the foundation for children's learning and for the development of valid and reliable screening and assessment instruments for the early identification of all children at risk for reading failure. The agenda also called for large-scale longitudinal studies to determine optimal environments and experiences that foster learning and reading success. This research agenda and key papers from that workshop were published in a special issue of the journal *Learning Disabilities Research and Practice* (McCardle, Cooper, Houle, Karp, & Paul-Brown, 2001).

Within a year after the publication of the workshop papers, First Lady Laura Bush, who has a strong interest in reading and in early child development, hosted the National Summit on Early Cognitive Development at Georgetown University. At that landmark meeting, Dr. G. Reid Lyon announced a large joint research effort between the NICHD, the U.S. Department of Education, and the Administration for Children and Families within the U.S. Department of Health and Human Services to develop rigorous scientific studies of the effectiveness of integrative early childhood interventions and programs across a variety of early childhood settings in promoting school readiness for children from birth to age 5 who are at risk of later school difficulties. Thus the preschool period is now included in the life-span research on reading and reading-related abilities.

In addition, several national reports have been published that emphasize the importance of learning in the preschool period. The National Research Council's reports *Eager to Learn: Educating Our Preschoolers* (Bowman, Donovan, & Burns, 2001) and *From Neurons to Neighborhoods: The Science of Early Childhood Development* (Shonkoff & Phillips, 2000) summarized the role of early experience in development. In addition, reports about the impact of Head Start and Early Head Start (U.S. Department of Health and Human Services, n.d.) have been published, as have evaluations of the Even Start program (U.S. Department of Education, 2003). Although all of these reports argue for the importance of high-quality preschool programs, more research evidence is needed about the most effective programs and curricula for preparing preschool children to enter kindergarten ready to learn.

National Early Literacy Panel

In addition, a new panel was formed to review, analyze, and synthesize existing research studies. The National Early Literacy Panel was charged to conduct an objective synthesis of the research literature on the development of early literacy in children ages birth to 5 years. Whereas the National Research Council reports (Bowman et al., 2001; Shonkoff & Phillips, 2000) had focused more broadly on early childhood development, the goal of the National Early Literacy Panel was to capture the scientific evidence that supports early literacy development and home and family influences on that development. Supported by a contract from the National Institute for Literacy to the National Center for Family Literacy, the panel consisted of research experts with diverse backgrounds and broad experience in addressing young children's early literacy and related areas of early development. A rigorous research process, similar to the one used by the NRP (NICHD, 2000), was adopted to answer important research questions such as the following: What are young children's (ages birth to 5 years) skills and abilities that predict later reading outcomes? What environments and settings contribute to or inhibit gains in these children's skills and abilities that are linked to later outcomes in reading? What child characteristics contribute to or inhibit gains in these children's skills and abilities that are linked to later outcomes in reading? What programs and interventions contribute to or inhibit gains in these children's skills and abilities that are linked to later outcomes in reading? Their report adds to the evidence of what factors influence early literacy development and ultimately will help researchers and educators identify the processes necessary for a child to not only learn to read but also to succeed in life.

The Research

As a result of the workshops and meetings on the topics of emergent and early literacy and early cognitive development and because of the clear need for research evidence, the Interagency Early Childhood

Research Initiative was established in 2001. This group, made up of the NICHD, OSERS, and the Administration for Children and Families and the Office of the Assistant Secretary for Planning and Evaluation within the U.S. Department of Health and Human Services, funded planning grants in 2002 and major research grants in 2003 for studies of this crucially important area of preschool development. The projects funded under the Interagency Early Childhood Research Initiative are studying the effectiveness of interventions, curricula, or programs intended to prepare children to enter kindergarten ready to learn. These studies integrate several cognitive areas (e.g., language and communication, early and emergent literacy, early mathematics, early science knowledge and skills) with social-emotional areas (e.g., social competency, the regulation of attention, behavior, and emotion).

The Future

Again, as the research progresses, the findings will hopefully provide convergent evidence on effective approaches to group and individual activities to ready infants and children up to the age of 5 years for successful entry to kindergarten and will provide information on which methods and approaches work best for which young children to foster not only their readiness to read but also their overall readiness to learn.

PREADOLESCENTS AND ADOLESCENTS

Another group that until this decade has been largely overlooked in reading instruction and reading research is preadolescents and adolescents, those students in the upper elementary grades (4–6) and middle and high school. Students in these grades who have difficulty learning to read are often referred to as "struggling readers." It is clear from epidemiological studies that learning to read is more difficult after 9 years of age, but the factors that might explain this decreased learning ability are not well understood. Since the late 1990s, both educational programs and publicity have focused on the important goal of having all children reading by the end of the third grade, reading by age 9. However, there has also been frequent reference to the "fourth-grade slump," in which students who seem to be progressing on reading begin to fail in fourth grade when the reading task becomes more complex.

Researchers know that children who have not developed foundational reading abilities by the time they are 9 years old are highly likely to struggle with reading all of the way through high school and beyond and that they may never read so efficiently that they will read for pleasure. This means that most middle and high school students who are poor or failing readers could be left behind as they continue through school and move into the workplace. The numbers underscore this finding. As many as one third of boys and one fifth of girls in high school cannot read at the basic level, and the percentages are greater than 40 percent for African American and Hispanic youth (National Center for Education Statistics [NCES], 1998).

Even those adolescents who score at the proficient level on NAEP (NCES, 1998) require continuing instruction as they are faced with increasingly complex text to decipher and understand. Yet, fewer than 5% of adolescents were able to extend or elaborate the meaning of the materials they read on the 1998 NAEP.

Writing ability can also be problematic. The NAEP writing assessment (NCES, 1998) data indicated that few adolescents could write effectively with enough detail to support main points. And the NAEP data are clearly an underestimate of the problem because they do not include those students who have dropped out of school; approximately 1.4 million students each year drop out of school between grades 9 and 12 (National Center for Education Statistics, as cited in U.S. Department of Education, 2002b). These data make two things clear—a focus is needed on reading and writing in the preadolescent and adolescent periods, and a focus on reading comprehension is needed. Much of instruction for adolescents focuses on teaching content—science, math, literature, and so forth—and does not focus on teaching students how to read and write effectively. In addition, the large number of high school dropouts, the large numbers of students in high-poverty schools who have reading difficulty, the large numbers of students requiring remedial courses at college entry, and the low proportions of minority students successfully completing college emphasize the need to focus on this age group.

Reading disabilities persist over time—they do not go away. Research has indicated that as many as 74% of children with reading disabilities in third grade have reading impairments at follow-up in ninth grade (Shaywitz & Shaywitz, 1996). Thus, the long-term implications of low literacy levels among preadolescents and adolescents are serious. Therefore, once again, an interagency effort is focusing on funding research to address literacy, this time for struggling readers in grades 4–12.

Based on a concern that middle and high school students should not be left behind in the national focus on reading, several professional associations worked with federal agencies to mount an effort to call attention to the research and practice needs of teenagers. During the spring of 2001, these groups held a series of workshops that included both researchers and practitioners. Summary documents are available on the National Institute for Literacy web site (http://www.nifl.gov/partnershipforreading/adolescent/). The consensus from those workshops was that despite the significant advances in the understanding of the abilities that children must acquire to become successful readers and the conditions under which the necessary skills are most effectively taught, very little converging evidence addresses how best to teach literacy—reading and writing—to middle and high school students. We need to know the extent to which current evidence about early reading instruction holds true for older students who fail to acquire the basic foundational skills for literacy. Why does it seem that learning to read is more difficult after age 9, and how can we best intervene after that age? Which specific reading abilities are more predictive of reading difficulties in adolescents? Do the relationships among phonemic awareness, phonics, fluency, vocabulary, and reading comprehension that predict age-appropriate reading development for children in kindergarten to third grade also apply to older students who are having reading difficulties? How can researchers and educators best identify, prevent, and remediate reading and writing difficulties? And how do educators motivate middle and high school students who have experienced failure in literacy to reengage in this all-important learning task? These are questions that need to be addressed. And they must be addressed both in terms of preventive intervention in the later elementary grades (the preadolescent period) and in terms of intervention at the middle and high school levels (adolescent period).

The RAND Report

As attention focused increasingly on the preadolescent and adolescent periods, the U.S. Department of Education initiated efforts to address the important area of reading comprehension in greater depth. First, the department commissioned a major report dedicated exclusively to reading comprehension: the RAND Reading Study

Group's (2002) report. In its executive summary, the RAND report indicated that although basic reading processes are well understood, the current state of knowledge in reading comprehension was not sufficient. Existing research, although sizable, was termed sketchy, unfocused, and inadequate as a basis for reform in reading comprehension instruction. The report indicated clearly that teachers must teach comprehension, beginning in but not limited to the primary grades; that reading comprehension instruction must continue throughout high school; and that instruction must be addressed both in language arts or English classes and in content areas.

The Research

Based on the findings and recommendations of the RAND Reading Study Group (2002) report, the U.S. Department of Education solicited research in the area of reading comprehension. Under the title Program of Research on Reading Comprehension, the department started awarding grants in 2002. Grover J. Whitehurst, Assistant Secretary of the U.S. Department of Education's Office of Educational Research Improvement (now Director of IES), described the programmatic goal: "to establish a scientific foundation for educational practice by supporting research on reading comprehension that is likely to produce substantial gains in academic achievement" (U.S. Department of Education, 2002a). That program, designed to expand scientific knowledge of how students develop proficient reading comprehension, how it is most effectively taught, and how it can be assessed, continued with a new solicitation in 2003 from the IES for studies in reading comprehension research.

In addition, to more generally address the need for evidence on adolescent literacy and on intervention with the struggling reader in grades 4–12 the NICHD, the U.S. Department of Education's Office of Vocational and Adult Education, and OSERS solicited and funded research grant applications on adolescent literacy in the fall of 2003.

The Future

As all of these newly funded projects begin to bear fruit, the findings on the best approaches and methods of reading and writing instruction for students older than age 9 and interventions for those who are struggling readers in grades 4–12 will be published in scholarly journals. But when it is clear that there is convergent evidence, it will be critical that these findings be shared with the practitioners who are working hard to ensure that our preadolescent and adolescent students are able to use their reading and writing skills to gain greater knowledge and education and to be successful in the nation's workforce.

ADULTS

Although reading instruction, learning to read, and reading disabilities are usually discussed in terms of children, a large number of adults in the United States cannot read and write effectively. To determine the literacy skills of American adults, the 1992 National Adult Literacy Survey (Kirsch, Jungeblut, Jenkins, & Kolstad, 1993) used test items resembling tasks of daily life that involved reading documents and using simple quantitative skills. Results were used to classify people taking the assessment in five literacy levels. Those placing at Level 1 do not read well enough to fill out an application, read a food label, or read a simple story to a child. Adults with Level 2 skills usually can draw comparisons and contrasts and integrate information but do not perform higher-level reading and problem-solving tasks. Adults with skills at Levels 1 and 2 lack a sufficient foundation of basic skills to function successfully in our society. Adults in Levels 3 through 5 usually can perform complex tasks with long and dense documents. Although few adults in the United States are truly illiterate, many adults with low literacy skills lack the foundation they need to find and keep well-paying jobs, support their children's education, and participate in civic life. Nearly one fourth of the U.S. adult population, or approximately 44 million people, scored in the lowest literacy level on the survey. Another 25%–28% of the U.S. adult population, or between 45 and 50 million people, scored at Level 2. Despite the clear need for adult literacy education, adult basic education programs throughout the country typically operate on much smaller budgets and face difficult issues such as student and teacher mobility to an even greater degree than do elementary and high school programs. In addition, adult literacy instruction has been a seriously underresearched area. Nevertheless, it is just as important to be able to identify effective approaches and programs in adult literacy if we are to succeed in having a fully literate nation.

The Reports

Since the 1990s, documents had been published indicating the need for research on adult literacy. Both the 1992 National Adult Literacy Survey (Kirsch et al., 1993) and the International Adult Literacy Survey (Human Resources Development Canada, 2002) provide interesting information about the demographics of adult literacy in the United States and clearly indicate the need for and importance of adult literacy instruction. However, little research has directly addressed instructional or program effectiveness in this area. In 2000, the National Institute for Literacy and the National Center for the Study of Adult Learning and Literacy at the Harvard Graduate School of Education formed an Adult Literacy Reading Research Working Group, which emphasized the centrality of reading and writing to adult basic education and indicated that research was needed that would focus on the complex, integrated process of reading in adults. Related to this activity, the National Institute for Literacy commissioned a synthesis of extant literature on adult literacy, using criteria similar to that used by the NRP (NICHD, 2000). So little experimental research has been reported in the literature that meta-analyses were impossible, but a review of the available literature was produced, clearly highlighting the need for additional research (Kruidenier, 2002).

The Research

To address the need for research on adult literacy, the NICHD, the National Institute for Literacy, and the U.S. Department of Education's Office of Vocational and Adult Education and Office of Elementary and Secondary Education convened an expert panel that produced a summary document outlining a research agenda (NICHD, 2002). Based on all of these activities and reports, in 2001 the NICHD, the National Institute for Literacy, and the Office of Vocational and Adult Education solicited research projects on adult literacy to form an Adult Literacy Research Network.

In the fall of 2002, six major studies were funded under this initiative, and these agencies hope to fund additional studies over the coming years. The network studies are currently working to design, develop, implement, and study the effectiveness of interventions for adults with low literacy skills, including investigation of the role of decoding, vocabulary, fluency, and comprehension instruction in adult literacy and explicitness of instruction. Over the 5-year funding period (2002–2006), these research teams will have screened nearly 73,000 adults with low literacy skills to identify the more than 3,800 research participants for these studies. All six projects use experimental designs, and at least four of these use combined quantitative and qualitative methods. It is estimated that more than 60% of those taking part in the studies will come from minority ethnic groups; most studies will have 30%–60% African American participants and 20%–50% Hispanic or Latino participants, many of whom are not native speakers of English. The investigators will be conducting this research in more than 80 sites in 16 different states.

The Future

As is the case with research on literacy development in ELLs, not enough is known about the identification of learning disabilities among adults. Therefore, NICHD, the National Institute for Literacy, and the U.S. Department of Education's Office of Vocational and Adult Education and OSERS are launching an effort to focus on the identification and remediation of learning disabilities in adults.

MOVING FORWARD

A great deal is known about reading instruction, given the findings of the Committee on Preventing Reading Difficulties in Young Children (Snow et al., 1998), the NRP (NICHD, 2000), and the RAND Reading Study Group (2002) report. Of course, there is always more to know, so the research will continue. But researchers have also gotten better at finding out reliably what is already known, and in particular how to establish the state of the science in a particular area, with high-quality, rigorously performed meta-analyses and research syntheses, such as those being performed by the National

Literacy Panel and the National Early Literacy Panel. The rigorous methodology is a legacy of the NRP (NICHD, 2000), and as with any valuable legacy, this methodology has been built upon, expanded, and extended. These new panels, not limited by a directive to ask only questions of effectiveness, are casting the net more broadly, often to include not only experimental but also correlational and qualitative research literature.

Since the publication of the NRP report in 2000, much research has been produced on reading instruction in the elementary school years, and this is not being overlooked. The National Institute for Literacy, under the auspices of The Partnership for Reading, is establishing a new panel, the Reading Research Panel, to carry on and expand the work of the NRP and to review, analyze, and synthesize both quantitative and qualitative research using the methodologies developed by previous panels, adapting and extending them when necessary. When that information is provided, the field must continue to build on what is known, to add to it and expand it, because these findings are based on multiple rigorously conducted studies that are trustworthy. Although we do not know everything, what we do know is information in which we can have confidence.

Literacy researchers must continue to produce high-quality research on what works in teaching students to read and write and in improving abilities for those who are struggling. We need to know what works, for whom, and under what conditions, as well as how and why it works, for all individuals across the life span and for all populations in this diverse nation of ours. But funding and conducting the research is not enough. When the research provides convergent evidence of what works, for whom, under what conditions, it is important that that information be put into practice. The role of teachers and others who play a significant role in shaping a child's academic success is a difficult one. Research is a tool that they can and must use to help them carve out the fundamentals of reading instruction. Research empowers us all—teachers, parents, administrators, and researchers—to reach the ultimate goal of ensuring that our children, teenagers, and adults have the most accurate, scientifically based information on effective instruction in reading and writing. This volume is meant for them.

REFERENCES

Bowman, B.T., Donovan, M.S., & Burns, M.S. (Eds.). (2001). *Eager to learn: Educating our preschoolers.* Washington, DC: National Academies Press.

Center for Applied Linguistics. (2003, May 22). *Development of English literacy in Spanish-speaking children: A biliteracy research initiative sponsored by the National Institute of Child Health and Human Development and the Institute of Education Sciences of the Department of Education.* Retrieved October 23, 2003, from http://www.cal.org/delss/

Center for Applied Linguistics. (n.d.). *National Literacy Panel for Language Minority Children and Youth.* Retrieved October 23, 2003, from http://www.cal.org/natl-lit-panel/index.html

Human Resources Development Canada. (2002, October 15). *International Adult Literacy Survey (IALS).* Retrieved October 23, 2003, from http://www.nald.ca/nls/ials/introduc.htm

Kirsch, I.S., Jungeblut, A., Jenkins, L., & Kolstad, A. (1993). *Adult literacy in America: A first look at the results of the National Adult Literacy Survey* (Report 16-PL-02). Princeton, NJ: Educational Testing Service.

Kruidenier, J. (2002). *Research-based principles for adult basic education reading instruction* (NIFL Contract No. ED-01-PO-1037). Portsmouth, NH: RMC Research Corporation.

McCardle, P., Cooper, J., Houle, G., Karp, N., & Paul-Brown, D. (Eds.). (2001). Emergent and early literacy: Current status and research directions [Special issue]. *Learning Disabilities Research and Practice, 16*(4).

National Center for Education Statistics (NCES). (1998). *The nation's report card: National Assessment of Educational Progress.* Washington, DC: U.S. Department of Education.

National Institute of Child Health and Human Development (NICHD). (2000). *Report of the National Reading Panel. Teaching children to read: An evidence-based assessment of the scientific research literature on reading and its implications for reading instruction. Reports of the subgroups* (NIH Publication No. 00-4754). Washington, DC: U.S. Government Printing Office. Also available on-line: http://www.nichd.nih.gov/publications/nrp/report.htm

National Institute of Child Health and Human Development (NICHD). (2002, September 4). *Adult and family literacy: Current research and future directions. A workshop summary.* Retrieved October 23, 2003, from http://www.nichd.nih.gov/crmc/cdb/AFL_workshop.htm

RAND Reading Study Group. (2002). *Reading for understanding: Toward a R&D program in reading comprehension.* Retrieved October 23, 2003, from http://www.rand.org/multi/achievementforall/reading/readreport.html

Shaywitz, S.E., & Shaywitz, B.A. (1996). Unlocking learning disabilities: The neurological basis. In S.C. Cramer & W. Ellis (Eds.), *Learning disabilities: Lifelong issues* (pp. 255–260). Baltimore: Paul H. Brookes Publishing Co.

Shonkoff, J.P., & Phillips, D.A. (Eds.). (2000). *From neurons to neighborhoods: The science of early childhood development.* Washington, DC: National Academies Press.

Snow, C.E., Burns, M.S., & Griffin, P. (Eds.). (1998). *Preventing reading difficulties in young children.* Washington, DC: National Academies Press.

U.S. Census Bureau. (2001, September). *The Hispanic population: 2000. Percent of population for one or more races.* Retrieved October 23, 2003, from http://www.census.gov/prod/2001pubs/mso01-hp.pdf

U.S. Census Bureau, Population Division, Education and Social Stratification Branch. (2003). *Summary tables on language use and English ability: 2000 (PHC-T-20).* Retrieved October 23, 2003, from http://www.census .gov/population/www/cen2000/phc-t20.html

U.S. Department of Education. (2002a, September 16). *Department awards grants on research for reading comprehension* (Press release). Retrieved October 23, 2003, from http://www.ed.gov/news/pressreleases/2002/09/ 09162002a.html

U.S. Department of Education, Office of Vocational and Adult Education, Office of the Assistant Secretary. (2002b, March). Key issue brief: High school reading. Retrieved October 23, 2003, from http://www.ed.gov/ about/offices/list/ovae/pi/hs/reading.doc.

U.S. Department of Education. (2003, March 6). *Third national Even Start evaluation: Program impacts and implications for improvement.* Retrieved October 23, 2003, from http://www.ed.gov/offices/OUS/PES/ ed_for_disadvantaged.html#evenstart

U.S. Department of Health and Human Services, Administration for Children and Families. (n.d.). *ACF child outcomes research and evaluation.* Retrieved October 23, 2003, from http://www.acf.hhs.gov/programs/ core/index.html

Closing Comments from G. Reid Lyon

When I was asked to write the closing comments for *The Voice of Evidence in Reading Research*, edited by my colleagues Peggy McCardle and Vinita Chhabra, I was both pleased by the outstanding quality of the chapters in the volume and honored by their request. In my review of the book, I was startled to read that this volume had been dedicated to me. Humbled would be a better description. While it is the case that we all work hard here at the National Institute of Child Health and Human Development (NICHD) to build and support highly productive research programs that can inform educational policies and practices, the fact that strong converging evidence is now being used to inform professional development and reading instruction is a testament to the lifelong work of many scientists, teachers, and policy makers around the country— many of whom have received NICHD funding and many of whom have contributed to this book. I have played a limited role. We have accomplished a great deal, together, however, and we have done it through an unremitting focus on answering four basic questions:

1. How do children learn to read? Specifically, what are the critical skills, environments, genetic factors, neurobiological factors, and instructional interactions alone and in combination that influence the development of the ability to read with robust comprehension?

2. Given that many of our nation's children fail to learn to read, which of these factors, if not optimal, impede the process?

3. How can we prevent reading failure?

4. How can we help struggling readers learn to read at older ages?

Given these questions as our focus, we have been persistent. It is very difficult to answer these four questions if you do not walk with children through their lives and study them as they grow, change, and respond to different interactions in life, including class-room instruction. Thus, we have tried to support research that allows reading scientists to study youngsters over time and to work with them in the contexts that characterize their lives.

This focus and persistence has produced a converging body of scientific evidence relevant to reading development and reading instruction that is ready for implementation in the classroom. And this is what this book is about. The information presented in this volume is not only timely for teachers but also critical to their future practice. It is almost an understatement to say that teachers do not use specific evidence to guide their instruction in reading. Why should they? Typically teachers in training or interacting in ongoing professional development activities learn little about what consti-tutes different types of evidence and which types of evidence are most relevant to determining the effectiveness of a particular approach or strategy. More often, teachers are exposed to information that forces complex dimensional concepts into simple polarized dichotomies. Indeed, many of our teachers have been taught that learning basic reading skills is in conflict with developing reading comprehension strategies, instead of being given the basic underlying knowledge to understand that different reading skills are salient at different points of reading development. Many of the teachers who work with us tell us that research information is frequently presented to them in a disconnected, jargon-filled manner. And many tell us that there are so many perspectives and theories about reading and reading instruction, with more coming on the scene every year, that they cannot separate the wheat from the chaff. After a while, many cease to even try.

The chapters in this book provide a clear and compelling case for how scientific evidence, rather than beliefs and philosophical positions, can help teachers make informed instructional decisions. The information presented can help teachers and others begin to communicate in a common language about what works with differ-ent types of learners. We continue to see more than one third of our nation's children failing to learn to read, with reading failure reaching epidemic proportions in disadvantaged communities. As the content of this volume clearly points out, it does not have to be this way.

As I have said in testimony before the House Science Commit-tee, Subcommittee on Basic Research, education is at a crossroads. We can choose to be part of a modern scientific community and base our work with children on converging evidence of what works or we can continue to bring instruction to our youngsters based upon untested assumptions and philosophical beliefs. The first path leads to successful readers with far better future prospects. The second will invariably lead to failure and wasted lives. This book should help you make the right choice.

G. Reid Lyon, Ph.D.
Chief, Child Development and Behavior Branch
National Institute of Child Health and Human Development
National Institutes of Health
U.S. Department of Health and Human Services

Index

Page numbers followed by *f, t,* and *n*
indicate figures, tables, and footnotes, respectively.